The ONE YEAR® *Seasonal* BIBLE

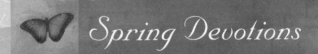

Spring Devotions

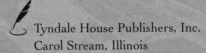

Tyndale House Publishers, Inc.
Carol Stream, Illinois

Tyndale House Publishers and Wycliffe Bible Translators share the vision for an understandable, accurate translation of the Bible for every person in the world. Each sale of the *Holy Bible,* New Living Translation, benefits Wycliffe Bible Translators. Wycliffe is working with partners around the world to accomplish Vision 2025—an initiative to start a Bible translation program in every language group that needs it by the year 2025.

CONTENTS

Genesis / *January 1* . . . . Vol 1 / 1

Exodus / *January 25* . . . . Vol 1 / 91

Leviticus / *February 16* . . . . . . Vol 1 / 172

Numbers / *March 3* . . . . Vol 1 / 229

Deuteronomy / *March 23* . . . . . Vol 1 / 307

Joshua / *April 10* . . . . Vol 2 / 35

Judges / *April 23* . . . . Vol 2 / 81

Ruth / *May 5* . . . . Vol 2 / 128

1 Samuel / *May 7* . . . . Vol 2 / 134

2 Samuel / *May 22* . . . . Vol 2 / 190

1 Kings / *June 6* . . . . Vol 2 / 245

2 Kings / *June 21* . . . . Vol 2 / 300

1 Chronicles / *July 5* . . . . Vol 3 / 16

2 Chronicles / *July 20* . . . . Vol 3 / 71

Ezra / *August 5* . . . . Vol 3 / 133

Nehemiah / *August 11* . . . . Vol 3 / 152

Esther / *August 18* . . . . Vol 3 / 178

Job / *August 21* . . . . Vol 3 / 190

Psalms / *January 1*

   and *July 3* . . . . Vol 1 / 4; Vol 3 / 12

Proverbs / *January 1* . . . . Vol 1 / 5

Ecclesiastes / *September 2* . . . . Vol 3 / 242

Song of Songs / *September 6* . . . Vol 3 / 255

Isaiah / *September 8* . . . . Vol 3 / 264

Jeremiah / *October 3* . . . . Vol 4 / 10

Lamentations / *October 29* . . . . Vol 4 / 118

Ezekiel / *November 1* . . . . Vol 4 / 131

Daniel / *November 25* . . . . Vol 4 / 220

Hosea / *December 5* . . . . Vol 4 / 251

Joel / *December 9* . . . . Vol 4 / 268

Amos / *December 10* . . . . Vol 4 / 273

Obadiah / *December 13* . . . . . . Vol 4 / 286

Jonah / *December 14* . . . . Vol 4 / 289

Micah / *December 15* . . . . Vol 4 / 292

Nahum / *December 17* . . . . Vol 4 / 301

Habakkuk / *December 18* . . . . . Vol 4 / 305

Zephaniah / *December 19* . . . . . Vol 4 / 310

Haggai / *December 20* . . . . Vol 4 / 314

Zechariah / *December 21* . . . . . Vol 4 / 318

Malachi / *December 30* . . . . . . Vol 4 / 342

Matthew / *January 1* . . . . Vol 1 / 3

Mark / *February 15* . . . . Vol 1 / 171

Luke / *March 13* . . . . Vol 1 / 272

John / *April 30* . . . . Vol 2 / 108

Acts / *June 3* . . . . Vol 2 / 236

Romans / *July 12* . . . . Vol 3 / 45

1 Corinthians / *August 4* . . . . . Vol 3 / 132

2 Corinthians / *August 26* . . . . . Vol 3 / 216

Galatians / *September 14* . . . . . Vol 3 / 290

Ephesians / *September 22* . . . . . Vol 3 / 326

Philippians / *September 29* . . . . Vol 3 / 359

Colossians / *October 4* . . . . Vol 4 / 17

1 Thessalonians / October 9 . . . . Vol 4 / 39

2 Thessalonians / October 13 . . . Vol 4 / 56

1 Timothy / *October 16* . . . . Vol 4 / 67

2 Timothy / *October 22* . . . . Vol 4 / 89

Titus / *October 26* . . . . Vol 4 / 109

Philemon / *October 29* . . . . Vol 4 / 122

Hebrews / *October 30* . . . . Vol 4 / 125

James / *November 17* . . . . Vol 4 / 194

1 Peter / *November 22* . . . . Vol 4 / 211

2 Peter / *November 27* . . . . Vol 4 / 229

1 John / *November 30* . . . . Vol 4 / 238

2 John / *December 6* . . . . Vol 4 / 257

3 John / *December 7* . . . . Vol 4 / 261

Jude / *December 8* . . . . Vol 4 / 266

Revelation / *December 9* . . . . . Vol 4 / 272

DEUTERONOMY 18:1–20:20

"Remember that the Levitical priests—that is, the whole of the tribe of Levi—will receive no allotment of land among the other tribes in Israel. Instead, the priests and Levites will eat from the special gifts given to the LORD, for that is their share. ²They will have no land of their own among the Israelites. The LORD himself is their special possession, just as he promised them.

³"These are the parts the priests may claim as their share from the cattle, sheep, and goats that the people bring as offerings: the shoulder, the cheeks, and the stomach. ⁴You must also give to the priests the first share of the grain, the new wine, the olive oil, and the wool at shearing time. ⁵For the LORD your God chose the tribe of Levi out of all your tribes to minister in the LORD's name forever.

⁶"Suppose a Levite chooses to move from his town in Israel, wherever he is living, to the place the LORD chooses for worship. ⁷He may minister there in the name of the LORD his God, just like all his fellow Levites who are serving the LORD there. ⁸He may eat his share of the sacrifices and offerings, even if he also receives support from his family.

⁹"When you enter the land the LORD your God is giving you, be very careful not to imitate the detestable customs of those nations living there. ¹⁰For example, never sacrifice your son or daughter as a burnt offering.* And do not let your people practice fortune-telling, or use sorcery, or interpret omens, or engage in witchcraft, ¹¹or cast spells, or function as mediums or psychics, or call

forth the spirits of the dead. ¹²Anyone who does these things is detestable to the LORD. It is because the other nations have done these detestable things that the LORD your God will drive them out ahead of you. ¹³But you must be blameless before the LORD your God. ¹⁴The nations you are about to displace consult sorcerers and fortune-tellers, but the LORD your God forbids you to do such things."

¹⁵Moses continued, "The LORD your God will raise up for you a prophet like me from among your fellow Israelites. You must listen to him. ¹⁶For this is what you yourselves requested of the LORD your God when you were assembled at Mount Sinai.* You said, 'Don't let us hear the voice of the LORD our God anymore or see this blazing fire, for we will die.'

¹⁷"Then the LORD said to me, 'What they have said is right. ¹⁸I will raise up a prophet like you from among their fellow Israelites. I will put my words in his mouth, and he will tell the people everything I command him. ¹⁹I will personally deal with anyone who will not listen to the messages the prophet proclaims on my behalf. ²⁰But any prophet who falsely claims to speak in my name or who speaks in the name of another god must die.'

²¹"But you may wonder, 'How will we know whether or not a prophecy is from the LORD?' ²²If the prophet speaks in the LORD's name but his prediction does not happen or come true, you will know that the LORD did not give that message. That prophet has spoken without my authority and need not be feared.

¹⁹:¹"WHEN the LORD your God destroys the nations whose land he is giving you, you will take over their land and settle in their towns and homes. ²Then you must set apart three cities of refuge in the land the LORD your God is giving

you. [3] Survey the territory,* and divide the land the LORD your God is giving you into three districts, with one of these cities in each district. Then anyone who has killed someone can flee to one of the cities of refuge for safety.

[4] "If someone kills another person unintentionally, without previous hostility, the slayer may flee to any of these cities to live in safety. [5] For example, suppose someone goes into the forest with a neighbor to cut wood. And suppose one of them swings an ax to chop down a tree, and the ax head flies off the handle, killing the other person. In such cases, the slayer may flee to one of the cities of refuge to live in safety.

[6] "If the distance to the nearest city of refuge is too far, an enraged avenger might be able to chase down and kill the person who caused the death. Then the slayer would die unfairly, since he had never shown hostility toward the person who died. [7] That is why I am commanding you to set aside three cities of refuge.

[8] "And if the LORD your God enlarges your territory, as he swore to your ancestors, and gives you all the land he promised them, [9] you must designate three additional cities of refuge. (He will give you this land if you are careful to obey all the commands I have given you—if you always love the LORD your God and walk in his ways.) [10] That way you will prevent the death of innocent people in the land the LORD your God is giving you as your special possession. You will not be held responsible for the death of innocent people.

[11] "But suppose someone is hostile toward a neighbor and deliberately ambushes and murders him and then flees to one of the cities of refuge. [12] In that case, the elders of the murderer's hometown must send agents to the city of refuge to bring him back and hand him over to the dead person's avenger to be put to death. [13] Do not feel sorry for that murderer! Purge from Israel the guilt of murdering innocent people; then all will go well with you.

[14] "When you arrive in the land the

LORD your God is giving you as your special possession, you must never steal anyone's land by moving the boundary markers your ancestors set up to mark their property.

[15] "You must not convict anyone of a crime on the testimony of only one witness. The facts of the case must be established by the testimony of two or three witnesses.

[16] "If a malicious witness comes forward and accuses someone of a crime, [17] then both the accuser and accused must appear before the LORD by coming to the priests and judges in office at that time. [18] The judges must investigate the case thoroughly. If the accuser has brought false charges against his fellow Israelite, [19] you must impose on the accuser the sentence he intended for the other person. In this way, you will purge such evil from among you. [20] Then the rest of the people will hear about it and be afraid to do such an evil thing. [21] You must show no pity for the guilty! Your rule should be life for life, eye for eye, tooth for tooth, hand for hand, foot for foot.

[20:1] "WHEN you go out to fight your enemies and you face horses and chariots and an army greater than your own, do not be afraid. The LORD your God, who brought you out of the land of Egypt, i with you! [2] When you prepare for battl the priest must come forward to spe to the troops. [3] He will say to them, " ten to me, all you men of Israel! Dc be afraid as you go out to fight you' mies today! Do not lose heart or p; tremble before them. [4] For th' your God is going with you! He for you against your enemie' will give you victory!'

[5] "Then the officers of the address the troops and say, here just built a new hous dedicated it? If so, you may might be killed in the ba one else would dedicate anyone here just plant not yet eaten any of i'

may go home! You might die in battle, and someone else would eat the first fruit. [7]Has anyone here just become engaged to a woman but not yet married her? Well, you may go home and get married! You might die in the battle, and someone else would marry her.'

[8]"Then the officers will also say, 'Is anyone here afraid or worried? If you are, you may go home before you frighten anyone else.' [9]When the officers have finished speaking to their troops, they will appoint the unit commanders.

[10]"As you approach a town to attack it, you must first offer its people terms for peace. [11]If they accept your terms and open the gates to you, then all the people inside will serve you in forced labor. [12]But if they refuse to make peace and prepare to fight, you must attack the town. [13]When the LORD your God hands the town over to you, use your swords to kill every man in the town. [14]But you may keep for yourselves all the women, children, livestock, and other plunder. You may enjoy the plunder from your enemies that the LORD your God has given you.

[15]"But these instructions apply only to distant towns, not to the towns of the nations in the land you will enter. [16]In those towns that the LORD your God is giving you as a special possession, destroy every living thing. [17]You must completely destroy* the Hittites, Amorites, Canaanites, Perizzites, Hivites, and Jebusites, just as the LORD your God has commanded you. [18]This will prevent the people of the land from teaching you to imitate their detestable customs in the worship of their gods, which would cause you to sin deeply against the LORD your God.

[19]"When you are attacking a town and the war drags on, you must not cut down the trees with your axes. You may eat the fruit, but do not cut down the trees. Are the trees your enemies, that you should attack them? [20]You may only cut down trees that you know are not valuable for food. Use them to make

the equipment you need to attack the enemy town until it falls."

18:10 Or *never make your son or daughter pass through the fire.*   **18:16** Hebrew *Horeb,* another name for Sinai.   **19:3** Or *Keep the roads in good repair.*   **20:17** The Hebrew term used here refers to the complete consecration of things or people to the LORD, either by destroying them or by giving them as an offering.

LUKE 9:28-50

About eight days later Jesus took Peter, James, and John up on a mountain to pray. [29]And as he was praying, the appearance of his face was transformed, and his clothes became dazzling white. [30]Then two men, Moses and Elijah, appeared and began talking with Jesus. [31]They were glorious to see. And they were speaking about his exodus from this world, which was about to be fulfilled in Jerusalem.

[32]Peter and the others had fallen asleep. When they woke up, they saw Jesus' glory and the two men standing with him. [33]As Moses and Elijah were starting to leave, Peter, not even knowing what he was saying, blurted out, "Master, it's wonderful for us to be here! Let's make three shelters as memorials*—one for you, one for Moses, and one for Elijah." [34]But even as he was saying this, a cloud came over them, and terror gripped them as the cloud covered them.

[35]Then a voice from the cloud said, "This is my Son, my Chosen One.* Listen to him." [36]When the voice finished, Jesus was there alone. They didn't tell anyone at that time what they had seen.

[37]The next day, after they had come down the mountain, a large crowd met Jesus. [38]A man in the crowd called out to him, "Teacher, I beg you to look at my son, my only child. [39]An evil spirit keeps seizing him, making him scream. It throws him into convulsions so that he foams at the mouth. It batters him and hardly ever leaves him alone. [40]I begged your disciples to cast out the spirit, but they couldn't do it."

[41]"You faithless and corrupt people," Jesus said, "how long must I be with you and put up with you?" Then he said to the man, "Bring your son here."

⁴²As the boy came forward, the demon knocked him to the ground and threw him into a violent convulsion. But Jesus rebuked the evil* spirit and healed the boy. Then he gave him back to his father. ⁴³Awe gripped the people as they saw this majestic display of God's power.

While everyone was marveling at everything he was doing, Jesus said to his disciples, ⁴⁴"Listen to me and remember what I say. The Son of Man is going to be betrayed into the hands of his enemies." ⁴⁵But they didn't know what he meant. Its significance was hidden from them, so they couldn't understand it, and they were afraid to ask him about it.

⁴⁶Then his disciples began arguing about which of them was the greatest. ⁴⁷But Jesus knew their thoughts, so he brought a little child to his side. ⁴⁸**Then he said to them, "Anyone who welcomes a little child like this on my behalf* welcomes me, and anyone who welcomes me also welcomes my Father who sent me. Whoever is the least among you is the greatest."**

⁴⁹John said to Jesus, "Master, we saw someone using your name to cast out demons, but we told him to stop because he isn't in our group."

⁵⁰But Jesus said, "Don't stop him! Anyone who is not against you is for you."

9:33 Greek *three tabernacles.*   **9:35** Some manuscripts read *This is my dearly loved Son.*   **9:42** Greek *unclean.* **9:48** Greek *in my name.*

PSALM 73:1-28
A psalm of Asaph.

¹ **T**ruly God is good to Israel,
  to those whose hearts are pure.
² But as for me, I almost lost
    my footing.
  My feet were slipping, and I was
    almost gone.
³ For I envied the proud
    when I saw them prosper
    despite their wickedness.
⁴ They seem to live such painless lives;
    their bodies are so healthy
    and strong.
⁵ They don't have troubles like other
    people;

  they're not plagued with
    problems like everyone else.
⁶ They wear pride like a jeweled
    necklace
  and clothe themselves with
    cruelty.
⁷ These fat cats have everything
    their hearts could ever wish for!
⁸ They scoff and speak only evil;
  in their pride they seek to crush
    others.
⁹ They boast against the very heavens,
  and their words strut throughout
    the earth.
¹⁰ And so the people are dismayed
    and confused,
  drinking in all their words.
¹¹ "What does God know?" they ask.
  "Does the Most High even know
    what's happening?"
¹² Look at these wicked people—
  enjoying a life of ease while their
    riches multiply.

¹³ Did I keep my heart pure
    for nothing?
  Did I keep myself innocent
    for no reason?
¹⁴ I get nothing but trouble all
    day long;
  every morning brings me pain.
¹⁵ If I had really spoken this way
    to others,
  I would have been a traitor
    to your people.
¹⁶ So I tried to understand why the
    wicked prosper.
  But what a difficult task it is!
¹⁷ Then I went into your sanctuary,
    O God,
  and I finally understood the
    destiny of the wicked.
¹⁸ Truly, you put them on a slippery
    path
  and send them sliding over the
    cliff to destruction.
¹⁹ In an instant they are destroyed,
  completely swept away by terrors.
²⁰ When you arise, O Lord,
  you will laugh at their silly ideas
  as a person laughs at dreams
    in the morning.

21 Then I realized that my heart
      was bitter,
      and I was all torn up inside.
22 I was so foolish and ignorant—
      I must have seemed like a
      senseless animal to you.
23 Yet I still belong to you;
      you hold my right hand.
24 You guide me with your counsel,
      leading me to a glorious destiny.
25 Whom have I in heaven but you?
      I desire you more than anything
      on earth.
26 My health may fail, and my spirit
      may grow weak,
      but God remains the strength
      of my heart;
      he is mine forever.

27 Those who desert him will perish,
      for you destroy those who
      abandon you.
28 But as for me, how good it is
      to be near God!
      I have made the Sovereign LORD
      my shelter,
      and I will tell everyone about the
      wonderful things you do.

PROVERBS 12:10
The godly care for their animals, but the
wicked are always cruel.

APRIL
2

DEUTERONOMY 21:1–22:30
"When you are in the land the LORD your
God is giving you, someone may be found
murdered in a field, and you don't know
who committed the murder. 2In such a
case, your elders and judges must measure the distance from the site of the
crime to the nearby towns. 3When the
nearest town has been determined, that
town's elders must select from the herd a
young cow that has never been trained or
yoked to a plow. 4They must lead it down
to a valley that has not been plowed or
planted and that has a stream running
through it. There in the valley they must
break the young cow's neck. 5Then the
Levitical priests must step forward, for
the LORD your God has chosen them to
minister before him and to pronounce
blessings in the LORD's name. They are to
decide all legal and criminal cases.

6"The elders of the town must wash
their hands over the young cow whose
neck was broken. 7Then they must say,
'Our hands did not shed this person's
blood, nor did we see it happen. 8O LORD,
forgive your people Israel whom you
have redeemed. Do not charge your people with the guilt of murdering an innocent person.' Then they will be absolved
of the guilt of this person's blood. 9By
following these instructions, you will do
what is right in the LORD's sight and will
cleanse the guilt of murder from your
community.

10"Suppose you go out to war against
your enemies and the LORD your God
hands them over to you, and you take
some of them as captives. 11And suppose
you see among the captives a beautiful
woman, and you are attracted to her and
want to marry her. 12If this happens, you
may take her to your home, where she
must shave her head, cut her nails, 13and
change the clothes she was wearing
when she was captured. She will stay in
your home, but let her mourn for her father and mother for a full month. Then
you may marry her, and you will be her
husband and she will be your wife. 14But
if you marry her and she does not please
you, you must let her go free. You may
not sell her or treat her as a slave, for you
have humiliated her.

15"Suppose a man has two wives, but
he loves one and not the other, and both
have given him sons. And suppose the
firstborn son is the son of the wife he
does not love. 16When the man divides
his inheritance, he may not give the
larger inheritance to his younger son,
the son of the wife he loves, as if he were
the firstborn son. 17He must recognize

the rights of his oldest son, the son of the wife he does not love, by giving him a double portion. He is the first son of his father's virility, and the rights of the firstborn belong to him.

18"Suppose a man has a stubborn and rebellious son who will not obey his father or mother, even though they discipline him. 19 In such a case, the father and mother must take the son to the elders as they hold court at the town gate. 20The parents must say to the elders, 'This son of ours is stubborn and rebellious and refuses to obey. He is a glutton and a drunkard.' 21Then all the men of his town must stone him to death. In this way, you will purge this evil from among you, and all Israel will hear about it and be afraid.

22"If someone has committed a crime worthy of death and is executed and hung on a tree,* 23 the body must not remain hanging from the tree overnight. You must bury the body that same day, for anyone who is hung* is cursed in the sight of God. In this way, you will prevent the defilement of the land the LORD your God is giving you as your special possession.

22:1"IF you see your neighbor's ox or sheep or goat wandering away, don't ignore your responsibility.* Take it back to its owner. 2If its owner does not live nearby or you don't know who the owner is, take it to your place and keep it until the owner comes looking for it. Then you must return it. 3Do the same if you find your neighbor's donkey, clothing, or anything else your neighbor loses. Don't ignore your responsibility.

4"If you see that your neighbor's donkey or ox has collapsed on the road, do not look the other way. Go and help your neighbor get it back on its feet!

5"A woman must not put on men's clothing, and a man must not wear women's clothing. Anyone who does this is detestable in the sight of the LORD your God.

6"If you happen to find a bird's nest in a tree or on the ground, and there are young ones or eggs in it with the mother sitting in the nest, do not take the mother with the young. 7 You may take the young, but let the mother go, so that you may prosper and enjoy a long life.

8"When you build a new house, you must build a railing around the edge of its flat roof. That way you will not be considered guilty of murder if someone falls from the roof.

9"You must not plant any other crop between the rows of your vineyard. If you do, you are forbidden to use either the grapes from the vineyard or the other crop.

10"You must not plow with an ox and a donkey harnessed together.

11"You must not wear clothing made of wool and linen woven together.

12"You must put four tassels on the hem of the cloak with which you cover yourself—on the front, back, and sides.

13"Suppose a man marries a woman, but after sleeping with her, he turns against her 14 and publicly accuses her of shameful conduct, saying, 'When I married this woman, I discovered she was not a virgin.' 15Then the woman's father and mother must bring the proof of her virginity to the elders as they hold court at the town gate. 16Her father must say to them, 'I gave my daughter to this man to be his wife, and now he has turned against her. 17He has accused her of shameful conduct, saying, "I discovered that your daughter was not a virgin." But here is the proof of my daughter's virginity.' Then they must spread her bed sheet before the elders. 18The elders must then take the man and punish him. 19They must also fine him 100 pieces of silver,* which he must pay to the woman's father because he publicly accused a virgin of Israel of shameful conduct. The woman will then remain the man's wife, and he may never divorce her.

20"But suppose the man's accusations are true, and he can show that she was not a virgin. 21The woman must be taken to the door of her father's home, and there the men of the town must stone her to death, for she has committed a disgraceful crime in Israel by being promiscuous while living in her parents' home. In this way, you will purge this evil from among you.

²²"If a man is discovered committing adultery, both he and the woman must die. In this way, you will purge Israel of such evil.

²³"Suppose a man meets a young woman, a virgin who is engaged to be married, and he has sexual intercourse with her. If this happens within a town, ²⁴you must take both of them to the gates of that town and stone them to death. The woman is guilty because she did not scream for help. The man must die because he violated another man's wife. In this way, you will purge this evil from among you.

²⁵"But if the man meets the engaged woman out in the country, and he rapes her, then only the man must die. ²⁶Do nothing to the young woman; she has committed no crime worthy of death. She is as innocent as a murder victim. ²⁷Since the man raped her out in the country, it must be assumed that she screamed, but there was no one to rescue her.

²⁸"Suppose a man has intercourse with a young woman who is a virgin but is not engaged to be married. If they are discovered, ²⁹he must pay her father fifty pieces of silver.* Then he must marry the young woman because he violated her, and he may never divorce her as long as he lives.

³⁰*"A man must not marry his father's former wife, for this would violate his father."

21:22 Or *impaled on a pole;* similarly in 21:23.
21:23 Greek version reads *for everyone who is hung on a tree.* Compare Gal 3:13.   22:1 Hebrew *don't hide yourself;* similarly in 22:3.   22:19 Hebrew *100 shekels of silver,* about 2.5 pounds or 1.1 kilograms in weight.
22:29 Hebrew *50 shekels of silver,* about 1.25 pounds or 570 grams in weight.   22:30 Verse 22:30 is numbered 23:1 in Hebrew text.

LUKE 9:51–10:12

As the time drew near for him to ascend to heaven, Jesus resolutely set out for Jerusalem. ⁵²He sent messengers ahead to a Samaritan village to prepare for his arrival. ⁵³But the people of the village did not welcome Jesus because he was on his way to Jerusalem. ⁵⁴When James and John saw this, they said to Jesus, "Lord, should we call down fire from heaven to burn them up*?" ⁵⁵But Jesus turned and rebuked them.* ⁵⁶So they went on to another village.

⁵⁷As they were walking along, someone said to Jesus, "I will follow you wherever you go."

⁵⁸But Jesus replied, "Foxes have dens to live in, and birds have nests, but the Son of Man has no place even to lay his head."

⁵⁹He said to another person, "Come, follow me."

The man agreed, but he said, "Lord, first let me return home and bury my father."

⁶⁰But Jesus told him, "Let the spiritually dead bury their own dead!* Your duty is to go and preach about the Kingdom of God."

⁶¹Another said, "Yes, Lord, I will follow you, but first let me say good-bye to my family."

⁶²**But Jesus told him, "Anyone who puts a hand to the plow and then looks back is not fit for the Kingdom of God."**

¹⁰:¹THE Lord now chose seventy-two* other disciples and sent them ahead in pairs to all the towns and places he planned to visit. ²These were his instructions to them: "The harvest is great, but the workers are few. So pray to the Lord who is in charge of the harvest; ask him to send more workers into his fields. ³Now go, and remember that I am sending you out as lambs among wolves. ⁴Don't take any money with you, nor a traveler's bag, nor an extra pair of sandals. And don't stop to greet anyone on the road.

⁵"Whenever you enter someone's home, first say, 'May God's peace be on this house.' ⁶If those who live there are peaceful, the blessing will stand; if they are not, the blessing will return to you. ⁷Don't move around from home to home. Stay in one place, eating and

drinking what they provide. Don't hesitate to accept hospitality, because those who work deserve their pay.

8"If you enter a town and it welcomes you, eat whatever is set before you. 9Heal the sick, and tell them, 'The Kingdom of God is near you now.' 10But if a town refuses to welcome you, go out into its streets and say, 11'We wipe even the dust of your town from our feet to show that we have abandoned you to your fate. And know this—the Kingdom of God is near!' 12I assure you, even wicked Sodom will be better off than such a town on judgment day."

9:54 Some manuscripts add *as Elijah did.*   **9:55** Some manuscripts add *And he said, "You don't realize what your hearts are like.* 56*For the Son of Man has not come to destroy people's lives, but to save them."*   **9:60** Greek *Let the dead bury their own dead.*   **10:1** Some manuscripts read *seventy;* also in 10:17.

PSALM 74:1-23
A psalm* of Asaph.

1 ● God, why have you rejected
     us so long?
   Why is your anger so intense
     against the sheep of your
     own pasture?
2 Remember that we are the
     people you chose long ago,
   the tribe you redeemed as
     your own special possession!
   And remember Jerusalem,* your
     home here on earth.
3 Walk through the awful ruins
     of the city;
   see how the enemy has destroyed
     your sanctuary.

4 There your enemies shouted their
     victorious battle cries;
   there they set up their battle
     standards.
5 They swung their axes
     like woodcutters in a forest.
6 With axes and picks,
     they smashed the carved
     paneling.
7 They burned your sanctuary
     to the ground.
   They defiled the place that bears
     your name.

8 Then they thought, "Let's destroy
     everything!"
   So they burned down all the
     places where God was
     worshiped.

9 We no longer see your miraculous
     signs.
   All the prophets are gone,
   and no one can tell us when
     it will end.
10 How long, O God, will you allow
     our enemies to insult you?
   Will you let them dishonor your
     name forever?
11 Why do you hold back your strong
     right hand?
   Unleash your powerful fist and
     destroy them.

12 You, O God, are my king from
     ages past,
   bringing salvation to the earth.
13 You split the sea by your strength
     and smashed the heads of the
     sea monsters.
14 You crushed the heads of
     Leviathan*
   and let the desert animals
     eat him.
15 You caused the springs and streams
     to gush forth,
   and you dried up rivers that
     never run dry.
16 Both day and night belong to you;
     you made the starlight* and
     the sun.
17 You set the boundaries of the earth,
     and you made both summer
     and winter.

18 See how these enemies insult
     you, LORD.
   A foolish nation has dishonored
     your name.
19 Don't let these wild beasts destroy
     your turtledoves.
   Don't forget your suffering
     people forever.

20 Remember your covenant promises,
     for the land is full of darkness
     and violence!

21 Don't let the downtrodden
    be humiliated again.
    Instead, let the poor and needy
    praise your name.

22 Arise, O God, and defend your cause.
    Remember how these fools insult
    you all day long.
23 Don't overlook what your enemies
    have said
    or their growing uproar.

74:TITLE Hebrew *maskil*. This may be a literary or musical
term. 74:2 Hebrew *Mount Zion*. 74:14 The
identification of Leviathan is disputed, ranging from an
earthly creature to a mythical sea monster in ancient
literature. 74:16 Or *moon;* Hebrew reads *light.*

PROVERBS 12:11
A hard worker has plenty of food, but a
person who chases fantasies has no
sense.

APRIL 3

DEUTERONOMY 23:1–25:19
1*"**I**f a man's testicles are crushed or his
penis is cut off, he may not be admitted
to the assembly of the LORD.

2"If a person is illegitimate by birth,
neither he nor his descendants for ten
generations may be admitted to the assembly of the LORD.

3"No Ammonite or Moabite or any of
their descendants for ten generations
may be admitted to the assembly of the
LORD. 4These nations did not welcome
you with food and water when you came
out of Egypt. Instead, they hired Balaam
son of Beor from Pethor in distant Aram-
naharaim to curse you. 5But the LORD
your God refused to listen to Balaam. He
turned the intended curse into a blessing
because the LORD your God loves you.
6As long as you live, you must never pro-
mote the welfare and prosperity of the
Ammonites or Moabites.

7"Do not detest the Edomites or the
Egyptians, because the Edomites are
your relatives and you lived as foreigners among the Egyptians. 8The third
generation of Edomites and Egyptians
may enter the assembly of the LORD.

9"When you go to war against your
enemies, be sure to stay away from anything that is impure.

10"Any man who becomes ceremonially defiled because of a nocturnal
emission must leave the camp and stay
away all day. 11Toward evening he must
bathe himself, and at sunset he may return to the camp.

12"You must have a designated area
outside the camp where you can go to relieve yourself. 13Each of you must have a
spade as part of your equipment. Whenever you relieve yourself, dig a hole with
the spade and cover the excrement.
14The camp must be holy, for the LORD
your God moves around in your camp to
protect you and to defeat your enemies.
He must not see any shameful thing
among you, or he will turn away from
you.

15"If slaves should escape from their
masters and take refuge with you, you
must not hand them over to their masters. 16Let them live among you in any
town they choose, and do not oppress
them.

17"No Israelite, whether man or
woman, may become a temple prostitute. 18When you are bringing an offering to fulfill a vow, you must not bring to
the house of the LORD your God any offering from the earnings of a prostitute,
whether a man* or a woman, for both
are detestable to the LORD your God.

19"Do not charge interest on the loans
you make to a fellow Israelite, whether
you loan money, or food, or anything
else. 20You may charge interest to foreigners, but you may not charge interest
to Israelites, so that the LORD your God
may bless you in everything you do in the
land you are about to enter and occupy.

21"When you make a vow to the LORD
your God, be prompt in fulfilling whatever you promised him. For the LORD
your God demands that you promptly

fulfill all your vows, or you will be guilty of sin. [22]However, it is not a sin to refrain from making a vow. [23]But once you have voluntarily made a vow, be careful to fulfill your promise to the LORD your God.

[24]"When you enter your neighbor's vineyard, you may eat your fill of grapes, but you must not carry any away in a basket. [25]And when you enter your neighbor's field of grain, you may pluck the heads of grain with your hand, but you must not harvest it with a sickle.

[24:1]"SUPPOSE a man marries a woman but she does not please him. Having discovered something wrong with her, he writes her a letter of divorce, hands it to her, and sends her away from his house. [2]When she leaves his house, she is free to marry another man. [3]But if the second husband also turns against her and divorces her, or if he dies, [4]the first husband may not marry her again, for she has been defiled. That would be detestable to the LORD. You must not bring guilt upon the land the LORD your God is giving you as a special possession.

[5]"A newly married man must not be drafted into the army or be given any other official responsibilities. He must be free to spend one year at home, bringing happiness to the wife he has married.

[6]"It is wrong to take a set of millstones, or even just the upper millstone, as security for a loan, for the owner uses it to make a living.

[7]"If anyone kidnaps a fellow Israelite and treats him as a slave or sells him, the kidnapper must die. In this way, you will purge the evil from among you.

[8]"In all cases involving serious skin diseases,* be careful to follow the instructions of the Levitical priests; obey all the commands I have given them. [9]Remember what the LORD your God did to Miriam as you were coming from Egypt.

[10]"If you lend anything to your neighbor, do not enter his house to pick up the item he is giving as security. [11]You

must wait outside while he goes in and brings it out to you. [12]If your neighbor is poor and gives you his cloak as security for a loan, do not keep the cloak overnight. [13]Return the cloak to its owner by sunset so he can stay warm through the night and bless you, and the LORD your God will count you as righteous.

[14]"Never take advantage of poor and destitute laborers, whether they are fellow Israelites or foreigners living in your towns. [15]You must pay them their wages each day before sunset because they are poor and are counting on it. If you don't, they might cry out to the LORD against you, and it would be counted against you as sin.

[16]"Parents must not be put to death for the sins of their children, nor children for the sins of their parents. Those deserving to die must be put to death for their own crimes.

[17]"True justice must be given to foreigners living among you and to orphans, and you must never accept a widow's garment as security for her debt. [18]Always remember that you were slaves in Egypt and that the LORD your God redeemed you from your slavery. That is why I have given you this command.

[19]"When you are harvesting your crops and forget to bring in a bundle of grain from your field, don't go back to get it. Leave it for the foreigners, orphans, and widows. Then the LORD your God will bless you in all you do. [20]When you beat the olives from your olive trees, don't go over the boughs twice. Leave the remaining olives for the foreigners, orphans, and widows. [21]When you gather the grapes in your vineyard, don't glean the vines after they are picked. Leave the remaining grapes for the foreigners, orphans, and widows. [22]Remember that you were slaves in the land of Egypt. That is why I am giving you this command.

[25:1]"SUPPOSE two people take a dispute to court, and the judges declare that one is right and the other is wrong. [2]If the person in the wrong is sentenced to be flogged, the judge must command him to lie down and be beaten in his presence with the number of lashes appropriate to the crime. ³But never give more than forty lashes; more than forty lashes would publicly humiliate your neighbor.

⁴"You must not muzzle an ox to keep it from eating as it treads out the grain.

⁵"If two brothers are living together on the same property and one of them dies without a son, his widow may not be married to anyone from outside the family. Instead, her husband's brother should marry her and have intercourse with her to fulfill the duties of a brother-in-law. ⁶The first son she bears to him will be considered the son of the dead brother, so that his name will not be forgotten in Israel.

⁷"But if the man refuses to marry his brother's widow, she must go to the town gate and say to the elders assembled there, 'My husband's brother refuses to preserve his brother's name in Israel—he refuses to fulfill the duties of a brother-in-law by marrying me.' ⁸The elders of the town will then summon him and talk with him. If he still refuses and says, 'I don't want to marry her,' ⁹the widow must walk over to him in the presence of the elders, pull his sandal from his foot, and spit in his face. Then she must declare, 'This is what happens to a man who refuses to provide his brother with children.' ¹⁰Ever afterward in Israel his family will be referred to as 'the family of the man whose sandal was pulled off'!

¹¹"If two Israelite men get into a fight and the wife of one tries to rescue her husband by grabbing the testicles of the other man, ¹²you must cut off her hand. Show her no pity.

¹³"You must use accurate scales when you weigh out merchandise, ¹⁴and you must use full and honest measures. ¹⁵Yes, always use honest weights and measures, so that you may enjoy a long life in the land the Lord your God is giving you. ¹⁶All who cheat with dishonest weights and measures are detestable to the Lord your God.

¹⁷"Never forget what the Amalekites did to you as you came from Egypt. ¹⁸They attacked you when you were exhausted and weary, and they struck down those who were straggling behind. They had no fear of God. ¹⁹Therefore, when the Lord your God has given you rest from all your enemies in the land he is giving you as a special possession, you must destroy the Amalekites and erase their memory from under heaven. Never forget this!"

23:1 Verses 23:1-25 are numbered 23:2-26 in Hebrew text.　23:18 Hebrew *a dog*.　24:8 Traditionally rendered *leprosy*. The Hebrew word used here can describe various skin diseases.

LUKE 10:13-37

"**W**hat sorrow awaits you, Korazin and Bethsaida! For if the miracles I did in you had been done in wicked Tyre and Sidon, their people would have repented of their sins long ago, clothing themselves in burlap and throwing ashes on their heads to show their remorse. ¹⁴Yes, Tyre and Sidon will be better off on judgment day than you. ¹⁵And you people of Capernaum, will you be honored in heaven? No, you will go down to the place of the dead.*"

¹⁶Then he said to the disciples, "Anyone who accepts your message is also accepting me. And anyone who rejects you is rejecting me. And anyone who rejects me is rejecting God, who sent me."

¹⁷When the seventy-two disciples returned, they joyfully reported to him, "Lord, even the demons obey us when we use your name!"

¹⁸"Yes," he told them, "I saw Satan fall from heaven like lightning! ¹⁹Look, I have given you authority over all the power of the enemy, and you can walk among snakes and scorpions and crush them. Nothing will injure you. ²⁰But don't rejoice because evil spirits obey you; rejoice because your names are registered in heaven."

²¹At that same time Jesus was filled with the joy of the Holy Spirit, and he said, "O Father, Lord of heaven and earth, thank you for hiding these things from those who think themselves wise and clever, and for revealing them to

the childlike. Yes, Father, it pleased you to do it this way.

22"My Father has entrusted everything to me. No one truly knows the Son except the Father, and no one truly knows the Father except the Son and those to whom the Son chooses to reveal him."

23**Then when they were alone, he turned to the disciples and said, "Blessed are the eyes that see what you have seen.** 24**I tell you, many prophets and kings longed to see what you see, but they didn't see it. And they longed to hear what you hear, but they didn't hear it."**

25One day an expert in religious law stood up to test Jesus by asking him this question: "Teacher, what should I do to inherit eternal life?"

26Jesus replied, "What does the law of Moses say? How do you read it?"

27The man answered, "'You must love the LORD your God with all your heart, all your soul, all your strength, and all your mind.' And, 'Love your neighbor as yourself.'"*

28"Right!" Jesus told him. "Do this and you will live!"

29The man wanted to justify his actions, so he asked Jesus, "And who is my neighbor?"

30Jesus replied with a story: "A Jewish man was traveling on a trip from Jerusalem to Jericho, and he was attacked by bandits. They stripped him of his clothes, beat him up, and left him half dead beside the road.

31"By chance a priest came along. But when he saw the man lying there, he crossed to the other side of the road and passed him by. 32A Temple assistant* walked over and looked at him lying there, but he also passed by on the other side.

33"Then a despised Samaritan came along, and when he saw the man, he felt compassion for him. 34Going over to him, the Samaritan soothed his wounds with olive oil and wine and bandaged them. Then he put the man on his own donkey and took him to an inn, where he took care of him. 35The next day he handed the innkeeper two silver coins,* telling him, 'Take care of this man. If his bill runs higher than this, I'll pay you the next time I'm here.'

36"Now which of these three would you say was a neighbor to the man who was attacked by bandits?" Jesus asked.

37The man replied, "The one who showed him mercy."

Then Jesus said, "Yes, now go and do the same."

10:15 Greek *to Hades.*   10:27 Deut 6:5; Lev 19:18.
10:32 Greek *A Levite.*   10:35 Greek *two denarii.* A denarius was equivalent to a laborer's full day's wage.

PSALM 75:1-10
For the choir director: A psalm of Asaph.
A song to be sung to the tune "Do Not Destroy!"

¹ **W**e thank you, O God!
    We give thanks because
        you are near.
    People everywhere tell of your
        wonderful deeds.

² God says, "At the time I have planned,
    I will bring justice against the
        wicked.
³ When the earth quakes and its
        people live in turmoil,
    I am the one who keeps its
        foundations firm.   *Interlude*

⁴ "I warned the proud, 'Stop your
        boasting!'
    I told the wicked, 'Don't raise
        your fists!
⁵ Don't raise your fists in defiance
        at the heavens
    or speak with such arrogance.'"
⁶ For no one on earth—from east
        or west,
    or even from the wilderness—
    should raise a defiant fist.*
⁷ It is God alone who judges;
    he decides who will rise and
        who will fall.
⁸ For the LORD holds a cup in his hand
    that is full of foaming wine mixed
        with spices.
    He pours out the wine in judgment,
    and all the wicked must drink it,
        draining it to the dregs.

⁹ But as for me, I will always proclaim
   what God has done;
 I will sing praises to the God
   of Jacob.
¹⁰ For God says, "I will break the
    strength of the wicked,
  but I will increase the power
    of the godly."

75:6 Hebrew *should lift.*

PROVERBS 12:12-14
Thieves are jealous of each other's loot,
but the godly are well rooted and bear
their own fruit. □ The wicked are
trapped by their own words, but the
godly escape such trouble. □ Wise
words bring many benefits, and hard
work brings rewards.

APRIL
4

DEUTERONOMY 26:1–27:26
"When you enter the land the Lord
your God is giving you as a special possession and you have conquered it and
settled there, ²put some of the first
produce from each crop you harvest
into a basket and bring it to the designated place of worship—the place the
Lord your God chooses for his name to
be honored. ³Go to the priest in charge
at that time and say to him, 'With this
gift I acknowledge to the Lord your
God that I have entered the land he
swore to our ancestors he would give
us.' ⁴The priest will then take the basket from your hand and set it before
the altar of the Lord your God.

⁵"You must then say in the presence
of the Lord your God, 'My ancestor Jacob was a wandering Aramean who
went to live as a foreigner in Egypt. His
family arrived few in number, but in
Egypt they became a large and mighty
nation. ⁶When the Egyptians oppressed

and humiliated us by making us their
slaves, ⁷we cried out to the Lord, the
God of our ancestors. He heard our
cries and saw our hardship, toil, and oppression. ⁸So the Lord brought us out
of Egypt with a strong hand and powerful arm, with overwhelming terror, and
with miraculous signs and wonders.
⁹He brought us to this place and gave us
this land flowing with milk and honey!
¹⁰And now, O Lord, I have brought you
the first portion of the harvest you have
given me from the ground.' Then place
the produce before the Lord your God,
and bow to the ground in worship before him. ¹¹Afterward you may go and
celebrate because of all the good things
the Lord your God has given to you and
your household. Remember to include
the Levites and the foreigners living
among you in the celebration.

¹²"Every third year you must offer a
special tithe of your crops. In this year of
the special tithe you must give your tithes
to the Levites, foreigners, orphans, and
widows, so that they will have enough to
eat in your towns. ¹³Then you must declare in the presence of the Lord your
God, 'I have taken the sacred gift from my
house and have given it to the Levites,
foreigners, orphans, and widows, just as
you commanded me. I have not violated
or forgotten any of your commands. ¹⁴I
have not eaten any of it while in mourning; I have not handled it while I was ceremonially unclean; and I have not offered
any of it to the dead. I have obeyed the
Lord my God and have done everything
you commanded me. ¹⁵Now look down
from your holy dwelling place in heaven
and bless your people Israel and the land
you swore to our ancestors to give us—a
land flowing with milk and honey.'

¹⁶"Today the Lord your God has
commanded you to obey all these decrees and regulations. So be careful to
obey them wholeheartedly. ¹⁷You have
declared today that the Lord is your
God. And you have promised to walk in
his ways, and to obey his decrees, commands, and regulations, and to do
everything he tells you. ¹⁸The Lord has

declared today that you are his people, his own special treasure, just as he promised, and that you must obey all his commands. [19]And if you do, he will set you high above all the other nations he has made. Then you will receive praise, honor, and renown. You will be a nation that is holy to the LORD your God, just as he promised."

[27:1]THEN Moses and the leaders of Israel gave this charge to the people: "Obey all these commands that I am giving you today. [2]When you cross the Jordan River and enter the land the LORD your God is giving you, set up some large stones and coat them with plaster. [3]Write this whole body of instruction on them when you cross the river to enter the land the LORD your God is giving you—a land flowing with milk and honey, just as the LORD, the God of your ancestors, promised you. [4]When you cross the Jordan, set up these stones at Mount Ebal and coat them with plaster, as I am commanding you today.

[5]"Then build an altar there to the LORD your God, using natural, uncut stones. You must not shape the stones with an iron tool. [6]Build the altar of uncut stones, and use it to offer burnt offerings to the LORD your God. [7]Also sacrifice peace offerings on it, and celebrate by feasting there before the LORD your God. [8]You must clearly write all these instructions on the stones coated with plaster."

[9]Then Moses and the Levitical priests addressed all Israel as follows: "O Israel, be quiet and listen! Today you have become the people of the LORD your God. [10]So you must obey the LORD your God by keeping all these commands and decrees that I am giving you today."

[11]That same day Moses also gave this charge to the people: [12]"When you cross the Jordan River, the tribes of Simeon, Levi, Judah, Issachar, Joseph, and Benjamin must stand on Mount Gerizim to proclaim a blessing over the people. [13]And the tribes of Reuben, Gad, Asher, Zebulun, Dan, and Naphtali must stand on Mount Ebal to proclaim a curse.

[14]"Then the Levites will shout to all the people of Israel:

[15]'Cursed is anyone who carves or casts an idol and secretly sets it up. These idols, the work of craftsmen, are detestable to the LORD.'

And all the people will reply, 'Amen.'"

[16]'Cursed is anyone who dishonors father or mother.'

And all the people will reply, 'Amen.'

[17]'Cursed is anyone who steals property from a neighbor by moving a boundary marker.'

And all the people will reply, 'Amen.'

[18]'Cursed is anyone who leads a blind person astray on the road.'

And all the people will reply, 'Amen.'

[19]'Cursed is anyone who denies justice to foreigners, orphans, or widows.'

And all the people will reply, 'Amen.'

[20]'Cursed is anyone who has sexual intercourse with one of his father's wives, for he has violated his father.'

And all the people will reply, 'Amen.'

[21]'Cursed is anyone who has sexual intercourse with an animal.'

And all the people will reply, 'Amen.'

[22]'Cursed is anyone who has sexual intercourse with his sister, whether she is the daughter of his father or his mother.'

And all the people will reply, 'Amen.'

[23]'Cursed is anyone who has sexual intercourse with his mother-in-law.'

And all the people will reply,
'Amen.'

24'Cursed is anyone who attacks a
neighbor in secret.'
     And all the people will reply,
'Amen.'

25'Cursed is anyone who accepts
payment to kill an innocent
person.'
     And all the people will reply,
'Amen.'

26'Cursed is anyone who does not
affirm and obey the terms of these
instructions.'
     And all the people will reply,
'Amen.'"

LUKE 10:38–11:13

As Jesus and the disciples continued on
their way to Jerusalem, they came to a
certain village where a woman named
Martha welcomed them into her home.
39Her sister, Mary, sat at the Lord's feet,
listening to what he taught. 40But Martha
was distracted by the big dinner she was
preparing. She came to Jesus and said,
"Lord, doesn't it seem unfair to you that
my sister just sits here while I do all the
work? Tell her to come and help me."

41But the Lord said to her, "My dear
Martha, you are worried and upset over
all these details! 42There is only one
thing worth being concerned about.
Mary has discovered it, and it will not be
taken away from her."

11:1Once Jesus was in a certain place
praying. As he finished, one of his disciples came to him and said, "Lord, teach
us to pray, just as John taught his disciples."

2Jesus said, "This is how you should
pray:*

"Father, may your name be
     kept holy.
     May your Kingdom come soon.
3 Give us each day the food we need,*
4 and forgive us our sins,
     as we forgive those who sin
          against us.

And don't let us yield to
          temptation.*"

5Then, teaching them more about
prayer, he used this story: "Suppose you
went to a friend's house at midnight,
wanting to borrow three loaves of bread.
You say to him, 6'A friend of mine has
just arrived for a visit, and I have nothing
for him to eat.' 7And suppose he calls
out from his bedroom, 'Don't bother
me. The door is locked for the night, and
my family and I are all in bed. I can't help
you.' 8But I tell you this—though he
won't do it for friendship's sake, if you
keep knocking long enough, he will get
up and give you whatever you need because of your shameless persistence.*

9"And so I tell you, keep on asking,
and you will receive what you ask for.
Keep on seeking, and you will find.
Keep on knocking, and the door will
be opened to you. 10For everyone who
asks, receives. Everyone who seeks,
finds. And to everyone who knocks,
the door will be opened.

11"You fathers—if your children ask*
for a fish, do you give them a snake instead? 12Or if they ask for an egg, do you
give them a scorpion? Of course not!
13So if you sinful people know how to
give good gifts to your children, how
much more will your heavenly Father
give the Holy Spirit to those who ask
him."

11:2 Some manuscripts add additional phrases from the
Lord's Prayer as it reads in Matt 6:9-13.   11:3 Or *Give us
each day our food for the day;* or *Give us each day our food
for tomorrow.*   11:4 Or *And keep us from being tested.*
11:8 Or *in order to avoid shame,* or *so his reputation won't
be damaged.*   11:11 Some manuscripts add *for bread, do
you give them a stone? Or if they ask.*

PSALM 76:1-12

*For the choir director: A psalm of Asaph.
A song to be accompanied by stringed
instruments.*

1 God is honored in Judah;
     his name is great in Israel.
2 Jerusalem* is where he lives;
     Mount Zion is his home.
3 There he has broken the fiery
     arrows of the enemy,

the shields and swords and
weapons of war.   *Interlude*

⁴ You are glorious and more majestic
than the everlasting mountains.*
⁵ Our boldest enemies have been
plundered.
They lie before us in the sleep
of death.
No warrior could lift a hand
against us.
⁶ At the blast of your breath,
O God of Jacob,
their horses and chariots lay still.

⁷ No wonder you are greatly feared!
Who can stand before you when
your anger explodes?
⁸ From heaven you sentenced your
enemies;
the earth trembled and stood
silent before you.
⁹ You stand up to judge those who
do evil, O God,
and to rescue the oppressed
of the earth.   *Interlude*
¹⁰ Human defiance only enhances
your glory,
for you use it as a weapon.*

¹¹ Make vows to the LORD your God,
and keep them.
Let everyone bring tribute to the
Awesome One.
¹² For he breaks the pride of princes,
and the kings of the earth
fear him.

76:2 Hebrew *Salem,* another name for Jerusalem.   76:4 As
in Greek version; Hebrew reads *than mountains filled with
beasts of prey.*   76:10 The meaning of the Hebrew is
uncertain.

PROVERBS 12:15-17
Fools think their own way is right, but
the wise listen to others. □ A fool is
quick-tempered, but a wise person
stays calm when insulted. □ An honest
witness tells the truth; a false witness
tells lies.

APRIL
5

DEUTERONOMY 28:1-68
"**I**f you fully obey the LORD your God and
carefully keep all his commands that I
am giving you today, the LORD your God
will set you high above all the nations of
the world. ²You will experience all these
blessings if you obey the LORD your God:

³ Your towns and your fields
will be blessed.
⁴ Your children and your crops
will be blessed.
The offspring of your herds
and flocks
will be blessed.
⁵ Your fruit baskets and breadboards
will be blessed.
⁶ Wherever you go and whatever
you do,
you will be blessed.

⁷"The LORD will conquer your enemies when they attack you. They will attack you from one direction, but they
will scatter from you in seven!
⁸"The LORD will guarantee a blessing
on everything you do and will fill your
storehouses with grain. The LORD your
God will bless you in the land he is giving you.
⁹"If you obey the commands of the
LORD your God and walk in his ways, the
LORD will establish you as his holy people as he swore he would do. ¹⁰Then all
the nations of the world will see that
you are a people claimed by the LORD,
and they will stand in awe of you.
¹¹"The LORD will give you prosperity
in the land he swore to your ancestors to
give you, blessing you with many children, numerous livestock, and abundant
crops. ¹²The LORD will send rain at the
proper time from his rich treasury in the
heavens and will bless all the work you
do. You will lend to many nations, but
you will never need to borrow from
them. ¹³If you listen to these commands

of the Lord your God that I am giving you today, and if you carefully obey them, the Lord will make you the head and not the tail, and you will always be on top and never at the bottom. [14]You must not turn away from any of the commands I am giving you today, nor follow after other gods and worship them.

[15]"But if you refuse to listen to the Lord your God and do not obey all the commands and decrees I am giving you today, all these curses will come and overwhelm you:

[16] Your towns and your fields
    will be cursed.
[17] Your fruit baskets and breadboards
    will be cursed.
[18] Your children and your crops
    will be cursed.
    The offspring of your herds
        and flocks
    will be cursed.
[19] Wherever you go and whatever
        you do,
    you will be cursed.

[20]"The Lord himself will send on you curses, confusion, and frustration in everything you do, until at last you are completely destroyed for doing evil and abandoning me. [21]The Lord will afflict you with diseases until none of you are left in the land you are about to enter and occupy. [22]The Lord will strike you with wasting diseases, fever, and inflammation, with scorching heat and drought, and with blight and mildew. These disasters will pursue you until you die. [23]The skies above will be as unyielding as bronze, and the earth beneath will be as hard as iron. [24]The Lord will change the rain that falls on your land into powder, and dust will pour down from the sky until you are destroyed.

[25]"The Lord will cause you to be defeated by your enemies. You will attack your enemies from one direction, but you will scatter from them in seven! You will be an object of horror to all the kingdoms of the earth. [26]Your corpses will be food for all the scavenging birds

and wild animals, and no one will be there to chase them away.

[27]"The Lord will afflict you with the boils of Egypt and with tumors, scurvy, and the itch, from which you cannot be cured. [28]The Lord will strike you with madness, blindness, and panic. [29]You will grope around in broad daylight like a blind person groping in the darkness, but you will not find your way. You will be oppressed and robbed continually, and no one will come to save you.

[30]"You will be engaged to a woman, but another man will sleep with her. You will build a house, but someone else will live in it. You will plant a vineyard, but you will never enjoy its fruit. [31]Your ox will be butchered before your eyes, but you will not eat a single bite of the meat. Your donkey will be taken from you, never to be returned. Your sheep and goats will be given to your enemies, and no one will be there to help you. [32]You will watch as your sons and daughters are taken away as slaves. Your heart will break for them, but you won't be able to help them. [33]A foreign nation you have never heard about will eat the crops you worked so hard to grow. You will suffer under constant oppression and harsh treatment. [34]You will go mad because of all the tragedy you see around you. [35]The Lord will cover your knees and legs with incurable boils. In fact, you will be covered from head to foot.

[36]"The Lord will exile you and your king to a nation unknown to you and your ancestors. There in exile you will worship gods of wood and stone! [37]You will become an object of horror, ridicule, and mockery among all the nations to which the Lord sends you.

[38]"You will plant much but harvest little, for locusts will eat your crops. [39]You will plant vineyards and care for them, but you will not drink the wine or eat the grapes, for worms will destroy the vines. [40]You will grow olive trees throughout your land, but you will never use the olive oil, for the fruit will drop before it ripens. [41]You will have sons and daughters, but you will lose them, for they will be

led away into captivity. [42]Swarms of insects will destroy your trees and crops.

[43]"The foreigners living among you will become stronger and stronger, while you become weaker and weaker. [44]They will lend money to you, but you will not lend to them. They will be the head, and you will be the tail!

[45]"If you refuse to listen to the Lord your God and to obey the commands and decrees he has given you, all these curses will pursue and overtake you until you are destroyed. [46]These horrors will serve as a sign and warning among you and your descendants forever. [47]If you do not serve the Lord your God with joy and enthusiasm for the abundant benefits you have received, [48]you will serve your enemies whom the Lord will send against you. You will be left hungry, thirsty, naked, and lacking in everything. The Lord will put an iron yoke on your neck, oppressing you harshly until he has destroyed you.

[49]"The Lord will bring a distant nation against you from the end of the earth, and it will swoop down on you like a vulture. It is a nation whose language you do not understand, [50]a fierce and heartless nation that shows no respect for the old and no pity for the young. [51]Its armies will devour your livestock and crops, and you will be destroyed. They will leave you no grain, new wine, olive oil, calves, or lambs, and you will starve to death. [52]They will attack your cities until all the fortified walls in your land—the walls you trusted to protect you—are knocked down. They will attack all the towns in the land the Lord your God has given you.

[53]"The siege and terrible distress of the enemy's attack will be so severe that you will eat the flesh of your own sons and daughters, whom the Lord your God has given you. [54]The most tenderhearted man among you will have no compassion for his own brother, his beloved wife, and his surviving children. [55]He will refuse to share with them the flesh he is devouring—the flesh of one of his own children—because he has nothing

else to eat during the siege and terrible distress that your enemy will inflict on all your towns. [56]The most tender and delicate woman among you—so delicate she would not so much as touch the ground with her foot—will be selfish toward the husband she loves and toward her own son or daughter. [57]She will hide from them the afterbirth and the new baby she has borne, so that she herself can secretly eat them. She will have nothing else to eat during the siege and terrible distress that your enemy will inflict on all your towns.

[58]"If you refuse to obey all the words of instruction that are written in this book, and if you do not fear the glorious and awesome name of the Lord your God, [59]then the Lord will overwhelm you and your children with indescribable plagues. These plagues will be intense and without relief, making you miserable and unbearably sick. [60]He will afflict you with all the diseases of Egypt that you feared so much, and you will have no relief. [61]The Lord will afflict you with every sickness and plague there is, even those not mentioned in this Book of Instruction, until you are destroyed. [62]Though you become as numerous as the stars in the sky, few of you will be left because you would not listen to the Lord your God.

[63]"Just as the Lord has found great pleasure in causing you to prosper and multiply, the Lord will find pleasure in destroying you. You will be torn from the land you are about to enter and occupy. [64]For the Lord will scatter you among all the nations from one end of the earth to the other. There you will worship foreign gods that neither you nor your ancestors have known, gods made of wood and stone! [65]There among those nations you will find no peace or place to rest. And the Lord will cause your heart to tremble, your eyesight to fail, and your soul to despair. [66]Your life will constantly hang in the balance. You will live night and day in fear, unsure if you will survive. [67]In the morning you will say, 'If only it were night!' And in the evening

you will say, 'If only it were morning!' For you will be terrified by the awful horrors you see around you. [68]Then the LORD will send you back to Egypt in ships, to a destination I promised you would never see again. There you will offer to sell yourselves to your enemies as slaves, but no one will buy you."

LUKE 11:14-36

One day Jesus cast out a demon from a man who couldn't speak, and when the demon was gone, the man began to speak. The crowds were amazed, [15]but some of them said, "No wonder he can cast out demons. He gets his power from Satan,* the prince of demons." [16]Others, trying to test Jesus, demanded that he show them a miraculous sign from heaven to prove his authority.

[17]He knew their thoughts, so he said, "Any kingdom divided by civil war is doomed. A family splintered by feuding will fall apart. [18]You say I am empowered by Satan. But if Satan is divided and fighting against himself, how can his kingdom survive? [19]And if I am empowered by Satan, what about your own exorcists? They cast out demons, too, so they will condemn you for what you have said. [20]But if I am casting out demons by the power of God,* then the Kingdom of God has arrived among you. [21]For when a strong man like Satan is fully armed and guards his palace, his possessions are safe— [22]until someone even stronger attacks and overpowers him, strips him of his weapons, and carries off his belongings.

[23]"Anyone who isn't with me opposes me, and anyone who isn't working with me is actually working against me.

[24]"When an evil* spirit leaves a person, it goes into the desert, searching for rest. But when it finds none, it says, 'I will return to the person I came from.' [25]So it returns and finds that its former home is all swept and in order. [26]Then the spirit finds seven other spirits more evil than itself, and they all enter the person and live there. And so that person is worse off than before."

[27]As he was speaking, a woman in the crowd called out, "God bless your mother—the womb from which you came, and the breasts that nursed you!"

[28]Jesus replied, "But even more blessed are all who hear the word of God and put it into practice."

[29]As the crowd pressed in on Jesus, he said, "This evil generation keeps asking me to show them a miraculous sign. But the only sign I will give them is the sign of Jonah. [30]What happened to him was a sign to the people of Nineveh that God had sent him. What happens to the Son of Man* will be a sign to these people that he was sent by God.

[31]"The queen of Sheba* will stand up against this generation on judgment day and condemn it, for she came from a distant land to hear the wisdom of Solomon. Now someone greater than Solomon is here—but you refuse to listen. [32]The people of Nineveh will also stand up against this generation on judgment day and condemn it, for they repented of their sins at the preaching of Jonah. Now someone greater than Jonah is here—but you refuse to repent.

[33]"No one lights a lamp and then hides it or puts it under a basket.* Instead, a lamp is placed on a stand, where its light can be seen by all who enter the house.

[34]"Your eye is a lamp that provides light for your body. When your eye is good, your whole body is filled with light. But when it is bad, your body is filled with darkness. [35]Make sure that the light you think you have is not actually darkness. [36]If you are filled with light, with no dark corners, then your whole life will be radiant, as though a floodlight were filling you with light."

11:15 Greek *Beelzeboul;* also in 11:18, 19. Other manuscripts read *Beezeboul;* Latin version reads *Beelzebub.*   11:20 Greek *by the finger of God.* 11:24 Greek *unclean.*   11:30 "Son of Man" is a title Jesus used for himself.   11:31 Greek *The queen of the south.* 11:33 Some manuscripts omit *or puts it under a basket.*

PSALM 77:1-20
For Jeduthun, the choir director: A psalm of Asaph.

[1] I cry out to God; yes, I shout.
    Oh, that God would listen to me!

² When I was in deep trouble,
  I searched for the Lord.
All night long I prayed, with
    hands lifted toward heaven,
  but my soul was not comforted.
³ I think of God, and I moan,
  overwhelmed with longing
    for his help.   *Interlude*

⁴ You don't let me sleep.
  I am too distressed even to pray!
⁵ I think of the good old days,
  long since ended,
⁶ when my nights were filled with
    joyful songs.
  I search my soul and ponder
    the difference now.
⁷ Has the Lord rejected me forever?
  Will he never again be kind to me?
⁸ Is his unfailing love gone forever?
  Have his promises permanently
    failed?
⁹ Has God forgotten to be gracious?
  Has he slammed the door
    on his compassion?   *Interlude*

¹⁰ And I said, "This is my fate;
  the Most High has turned his
    hand against me."
¹¹ But then I recall all you have done,
  O Lord;
  I remember your wonderful
    deeds of long ago.
¹² They are constantly in my thoughts.
  I cannot stop thinking about your
    mighty works.

¹³ O God, your ways are holy.
  Is there any god as mighty as you?
¹⁴ You are the God of great wonders!
  You demonstrate your awesome
    power among the nations.
¹⁵ By your strong arm, you redeemed
    your people,
  the descendants of Jacob
    and Joseph.   *Interlude*

¹⁶ When the Red Sea* saw you, O God,
  its waters looked and trembled!
  The sea quaked to its very depths.
¹⁷ The clouds poured down rain;
  the thunder rumbled in the sky.
  Your arrows of lightning flashed.

¹⁸ Your thunder roared from
    the whirlwind;
  the lightning lit up the world!
  The earth trembled and shook.
¹⁹ Your road led through the sea,
  your pathway through the
    mighty waters—
  a pathway no one knew
    was there!
²⁰ You led your people along that road
    like a flock of sheep,
  with Moses and Aaron as their
    shepherds.

77:16 Hebrew *the waters.*

PROVERBS 12:18
Some people make cutting remarks,
but the words of the wise bring healing.

APRIL 6

DEUTERONOMY 29:1–30:20
¹***T**hese are the terms of the covenant
the Lord commanded Moses to make
with the Israelites while they were in
the land of Moab, in addition to the covenant he had made with them at Mount
Sinai.*

²*Moses summoned all the Israelites
and said to them, "You have seen with
your own eyes everything the Lord did
in the land of Egypt to Pharaoh and to
all his servants and to his whole country—³all the great tests of strength, the
miraculous signs, and the amazing
wonders. ⁴But to this day the Lord has
not given you minds that understand,
nor eyes that see, nor ears that hear!
⁵For forty years I led you through the
wilderness, yet your clothes and sandals
did not wear out. ⁶You ate no bread and
drank no wine or other alcoholic drink,
but he gave you food so you would know
that he is the Lord your God.

⁷"When we came here, King Sihon of
Heshbon and King Og of Bashan came

out to fight against us, but we defeated them. [8]We took their land and gave it to the tribes of Reuben and Gad and to the half-tribe of Manasseh as their grant of land.

[9]"Therefore, obey the terms of this covenant so that you will prosper in everything you do. [10]All of you—tribal leaders, elders, officers, all the men of Israel—are standing today in the presence of the LORD your God. [11]Your little ones and your wives are with you, as well as the foreigners living among you who chop your wood and carry your water. [12]You are standing here today to enter into the covenant of the LORD your God. The LORD is making this covenant, including the curses. [13]By entering into the covenant today, he will establish you as his people and confirm that he is your God, just as he promised you and as he swore to your ancestors Abraham, Isaac, and Jacob.

[14]"But you are not the only ones with whom I am making this covenant with its curses. [15]I am making this covenant both with you who stand here today in the presence of the LORD our God, and also with the future generations who are not standing here today.

[16]"You remember how we lived in the land of Egypt and how we traveled through the lands of enemy nations as we left. [17]You have seen their detestable practices and their idols* made of wood, stone, silver, and gold. [18]I am making this covenant with you so that no one among you—no man, woman, clan, or tribe—will turn away from the LORD our God to worship these gods of other nations, and so that no root among you bears bitter and poisonous fruit.

[19]"Those who hear the warnings of this curse should not congratulate themselves, thinking, 'I am safe, even though I am following the desires of my own stubborn heart.' This would lead to utter ruin! [20]The LORD will never pardon such people. Instead his anger and jealousy will burn against them. All the curses written in this book will come down on them, and the LORD will erase their names from under heaven. [21]The LORD will separate them from all the tribes of Israel, to pour out on them all the curses of the covenant recorded in this Book of Instruction.

[22]"Then the generations to come, both your own descendants and the foreigners who come from distant lands, will see the devastation of the land and the diseases the LORD inflicts on it. [23]They will exclaim, 'The whole land is devastated by sulfur and salt. It is a wasteland with nothing planted and nothing growing, not even a blade of grass. It is like the cities of Sodom and Gomorrah, Admah and Zeboiim, which the LORD destroyed in his intense anger.'

[24]"And all the surrounding nations will ask, 'Why has the LORD done this to this land? Why was he so angry?'

[25]"And the answer will be, 'This happened because the people of the land abandoned the covenant that the LORD, the God of their ancestors, made with them when he brought them out of the land of Egypt. [26]Instead, they turned away to serve and worship gods they had not known before, gods that were not from the LORD. [27]That is why the LORD's anger has burned against this land, bringing down on it every curse recorded in this book. [28]In great anger and fury the LORD uprooted his people from their land and banished them to another land, where they still live today!'

[29]"The LORD our God has secrets known to no one. We are not accountable for them, but we and our children are accountable forever for all that he has revealed to us, so that we may obey all the terms of these instructions.

[30:1]"In the future, when you experience all these blessings and curses I have listed for you, and when you are living among the nations to which the LORD your God has exiled you, take to heart all these instructions. [2]If at that time you and your children return to the LORD your God, and if you obey with all your heart and all your soul all the commands I have given you today, [3]then the LORD your God will restore your fortunes. He will have mercy on you and gather you back from all the nations where he has scattered you. [4]Even though you are banished to the ends of the earth, the LORD your God will gather you from there and bring you back again. [5]The LORD your God will return you to the land that belonged to your ancestors, and you will possess that land again. Then he will make you even more prosperous and numerous than your ancestors!

[6]"The LORD your God will change your heart* and the hearts of all your descendants, so that you will love him with all your heart and soul and so you may live! [7]The LORD your God will inflict all these curses on your enemies and on those who hate and persecute you. [8]Then you will again obey the LORD and keep all his commands that I am giving you today.

[9]"The LORD your God will then make you successful in everything you do. He will give you many children and numerous livestock, and he will cause your fields to produce abundant harvests, for the LORD will again delight in being good to you as he was to your ancestors. [10]The LORD your God will delight in you if you obey his voice and keep the commands and decrees written in this Book of Instruction, and if you turn to the LORD your God with all your heart and soul.

[11]"This command I am giving you today is not too difficult for you to understand, and it is not beyond your reach. [12]It is not kept in heaven, so distant that you must ask, 'Who will go up to heaven and bring it down so we can hear it and obey?' [13]It is not kept beyond the sea, so far away that you must ask, 'Who will cross the sea to bring it to us so we can hear it and obey?' [14]No, the message is very close at hand; it is on your lips and in your heart so that you can obey it.

[15]"Now listen! Today I am giving you a choice between life and death, between prosperity and disaster. [16]For I command you this day to love the LORD your God and to keep his commands, decrees, and regulations by walking in his ways. If you do this, you will live and multiply, and the LORD your God will bless you and the land you are about to enter and occupy.

[17]"But if your heart turns away and you refuse to listen, and if you are drawn away to serve and worship other gods, [18]then I warn you now that you will certainly be destroyed. You will not live a long, good life in the land you are crossing the Jordan to occupy.

[19]**"Today I have given you the choice between life and death, between blessings and curses. Now I call on heaven and earth to witness the choice you make. Oh, that you would choose life, so that you and your descendants might live! [20]You can make this choice by loving the LORD your God, obeying him, and committing yourself firmly to him. This* is the key to your life. And if you love and obey the LORD, you will live long in the land the LORD swore to give your ancestors Abraham, Isaac, and Jacob."**

29:1a Verse 29:1 is numbered 28:69 in Hebrew text.
29:1b Hebrew *Horeb*, another name for Sinai.
29:2 Verses 29:2-29 are numbered 29:1-28 in Hebrew text.   29:17 The Hebrew term (literally *round things*) probably alludes to dung.   30:6 Hebrew *circumcise your heart*.   30:20 Or *He*.

LUKE 11:37–12:7

As Jesus was speaking, one of the Pharisees invited him home for a meal. So he went in and took his place at the table.* [38]His host was amazed to see that he sat down to eat without first performing the hand-washing ceremony required by Jewish custom. [39]Then the Lord said to him, "You Pharisees are so careful to clean the outside of the cup and the dish, but inside you are filthy—full of greed and wickedness! [40]Fools! Didn't God make the inside as well as the outside? [41]So clean the inside by giving gifts to the poor, and you will be clean all over.

[42]"What sorrow awaits you Pharisees! For you are careful to tithe even the tiniest income from your herb gardens,* but you ignore justice and the love of God. You should tithe, yes, but do not neglect the more important things.

43"What sorrow awaits you Pharisees! For you love to sit in the seats of honor in the synagogues and receive respectful greetings as you walk in the marketplaces. 44Yes, what sorrow awaits you! For you are like hidden graves in a field. People walk over them without knowing the corruption they are stepping on."

45"Teacher," said an expert in religious law, "you have insulted us, too, in what you just said."

46"Yes," said Jesus, "what sorrow also awaits you experts in religious law! For you crush people with impossible religious demands, and you never lift a finger to ease the burden. 47What sorrow awaits you! For you build monuments for the prophets your own ancestors killed long ago. 48But in fact, you stand as witnesses who agree with what your ancestors did. They killed the prophets, and you join in their crime by building the monuments! 49This is what God in his wisdom said about you:* 'I will send prophets and apostles to them, but they will kill some and persecute the others.'

50"As a result, this generation will be held responsible for the murder of all God's prophets from the creation of the world—51from the murder of Abel to the murder of Zechariah, who was killed between the altar and the sanctuary. Yes, it will certainly be charged against this generation.

52"What sorrow awaits you experts in religious law! For you remove the key to knowledge from the people. You don't enter the Kingdom yourselves, and you prevent others from entering."

53As Jesus was leaving, the teachers of religious law and the Pharisees became hostile and tried to provoke him with many questions. 54They wanted to trap him into saying something they could use against him.

12:1MEANWHILE, the crowds grew until thousands were milling about and stepping on each other. Jesus turned first to his disciples and warned them, "Beware of the yeast of the Pharisees—their hypocrisy. 2The time is coming when everything that is covered up will be revealed, and all that is secret will be made known to all. 3Whatever you have said in the dark will be heard in the light, and what you have whispered behind closed doors will be shouted from the housetops for all to hear!

4"Dear friends, don't be afraid of those who want to kill your body; they cannot do any more to you after that. 5But I'll tell you whom to fear. Fear God, who has the power to kill you and then throw you into hell.* Yes, he's the one to fear.

6"What is the price of five sparrows—two copper coins*? Yet God does not forget a single one of them. 7And the very hairs on your head are all numbered. So don't be afraid; you are more valuable to God than a whole flock of sparrows."

11:37 Or *and reclined.* 11:42 Greek *tithe the mint, the rue, and every herb.* 11:49 Greek *Therefore, the wisdom of God said.* 12:5 Greek *Gehenna.* 12:6 Greek *two assaria* [Roman coins equal to ⅟₁₆ of a denarius].

PSALM 78:1-31
A psalm of Asaph.

1 **O** my people, listen to my
      instructions.
   Open your ears to what
      I am saying,
2   for I will speak to you in
      a parable.
   I will teach you hidden lessons
      from our past—
3   stories we have heard and
      known,
   stories our ancestors handed
      down to us.
4 We will not hide these truths from
      our children;
   we will tell the next generation
   about the glorious deeds
      of the LORD,
   about his power and his mighty
      wonders.
5 For he issued his laws to Jacob;
   he gave his instructions to Israel.
   He commanded our ancestors
      to teach them to their children,
6 so the next generation might
      know them—

even the children not yet born—
and they in turn will teach their
own children.
7 So each generation should set its
hope anew on God,
not forgetting his glorious
miracles
and obeying his commands.
8 Then they will not be like their
ancestors—
stubborn, rebellious, and
unfaithful,
refusing to give their hearts to God.

9 The warriors of Ephraim, though
armed with bows,
turned their backs and fled on
the day of battle.
10 They did not keep God's covenant
and refused to live by his
instructions.
11 They forgot what he had done—
the great wonders he had shown
them,
12 the miracles he did for their
ancestors
on the plain of Zoan in the land
of Egypt.
13 For he divided the sea and led them
through,
making the water stand up like
walls!
14 In the daytime he led them
by a cloud,
and all night by a pillar of fire.
15 He split open the rocks in the
wilderness
to give them water, as from
a gushing spring.
16 He made streams pour from
the rock,
making the waters flow down
like a river!

17 Yet they kept on sinning against
him,
rebelling against the Most High
in the desert.
18 They stubbornly tested God in
their hearts,
demanding the foods they craved.
19 They even spoke against God
himself, saying,

"God can't give us food in the
wilderness.
20 Yes, he can strike a rock so water
gushes out,
but he can't give his people bread
and meat."
21 When the LORD heard them, he was
furious.
The fire of his wrath burned
against Jacob.
Yes, his anger rose against Israel,
22 for they did not believe God
or trust him to care for them.
23 But he commanded the skies
to open;
he opened the doors of heaven.
24 He rained down manna for them
to eat;
he gave them bread from heaven.
25 They ate the food of angels!
God gave them all they could
hold.
26 He released the east wind in the
heavens
and guided the south wind
by his mighty power.
27 He rained down meat as thick
as dust—
birds as plentiful as the sand
on the seashore!
28 He caused the birds to fall within
their camp
and all around their tents.
29 The people ate their fill.
He gave them what they craved.
30 But before they satisfied their
craving,
while the meat was yet in their
mouths,
31 the anger of God rose against them,
and he killed their strongest men.
He struck down the finest of
Israel's young men.

78:TITLE Hebrew *maskil*. This may be a literary or musical term.

PROVERBS 12:19-20

Truthful words stand the test of time,
but lies are soon exposed. □ Deceit fills
hearts that are plotting evil; joy fills
hearts that are planning peace!

APRIL 7

DEUTERONOMY 31:1–32:27

When Moses had finished giving these instructions* to all the people of Israel, [2] he said, "I am now 120 years old, and I am no longer able to lead you. The Lord has told me, 'You will not cross the Jordan River.' [3] But the Lord your God himself will cross over ahead of you. He will destroy the nations living there, and you will take possession of their land. Joshua will lead you across the river, just as the Lord promised.

[4] "The Lord will destroy the nations living in the land, just as he destroyed Sihon and Og, the kings of the Amorites. [5] The Lord will hand over to you the people who live there, and you must deal with them as I have commanded you. [6] So be strong and courageous! Do not be afraid and do not panic before them. For the Lord your God will personally go ahead of you. He will neither fail you nor abandon you."

[7] Then Moses called for Joshua, and as all Israel watched, he said to him, "Be strong and courageous! For you will lead these people into the land that the Lord swore to their ancestors he would give them. You are the one who will divide it among them as their grants of land. [8] Do not be afraid or discouraged, for the Lord will personally go ahead of you. He will be with you; he will neither fail you nor abandon you."

[9] So Moses wrote this entire body of instruction in a book and gave it to the priests, who carried the Ark of the Lord's Covenant, and to the elders of Israel. [10] Then Moses gave them this command: "At the end of every seventh year, the Year of Release, during the Festival of Shelters, [11] you must read this Book of Instruction to all the people of Israel when they assemble before the Lord your God at the place he chooses. [12] Call them all together—men, women, children, and the foreigners living in your towns—so they may hear this Book of Instruction and learn to fear the Lord your God and carefully obey all the terms of these instructions. [13] Do this so that your children who have not known these instructions will hear them and will learn to fear the Lord your God. Do this as long as you live in the land you are crossing the Jordan to occupy."

[14] Then the Lord said to Moses, "The time has come for you to die. Call Joshua and present yourselves at the Tabernacle,* so that I may commission him there." So Moses and Joshua went and presented themselves at the Tabernacle. [15] And the Lord appeared to them in a pillar of cloud that stood at the entrance to the sacred tent.

[16] The Lord said to Moses, "You are about to die and join your ancestors. After you are gone, these people will begin to worship foreign gods, the gods of the land where they are going. They will abandon me and break my covenant that I have made with them. [17] Then my anger will blaze forth against them. I will abandon them, hiding my face from them, and they will be devoured. Terrible trouble will come down on them, and on that day they will say, 'These disasters have come down on us because God is no longer among us!' [18] At that time I will hide my face from them on account of all the evil they commit by worshiping other gods.

[19] "So write down the words of this song, and teach it to the people of Israel. Help them learn it, so it may serve as a witness for me against them. [20] For I will bring them into the land I swore to give their ancestors—a land flowing with milk and honey. There they will become prosperous, eat all the food they want, and become fat. But they will begin to worship other gods; they will despise me and break my covenant. [21] And when great disasters come down on them, this song will stand as evidence against them, for it will never be forgotten by their descendants. I know the intentions of these people, even now before

they have entered the land I swore to give them."

²²So that very day Moses wrote down the words of the song and taught it to the Israelites.

²³Then the Lord commissioned Joshua son of Nun with these words: "Be strong and courageous, for you must bring the people of Israel into the land I swore to give them. I will be with you."

²⁴When Moses had finished writing this entire body of instruction in a book, ²⁵he gave this command to the Levites who carried the Ark of the Lord's Covenant: ²⁶"Take this Book of Instruction and place it beside the Ark of the Covenant of the Lord your God, so it may remain there as a witness against the people of Israel. ²⁷For I know how rebellious and stubborn you are. Even now, while I am still alive and am here with you, you have rebelled against the Lord. How much more rebellious will you be after my death!

²⁸"Now summon all the elders and officials of your tribes, so that I can speak to them directly and call heaven and earth to witness against them. ²⁹I know that after my death you will become utterly corrupt and will turn from the way I have commanded you to follow. In the days to come, disaster will come down on you, for you will do what is evil in the Lord's sight, making him very angry with your actions."

³⁰So Moses recited this entire song publicly to the assembly of Israel:

³²:¹"Listen, O heavens, and I will speak!
    Hear, O earth, the words that I say!
² Let my teaching fall on you like rain;
    let my speech settle like dew.
  Let my words fall like rain on
      tender grass,
    like gentle showers on young
      plants.
³ I will proclaim the name
      of the Lord;
    how glorious is our God!
⁴ He is the Rock; his deeds
      are perfect.
    Everything he does is just and fair.

He is a faithful God who does
      no wrong;
    how just and upright he is!

⁵ "But they have acted corruptly
      toward him;
    when they act so perversely,
  are they really his children?*
    They are a deceitful and twisted
      generation.
⁶ Is this the way you repay the Lord,
    you foolish and senseless people?
  Isn't he your Father who created
      you?
    Has he not made you and
      established you?
⁷ Remember the days of long ago;
    think about the generations past.
  Ask your father, and he will inform
      you.
    Inquire of your elders, and they
      will tell you.
⁸ When the Most High assigned lands
      to the nations,
    when he divided up the human
      race,
  he established the boundaries
      of the peoples
    according to the number in
      his heavenly court.*

⁹ "For the people of Israel belong
      to the Lord;
    Jacob is his special possession.
¹⁰ He found them in a desert land,
    in an empty, howling wasteland.
  He surrounded them and watched
      over them;
    he guarded them as he would
      guard his own eyes.*
¹¹ Like an eagle that rouses her chicks
    and hovers over her young,
  so he spread his wings to take
      them up
    and carried them safely on
      his pinions.
¹² The Lord alone guided them;
    they followed no foreign gods.
¹³ He let them ride over the highlands
    and feast on the crops of the
      fields.
  He nourished them with honey
      from the rock

and olive oil from the stony
ground.
14 He fed them yogurt from the herd
and milk from the flock,
together with the fat of lambs.
He gave them choice rams from
Bashan, and goats,
together with the choicest wheat.
You drank the finest wine,
made from the juice of grapes.

15 "But Israel* soon became fat and
unruly;
the people grew heavy, plump,
and stuffed!
Then they abandoned the God who
had made them;
they made light of the Rock
of their salvation.
16 They stirred up his jealousy by
worshiping foreign gods;
they provoked his fury with
detestable deeds.
17 They offered sacrifices to demons,
which are not God,
to gods they had not known
before,
to new gods only recently arrived,
to gods their ancestors had never
feared.
18 You neglected the Rock who had
fathered you;
you forgot the God who had given
you birth.

19 "The LORD saw this and drew back,
provoked to anger by his own
sons and daughters.
20 He said, 'I will abandon them;
then see what becomes of them.
For they are a twisted generation,
children without integrity.
21 They have roused my jealousy by
worshiping things that are
not God;
they have provoked my anger
with their useless idols.
Now I will rouse their jealousy
through people who are not
even a people;
I will provoke their anger through
the foolish Gentiles.
22 For my anger blazes forth like fire

and burns to the depths
of the grave.*
It devours the earth and all its crops
and ignites the foundations of the
mountains.
23 I will heap disasters upon them
and shoot them down with my
arrows.
24 I will weaken them with famine,
burning fever, and deadly disease.
I will send the fangs of wild beasts
and poisonous snakes that glide
in the dust.
25 Outside, the sword will bring death,
and inside, terror will strike
both young men and young women,
both infants and the aged.
26 I would have annihilated them,
wiping out even the memory
of them.
27 But I feared the taunt of Israel's
enemy,
who might misunderstand
and say,
"Our own power has triumphed!
The LORD had nothing to do
with this!"'"

31:1 As in Dead Sea Scrolls and Greek version; Masoretic
Text reads *Moses went and spoke*. 31:14 Hebrew *Tent of
Meeting;* also in 31:14b. 32:5 The meaning of the
Hebrew is uncertain. 32:8 As in Dead Sea Scrolls, which
read *the number of the sons of God,* and Greek version,
which reads *the number of the angels of God;* Masoretic
Text reads *the number of the sons of Israel.* 32:10 Hebrew
as the pupil of his eye. 32:15 Hebrew *Jeshurun,* a term of
endearment for Israel. 32:22 Hebrew *of Sheol.*

LUKE 12:8-34
"I tell you the truth, everyone who ac-
knowledges me publicly here on earth,
the Son of Man* will also acknowledge
in the presence of God's angels. 9But
anyone who denies me here on earth will
be denied before God's angels. 10Anyone
who speaks against the Son of Man can
be forgiven, but anyone who blasphemes
the Holy Spirit will not be forgiven.

11"And when you are brought to trial
in the synagogues and before rulers and
authorities, don't worry about how to
defend yourself or what to say, 12for the
Holy Spirit will teach you at that time
what needs to be said."

13Then someone called from the

crowd, "Teacher, please tell my brother to divide our father's estate with me."

[14]Jesus replied, "Friend, who made me a judge over you to decide such things as that?" [15]Then he said, "Beware! Guard against every kind of greed. Life is not measured by how much you own."

[16]Then he told them a story: "A rich man had a fertile farm that produced fine crops. [17]He said to himself, 'What should I do? I don't have room for all my crops.' [18]Then he said, 'I know! I'll tear down my barns and build bigger ones. Then I'll have room enough to store all my wheat and other goods. [19]And I'll sit back and say to myself, "My friend, you have enough stored away for years to come. Now take it easy! Eat, drink, and be merry!"'

[20]"But God said to him, 'You fool! You will die this very night. Then who will get everything you worked for?'

[21]"Yes, a person is a fool to store up earthly wealth but not have a rich relationship with God."

[22]Then, turning to his disciples, Jesus said, "That is why I tell you not to worry about everyday life—whether you have enough food to eat or enough clothes to wear. [23]For life is more than food, and your body more than clothing. [24]Look at the ravens. They don't plant or harvest or store food in barns, for God feeds them. And you are far more valuable to him than any birds! [25]Can all your worries add a single moment to your life? [26]And if worry can't accomplish a little thing like that, what's the use of worrying over bigger things?

[27]"Look at the lilies and how they grow. They don't work or make their clothing, yet Solomon in all his glory was not dressed as beautifully as they are. [28]And if God cares so wonderfully for flowers that are here today and thrown into the fire tomorrow, he will certainly care for you. Why do you have so little faith?

[29]"And don't be concerned about what to eat and what to drink. Don't worry about such things. [30]These things dominate the thoughts of unbelievers all over the world, but your Father already knows your needs. [31]Seek the Kingdom of God above all else, and he will give you everything you need.

[32]"So don't be afraid, little flock. For it gives your Father great happiness to give you the Kingdom.

[33]"Sell your possessions and give to those in need. This will store up treasure for you in heaven! And the purses of heaven never get old or develop holes. Your treasure will be safe; no thief can steal it and no moth can destroy it. [34]Wherever your treasure is, there the desires of your heart will also be."

12:8 "Son of Man" is a title Jesus used for himself.

PSALM 78:32-55

But in spite of this, the people
        kept sinning.
    Despite his wonders, they refused
        to trust him.
[33] So he ended their lives in failure,
        their years in terror.
[34] When God began killing them,
        they finally sought him.
    They repented and took God
        seriously.
[35] Then they remembered that God
        was their rock,
    that God Most High* was
        their redeemer.
[36] But all they gave him was lip
        service;
    they lied to him with their
        tongues.
[37] Their hearts were not loyal to him.
    They did not keep his covenant.
[38] Yet he was merciful and forgave
        their sins
    and did not destroy them all.
    Many times he held back his
        anger
    and did not unleash his fury!
[39] For he remembered that they were
        merely mortal,
    gone like a breath of wind that
        never returns.

[40] Oh, how often they rebelled against
        him in the wilderness

and grieved his heart in that dry
 wasteland.
⁴¹ Again and again they tested God's
 patience
 and provoked the Holy One
 of Israel.
⁴² They did not remember his power
 and how he rescued them from
 their enemies.
⁴³ They did not remember his
 miraculous signs in Egypt,
 his wonders on the plain of Zoan.
⁴⁴ For he turned their rivers into
 blood,
 so no one could drink from
 the streams.
⁴⁵ He sent vast swarms of flies to
 consume them
 and hordes of frogs to ruin them.
⁴⁶ He gave their crops to caterpillars;
 their harvest was consumed
 by locusts.
⁴⁷ He destroyed their grapevines
 with hail
 and shattered their sycamore-figs
 with sleet.
⁴⁸ He abandoned their cattle to
 the hail,
 their livestock to bolts of
 lightning.
⁴⁹ He loosed on them his fierce
 anger—
 all his fury, rage, and hostility.
 He dispatched against them
 a band of destroying angels.
⁵⁰ He turned his anger against them;
 he did not spare the Egyptians'
 lives
 but ravaged them with the plague.
⁵¹ He killed the oldest son in each
 Egyptian family,
 the flower of youth throughout
 the land of Egypt.*
⁵² But he led his own people like
 a flock of sheep,
 guiding them safely through
 the wilderness.
⁵³ He kept them safe so they were
 not afraid;
 but the sea covered their enemies.
⁵⁴ He brought them to the border
 of his holy land,

to this land of hills he had won
 for them.
⁵⁵ He drove out the nations before
 them;
 he gave them their inheritance
 by lot.
 He settled the tribes of Israel into
 their homes.

78:35 Hebrew *El-Elyon.*   **78:51** Hebrew *in the tents of Ham.*

PROVERBS 12:21-23
No harm comes to the godly, but the wicked have their fill of trouble. □ The LORD detests lying lips, but he delights in those who tell the truth. □ The wise don't make a show of their knowledge, but fools broadcast their foolishness.

APRIL
8

DEUTERONOMY 32:28-52
 "**B**ut Israel is a senseless nation;
 the people are foolish, without
 understanding.
²⁹ Oh, that they were wise and could
 understand this!
 Oh, that they might know their
 fate!
³⁰ How could one person chase
 a thousand of them,
 and two people put ten thousand
 to flight,
 unless their Rock had sold them,
 unless the LORD had given
 them up?
³¹ But the rock of our enemies is not
 like our Rock,
 as even they recognize.*
³² Their vine grows from the vine
 of Sodom,
 from the vineyards of Gomorrah.
 Their grapes are poison,
 and their clusters are bitter.
³³ Their wine is the venom of serpents,
 the deadly poison of cobras.

³⁴ "The LORD says, 'Am I not storing
        up these things,
    sealing them away in my treasury?
³⁵ I will take revenge; I will pay
        them back.
    In due time their feet will slip.
    Their day of disaster will arrive,
        and their destiny will overtake
        them.'

³⁶ "Indeed, the LORD will give justice
        to his people,
    and he will change his mind
        about* his servants,
    when he sees their strength is gone
        and no one is left, slave or free.
³⁷ Then he will ask, 'Where are
        their gods,
    the rocks they fled to for refuge?
³⁸ Where now are those gods,
        who ate the fat of their sacrifices
        and drank the wine of their
        offerings?
    Let those gods arise and help you!
    Let them provide you with shelter!
³⁹ Look now; I myself am he!
    There is no other god but me!
    I am the one who kills and gives life;
    I am the one who wounds
        and heals;
        no one can be rescued from my
        powerful hand!
⁴⁰ Now I raise my hand to heaven
        and declare, "As surely as I live,
⁴¹ when I sharpen my flashing sword
        and begin to carry out justice,
    I will take revenge on my enemies
        and repay those who reject me.
⁴² I will make my arrows drunk with
        blood,
    and my sword will devour flesh—
    the blood of the slaughtered
        and the captives,
    and the heads of the enemy
        leaders."'

⁴³ "Rejoice with him, you heavens,
        and let all of God's angels worship
        him.*
    Rejoice with his people, you nations,
        and let all the angels be
        strengthened in him.*

For he will avenge the blood
        of his servants;
    he will take revenge against
        his enemies.
    He will repay those who hate him*
        and cleanse the land for his
        people."

⁴⁴So Moses came with Joshua* son of
Nun and recited all the words of this
song to the people.

⁴⁵When Moses had finished reciting
all these words to the people of Israel,
⁴⁶he added: "Take to heart all the words
of warning I have given you today. Pass
them on as a command to your children
so they will obey every word of these instructions. ⁴⁷These instructions are not
empty words—they are your life! By
obeying them you will enjoy a long life
in the land you will occupy when you
cross the Jordan River."

⁴⁸That same day the LORD said to
Moses, ⁴⁹"Go to Moab, to the mountains
east of the river,* and climb Mount Nebo,
which is across from Jericho. Look out
across the land of Canaan, the land I am
giving to the people of Israel as their own
special possession. ⁵⁰Then you will die
there on the mountain. You will join your
ancestors, just as Aaron, your brother,
died on Mount Hor and joined his ancestors. ⁵¹For both of you betrayed me with
the Israelites at the waters of Meribah at
Kadesh* in the wilderness of Zin. You
failed to demonstrate my holiness to the
people of Israel there. ⁵²So you will see
the land from a distance, but you may not
enter the land I am giving to the people of
Israel."

32:31 The meaning of the Hebrew is uncertain. Greek
version reads *our enemies are fools.*   32:36 Or *will take
revenge for.*   32:43a As in Dead Sea Scrolls and Greek
version; Masoretic Text lacks the first two lines. Compare
Heb 1:6.   32:43b As in Greek version; Hebrew text lacks
this line.   32:43c As in Dead Sea Scrolls and Greek version;
Masoretic Text lacks this line.   32:44 Hebrew *Hoshea,* a
variant name for Joshua.   32:49 Hebrew *the mountains of
Abarim.*   32:51 Hebrew *waters of Meribath-kadesh.*

LUKE 12:35-59
"**B**e dressed for service and keep your
lamps burning, ³⁶as though you were
waiting for your master to return from
the wedding feast. Then you will be

ready to open the door and let him in the moment he arrives and knocks. [37] The servants who are ready and waiting for his return will be rewarded. I tell you the truth, he himself will seat them, put on an apron, and serve them as they sit and eat! [38] He may come in the middle of the night or just before dawn.* But whenever he comes, he will reward the servants who are ready.

[39] **"Understand this: If a homeowner knew exactly when a burglar was coming, he would not permit his house to be broken into.** [40] **You also must be ready all the time, for the Son of Man will come when least expected."**

[41] Peter asked, "Lord, is that illustration just for us or for everyone?"

[42] And the Lord replied, "A faithful, sensible servant is one to whom the master can give the responsibility of managing his other household servants and feeding them. [43] If the master returns and finds that the servant has done a good job, there will be a reward. [44] I tell you the truth, the master will put that servant in charge of all he owns. [45] But what if the servant thinks, 'My master won't be back for a while,' and he begins beating the other servants, partying, and getting drunk? [46] The master will return unannounced and unexpected, and he will cut the servant in pieces and banish him with the unfaithful.

[47] "And a servant who knows what the master wants, but isn't prepared and doesn't carry out those instructions, will be severely punished. [48] But someone who does not know, and then does something wrong, will be punished only lightly. When someone has been given much, much will be required in return; and when someone has been entrusted with much, even more will be required.

[49] "I have come to set the world on fire, and I wish it were already burning! [50] I have a terrible baptism of suffering ahead of me, and I am under a heavy burden until it is accomplished. [51] Do you think I have come to bring peace to the earth? No, I have come to divide people against each other! [52] From now on families will be split apart, three in favor of me, and two against—or two in favor and three against.

[53] 'Father will be divided against
        son
    and son against father;
  mother against daughter
    and daughter against mother;
  and mother-in-law against
        daughter-in-law
    and daughter-in-law against
        mother-in-law.'*"

[54] Then Jesus turned to the crowd and said, "When you see clouds beginning to form in the west, you say, 'Here comes a shower.' And you are right. [55] When the south wind blows, you say, 'Today will be a scorcher.' And it is. [56] You fools! You know how to interpret the weather signs of the earth and sky, but you don't know how to interpret the present times.

[57] "Why can't you decide for yourselves what is right? [58] When you are on the way to court with your accuser, try to settle the matter before you get there. Otherwise, your accuser may drag you before the judge, who will hand you over to an officer, who will throw you into prison. [59] And if that happens, you won't be free again until you have paid the very last penny.*"

12:38 Greek *in the second or third watch.*   12:53 Mic 7:6.
12:59 Greek *last lepton* [the smallest Jewish coin].

PSALM 78:56-64

  But they kept testing and rebelling
        against God Most High.
    They did not obey his laws.
[57] They turned back and were as
        faithless as their parents.
    They were as undependable
        as a crooked bow.
[58] They angered God by building
        shrines to other gods;
    they made him jealous with
        their idols.
[59] When God heard them, he was
        very angry,
    and he completely rejected
        Israel.

⁶⁰ Then he abandoned his dwelling
at Shiloh,
the Tabernacle where he had
lived among the people.
⁶¹ He allowed the Ark of his might
to be captured;
he surrendered his glory into
enemy hands.
⁶² He gave his people over to be
butchered by the sword,
because he was so angry with his
own people—his special
possession.
⁶³ Their young men were killed by fire;
their young women died before
singing their wedding songs.
⁶⁴ Their priests were slaughtered,
and their widows could not
mourn their deaths.

PROVERBS 12:24
Work hard and become a leader; be
lazy and become a slave.

APRIL 9

DEUTERONOMY 33:1-29
This is the blessing that Moses, the man
of God, gave to the people of Israel before his death:

² "The LORD came from Mount Sinai
and dawned upon us* from
Mount Seir;
he shone forth from Mount Paran
and came from Meribah-kadesh
with flaming fire at his right
hand.*
³ Indeed, he loves his people;*
all his holy ones are in his hands.
They follow in his steps
and accept his teaching.
⁴ Moses gave us the LORD's
instruction,
the special possession of the
people of Israel.*

⁵ The LORD became king in Israel*—
when the leaders of the people
assembled,
when the tribes of Israel gathered
as one."

⁶Moses said this about the tribe of Reuben:*

"Let the tribe of Reuben live and
not die out,
though they are few in number."

⁷Moses said this about the tribe of Judah:

"O LORD, hear the cry of Judah
and bring them together as
a people.
Give them strength to defend
their cause;
help them against their
enemies!"

⁸Moses said this about the tribe of Levi:

"O LORD, you have given your
Thummim and Urim—the
sacred lots—
to your faithful servants the
Levites.*
You put them to the test at Massah
and struggled with them at the
waters of Meribah.
⁹ The Levites obeyed your word
and guarded your covenant.
They were more loyal to you
than to their own parents.
They ignored their relatives
and did not acknowledge their
own children.
¹⁰ They teach your regulations
to Jacob;
they give your instructions
to Israel.
They present incense before you
and offer whole burnt offerings
on the altar.
¹¹ Bless the ministry of the Levites,
O LORD,
and accept all the work
of their hands.
Hit their enemies where it hurts
the most;

strike down their foes so they
never rise again."

¹²Moses said this about the tribe of Benjamin:

"The people of Benjamin are loved
by the LORD
and live in safety beside him.
He surrounds them continuously
and preserves them from every
harm."

¹³Moses said this about the tribes of Joseph:

"May their land be blessed by the
LORD
with the precious gift of dew
from the heavens
and water from beneath the earth;
¹⁴ with the rich fruit that grows
in the sun,
and the rich harvest produced
each month;
¹⁵ with the finest crops of the ancient
mountains,
and the abundance from the
everlasting hills;
¹⁶ with the best gifts of the earth and
its bounty,
and the favor of the one who
appeared in the burning bush.
May these blessings rest on Joseph's
head,
crowning the brow of the prince
among his brothers.
¹⁷ Joseph has the majesty of a young
bull;
he has the horns of a wild ox.
He will gore distant nations,
driving them to the ends of
the earth.
This is my blessing for the
multitudes of Ephraim
and the thousands of Manasseh."

¹⁸Moses said this about the tribes of
Zebulun and Issachar*:

"May the people of Zebulun prosper
in their travels.
May the people of Issachar
prosper at home in
their tents.

¹⁹ They summon the people to the
mountain
to offer proper sacrifices there.
They benefit from the riches
of the sea
and the hidden treasures
in the sand."

²⁰Moses said this about the tribe of
Gad:

"Blessed is the one who enlarges
Gad's territory!
Gad is poised there like a lion
to tear off an arm or a head.
²¹ The people of Gad took the best
land for themselves;
a leader's share was assigned
to them.
When the leaders of the people
were assembled,
they carried out the LORD's
justice
and obeyed his regulations for
Israel."

²²Moses said this about the tribe of Dan:

"Dan is a lion's cub,
leaping out from Bashan."

²³Moses said this about the tribe of
Naphtali:

"O Naphtali, you are rich in favor
and full of the LORD's blessings;
may you possess the west and the
south."

²⁴Moses said this about the tribe of
Asher:

"May Asher be blessed above
other sons;
may he be esteemed by his
brothers;
may he bathe his feet in olive oil.
²⁵ May the bolts of your gates be
of iron and bronze;
may you be secure all your days."

²⁶ "There is no one like the God
of Israel.*
He rides across the heavens
to help you,

across the skies in majestic
splendor.
27 The eternal God is your refuge,
and his everlasting arms are
under you.
He drives out the enemy before you;
he cries out, 'Destroy them!'
28 So Israel will live in safety,
prosperous Jacob in security,
in a land of grain and new wine,
while the heavens drop down
dew.
29 How blessed you are, O Israel!
Who else is like you, a people
saved by the LORD?
He is your protecting shield
and your triumphant sword!
Your enemies will cringe before you,
and you will stomp on their backs!"

33:2a As in Greek and Syriac versions; Hebrew reads *upon them.* 33:2b Or *came from myriads of holy ones, from the south, from his mountain slopes.* The meaning of the Hebrew is uncertain. 33:3 As in Greek version; Hebrew reads *Indeed, lover of the peoples.* 33:4 Hebrew *of Jacob.* The names "Jacob" and "Israel" are often interchanged throughout the Old Testament, referring sometimes to the individual patriarch and sometimes to the nation. 33:5 Hebrew *in Jeshurun,* a term of endearment for Israel. 33:6 Hebrew lacks *Moses said this about the tribe of Reuben.* 33:8 As in Greek version; Hebrew lacks *the Levites.* 33:18 Hebrew lacks *and Issachar.* 33:26 Hebrew *of Jeshurun,* a term of endearment for Israel.

LUKE 13:1-21

About this time Jesus was informed that Pilate had murdered some people from Galilee as they were offering sacrifices at the Temple. 2"Do you think those Galileans were worse sinners than all the other people from Galilee?" Jesus asked. "Is that why they suffered? 3Not at all! And you will perish, too, unless you repent of your sins and turn to God. 4And what about the eighteen people who died when the tower in Siloam fell on them? Were they the worst sinners in Jerusalem? 5No, and I tell you again that unless you repent, you will perish, too."

6Then Jesus told this story: "A man planted a fig tree in his garden and came again and again to see if there was any fruit on it, but he was always disapointed. 7Finally, he said to his gardener, 'I've waited three years, and there hasn't been a single fig! Cut it down. It's just taking up space in the garden.'

8"The gardener answered, 'Sir, give it one more chance. Leave it another year, and I'll give it special attention and plenty of fertilizer. 9If we get figs next year, fine. If not, then you can cut it down.'"

10One Sabbath day as Jesus was teaching in a synagogue, 11he saw a woman who had been crippled by an evil spirit. She had been bent double for eighteen years and was unable to stand up straight. 12When Jesus saw her, he called her over and said, "Dear woman, you are healed of your sickness!" 13Then he touched her, and instantly she could stand straight. How she praised God!

14But the leader in charge of the synagogue was indignant that Jesus had healed her on the Sabbath day. "There are six days of the week for working," he said to the crowd. "Come on those days to be healed, not on the Sabbath."

15But the Lord replied, "You hypocrites! Each of you works on the Sabbath day! Don't you untie your ox or your donkey from its stall on the Sabbath and lead it out for water? 16This dear woman, a daughter of Abraham, has been held in bondage by Satan for eighteen years. Isn't it right that she be released, even on the Sabbath?"

17This shamed his enemies, but all the people rejoiced at the wonderful things he did.

18Then Jesus said, "What is the Kingdom of God like? How can I illustrate it? 19It is like a tiny mustard seed that a man planted in a garden; it grows and becomes a tree, and the birds make nests in its branches."

20He also asked, "What else is the Kingdom of God like? 21It is like the yeast a woman used in making bread. Even though she put only a little yeast in three measures of flour, it permeated every part of the dough."

PSALM 78:65-72

Then the Lord rose up as though
waking from sleep,
like a warrior aroused from
a drunken stupor.
66 He routed his enemies

and sent them to eternal shame.
⁶⁷ But he rejected Joseph's
    descendants;
  he did not choose the tribe
    of Ephraim.
⁶⁸ He chose instead the tribe of Judah,
  and Mount Zion, which he loved.
⁶⁹ There he built his sanctuary as high
    as the heavens,
  as solid and enduring as the earth.
⁷⁰ He chose his servant David,
  calling him from the sheep pens.
⁷¹ He took David from tending the
    ewes and lambs
  and made him the shepherd of
    Jacob's descendants—
  God's own people, Israel.
⁷² He cared for them with a true heart
  and led them with skillful hands.

PROVERBS 12:25
Worry weighs a person down; an encouraging word cheers a person up.

APRIL 10

DEUTERONOMY 34:1—JOSHUA 2:24
Then Moses went up to Mount Nebo from the plains of Moab and climbed Pisgah Peak, which is across from Jericho. And the LORD showed him the whole land, from Gilead as far as Dan; ²all the land of Naphtali; the land of Ephraim and Manasseh; all the land of Judah, extending to the Mediterranean Sea*; ³the Negev; the Jordan Valley with Jericho—the city of palms—as far as Zoar. ⁴Then the LORD said to Moses, "This is the land I promised on oath to Abraham, Isaac, and Jacob when I said, 'I will give it to your descendants.' I have now allowed you to see it with your own eyes, but you will not enter the land."

⁵So Moses, the servant of the LORD, died there in the land of Moab, just as the LORD had said. ⁶The LORD buried him* in a valley near Beth-peor in Moab, but to this day no one knows the exact place. ⁷Moses was 120 years old when he died, yet his eyesight was clear, and he was as strong as ever. ⁸The people of Israel mourned for Moses on the plains of Moab for thirty days, until the customary period of mourning was over.

⁹Now Joshua son of Nun was full of the spirit of wisdom, for Moses had laid his hands on him. So the people of Israel obeyed him, doing just as the LORD had commanded Moses.

¹⁰**There has never been another prophet in Israel like Moses, whom the LORD knew face to face. ¹¹The LORD sent him to perform all the miraculous signs and wonders in the land of Egypt against Pharaoh, and all his servants, and his entire land.** ¹²With mighty power, Moses performed terrifying acts in the sight of all Israel.

¹:¹AFTER the death of Moses the LORD's servant, the LORD spoke to Joshua son of Nun, Moses' assistant. He said, ²"Moses my servant is dead. Therefore, the time has come for you to lead these people, the Israelites, across the Jordan River into the land I am giving them. ³I promise you what I promised Moses: 'Wherever you set foot, you will be on land I have given you—⁴from the Negev wilderness in the south to the Lebanon mountains in the north, from the Euphrates River in the east to the Mediterranean Sea* in the west, including all the land of the Hittites.' ⁵No one will be able to stand against you as long as you live. For I will be with you as I was with Moses. I will not fail you or abandon you.

⁶"Be strong and courageous, for you are the one who will lead these people to possess all the land I swore to their ancestors I would give them. ⁷Be strong and very courageous. Be careful to obey all the instructions Moses gave you. Do not deviate from them, turning either to the right or to the left. Then you will be successful in everything you do. ⁸Study this Book of Instruction continually. Meditate on it day and night so you will

be sure to obey everything written in it. Only then will you prosper and succeed in all you do. 9 This is my command—be strong and courageous! Do not be afraid or discouraged. For the LORD your God is with you wherever you go."

10 Joshua then commanded the officers of Israel, 11 "Go through the camp and tell the people to get their provisions ready. In three days you will cross the Jordan River and take possession of the land the LORD your God is giving you."

12 Then Joshua called together the tribes of Reuben, Gad, and the half-tribe of Manasseh. He told them, 13 "Remember what Moses, the servant of the LORD, commanded you: 'The LORD your God is giving you a place of rest. He has given you this land.' 14 Your wives, children, and livestock may remain here in the land Moses assigned to you on the east side of the Jordan River. But your strong warriors, fully armed, must lead the other tribes across the Jordan to help them conquer their territory. Stay with them 15 until the LORD gives them rest, as he has given you rest, and until they, too, possess the land the LORD your God is giving them. Only then may you return and settle here on the east side of the Jordan River in the land that Moses, the servant of the LORD, assigned to you."

16 They answered Joshua, "We will do whatever you command us, and we will go wherever you send us. 17 We will obey you just as we obeyed Moses. And may the LORD your God be with you as he was with Moses. 18 Anyone who rebels against your orders and does not obey your words and everything you command will be put to death. So be strong and courageous!"

2:1 THEN Joshua secretly sent out two spies from the Israelite camp at Acacia Grove.* He instructed them, "Scout out the land on the other side of the Jordan River, especially around Jericho." So the two men set out and came to the house of a prostitute named Rahab and stayed there that night.

2 But someone told the king of Jericho, "Some Israelites have come here tonight to spy out the land." 3 So the king of Jericho sent orders to Rahab: "Bring out the men who have come into your house, for they have come here to spy out the whole land."

4 Rahab had hidden the two men, but she replied, "Yes, the men were here earlier, but I didn't know where they were from. 5 They left the town at dusk, as the gates were about to close. I don't know where they went. If you hurry, you can probably catch up with them." 6 (Actually, she had taken them up to the roof and hidden them beneath bundles of flax she had laid out.) 7 So the king's men went looking for the spies along the road leading to the shallow crossings of the Jordan River. And as soon as the king's men had left, the gate of Jericho was shut.

8 Before the spies went to sleep that night, Rahab went up on the roof to talk with them. 9 "I know the LORD has given you this land," she told them. "We are all afraid of you. Everyone in the land is living in terror. 10 For we have heard how the LORD made a dry path for you through the Red Sea* when you left Egypt. And we know what you did to Sihon and Og, the two Amorite kings east of the Jordan River, whose people you completely destroyed.* 11 No wonder our hearts have melted in fear! No one has the courage to fight after hearing such things. For the LORD your God is the supreme God of the heavens above and the earth below.

12 "Now swear to me by the LORD that you will be kind to me and my family since I have helped you. Give me some guarantee that 13 when Jericho is conquered, you will let me live, along with my father and mother, my brothers and sisters, and all their families."

14 "We offer our own lives as a guarantee for your safety," the men agreed. "If you don't betray us, we will keep our promise and be kind to you when the LORD gives us the land."

15 Then, since Rahab's house was built into the town wall, she let them down by

a rope through the window. ¹⁶"Escape to the hill country," she told them. "Hide there for three days from the men searching for you. Then, when they have returned, you can go on your way."

¹⁷Before they left, the men told her, "We will be bound by the oath we have taken only if you follow these instructions. ¹⁸When we come into the land, you must leave this scarlet rope hanging from the window through which you let us down. And all your family members—your father, mother, brothers, and all your relatives—must be here inside the house. ¹⁹If they go out into the street and are killed, it will not be our fault. But if anyone lays a hand on people inside this house, we will accept the responsibility for their death. ²⁰If you betray us, however, we are not bound by this oath in any way."

²¹"I accept your terms," she replied. And she sent them on their way, leaving the scarlet rope hanging from the window.

²²The spies went up into the hill country and stayed there three days. The men who were chasing them searched everywhere along the road, but they finally returned without success.

²³Then the two spies came down from the hill country, crossed the Jordan River, and reported to Joshua all that had happened to them. ²⁴"The LORD has given us the whole land," they said, "for all the people in the land are terrified of us."

34:2 Hebrew *the western sea.*   34:6 Hebrew *He buried him;* Samaritan Pentateuch and some Greek manuscripts read *They buried him.*   1:4 Hebrew *the Great Sea.* 2:1 Hebrew *Shittim.*   2:10a Hebrew *sea of reeds.* 2:10b The Hebrew term used here refers to the complete consecration of things or people to the LORD, either by destroying them or by giving them as an offering.

LUKE 13:22-14:6

Jesus went through the towns and villages, teaching as he went, always pressing on toward Jerusalem. ²³Someone asked him, "Lord, will only a few be saved?"

He replied, ²⁴"Work hard to enter the narrow door to God's Kingdom, for many will try to enter but will fail.

²⁵When the master of the house has locked the door, it will be too late. You will stand outside knocking and pleading, 'Lord, open the door for us!' But he will reply, 'I don't know you or where you come from.' ²⁶Then you will say, 'But we ate and drank with you, and you taught in our streets.' ²⁷And he will reply, 'I tell you, I don't know you or where you come from. Get away from me, all you who do evil.'

²⁸"There will be weeping and gnashing of teeth, for you will see Abraham, Isaac, Jacob, and all the prophets in the Kingdom of God, but you will be thrown out. ²⁹And people will come from all over the world—from east and west, north and south—to take their places in the Kingdom of God. ³⁰And note this: Some who seem least important now will be the greatest then, and some who are the greatest now will be least important then.*"

³¹At that time some Pharisees said to him, "Get away from here if you want to live! Herod Antipas wants to kill you!"

³²Jesus replied, "Go tell that fox that I will keep on casting out demons and healing people today and tomorrow; and the third day I will accomplish my purpose. ³³Yes, today, tomorrow, and the next day I must proceed on my way. For it wouldn't do for a prophet of God to be killed except in Jerusalem!

³⁴"O Jerusalem, Jerusalem, the city that kills the prophets and stones God's messengers! How often I have wanted to gather your children together as a hen protects her chicks beneath her wings, but you wouldn't let me. ³⁵And now, look, your house is abandoned. And you will never see me again until you say, 'Blessings on the one who comes in the name of the LORD!'*"

¹⁴:¹ONE Sabbath day Jesus went to eat dinner in the home of a leader of the Pharisees, and the people were watching him closely. ²There was a man there whose arms and legs were swollen.* ³Jesus asked the Pharisees and experts in religious law, "Is it permitted in the

law to heal people on the Sabbath day, or not?" ⁴When they refused to answer, Jesus touched the sick man and healed him and sent him away. ⁵Then he turned to them and said, "Which of you doesn't work on the Sabbath? If your son* or your cow falls into a pit, don't you rush to get him out?" ⁶Again they could not answer.

13:30 Greek *Some are last who will be first, and some are first who will be last.*   13:35 Ps 118:26.   14:2 Or *who had dropsy.*   14:5 Some manuscripts read *donkey.*

PSALM 79:1-13
A psalm of Asaph.

¹ O God, pagan nations have
    conquered your land,
    your special possession.
  They have defiled your holy Temple
    and made Jerusalem a heap
    of ruins.
² They have left the bodies of your
    servants
    as food for the birds of heaven.
  The flesh of your godly ones
    has become food for the wild
    animals.
³ Blood has flowed like water all
    around Jerusalem;
    no one is left to bury the dead.
⁴ We are mocked by our neighbors,
    an object of scorn and derision
    to those around us.

⁵ O LORD, how long will you be angry
    with us? Forever?
  How long will your jealousy burn
    like fire?
⁶ Pour out your wrath on the nations
    that refuse to acknowledge
    you—
  on kingdoms that do not call
    upon your name.
⁷ For they have devoured your
    people Israel,*
    making the land a desolate
    wilderness.
⁸ Do not hold us guilty for the sins
    of our ancestors!
  Let your compassion quickly
    meet our needs,
    for we are on the brink of despair.

⁹ Help us, O God of our salvation!
  Help us for the glory
    of your name.
  Save us and forgive our sins
    for the honor of your name.
¹⁰ Why should pagan nations be
    allowed to scoff,
    asking, "Where is their God?"
  Show us your vengeance against
    the nations,
    for they have spilled the blood
    of your servants.
¹¹ Listen to the moaning of the
    prisoners.
  Demonstrate your great power by
    saving those condemned to die.

¹² O Lord, pay back our neighbors
    seven times
    for the scorn they have hurled
    at you.
¹³ Then we your people, the sheep
    of your pasture,
    will thank you forever and ever,
    praising your greatness from
    generation to generation.

79:7 Hebrew *devoured Jacob.* See note on 44:4.

PROVERBS 12:26
The godly give good advice to their friends;* the wicked lead them astray.

12:26 Or *The godly are cautious in friendship;* or *The godly are freed from evil.* The meaning of the Hebrew is uncertain.

APRIL 11

JOSHUA 3:1–4:24
Early the next morning Joshua and all the Israelites left Acacia Grove* and arrived at the banks of the Jordan River, where they camped before crossing. ²Three days later the Israelite officers went through the camp, ³giving these instructions to the people: "When you see the Levitical priests carrying the Ark of the

Covenant of the LORD your God, move out from your positions and follow them. ⁴Since you have never traveled this way before, they will guide you. Stay about a half mile* behind them, keeping a clear distance between you and the Ark. Make sure you don't come any closer."

⁵Then Joshua told the people, "Purify yourselves, for tomorrow the LORD will do great wonders among you."

⁶In the morning Joshua said to the priests, "Lift up the Ark of the Covenant and lead the people across the river." And so they started out and went ahead of the people.

⁷The LORD told Joshua, "Today I will begin to make you a great leader in the eyes of all the Israelites. They will know that I am with you, just as I was with Moses. ⁸Give this command to the priests who carry the Ark of the Covenant: 'When you reach the banks of the Jordan River, take a few steps into the river and stop there.'"

⁹So Joshua told the Israelites, "Come and listen to what the LORD your God says. ¹⁰Today you will know that the living God is among you. He will surely drive out the Canaanites, Hittites, Hivites, Perizzites, Girgashites, Amorites, and Jebusites ahead of you. ¹¹Look, the Ark of the Covenant, which belongs to the Lord of the whole earth, will lead you across the Jordan River! ¹²Now choose twelve men from the tribes of Israel, one from each tribe. ¹³The priests will carry the Ark of the LORD, the Lord of all the earth. As soon as their feet touch the water, the flow of water will be cut off upstream, and the river will stand up like a wall."

¹⁴So the people left their camp to cross the Jordan, and the priests who were carrying the Ark of the Covenant went ahead of them. ¹⁵It was the harvest season, and the Jordan was overflowing its banks. But as soon as the feet of the priests who were carrying the Ark touched the water at the river's edge, ¹⁶the water above that point began backing up a great distance away at a town called Adam, which is near Zarethan. And the water below that point

flowed on to the Dead Sea* until the riverbed was dry. Then all the people crossed over near the town of Jericho.

¹⁷Meanwhile, the priests who were carrying the Ark of the LORD's Covenant stood on dry ground in the middle of the riverbed as the people passed by. They waited there until the whole nation of Israel had crossed the Jordan on dry ground.

^{4:1}WHEN all the people had crossed the Jordan, the LORD said to Joshua, ²"Now choose twelve men, one from each tribe. ³Tell them, 'Take twelve stones from the very place where the priests are standing in the middle of the Jordan. Carry them out and pile them up at the place where you will camp tonight.'"

⁴So Joshua called together the twelve men he had chosen—one from each of the tribes of Israel. ⁵He told them, "Go into the middle of the Jordan, in front of the Ark of the LORD your God. Each of you must pick up one stone and carry it out on your shoulder—twelve stones in all, one for each of the twelve tribes of Israel. ⁶We will use these stones to build a memorial. In the future your children will ask you, 'What do these stones mean?' ⁷Then you can tell them, 'They remind us that the Jordan River stopped flowing when the Ark of the LORD's Covenant went across.' These stones will stand as a memorial among the people of Israel forever."

⁸So the men did as Joshua had commanded them. They took twelve stones from the middle of the Jordan River, one for each tribe, just as the LORD had told Joshua. They carried them to the place where they camped for the night and constructed the memorial there.

⁹Joshua also set up another pile of twelve stones in the middle of the Jordan, at the place where the priests who carried the Ark of the Covenant were standing. And they are there to this day.

¹⁰The priests who were carrying the Ark stood in the middle of the river until all of the LORD's commands that Moses had given to Joshua were carried

out. Meanwhile, the people hurried across the riverbed. [11]And when everyone was safely on the other side, the priests crossed over with the Ark of the LORD as the people watched.

[12]The armed warriors from the tribes of Reuben, Gad, and the half-tribe of Manasseh led the Israelites across the Jordan, just as Moses had directed. [13]These armed men—about 40,000 strong—were ready for battle, and the LORD was with them as they crossed over to the plains of Jericho.

[14]That day the LORD made Joshua a great leader in the eyes of all the Israelites, and for the rest of his life they revered him as much as they had revered Moses.

[15]The LORD had said to Joshua, [16]"Command the priests carrying the Ark of the Covenant* to come up out of the riverbed." [17]So Joshua gave the command. [18]As soon as the priests carrying the Ark of the LORD's Covenant came up out of the riverbed and their feet were on high ground, the water of the Jordan returned and overflowed its banks as before.

[19]The people crossed the Jordan on the tenth day of the first month.* Then they camped at Gilgal, just east of Jericho. [20]It was there at Gilgal that Joshua piled up the twelve stones taken from the Jordan River.

[21]Then Joshua said to the Israelites, "In the future your children will ask, 'What do these stones mean?' [22]Then you can tell them, 'This is where the Israelites crossed the Jordan on dry ground.' [23]For the LORD your God dried up the river right before your eyes, and he kept it dry until you were all across, just as he did at the Red Sea* when he dried it up until we had all crossed over. [24]He did this so all the nations of the earth might know that the LORD's hand is powerful, and so you might fear the LORD your God forever."

3:1 Hebrew *Shittim.*   3:4 Hebrew *about 2,000 cubits* [920 meters].   3:16 Hebrew *the sea of the Arabah, the Salt Sea.*   4:16 Hebrew *Ark of the Testimony.*   4:19 This day in the ancient Hebrew lunar calendar occurred in late March, April, or early May.   4:23 Hebrew *sea of reeds.*

LUKE 14:7-35

When Jesus noticed that all who had come to the dinner were trying to sit in the seats of honor near the head of the table, he gave them this advice: [8]"When you are invited to a wedding feast, don't sit in the seat of honor. What if someone who is more distinguished than you has also been invited? [9]The host will come and say, 'Give this person your seat.' Then you will be embarrassed, and you will have to take whatever seat is left at the foot of the table!

[10]"Instead, take the lowest place at the foot of the table. Then when your host sees you, he will come and say, 'Friend, we have a better place for you!' Then you will be honored in front of all the other guests. [11]For those who exalt themselves will be humbled, and those who humble themselves will be exalted."

[12]Then he turned to his host. "When you put on a luncheon or a banquet," he said, "don't invite your friends, brothers, relatives, and rich neighbors. For they will invite you back, and that will be your only reward. [13]Instead, invite the poor, the crippled, the lame, and the blind. [14]Then at the resurrection of the righteous, God will reward you for inviting those who could not repay you."

[15]Hearing this, a man sitting at the table with Jesus exclaimed, "What a blessing it will be to attend a banquet* in the Kingdom of God!"

[16]Jesus replied with this story: "A man prepared a great feast and sent out many invitations. [17]When the banquet was ready, he sent his servant to tell the guests, 'Come, the banquet is ready.' [18]But they all began making excuses. One said, 'I have just bought a field and must inspect it. Please excuse me.' [19]Another said, 'I have just bought five pairs of oxen, and I want to try them out. Please excuse me.' [20]Another said, 'I now have a wife, so I can't come.'

[21]"The servant returned and told his master what they had said. His master was furious and said, 'Go quickly into the streets and alleys of the town and invite the poor, the crippled, the blind, and the

lame.' ²²After the servant had done this, he reported, 'There is still room for more.' ²³So his master said, 'Go out into the country lanes and behind the hedges and urge anyone you find to come, so that the house will be full. ²⁴For none of those I first invited will get even the smallest taste of my banquet.'"

²⁵A large crowd was following Jesus. He turned around and said to them, ²⁶"If you want to be my disciple, you must hate everyone else by comparison—your father and mother, wife and children, brothers and sisters—yes, even your own life. Otherwise, you cannot be my disciple. ²⁷And if you do not carry your own cross and follow me, you cannot be my disciple.

²⁸"But don't begin until you count the cost. For who would begin construction of a building without first calculating the cost to see if there is enough money to finish it? ²⁹Otherwise, you might complete only the foundation before running out of money, and then everyone would laugh at you. ³⁰They would say, 'There's the person who started that building and couldn't afford to finish it!'

³¹"Or what king would go to war against another king without first sitting down with his counselors to discuss whether his army of 10,000 could defeat the 20,000 soldiers marching against him? ³²And if he can't, he will send a delegation to discuss terms of peace while the enemy is still far away. ³³**So you cannot become my disciple without giving up everything you own.**

³⁴"Salt is good for seasoning. But if it loses its flavor, how do you make it salty again? ³⁵Flavorless salt is good neither for the soil nor for the manure pile. It is thrown away. Anyone with ears to hear should listen and understand!"

14:15 Greek *to eat bread.*

PSALM 80:1-19

For the choir director: A psalm of Asaph, to be sung to the tune "Lilies of the Covenant."

¹ **P**lease listen, O Shepherd of Israel,
    you who lead Joseph's
        descendants like a flock.

O God, enthroned above the
        cherubim,
    display your radiant glory
² to Ephraim, Benjamin, and
        Manasseh.
Show us your mighty power.
    Come to rescue us!

³ Turn us again to yourself, O God.
    Make your face shine down
        upon us.
    Only then will we be saved.
⁴ O LORD God of Heaven's Armies,
    how long will you be angry with
        our prayers?
⁵ You have fed us with sorrow
    and made us drink tears
        by the bucketful.
⁶ You have made us the scorn*
    of neighboring nations.
    Our enemies treat us as a joke.

⁷ Turn us again to yourself, O God
        of Heaven's Armies.
    Make your face shine down
        upon us.
    Only then will we be saved.
⁸ You brought us from Egypt like
        a grapevine;
    you drove away the pagan nations
        and transplanted us into
        your land.
⁹ You cleared the ground for us,
    and we took root and filled
        the land.
¹⁰ Our shade covered the mountains;
    our branches covered the mighty
        cedars.
¹¹ We spread our branches west to the
        Mediterranean Sea;
    our shoots spread east to the
        Euphrates River.*
¹² But now, why have you broken down
        our walls
    so that all who pass by may steal
        our fruit?
¹³ The wild boar from the forest
        devours it,
    and the wild animals feed on it.

¹⁴ Come back, we beg you, O God
        of Heaven's Armies.

Look down from heaven and see
our plight.
Take care of this grapevine
15   that you yourself have planted,
this son you have raised for
yourself.
16 For we are chopped up and burned
by our enemies.
May they perish at the sight
of your frown.
17 Strengthen the man you love,
the son of your choice.
18 Then we will never abandon you
again.
Revive us so we can call on your
name once more.

19 Turn us again to yourself, O LORD
God of Heaven's Armies.
Make your face shine down
upon us.
Only then will we be saved.

80:6 As in Syriac version; Hebrew reads *the strife.*
80:11 Hebrew *west to the sea, . . . east to the river.*

PROVERBS 12:27-28
Lazy people don't even cook the game
they catch, but the diligent make use of
everything they find. □ The way of the
godly leads to life; that path does not
lead to death.

APRIL

12

JOSHUA 5:1–7:15
When all the Amorite kings west of the
Jordan and all the Canaanite kings who
lived along the Mediterranean coast*
heard how the LORD had dried up the
Jordan River so the people of Israel
could cross, they lost heart and were
paralyzed with fear because of them.

²At that time the LORD told Joshua,
"Make flint knives and circumcise this
second generation of Israelites.*" ³So
Joshua made flint knives and circum-

cised the entire male population of
Israel at Gibeath-haaraloth.*

⁴Joshua had to circumcise them because all the men who were old enough
to fight in battle when they left Egypt
had died in the wilderness. ⁵Those who
left Egypt had all been circumcised, but
none of those born after the Exodus,
during the years in the wilderness, had
been circumcised. ⁶The Israelites had
traveled in the wilderness for forty years
until all the men who were old enough to
fight in battle when they left Egypt had
died. For they had disobeyed the LORD,
and the LORD vowed he would not let
them enter the land he had sworn to give
us—a land flowing with milk and honey.
⁷So Joshua circumcised their sons—
those who had grown up to take their fathers' places—for they had not been circumcised on the way to the Promised
Land. ⁸After all the males had been circumcised, they rested in the camp until
they were healed.

⁹Then the LORD said to Joshua, "Today I have rolled away the shame of
your slavery in Egypt." So that place has
been called Gilgal* to this day.

¹⁰While the Israelites were camped
at Gilgal on the plains of Jericho, they
celebrated Passover on the evening of
the fourteenth day of the first month.*
¹¹The very next day they began to eat
unleavened bread and roasted grain
harvested from the land. ¹²No manna
appeared on the day they first ate from
the crops of the land, and it was never
seen again. So from that time on the Israelites ate from the crops of Canaan.

¹³When Joshua was near the town of
Jericho, he looked up and saw a man
standing in front of him with sword in
hand. Joshua went up to him and demanded, "Are you friend or foe?"

¹⁴"Neither one," he replied. "I am the
commander of the LORD's army."

At this, Joshua fell with his face to the
ground in reverence. "I am at your command," Joshua said. "What do you want
your servant to do?"

¹⁵The commander of the LORD's
army replied, "Take off your sandals,

for the place where you are standing is holy." And Joshua did as he was told.

6:1Now the gates of Jericho were tightly shut because the people were afraid of the Israelites. No one was allowed to go out or in. 2But the Lord said to Joshua, "I have given you Jericho, its king, and all its strong warriors. 3You and your fighting men should march around the town once a day for six days. 4Seven priests will walk ahead of the Ark, each carrying a ram's horn. On the seventh day you are to march around the town seven times, with the priests blowing the horns. 5When you hear the priests give one long blast on the rams' horns, have all the people shout as loud as they can. Then the walls of the town will collapse, and the people can charge straight into the town."

6So Joshua called together the priests and said, "Take up the Ark of the Lord's Covenant, and assign seven priests to walk in front of it, each carrying a ram's horn." 7Then he gave orders to the people: "March around the town, and the armed men will lead the way in front of the Ark of the Lord."

8After Joshua spoke to the people, the seven priests with the rams' horns started marching in the presence of the Lord, blowing the horns as they marched. And the Ark of the Lord's Covenant followed behind them. 9Some of the armed men marched in front of the priests with the horns and some behind the Ark, with the priests continually blowing the horns. 10"Do not shout; do not even talk," Joshua commanded. "Not a single word from any of you until I tell you to shout. Then shout!" 11So the Ark of the Lord was carried around the town once that day, and then everyone returned to spend the night in the camp.

12Joshua got up early the next morning, and the priests again carried the Ark of the Lord. 13The seven priests with the rams' horns marched in front of the Ark of the Lord, blowing their horns. Again the armed men marched both in front of the priests with the horns and behind the Ark of the Lord. All this time the priests were blowing their horns. 14On the second day they again marched around the town once and returned to the camp. They followed this pattern for six days.

15On the seventh day the Israelites got up at dawn and marched around the town as they had done before. But this time they went around the town seven times. 16The seventh time around, as the priests sounded the long blast on their horns, Joshua commanded the people, "Shout! For the Lord has given you the town! 17Jericho and everything in it must be completely destroyed* as an offering to the Lord. Only Rahab the prostitute and the others in her house will be spared, for she protected our spies.

18"Do not take any of the things set apart for destruction, or you yourselves will be completely destroyed, and you will bring trouble on the camp of Israel. 19Everything made from silver, gold, bronze, or iron is sacred to the Lord and must be brought into his treasury."

20When the people heard the sound of the rams' horns, they shouted as loud as they could. Suddenly, the walls of Jericho collapsed, and the Israelites charged straight into the town and captured it. 21They completely destroyed everything in it with their swords—men and women, young and old, cattle, sheep, goats, and donkeys.

22Meanwhile, Joshua said to the two spies, "Keep your promise. Go to the prostitute's house and bring her out, along with all her family."

23The men who had been spies went in and brought out Rahab, her father, mother, brothers, and all the other relatives who were with her. They moved her whole family to a safe place near the camp of Israel.

24Then the Israelites burned the town and everything in it. Only the things made from silver, gold, bronze, or iron were kept for the treasury of the Lord's house. 25So Joshua spared Rahab the prostitute and her relatives who were with her in the house, because she had hidden the spies Joshua sent to Jericho. And she lives among the Israelites to this day.

²⁶At that time Joshua invoked this curse:

"May the curse of the LORD fall
    on anyone
who tries to rebuild the town
    of Jericho.
At the cost of his firstborn son,
    he will lay its foundation.
At the cost of his youngest son,
    he will set up its gates."

²⁷So the LORD was with Joshua, and his reputation spread throughout the land.

⁷:¹BUT Israel violated the instructions about the things set apart for the LORD.* A man named Achan had stolen some of these dedicated things, so the LORD was very angry with the Israelites. Achan was the son of Carmi, a descendant of Zimri* son of Zerah, of the tribe of Judah.

²Joshua sent some of his men from Jericho to spy out the town of Ai, east of Bethel, near Beth-aven. ³When they returned, they told Joshua, "There's no need for all of us to go up there; it won't take more than two or three thousand men to attack Ai. Since there are so few of them, don't make all our people struggle to go up there."

⁴So approximately 3,000 warriors were sent, but they were soundly defeated. The men of Ai ⁵chased the Israelites from the town gate as far as the quarries,* and they killed about thirty-six who were retreating down the slope. The Israelites were paralyzed with fear at this turn of events, and their courage melted away.

⁶Joshua and the elders of Israel tore their clothing in dismay, threw dust on their heads, and bowed face down to the ground before the Ark of the LORD until evening. ⁷Then Joshua cried out, "Oh, Sovereign LORD, why did you bring us across the Jordan River if you are going to let the Amorites kill us? If only we had been content to stay on the other side!

⁸Lord, what can I say now that Israel has fled from its enemies? ⁹For when the Canaanites and all the other people living in the land hear about it, they will surround us and wipe our name off the face of the earth. And then what will happen to the honor of your great name?"

¹⁰But the LORD said to Joshua, "Get up! Why are you lying on your face like this? ¹¹Israel has sinned and broken my covenant! They have stolen some of the things that I commanded must be set apart for me. And they have not only stolen them but have lied about it and hidden the things among their own belongings. ¹²That is why the Israelites are running from their enemies in defeat. For now Israel itself has been set apart for destruction. I will not remain with you any longer unless you destroy the things among you that were set apart for destruction.

¹³"Get up! Command the people to purify themselves in preparation for tomorrow. For this is what the LORD, the God of Israel, says: Hidden among you, O Israel, are things set apart for the LORD. You will never defeat your enemies until you remove these things from among you.

¹⁴"In the morning you must present yourselves by tribes, and the LORD will point out the tribe to which the guilty man belongs. That tribe must come forward with its clans, and the LORD will point out the guilty clan. That clan will then come forward, and the LORD will point out the guilty family. Finally, each member of the guilty family must come forward one by one. ¹⁵The one who has stolen what was set apart for destruction will himself be burned with fire, along with everything he has, for he has broken the covenant of the LORD and has done a horrible thing in Israel."

5:1 Hebrew *along the sea.*   5:2 Or *circumcise the Israelites a second time.*   5:3 *Gibeath-haaraloth* means "hill of foreskins."   5:9 *Gilgal* sounds like the Hebrew word *galal,* meaning "to roll."   5:10 This day in the ancient Hebrew lunar calendar occurred in late March, April, or early May.   6:17 The Hebrew term used here refers to the complete consecration of things or people to the LORD, either by destroying them or by giving them as an offering; similarly in 6:18, 21.   7:1a The Hebrew term used here refers to the complete consecration of things or people to the LORD,

either by destroying them or by giving them as an offering;
similarly in 7:11, 12, 13, 15.   **7:1b** As in Greek version (see
also 1 Chr 2:6); Hebrew reads *Zabdi*. Also in 7:17, 18.
7:5 Or *as far as Shebarim.*

LUKE 15:1-32

Tax collectors and other notorious sinners often came to listen to Jesus teach. [2] This made the Pharisees and teachers of religious law complain that he was associating with such sinful people— even eating with them!

[3] So Jesus told them this story: [4] "If a man has a hundred sheep and one of them gets lost, what will he do? Won't he leave the ninety-nine others in the wilderness and go to search for the one that is lost until he finds it? [5] And when he has found it, he will joyfully carry it home on his shoulders. [6] When he arrives, he will call together his friends and neighbors, saying, 'Rejoice with me because I have found my lost sheep.' [7] **In the same way, there is more joy in heaven over one lost sinner who repents and returns to God than over ninety-nine others who are righteous and haven't strayed away!**

[8] "Or suppose a woman has ten silver coins* and loses one. Won't she light a lamp and sweep the entire house and search carefully until she finds it? [9] And when she finds it, she will call in her friends and neighbors and say, 'Rejoice with me because I have found my lost coin.' [10] In the same way, there is joy in the presence of God's angels when even one sinner repents."

[11] To illustrate the point further, Jesus told them this story: "A man had two sons. [12] The younger son told his father, 'I want my share of your estate now before you die.' So his father agreed to divide his wealth between his sons.

[13] "A few days later this younger son packed all his belongings and moved to a distant land, and there he wasted all his money in wild living. [14] About the time his money ran out, a great famine swept over the land, and he began to starve. [15] He persuaded a local farmer to hire him, and the man sent him into his fields to feed the pigs. [16] The young man became so hungry that even the pods he was feeding the pigs looked good to him. But no one gave him anything.

[17] "When he finally came to his senses, he said to himself, 'At home even the hired servants have food enough to spare, and here I am dying of hunger! [18] I will go home to my father and say, "Father, I have sinned against both heaven and you, [19] and I am no longer worthy of being called your son. Please take me on as a hired servant."'

[20] "So he returned home to his father. And while he was still a long way off, his father saw him coming. Filled with love and compassion, he ran to his son, embraced him, and kissed him. [21] His son said to him, 'Father, I have sinned against both heaven and you, and I am no longer worthy of being called your son.*'

[22] "But his father said to the servants, 'Quick! Bring the finest robe in the house and put it on him. Get a ring for his finger and sandals for his feet. [23] And kill the calf we have been fattening. We must celebrate with a feast, [24] for this son of mine was dead and has now returned to life. He was lost, but now he is found.' So the party began.

[25] "Meanwhile, the older son was in the fields working. When he returned home, he heard music and dancing in the house, [26] and he asked one of the servants what was going on. [27] 'Your brother is back,' he was told, 'and your father has killed the fattened calf. We are celebrating because of his safe return.'

[28] "The older brother was angry and wouldn't go in. His father came out and begged him, [29] but he replied, 'All these years I've slaved for you and never once refused to do a single thing you told me to. And in all that time you never gave me even one young goat for a feast with my friends. [30] Yet when this son of yours comes back after squandering your money on prostitutes, you celebrate by killing the fattened calf!'

[31] "His father said to him, 'Look, dear son, you have always stayed by me, and everything I have is yours. [32] We had to celebrate this happy day. For your

brother was dead and has come back to life! He was lost, but now he is found!'"

15:8 Greek *ten drachmas*. A drachma was the equivalent of a full day's wage.   15:21 Some manuscripts add *Please take me on as a hired servant.*

PSALM 81:1-16

For the choir director: A psalm of Asaph, to be accompanied by a stringed instrument.*

¹ **S**ing praises to God, our strength.
  Sing to the God of Jacob.
² Sing! Beat the tambourine.
  Play the sweet lyre and the harp.
³ Blow the ram's horn at new moon,
  and again at full moon to call
  a festival!
⁴ For this is required by the decrees
  of Israel;
  it is a regulation of the God
  of Jacob.
⁵ He made it a law for Israel*
  when he attacked Egypt to set
  us free.

I heard an unknown voice say,
⁶ "Now I will take the load from your
  shoulders;
  I will free your hands from their
  heavy tasks.
⁷ You cried to me in trouble, and
  I saved you;
  I answered out of the thundercloud
  and tested your faith when there
  was no water at Meribah.
                                    Interlude

⁸ "Listen to me, O my people, while
  I give you stern warnings.
  O Israel, if you would only listen
  to me!
⁹ You must never have a foreign god;
  you must not bow down before
  a false god.
¹⁰ For it was I, the Lord your God,
  who rescued you from the land
  of Egypt.
  Open your mouth wide, and I will
  fill it with good things.

¹¹ "But no, my people wouldn't listen.
  Israel did not want me around.
¹² So I let them follow their own
  stubborn desires,

living according to their own
  ideas.
¹³ Oh, that my people would listen
  to me!
  Oh, that Israel would follow me,
  walking in my paths!
¹⁴ How quickly I would then subdue
  their enemies!
  How soon my hands would be
  upon their foes!
¹⁵ Those who hate the Lord would
  cringe before him;
  they would be doomed forever.
¹⁶ But I would feed you with the
  finest wheat.
  I would satisfy you with wild
  honey from the rock."

81:TITLE Hebrew *according to the gittith.*   81:5 Hebrew *for Joseph.*

PROVERBS 13:1

A wise child accepts a parent's discipline;* a mocker refuses to listen to correction.

13:1 Hebrew *A wise son accepts his father's discipline.*

APRIL 13

JOSHUA 7:16–9:2

Early the next morning Joshua brought the tribes of Israel before the Lord, and the tribe of Judah was singled out. ¹⁷Then the clans of Judah came forward, and the clan of Zerah was singled out. Then the families of Zerah came forward, and the family of Zimri was singled out. ¹⁸Every member of Zimri's family was brought forward person by person, and Achan was singled out.

¹⁹Then Joshua said to Achan, "My son, give glory to the Lord, the God of Israel, by telling the truth. Make your confession and tell me what you have done. Don't hide it from me."

²⁰Achan replied, "It is true! I have sinned against the Lord, the God of Is-

rael. ²¹Among the plunder I saw a beautiful robe from Babylon,* 200 silver coins,* and a bar of gold weighing more than a pound.* I wanted them so much that I took them. They are hidden in the ground beneath my tent, with the silver buried deeper than the rest."

²²So Joshua sent some men to make a search. They ran to the tent and found the stolen goods hidden there, just as Achan had said, with the silver buried beneath the rest. ²³They took the things from the tent and brought them to Joshua and all the Israelites. Then they laid them on the ground in the presence of the LORD.

²⁴Then Joshua and all the Israelites took Achan, the silver, the robe, the bar of gold, his sons, daughters, cattle, donkeys, sheep, goats, tent, and everything he had, and they brought them to the valley of Achor. ²⁵Then Joshua said to Achan, "Why have you brought trouble on us? The LORD will now bring trouble on you." And all the Israelites stoned Achan and his family and burned their bodies. ²⁶They piled a great heap of stones over Achan, which remains to this day. That is why the place has been called the Valley of Trouble* ever since. So the LORD was no longer angry.

^{8:1}THEN the LORD said to Joshua, "Do not be afraid or discouraged. Take all your fighting men and attack Ai, for I have given you the king of Ai, his people, his town, and his land. ²You will destroy them as you destroyed Jericho and its king. But this time you may keep the plunder and the livestock for yourselves. Set an ambush behind the town."

³So Joshua and all the fighting men set out to attack Ai. Joshua chose 30,000 of his best warriors and sent them out at night ⁴with these orders: "Hide in ambush close behind the town and be ready for action. ⁵When our main army attacks, the men of Ai will come out to fight as they did before, and we will run away from them. ⁶We will let them chase us until we have drawn them away from the town. For they will say, 'The Israelites

are running away from us as they did before.' Then, while we are running from them, ⁷you will jump up from your ambush and take possession of the town, for the LORD your God will give it to you. ⁸Set the town on fire, as the LORD has commanded. You have your orders."

⁹So they left and went to the place of ambush between Bethel and the west side of Ai. But Joshua remained among the people in the camp that night. ¹⁰Early the next morning Joshua roused his men and started toward Ai, accompanied by the elders of Israel. ¹¹All the fighting men who were with Joshua marched in front of the town and camped on the north side of Ai, with a valley between them and the town. ¹²That night Joshua sent 5,000 men to lie in ambush between Bethel and Ai, on the west side of the town. ¹³So they stationed the main army north of the town and the ambush west of the town. Joshua himself spent that night in the valley.

¹⁴When the king of Ai saw the Israelites across the valley, he and all his army hurried out early in the morning and attacked the Israelites at a place overlooking the Jordan Valley.* But he didn't realize there was an ambush behind the town. ¹⁵Joshua and the Israelite army fled toward the wilderness as though they were badly beaten. ¹⁶Then all the men in the town were called out to chase after them. In this way, they were lured away from the town. ¹⁷There was not a man left in Ai or Bethel* who did not chase after the Israelites, and the town was left wide open.

¹⁸Then the LORD said to Joshua, "Point the spear in your hand toward Ai, for I will hand the town over to you." Joshua did as he was commanded. ¹⁹As soon as Joshua gave this signal, all the men in ambush jumped up from their position and poured into the town. They quickly captured it and set it on fire.

²⁰When the men of Ai looked behind them, smoke from the town was filling the sky, and they had nowhere to go. For the Israelites who had fled in the direction of the wilderness now turned on

their pursuers. ²¹When Joshua and all the other Israelites saw that the ambush had succeeded and that smoke was rising from the town, they turned and attacked the men of Ai. ²²Meanwhile, the Israelites who were inside the town came out and attacked the enemy from the rear. So the men of Ai were caught in the middle, with Israelite fighters on both sides. Israel attacked them, and not a single person survived or escaped. ²³Only the king of Ai was taken alive and brought to Joshua.

²⁴When the Israelite army finished chasing and killing all the men of Ai in the open fields, they went back and finished off everyone inside. ²⁵So the entire population of Ai, including men and women, was wiped out that day—12,000 in all. ²⁶For Joshua kept holding out his spear until everyone who had lived in Ai was completely destroyed.* ²⁷Only the livestock and the treasures of the town were not destroyed, for the Israelites kept these as plunder for themselves, as the LORD had commanded Joshua. ²⁸So Joshua burned the town of Ai,* and it became a permanent mound of ruins, desolate to this very day.

²⁹Joshua impaled the king of Ai on a sharpened pole and left him there until evening. At sunset the Israelites took down the body, as Joshua commanded, and threw it in front of the town gate. They piled a great heap of stones over him that can still be seen today.

³⁰Then Joshua built an altar to the LORD, the God of Israel, on Mount Ebal. ³¹He followed the commands that Moses the LORD's servant had written in the Book of Instruction: "Make me an altar from stones that are uncut and have not been shaped with iron tools."* Then on the altar they presented burnt offerings and peace offerings to the LORD. ³²And as the Israelites watched, Joshua copied onto the stones of the altar* the instructions Moses had given them.

³³Then all the Israelites—foreigners and native-born alike—along with the elders, officers, and judges, were divided into two groups. One group stood in front of Mount Gerizim, the other in front of Mount Ebal. Each group faced the other, and between them stood the Levitical priests carrying the Ark of the LORD's Covenant. This was all done according to the commands that Moses, the servant of the LORD, had previously given for blessing the people of Israel.

³⁴Joshua then read to them all the blessings and curses Moses had written in the Book of Instruction. ³⁵Every word of every command that Moses had ever given was read to the entire assembly of Israel, including the women and children and the foreigners who lived among them.

^{9:1}Now all the kings west of the Jordan River heard about what had happened. These were the kings of the Hittites, Amorites, Canaanites, Perizzites, Hivites, and Jebusites, who lived in the hill country, in the western foothills,* and along the coast of the Mediterranean Sea* as far north as the Lebanon mountains. ²These kings combined their armies to fight as one against Joshua and the Israelites.

7:21a Hebrew *Shinar.*   7:21b Hebrew *200 shekels of silver,* about 5 pounds or 2.3 kilograms in weight.
7:21c Hebrew *50 shekels,* about 20 ounces or 570 grams in weight.   7:26 Hebrew *valley of Achor.*   8:14 Hebrew *the Arabah.*   8:17 Some manuscripts lack *or Bethel.*
8:26 The Hebrew term used here refers to the complete consecration of things or people to the LORD, either by destroying them or by giving them as an offering.   8:28 *Ai* means "ruin."   8:31 Exod 20:25; Deut 27:5-6.   8:32 Or *onto stones.*   9:1a Hebrew *the Shephelah.*   9:1b Hebrew *the Great Sea.*

LUKE 16:1-18

Jesus told this story to his disciples: "There was a certain rich man who had a manager handling his affairs. One day a report came that the manager was wasting his employer's money. ²So the employer called him in and said, 'What's this I hear about you? Get your report in order, because you are going to be fired.'

³"The manager thought to himself, 'Now what? My boss has fired me. I don't have the strength to dig ditches, and I'm too proud to beg. ⁴Ah, I know how to ensure that I'll have plenty of friends who will give me a home when I am fired.'

⁵"So he invited each person who owed money to his employer to come

and discuss the situation. He asked the first one, 'How much do you owe him?' ⁶The man replied, 'I owe him 800 gallons of olive oil.' So the manager told him, 'Take the bill and quickly change it to 400 gallons.*'

⁷"'And how much do you owe my employer?' he asked the next man. 'I owe him 1,000 bushels of wheat,' was the reply. 'Here,' the manager said, 'take the bill and change it to 800 bushels.*'

⁸"The rich man had to admire the dishonest rascal for being so shrewd. And it is true that the children of this world are more shrewd in dealing with the world around them than are the children of the light. ⁹Here's the lesson: Use your worldly resources to benefit others and make friends. Then, when your earthly possessions are gone, they will welcome you to an eternal home.*

¹⁰"If you are faithful in little things, you will be faithful in large ones. But if you are dishonest in little things, you won't be honest with greater responsibilities. ¹¹And if you are untrustworthy about worldly wealth, who will trust you with the true riches of heaven? ¹²And if you are not faithful with other people's things, why should you be trusted with things of your own?

¹³"No one can serve two masters. For you will hate one and love the other; you will be devoted to one and despise the other. You cannot serve both God and money."

¹⁴The Pharisees, who dearly loved their money, heard all this and scoffed at him. ¹⁵Then he said to them, "You like to appear righteous in public, but God knows your hearts. What this world honors is detestable in the sight of God.

¹⁶"Until John the Baptist, the law of Moses and the messages of the prophets were your guides. But now the Good News of the Kingdom of God is preached, and everyone is eager to get in.* ¹⁷But that doesn't mean that the law has lost its force. It is easier for heaven and earth to disappear than for the smallest point of God's law to be overturned.

¹⁸"For example, a man who divorces his wife and marries someone else commits adultery. And anyone who marries a woman divorced from her husband commits adultery."

16:6 Greek *100 baths . . . 50 (baths).*   16:7 Greek *100 korous . . . 80 (korous).*   16:9 Or *you will be welcomed into eternal homes.*   16:16 Or *everyone is urged to enter in.*

PSALM 82:1-8
A psalm of Asaph.

¹ **G**od presides over heaven's court;
   he pronounces judgment on the
      heavenly beings:
² "How long will you hand down
      unjust decisions
   by favoring the wicked?
                        Interlude

³ "Give justice to the poor and
      the orphan;
   uphold the rights of the
      oppressed and the destitute.
⁴ Rescue the poor and helpless;
   deliver them from the grasp
      of evil people.
⁵ But these oppressors know nothing;
      they are so ignorant!
   They wander about in darkness,
      while the whole world is shaken
         to the core.
⁶ I say, 'You are gods;
   you are all children of the
      Most High.
⁷ But you will die like mere mortals
   and fall like every other ruler.'"

⁸ Rise up, O God, and judge the earth,
   for all the nations belong to you.

PROVERBS 13:2-3
Wise words will win you a good meal, but treacherous people have an appetite for violence. □ Those who control their tongue will have a long life; opening your mouth can ruin everything.

APRIL 14

JOSHUA 9:3–10:43

But when the people of Gibeon heard what Joshua had done to Jericho and Ai, 4they resorted to deception to save themselves. They sent ambassadors to Joshua, loading their donkeys with weathered saddlebags and old, patched wineskins. 5They put on worn-out, patched sandals and ragged clothes. And the bread they took with them was dry and moldy. 6When they arrived at the camp of Israel at Gilgal, they told Joshua and the men of Israel, "We have come from a distant land to ask you to make a peace treaty with us."

7The Israelites replied to these Hivites, "How do we know you don't live nearby? For if you do, we cannot make a treaty with you."

8They replied, "We are your servants." "But who are you?" Joshua demanded. "Where do you come from?"

9They answered, "Your servants have come from a very distant country. We have heard of the might of the LORD your God and of all he did in Egypt. 10We have also heard what he did to the two Amorite kings east of the Jordan River—King Sihon of Heshbon and King Og of Bashan (who lived in Ashtaroth). 11So our elders and all our people instructed us, 'Take supplies for a long journey. Go meet with the people of Israel and tell them, "We are your servants; please make a treaty with us."'

12"This bread was hot from the ovens when we left our homes. But now, as you can see, it is dry and moldy. 13These wineskins were new when we filled them, but now they are old and split open. And our clothing and sandals are worn out from our very long journey."

14So the Israelites examined their food, but they did not consult the LORD. 15Then Joshua made a peace treaty with them and guaranteed their safety, and the leaders of the community ratified their agreement with a binding oath.

16Three days after making the treaty, they learned that these people actually lived nearby! 17The Israelites set out at once to investigate and reached their towns in three days. The names of these towns were Gibeon, Kephirah, Beeroth, and Kiriath-jearim. 18But the Israelites did not attack the towns, for the Israelite leaders had made a vow to them in the name of the LORD, the God of Israel.

The people of Israel grumbled against their leaders because of the treaty. 19But the leaders replied, "Since we have sworn an oath in the presence of the LORD, the God of Israel, we cannot touch them. 20This is what we must do. We must let them live, for divine anger would come upon us if we broke our oath. 21Let them live." So they made them woodcutters and water carriers for the entire community, as the Israelite leaders directed.

22Joshua called together the Gibeonites and said, "Why did you lie to us? Why did you say that you live in a distant land when you live right here among us? 23May you be cursed! From now on you will always be servants who cut wood and carry water for the house of my God."

24They replied, "We did it because we—your servants—were clearly told that the LORD your God commanded his servant Moses to give you this entire land and to destroy all the people living in it. So we feared greatly for our lives because of you. That is why we have done this. 25Now we are at your mercy—do to us whatever you think is right."

26So Joshua did not allow the people of Israel to kill them. 27But that day he made the Gibeonites the woodcutters and water carriers for the community of Israel and for the altar of the LORD—wherever the LORD would choose to build it. And that is what they do to this day.

10:1ADONI-ZEDEK, king of Jerusalem, heard that Joshua had captured and completely destroyed* Ai and killed its king, just as he had destroyed the town of Jericho and killed its king. He also learned that the Gibeonites had made peace with Israel and were now their allies. ²He and his people became very afraid when they heard all this because Gibeon was a large town—as large as the royal cities and larger than Ai. And the Gibeonite men were strong warriors.

³So King Adoni-zedek of Jerusalem sent messengers to several other kings: Hoham of Hebron, Piram of Jarmuth, Japhia of Lachish, and Debir of Eglon. ⁴"Come and help me destroy Gibeon," he urged them, "for they have made peace with Joshua and the people of Israel." ⁵So these five Amorite kings combined their armies for a united attack. They moved all their troops into place and attacked Gibeon.

⁶The men of Gibeon quickly sent messengers to Joshua at his camp in Gilgal. "Don't abandon your servants now!" they pleaded. "Come at once! Save us! Help us! For all the Amorite kings who live in the hill country have joined forces to attack us."

⁷So Joshua and his entire army, including his best warriors, left Gilgal and set out for Gibeon. ⁸"Do not be afraid of them," the LORD said to Joshua, "for I have given you victory over them. Not a single one of them will be able to stand up to you."

⁹Joshua traveled all night from Gilgal and took the Amorite armies by surprise. ¹⁰The LORD threw them into a panic, and the Israelites slaughtered great numbers of them at Gibeon. Then the Israelites chased the enemy along the road to Beth-horon, killing them all along the way to Azekah and Makkedah. ¹¹As the Amorites retreated down the road from Beth-horon, the LORD destroyed them with a terrible hailstorm from heaven that continued until they reached Azekah. The hail killed more of the enemy than the Israelites killed with the sword.

¹²On the day the LORD gave the Israelites victory over the Amorites, Joshua prayed to the LORD in front of all the people of Israel. He said,

"Let the sun stand still over Gibeon,
    and the moon over the valley
    of Aijalon."

¹³So the sun stood still and the moon stayed in place until the nation of Israel had defeated its enemies.

Is this event not recorded in *The Book of Jashar**? The sun stayed in the middle of the sky, and it did not set as on a normal day.* ¹⁴There has never been a day like this one before or since, when the LORD answered such a prayer. Surely the LORD fought for Israel that day!

¹⁵Then Joshua and the Israelite army returned to their camp at Gilgal.

¹⁶During the battle the five kings escaped and hid in a cave at Makkedah. ¹⁷When Joshua heard that they had been found, ¹⁸he issued this command: "Cover the opening of the cave with large rocks, and place guards at the entrance to keep the kings inside. ¹⁹The rest of you continue chasing the enemy and cut them down from the rear. Don't give them a chance to get back to their towns, for the LORD your God has given you victory over them."

²⁰So Joshua and the Israelite army continued the slaughter and completely crushed the enemy. They totally wiped out the five armies except for a tiny remnant that managed to reach their fortified towns. ²¹Then the Israelites returned safely to Joshua in the camp at Makkedah. After that, no one dared to speak even a word against Israel.

²²Then Joshua said, "Remove the rocks covering the opening of the cave, and bring the five kings to me." ²³So they brought the five kings out of the cave—the kings of Jerusalem, Hebron, Jarmuth, Lachish, and Eglon. ²⁴When they brought them out, Joshua told the commanders of his army, "Come and put your feet on the kings' necks." And they did as they were told.

²⁵"Don't ever be afraid or discouraged," Joshua told his men. "Be strong and courageous, for the LORD is going to do this to all of your enemies." ²⁶Then Joshua killed each of the five kings and impaled them on five sharpened poles, where they hung until evening.

²⁷As the sun was going down, Joshua gave instructions for the bodies of the

kings to be taken down from the poles and thrown into the cave where they had been hiding. Then they covered the opening of the cave with a pile of large rocks, which remains to this very day.

²⁸That same day Joshua captured and destroyed the town of Makkedah. He killed everyone in it, including the king, leaving no survivors. He destroyed them all, and he killed the king of Makkedah as he had killed the king of Jericho. ²⁹Then Joshua and the Israelites went to Libnah and attacked it. ³⁰There, too, the LORD gave them the town and its king. He killed everyone in it, leaving no survivors. Then Joshua killed the king of Libnah as he had killed the king of Jericho.

³¹From Libnah, Joshua and the Israelites went to Lachish and attacked it. ³²Here again, the LORD gave them Lachish. Joshua took it on the second day and killed everyone in it, just as he had done at Libnah. ³³During the attack on Lachish, King Horam of Gezer arrived with his army to help defend the town. But Joshua's men killed him and his army, leaving no survivors.

³⁴Then Joshua and the Israelite army went on to Eglon and attacked it. ³⁵They captured it that day and killed everyone in it. He completely destroyed everyone, just as he had done at Lachish. ³⁶From Eglon, Joshua and the Israelite army went up to Hebron and attacked it. ³⁷They captured the town and killed everyone in it, including its king, leaving no survivors. They did the same thing to all of its surrounding villages. And just as he had done at Eglon, he completely destroyed the entire population.

³⁸Then Joshua and the Israelites turned back and attacked Debir. ³⁹He captured the town, its king, and all of its surrounding villages. He completely destroyed everyone in it, leaving no survivors. He did to Debir and its king just what he had done to Hebron and to Libnah and its king.

⁴⁰So Joshua conquered the whole region—the kings and people of the hill country, the Negev, the western foot-hills,* and the mountain slopes. He completely destroyed everyone in the land, leaving no survivors, just as the LORD, the God of Israel, had commanded. ⁴¹Joshua slaughtered them from Kadesh-barnea to Gaza and from the region around the town of Goshen up to Gibeon. ⁴²Joshua conquered all these kings and their land in a single campaign, for the LORD, the God of Israel, was fighting for his people.

⁴³Then Joshua and the Israelite army returned to their camp at Gilgal.

10:1 The Hebrew term used here refers to the complete consecration of things or people to the LORD, either by destroying them or by giving them as an offering; also in 10:28, 35, 37, 39, 40. 10:13a Or *The Book of the Upright.* 10:13b Or *did not set for about a whole day.* 10:40 Hebrew *the Shephelah.*

LUKE 16:19–17:10

Jesus said, "There was a certain rich man who was splendidly clothed in purple and fine linen and who lived each day in luxury. ²⁰At his gate lay a poor man named Lazarus who was covered with sores. ²¹As Lazarus lay there longing for scraps from the rich man's table, the dogs would come and lick his open sores.

²²"Finally, the poor man died and was carried by the angels to be with Abraham.* The rich man also died and was buried, ²³and his soul went to the place of the dead.* There, in torment, he saw Abraham in the far distance with Lazarus at his side.

²⁴"The rich man shouted, 'Father Abraham, have some pity! Send Lazarus over here to dip the tip of his finger in water and cool my tongue. I am in anguish in these flames.'

²⁵"But Abraham said to him, 'Son, remember that during your lifetime you had everything you wanted, and Lazarus had nothing. So now he is here being comforted, and you are in anguish. ²⁶And besides, there is a great chasm separating us. No one can cross over to you from here, and no one can cross over to us from there.'

²⁷"Then the rich man said, 'Please, Father Abraham, at least send him to my father's home. ²⁸For I have five brothers,

and I want him to warn them so they don't end up in this place of torment.'

²⁹"But Abraham said, 'Moses and the prophets have warned them. Your brothers can read what they wrote.'

³⁰"The rich man replied, 'No, Father Abraham! But if someone is sent to them from the dead, then they will repent of their sins and turn to God.'

³¹"But Abraham said, 'If they won't listen to Moses and the prophets, they won't listen even if someone rises from the dead.'"

¹⁷:¹ONE day Jesus said to his disciples, "There will always be temptations to sin, but what sorrow awaits the person who does the tempting! ²It would be better to be thrown into the sea with a millstone hung around your neck than to cause one of these little ones to fall into sin. ³So watch yourselves!

"If another believer* sins, rebuke that person; then if there is repentance, forgive. ⁴Even if that person wrongs you seven times a day and each time turns again and asks forgiveness, you must forgive."

⁵The apostles said to the Lord, "Show us how to increase our faith."

⁶The Lord answered, "If you had faith even as small as a mustard seed, you could say to this mulberry tree, 'May you be uprooted and thrown into the sea,' and it would obey you!

⁷"When a servant comes in from plowing or taking care of sheep, does his master say, 'Come in and eat with me'? ⁸No, he says, 'Prepare my meal, put on your apron, and serve me while I eat. Then you can eat later.' ⁹And does the master thank the servant for doing what he was told to do? Of course not. ¹⁰**In the same way, when you obey me you should say, 'We are unworthy servants who have simply done our duty.'"**

16:22 Greek *into Abraham's bosom.*   16:23 Greek *to Hades.*   17:3 Greek *If your brother.*

PSALM 83:1-18
A song. A psalm of Asaph.

¹ **O** God, do not be silent!
   Do not be deaf.

   Do not be quiet, O God.
² Don't you hear the uproar of your
      enemies?
   Don't you see that your arrogant
      enemies are rising up?
³ They devise crafty schemes against
      your people;
   they conspire against your
      precious ones.
⁴ "Come," they say, "let us wipe out
      Israel as a nation.
   We will destroy the very memory
      of its existence."
⁵ Yes, this was their unanimous
      decision.
   They signed a treaty as allies
      against you—
⁶ these Edomites and Ishmaelites;
      Moabites and Hagrites;
⁷ Gebalites, Ammonites, and
      Amalekites;
   and people from Philistia
      and Tyre.
⁸ Assyria has joined them, too,
   and is allied with the descendants
      of Lot.   *Interlude*

⁹ Do to them as you did to the
      Midianites
   and as you did to Sisera and Jabin
      at the Kishon River.
¹⁰ They were destroyed at Endor,
   and their decaying corpses
      fertilized the soil.
¹¹ Let their mighty nobles die as Oreb
      and Zeeb did.
   Let all their princes die like
      Zebah and Zalmunna,
¹² for they said, "Let us seize for
      our own use
   these pasturelands of God!"
¹³ O my God, scatter them like
      tumbleweed,
   like chaff before the wind!
¹⁴ As a fire burns a forest
   and as a flame sets mountains
      ablaze,
¹⁵ chase them with your fierce storm;
   terrify them with your tempest.
¹⁶ Utterly disgrace them
   until they submit to your name,
      O LORD.

¹⁷ Let them be ashamed and terrified forever.

Let them die in disgrace.

¹⁸ Then they will learn that you alone are called the LORD,

that you alone are the Most High, supreme over all the earth.

PROVERBS 13:4

Lazy people want much but get little, but those who work hard will prosper.

APRIL
15

JOSHUA 11:1–12:24

When King Jabin of Hazor heard what had happened, he sent messages to the following kings: King Jobab of Madon; the king of Shimron; the king of Acshaph; ²all the kings of the northern hill country; the kings in the Jordan Valley south of Galilee*; the kings in the Galilean foothills*; the kings of Naphoth-dor on the west; ³the kings of Canaan, both east and west; the kings of the Amorites, the Hittites, the Perizzites, the Jebusites in the hill country, and the Hivites in the towns on the slopes of Mount Hermon in the land of Mizpah.

⁴All these kings came out to fight. Their combined armies formed a vast horde. And with all their horses and chariots, they covered the landscape like the sand on the seashore. ⁵The kings joined forces and established their camp around the water near Merom to fight against Israel.

⁶Then the LORD said to Joshua, "Do not be afraid of them. By this time tomorrow I will hand all of them over to Israel as dead men. Then you must cripple their horses and burn their chariots."

⁷So Joshua and all his fighting men traveled to the water near Merom and attacked suddenly. ⁸And the LORD gave them victory over their enemies. The Israelites chased them as far as Greater Sidon and Misrephoth-maim, and eastward into the valley of Mizpah, until not one enemy warrior was left alive. ⁹Then Joshua crippled the horses and burned all the chariots, as the LORD had instructed.

¹⁰Joshua then turned back and captured Hazor and killed its king. (Hazor had at one time been the capital of all these kingdoms.) ¹¹The Israelites completely destroyed* every living thing in the city, leaving no survivors. Not a single person was spared. And then Joshua burned the city.

¹²Joshua slaughtered all the other kings and their people, completely destroying them, just as Moses, the servant of the LORD, had commanded. ¹³But the Israelites did not burn any of the towns built on mounds except Hazor, which Joshua burned. ¹⁴And the Israelites took all the plunder and livestock of the ravaged towns for themselves. But they killed all the people, leaving no survivors. ¹⁵As the LORD had commanded his servant Moses, so Moses commanded Joshua. And Joshua did as he was told, carefully obeying all the commands that the LORD had given to Moses.

¹⁶So Joshua conquered the entire region—the hill country, the entire Negev, the whole area around the town of Goshen, the western foothills, the Jordan Valley,* the mountains of Israel, and the Galilean foothills. ¹⁷The Israelite territory now extended all the way from Mount Halak, which leads up to Seir in the south, as far north as Baal-gad at the foot of Mount Hermon in the valley of Lebanon. Joshua killed all the kings of those territories, ¹⁸waging war for a long time to accomplish this. ¹⁹No one in this region made peace with the Israelites except the Hivites of Gibeon. All the others were defeated. ²⁰For the LORD hardened their hearts and caused them to fight the Israelites. So they were completely destroyed without mercy, as the LORD had commanded Moses.

²¹During this period Joshua destroyed

all the descendants of Anak, who lived in the hill country of Hebron, Debir, Anab, and the entire hill country of Judah and Israel. He killed them all and completely destroyed their towns. ²²None of the descendants of Anak were left in all the land of Israel, though some still remained in Gaza, Gath, and Ashdod.

²³So Joshua took control of the entire land, just as the LORD had instructed Moses. He gave it to the people of Israel as their special possession, dividing the land among the tribes. So the land finally had rest from war.

^{12:1}THESE are the kings east of the Jordan River who had been killed by the Israelites and whose land was taken. Their territory extended from the Arnon Gorge to Mount Hermon and included all the land east of the Jordan Valley.*

²King Sihon of the Amorites, who lived in Heshbon, was defeated. His kingdom included Aroer, on the edge of the Arnon Gorge, and extended from the middle of the Arnon Gorge to the Jabbok River, which serves as a border for the Ammonites. This territory included the southern half of the territory of Gilead. ³Sihon also controlled the Jordan Valley and regions to the east— from as far north as the Sea of Galilee to as far south as the Dead Sea,* including the road to Beth-jeshimoth and southward to the slopes of Pisgah.

⁴King Og of Bashan, the last of the Rephaites, lived at Ashtaroth and Edrei. ⁵He ruled a territory stretching from Mount Hermon to Salecah in the north and to all of Bashan in the east, and westward to the borders of the kingdoms of Geshur and Maacah. This territory included the northern half of Gilead, as far as the boundary of King Sihon of Heshbon.

⁶Moses, the servant of the LORD, and the Israelites had destroyed the people of King Sihon and King Og. And Moses gave their land as a possession to the tribes of Reuben, Gad, and the half-tribe of Manasseh.

⁷The following is a list of the kings that Joshua and the Israelite armies defeated on the west side of the Jordan, from Baal-gad in the valley of Lebanon to Mount Halak, which leads up to Seir. (Joshua gave this land to the tribes of Israel as their possession, ⁸including the hill country, the western foothills,* the Jordan Valley, the mountain slopes, the Judean wilderness, and the Negev. The people who lived in this region were the Hittites, the Amorites, the Canaanites, the Perizzites, the Hivites, and the Jebusites.) These are the kings Israel defeated:

⁹ The king of Jericho
    The king of Ai, near Bethel
¹⁰ The king of Jerusalem
    The king of Hebron
¹¹ The king of Jarmuth
    The king of Lachish
¹² The king of Eglon
    The king of Gezer
¹³ The king of Debir
    The king of Geder
¹⁴ The king of Hormah
    The king of Arad
¹⁵ The king of Libnah
    The king of Adullam
¹⁶ The king of Makkedah
    The king of Bethel
¹⁷ The king of Tappuah
    The king of Hepher
¹⁸ The king of Aphek
    The king of Lasharon
¹⁹ The king of Madon
    The king of Hazor
²⁰ The king of Shimron-meron
    The king of Acshaph
²¹ The king of Taanach
    The king of Megiddo
²² The king of Kedesh
    The king of Jokneam in Carmel
²³ The king of Dor in the town of
    Naphoth-dor*
    The king of Goyim in Gilgal*
²⁴ The king of Tirzah.

In all, thirty-one kings were defeated.

11:2a Hebrew *in the Arabah south of Kinnereth.*
11:2b Hebrew *the Shephelah;* also in 11:16.   11:11 The Hebrew term used here refers to the complete consecration of things or people to the LORD, either by destroying them or by giving them as an offering; also in 11:12, 20, 21.
11:16 Hebrew *the Shephelah, the Arabah.*   12:1 Hebrew *the Arabah;* also in 12:3, 8.   12:3 Hebrew *from the Sea of*

Kinnereth to the Sea of the Arabah, which is the Salt Sea.
12:8 Hebrew *the Shephelah*.   **12:23a** Hebrew *Naphath-dor*, a variant spelling of Naphoth-dor.   **12:23b** Greek version reads *Goyim in Galilee*.

LUKE 17:11-37

As Jesus continued on toward Jerusalem, he reached the border between Galilee and Samaria. ¹²As he entered a village there, ten lepers stood at a distance, ¹³crying out, "Jesus, Master, have mercy on us!"

¹⁴He looked at them and said, "Go show yourselves to the priests."* And as they went, they were cleansed of their leprosy.

¹⁵One of them, when he saw that he was healed, came back to Jesus, shouting, "Praise God!" ¹⁶He fell to the ground at Jesus' feet, thanking him for what he had done. This man was a Samaritan.

¹⁷Jesus asked, "Didn't I heal ten men? Where are the other nine? ¹⁸Has no one returned to give glory to God except this foreigner?" ¹⁹And Jesus said to the man, "Stand up and go. Your faith has healed you.*"

²⁰**One day the Pharisees asked Jesus, "When will the Kingdom of God come?"**

Jesus replied, "The Kingdom of God can't be detected by visible signs.* ²¹**You won't be able to say, 'Here it is!' or 'It's over there!' For the Kingdom of God is already among you.*"**

²²Then he said to his disciples, "The time is coming when you will long to see the day when the Son of Man returns,* but you won't see it. ²³People will tell you, 'Look, there is the Son of Man,' or 'Here he is,' but don't go out and follow them. ²⁴For as the lightning flashes and lights up the sky from one end to the other, so it will be on the day when the Son of Man comes. ²⁵But first the Son of Man must suffer terribly* and be rejected by this generation.

²⁶"When the Son of Man returns, it will be like it was in Noah's day. ²⁷In those days, the people enjoyed banquets and parties and weddings right up to the time Noah entered his boat

and the flood came and destroyed them all.

²⁸"And the world will be as it was in the days of Lot. People went about their daily business—eating and drinking, buying and selling, farming and building—²⁹until the morning Lot left Sodom. Then fire and burning sulfur rained down from heaven and destroyed them all. ³⁰Yes, it will be 'business as usual' right up to the day when the Son of Man is revealed. ³¹On that day a person out on the deck of a roof must not go down into the house to pack. A person out in the field must not return home. ³²Remember what happened to Lot's wife! ³³If you cling to your life, you will lose it, and if you let your life go, you will save it. ³⁴That night two people will be asleep in one bed; one will be taken, the other left. ³⁵Two women will be grinding flour together at the mill; one will be taken, the other left.*"

³⁷"Where will this happen, Lord?"* the disciples asked.

Jesus replied, "Just as the gathering of vultures shows there is a carcass nearby, so these signs indicate that the end is near."*

17:14 See Lev 14:2-32.   **17:19** Or *Your faith has saved you*.   **17:20** Or *by your speculations*.   **17:21** Or *is within you*, or *is in your grasp*.   **17:22** Or *long for even one day with the Son of Man*. "Son of Man" is a title Jesus used for himself.   **17:25** Or *suffer many things*.   **17:35** Some manuscripts add verse 36, *Two men will be working in the field; one will be taken, the other left*. Compare Matt 24:40.   **17:37a** Greek *"Where, Lord?"*   **17:37b** Greek *"Wherever the carcass is, the vultures gather."*

PSALM 84:1-12

For the choir director: A psalm of the descendants of Korah, to be accompanied by a stringed instrument.

¹ **H**ow lovely is your dwelling place,
  O Lord of Heaven's Armies.
² I long, yes, I faint with longing
  to enter the courts of the Lord.
 With my whole being, body and soul,
  I will shout joyfully to the living God.
³ Even the sparrow finds a home,
  and the swallow builds her nest
  and raises her young
 at a place near your altar,

O LORD of Heaven's Armies,
  my King and my God!
⁴ What joy for those who can live
  in your house,
  always singing your praises.
             Interlude

⁵ What joy for those whose strength
  comes from the LORD,
  who have set their minds on
  a pilgrimage to Jerusalem.
⁶ When they walk through the Valley
  of Weeping,*
  it will become a place of
  refreshing springs.
  The autumn rains will clothe
  it with blessings.
⁷ They will continue to grow stronger,
  and each of them will appear
  before God in Jerusalem.*

⁸ O LORD God of Heaven's Armies,
  hear my prayer.
  Listen, O God of Jacob. *Interlude*

⁹ O God, look with favor upon the
  king, our shield!
  Show favor to the one you
  have anointed.

¹⁰ A single day in your courts
  is better than a thousand
  anywhere else!
  I would rather be a gatekeeper
  in the house of my God
  than live the good life in the
  homes of the wicked.
¹¹ For the LORD God is our sun and
  our shield.
  He gives us grace and glory.
  The LORD will withhold no
  good thing
  from those who do what is right.
¹² O LORD of Heaven's Armies,
  what joy for those who trust
  in you.

84:TITLE Hebrew *according to the gittith.* 84:6 Or *Valley of Poplars;* Hebrew reads *valley of Baca.* 84:7 Hebrew *Zion.*

PROVERBS 13:5-6

The godly hate lies; the wicked cause shame and disgrace. ☐ Godliness guards the path of the blameless, but the evil are misled by sin.

APRIL 16

JOSHUA 13:1–14:15

When Joshua was an old man, the LORD said to him, "You are growing old, and much land remains to be conquered. ²This is the territory that remains: all the regions of the Philistines and the Geshurites, ³and the larger territory of the Canaanites, extending from the stream of Shihor on the border of Egypt, northward to the boundary of Ekron. It includes the territory of the five Philistine rulers of Gaza, Ashdod, Ashkelon, Gath, and Ekron. The land of the Avvites ⁴in the south also remains to be conquered. In the north, the following area has not yet been conquered: all the land of the Canaanites, including Mearah (which belongs to the Sidonians), stretching northward to Aphek on the border of the Amorites; ⁵the land of the Gebalites and all of the Lebanon mountain area to the east, from Baal-gad below Mount Hermon to Lebo-hamath; ⁶and all the hill country from Lebanon to Misrephoth-maim, including all the land of the Sidonians.

"I myself will drive these people out of the land ahead of the Israelites. So be sure to give this land to Israel as a special possession, just as I have commanded you. ⁷Include all this territory as Israel's possession when you divide this land among the nine tribes and the half-tribe of Manasseh."

⁸Half the tribe of Manasseh and the tribes of Reuben and Gad had already received their grants of land on the east side of the Jordan, for Moses, the servant of the LORD, had previously assigned this land to them.

⁹Their territory extended from Aroer on the edge of the Arnon Gorge (including the town in the middle of the gorge) to the plain beyond Medeba, as far as Dibon.

¹⁰It also included all the towns of King Sihon of the Amorites, who had reigned in Heshbon, and extended as far as the borders of Ammon. ¹¹It included Gilead, the territory of the kingdoms of Geshur and Maacah, all of Mount Hermon, all of Bashan as far as Salecah, ¹²and all the territory of King Og of Bashan, who had reigned in Ashtaroth and Edrei. King Og was the last of the Rephaites, for Moses had attacked them and driven them out. ¹³But the Israelites failed to drive out the people of Geshur and Maacah, so they continue to live among the Israelites to this day.

¹⁴Moses did not assign any allotment of land to the tribe of Levi. Instead, as the LORD had promised them, their allotment came from the offerings burned on the altar to the LORD, the God of Israel.

¹⁵Moses had assigned the following area to the clans of the tribe of Reuben.

¹⁶Their territory extended from Aroer on the edge of the Arnon Gorge (including the town in the middle of the gorge) to the plain beyond Medeba. ¹⁷It included Heshbon and the other towns on the plain—Dibon, Bamoth-baal, Beth-baal-meon, ¹⁸Jahaz, Kedemoth, Mephaath, ¹⁹Kiriathaim, Sibmah, Zereth-shahar on the hill above the valley, ²⁰Beth-peor, the slopes of Pisgah, and Beth-jeshimoth.

²¹The land of Reuben also included all the towns of the plain and the entire kingdom of Sihon. Sihon was the Amorite king who had reigned in Heshbon and was killed by Moses along with the leaders of Midian—Evi, Rekem, Zur, Hur, and Reba—princes living in the region who were allied with Sihon. ²²The Israelites had also killed Balaam son of Beor, who used magic to tell the future. ²³The Jordan River marked the western boundary for the tribe of Reuben. The towns

and their surrounding villages in this area were given as a homeland to the clans of the tribe of Reuben.

²⁴Moses had assigned the following area to the clans of the tribe of Gad.

²⁵Their territory included Jazer, all the towns of Gilead, and half of the land of Ammon, as far as the town of Aroer just west of* Rabbah. ²⁶It extended from Heshbon to Ramath-mizpeh and Betonim, and from Mahanaim to Lo-debar.* ²⁷In the valley were Beth-haram, Beth-nimrah, Succoth, Zaphon, and the rest of the kingdom of King Sihon of Heshbon. The western boundary ran along the Jordan River, extended as far north as the tip of the Sea of Galilee,* and then turned eastward. ²⁸The towns and their surrounding villages in this area were given as a homeland to the clans of the tribe of Gad.

²⁹Moses had assigned the following area to the clans of the half-tribe of Manasseh.

³⁰Their territory extended from Mahanaim, including all of Bashan, all the former kingdom of King Og, and the sixty towns of Jair in Bashan. ³¹It also included half of Gilead and King Og's royal cities of Ashtaroth and Edrei. All this was given to the clans of the descendants of Makir, who was Manasseh's son.

³²These are the allotments Moses had made while he was on the plains of Moab, across the Jordan River, east of Jericho. ³³But Moses gave no allotment of land to the tribe of Levi, for the LORD, the God of Israel, had promised that he himself would be their allotment.

14:1THE remaining tribes of Israel received land in Canaan as allotted by Eleazar the priest, Joshua son of Nun, and the tribal leaders. ²These nine and a half tribes received their grants of land by means of sacred lots, in accordance with the LORD's command through Moses. ³Moses had already given a grant of land to the two and a half tribes on the east side of the Jordan River, but he had given the Levites no such allotment. ⁴The descendants of Joseph had become two separate tribes—Manasseh and Ephraim. And the Levites were given no land at all, only towns to live in with surrounding pasturelands for their livestock and all their possessions. ⁵So the land was distributed in strict accordance with the LORD's commands to Moses.

⁶A delegation from the tribe of Judah, led by Caleb son of Jephunneh the Kenizzite, came to Joshua at Gilgal. Caleb said to Joshua, "Remember what the LORD said to Moses, the man of God, about you and me when we were at Kadesh-barnea. ⁷I was forty years old when Moses, the servant of the LORD, sent me from Kadesh-barnea to explore the land of Canaan. I returned and gave an honest report, ⁸but my brothers who went with me frightened the people from entering the Promised Land. For my part, I wholeheartedly followed the LORD my God. ⁹So that day Moses solemnly promised me, 'The land of Canaan on which you were just walking will be your grant of land and that of your descendants forever, because you wholeheartedly followed the LORD my God.'

¹⁰"Now, as you can see, the LORD has kept me alive and well as he promised for all these forty-five years since Moses made this promise—even while Israel wandered in the wilderness. Today I am eighty-five years old. ¹¹I am as strong now as I was when Moses sent me on that journey, and I can still travel and fight as well as I could then. ¹²So give me the hill country that the LORD promised me. You will remember that as scouts we found the descendants of Anak living there in great, walled towns. But if the LORD is with me, I will drive them out of the land, just as the LORD said."

¹³So Joshua blessed Caleb son of Jephunneh and gave Hebron to him as his portion of land. ¹⁴Hebron still belongs to the descendants of Caleb son of Je-

phunneh the Kenizzite because he wholeheartedly followed the LORD, the God of Israel. ¹⁵(Previously Hebron had been called Kiriath-arba. It had been named after Arba, a great hero of the descendants of Anak.)

And the land had rest from war.

13:25 Hebrew *in front of.* 13:26 Or *to the territory of Debir.* 13:27 Hebrew *Sea of Kinnereth.*

LUKE 18:1-17

One day Jesus told his disciples a story to show that they should always pray and never give up. ²"There was a judge in a certain city," he said, "who neither feared God nor cared about people. ³A widow of that city came to him repeatedly, saying, 'Give me justice in this dispute with my enemy.' ⁴The judge ignored her for a while, but finally he said to himself, 'I don't fear God or care about people, ⁵but this woman is driving me crazy. I'm going to see that she gets justice, because she is wearing me out with her constant requests!'"

⁶**Then the Lord said, "Learn a lesson from this unjust judge. ⁷Even he rendered a just decision in the end. So don't you think God will surely give justice to his chosen people who cry out to him day and night? Will he keep putting them off? ⁸I tell you, he will grant justice to them quickly! But when the Son of Man* returns, how many will he find on the earth who have faith?"**

⁹Then Jesus told this story to some who had great confidence in their own righteousness and scorned everyone else: ¹⁰"Two men went to the Temple to pray. One was a Pharisee, and the other was a despised tax collector. ¹¹The Pharisee stood by himself and prayed this prayer*: 'I thank you, God, that I am not a sinner like everyone else. For I don't cheat, I don't sin, and I don't commit adultery. I'm certainly not like that tax collector! ¹²I fast twice a week, and I give you a tenth of my income.'

¹³"But the tax collector stood at a distance and dared not even lift his eyes to heaven as he prayed. Instead, he beat his

chest in sorrow, saying, 'O God, be merciful to me, for I am a sinner.' [14]I tell you, this sinner, not the Pharisee, returned home justified before God. For those who exalt themselves will be humbled, and those who humble themselves will be exalted."

[15]One day some parents brought their little children to Jesus so he could touch and bless them. But when the disciples saw this, they scolded the parents for bothering him.

[16]Then Jesus called for the children and said to the disciples, "Let the children come to me. Don't stop them! For the Kingdom of God belongs to those who are like these children. [17]I tell you the truth, anyone who doesn't receive the Kingdom of God like a child will never enter it."

18:8 "Son of Man" is a title Jesus used for himself.
18:11 Some manuscripts read *stood and prayed this prayer to himself.*

PSALM 85:1-13
For the choir director: A psalm of the descendants of Korah.

[1] **L**ORD, you poured out blessings
        on your land!
    You restored the fortunes
        of Israel.*
[2] You forgave the guilt of your
        people—
    yes, you covered all their sins.
                              Interlude

[3] You held back your fury.
    You kept back your blazing
        anger.

[4] Now restore us again, O God of
        our salvation.
    Put aside your anger against us
        once more.
[5] Will you be angry with us always?
    Will you prolong your wrath
        to all generations?
[6] Won't you revive us again,
    so your people can rejoice
        in you?
[7] Show us your unfailing love,
        O LORD,
    and grant us your salvation.

[8] I listen carefully to what God the
        LORD is saying,
    for he speaks peace to his faithful
        people.
    But let them not return to their
        foolish ways.
[9] Surely his salvation is near to those
        who fear him,
    so our land will be filled with
        his glory.

[10] Unfailing love and truth have
        met together.
    Righteousness and peace have
        kissed!
[11] Truth springs up from the earth,
    and righteousness smiles down
        from heaven.
[12] Yes, the LORD pours down his
        blessings.
    Our land will yield its bountiful
        harvest.
[13] Righteousness goes as a herald
        before him,
    preparing the way for his steps.

85:1 Hebrew *of Jacob.* See note on 44:4.

PROVERBS 13:7-8
Some who are poor pretend to be rich; others who are rich pretend to be poor.
□ The rich can pay a ransom for their lives, but the poor won't even get threatened.

APRIL 17

JOSHUA 15:1-63
The allotment for the clans of the tribe of Judah reached southward to the border of Edom, as far south as the wilderness of Zin.

[2]The southern boundary began at the south bay of the Dead Sea,* [3]ran south of Scorpion Pass* into the wilderness of Zin, and then went

south of Kadesh-barnea to Hezron. Then it went up to Addar, where it turned toward Karka. ⁴From there it passed to Azmon until it finally reached the Brook of Egypt, which it followed to the Mediterranean Sea.* This was their* southern boundary.

⁵The eastern boundary extended along the Dead Sea to the mouth of the Jordan River.

The northern boundary began at the bay where the Jordan River empties into the Dead Sea, ⁶went up from there to Beth-hoglah, then proceeded north of Beth-arabah to the Stone of Bohan. (Bohan was Reuben's son.) ⁷From that point it went through the valley of Achor to Debir, turning north toward Gilgal, which is across from the slopes of Adummim on the south side of the valley. From there the boundary extended to the springs at En-shemesh and on to En-rogel. ⁸The boundary then passed through the valley of Ben-Hinnom, along the southern slopes of the Jebusites, where the city of Jerusalem is located. Then it went west to the top of the mountain above the valley of Hinnom, and on up to the northern end of the valley of Rephaim. ⁹From there the boundary extended from the top of the mountain to the spring at the waters of Nephtoah,* and from there to the towns on Mount Ephron. Then it turned toward Baalah (that is, Kiriath-jearim). ¹⁰The boundary circled west of Baalah to Mount Seir, passed along to the town of Kesalon on the northern slope of Mount Jearim, and went down to Beth-shemesh and on to Timnah. ¹¹The boundary then proceeded to the slope of the hill north of Ekron, where it turned toward Shikkeron and Mount Baalah. It passed Jabneel and ended at the Mediterranean Sea.

¹²The western boundary was the shoreline of the Mediterranean Sea.*

These are the boundaries for the clans of the tribe of Judah.

¹³The LORD commanded Joshua to assign some of Judah's territory to Caleb son of Jephunneh. So Caleb was given the town of Kiriath-arba (that is, Hebron), which had been named after Anak's ancestor. ¹⁴Caleb drove out the three groups of Anakites—the descendants of Sheshai, Ahiman, and Talmai, the sons of Anak.

¹⁵From there he went to fight against the people living in the town of Debir (formerly called Kiriath-sepher). ¹⁶Caleb said, "I will give my daughter Acsah in marriage to the one who attacks and captures Kiriath-sepher." ¹⁷Othniel, the son of Caleb's brother Kenaz, was the one who conquered it, so Acsah became Othniel's wife.

¹⁸When Acsah married Othniel, she urged him* to ask her father for a field. As she got down off her donkey, Caleb asked her, "What's the matter?"

¹⁹She said, "Give me another gift. You have already given me land in the Negev; now please give me springs of water, too." So Caleb gave her the upper and lower springs.

²⁰This was the homeland allocated to the clans of the tribe of Judah.

²¹The towns of Judah situated along the borders of Edom in the extreme south were Kabzeel, Eder, Jagur, ²²Kinah, Dimonah, Adadah, ²³Kedesh, Hazor, Ithnan, ²⁴Ziph, Telem, Bealoth, ²⁵Hazor-hadattah, Kerioth-hezron (that is, Hazor), ²⁶Amam, Shema, Moladah, ²⁷Hazar-gaddah, Heshmon, Beth-pelet, ²⁸Hazar-shual, Beersheba, Biziothiah, ²⁹Baalah, Iim, Ezem, ³⁰Eltolad, Kesil, Hormah, ³¹Ziklag, Madmannah, Sansannah, ³²Lebaoth, Shilhim, Ain, and Rimmon—twenty-nine towns with their surrounding villages.

³³The following towns situated in the western foothills* were also

given to Judah: Eshtaol, Zorah, Ashnah, ³⁴Zanoah, En-gannim, Tappuah, Enam, ³⁵Jarmuth, Adullam, Socoh, Azekah, ³⁶Shaaraim, Adithaim, Gederah, and Gederothaim—fourteen towns with their surrounding villages.

³⁷Also included were Zenan, Hadashah, Migdal-gad, ³⁸Dilean, Mizpeh, Joktheel, ³⁹Lachish, Bozkath, Eglon, ⁴⁰Cabbon, Lahmam, Kitlish, ⁴¹Gederoth, Beth-dagon, Naamah, and Makkedah—sixteen towns with their surrounding villages.

⁴²Besides these, there were Libnah, Ether, Ashan, ⁴³Iphtah, Ashnah, Nezib, ⁴⁴Keilah, Aczib, and Mareshah—nine towns with their surrounding villages.

⁴⁵The territory of the tribe of Judah also included Ekron and its surrounding settlements and villages. ⁴⁶From Ekron the boundary extended west and included the towns near Ashdod with their surrounding villages. ⁴⁷It also included Ashdod with its surrounding settlements and villages and Gaza with its settlements and villages, as far as the Brook of Egypt and along the coast of the Mediterranean Sea.

⁴⁸Judah also received the following towns in the hill country: Shamir, Jattir, Socoh, ⁴⁹Dannah, Kiriath-sannah (that is, Debir), ⁵⁰Anab, Eshtemoh, Anim, ⁵¹Goshen, Holon, and Giloh—eleven towns with their surrounding villages.

⁵²Also included were the towns of Arab, Dumah, Eshan, ⁵³Janim, Beth-tappuah, Aphekah, ⁵⁴Humtah, Kiriath-arba (that is, Hebron), and Zior—nine towns with their surrounding villages.

⁵⁵Besides these, there were Maon, Carmel, Ziph, Juttah, ⁵⁶Jezreel, Jokdeam, Zanoah, ⁵⁷Kain, Gibeah, and Timnah—ten towns with their surrounding villages.

⁵⁸In addition, there were Halhul, Beth-zur, Gedor, ⁵⁹Maarath, Beth-anoth, and Eltekon—six towns with their surrounding villages.

⁶⁰There were also Kiriath-baal (that is, Kiriath-jearim) and Rabbah—two towns with their surrounding villages.

⁶¹In the wilderness there were the towns of Beth-arabah, Middin, Secacah, ⁶²Nibshan, the City of Salt, and En-gedi—six towns with their surrounding villages.

⁶³But the tribe of Judah could not drive out the Jebusites, who lived in the city of Jerusalem, so the Jebusites live there among the people of Judah to this day.

15:2 Hebrew *the Salt Sea;* also in 15:5.   15:3 Hebrew *Akrabbim.*   15:4a Hebrew *the sea;* also in 15:11. 15:4b Hebrew *your.*   15:9 Or *the spring at Me-nephtoah.* 15:12 Hebrew *the Great Sea;* also in 15:47.   15:18 Some Greek manuscripts read *he urged her.*   15:33 Hebrew *the Shephelah.*

LUKE 18:18-43

❶nce a religious leader asked Jesus this question: "Good Teacher, what should I do to inherit eternal life?"

¹⁹"Why do you call me good?" Jesus asked him. "Only God is truly good. ²⁰But to answer your question, you know the commandments: 'You must not commit adultery. You must not murder. You must not steal. You must not testify falsely. Honor your father and mother.'*"

²¹The man replied, "I've carefully obeyed all these commandments since I was young."

²²When Jesus heard his answer, he said, "There is still one thing you haven't done. Sell all your possessions and give the money to the poor, and you will have treasure in heaven. Then come, follow me."

²³But when the man heard this he became sad, for he was very rich.

²⁴When Jesus saw this,* he said, "How hard it is for the rich to enter the Kingdom of God! ²⁵In fact, it is easier for a camel to go through the eye of a needle than for a rich person to enter the Kingdom of God!"

²⁶Those who heard this said, "Then who in the world can be saved?"

²⁷He replied, "What is impossible for people is possible with God."

²⁸Peter said, "We've left our homes to follow you."

²⁹"Yes," Jesus replied, "and I assure you that everyone who has given up house or wife or brothers or parents or children, for the sake of the Kingdom of God, ³⁰will be repaid many times over in this life, and will have eternal life in the world to come."

³¹Taking the twelve disciples aside, Jesus said, "Listen, we're going up to Jerusalem, where all the predictions of the prophets concerning the Son of Man will come true. ³²He will be handed over to the Romans,* and he will be mocked, treated shamefully, and spit upon. ³³They will flog him with a whip and kill him, but on the third day he will rise again."

³⁴But they didn't understand any of this. The significance of his words was hidden from them, and they failed to grasp what he was talking about.

³⁵As Jesus approached Jericho, a blind beggar was sitting beside the road. ³⁶When he heard the noise of a crowd going past, he asked what was happening. ³⁷They told him that Jesus the Nazarene* was going by. ³⁸So he began shouting, "Jesus, Son of David, have mercy on me!"

³⁹"Be quiet!" the people in front yelled at him.

But he only shouted louder, "Son of David, have mercy on me!"

⁴⁰When Jesus heard him, he stopped and ordered that the man be brought to him. As the man came near, Jesus asked him, ⁴¹"What do you want me to do for you?"

"Lord," he said, "I want to see!"

⁴²And Jesus said, "All right, receive your sight! Your faith has healed you." ⁴³Instantly the man could see, and he followed Jesus, praising God. And all who saw it praised God, too.

18:20 Exod 20:12-16; Deut 5:16-20.   18:24 Some manuscripts read *When Jesus saw how sad the man was.* 18:32 Greek *the Gentiles.*   18:37 Or *Jesus of Nazareth.*

PSALM 86:1-17
A prayer of David.

¹ Bend down, O Lord, and hear
      my prayer;
   answer me, for I need your help.
² Protect me, for I am devoted to you.
      Save me, for I serve you and
         trust you.
      You are my God.
³ Be merciful to me, O Lord,
      for I am calling on you constantly.
⁴ Give me happiness, O Lord,
      for I give myself to you.
⁵ O Lord, you are so good, so ready
         to forgive,
      so full of unfailing love for all
         who ask for your help.
⁶ Listen closely to my prayer, O Lord;
      hear my urgent cry.
⁷ I will call to you whenever I'm
         in trouble,
      and you will answer me.

⁸ No pagan god is like you, O Lord.
      None can do what you do!
⁹ All the nations you made
      will come and bow before
         you, Lord;
      they will praise your holy name.
¹⁰ For you are great and perform
         wonderful deeds.
      You alone are God.

¹¹ **Teach me your ways, O Lord,**
      that I may live according to
         your truth!
   Grant me purity of heart,
      so that I may honor you.
¹² **With all my heart I will praise you,**
      O Lord my God.
   I will give glory to your name
      forever,
¹³ for your love for me is very great.
      You have rescued me from the
         depths of death.*

¹⁴ O God, insolent people rise up
         against me;
      a violent gang is trying to kill me.
      You mean nothing to them.
¹⁵ But you, O Lord,
      are a God of compassion and mercy,
      slow to get angry

and filled with unfailing love and
faithfulness.
16 Look down and have mercy on me.
    Give your strength to your servant;
    save me, the son of your servant.
17 Send me a sign of your favor.
    Then those who hate me will be
        put to shame,
    for you, O Lord, help and
        comfort me.

86:13 Hebrew *of Sheol.*

PROVERBS 13:9-10
The life of the godly is full of light and
joy, but the light of the wicked will be
snuffed out. □ Pride leads to conflict;
those who take advice are wise.

APRIL
18

JOSHUA 16:1–18:28
The allotment for the descendants
of Joseph extended from the Jordan
River near Jericho, east of the
springs of Jericho, through the wilderness and into the hill country of
Bethel. 2 From Bethel (that is, Luz)* it
ran over to Ataroth in the territory
of the Arkites. 3 Then it descended
westward to the territory of the
Japhletites as far as Lower Beth-
horon, then to Gezer and over to the
Mediterranean Sea.*

4 This was the homeland allocated to the
families of Joseph's sons, Manasseh and
Ephraim.

5 The following territory was given to
the clans of the tribe of Ephraim.

The boundary of their homeland
began at Ataroth-addar in the east.
From there it ran to Upper Beth-
horon, 6 then on to the Mediterranean Sea. From Micmethath on
the north, the boundary curved

eastward past Taanath-shiloh to the
east of Janoah. 7 From Janoah it
turned southward to Ataroth and
Naarah, touched Jericho, and ended
at the Jordan River. 8 From Tappuah
the boundary extended westward,
following the Kanah Ravine to the
Mediterranean Sea. This is the
homeland allocated to the clans of
the tribe of Ephraim.

9 In addition, some towns with
their surrounding villages in the
territory allocated to the half-tribe
of Manasseh were set aside for the
tribe of Ephraim. 10 They did not
drive the Canaanites out of Gezer,
however, so the people of Gezer live
as slaves among the people of
Ephraim to this day.

17:1 The next allotment of land was given
to the half-tribe of Manasseh, the descendants of Joseph's older son. Makir,
the firstborn son of Manasseh, was the
father of Gilead. Because his descendants were experienced soldiers, the regions of Gilead and Bashan on the east
side of the Jordan had already been
given to them. 2 So the allotment on the
west side of the Jordan was for the remaining families within the clans of the
tribe of Manasseh: Abiezer, Helek, Asri-
el, Shechem, Hepher, and Shemida.
These clans represent the male descendants of Manasseh son of Joseph.

3 However, Zelophehad, a descendant
of Hepher son of Gilead, son of Makir,
son of Manasseh, had no sons. He had
only daughters, whose names were
Mahlah, Noah, Hoglah, Milcah, and Tirzah. 4 These women came to Eleazar the
priest, Joshua son of Nun, and the Israelite leaders and said, "The Lord commanded Moses to give us a grant of land
along with the men of our tribe."

So Joshua gave them a grant of land
along with their uncles, as the Lord had
commanded. 5 As a result, Manasseh's
total allocation came to ten parcels of
land, in addition to the land of Gilead
and Bashan across the Jordan River,
6 because the female descendants of

Manasseh received a grant of land along with the male descendants. (The land of Gilead was given to the rest of the male descendants of Manasseh.)

7 The boundary of the tribe of Manasseh extended from the border of Asher to Micmethath, near Shechem. Then the boundary went south from Micmethath to the settlement near the spring of Tappuah. 8 The land surrounding Tappuah belonged to Manasseh, but the town of Tappuah itself, on the border of Manasseh's territory, belonged to the tribe of Ephraim. 9 From the spring of Tappuah, the boundary of Manasseh followed the Kanah Ravine to the Mediterranean Sea.* Several towns south of the ravine were inside Manasseh's territory, but they actually belonged to the tribe of Ephraim. 10 In general, however, the land south of the ravine belonged to Ephraim, and the land north of the ravine belonged to Manasseh. Manasseh's boundary ran along the northern side of the ravine and ended at the Mediterranean Sea. North of Manasseh was the territory of Asher, and to the east was the territory of Issachar.
11 The following towns within the territory of Issachar and Asher, however, were given to Manasseh: Beth-shan,* Ibleam, Dor (that is, Naphoth-dor),* Endor, Taanach, and Megiddo, each with their surrounding settlements.

12 But the descendants of Manasseh were unable to occupy these towns. They could not drive out the Canaanites who continued to live there. 13 Later, however, when the Israelites became strong enough, they forced the Canaanites to work as slaves. But they did not drive them out of the land.

14 The descendants of Joseph came to Joshua and asked, "Why have you given us only one portion of land as our homeland when the LORD has blessed us with so many people?"

15 Joshua replied, "If there are so many of you, and if the hill country of Ephraim is not large enough for you, clear out land for yourselves in the forest where the Perizzites and Rephaites live."

16 The descendants of Joseph responded, "It's true that the hill country is not large enough for us. But all the Canaanites in the lowlands have iron chariots, both those in Beth-shan and its surrounding settlements and those in the valley of Jezreel. They are too strong for us."

17 Then Joshua said to the tribes of Ephraim and Manasseh, the descendants of Joseph, "Since you are so large and strong, you will be given more than one portion. 18 The forests of the hill country will be yours as well. Clear as much of the land as you wish, and take possession of its farthest corners. And you will drive out the Canaanites from the valleys, too, even though they are strong and have iron chariots."

18:1 Now that the land was under Israelite control, the entire community of Israel gathered at Shiloh and set up the Tabernacle.* 2 But there remained seven tribes who had not yet been allotted their grants of land.

3 Then Joshua asked them, "How long are you going to wait before taking possession of the remaining land the LORD, the God of your ancestors, has given to you? 4 Select three men from each tribe, and I will send them out to explore the land and map it out. They will then return to me with a written report of their proposed divisions of their new homeland. 5 Let them divide the land into seven sections, excluding Judah's territory in the south and Joseph's territory in the north. 6 And when you record the seven divisions of the land and bring them to me, I will cast sacred lots in the presence of the LORD our God to assign land to each tribe.

7 "The Levites, however, will not receive any allotment of land. Their role as priests of the LORD is their allotment. And the tribes of Gad, Reuben, and the half-tribe of Manasseh won't receive

any more land, for they have already received their grant of land, which Moses, the servant of the LORD, gave them on the east side of the Jordan River."

8As the men started on their way to map out the land, Joshua commanded them, "Go and explore the land and write a description of it. Then return to me, and I will assign the land to the tribes by casting sacred lots here in the presence of the LORD at Shiloh." 9The men did as they were told and mapped the entire territory into seven sections, listing the towns in each section. They made a written record and then returned to Joshua in the camp at Shiloh. 10And there at Shiloh, Joshua cast sacred lots in the presence of the LORD to determine which tribe should have each section.

11The first allotment of land went to the clans of the tribe of Benjamin. It lay between the territory assigned to the tribes of Judah and Joseph.

12The northern boundary of Benjamin's land began at the Jordan River, went north of the slope of Jericho, then west through the hill country and the wilderness of Beth-aven. 13From there the boundary went south to Luz (that is, Bethel) and proceeded down to Ataroth-addar on the hill that lies south of Lower Beth-horon.

14The boundary then made a turn and swung south along the western edge of the hill facing Beth-horon, ending at the village of Kiriath-baal (that is, Kiriath-jearim), a town belonging to the tribe of Judah. This was the western boundary.

15The southern boundary began at the outskirts of Kiriath-jearim. From that western point it ran* to the spring at the waters of Neph-toah,* 16and down to the base of the mountain beside the valley of Ben-Hinnom, at the northern end of the valley of Rephaim. From there it went down the valley of Hinnom, crossing south of the slope where the Jebusites lived, and continued

down to En-rogel. 17From En-rogel the boundary proceeded in a northerly direction and came to En-shemesh and on to Geliloth (which is across from the slopes of Adummim). Then it went down to the Stone of Bohan. (Bohan was Reuben's son.) 18From there it passed along the north side of the slope overlooking the Jordan Valley.* The border then went down into the valley, 19ran past the north slope of Beth-hoglah, and ended at the north bay of the Dead Sea,* which is the southern end of the Jordan River. This was the southern boundary.

20The eastern boundary was the Jordan River.

These were the boundaries of the homeland allocated to the clans of the tribe of Benjamin.

21These were the towns given to the clans of the tribe of Benjamin.

Jericho, Beth-hoglah, Emek-keziz, 22Beth-arabah, Zemaraim, Bethel, 23Avvim, Parah, Ophrah, 24Kephar-ammoni, Ophni, and Geba—twelve towns with their surrounding villages. 25Also Gibeon, Ramah, Beeroth, 26Mizpeh, Kephirah, Mozah, 27Rekem, Irpeel, Taralah, 28Zela, Haeleph, Jebus (that is, Jerusalem), Gibeah, and Kiriath-jearim*—fourteen towns with their surrounding villages.

This was the homeland allocated to the clans of the tribe of Benjamin.

16:2 As in Greek version (also see 18:13); Hebrew reads *From Bethel to Luz.*   16:3 Hebrew *the sea;* also in 16:6, 8.   17:9 Hebrew *the sea;* also in 17:10.   17:11a Hebrew *Beth-shean,* a variant spelling of Beth-shan; also in 17:16.   17:11b The meaning of the Hebrew is uncertain.   18:1 Hebrew *Tent of Meeting.*   18:15a Or *From there it went to Mozah.* The meaning of the Hebrew is uncertain.   18:15b Or *the spring at Me-nephtoah.*   18:18 Hebrew *overlooking the Arabah,* or *overlooking Beth-arabah.*   18:19 Hebrew *Salt Sea.*   18:28 As in Greek version; Hebrew reads *Kiriath.*

LUKE 19:1-27

Jesus entered Jericho and made his way through the town. 2There was a man there named Zacchaeus. He was the chief tax collector in the region, and he had become very rich. ³He tried to get a look at Jesus, but he was too short to see over the crowd. ⁴So he ran ahead and climbed a sycamore-fig tree beside the road, for Jesus was going to pass that way.

⁵When Jesus came by, he looked up at Zacchaeus and called him by name. "Zacchaeus!" he said. "Quick, come down! I must be a guest in your home today."

⁶Zacchaeus quickly climbed down and took Jesus to his house in great excitement and joy. ⁷But the people were displeased. "He has gone to be the guest of a notorious sinner," they grumbled.

⁸Meanwhile, Zacchaeus stood before the Lord and said, "I will give half my wealth to the poor, Lord, and if I have cheated people on their taxes, I will give them back four times as much!"

⁹**Jesus responded, "Salvation has come to this home today, for this man has shown himself to be a true son of Abraham. ¹⁰For the Son of Man* came to seek and save those who are lost."**

¹¹The crowd was listening to everything Jesus said. And because he was nearing Jerusalem, he told them a story to correct the impression that the Kingdom of God would begin right away. ¹²He said, "A nobleman was called away to a distant empire to be crowned king and then return. ¹³Before he left, he called together ten of his servants and divided among them ten pounds of silver,* saying, 'Invest this for me while I am gone.' ¹⁴But his people hated him and sent a delegation after him to say, 'We do not want him to be our king.'

¹⁵"After he was crowned king, he returned and called in the servants to whom he had given the money. He wanted to find out what their profits were. ¹⁶The first servant reported, 'Master, I invested your money and made ten times the original amount!'

¹⁷" 'Well done!' the king exclaimed. 'You are a good servant. You have been faithful with the little I entrusted to you, so you will be governor of ten cities as your reward.'

¹⁸"The next servant reported, 'Master, I invested your money and made five times the original amount.'

¹⁹"'Well done!' the king said. 'You will be governor over five cities.'

²⁰"But the third servant brought back only the original amount of money and said, 'Master, I hid your money and kept it safe. ²¹I was afraid because you are a hard man to deal with, taking what isn't yours and harvesting crops you didn't plant.'

²²" 'You wicked servant!' the king roared. 'Your own words condemn you. If you knew that I'm a hard man who takes what isn't mine and harvests crops I didn't plant, ²³why didn't you deposit my money in the bank? At least I could have gotten some interest on it.'

²⁴"Then, turning to the others standing nearby, the king ordered, 'Take the money from this servant, and give it to the one who has ten pounds.'

²⁵"'But, master,' they said, 'he already has ten pounds!'

²⁶"'Yes,' the king replied, 'and to those who use well what they are given, even more will be given. But from those who do nothing, even what little they have will be taken away. ²⁷And as for these enemies of mine who didn't want me to be their king—bring them in and execute them right here in front of me.'"

19:10 "Son of Man" is a title Jesus used for himself.
19:13 Greek *ten minas;* one mina was worth about three months' wages.

PSALM 87:1-7
A song. A psalm of the descendants of Korah.

¹ **O**n the holy mountain
        stands the city founded
            by the LORD.
² He loves the city of Jerusalem
        more than any other city in Israel.*
³ O city of God,
        what glorious things are
            said of you!   *Interlude*

⁴ I will count Egypt* and Babylon
        among those who know me—
        also Philistia and Tyre, and even
            distant Ethiopia.*

They have all become citizens
of Jerusalem!

⁵ Regarding Jerusalem* it will be said,
"Everyone enjoys the rights
of citizenship there."
And the Most High will personally
bless this city.

⁶ When the LORD registers the
nations, he will say,
"They have all become citizens
of Jerusalem."   *Interlude*

⁷ The people will play flutes* and sing,
"The source of my life springs
from Jerusalem!"

87:2 Hebrew *He loves the gates of Zion more than all the
dwellings of Jacob.* See note on 44:4.   87:4a Hebrew
Rahab, the name of a mythical sea monster that represents
chaos in ancient literature. The name is used here as a
poetic name for Egypt.   87:4b Hebrew *Cush.*
87:5 Hebrew *Zion.*   87:7 Or *will dance.*

PROVERBS 13:11
Wealth from get-rich-quick schemes
quickly disappears; wealth from hard
work grows over time.

APRIL 19

JOSHUA 19:1–20:9
The second allotment of land went to
the clans of the tribe of Simeon. Their
homeland was surrounded by Judah's
territory.

² Simeon's homeland included
Beersheba, Sheba, Moladah, ³ Hazar-
shual, Balah, Ezem, ⁴ Eltolad, Bethul,
Hormah, ⁵ Ziklag, Beth-marcaboth,
Hazar-susah, ⁶ Beth-lebaoth, and
Sharuhen—thirteen towns with
their surrounding villages. ⁷ It also
included Ain, Rimmon, Ether, and
Ashan—four towns with their
villages, ⁸ including all the
surrounding villages as far south as
Baalath-beer (also known as Ramah
of the Negev).

This was the homeland allocated to the
clans of the tribe of Simeon. ⁹ Their allocation of land came from part of what
had been given to Judah because Judah's
territory was too large for them. So the
tribe of Simeon received an allocation
within the territory of Judah.

¹⁰ The third allotment of land went to
the clans of the tribe of Zebulun.

The boundary of Zebulun's
homeland started at Sarid. ¹¹ From
there it went west, going past
Maralah, touching Dabbesheth, and
proceeding to the brook east of
Jokneam. ¹² In the other direction,
the boundary went east from Sarid
to the border of Kisloth-tabor, and
from there to Daberath and up to
Japhia. ¹³ Then it continued east to
Gath-hepher, Eth-kazin, and
Rimmon and turned toward Neah.
¹⁴ The northern boundary of
Zebulun passed Hannathon and
ended at the valley of Iphtah-el.
¹⁵ The towns in these areas included
Kattath, Nahalal, Shimron, Idalah,
and Bethlehem—twelve towns with
their surrounding villages.

¹⁶ The homeland allocated to the clans
of the tribe of Zebulun included these
towns and their surrounding villages.

¹⁷ The fourth allotment of land went
to the clans of the tribe of Issachar.

¹⁸ Its boundaries included the
following towns: Jezreel, Kesulloth,
Shunem, ¹⁹ Hapharaim, Shion,
Anaharath, ²⁰ Rabbith, Kishion, Ebez,
²¹ Remeth, En-gannim, En-haddah,
and Beth-pazzez. ²² The boundary
also touched Tabor, Shahazumah,
and Beth-shemesh, ending at the
Jordan River—sixteen towns with
their surrounding villages.

²³ The homeland allocated to the clans
of the tribe of Issachar included these
towns and their surrounding villages.

²⁴ The fifth allotment of land went to
the clans of the tribe of Asher.

25 Its boundaries included these towns: Helkath, Hali, Beten, Acshaph, 26 Allammelech, Amad, and Mishal. The boundary on the west touched Carmel and Shihor-libnath, 27 then it turned east toward Beth-dagon, and ran as far as Zebulun in the valley of Iphtah-el, going north to Beth-emek and Neiel. It then continued north to Cabul, 28 Abdon,* Rehob, Hammon, Kanah, and as far as Greater Sidon. 29 Then the boundary turned toward Ramah and the fortified city of Tyre, where it turned toward Hosah and came to the Mediterranean Sea.* The territory also included Mehebel, Aczib, 30 Ummah, Aphek, and Rehob—twenty-two towns with their surrounding villages.

31 The homeland allocated to the clans of the tribe of Asher included these towns and their surrounding villages.

32 The sixth allotment of land went to the clans of the tribe of Naphtali.

33 Its boundary ran from Heleph, from the oak at Zaanannim, and extended across to Adami-nekeb, Jabneel, and as far as Lakkum, ending at the Jordan River. 34 The western boundary ran past Aznoth-tabor, then to Hukkok, and touched the border of Zebulun in the south, the border of Asher on the west, and the Jordan River* on the east. 35 The fortified towns included in this territory were Ziddim, Zer, Hammath, Rakkath, Kinnereth, 36 Adamah, Ramah, Hazor, 37 Kedesh, Edrei, En-hazor, 38 Yiron, Migdal-el, Horem, Beth-anath, and Beth-shemesh—nineteen towns with their surrounding villages.

39 The homeland allocated to the clans of the tribe of Naphtali included these towns and their surrounding villages.

40 The seventh allotment of land went to the clans of the tribe of Dan.

41 The land allocated as their homeland included the following towns: Zorah, Eshtaol, Ir-shemesh, 42 Shaalabbin, Aijalon, Ithlah, 43 Elon, Timnah, Ekron, 44 Eltekeh, Gibbethon, Baalath, 45 Jehud, Bene-berak, Gath-rimmon, 46 Me-jarkon, Rakkon, and the territory across from Joppa.

47 But the tribe of Dan had trouble taking possession of their land,* so they attacked the town of Laish.* They captured it, slaughtered its people, and settled there. They renamed the town Dan after their ancestor.

48 The homeland allocated to the clans of the tribe of Dan included these towns and their surrounding villages.

49 After all the land was divided among the tribes, the Israelites gave a piece of land to Joshua as his allocation. 50 For the LORD had said he could have any town he wanted. He chose Timnath-serah in the hill country of Ephraim. He rebuilt the town and lived there.

51 These are the territories that Eleazar the priest, Joshua son of Nun, and the tribal leaders allocated as grants of land to the tribes of Israel by casting sacred lots in the presence of the LORD at the entrance of the Tabernacle* at Shiloh. So the division of the land was completed.

20:1 THE LORD said to Joshua, 2 "Now tell the Israelites to designate the cities of refuge, as I instructed Moses. 3 Anyone who kills another person accidentally and unintentionally can run to one of these cities; they will be places of refuge from relatives seeking revenge for the person who was killed.

4 "Upon reaching one of these cities, the one who caused the death will appear before the elders at the city gate and present his case. They must allow him to enter the city and give him a place to live among them. 5 If the relatives of the victim come to avenge the killing, the leaders must not release the slayer to them, for he killed the other person

unintentionally and without previous hostility. [6] But the slayer must stay in that city and be tried by the local assembly, which will render a judgment. And he must continue to live in that city until the death of the high priest who was in office at the time of the accident. After that, he is free to return to his own home in the town from which he fled."

[7] The following cities were designated as cities of refuge: Kedesh of Galilee, in the hill country of Naphtali; Shechem, in the hill country of Ephraim; and Kiriath-arba (that is, Hebron), in the hill country of Judah. [8] On the east side of the Jordan River, across from Jericho, the following cities were designated: Bezer, in the wilderness plain of the tribe of Reuben; Ramoth in Gilead, in the territory of the tribe of Gad; and Golan in Bashan, in the land of the tribe of Manasseh. [9] These cities were set apart for all the Israelites as well as the foreigners living among them. Anyone who accidentally killed another person could take refuge in one of these cities. In this way, they could escape being killed in revenge prior to standing trial before the local assembly.

19:28 As in some Hebrew manuscripts (see also 21:30); most Hebrew manuscripts read *Ebron.* 19:29 Hebrew *the sea.* 19:34 Hebrew *and Judah at the Jordan River.* 19:47a Or *had trouble holding onto their land.* 19:47b Hebrew *Leshem,* a variant spelling of Laish. 19:51 Hebrew *Tent of Meeting.*

LUKE 19:28-48

After telling this story, Jesus went on toward Jerusalem, walking ahead of his disciples. [29] As they came to the towns of Bethphage and Bethany on the Mount of Olives, he sent two disciples ahead. [30] "Go into that village over there," he told them. "As you enter it, you will see a young donkey tied there that no one has ever ridden. Untie it and bring it here. [31] If anyone asks, 'Why are you untying that colt?' just say, 'The Lord needs it.'"

[32] So they went and found the colt, just as Jesus had said. [33] And sure enough, as they were untying it, the owners asked them, "Why are you untying that colt?"

[34] And the disciples simply replied, "The Lord needs it." [35] So they brought the colt to Jesus and threw their garments over it for him to ride on.

[36] As he rode along, the crowds spread out their garments on the road ahead of him. [37] When they reached the place where the road started down the Mount of Olives, all of his followers began to shout and sing as they walked along, praising God for all the wonderful miracles they had seen.

[38] "Blessings on the King who comes in the name of the LORD!
Peace in heaven, and glory in highest heaven!"*

[39] But some of the Pharisees among the crowd said, "Teacher, rebuke your followers for saying things like that!"

[40] He replied, "If they kept quiet, the stones along the road would burst into cheers!"

[41] But as they came closer to Jerusalem and Jesus saw the city ahead, he began to weep. [42] "How I wish today that you of all people would understand the way to peace. But now it is too late, and peace is hidden from your eyes. [43] Before long your enemies will build ramparts against your walls and encircle you and close in on you from every side. [44] They will crush you into the ground, and your children with you. Your enemies will not leave a single stone in place, because you did not accept your opportunity for salvation."

[45] **Then Jesus entered the Temple and began to drive out the people selling animals for sacrifices. [46] He said to them, "The Scriptures declare, 'My Temple will be a house of prayer,' but you have turned it into a den of thieves.'"***

[47] After that, he taught daily in the Temple, but the leading priests, the teachers of religious law, and the other leaders of the people began planning how to kill him. [48] But they could think of nothing, because all the people hung on every word he said.

19:38 Pss 118:26; 148:1. 19:46 Isa 56:7; Jer 7:11.

PSALM 88:1-18

For the choir director: A psalm of the descendants of Korah. A song to be sung to the tune "The Suffering of Affliction." A psalm* of Heman the Ezrahite.

¹ O LORD, God of my salvation,
    I cry out to you by day.
    I come to you at night.
² Now hear my prayer;
    listen to my cry.
³ For my life is full of troubles,
    and death* draws near.
⁴ I am as good as dead,
    like a strong man with no
      strength left.
⁵ They have left me among
      the dead,
    and I lie like a corpse in a grave.
    I am forgotten,
      cut off from your care.
⁶ You have thrown me into the
      lowest pit,
    into the darkest depths.
⁷ Your anger weighs me down;
    with wave after wave you have
      engulfed me.   *Interlude*

⁸ You have driven my friends away
    by making me repulsive to them.
    I am in a trap with no way of escape.
⁹   My eyes are blinded by my tears.
    Each day I beg for your help,
    O LORD;
    I lift my hands to you for mercy.
¹⁰ Are your wonderful deeds of any
      use to the dead?
    Do the dead rise up and
      praise you?   *Interlude*

¹¹ Can those in the grave declare your
      unfailing love?
    Can they proclaim your
      faithfulness in the place
      of destruction?*
¹² Can the darkness speak of your
      wonderful deeds?
    Can anyone in the land of
      forgetfulness talk about your
      righteousness?
¹³ O LORD, I cry out to you.
    I will keep on pleading day by day.
¹⁴ O LORD, why do you reject me?

Why do you turn your face
    from me?

¹⁵ I have been sick and close to death
    since my youth.
    I stand helpless and desperate
    before your terrors.
¹⁶ Your fierce anger has overwhelmed
    me.
    Your terrors have paralyzed me.
¹⁷ They swirl around me like
      floodwaters all day long.
    They have engulfed me
      completely.
¹⁸ You have taken away my
      companions and loved ones.
    Darkness is my closest friend.

88:TITLE Hebrew *maskil*. This may be a literary or musical term.   **88:3** Hebrew *Sheol*.   **88:11** Hebrew *in Abaddon?*

PROVERBS 13:12-14

Hope deferred makes the heart sick, but a dream fulfilled is a tree of life. ☐ People who despise advice are asking for trouble; those who respect a command will succeed. ☐ The instruction of the wise is like a life-giving fountain; those who accept it avoid the snares of death.

APRIL
20

JOSHUA 21:1–22:20

Then the leaders of the tribe of Levi came to consult with Eleazar the priest, Joshua son of Nun, and the leaders of the other tribes of Israel. ² They came to them at Shiloh in the land of Canaan and said, "The LORD commanded Moses to give us towns to live in and pasturelands for our livestock." ³ So by the command of the LORD the people of Israel gave the Levites the following towns and pasturelands out of their own grants of land.

⁴ The descendants of Aaron, who were members of the Kohathite clan

within the tribe of Levi, were allotted thirteen towns that were originally assigned to the tribes of Judah, Simeon, and Benjamin. [5]The other families of the Kohathite clan were allotted ten towns from the tribes of Ephraim, Dan, and the half-tribe of Manasseh.

[6]The clan of Gershon was allotted thirteen towns from the tribes of Issachar, Asher, Naphtali, and the half-tribe of Manasseh in Bashan.

[7]The clan of Merari was allotted twelve towns from the tribes of Reuben, Gad, and Zebulun.

[8]So the Israelites obeyed the LORD's command to Moses and assigned these towns and pasturelands to the Levites by casting sacred lots.

[9]The Israelites gave the following towns from the tribes of Judah and Simeon [10]to the descendants of Aaron, who were members of the Kohathite clan within the tribe of Levi, since the sacred lot fell to them first: [11]Kiriath-arba (that is, Hebron), in the hill country of Judah, along with its surrounding pasturelands. (Arba was an ancestor of Anak.) [12]But the open fields beyond the town and the surrounding villages were given to Caleb son of Jephunneh as his possession.

[13]The following towns with their pasturelands were given to the descendants of Aaron the priest: Hebron (a city of refuge for those who accidentally killed someone), Libnah, [14]Jattir, Eshtemoa, [15]Holon, Debir, [16]Ain, Juttah, and Beth-shemesh—nine towns from these two tribes.

[17]From the tribe of Benjamin the priests were given the following towns with their pasturelands: Gibeon, Geba, [18]Anathoth, and Almon—four towns. [19]So in all, thirteen towns with their pasturelands were given to the priests, the descendants of Aaron.

[20]The rest of the Kohathite clan from the tribe of Levi was allotted the following towns and pasturelands from the tribe of Ephraim: [21]Shechem in the hill country of Ephraim (a city of refuge for those who accidentally killed someone), Gezer, [22]Kibzaim, and Beth-horon—four towns.

[23]The following towns and pasturelands were allotted to the priests from the tribe of Dan: Eltekeh, Gibbethon, [24]Aijalon, and Gath-rimmon—four towns.

[25]The half-tribe of Manasseh allotted the following towns with their pasturelands to the priests: Taanach and Gath-rimmon—two towns. [26]So in all, ten towns with their pasturelands were given to the rest of the Kohathite clan.

[27]The descendants of Gershon, another clan within the tribe of Levi, received the following towns with their pasturelands from the half-tribe of Manasseh: Golan in Bashan (a city of refuge for those who accidentally killed someone) and Be-eshterah—two towns.

[28]From the tribe of Issachar they received the following towns with their pasturelands: Kishion, Daberath, [29]Jarmuth, and En-gannim—four towns.

[30]From the tribe of Asher they received the following towns with their pasturelands: Mishal, Abdon, [31]Helkath, and Rehob—four towns.

[32]From the tribe of Naphtali they received the following towns with their pasturelands: Kedesh in Galilee (a city of refuge for those who accidentally killed someone), Hammoth-dor, and Kartan—three towns. [33]So in all, thirteen towns with their pasturelands were allotted to the clan of Gershon.

[34]The rest of the Levites—the Merari clan—were given the following towns with their pasturelands from the tribe of Zebulun: Jokneam, Kartah, [35]Dimnah, and Nahalal—four towns.

[36]From the tribe of Reuben they received the following towns with their pasturelands: Bezer, Jahaz,* [37]Kedemoth, and Mephaath—four towns.

[38]From the tribe of Gad they received the following towns with their pasturelands: Ramoth in Gilead (a city of refuge for those who accidentally killed someone), Mahanaim, [39]Heshbon, and Jazer—four towns. [40]So in all, twelve towns were allotted to the clan of Merari.

⁴¹The total number of towns and pasturelands within Israelite territory given to the Levites came to forty-eight. ⁴²Every one of these towns had pasturelands surrounding it.

⁴³So the LORD gave to Israel all the land he had sworn to give their ancestors, and they took possession of it and settled there. ⁴⁴And the LORD gave them rest on every side, just as he had solemnly promised their ancestors. None of their enemies could stand against them, for the LORD helped them conquer all their enemies. ⁴⁵Not a single one of all the good promises the LORD had given to the family of Israel was left unfulfilled; everything he had spoken came true.

22:1THEN Joshua called together the tribes of Reuben, Gad, and the half-tribe of Manasseh. ²He told them, "You have done as Moses, the servant of the LORD, commanded you, and you have obeyed every order I have given you. ³During all this time you have not deserted the other tribes. You have been careful to obey the commands of the LORD your God right up to the present day. ⁴And now the LORD your God has given the other tribes rest, as he promised them. So go back home to the land that Moses, the servant of the LORD, gave you as your possession on the east side of the Jordan River. ⁵But be very careful to obey all the commands and the instructions that Moses gave to you. Love the LORD your God, walk in all his ways, obey his commands, hold firmly to him, and serve him with all your heart and all your soul." ⁶So Joshua blessed them and sent them away, and they went home.

⁷Moses had given the land of Bashan, east of the Jordan River, to the half-tribe of Manasseh. (The other half of the tribe was given land west of the Jordan.) As Joshua sent them away and blessed them, ⁸he said to them, "Go back to your homes with the great wealth you have taken from your enemies—the vast herds of livestock, the silver, gold, bronze, and iron, and the large supply of clothing. Share the plunder with your relatives."

⁹So the men of Reuben, Gad, and the half-tribe of Manasseh left the rest of Israel at Shiloh in the land of Canaan. They started the journey back to their own land of Gilead, the territory that belonged to them according to the LORD's command through Moses.

¹⁰But while they were still in Canaan, and when they came to a place called Geliloth* near the Jordan River, the men of Reuben, Gad, and the half-tribe of Manasseh stopped to build a large and imposing altar.

¹¹The rest of Israel heard that the people of Reuben, Gad, and the half-tribe of Manasseh had built an altar at Geliloth at the edge of the land of Canaan, on the west side of the Jordan River. ¹²So the whole community of Israel gathered at Shiloh and prepared to go to war against them. ¹³First, however, they sent a delegation led by Phinehas son of Eleazar, the priest, to talk with the tribes of Reuben, Gad, and the half-tribe of Manasseh. ¹⁴In this delegation were ten leaders of Israel, one from each of the ten tribes, and each the head of his family within the clans of Israel.

¹⁵When they arrived in the land of Gilead, they said to the tribes of Reuben, Gad, and the half-tribe of Manasseh, ¹⁶"The whole community of the LORD demands to know why you are betraying the God of Israel. How could you turn away from the LORD and build an altar for yourselves in rebellion against him? ¹⁷Was our sin at Peor not enough? To this day we are not fully cleansed of it, even after the plague that struck the entire community of the LORD. ¹⁸And yet today you are turning away from following the LORD. If you rebel against the LORD today, he will be angry with all of us tomorrow.

¹⁹"If you need the altar because the land you possess is defiled, then join us in the LORD's land, where the Tabernacle of the LORD is situated, and share our land with us. But do not rebel against the

LORD or against us by building an altar other than the one true altar of the LORD our God. [20]Didn't divine anger fall on the entire community of Israel when Achan, a member of the clan of Zerah, sinned by stealing the things set apart for the LORD*? He was not the only one who died because of his sin."

21:36 Hebrew *Jahzah*, a variant spelling of Jahaz.
22:10 Or *to the circle of stones;* similarly in 22:11.
22:20 The Hebrew term used here refers to the complete consecration of things or people to the LORD, either by destroying them or by giving them as an offering.

LUKE 20:1-26

❶ne day as Jesus was teaching the people and preaching the Good News in the Temple, the leading priests, the teachers of religious law, and the elders came up to him. [2]They demanded, "By what authority are you doing all these things? Who gave you the right?"

[3]"Let me ask you a question first," he replied. [4]"Did John's authority to baptize come from heaven, or was it merely human?"

[5]They talked it over among themselves. "If we say it was from heaven, he will ask why we didn't believe John. [6]But if we say it was merely human, the people will stone us because they are convinced John was a prophet." [7]So they finally replied that they didn't know.

[8]And Jesus responded, "Then I won't tell you by what authority I do these things."

[9]Now Jesus turned to the people again and told them this story: "A man planted a vineyard, leased it to tenant farmers, and moved to another country to live for several years. [10]At the time of the grape harvest, he sent one of his servants to collect his share of the crop. But the farmers attacked the servant, beat him up, and sent him back empty-handed. [11]So the owner sent another servant, but they also insulted him, beat him up, and sent him away empty-handed. [12]A third man was sent, and they wounded him and chased him away.

[13]"'What will I do?' the owner asked himself. 'I know! I'll send my cherished son. Surely they will respect him.'

[14]"But when the tenant farmers saw his son, they said to each other, 'Here comes the heir to this estate. Let's kill him and get the estate for ourselves!' [15]So they dragged him out of the vineyard and murdered him.

"What do you suppose the owner of the vineyard will do to them?" Jesus asked. [16]"I'll tell you—he will come and kill those farmers and lease the vineyard to others."

"How terrible that such a thing should ever happen," his listeners protested.

[17]Jesus looked at them and said, "Then what does this Scripture mean?

'The stone that the builders rejected
has now become the cornerstone.'*

[18]Everyone who stumbles over that stone will be broken to pieces, and it will crush anyone it falls on."

[19]The teachers of religious law and the leading priests wanted to arrest Jesus immediately because they realized he was telling the story against them—they were the wicked farmers. But they were afraid of the people's reaction.

[20]Watching for their opportunity, the leaders sent spies pretending to be honest men. They tried to get Jesus to say something that could be reported to the Roman governor so he would arrest Jesus. [21]"Teacher," they said, "we know that you speak and teach what is right and are not influenced by what others think. You teach the way of God truthfully. [22]Now tell us—is it right for us to pay taxes to Caesar or not?"

[23]He saw through their trickery and said, [24]"Show me a Roman coin.* Whose picture and title are stamped on it?"

"Caesar's," they replied.

[25]"Well then," he said, "give to Caesar what belongs to Caesar, and give to God what belongs to God."

[26]So they failed to trap him by what he said in front of the people. Instead,

they were amazed by his answer, and they became silent.

20:17 Ps 118:22.   20:24 Greek *a denarius.*

PSALM 89:1-13
A psalm* of Ethan the Ezrahite.

¹ I will sing of the LORD's unfailing
    love forever!
  Young and old will hear of your
    faithfulness.
² Your unfailing love will last forever.
  Your faithfulness is as enduring
    as the heavens.

³ The LORD said, "I have made a
    covenant with David, my
    chosen servant.
  I have sworn this oath to him:
⁴ 'I will establish your descendants
    as kings forever;
  they will sit on your throne
    from now until eternity.'"
                                    Interlude
⁵ All heaven will praise your great
    wonders, LORD;
  myriads of angels will praise you
    for your faithfulness.
⁶ For who in all of heaven can
    compare with the LORD?
  What mightiest angel is anything
    like the LORD?
⁷ The highest angelic powers stand
    in awe of God.
  He is far more awesome than all
    who surround his throne.
⁸ O LORD God of Heaven's Armies!
  Where is there anyone as mighty
    as you, O LORD?
  You are entirely faithful.

⁹ You rule the oceans.
  You subdue their storm-tossed
    waves.
¹⁰ You crushed the great sea monster.*
  You scattered your enemies with
    your mighty arm.
¹¹ The heavens are yours, and the
    earth is yours;
  everything in the world is yours—
    you created it all.
¹² You created north and south.

  Mount Tabor and Mount Hermon
    praise your name.
¹³ Powerful is your arm!
  Strong is your hand!
  Your right hand is lifted high in
    glorious strength.

89:TITLE Hebrew *maskil.* This may be a literary or musical term.   89:10 Hebrew *Rahab,* the name of a mythical sea monster that represents chaos in ancient literature.

PROVERBS 13:15-16
A person with good sense is respected; a treacherous person is headed for destruction.* □ Wise people think before they act; fools don't—and even brag about their foolishness.

13:15 As in Greek version; Hebrew reads *the way of the treacherous is lasting.*

APRIL
21

JOSHUA 22:21–23:16
Then the people of Reuben, Gad, and the half-tribe of Manasseh answered the heads of the clans of Israel: ²²"The LORD, the Mighty One, is God! The LORD, the Mighty One, is God! He knows the truth, and may Israel know it, too! We have not built the altar in treacherous rebellion against the LORD. If we have done so, do not spare our lives this day. ²³If we have built an altar for ourselves to turn away from the LORD or to offer burnt offerings or grain offerings or peace offerings, may the LORD himself punish us.

²⁴"The truth is, we have built this altar because we fear that in the future your descendants will say to ours, 'What right do you have to worship the LORD, the God of Israel? ²⁵The LORD has placed the Jordan River as a barrier between our people and you people of Reuben and Gad. You have no claim to the LORD.' So your descendants may prevent our descendants from worshiping the LORD.

[26]"So we decided to build the altar, not for burnt offerings or sacrifices, [27]but as a memorial. It will remind our descendants and your descendants that we, too, have the right to worship the LORD at his sanctuary with our burnt offerings, sacrifices, and peace offerings. Then your descendants will not be able to say to ours, 'You have no claim to the LORD.'

[28]"If they say this, our descendants can reply, 'Look at this copy of the LORD's altar that our ancestors made. It is not for burnt offerings or sacrifices; it is a reminder of the relationship both of us have with the LORD.' [29]Far be it from us to rebel against the LORD or turn away from him by building our own altar for burnt offerings, grain offerings, or sacrifices. Only the altar of the LORD our God that stands in front of the Tabernacle may be used for that purpose."

[30]When Phinehas the priest and the leaders of the community—the heads of the clans of Israel—heard this from the tribes of Reuben, Gad, and the half-tribe of Manasseh, they were satisfied. [31]Phinehas son of Eleazar, the priest, replied to them, "Today we know the LORD is among us because you have not committed this treachery against the LORD as we thought. Instead, you have rescued Israel from being destroyed by the hand of the LORD."

[32]Then Phinehas son of Eleazar, the priest, and the other leaders left the tribes of Reuben and Gad in Gilead and returned to the land of Canaan to tell the Israelites what had happened. [33]And all the Israelites were satisfied and praised God and spoke no more of war against Reuben and Gad.

[34]The people of Reuben and Gad named the altar "Witness,"* for they said, "It is a witness between us and them that the LORD is our God, too."

[23:1]THE years passed, and the LORD had given the people of Israel rest from all their enemies. Joshua, who was now very old, [2]called together all the elders, leaders, judges, and officers of Israel. He said to them, "I am now a very old

man. [3]You have seen everything the LORD your God has done for you during my lifetime. The LORD your God has fought for you against your enemies. [4]I have allotted to you as your homeland all the land of the nations yet unconquered, as well as the land of those we have already conquered—from the Jordan River to the Mediterranean Sea* in the west. [5]This land will be yours, for the LORD your God will himself drive out all the people living there now. You will take possession of their land, just as the LORD your God promised you.

[6]"So be very careful to follow everything Moses wrote in the Book of Instruction. Do not deviate from it, turning either to the right or to the left. [7]Make sure you do not associate with the other people still remaining in the land. Do not even mention the names of their gods, much less swear by them or serve them or worship them. [8]Rather, cling tightly to the LORD your God as you have done until now.

[9]"For the LORD has driven out great and powerful nations for you, and no one has yet been able to defeat you. [10]Each one of you will put to flight a thousand of the enemy, for the LORD your God fights for you, just as he has promised. [11]So be very careful to love the LORD your God.

[12]"But if you turn away from him and cling to the customs of the survivors of these nations remaining among you, and if you intermarry with them, [13]then know for certain that the LORD your God will no longer drive them out of your land. Instead, they will be a snare and a trap to you, a whip for your backs and thorny brambles in your eyes, and you will vanish from this good land the LORD your God has given you.

[14]"Soon I will die, going the way of everything on earth. Deep in your hearts you know that every promise of the LORD your God has come true. Not a single one has failed! [15]But as surely as the LORD your God has given you the good things he promised, he will also bring disaster on you if you disobey

him. He will completely destroy you from this good land he has given you. [16]If you break the covenant of the Lord your God by worshiping and serving other gods, his anger will burn against you, and you will quickly vanish from the good land he has given you."

22:34 Some manuscripts lack this word.   23:4 Hebrew *the Great Sea.*

LUKE 20:27-47

Then Jesus was approached by some Sadducees—religious leaders who say there is no resurrection from the dead. [28]They posed this question: "Teacher, Moses gave us a law that if a man dies, leaving a wife but no children, his brother should marry the widow and have a child who will carry on the brother's name.* [29]Well, suppose there were seven brothers. The oldest one married and then died without children. [30]So the second brother married the widow, but he also died. [31]Then the third brother married her. This continued with all seven of them, who died without children. [32]Finally, the woman also died. [33]So tell us, whose wife will she be in the resurrection? For all seven were married to her!"

[34]Jesus replied, "Marriage is for people here on earth. [35]But in the age to come, those worthy of being raised from the dead will neither marry nor be given in marriage. [36]And they will never die again. In this respect they will be like angels. They are children of God and children of the resurrection.

[37]"But now, as to whether the dead will be raised—even Moses proved this when he wrote about the burning bush. Long after Abraham, Isaac, and Jacob had died, he referred to the Lord* as 'the God of Abraham, the God of Isaac, and the God of Jacob.'* [38]So he is the God of the living, not the dead, for they are all alive to him."

[39]"Well said, Teacher!" remarked some of the teachers of religious law who were standing there. [40]And then no one dared to ask him any more questions.

[41]Then Jesus presented them with a question. "Why is it," he asked, "that the Messiah is said to be the son of David? [42]For David himself wrote in the book of Psalms:

'The Lord said to my Lord,
    Sit in the place of honor
        at my right hand
[43] until I humble your enemies,
    making them a footstool under
        your feet.'*

[44]Since David called the Messiah 'Lord,' how can the Messiah be his son?"

[45]Then, with the crowds listening, he turned to his disciples and said, [46]"Beware of these teachers of religious law! For they like to parade around in flowing robes and love to receive respectful greetings as they walk in the marketplaces. And how they love the seats of honor in the synagogues and the head table at banquets. [47]Yet they shamelessly cheat widows out of their property and then pretend to be pious by making long prayers in public. Because of this, they will be severely punished."

20:28 See Deut 25:5-6.   20:37a Greek *when he wrote about the bush. He referred to the Lord.*   20:37b Exod 3:6.   20:42-43 Ps 110:1.

PSALM 89:14-37

Righteousness and justice are the
    foundation of your throne.
Unfailing love and truth walk
    before you as attendants.
[15] Happy are those who hear the
    joyful call to worship,
    for they will walk in the light
        of your presence, Lord.
[16] They rejoice all day long in your
    wonderful reputation.
    They exult in your righteousness.
[17] You are their glorious strength.
    It pleases you to make us strong.
[18] Yes, our protection comes from
        the Lord,
    and he, the Holy One of Israel,
        has given us our king.

[19] Long ago you spoke in a vision
        to your faithful people.
    You said, "I have raised up a warrior.

I have selected him from the
common people to be king.
²⁰ I have found my servant David.
I have anointed him with my
holy oil.
²¹ I will steady him with my hand;
with my powerful arm I will
make him strong.
²² His enemies will not defeat him,
nor will the wicked overpower
him.
²³ I will beat down his adversaries
before him
and destroy those who hate him.
²⁴ My faithfulness and unfailing love
will be with him,
and by my authority he will grow
in power.
²⁵ I will extend his rule over the sea,
his dominion over the rivers.
²⁶ And he will call out to me, 'You are
my Father,
my God, and the Rock of my
salvation.'
²⁷ I will make him my firstborn son,
the mightiest king on earth.
²⁸ I will love him and be kind to him
forever;
my covenant with him will
never end.
²⁹ I will preserve an heir for him;
his throne will be as endless
as the days of heaven.
³⁰ But if his descendants forsake
my instructions
and fail to obey my regulations,
³¹ if they do not obey my decrees
and fail to keep my commands,
³² then I will punish their sin
with the rod,
and their disobedience with
beating.
³³ But I will never stop loving him
nor fail to keep my promise
to him.
³⁴ No, I will not break my covenant;
I will not take back a single
word I said.
³⁵ I have sworn an oath to David,
and in my holiness I cannot lie:
³⁶ His dynasty will go on forever;

his kingdom will endure as
the sun.
³⁷ It will be as eternal as the moon,
my faithful witness in the sky!"

Interlude

PROVERBS 13:17-19

An unreliable messenger stumbles into trouble, but a reliable messenger brings healing. □ If you ignore criticism, you will end in poverty and disgrace; if you accept correction, you will be honored. □ It is pleasant to see dreams come true, but fools refuse to turn from evil to attain them.

APRIL
22

JOSHUA 24:1-33

Then Joshua summoned all the tribes of Israel to Shechem, including their elders, leaders, judges, and officers. So they came and presented themselves to God.

²Joshua said to the people, "This is what the LORD, the God of Israel, says: Long ago your ancestors, including Terah, the father of Abraham and Nahor, lived beyond the Euphrates River,* and they worshiped other gods. ³But I took your ancestor Abraham from the land beyond the Euphrates and led him into the land of Canaan. I gave him many descendants through his son Isaac. ⁴To Isaac I gave Jacob and Esau. To Esau I gave the mountains of Seir, while Jacob and his children went down into Egypt.

⁵"Then I sent Moses and Aaron, and I brought terrible plagues on Egypt; and afterward I brought you out as a free people. ⁶But when your ancestors arrived at the Red Sea,* the Egyptians chased after you with chariots and charioteers. ⁷When your ancestors cried out to the LORD, I put darkness between you and the Egyptians. I brought the sea

crashing down on the Egyptians, drowning them. With your very own eyes you saw what I did. Then you lived in the wilderness for many years.

8"Finally, I brought you into the land of the Amorites on the east side of the Jordan. They fought against you, but I destroyed them before you. I gave you victory over them, and you took possession of their land. 9Then Balak son of Zippor, king of Moab, started a war against Israel. He summoned Balaam son of Beor to curse you, 10but I would not listen to him. Instead, I made Balaam bless you, and so I rescued you from Balak.

11"When you crossed the Jordan River and came to Jericho, the men of Jericho fought against you, as did the Amorites, the Perizzites, the Canaanites, the Hittites, the Girgashites, the Hivites, and the Jebusites. But I gave you victory over them. 12And I sent terror* ahead of you to drive out the two kings of the Amorites. It was not your swords or bows that brought you victory. 13I gave you land you had not worked on, and I gave you towns you did not build— the towns where you are now living. I gave you vineyards and olive groves for food, though you did not plant them.

14"So fear the Lord and serve him wholeheartedly. Put away forever the idols your ancestors worshiped when they lived beyond the Euphrates River and in Egypt. Serve the Lord alone. 15**But if you refuse to serve the Lord, then choose today whom you will serve. Would you prefer the gods your ancestors served beyond the Euphrates? Or will it be the gods of the Amorites in whose land you now live? But as for me and my family, we will serve the Lord."**

16The people replied, "We would never abandon the Lord and serve other gods. 17For the Lord our God is the one who rescued us and our ancestors from slavery in the land of Egypt. He performed mighty miracles before our very eyes. As we traveled through the wilderness among our enemies, he preserved us. 18It was the Lord who drove out the Amorites and the other nations living here in the land. So we, too, will serve the Lord, for he alone is our God."

19Then Joshua warned the people, "You are not able to serve the Lord, for he is a holy and jealous God. He will not forgive your rebellion and your sins. 20If you abandon the Lord and serve other gods, he will turn against you and destroy you, even though he has been so good to you."

21But the people answered Joshua, "No, we will serve the Lord!"

22"You are a witness to your own decision," Joshua said. "You have chosen to serve the Lord."

"Yes," they replied, "we are witnesses to what we have said."

23"All right then," Joshua said, "destroy the idols among you, and turn your hearts to the Lord, the God of Israel."

24The people said to Joshua, "We will serve the Lord our God. We will obey him alone."

25So Joshua made a covenant with the people that day at Shechem, committing them to follow the decrees and regulations of the Lord. 26Joshua recorded these things in the Book of God's Instructions. As a reminder of their agreement, he took a huge stone and rolled it beneath the terebinth tree beside the Tabernacle of the Lord.

27Joshua said to all the people, "This stone has heard everything the Lord said to us. It will be a witness to testify against you if you go back on your word to God."

28Then Joshua sent all the people away to their own homelands.

29After this, Joshua son of Nun, the servant of the Lord, died at the age of 110. 30They buried him in the land he had been allocated, at Timnath-serah in the hill country of Ephraim, north of Mount Gaash.

31The people of Israel served the Lord throughout the lifetime of Joshua and of the elders who outlived him— those who had personally experienced all that the Lord had done for Israel.

32The bones of Joseph, which the Israelites had brought along with them when they left Egypt, were buried at Shechem, in the parcel of ground Jacob had bought from the sons of Hamor for 100 pieces of silver.* This land was located in the territory allotted to the descendants of Joseph.

33Eleazar son of Aaron also died. He was buried in the hill country of Ephraim, in the town of Gibeah, which had been given to his son Phinehas.

24:2 Hebrew *the river;* also in 24:3, 14, 15.   24:6 Hebrew *sea of reeds.*   24:12 Often rendered *the hornet.* The meaning of the Hebrew is uncertain.   24:32 Hebrew *100 kesitahs;* the value or weight of the kesitah is no longer known.

LUKE 21:1-28

While Jesus was in the Temple, he watched the rich people dropping their gifts in the collection box. 2Then a poor widow came by and dropped in two small coins.*

3"I tell you the truth," Jesus said, "this poor widow has given more than all the rest of them. 4For they have given a tiny part of their surplus, but she, poor as she is, has given everything she has."

5Some of his disciples began talking about the majestic stonework of the Temple and the memorial decorations on the walls. But Jesus said, 6"The time is coming when all these things will be completely demolished. Not one stone will be left on top of another!"

7"Teacher," they asked, "when will all this happen? What sign will show us that these things are about to take place?"

8He replied, "Don't let anyone mislead you, for many will come in my name, claiming, 'I am the Messiah,'* and saying, 'The time has come!' But don't believe them. 9And when you hear of wars and insurrections, don't panic. Yes, these things must take place first, but the end won't follow immediately."

10Then he added, "Nation will go to war against nation, and kingdom against kingdom. 11There will be great earthquakes, and there will be famines and plagues in many lands, and there will be terrifying things and great miraculous signs from heaven.

12"But before all this occurs, there

will be a time of great persecution. You will be dragged into synagogues and prisons, and you will stand trial before kings and governors because you are my followers. 13But this will be your opportunity to tell them about me.* 14So don't worry in advance about how to answer the charges against you, 15for I will give you the right words and such wisdom that none of your opponents will be able to reply or refute you! 16Even those closest to you—your parents, brothers, relatives, and friends—will betray you. They will even kill some of you. 17And everyone will hate you because you are my followers.* 18But not a hair of your head will perish! 19By standing firm, you will win your souls.

20"And when you see Jerusalem surrounded by armies, then you will know that the time of its destruction has arrived. 21Then those in Judea must flee to the hills. Those in Jerusalem must get out, and those out in the country should not return to the city. 22For those will be days of God's vengeance, and the prophetic words of the Scriptures will be fulfilled. 23How terrible it will be for pregnant women and for nursing mothers in those days. For there will be disaster in the land and great anger against this people. 24They will be killed by the sword or sent away as captives to all the nations of the world. And Jerusalem will be trampled down by the Gentiles until the period of the Gentiles comes to an end.

25"And there will be strange signs in the sun, moon, and stars. And here on earth the nations will be in turmoil, perplexed by the roaring seas and strange tides. 26People will be terrified at what they see coming upon the earth, for the powers in the heavens will be shaken. 27Then everyone will see the Son of Man* coming on a cloud with power and great glory.* 28So when all these things begin to happen, stand and look up, for your salvation is near!"

21:2 Greek *two lepta* (the smallest of Jewish coins). 21:8 Greek *claiming, 'I am.'*   21:13 Or *This will be your testimony against them.*   21:17 Greek *on account of my name.*   21:27a "Son of Man" is a title Jesus used for himself.   21:27b See Dan 7:13.

PSALM 89:38-52

But now you have rejected him
   and cast him off.
   You are angry with your anointed
      king.
39 You have renounced your covenant
      with him;
   you have thrown his crown in
      the dust.
40 You have broken down the walls
      protecting him
   and ruined every fort defending
      him.
41 Everyone who comes along has
      robbed him,
   and he has become a joke to his
      neighbors.
42 You have strengthened his enemies
   and made them all rejoice.
43 You have made his sword useless
   and refused to help him in battle.
44 You have ended his splendor
   and overturned his throne.
45 You have made him old before
      his time
   and publicly disgraced him.
                              Interlude

46 O LORD, how long will this go on?
   Will you hide yourself forever?
   How long will your anger burn
      like fire?
47 Remember how short my life is,
   how empty and futile this human
      existence!
48 No one can live forever; all
      will die.
   No one can escape the power
      of the grave.*   *Interlude*

49 Lord, where is your unfailing
      love?
   You promised it to David with
      a faithful pledge.
50 Consider, Lord, how your servants
      are disgraced!
   I carry in my heart the insults
      of so many people.
51 Your enemies have mocked me,
      O LORD;
   they mock your anointed king
      wherever he goes.

52 Praise the LORD forever!
   Amen and amen!

89:48 Hebrew *of Sheol.*

PROVERBS 13:20-23

Walk with the wise and become wise; associate with fools and get in trouble. □ Trouble chases sinners, while blessings reward the righteous. □ Good people leave an inheritance to their grandchildren, but the sinner's wealth passes to the godly. □ A poor person's farm may produce much food, but injustice sweeps it all away.

JUDGES 1:1–2:9

After the death of Joshua, the Israelites asked the LORD, "Which tribe should go first to attack the Canaanites?"

2 The LORD answered, "Judah, for I have given them victory over the land."

3 The men of Judah said to their relatives from the tribe of Simeon, "Join with us to fight against the Canaanites living in the territory allotted to us. Then we will help you conquer your territory." So the men of Simeon went with Judah.

4 When the men of Judah attacked, the LORD gave them victory over the Canaanites and Perizzites, and they killed 10,000 enemy warriors at the town of Bezek. 5 While at Bezek they encountered King Adoni-bezek and fought against him, and the Canaanites and Perizzites were defeated. 6 Adoni-bezek escaped, but the Israelites soon captured him and cut off his thumbs and big toes.

7 Adoni-bezek said, "I once had seventy kings with their thumbs and big toes cut off, eating scraps from under my table. Now God has paid me back for

what I did to them." They took him to Jerusalem, and he died there.

8The men of Judah attacked Jerusalem and captured it, killing all its people and setting the city on fire. 9Then they went down to fight the Canaanites living in the hill country, the Negev, and the western foothills.* 10Judah marched against the Canaanites in Hebron (formerly called Kiriath-arba), defeating the forces of Sheshai, Ahiman, and Talmai.

11From there they went to fight against the people living in the town of Debir (formerly called Kiriath-sepher). 12Caleb said, "I will give my daughter Acsah in marriage to the one who attacks and captures Kiriath-sepher." 13Othniel, the son of Caleb's younger brother, Kenaz, was the one who conquered it, so Acsah became Othniel's wife.

14When Acsah married Othniel, she urged him* to ask her father for a field. As she got down off her donkey, Caleb asked her, "What's the matter?"

15She said, "Let me have another gift. You have already given me land in the Negev; now please give me springs of water, too." So Caleb gave her the upper and lower springs.

16When the tribe of Judah left Jericho—the city of palms—the Kenites, who were descendants of Moses' father-in-law, traveled with them into the wilderness of Judah. They settled among the people there, near the town of Arad in the Negev.

17Then Judah joined with Simeon to fight against the Canaanites living in Zephath, and they completely destroyed* the town. So the town was named Hormah.* 18In addition, Judah captured the towns of Gaza, Ashkelon, and Ekron, along with their surrounding territories.

19The LORD was with the people of Judah, and they took possession of the hill country. But they failed to drive out the people living in the plains, who had iron chariots. 20The town of Hebron was given to Caleb as Moses had promised. And Caleb drove out the people living there, who were descendants of the three sons of Anak.

21The tribe of Benjamin, however, failed to drive out the Jebusites, who were living in Jerusalem. So to this day the Jebusites live in Jerusalem among the people of Benjamin.

22The descendants of Joseph attacked the town of Bethel, and the LORD was with them. 23They sent men to scout out Bethel (formerly known as Luz). 24They confronted a man coming out of the town and said to him, "Show us a way into the town, and we will have mercy on you." 25So he showed them a way in, and they killed everyone in the town except that man and his family. 26Later the man moved to the land of the Hittites, where he built a town. He named it Luz, which is its name to this day.

27The tribe of Manasseh failed to drive out the people living in Bethshan,* Taanach, Dor, Ibleam, Megiddo, and all their surrounding settlements, because the Canaanites were determined to stay in that region. 28When the Israelites grew stronger, they forced the Canaanites to work as slaves, but they never did drive them completely out of the land.

29The tribe of Ephraim failed to drive out the Canaanites living in Gezer, so the Canaanites continued to live there among them.

30The tribe of Zebulun failed to drive out the residents of Kitron and Nahalol, so the Canaanites continued to live among them. But the Canaanites were forced to work as slaves for the people of Zebulun.

31The tribe of Asher failed to drive out the residents of Acco, Sidon, Ahlab, Aczib, Helbah, Aphik, and Rehob. 32Instead, the people of Asher moved in among the Canaanites, who controlled the land, for they failed to drive them out.

33Likewise, the tribe of Naphtali failed to drive out the residents of Bethshemesh and Beth-anath. Instead, they moved in among the Canaanites, who controlled the land. Nevertheless, the people of Beth-shemesh and Bethanath were forced to work as slaves for the people of Naphtali.

34As for the tribe of Dan, the Amorites forced them back into the hill country and would not let them come down into the plains. 35The Amorites were determined to stay in Mount Heres, Aijalon, and Shaalbim, but when the descendants of Joseph became stronger, they forced the Amorites to work as slaves. 36The boundary of the Amorites ran from Scorpion Pass* to Sela and continued upward from there.

2:1THE angel of the LORD went up from Gilgal to Bokim and said to the Israelites, "I brought you out of Egypt into this land that I swore to give your ancestors, and I said I would never break my covenant with you. 2For your part, you were not to make any covenants with the people living in this land; instead, you were to destroy their altars. But you disobeyed my command. Why did you do this? 3So now I declare that I will no longer drive out the people living in your land. They will be thorns in your sides,* and their gods will be a constant temptation to you."

4When the angel of the LORD finished speaking to all the Israelites, the people wept loudly. 5So they called the place Bokim (which means "weeping"), and they offered sacrifices there to the LORD.

6After Joshua sent the people away, each of the tribes left to take possession of the land allotted to them. 7And the Israelites served the LORD throughout the lifetime of Joshua and the leaders who outlived him—those who had seen all the great things the LORD had done for Israel.

8Joshua son of Nun, the servant of the LORD, died at the age of 110. 9They buried him in the land he had been allocated, at Timnath-serah* in the hill country of Ephraim, north of Mount Gaash.

1:9 Hebrew the Shephelah.   1:14 Greek version and Latin Vulgate read he urged her.   1:17a The Hebrew term used here refers to the complete consecration of things or people to the LORD, either by destroying them or by giving them as an offering.   1:17b Hormah means "destruction."   1:27 Hebrew Beth-shean, a variant spelling of Beth-shan.   1:36 Hebrew Akrabbim.   2:3 Hebrew They will be in your sides; compare Num 33:55.   2:9 As in parallel text at Josh 24:30; Hebrew reads Timnath-heres, a variant spelling of Timnath-serah.

LUKE 21:29–22:13
Then he gave them this illustration: "Notice the fig tree, or any other tree. 30When the leaves come out, you know without being told that summer is near. 31In the same way, when you see all these things taking place, you can know that the Kingdom of God is near. 32I tell you the truth, this generation will not pass from the scene until all these things have taken place. 33Heaven and earth will disappear, but my words will never disappear.

34"Watch out! Don't let your hearts be dulled by carousing and drunkenness, and by the worries of this life. Don't let that day catch you unaware, 35like a trap. For that day will come upon everyone living on the earth. 36Keep alert at all times. And pray that you might be strong enough to escape these coming horrors and stand before the Son of Man."

37Every day Jesus went to the Temple to teach, and each evening he returned to spend the night on the Mount of Olives. 38The crowds gathered at the Temple early each morning to hear him.

22:1THE Festival of Unleavened Bread, which is also called Passover, was approaching. 2The leading priests and teachers of religious law were plotting how to kill Jesus, but they were afraid of the people's reaction.

3Then Satan entered into Judas Iscariot, who was one of the twelve disciples, 4and he went to the leading priests and captains of the Temple guard to discuss the best way to betray Jesus to them. 5They were delighted, and they promised to give him money. 6So he agreed and began looking for an opportunity to betray Jesus so they could arrest him when the crowds weren't around.

7Now the Festival of Unleavened Bread arrived, when the Passover lamb is sacrificed. 8Jesus sent Peter and John ahead and said, "Go and prepare the Passover meal, so we can eat it together."

9"Where do you want us to prepare it?" they asked him.

10He replied, "As soon as you enter

Jerusalem, a man carrying a pitcher of water will meet you. Follow him. At the house he enters, [11] say to the owner, 'The Teacher asks: Where is the guest room where I can eat the Passover meal with my disciples?' [12] He will take you upstairs to a large room that is already set up. That is where you should prepare our meal." [13] They went off to the city and found everything just as Jesus had said, and they prepared the Passover meal there.

PSALM 90:1–91:16
A prayer of Moses, the man of God.

[1] Lord, through all the generations
    you have been our home!
[2] Before the mountains were born,
    before you gave birth to the earth
        and the world,
        from beginning to end, you are God.

[3] You turn people back to dust,
        saying,
    "Return to dust, you mortals!"
[4] For you, a thousand years are
        as a passing day,
    as brief as a few night hours.
[5] You sweep people away like dreams
        that disappear.
    They are like grass that springs
        up in the morning.
[6] In the morning it blooms and
        flourishes,
    but by evening it is dry and
        withered.
[7] We wither beneath your anger;
    we are overwhelmed by your fury.
[8] You spread out our sins before you—
    our secret sins—and you see
        them all.
[9] We live our lives beneath your wrath,
    ending our years with a groan.

[10] Seventy years are given to us!
    Some even live to eighty.
    But even the best years are filled
        with pain and trouble;
        soon they disappear, and we
        fly away.
[11] Who can comprehend the power
        of your anger?

Your wrath is as awesome as the
        fear you deserve.
[12] Teach us to realize the brevity
        of life,
    so that we may grow in wisdom.

[13] O LORD, come back to us!
    How long will you delay?
    Take pity on your servants!
[14] Satisfy us each morning with your
        unfailing love,
    so we may sing for joy to the end
        of our lives.
[15] Give us gladness in proportion to
        our former misery!
    Replace the evil years with good.
[16] Let us, your servants, see you
        work again;
    let our children see your glory.
[17] And may the Lord our God show us
        his approval
    and make our efforts successful.
    Yes, make our efforts successful!

[91:1] THOSE **who live in the shelter
        of the Most High
    will find rest in the shadow
        of the Almighty.**
[2] **This I declare about the LORD:
    He alone is my refuge, my place
        of safety;
    he is my God, and I trust him.**
[3] For he will rescue you from
        every trap
    and protect you from deadly
        disease.
[4] He will cover you with his feathers.
    He will shelter you with his wings.
    His faithful promises are your
        armor and protection.
[5] Do not be afraid of the terrors
        of the night,
    nor the arrow that flies in the day.
[6] Do not dread the disease that stalks
        in darkness,
    nor the disaster that strikes
        at midday.
[7] Though a thousand fall at your side,
    though ten thousand are dying
        around you,
    these evils will not touch you.
[8] Just open your eyes,

and see how the wicked are
punished.

9 If you make the LORD your refuge,
   if you make the Most High your
   shelter,
10 no evil will conquer you;
   no plague will come near your
   home.
11 For he will order his angels
   to protect you wherever you go.
12 They will hold you up with
   their hands
   so you won't even hurt your foot
   on a stone.
13 You will trample upon lions
   and cobras;
   you will crush fierce lions and
   serpents under your feet!

14 The LORD says, "I will rescue those
   who love me.
   I will protect those who trust in
   my name.
15 When they call on me, I will
   answer;
   I will be with them in trouble.
   I will rescue and honor them.
16 I will reward them with a long life
   and give them my salvation."

PROVERBS 13:24-25
Those who spare the rod of discipline
hate their children. Those who love
their children care enough to discipline
them. □ The godly eat to their hearts'
content, but the belly of the wicked
goes hungry.

APRIL
24

JUDGES 2:10–3:31
After that generation died, another
generation grew up who did not acknowledge the LORD or remember the
mighty things he had done for Israel.
11The Israelites did evil in the LORD's

sight and served the images of Baal.
12They abandoned the LORD, the God of
their ancestors, who had brought them
out of Egypt. They went after other gods,
worshiping the gods of the people
around them. And they angered the
LORD. 13They abandoned the LORD to
serve Baal and the images of Ashtoreth.
14This made the LORD burn with anger
against Israel, so he handed them over to
raiders who stole their possessions. He
turned them over to their enemies all
around, and they were no longer able to
resist them. 15Every time Israel went out
to battle, the LORD fought against them,
causing them to be defeated, just as he
had warned. And the people were in
great distress.

16Then the LORD raised up judges to
rescue the Israelites from their attackers. 17Yet Israel did not listen to the
judges but prostituted themselves by
worshiping other gods. How quickly
they turned away from the path of their
ancestors, who had walked in obedience to the LORD's commands.

18Whenever the LORD raised up a
judge over Israel, he was with that judge
and rescued the people from their enemies throughout the judge's lifetime.
For the LORD took pity on his people,
who were burdened by oppression and
suffering. 19But when the judge died,
the people returned to their corrupt
ways, behaving worse than those who
had lived before them. They went after
other gods, serving and worshiping
them. And they refused to give up their
evil practices and stubborn ways.

20So the LORD burned with anger
against Israel. He said, "Because these
people have violated my covenant,
which I made with their ancestors, and
have ignored my commands, 21I will no
longer drive out the nations that Joshua
left unconquered when he died. 22I did
this to test Israel—to see whether or not
they would follow the ways of the LORD
as their ancestors did." 23That is why
the LORD left those nations in place. He
did not quickly drive them out or allow
Joshua to conquer them all.

3:1THESE are the nations that the LORD left in the land to test those Israelites who had not experienced the wars of Canaan. 2He did this to teach warfare to generations of Israelites who had no experience in battle. 3These are the nations: the Philistines (those living under the five Philistine rulers), all the Canaanites, the Sidonians, and the Hivites living in the mountains of Lebanon from Mount Baal-hermon to Lebo-hamath. 4These people were left to test the Israelites—to see whether they would obey the commands the LORD had given to their ancestors through Moses.

5So the people of Israel lived among the Canaanites, Hittites, Amorites, Perizzites, Hivites, and Jebusites, 6and they intermarried with them. Israelite sons married their daughters, and Israelite daughters were given in marriage to their sons. And the Israelites served their gods.

7The Israelites did evil in the LORD's sight. They forgot about the LORD their God, and they served the images of Baal and the Asherah poles. 8Then the LORD burned with anger against Israel, and he turned them over to King Cushan-rishathaim of Aram-naharaim.* And the Israelites served Cushan-rishathaim for eight years.

9But when the people of Israel cried out to the LORD for help, the LORD raised up a rescuer to save them. His name was Othniel, the son of Caleb's younger brother, Kenaz. 10The Spirit of the LORD came upon him, and he became Israel's judge. He went to war against King Cushan-rishathaim of Aram, and the LORD gave Othniel victory over him. 11So there was peace in the land for forty years. Then Othniel son of Kenaz died.

12Once again the Israelites did evil in the LORD's sight, and the LORD gave King Eglon of Moab control over Israel because of their evil. 13Eglon enlisted the Ammonites and Amalekites as allies, and then he went out and defeated Israel, taking possession of Jericho, the city of palms. 14And the Israelites served Eglon of Moab for eighteen years.

15But when the people of Israel cried out to the LORD for help, the LORD again raised up a rescuer to save them. His name was Ehud son of Gera, a left-handed man of the tribe of Benjamin. The Israelites sent Ehud to deliver their tribute money to King Eglon of Moab. 16So Ehud made a double-edged dagger that was about a foot* long, and he strapped it to his right thigh, keeping it hidden under his clothing. 17He brought the tribute money to Eglon, who was very fat.

18After delivering the payment, Ehud started home with those who had helped carry the tribute. 19But when Ehud reached the stone idols near Gilgal, he turned back. He came to Eglon and said, "I have a secret message for you."

So the king commanded his servants, "Be quiet!" and he sent them all out of the room.

20Ehud walked over to Eglon, who was sitting alone in a cool upstairs room. And Ehud said, "I have a message from God for you!" As King Eglon rose from his seat, 21Ehud reached with his left hand, pulled out the dagger strapped to his right thigh, and plunged it into the king's belly. 22The dagger went so deep that the handle disappeared beneath the king's fat. So Ehud did not pull out the dagger, and the king's bowels emptied.* 23Then Ehud closed and locked the doors of the room and escaped down the latrine.*

24After Ehud was gone, the king's servants returned and found the doors to the upstairs room locked. They thought he might be using the latrine in the room, 25so they waited. But when the king didn't come out after a long delay, they became concerned and got a key. And when they opened the doors, they found their master dead on the floor.

26While the servants were waiting, Ehud escaped, passing the stone idols on his way to Seirah. 27When he arrived in the hill country of Ephraim, Ehud sounded a call to arms. Then he led a band of Israelites down from the hills.

28"Follow me," he said, "for the LORD has given you victory over Moab your enemy." So they followed him. And the Israelites took control of the shallow crossings of the Jordan River across from Moab, preventing anyone from crossing.

29They attacked the Moabites and killed about 10,000 of their strongest and most able-bodied warriors. Not one of them escaped. 30So Moab was conquered by Israel that day, and there was peace in the land for eighty years.

31After Ehud, Shamgar son of Anath rescued Israel. He once killed 600 Philistines with an ox goad.

3:8 *Aram-naharaim* means "Aram of the two rivers," thought to have been located between the Euphrates and Balih Rivers in northwestern Mesopotamia.   3:16 Hebrew *gomed*, the length of which is uncertain.   3:22 Or *and it came out behind*.   3:23 Or *and went out through the porch*; the meaning of the Hebrew is uncertain.

LUKE 22:14-34

When the time came, Jesus and the apostles sat down together at the table.* 15Jesus said, "I have been very eager to eat this Passover meal with you before my suffering begins. 16For I tell you now that I won't eat this meal again until its meaning is fulfilled in the Kingdom of God."

17Then he took a cup of wine, and gave thanks to God for it. Then he said, "Take this and share it among yourselves. 18For I will not drink wine again until the Kingdom of God has come."

19He took some bread and gave thanks to God for it. Then he broke it in pieces and gave it to the disciples, saying, "This is my body, which is given for you. Do this to remember me."

20After supper he took another cup of wine and said, "This cup is the new covenant between God and his people—an agreement confirmed with my blood, which is poured out as a sacrifice for you.*

21"But here at this table, sitting among us as a friend, is the man who will betray me. 22For it has been determined that the Son of Man* must die. But what sorrow awaits the one who betrays him." 23The disciples began to ask

each other which of them would ever do such a thing.

24Then they began to argue among themselves about who would be the greatest among them. 25Jesus told them, "In this world the kings and great men lord it over their people, yet they are called 'friends of the people.' 26But among you it will be different. Those who are the greatest among you should take the lowest rank, and the leader should be like a servant. 27Who is more important, the one who sits at the table or the one who serves? The one who sits at the table, of course. But not here! For I am among you as one who serves.

28"You have stayed with me in my time of trial. 29And just as my Father has granted me a Kingdom, I now grant you the right 30to eat and drink at my table in my Kingdom. And you will sit on thrones, judging the twelve tribes of Israel.

31"Simon, Simon, Satan has asked to sift each of you like wheat. 32But I have pleaded in prayer for you, Simon, that your faith should not fail. So when you have repented and turned to me again, strengthen your brothers."

33Peter said, "Lord, I am ready to go to prison with you, and even to die with you."

34But Jesus said, "Peter, let me tell you something. Before the rooster crows tomorrow morning, you will deny three times that you even know me."

22:14 Or *reclined together*.   22:19-20 Some manuscripts omit 22:19b-20, *which is given for you . . . which is poured out as a sacrifice for you*.   22:22 "Son of Man" is a title Jesus used for himself.

PSALM 92:1–93:5

A psalm. A song to be sung on the Sabbath Day.

1 **It is good to give thanks to the LORD,
    to sing praises to the Most High.**
2 **It is good to proclaim your
        unfailing love in the morning,
    your faithfulness in the
        evening,**
3 **accompanied by the ten-stringed
        harp
    and the melody of the lyre.**

4 You thrill me, LORD, with all you
   have done for me!
   I sing for joy because of what you
   have done.
5 O LORD, what great works you do!
   And how deep are your
   thoughts.
6 Only a simpleton would not know,
   and only a fool would not
   understand this:
7 Though the wicked sprout like
   weeds
   and evildoers flourish,
   they will be destroyed forever.

8 But you, O LORD, will be exalted
   forever.
9 Your enemies, LORD, will surely
   perish;
   all evildoers will be scattered.
10 But you have made me as strong
   as a wild ox.
   You have anointed me with the
   finest oil.
11 My eyes have seen the downfall
   of my enemies;
   my ears have heard the defeat
   of my wicked opponents.
12 But the godly will flourish like palm
   trees
   and grow strong like the cedars
   of Lebanon.
13 For they are transplanted to the
   LORD's own house.
   They flourish in the courts
   of our God.
14 Even in old age they will still
   produce fruit;
   they will remain vital and green.
15 They will declare, "The LORD is just!
   He is my rock!
   There is no evil in him!"

93:1 THE LORD is king! He is robed in
   majesty.
   Indeed, the LORD is robed in
   majesty and armed with
   strength.
   The world stands firm
   and cannot be shaken.

2 Your throne, O LORD, has stood from
   time immemorial.

   You yourself are from the
   everlasting past.
3 The floods have risen up, O LORD.
   The floods have roared like
   thunder;
   the floods have lifted their
   pounding waves.
4 But mightier than the violent raging
   of the seas,
   mightier than the breakers on the
   shore—
   the LORD above is mightier than
   these!
5 Your royal laws cannot be changed.
   Your reign, O LORD, is holy forever
   and ever.

PROVERBS 14:1-2
A wise woman builds her home, but a
foolish woman tears it down with her
own hands. □ Those who follow the
right path fear the LORD; those who take
the wrong path despise him.

JUDGES 4:1–5:31
After Ehud's death, the Israelites again
did evil in the LORD's sight. 2 So the LORD
turned them over to King Jabin of Hazor,
a Canaanite king. The commander of his
army was Sisera, who lived in Harosheth-
haggoyim. 3 Sisera, who had 900 iron
chariots, ruthlessly oppressed the Israelites for twenty years. Then the people of
Israel cried out to the LORD for help.

4 Deborah, the wife of Lappidoth, was a
prophet who was judging Israel at that
time. 5 She would sit under the Palm of
Deborah, between Ramah and Bethel in
the hill country of Ephraim, and the Israelites would go to her for judgment. 6 One
day she sent for Barak son of Abinoam,
who lived in Kedesh in the land of Naphtali. She said to him, "This is what the
LORD, the God of Israel, commands you:

Call out 10,000 warriors from the tribes of Naphtali and Zebulun at Mount Tabor. ⁷And I will call out Sisera, commander of Jabin's army, along with his chariots and warriors, to the Kishon River. There I will give you victory over him."

⁸Barak told her, "I will go, but only if you go with me."

⁹"Very well," she replied, "I will go with you. But you will receive no honor in this venture, for the LORD's victory over Sisera will be at the hands of a woman." So Deborah went with Barak to Kedesh. ¹⁰At Kedesh, Barak called together the tribes of Zebulun and Naphtali, and 10,000 warriors went up with him. Deborah also went with him.

¹¹Now Heber the Kenite, a descendant of Moses' brother-in-law* Hobab, had moved away from the other members of his tribe and pitched his tent by the oak of Zaanannim near Kedesh.

¹²When Sisera was told that Barak son of Abinoam had gone up to Mount Tabor, ¹³he called for all 900 of his iron chariots and all of his warriors, and they marched from Harosheth-haggoyim to the Kishon River.

¹⁴Then Deborah said to Barak, "Get ready! This is the day the LORD will give you victory over Sisera, for the LORD is marching ahead of you." So Barak led his 10,000 warriors down the slopes of Mount Tabor into battle. ¹⁵When Barak attacked, the LORD threw Sisera and all his chariots and warriors into a panic. Sisera leaped down from his chariot and escaped on foot. ¹⁶Then Barak chased the chariots and the enemy army all the way to Harosheth-haggoyim, killing all of Sisera's warriors. Not a single one was left alive.

¹⁷Meanwhile, Sisera ran to the tent of Jael, the wife of Heber the Kenite, because Heber's family was on friendly terms with King Jabin of Hazor. ¹⁸Jael went out to meet Sisera and said to him, "Come into my tent, sir. Come in. Don't be afraid." So he went into her tent, and she covered him with a blanket.

¹⁹"Please give me some water," he said.

"I'm thirsty." So she gave him some milk from a leather bag and covered him again.

²⁰"Stand at the door of the tent," he told her. "If anybody comes and asks you if there is anyone here, say no."

²¹But when Sisera fell asleep from exhaustion, Jael quietly crept up to him with a hammer and tent peg in her hand. Then she drove the tent peg through his temple and into the ground, and so he died.

²²When Barak came looking for Sisera, Jael went out to meet him. She said, "Come, and I will show you the man you are looking for." So he followed her into the tent and found Sisera lying there dead, with the tent peg through his temple.

²³So on that day Israel saw God defeat Jabin, the Canaanite king. ²⁴And from that time on Israel became stronger and stronger against King Jabin until they finally destroyed him.

⁵:¹ON that day Deborah and Barak son of Abinoam sang this song:

² "Israel's leaders took charge,
        and the people gladly followed.
   Praise the LORD!

³ "Listen, you kings!
        Pay attention, you mighty rulers!
   For I will sing to the LORD.
        I will make music to the LORD,
        the God of Israel.

⁴ "LORD, when you set out from Seir
        and marched across the fields
        of Edom,
   the earth trembled,
        and the cloudy skies poured
        down rain.

⁵ The mountains quaked in the
        presence of the LORD,
        the God of Mount Sinai—
   in the presence of the LORD,
        the God of Israel.

⁶ "In the days of Shamgar son
        of Anath,
        and in the days of Jael,
   people avoided the main roads,

and travelers stayed on winding
pathways.
⁷ There were few people left in the
villages of Israel*—
until Deborah arose as a mother
for Israel.
⁸ When Israel chose new gods,
war erupted at the city gates.
Yet not a shield or spear could be
seen
among forty thousand warriors
in Israel!
⁹ My heart is with the commanders
of Israel,
with those who volunteered
for war.
Praise the LORD!

¹⁰ "Consider this, you who ride on fine
donkeys,
you who sit on fancy saddle
blankets,
and you who walk along the road.
¹¹ Listen to the village musicians*
gathered at the watering holes.
They recount the righteous victories
of the LORD
and the victories of his villagers
in Israel.
Then the people of the LORD
marched down to the city gates.

¹² "Wake up, Deborah, wake up!
Wake up, wake up, and sing
a song!
Arise, Barak!
Lead your captives away,
son of Abinoam!

¹³ "Down from Tabor marched the
few against the nobles.
The people of the LORD marched
down against mighty warriors.
¹⁴ They came down from Ephraim—
a land that once belonged to
the Amalekites;
they followed you, Benjamin,
with your troops.
From Makir the commanders
marched down;
from Zebulun came those who
carry a commander's staff.

¹⁵ The princes of Issachar were with
Deborah and Barak.
They followed Barak, rushing into
the valley.
But in the tribe of Reuben
there was great indecision.
¹⁶ Why did you sit at home among
the sheepfolds—
to hear the shepherds whistle
for their flocks?
Yes, in the tribe of Reuben
there was great indecision.
¹⁷ Gilead remained east of the Jordan.
And why did Dan stay home?
Asher sat unmoved at the seashore,
remaining in his harbors.
¹⁸ But Zebulun risked his life,
as did Naphtali, on the heights
of the battlefield.

¹⁹ "The kings of Canaan came and
fought,
at Taanach near Megiddo's
springs,
but they carried off no silver
treasures.
²⁰ The stars fought from heaven.
The stars in their orbits fought
against Sisera.
²¹ The Kishon River swept them
away—
that ancient torrent, the Kishon.
March on with courage, my soul!
²² Then the horses' hooves hammered
the ground,
the galloping, galloping of Sisera's
mighty steeds.
²³ 'Let the people of Meroz be cursed,'
said the angel of the LORD.
'Let them be utterly cursed,
because they did not come to help
the LORD—
to help the LORD against the
mighty warriors.'

²⁴ "Most blessed among women
is Jael,
the wife of Heber the Kenite.
May she be blessed above all
women who live in tents.
²⁵ Sisera asked for water,
and she gave him milk.
In a bowl fit for nobles,

she brought him yogurt.

26 Then with her left hand she reached
for a tent peg,
and with her right hand for the
workman's hammer.
She struck Sisera with the hammer,
crushing his head.
With a shattering blow, she
pierced his temples.

27 He sank, he fell,
he lay still at her feet.
And where he sank,
there he died.

28 "From the window Sisera's mother
looked out.
Through the window she watched
for his return, saying,
'Why is his chariot so long
in coming?
Why don't we hear the sound
of chariot wheels?'

29 "Her wise women answer,
and she repeats these words
to herself:

30 'They must be dividing the captured
plunder—
with a woman or two for
every man.
There will be colorful robes
for Sisera,
and colorful, embroidered robes
for me.
Yes, the plunder will include
colorful robes embroidered
on both sides.'

31 "LORD, may all your enemies die
like Sisera!
But may those who love you rise
like the sun in all its power!"

Then there was peace in the land for
forty years.

4:11 Or *father-in-law.*   5:7 The meaning of the Hebrew is
uncertain.   5:11 The meaning of the Hebrew is uncertain.

LUKE 22:35-53
Then Jesus asked them, "When I sent you
out to preach the Good News and you did
not have money, a traveler's bag, or extra
clothing, did you need anything?"
"No," they replied.

36 "But now," he said, "take your
money and a traveler's bag. And if you
don't have a sword, sell your cloak and
buy one! 37 For the time has come for
this prophecy about me to be fulfilled:
'He was counted among the rebels.'*
Yes, everything written about me by the
prophets will come true."
38 "Look, Lord," they replied, "we have
two swords among us."
"That's enough," he said.
39 Then, accompanied by the disciples, Jesus left the upstairs room and
went as usual to the Mount of Olives.
40 There he told them, "Pray that you will
not give in to temptation."
41 **He walked away, about a stone's
throw, and knelt down and prayed,**
42 **"Father, if you are willing, please
take this cup of suffering away from
me. Yet I want your will to be done,
not mine."** 43 Then an angel from
heaven appeared and strengthened
him. 44 He prayed more fervently, and
he was in such agony of spirit that his
sweat fell to the ground like great drops
of blood.*
45 At last he stood up again and returned to the disciples, only to find them
asleep, exhausted from grief. 46 "Why are
you sleeping?" he asked them. "Get up
and pray, so that you will not give in to
temptation."
47 But even as Jesus said this, a crowd
approached, led by Judas, one of his
twelve disciples. Judas walked over to
Jesus to greet him with a kiss. 48 But
Jesus said, "Judas, would you betray the
Son of Man with a kiss?"
49 When the other disciples saw what
was about to happen, they exclaimed,
"Lord, should we fight? We brought the
swords!" 50 And one of them struck at
the high priest's slave, slashing off his
right ear.
51 But Jesus said, "No more of this."
And he touched the man's ear and
healed him.
52 Then Jesus spoke to the leading
priests, the captains of the Temple guard,
and the elders who had come for him. "Am
I some dangerous revolutionary," he asked,

"that you come with swords and clubs to arrest me? [53] Why didn't you arrest me in the Temple? I was there every day. But this is your moment, the time when the power of darkness reigns."

22:37 Isa 53:12.   **22:43-44** Verses 43 and 44 are not included in many ancient manuscripts.

PSALM 94:1-23

⊙ Lord, the God of vengeance,
    O God of vengeance, let your
        glorious justice shine forth!
[2] Arise, O judge of the earth.
    Give the proud what they
        deserve.
[3] How long, O Lord?
    How long will the wicked be
        allowed to gloat?
[4] How long will they speak with
        arrogance?
    How long will these evil people
        boast?
[5] They crush your people, Lord,
    hurting those you claim as your
        own.
[6] They kill widows and foreigners
    and murder orphans.
[7] "The Lord isn't looking," they say,
    "and besides, the God of Israel*
        doesn't care."

[8] Think again, you fools!
    When will you finally catch on?
[9] Is he deaf—the one who made
        your ears?
    Is he blind—the one who formed
        your eyes?
[10] He punishes the nations—won't he
        also punish you?
    He knows everything—doesn't
        he also know what you are
        doing?
[11] The Lord knows people's thoughts;
    he knows they are worthless!

[12] Joyful are those you discipline,
        Lord,
    those you teach with your
        instructions.
[13] You give them relief from troubled
        times
    until a pit is dug to capture
        the wicked.

[14] The Lord will not reject his people;
    he will not abandon his special
        possession.
[15] Judgment will again be founded on
        justice,
    and those with virtuous hearts
        will pursue it.

[16] Who will protect me from the
        wicked?
    Who will stand up for me against
        evildoers?
[17] Unless the Lord had helped me,
    I would soon have settled in the
        silence of the grave.
[18] I cried out, "I am slipping!"
    but your unfailing love, O Lord,
        supported me.
[19] When doubts filled my mind,
    your comfort gave me renewed
        hope and cheer.

[20] Can unjust leaders claim that God
        is on their side—
    leaders whose decrees permit
        injustice?
[21] They gang up against the righteous
    and condemn the innocent to
        death.
[22] But the Lord is my fortress;
    my God is the mighty rock where
        I hide.
[23] God will turn the sins of evil people
        back on them.
    He will destroy them for their
        sins.
    The Lord our God will destroy
        them.

94:7 Hebrew *of Jacob*. See note on 44:4.

PROVERBS 14:3-4

A fool's proud talk becomes a rod that beats him, but the words of the wise keep them safe. ☐ Without oxen a stable stays clean, but you need a strong ox for a large harvest.

APRIL 26

JUDGES 6:1-40

The Israelites did evil in the LORD's sight. So the LORD handed them over to the Midianites for seven years. ²The Midianites were so cruel that the Israelites made hiding places for themselves in the mountains, caves, and strongholds. ³Whenever the Israelites planted their crops, marauders from Midian, Amalek, and the people of the east would attack Israel, ⁴camping in the land and destroying crops as far away as Gaza. They left the Israelites with nothing to eat, taking all the sheep, goats, cattle, and donkeys. ⁵These enemy hordes, coming with their livestock and tents, were as thick as locusts; they arrived on droves of camels too numerous to count. And they stayed until the land was stripped bare. ⁶So Israel was reduced to starvation by the Midianites. Then the Israelites cried out to the LORD for help.

⁷When they cried out to the LORD because of Midian, ⁸the LORD sent a prophet to the Israelites. He said, "This is what the LORD, the God of Israel, says: I brought you up out of slavery in Egypt. ⁹I rescued you from the Egyptians and from all who oppressed you. I drove out your enemies and gave you their land. ¹⁰I told you, 'I am the LORD your God. You must not worship the gods of the Amorites, in whose land you now live.' But you have not listened to me."

¹¹Then the angel of the LORD came and sat beneath the great tree at Ophrah, which belonged to Joash of the clan of Abiezer. Gideon son of Joash was threshing wheat at the bottom of a winepress to hide the grain from the Midianites. ¹²The angel of the LORD appeared to him and said, "Mighty hero, the LORD is with you!"

¹³"Sir," Gideon replied, "if the LORD is with us, why has all this happened to us? And where are all the miracles our ancestors told us about? Didn't they say, 'The LORD brought us up out of Egypt'? But now the LORD has abandoned us and handed us over to the Midianites."

¹⁴Then the LORD turned to him and said, "Go with the strength you have, and rescue Israel from the Midianites. I am sending you!"

¹⁵"But Lord," Gideon replied, "how can I rescue Israel? My clan is the weakest in the whole tribe of Manasseh, and I am the least in my entire family!"

¹⁶The LORD said to him, "I will be with you. And you will destroy the Midianites as if you were fighting against one man."

¹⁷Gideon replied, "If you are truly going to help me, show me a sign to prove that it is really the LORD speaking to me. ¹⁸Don't go away until I come back and bring my offering to you."

He answered, "I will stay here until you return."

¹⁹Gideon hurried home. He cooked a young goat, and with a basket* of flour he baked some bread without yeast. Then, carrying the meat in a basket and the broth in a pot, he brought them out and presented them to the angel, who was under the great tree.

²⁰The angel of God said to him, "Place the meat and the unleavened bread on this rock, and pour the broth over it." And Gideon did as he was told. ²¹Then the angel of the LORD touched the meat and bread with the tip of the staff in his hand, and fire flamed up from the rock and consumed all he had brought. And the angel of the LORD disappeared.

²²When Gideon realized that it was the angel of the LORD, he cried out, "Oh, Sovereign LORD, I'm doomed! I have seen the angel of the LORD face to face!"

²³"It is all right," the LORD replied. "Do not be afraid. You will not die." ²⁴And Gideon built an altar to the LORD there and named it Yahweh-Shalom (which means "the LORD is peace"). The altar remains in Ophrah in the land of the clan of Abiezer to this day.

²⁵That night the LORD said to Gideon, "Take the second bull from your father's

herd, the one that is seven years old. Pull down your father's altar to Baal, and cut down the Asherah pole standing beside it. 26Then build an altar to the LORD your God here on this hilltop sanctuary, laying the stones carefully. Sacrifice the bull as a burnt offering on the altar, using as fuel the wood of the Asherah pole you cut down."

27So Gideon took ten of his servants and did as the LORD had commanded. But he did it at night because he was afraid of the other members of his father's household and the people of the town.

28Early the next morning, as the people of the town began to stir, someone discovered that the altar of Baal had been broken down and that the Asherah pole beside it had been cut down. In their place a new altar had been built, and on it were the remains of the bull that had been sacrificed. 29The people said to each other, "Who did this?" And after asking around and making a careful search, they learned that it was Gideon, the son of Joash.

30"Bring out your son," the men of the town demanded of Joash. "He must die for destroying the altar of Baal and for cutting down the Asherah pole."

31But Joash shouted to the mob that confronted him, "Why are you defending Baal? Will you argue his case? Whoever pleads his case will be put to death by morning! If Baal truly is a god, let him defend himself and destroy the one who broke down his altar!" 32From then on Gideon was called Jerub-baal, which means "Let Baal defend himself," because he broke down Baal's altar.

33Soon afterward the armies of Midian, Amalek, and the people of the east formed an alliance against Israel and crossed the Jordan, camping in the valley of Jezreel. 34Then the Spirit of the LORD took possession of Gideon. He blew a ram's horn as a call to arms, and the men of the clan of Abiezer came to him. 35He also sent messengers throughout Manasseh, Asher, Zebulun, and Naphtali, summoning their warriors, and all of them responded.

36Then Gideon said to God, "If you are truly going to use me to rescue Israel as you promised, 37prove it to me in this way. I will put a wool fleece on the threshing floor tonight. If the fleece is wet with dew in the morning but the ground is dry, then I will know that you are going to help me rescue Israel as you promised." 38And that is just what happened. When Gideon got up early the next morning, he squeezed the fleece and wrung out a whole bowlful of water.

39Then Gideon said to God, "Please don't be angry with me, but let me make one more request. Let me use the fleece for one more test. This time let the fleece remain dry while the ground around it is wet with dew." 40So that night God did as Gideon asked. The fleece was dry in the morning, but the ground was covered with dew.

6:19 Hebrew *an ephah* [20 quarts or 22 liters].

LUKE 22:54–23:12

So they arrested him and led him to the high priest's home. And Peter followed at a distance. 55The guards lit a fire in the middle of the courtyard and sat around it, and Peter joined them there. 56A servant girl noticed him in the firelight and began staring at him. Finally she said, "This man was one of Jesus' followers!"

57But Peter denied it. "Woman," he said, "I don't even know him!"

58After a while someone else looked at him and said, "You must be one of them!"

"No, man, I'm not!" Peter retorted.

59About an hour later someone else insisted, "This must be one of them, because he is a Galilean, too."

60But Peter said, "Man, I don't know what you are talking about." And immediately, while he was still speaking, the rooster crowed.

61At that moment the Lord turned and looked at Peter. Then Peter remembered that the Lord had said, "Before the rooster crows tomorrow morning, you will deny three times that you even know me." 62And Peter left the courtyard, weeping bitterly.

63The guards in charge of Jesus began mocking and beating him. 64They blindfolded him and said, "Prophesy to us! Who hit you that time?" 65And they hurled all sorts of terrible insults at him.

66At daybreak all the elders of the people assembled, including the leading priests and the teachers of religious law. Jesus was led before this high council,* 67and they said, "Tell us, are you the Messiah?"

But he replied, "If I tell you, you won't believe me. 68And if I ask you a question, you won't answer. 69But from now on the Son of Man will be seated in the place of power at God's right hand.*"

70They all shouted, "So, are you claiming to be the Son of God?"

And he replied, "You say that I am."

71"Why do we need other witnesses?" they said. "We ourselves heard him say it."

23:1THEN the entire council took Jesus to Pilate, the Roman governor. 2They began to state their case: "This man has been leading our people astray by telling them not to pay their taxes to the Roman government and by claiming he is the Messiah, a king."

3So Pilate asked him, "Are you the king of the Jews?"

Jesus replied, "You have said it."

4Pilate turned to the leading priests and to the crowd and said, "I find nothing wrong with this man!"

5Then they became insistent. "But he is causing riots by his teaching wherever he goes—all over Judea, from Galilee to Jerusalem!"

6"Oh, is he a Galilean?" Pilate asked. 7When they said that he was, Pilate sent him to Herod Antipas, because Galilee was under Herod's jurisdiction, and Herod happened to be in Jerusalem at the time.

8Herod was delighted at the opportunity to see Jesus, because he had heard about him and had been hoping for a long time to see him perform a miracle. 9He asked Jesus question after question, but Jesus refused to answer. 10Meanwhile, the leading priests and the teachers of religious law stood there shouting their accusations. 11Then Herod and his soldiers began mocking and ridiculing Jesus. Finally, they put a royal robe on him and sent him back to Pilate. 12(Herod and Pilate, who had been enemies before, became friends that day.)

22:66 Greek *before their Sanhedrin.*   22:69 See Ps 110:1.

PSALM 95:1–96:13

Come, let us sing to the LORD!
  Let us shout joyfully to the Rock
    of our salvation.
2 Let us come to him with
    thanksgiving.
  Let us sing psalms of praise
    to him.
3 For the LORD is a great God,
  a great King above all gods.
4 He holds in his hands the depths
    of the earth
  and the mightiest mountains.
5 The sea belongs to him, for he
    made it.
  His hands formed the dry
    land, too.

6 **Come, let us worship and
    bow down.
  Let us kneel before the
    LORD our maker,**
7 **for he is our God.
  We are the people he watches over,
    the flock under his care.**

  If only you would listen to his
    voice today!
8 The LORD says, "Don't harden your
    hearts as Israel did at Meribah,
  as they did at Massah in the
    wilderness.
9 For there your ancestors tested and
    tried my patience,
  even though they saw everything
    I did.
10 For forty years I was angry with
    them, and I said,
  'They are a people whose hearts turn
    away from me.

They refuse to do what I tell
them.'
[11] So in my anger I took an oath:
'They will never enter my place
of rest.'"

96:1 SING a new song to the LORD!
Let the whole earth sing to the
LORD!
[2] Sing to the LORD; praise his name.
Each day proclaim the good news
that he saves.
[3] Publish his glorious deeds among
the nations.
Tell everyone about the amazing
things he does.
[4] Great is the LORD! He is most worthy
of praise!
He is to be feared above all gods.
[5] The gods of other nations are mere
idols,
but the LORD made the heavens!
[6] Honor and majesty surround him;
strength and beauty fill his
sanctuary.
[7] O nations of the world, recognize
the LORD;
recognize that the LORD is
glorious and strong.
[8] Give to the LORD the glory he
deserves!
Bring your offering and come into
his courts.
[9] Worship the LORD in all his holy
splendor.
Let all the earth tremble before
him.
[10] Tell all the nations, "The LORD
reigns!"
The world stands firm and cannot
be shaken.
He will judge all peoples fairly.
[11] Let the heavens be glad, and the
earth rejoice!
Let the sea and everything in it
shout his praise!
[12] Let the fields and their crops burst
out with joy!
Let the trees of the forest rustle
with praise
[13] before the LORD, for he is coming!

He is coming to judge the earth.
He will judge the world with justice,
and the nations with his truth.

PROVERBS 14:5-6
An honest witness does not lie; a false
witness breathes lies. □ A mocker seeks
wisdom and never finds it, but knowledge comes easily to those with understanding.

APRIL
27

JUDGES 7:1–8:17
So Jerub-baal (that is, Gideon) and his
army got up early and went as far as the
spring of Harod. The armies of Midian
were camped north of them in the valley near the hill of Moreh. [2] The LORD
said to Gideon, "You have too many warriors with you. If I let all of you fight the
Midianites, the Israelites will boast to
me that they saved themselves by their
own strength. [3] Therefore, tell the people, 'Whoever is timid or afraid may
leave this mountain* and go home.'" So
22,000 of them went home, leaving
only 10,000 who were willing to fight.

[4] But the LORD told Gideon, "There are
still too many! Bring them down to the
spring, and I will test them to determine
who will go with you and who will not."
[5] When Gideon took his warriors down
to the water, the LORD told him, "Divide
the men into two groups. In one group
put all those who cup water in their
hands and lap it up with their tongues
like dogs. In the other group put all those
who kneel down and drink with their
mouths in the stream." [6] Only 300 of the
men drank from their hands. All the others got down on their knees and drank
with their mouths in the stream.

[7] The LORD told Gideon, "With these
300 men I will rescue you and give you
victory over the Midianites. Send all the

others home." ⁸So Gideon collected the provisions and rams' horns of the other warriors and sent them home. But he kept the 300 men with him.

The Midianite camp was in the valley just below Gideon. ⁹That night the LORD said, "Get up! Go down into the Midianite camp, for I have given you victory over them! ¹⁰But if you are afraid to attack, go down to the camp with your servant Purah. ¹¹Listen to what the Midianites are saying, and you will be greatly encouraged. Then you will be eager to attack."

So Gideon took Purah and went down to the edge of the enemy camp. ¹²The armies of Midian, Amalek, and the people of the east had settled in the valley like a swarm of locusts. Their camels were like grains of sand on the seashore—too many to count! ¹³Gideon crept up just as a man was telling his companion about a dream. The man said, "I had this dream, and in my dream a loaf of barley bread came tumbling down into the Midianite camp. It hit a tent, turned it over, and knocked it flat!"

¹⁴His companion answered, "Your dream can mean only one thing—God has given Gideon son of Joash, the Israelite, victory over Midian and all its allies!"

¹⁵When Gideon heard the dream and its interpretation, he bowed in worship before the LORD.* Then he returned to the Israelite camp and shouted, "Get up! For the LORD has given you victory over the Midianite hordes!" ¹⁶He divided the 300 men into three groups and gave each man a ram's horn and a clay jar with a torch in it.

¹⁷Then he said to them, "Keep your eyes on me. When I come to the edge of the camp, do just as I do. ¹⁸As soon as I and those with me blow the rams' horns, blow your horns, too, all around the entire camp, and shout, 'For the LORD and for Gideon!'"

¹⁹It was just after midnight,* after the changing of the guard, when Gideon and the 100 men with him reached the edge of the Midianite camp. Suddenly, they blew the rams' horns and broke their clay jars. ²⁰Then all three groups blew their horns and broke their jars. They held the blazing torches in their left hands and the horns in their right hands, and they all shouted, "A sword for the LORD and for Gideon!"

²¹Each man stood at his position around the camp and watched as all the Midianites rushed around in a panic, shouting as they ran to escape. ²²When the 300 Israelites blew their rams' horns, the LORD caused the warriors in the camp to fight against each other with their swords. Those who were not killed fled to places as far away as Beth-shittah near Zererah and to the border of Abel-meholah near Tabbath.

²³Then Gideon sent for the warriors of Naphtali, Asher, and Manasseh, who joined in chasing the army of Midian. ²⁴Gideon also sent messengers throughout the hill country of Ephraim, saying, "Come down to attack the Midianites. Cut them off at the shallow crossings of the Jordan River at Beth-barah."

So all the men of Ephraim did as they were told. ²⁵They captured Oreb and Zeeb, the two Midianite commanders, killing Oreb at the rock of Oreb, and Zeeb at the winepress of Zeeb. And they continued to chase the Midianites. Afterward the Israelites brought the heads of Oreb and Zeeb to Gideon, who was by the Jordan River.

⁸:¹THEN the people of Ephraim asked Gideon, "Why have you treated us this way? Why didn't you send for us when you first went out to fight the Midianites?" And they argued heatedly with Gideon.

²But Gideon replied, "What have I accomplished compared to you? Aren't even the leftover grapes of Ephraim's harvest better than the entire crop of my little clan of Abiezer? ³God gave you victory over Oreb and Zeeb, the commanders of the Midianite army. What have I accomplished compared to that?" When the men of Ephraim heard Gideon's answer, their anger subsided.

⁴Gideon then crossed the Jordan River with his 300 men, and though

exhausted, they continued to chase the enemy. [5]When they reached Succoth, Gideon asked the leaders of the town, "Please give my warriors some food. They are very tired. I am chasing Zebah and Zalmunna, the kings of Midian."

[6]But the officials of Succoth replied, "Catch Zebah and Zalmunna first, and then we will feed your army."

[7]So Gideon said, "After the LORD gives me victory over Zebah and Zalmunna, I will return and tear your flesh with the thorns and briers from the wilderness."

[8]From there Gideon went up to Peniel* and again asked for food, but he got the same answer. [9]So he said to the people of Peniel, "After I return in victory, I will tear down this tower."

[10]By this time Zebah and Zalmunna were in Karkor with 15,000 warriors—all that remained of the allied armies of the east, for 120,000 had already been killed. [11]Gideon circled around by the caravan route east of Nobah and Jogbehah, taking the Midianite army by surprise. [12]Zebah and Zalmunna, the two Midianite kings, fled, but Gideon chased them down and captured all their warriors.

[13]After this, Gideon returned from the battle by way of Heres Pass. [14]There he captured a young man from Succoth and demanded that he write down the names of all the seventy-seven officials and elders in the town. [15]Gideon then returned to Succoth and said to the leaders, "Here are Zebah and Zalmunna. When we were here before, you taunted me, saying, 'Catch Zebah and Zalmunna first, and then we will feed your exhausted army.'" [16]Then Gideon took the elders of the town and taught them a lesson, punishing them with thorns and briers from the wilderness. [17]He also tore down the tower of Peniel and killed all the men in the town.

7:3 Hebrew *may leave Mount Gilead.* The identity of Mount Gilead is uncertain in this context. It is perhaps used here as another name for Mount Gilboa. **7:15** As in Greek version; Hebrew reads *he bowed.* **7:19** Hebrew *at the beginning of the second watch.* **8:8** Hebrew *Penuel,* a variant spelling of Peniel; also in 8:9, 17.

LUKE 23:13-43

Then Pilate called together the leading priests and other religious leaders, along with the people, [14]and he announced his verdict. "You brought this man to me, accusing him of leading a revolt. I have examined him thoroughly on this point in your presence and find him innocent. [15]Herod came to the same conclusion and sent him back to us. Nothing this man has done calls for the death penalty. [16]So I will have him flogged, and then I will release him."*

[18]Then a mighty roar rose from the crowd, and with one voice they shouted, "Kill him, and release Barabbas to us!" [19](Barabbas was in prison for taking part in an insurrection in Jerusalem against the government, and for murder.) [20]Pilate argued with them, because he wanted to release Jesus. [21]But they kept shouting, "Crucify him! Crucify him!"

[22]For the third time he demanded, "Why? What crime has he committed? I have found no reason to sentence him to death. So I will have him flogged, and then I will release him."

[23]But the mob shouted louder and louder, demanding that Jesus be crucified, and their voices prevailed. [24]So Pilate sentenced Jesus to die as they demanded. [25]As they had requested, he released Barabbas, the man in prison for insurrection and murder. But he turned Jesus over to them to do as they wished.

[26]As they led Jesus away, a man named Simon, who was from Cyrene,* happened to be coming in from the countryside. The soldiers seized him and put the cross on him and made him carry it behind Jesus. [27]A large crowd trailed behind, including many grief-stricken women. [28]But Jesus turned and said to them, "Daughters of Jerusalem, don't weep for me, but weep for yourselves and for your children. [29]For the days are coming when they will say, 'Fortunate indeed are the women who are childless, the wombs that have not borne a child and the breasts that have never nursed.' [30]People will beg the mountains, 'Fall on us,' and plead with the hills, 'Bury us.'*

³¹For if these things are done when the tree is green, what will happen when it is dry?*"

³²Two others, both criminals, were led out to be executed with him. ³³When they came to a place called The Skull,* they nailed him to the cross. And the criminals were also crucified—one on his right and one on his left.

³⁴Jesus said, "Father, forgive them, for they don't know what they are doing."* And the soldiers gambled for his clothes by throwing dice.*

³⁵The crowd watched and the leaders scoffed. "He saved others," they said, "let him save himself if he is really God's Messiah, the Chosen One." ³⁶The soldiers mocked him, too, by offering him a drink of sour wine. ³⁷They called out to him, "If you are the King of the Jews, save yourself!" ³⁸A sign was fastened to the cross above him with these words: "This is the King of the Jews."

³⁹One of the criminals hanging beside him scoffed, "So you're the Messiah, are you? Prove it by saving yourself—and us, too, while you're at it!"

⁴⁰But the other criminal protested, "Don't you fear God even when you have been sentenced to die? ⁴¹We deserve to die for our crimes, but this man hasn't done anything wrong." ⁴²Then he said, "Jesus, remember me when you come into your Kingdom."

⁴³And Jesus replied, "I assure you, today you will be with me in paradise."

23:16 Some manuscripts add verse 17, *Now it was necessary for him to release one prisoner to them during the Passover celebration.* Compare Matt 27:15; Mark 15:6; John 18:39.   23:26 *Cyrene* was a city in northern Africa.   23:30 Hos 10:8.   23:31 Or *If these things are done to me, the living tree, what will happen to you, the dry tree?*   23:33 Sometimes rendered *Calvary,* which comes from the Latin word for "skull."   23:34a This sentence is not included in many ancient manuscripts.   23:34b Greek *by casting lots.* See Ps 22:18.

PSALM 97:1–98:9

The LORD is king!
　　Let the earth rejoice!
　　Let the farthest coastlands be glad.
² Dark clouds surround him.
　　Righteousness and justice are the
　　　　foundation of his throne.
³ Fire spreads ahead of him

and burns up all his foes.
⁴ His lightning flashes out across
　　the world.
　　The earth sees and trembles.
⁵ The mountains melt like wax
　　before the LORD,
　　before the Lord of all the earth.
⁶ The heavens proclaim his
　　righteousness;
　　every nation sees his glory.
⁷ Those who worship idols are
　　disgraced—
　　all who brag about their worthless
　　　　gods—
　　for every god must bow to him.
⁸ Jerusalem* has heard and rejoiced,
　　and all the towns of Judah
　　　　are glad
　　because of your justice, O LORD!
⁹ For you, O LORD, are supreme over
　　all the earth;
　　you are exalted far above all gods.

¹⁰ You who love the LORD, hate evil!
　　He protects the lives of his
　　　　godly people
　　and rescues them from the power
　　　　of the wicked.
¹¹ Light shines on the godly,
　　and joy on those whose hearts
　　　　are right.
¹² May all who are godly rejoice
　　in the LORD
　　and praise his holy name!

98:1 SING a new song to the LORD,
　　for he has done wonderful deeds.
　His right hand has won a mighty
　　　　victory;
　　his holy arm has shown his
　　　　saving power!
² The LORD has announced his victory
　　and has revealed his
　　　　righteousness to every nation!
³ He has remembered his promise to
　　love and be faithful to Israel.
　　The ends of the earth have seen
　　　　the victory of our God.

⁴ **Shout to the LORD, all the earth;**
　　break out in praise and sing
　　　　for joy!

⁵ Sing your praise to the Lᴏʀᴅ with
     the harp,
   with the harp and melodious
     song,
⁶ with trumpets and the sound
     of the ram's horn.
   Make a joyful symphony before
     the Lᴏʀᴅ, the King!

⁷ Let the sea and everything in it
     shout his praise!
   Let the earth and all living
     things join in.
⁸ Let the rivers clap their hands
     in glee!
   Let the hills sing out their songs
     of joy
⁹ before the Lᴏʀᴅ.
   For the Lᴏʀᴅ is coming to judge
     the earth.
   He will judge the world with justice,
     and the nations with fairness.

97:8 Hebrew *Zion.*

PROVERBS 14:7-8

Stay away from fools, for you won't find
knowledge on their lips. □ The prudent
understand where they are going, but
fools deceive themselves.

APRIL
28

JUDGES 8:18–9:21

Then Gideon asked Zebah and Zalmunna, "The men you killed at Tabor—what
were they like?"

"Like you," they replied. "They all had
the look of a king's son."

¹⁹"They were my brothers, the sons
of my own mother!" Gideon exclaimed.
"As surely as the Lᴏʀᴅ lives, I wouldn't
kill you if you hadn't killed them."

²⁰Turning to Jether, his oldest son, he
said, "Kill them!" But Jether did not
draw his sword, for he was only a boy
and was afraid.

²¹Then Zebah and Zalmunna said to
Gideon, "Be a man! Kill us yourself!" So
Gideon killed them both and took the
royal ornaments from the necks of their
camels.

²²Then the Israelites said to Gideon,
"Be our ruler! You and your son and
your grandson will be our rulers, for you
have rescued us from Midian."

²³But Gideon replied, "I will not rule
over you, nor will my son. The Lᴏʀᴅ will
rule over you! ²⁴However, I do have one
request—that each of you give me an
earring from the plunder you collected
from your fallen enemies." (The enemies, being Ishmaelites, all wore gold
earrings.)

²⁵"Gladly!" they replied. They spread
out a cloak, and each one threw in a gold
earring he had gathered from the plunder. ²⁶The weight of the gold earrings
was forty-three pounds,* not including
the royal ornaments and pendants, the
purple clothing worn by the kings of
Midian, or the chains around the necks
of their camels.

²⁷Gideon made a sacred ephod from
the gold and put it in Ophrah, his hometown. But soon all the Israelites prostituted themselves by worshiping it, and
it became a trap for Gideon and his
family.

²⁸That is the story of how the people
of Israel defeated Midian, which never
recovered. Throughout the rest of Gideon's lifetime—about forty years—there
was peace in the land.

²⁹Then Gideon* son of Joash returned
home. ³⁰He had seventy sons born to
him, for he had many wives. ³¹He also
had a concubine in Shechem, who gave
birth to a son, whom he named Abimelech. ³²Gideon died when he was very
old, and he was buried in the grave of his
father, Joash, at Ophrah in the land of the
clan of Abiezer.

³³As soon as Gideon died, the Israelites
prostituted themselves by worshiping
the images of Baal, making Baal-berith
their god. ³⁴They forgot the Lᴏʀᴅ their
God, who had rescued them from all
their enemies surrounding them. ³⁵Nor

did they show any loyalty to the family of Jerub-baal (that is, Gideon), despite all the good he had done for Israel.

⁹:¹ONE day Gideon's* son Abimelech went to Shechem to visit his uncles—his mother's brothers. He said to them and to the rest of his mother's family, ²"Ask the leading citizens of Shechem whether they want to be ruled by all seventy of Gideon's sons or by one man. And remember that I am your own flesh and blood!"

³So Abimelech's uncles gave his message to all the citizens of Shechem on his behalf. And after listening to this proposal, the people of Shechem decided in favor of Abimelech because he was their relative. ⁴They gave him seventy silver coins from the temple of Baal-berith, which he used to hire some reckless troublemakers who agreed to follow him. ⁵He went to his father's home at Ophrah, and there, on one stone, they killed all seventy of his half brothers, the sons of Gideon.* But the youngest brother, Jotham, escaped and hid.

⁶Then all the leading citizens of Shechem and Beth-millo called a meeting under the oak beside the pillar* at Shechem and made Abimelech their king.

⁷When Jotham heard about this, he climbed to the top of Mount Gerizim and shouted,

"Listen to me, citizens of Shechem!
    Listen to me if you want God to
       listen to you!
⁸ Once upon a time the trees decided
       to elect a king.
    First they said to the olive tree,
       'Be our king!'
⁹ But the olive tree refused, saying,
    'Should I quit producing the olive oil
       that blesses both God and people,
    just to wave back and forth
       over the trees?'

¹⁰ "Then they said to the fig tree,
       'You be our king!'
¹¹ But the fig tree also refused, saying,
    'Should I quit producing my
       sweet fruit

    just to wave back and forth over
       the trees?'

¹² "Then they said to the grapevine,
       'You be our king!'
¹³ But the grapevine also refused,
       saying,
    'Should I quit producing the wine
       that cheers both God and people,
    just to wave back and forth over
       the trees?'

¹⁴ "Then all the trees finally turned to
       the thornbush and said,
    'Come, you be our king!'
¹⁵ And the thornbush replied to the
       trees,
    'If you truly want to make me your
       king,
    come and take shelter in my shade.
    If not, let fire come out from me
    and devour the cedars of Lebanon.'"

¹⁶Jotham continued, "Now make sure you have acted honorably and in good faith by making Abimelech your king, and that you have done right by Gideon and all of his descendants. Have you treated him with the honor he deserves for all he accomplished? ¹⁷For he fought for you and risked his life when he rescued you from the Midianites. ¹⁸But today you have revolted against my father and his descendants, killing his seventy sons on one stone. And you have chosen his slave woman's son, Abimelech, to be your king just because he is your relative.

¹⁹"If you have acted honorably and in good faith toward Gideon and his descendants today, then may you find joy in Abimelech, and may he find joy in you. ²⁰But if you have not acted in good faith, then may fire come out from Abimelech and devour the leading citizens of Shechem and Beth-millo; and may fire come out from the citizens of Shechem and Beth-millo and devour Abimelech!"

²¹Then Jotham escaped and lived in Beer because he was afraid of his brother Abimelech.

8:26 Hebrew *1,700 shekels* [19.4 kilograms].   8:29 Hebrew *Jerub-baal;* see 6:32.   9:1 Hebrew *Jerub-baal's* (see 6:32); also in 9:2, 24.   9:5 Hebrew *Jerub-baal* (see 6:32); also in 9:16, 19, 28, 57.   9:6 The meaning of the Hebrew is uncertain.

LUKE 23:44–24:12

By this time it was noon, and darkness fell across the whole land until three o'clock. [45] The light from the sun was gone. And suddenly, the curtain in the sanctuary of the Temple was torn down the middle. [46] Then Jesus shouted, "Father, I entrust my spirit into your hands!"* And with those words he breathed his last.

[47] When the Roman officer* overseeing the execution saw what had happened, he worshiped God and said, "Surely this man was innocent.*" [48] And when all the crowd that came to see the crucifixion saw what had happened, they went home in deep sorrow.* [49] But Jesus' friends, including the women who had followed him from Galilee, stood at a distance watching.

[50] Now there was a good and righteous man named Joseph. He was a member of the Jewish high council, [51] but he had not agreed with the decision and actions of the other religious leaders. He was from the town of Arimathea in Judea, and he was waiting for the Kingdom of God to come. [52] He went to Pilate and asked for Jesus' body. [53] Then he took the body down from the cross and wrapped it in a long sheet of linen cloth and laid it in a new tomb that had been carved out of rock. [54] This was done late on Friday afternoon, the day of preparation,* as the Sabbath was about to begin.

[55] As his body was taken away, the women from Galilee followed and saw the tomb where his body was placed. [56] Then they went home and prepared spices and ointments to anoint his body. But by the time they were finished the Sabbath had begun, so they rested as required by the law.

[24:1] BUT very early on Sunday morning* the women went to the tomb, taking the spices they had prepared. [2] They found that the stone had been rolled away from the entrance. [3] So they went in, but they didn't find the body of the Lord Jesus. [4] As they stood there puzzled, two men suddenly appeared to them, clothed in dazzling robes.

[5] **The women were terrified and bowed with their faces to the ground. Then the men asked, "Why are you looking among the dead for someone who is alive? [6] He isn't here! He is risen from the dead! Remember what he told you back in Galilee, [7] that the Son of Man* must be betrayed into the hands of sinful men and be crucified, and that he would rise again on the third day."**

[8] Then they remembered that he had said this. [9] So they rushed back from the tomb to tell his eleven disciples—and everyone else—what had happened. [10] It was Mary Magdalene, Joanna, Mary the mother of James, and several other women who told the apostles what had happened. [11] But the story sounded like nonsense to the men, so they didn't believe it. [12] However, Peter jumped up and ran to the tomb to look. Stooping, he peered in and saw the empty linen wrappings; then he went home again, wondering what had happened.

23:46 Ps 31:5.   **23:47a** Greek *the centurion.*   **23:47b** Or *righteous.*   **23:48** Greek *went home beating their breasts.*   **23:54** Greek *It was the day of preparation.*   **24:1** Greek *But on the first day of the week, very early in the morning.*   **24:7** "Son of Man" is a title Jesus used for himself.

PSALM 99:1-9

The LORD is king!
  Let the nations tremble!
He sits on his throne between the
    cherubim.
  Let the whole earth quake!
[2] The LORD sits in majesty in
      Jerusalem,*
  exalted above all the nations.
[3] Let them praise your great and
      awesome name.
  Your name is holy!
[4] Mighty King, lover of justice,
    you have established fairness.
  You have acted with justice
    and righteousness throughout
      Israel.*
[5] Exalt the LORD our God!
  Bow low before his feet, for he
    is holy!

⁶ Moses and Aaron were among
   his priests;
   Samuel also called on his name.
They cried to the LORD for help,
   and he answered them.
⁷ He spoke to Israel from the pillar
   of cloud,
   and they followed the laws and
   decrees he gave them.
⁸ O LORD our God, you answered
   them.
   You were a forgiving God to them,
   but you punished them when they
   went wrong.

⁹ Exalt the LORD our God,
   and worship at his holy mountain
   in Jerusalem,
   for the LORD our God is holy!

99:2 Hebrew *Zion.*   **99:4** Hebrew *Jacob.* See note on 44:4.

PROVERBS 14:9-10
Fools make fun of guilt, but the godly
acknowledge it and seek reconciliation.
□Each heart knows its own bitterness,
and no one else can fully share its joy.

APRIL
29

JUDGES 9:22–10:18
After Abimelech had ruled over Israel
for three years, ²³God sent a spirit that
stirred up trouble between Abimelech
and the leading citizens of Shechem,
and they revolted. ²⁴God was punishing
Abimelech for murdering Gideon's seventy sons, and the citizens of Shechem
for supporting him in this treachery of
murdering his brothers. ²⁵The citizens
of Shechem set an ambush for Abimelech on the hilltops and robbed everyone who passed that way. But someone
warned Abimelech about their plot.

²⁶One day Gaal son of Ebed moved to
Shechem with his brothers and gained
the confidence of the leading citizens of
Shechem. ²⁷During the annual harvest
festival at Shechem, held in the temple of
the local god, the wine flowed freely, and
everyone began cursing Abimelech.
²⁸"Who is Abimelech?" Gaal shouted.
"He's not a true son of Shechem,* so why
should we be his servants? He's merely
the son of Gideon, and this Zebul is
merely his deputy. Serve the true sons of
Hamor, the founder of Shechem. Why
should we serve Abimelech? ²⁹If I were
in charge here, I would get rid of Abimelech. I would say* to him, 'Get some soldiers, and come out and fight!'"

³⁰But when Zebul, the leader of the
city, heard what Gaal was saying, he was
furious. ³¹He sent messengers to Abimelech in Arumah,* telling him, "Gaal son
of Ebed and his brothers have come to
live in Shechem, and now they are incit-
ing the city to rebel against you. ³²Come
by night with an army and hide out in the
fields. ³³In the morning, as soon as it is
daylight, attack the city. When Gaal and
those who are with him come out against
you, you can do with them as you wish."

³⁴So Abimelech and all his men went
by night and split into four groups, sta-
tioning themselves around Shechem.
³⁵Gaal was standing at the city gates
when Abimelech and his army came out
of hiding. ³⁶When Gaal saw them, he
said to Zebul, "Look, there are people
coming down from the hilltops!"

Zebul replied, "It's just the shadows
on the hills that look like men."

³⁷But again Gaal said, "No, people are
coming down from the hills.* And another group is coming down the road
past the Diviners' Oak.*"

³⁸Then Zebul turned on him and
asked, "Now where is that big mouth of
yours? Wasn't it you that said, 'Who is
Abimelech, and why should we be his
servants?' The men you mocked are right
outside the city! Go out and fight them!"

³⁹So Gaal led the leading citizens of
Shechem into battle against Abimelech.
⁴⁰But Abimelech chased him, and many
of Shechem's men were wounded and
fell along the road as they retreated to
the city gate. ⁴¹Abimelech returned to

Arumah, and Zebul drove Gaal and his brothers out of Shechem.

42The next day the people of Shechem went out into the fields to battle. When Abimelech heard about it, 43he divided his men into three groups and set an ambush in the fields. When Abimelech saw the people coming out of the city, he and his men jumped up from their hiding places and attacked them. 44Abimelech and his group stormed the city gate to keep the men of Shechem from getting back in, while Abimelech's other two groups cut them down in the fields. 45The battle went on all day before Abimelech finally captured the city. He killed the people, leveled the city, and scattered salt all over the ground.

46When the leading citizens who lived in the tower of Shechem heard what had happened, they ran and hid in the temple of Baal-berith.* 47Someone reported to Abimelech that the citizens had gathered in the temple, 48so he led his forces to Mount Zalmon. He took an ax and chopped some branches from a tree, then put them on his shoulder. "Quick, do as I have done!" he told his men. 49So each of them cut down some branches, following Abimelech's example. They piled the branches against the walls of the temple and set them on fire. So all the people who had lived in the tower of Shechem died—about 1,000 men and women.

50Then Abimelech attacked the town of Thebez and captured it. 51But there was a strong tower inside the town, and all the men and women—the entire population—fled to it. They barricaded themselves in and climbed up to the roof of the tower. 52Abimelech followed them to attack the tower. But as he prepared to set fire to the entrance, 53a woman on the roof dropped a millstone that landed on Abimelech's head and crushed his skull. 54He quickly said to his young armor bearer, "Draw your sword and kill me! Don't let it be said that a woman killed Abimelech!" So the young man ran him through with his sword, and he died. 55When Abimelech's men saw that he

was dead, they disbanded and returned to their homes.

56In this way, God punished Abimelech for the evil he had done against his father by murdering his seventy brothers. 57God also punished the men of Shechem for all their evil. So the curse of Jotham son of Gideon was fulfilled.

10:1AFTER Abimelech died, Tola son of Puah, son of Dodo, was the next person to rescue Israel. He was from the tribe of Issachar but lived in the town of Shamir in the hill country of Ephraim. 2He judged Israel for twenty-three years. When he died, he was buried in Shamir.

3After Tola died, Jair from Gilead judged Israel for twenty-two years. 4His thirty sons rode around on thirty donkeys, and they owned thirty towns in the land of Gilead, which are still called the Towns of Jair.* 5When Jair died, he was buried in Kamon.

6Again the Israelites did evil in the LORD's sight. They served the images of Baal and Ashtoreth, and the gods of Aram, Sidon, Moab, Ammon, and Philistia. They abandoned the LORD and no longer served him at all. 7So the LORD burned with anger against Israel, and he turned them over to the Philistines and the Ammonites, 8who began to oppress them that year. For eighteen years they oppressed all the Israelites east of the Jordan River in the land of the Amorites (that is, in Gilead). 9The Ammonites also crossed to the west side of the Jordan and attacked Judah, Benjamin, and Ephraim.

The Israelites were in great distress. 10Finally, they cried out to the LORD for help, saying, "We have sinned against you because we have abandoned you as our God and have served the images of Baal."

11The LORD replied, "Did I not rescue you from the Egyptians, the Amorites, the Ammonites, the Philistines, 12the Sidonians, the Amalekites, and the Maonites? When they oppressed you, you cried out to me for help, and I rescued you. 13Yet you have abandoned me and served other gods. So I will not rescue you anymore. 14Go and cry out to the gods you have chosen! Let them rescue you in your hour of distress!"

15But the Israelites pleaded with the LORD and said, "We have sinned. Punish us as you see fit, only rescue us today from our enemies." 16Then the Israelites put aside their foreign gods and served the LORD. And he was grieved by their misery.

17At that time the armies of Ammon had gathered for war and were camped in Gilead, and the people of Israel assembled and camped at Mizpah. 18The leaders of Gilead said to each other, "Whoever attacks the Ammonites first will become ruler over all the people of Gilead."

9:28 Hebrew *Who is Shechem?* 9:29 As in Greek version; Hebrew reads *And he said.* 9:31 Or *in secret;* Hebrew reads *in Tormah;* compare 9:41. 9:37a Or *the center of the land.* 9:37b Hebrew *Elon-meonenim.* 9:46 Hebrew *El-berith,* another name for Baal-berith; compare 9:4. 10:4 Hebrew *Havvoth-jair.*

LUKE 24:13-53

That same day two of Jesus' followers were walking to the village of Emmaus, seven miles* from Jerusalem. 14As they walked along they were talking about everything that had happened. 15As they talked and discussed these things, Jesus himself suddenly came and began walking with them. 16But God kept them from recognizing him.

17He asked them, "What are you discussing so intently as you walk along?"

They stopped short, sadness written across their faces. 18Then one of them, Cleopas, replied, "You must be the only person in Jerusalem who hasn't heard about all the things that have happened there the last few days."

19"What things?" Jesus asked.

"The things that happened to Jesus, the man from Nazareth," they said. "He was a prophet who did powerful miracles, and he was a mighty teacher in the eyes of God and all the people. 20But our leading priests and other religious leaders handed him over to be condemned to death, and they crucified him. 21We had hoped he was the Messiah who had come to rescue Israel. This all happened three days ago.

22"Then some women from our group of his followers were at his tomb early this morning, and they came back with an amazing report. 23They said his body was missing, and they had seen angels who told them Jesus is alive! 24Some of our men ran out to see, and sure enough, his body was gone, just as the women had said."

25Then Jesus said to them, "You foolish people! You find it so hard to believe all that the prophets wrote in the Scriptures. 26Wasn't it clearly predicted that the Messiah would have to suffer all these things before entering his glory?" 27Then Jesus took them through the writings of Moses and all the prophets, explaining from all the Scriptures the things concerning himself.

28By this time they were nearing Emmaus and the end of their journey. Jesus acted as if he were going on, 29but they begged him, "Stay the night with us, since it is getting late." So he went home with them. 30As they sat down to eat,* he took the bread and blessed it. Then he broke it and gave it to them. 31Suddenly, their eyes were opened, and they recognized him. And at that moment he disappeared!

32They said to each other, "Didn't our hearts burn within us as he talked with us on the road and explained the Scriptures to us?" 33And within the hour they were on their way back to Jerusalem. There they found the eleven disciples and the others who had gathered with them, 34who said, "The Lord has really risen! He appeared to Peter.*"

35Then the two from Emmaus told their story of how Jesus had appeared to them as they were walking along the road, and how they had recognized him as he was breaking the bread. 36And just as they were telling about it, Jesus himself was suddenly standing there among them. "Peace be with you," he said. 37But the whole group was startled and frightened, thinking they were seeing a ghost!

38"Why are you frightened?" he asked. "Why are your hearts filled with doubt? 39Look at my hands. Look at my feet. You can see that it's really me. Touch me and make sure that I am not a ghost, because ghosts don't have bodies, as you see that I do." [40]As he spoke, he showed them his hands and his feet.

[41]Still they stood there in disbelief, filled with joy and wonder. Then he asked them, "Do you have anything here to eat?" [42]They gave him a piece of broiled fish, [43]and he ate it as they watched.

[44]Then he said, "When I was with you before, I told you that everything written about me in the law of Moses and the prophets and in the Psalms must be fulfilled." [45]Then he opened their minds to understand the Scriptures. [46]**And he said, "Yes, it was written long ago that the Messiah would suffer and die and rise from the dead on the third day.** [47]**It was also written that this message would be proclaimed in the authority of his name to all the nations,* beginning in Jerusalem: 'There is forgiveness of sins for all who repent.'** [48]You are witnesses of all these things.

[49]"And now I will send the Holy Spirit, just as my Father promised. But stay here in the city until the Holy Spirit comes and fills you with power from heaven."

[50]Then Jesus led them to Bethany, and lifting his hands to heaven, he blessed them. [51]While he was blessing them, he left them and was taken up to heaven.* [52]So they worshiped him and then returned to Jerusalem filled with great joy. [53]And they spent all of their time in the Temple, praising God.

24:13 Greek *60 stadia* [11.1 kilometers].   24:30 Or *As they reclined.*   24:34 Greek *Simon.*   24:47 Or *all peoples.* 24:51 Some manuscripts do not include *and was taken up to heaven.*

PSALM 100:1-5
A psalm of thanksgiving.

[1] **S**hout with joy to the Lord, all the earth!
[2]   Worship the Lord with gladness. Come before him, singing with joy.
[3] Acknowledge that the Lord is God! He made us, and we are his. We are his people, the sheep of his pasture.

[4] Enter his gates with thanksgiving; go into his courts with praise. Give thanks to him and praise his name.
[5] For the Lord is good. His unfailing love continues forever, and his faithfulness continues to each generation.

PROVERBS 14:11-12
The house of the wicked will be destroyed, but the tent of the godly will flourish. □ There is a path before each person that seems right, but it ends in death.

APRIL
30

JUDGES 11:1–12:15
Now Jephthah of Gilead was a great warrior. He was the son of Gilead, but his mother was a prostitute. [2]Gilead's wife also had several sons, and when these half brothers grew up, they chased Jephthah off the land. "You will not get any of our father's inheritance," they said, "for you are the son of a prostitute." [3]So Jephthah fled from his brothers and lived in the land of Tob. Soon he had a band of worthless rebels following him.

[4]At about this time, the Ammonites began their war against Israel. [5]When the Ammonites attacked, the elders of Gilead sent for Jephthah in the land of Tob. The elders said, [6]"Come and be our commander! Help us fight the Ammonites!"

[7]But Jephthah said to them, "Aren't you the ones who hated me and drove me from my father's house? Why do you come to me now when you're in trouble?"

[8]"Because we need you," the elders replied. "If you lead us in battle against the Ammonites, we will make you ruler over all the people of Gilead."

[9]Jephthah said to the elders, "Let me

get this straight. If I come with you and if the LORD gives me victory over the Ammonites, will you really make me ruler over all the people?"

¹⁰"The LORD is our witness," the elders replied. "We promise to do whatever you say."

¹¹So Jephthah went with the elders of Gilead, and the people made him their ruler and commander of the army. At Mizpah, in the presence of the LORD, Jephthah repeated what he had said to the elders.

¹²Then Jephthah sent messengers to the king of Ammon, asking, "Why have you come out to fight against my land?"

¹³The king of Ammon answered Jephthah's messengers, "When the Israelites came out of Egypt, they stole my land from the Arnon River to the Jabbok River and all the way to the Jordan. Now then, give back the land peaceably."

¹⁴Jephthah sent this message back to the Ammonite king:

¹⁵"This is what Jephthah says: Israel did not steal any land from Moab or Ammon. ¹⁶When the people of Israel arrived at Kadesh on their journey from Egypt after crossing the Red Sea,* ¹⁷they sent messengers to the king of Edom asking for permission to pass through his land. But their request was denied. Then they asked the king of Moab for similar permission, but he wouldn't let them pass through either. So the people of Israel stayed in Kadesh.

¹⁸"Finally, they went around Edom and Moab through the wilderness. They traveled along Moab's eastern border and camped on the other side of the Arnon River. But they never once crossed the Arnon River into Moab, for the Arnon was the border of Moab.

¹⁹"Then Israel sent messengers to King Sihon of the Amorites, who ruled from Heshbon, asking for permission to cross through his land to get to their destination. ²⁰But King Sihon didn't trust Israel to pass

through his land. Instead, he mobilized his army at Jahaz and attacked them. ²¹But the LORD, the God of Israel, gave his people victory over King Sihon. So Israel took control of all the land of the Amorites, who lived in that region, ²²from the Arnon River to the Jabbok River, and from the eastern wilderness to the Jordan.

²³"So you see, it was the LORD, the God of Israel, who took away the land from the Amorites and gave it to Israel. Why, then, should we give it back to you? ²⁴You keep whatever your god Chemosh gives you, and we will keep whatever the LORD our God gives us. ²⁵Are you any better than Balak son of Zippor, king of Moab? Did he try to make a case against Israel for disputed land? Did he go to war against them?

²⁶"Israel has been living here for 300 years, inhabiting Heshbon and its surrounding settlements, all the way to Aroer and its settlements, and in all the towns along the Arnon River. Why have you made no effort to recover it before now? ²⁷Therefore, I have not sinned against you. Rather, you have wronged me by attacking me. Let the LORD, who is judge, decide today which of us is right—Israel or Ammon."

²⁸But the king of Ammon paid no attention to Jephthah's message.

²⁹At that time the Spirit of the LORD came upon Jephthah, and he went throughout the land of Gilead and Manasseh, including Mizpah in Gilead, and from there he led an army against the Ammonites. ³⁰And Jephthah made a vow to the LORD. He said, "If you give me victory over the Ammonites, ³¹I will give to the LORD whatever comes out of my house to meet me when I return in triumph. I will sacrifice it as a burnt offering."

³²So Jephthah led his army against the Ammonites, and the LORD gave him victory. ³³He crushed the Ammonites,

devastating about twenty towns from Aroer to an area near Minnith and as far away as Abel-keramim. In this way Israel defeated the Ammonites.

34When Jephthah returned home to Mizpah, his daughter came out to meet him, playing on a tambourine and dancing for joy. She was his one and only child; he had no other sons or daughters. 35When he saw her, he tore his clothes in anguish. "Oh, my daughter!" he cried out. "You have completely destroyed me! You've brought disaster on me! For I have made a vow to the LORD, and I cannot take it back."

36And she said, "Father, if you have made a vow to the LORD, you must do to me what you have vowed, for the LORD has given you a great victory over your enemies, the Ammonites. 37But first let me do this one thing: Let me go up and roam in the hills and weep with my friends for two months, because I will die a virgin."

38"You may go," Jephthah said. And he sent her away for two months. She and her friends went into the hills and wept because she would never have children. 39When she returned home, her father kept the vow he had made, and she died a virgin.

So it has become a custom in Israel 40for young Israelite women to go away for four days each year to lament the fate of Jephthah's daughter.

12:1THEN the people of Ephraim mobilized an army and crossed over the Jordan River to Zaphon. They sent this message to Jephthah: "Why didn't you call for us to help you fight against the Ammonites? We are going to burn down your house with you in it!"

2Jephthah replied, "I summoned you at the beginning of the dispute, but you refused to come! You failed to help us in our struggle against Ammon. 3So when I realized you weren't coming, I risked my life and went to battle without you, and the LORD gave me victory over the Ammonites. So why have you now come to fight me?"

4The people of Ephraim responded, "You men of Gilead are nothing more than fugitives from Ephraim and Manasseh." So Jephthah gathered all the men of Gilead and attacked the men of Ephraim and defeated them.

5Jephthah captured the shallow crossings of the Jordan River, and whenever a fugitive from Ephraim tried to go back across, the men of Gilead would challenge him. "Are you a member of the tribe of Ephraim?" they would ask. If the man said, "No, I'm not," 6they would tell him to say "Shibboleth." If he was from Ephraim, he would say "Sibboleth," because people from Ephraim cannot pronounce the word correctly. Then they would take him and kill him at the shallow crossings of the Jordan. In all, 42,000 Ephraimites were killed at that time.

7Jephthah judged Israel for six years. When he died, he was buried in one of the towns of Gilead.

8After Jephthah died, Ibzan from Bethlehem judged Israel. 9He had thirty sons and thirty daughters. He sent his daughters to marry men outside his clan, and he brought in thirty young women from outside his clan to marry his sons. Ibzan judged Israel for seven years. 10When he died, he was buried at Bethlehem.

11After Ibzan died, Elon from the tribe of Zebulun judged Israel for ten years. 12When he died, he was buried at Aijalon in Zebulun.

13After Elon died, Abdon son of Hillel, from Pirathon, judged Israel. 14He had forty sons and thirty grandsons, who rode on seventy donkeys. He judged Israel for eight years. 15When he died, he was buried at Pirathon in Ephraim, in the hill country of the Amalekites.

11:16 Hebrew *sea of reeds.*

JOHN 1:1-28

In the beginning the Word already
    existed.
    The Word was with God,
    and the Word was God.

2 He existed in the beginning with God.

3 God created everything through him, and nothing was created except through him.

4 The Word gave life to everything that was created,*
and his life brought light to everyone.

5 The light shines in the darkness, and the darkness can never extinguish it.*

6 God sent a man, John the Baptist,* 7 to tell about the light so that everyone might believe because of his testimony. 8 John himself was not the light; he was simply a witness to tell about the light. 9 The one who is the true light, who gives light to everyone, was coming into the world.

10 He came into the very world he created, but the world didn't recognize him. 11 He came to his own people, and even they rejected him. 12 **But to all who believed him and accepted him, he gave the right to become children of God.** 13 **They are reborn—not with a physical birth resulting from human passion or plan, but a birth that comes from God.**

14 So the Word became human* and made his home among us. He was full of unfailing love and faithfulness.* And we have seen his glory, the glory of the Father's one and only Son.

15 John testified about him when he shouted to the crowds, "This is the one I was talking about when I said, 'Someone is coming after me who is far greater than I am, for he existed long before me.'"

16 From his abundance we have all received one gracious blessing after another.* 17 For the law was given through Moses, but God's unfailing love and faithfulness came through Jesus Christ. 18 No one has ever seen God. But the one and only Son is himself God and* is near to the Father's heart. He has revealed God to us.

19 This was John's testimony when the Jewish leaders sent priests and Temple assistants* from Jerusalem to ask John, "Who are you?" 20 He came right out and said, "I am not the Messiah."

21 "Well then, who are you?" they asked. "Are you Elijah?"

"No," he replied.

"Are you the Prophet we are expecting?"*

"No."

22 "Then who are you? We need an answer for those who sent us. What do you have to say about yourself?"

23 John replied in the words of the prophet Isaiah:

"I am a voice shouting in the wilderness,
'Clear the way for the LORD's coming!'"*

24 Then the Pharisees who had been sent 25 asked him, "If you aren't the Messiah or Elijah or the Prophet, what right do you have to baptize?"

26 John told them, "I baptize with* water, but right here in the crowd is someone you do not recognize. 27 Though his ministry follows mine, I'm not even worthy to be his slave and untie the straps of his sandal."

28 This encounter took place in Bethany, an area east of the Jordan River, where John was baptizing.

1:3-4 Or *and nothing that was created was created except through him. The Word gave life to everything.* 1:5 Or *and the darkness has not understood it.* 1:6 Greek *a man named John.* 1:14a Greek *became flesh.* 1:14b Or *grace and truth;* also in 1:17. 1:16 Or *received the grace of Christ rather than the grace of the law;* Greek reads *received grace upon grace.* 1:18 Greek *But [the] one and only God;* other manuscripts read *But the one and only Son.* 1:19 Greek *and Levites.* 1:21 Greek *Are you the Prophet?* See Deut 18:15, 18; Mal 4:5-6. 1:23 Isa 40:3. 1:26 Or *in;* also in 1:31, 33.

PSALM 101:1-8
A psalm of David.

1 I will sing of your love and justice,
LORD.
I will praise you with songs.
2 I will be careful to live a blameless life—
when will you come to help me?
I will lead a life of integrity

in my own home.
³ I will refuse to look at
     anything vile and vulgar.
  I hate all who deal crookedly;
     I will have nothing to do
          with them.
⁴ I will reject perverse ideas
     and stay away from every evil.
⁵ I will not tolerate people who
          slander their neighbors.
     I will not endure conceit
          and pride.

⁶ I will search for faithful people
     to be my companions.
  Only those who are above reproach
will be allowed to serve me.
⁷ I will not allow deceivers to serve
     in my house,
     and liars will not stay in
          my presence.
⁸ My daily task will be to ferret
          out the wicked
     and free the city of the LORD
          from their grip.

PROVERBS 14:13-14
Laughter can conceal a heavy heart, but when the laughter ends, the grief remains. □ Backsliders get what they deserve; good people receive their reward.

MAY 1

JUDGES 13:1–14:20

Again the Israelites did evil in the LORD's sight, so the LORD handed them over to the Philistines, who oppressed them for forty years.

²In those days a man named Manoah from the tribe of Dan lived in the town of Zorah. His wife was unable to become pregnant, and they had no children. ³The angel of the LORD appeared to Manoah's wife and said, "Even though you have been unable to have children, you will soon become pregnant and give birth to a son. ⁴So be careful; you must not drink wine or any other alcoholic drink nor eat any forbidden food.* ⁵You will become pregnant and give birth to a son, and his hair must never be cut. For he will be dedicated to God as a Nazirite from birth. He will begin to rescue Israel from the Philistines."

⁶The woman ran and told her husband, "A man of God appeared to me! He looked like one of God's angels, terrifying to see. I didn't ask where he was from, and he didn't tell me his name. ⁷But he told me, 'You will become pregnant and give birth to a son. You must not drink wine or any other alcoholic drink nor eat any forbidden food. For your son will be dedicated to God as a Nazirite from the moment of his birth until the day of his death.'"

⁸Then Manoah prayed to the LORD, saying, "Lord, please let the man of God come back to us again and give us more instructions about this son who is to be born."

⁹God answered Manoah's prayer, and the angel of God appeared once again to his wife as she was sitting in the field. But her husband, Manoah, was not with her. ¹⁰So she quickly ran and told her husband, "The man who appeared to me the other day is here again!"

¹¹Manoah ran back with his wife and asked, "Are you the man who spoke to my wife the other day?"

"Yes," he replied, "I am."

¹²So Manoah asked him, "When your words come true, what kind of rules should govern the boy's life and work?"

¹³The angel of the LORD replied, "Be sure your wife follows the instructions I gave her. ¹⁴She must not eat grapes or raisins, drink wine or any other alcoholic drink, or eat any forbidden food."

¹⁵Then Manoah said to the angel of the LORD, "Please stay here until we can prepare a young goat for you to eat."

¹⁶"I will stay," the angel of the LORD replied, "but I will not eat anything. However, you may prepare a burnt offering as a sacrifice to the LORD." (Manoah didn't realize it was the angel of the LORD.)

¹⁷Then Manoah asked the angel of the LORD, "What is your name? For when all this comes true, we want to honor you."

¹⁸"Why do you ask my name?" the angel of the LORD replied. "It is too wonderful for you to understand."

¹⁹Then Manoah took a young goat and a grain offering and offered it on a rock as a sacrifice to the LORD. And as Manoah and his wife watched, the LORD did an amazing thing. ²⁰As the flames from the altar shot up toward the sky, the angel of the LORD ascended in the fire. When Manoah and his wife saw this, they fell with their faces to the ground.

²¹The angel did not appear again to Manoah and his wife. Manoah finally realized it was the angel of the LORD, ²²and he said to his wife, "We will certainly die, for we have seen God!"

²³But his wife said, "If the LORD were going to kill us, he wouldn't have accepted our burnt offering and grain offering. He wouldn't have appeared to us and told us this wonderful thing and done these miracles."

²⁴When her son was born, she named him Samson. And the LORD blessed him as he grew up. ²⁵And the Spirit of the LORD began to stir him while he lived in Mahaneh-dan, which is located between the towns of Zorah and Eshtaol.

¹⁴:¹ONE day when Samson was in Timnah, one of the Philistine women caught his eye. ²When he returned home, he told his father and mother, "A young Philistine woman in Timnah caught my eye. I want to marry her. Get her for me."

³His father and mother objected. "Isn't there even one woman in our tribe or among all the Israelites you could marry?" they asked. "Why must you go to the pagan Philistines to find a wife?"

But Samson told his father, "Get her for me! She looks good to me." ⁴His father and mother didn't realize the LORD was at work in this, creating an opportunity to work against the Philistines, who ruled over Israel at that time.

⁵As Samson and his parents were going down to Timnah, a young lion suddenly attacked Samson near the vineyards of Timnah. ⁶At that moment the Spirit of the LORD came powerfully upon him, and he ripped the lion's jaws apart with his bare hands. He did it as easily as if it were a young goat. But he didn't tell his father or mother about it. ⁷When Samson arrived in Timnah, he talked with the woman and was very pleased with her.

⁸Later, when he returned to Timnah for the wedding, he turned off the path to look at the carcass of the lion. And he found that a swarm of bees had made some honey in the carcass. ⁹He scooped some of the honey into his hands and ate it along the way. He also gave some to his father and mother, and they ate it.

But he didn't tell them he had taken the honey from the carcass of the lion.

¹⁰As his father was making final arrangements for the marriage, Samson threw a party at Timnah, as was the custom for elite young men. ¹¹When the bride's parents* saw him, they selected thirty young men from the town to be his companions.

¹²Samson said to them, "Let me tell you a riddle. If you solve my riddle during these seven days of the celebration, I will give you thirty fine linen robes and thirty sets of festive clothing. ¹³But if you can't solve it, then you must give me thirty fine linen robes and thirty sets of festive clothing."

"All right," they agreed, "let's hear your riddle."

¹⁴So he said:

"Out of the one who eats came
        something to eat;
    out of the strong came
        something sweet."

Three days later they were still trying to figure it out. ¹⁵On the fourth* day they said to Samson's wife, "Entice your husband to explain the riddle for us, or we will burn down your father's house with you in it. Did you invite us to this party just to make us poor?"

¹⁶So Samson's wife came to him in tears and said, "You don't love me; you hate me! You have given my people a riddle, but you haven't told me the answer."

"I haven't even given the answer to my father or mother," he replied. "Why should I tell you?" ¹⁷So she cried whenever she was with him and kept it up for the rest of the celebration. At last, on the seventh day he told her the answer because she was tormenting him with her nagging. Then she explained the riddle to the young men.

¹⁸So before sunset of the seventh day, the men of the town came to Samson with their answer:

"What is sweeter than honey?
    What is stronger than a lion?"

Samson replied, "If you hadn't plowed with my heifer, you wouldn't have solved my riddle!"

19 Then the Spirit of the LORD came powerfully upon him. He went down to the town of Ashkelon, killed thirty men, took their belongings, and gave their clothing to the men who had solved his riddle. But Samson was furious about what had happened, and he went back home to live with his father and mother. 20 So his wife was given in marriage to the man who had been Samson's best man at the wedding.

13:4 Hebrew *any unclean thing;* also in 13:7, 14.
14:11 Hebrew *they.*   14:15 As in Greek version; Hebrew reads *seventh.*

JOHN 1:29-51

The next day John saw Jesus coming toward him and said, "Look! The Lamb of God who takes away the sin of the world! 30 He is the one I was talking about when I said, 'A man is coming after me who is far greater than I am, for he existed long before me.' 31 I did not recognize him as the Messiah, but I have been baptizing with water so that he might be revealed to Israel."

32 Then John testified, "I saw the Holy Spirit descending like a dove from heaven and resting upon him. 33 I didn't know he was the one, but when God sent me to baptize with water, he told me, 'The one on whom you see the Spirit descend and rest is the one who will baptize with the Holy Spirit.' 34 I saw this happen to Jesus, so I testify that he is the Chosen One of God.*"

35 The following day John was again standing with two of his disciples. 36 As Jesus walked by, John looked at him and declared, "Look! There is the Lamb of God!" 37 When John's two disciples heard this, they followed Jesus.

38 Jesus looked around and saw them following. "What do you want?" he asked them.

They replied, "Rabbi" (which means "Teacher"), "where are you staying?"

39 "Come and see," he said. It was about four o'clock in the afternoon when they went with him to the place where he was staying, and they remained with him the rest of the day.

40 Andrew, Simon Peter's brother, was one of these men who heard what John said and then followed Jesus. 41 Andrew went to find his brother, Simon, and told him, "We have found the Messiah" (which means "Christ"*).

42 Then Andrew brought Simon to meet Jesus. Looking intently at Simon, Jesus said, "Your name is Simon, son of John—but you will be called Cephas" (which means "Peter"*).

43 The next day Jesus decided to go to Galilee. He found Philip and said to him, "Come, follow me." 44 Philip was from Bethsaida, Andrew and Peter's hometown.

45 Philip went to look for Nathanael and told him, "We have found the very person Moses* and the prophets wrote about! His name is Jesus, the son of Joseph from Nazareth."

46 "Nazareth!" exclaimed Nathanael. "Can anything good come from Nazareth?"

"Come and see for yourself," Philip replied.

47 As they approached, Jesus said, "Now here is a genuine son of Israel—a man of complete integrity."

48 "How do you know about me?" Nathanael asked.

Jesus replied, "I could see you under the fig tree before Philip found you."

49 Then Nathanael exclaimed, "Rabbi, you are the Son of God—the King of Israel!"

50 Jesus asked him, "Do you believe this just because I told you I had seen you under the fig tree? You will see greater things than this." 51 Then he said, "I tell you the truth, you will all see heaven open and the angels of God going up and down on the Son of Man, the one who is the stairway between heaven and earth.*"

1:34 Some manuscripts read *the Son of God.*   1:41 *Messiah* (a Hebrew term) and *Christ* (a Greek term) both mean "the anointed one."   1:42 The names *Cephas* (from Aramaic) and *Peter* (from Greek) both mean "rock."   1:45 Greek *Moses in the law.*   1:51 Greek *going up and down on the Son of Man;* see Gen 28:10-17. "Son of Man" is a title Jesus used for himself.

PSALM 102:1-28

A prayer of one overwhelmed with trouble,
pouring out problems before the LORD.

¹ **L**ORD, hear my prayer!
   Listen to my plea!
² Don't turn away from me
   in my time of distress.
   Bend down to listen,
      and answer me quickly when
         I call to you.
³ For my days disappear like smoke,
   and my bones burn like red-hot
      coals.
⁴ My heart is sick, withered like
      grass,
   and I have lost my appetite.
⁵ Because of my groaning,
   I am reduced to skin and bones.
⁶ I am like an owl in the desert,
   like a little owl in a far-off
      wilderness.
⁷ I lie awake,
   lonely as a solitary bird
      on the roof.
⁸ My enemies taunt me day after day.
   They mock and curse me.
⁹ I eat ashes for food.
   My tears run down into my
      drink
¹⁰ because of your anger and wrath.
   For you have picked me up and
      thrown me out.
¹¹ My life passes as swiftly as the
      evening shadows.
   I am withering away like grass.

¹² But you, O LORD, will sit on your
      throne forever.
   Your fame will endure to every
      generation.
¹³ You will arise and have mercy
      on Jerusalem*—
   and now is the time to pity her,
   now is the time you promised
      to help.
¹⁴ For your people love every stone
      in her walls
   and cherish even the dust
      in her streets.
¹⁵ Then the nations will tremble
      before the LORD.

The kings of the earth will
      tremble before his glory.
¹⁶ For the LORD will rebuild Jerusalem.
   He will appear in his glory.
¹⁷ He will listen to the prayers
      of the destitute.
   He will not reject their pleas.

¹⁸ Let this be recorded for future
      generations,
   so that a people not yet born will
      praise the LORD.
¹⁹ Tell them the LORD looked down
      from his heavenly sanctuary.
   He looked down to earth from
      heaven
²⁰   to hear the groans of
         the prisoners,
      to release those condemned
         to die.
²¹ And so the LORD's fame will be
      celebrated in Zion,
   his praises in Jerusalem,
²² when multitudes gather together
   and kingdoms come to worship
      the LORD.

²³ He broke my strength in midlife,
   cutting short my days.
²⁴ But I cried to him, "O my God,
      who lives forever,
   don't take my life while I am
      so young!
²⁵ Long ago you laid the foundation
      of the earth
   and made the heavens with
      your hands.
²⁶ They will perish, but you remain
      forever;
   they will wear out like old
      clothing.
   You will change them like
         a garment
   and discard them.
²⁷ But you are always the same;
   you will live forever.
²⁸ The children of your people
      will live in security.
   Their children's children
      will thrive in your
         presence."

102:13 Hebrew *Zion;* also in 102:16.

PROVERBS 14:15-16

Only simpletons believe everything they're told! The prudent carefully consider their steps. □ The wise are cautious* and avoid danger; fools plunge ahead with reckless confidence.

14:16 Hebrew *The wise fear.*

MAY 2

JUDGES 15:1–16:31

Later on, during the wheat harvest, Samson took a young goat as a present to his wife. He said, "I'm going into my wife's room to sleep with her," but her father wouldn't let him in.

²"I truly thought you must hate her," her father explained, "so I gave her in marriage to your best man. But look, her younger sister is even more beautiful than she is. Marry her instead."

³Samson said, "This time I cannot be blamed for everything I am going to do to you Philistines." ⁴Then he went out and caught 300 foxes. He tied their tails together in pairs, and he fastened a torch to each pair of tails. ⁵Then he lit the torches and let the foxes run through the grain fields of the Philistines. He burned all their grain to the ground, including the sheaves and the uncut grain. He also destroyed their vineyards and olive groves.

⁶"Who did this?" the Philistines demanded.

"Samson," was the reply, "because his father-in-law from Timnah gave Samson's wife to be married to his best man." So the Philistines went and got the woman and her father and burned them to death.

⁷"Because you did this," Samson vowed, "I won't rest until I take my revenge on you!" ⁸So he attacked the Philistines with great fury and killed many of them. Then he went to live in a cave in the rock of Etam.

⁹The Philistines retaliated by setting up camp in Judah and spreading out near the town of Lehi. ¹⁰The men of Judah asked the Philistines, "Why are you attacking us?"

The Philistines replied, "We've come to capture Samson. We've come to pay him back for what he did to us."

¹¹So 3,000 men of Judah went down to get Samson at the cave in the rock of Etam. They said to Samson, "Don't you realize the Philistines rule over us? What are you doing to us?"

But Samson replied, "I only did to them what they did to me."

¹²But the men of Judah told him, "We have come to tie you up and hand you over to the Philistines."

"All right," Samson said. "But promise that you won't kill me yourselves."

¹³"We will only tie you up and hand you over to the Philistines," they replied. "We won't kill you." So they tied him up with two new ropes and brought him up from the rock.

¹⁴As Samson arrived at Lehi, the Philistines came shouting in triumph. But the Spirit of the LORD came powerfully upon Samson, and he snapped the ropes on his arms as if they were burnt strands of flax, and they fell from his wrists. ¹⁵Then he found the jawbone of a recently killed donkey. He picked it up and killed 1,000 Philistines with it. ¹⁶Then Samson said,

"With the jawbone of a donkey,
    I've piled them in heaps!
With the jawbone of a donkey,
    I've killed a thousand men!"

¹⁷When he finished his boasting, he threw away the jawbone; and the place was named Jawbone Hill.*

¹⁸Samson was now very thirsty, and he cried out to the LORD, "You have accomplished this great victory by the strength of your servant. Must I now die of thirst and fall into the hands of these pagans?" ¹⁹So God caused water to gush

out of a hollow in the ground at Lehi, and Samson was revived as he drank. Then he named that place "The Spring of the One Who Cried Out,"* and it is still in Lehi to this day.

²⁰Samson judged Israel for twenty years during the period when the Philistines dominated the land.

¹⁶:¹ONE day Samson went to the Philistine town of Gaza and spent the night with a prostitute. ²Word soon spread* that Samson was there, so the men of Gaza gathered together and waited all night at the town gates. They kept quiet during the night, saying to themselves, "When the light of morning comes, we will kill him."

³But Samson stayed in bed only until midnight. Then he got up, took hold of the doors of the town gate, including the two posts, and lifted them up, bar and all. He put them on his shoulders and carried them all the way to the top of the hill across from Hebron.

⁴Some time later Samson fell in love with a woman named Delilah, who lived in the valley of Sorek. ⁵The rulers of the Philistines went to her and said, "Entice Samson to tell you what makes him so strong and how he can be overpowered and tied up securely. Then each of us will give you 1,100 pieces* of silver."

⁶So Delilah said to Samson, "Please tell me what makes you so strong and what it would take to tie you up securely."

⁷Samson replied, "If I were tied up with seven new bowstrings that have not yet been dried, I would become as weak as anyone else."

⁸So the Philistine rulers brought Delilah seven new bowstrings, and she tied Samson up with them. ⁹She had hidden some men in one of the inner rooms of her house, and she cried out, "Samson! The Philistines have come to capture you!" But Samson snapped the bowstrings as a piece of string snaps when it is burned by a fire. So the secret of his strength was not discovered.

¹⁰Afterward Delilah said to him,

"You've been making fun of me and telling me lies! Now please tell me how you can be tied up securely."

¹¹Samson replied, "If I were tied up with brand-new ropes that had never been used, I would become as weak as anyone else."

¹²So Delilah took new ropes and tied him up with them. The men were hiding in the inner room as before, and again Delilah cried out, "Samson! The Philistines have come to capture you!" But again Samson snapped the ropes from his arms as if they were thread.

¹³Then Delilah said, "You've been making fun of me and telling me lies! Now tell me how you can be tied up securely."

Samson replied, "If you were to weave the seven braids of my hair into the fabric on your loom and tighten it with the loom shuttle, I would become as weak as anyone else."

So while he slept, Delilah wove the seven braids of his hair into the fabric. ¹⁴Then she tightened it with the loom shuttle.* Again she cried out, "Samson! The Philistines have come to capture you!" But Samson woke up, pulled back the loom shuttle, and yanked his hair away from the loom and the fabric.

¹⁵Then Delilah pouted, "How can you tell me, 'I love you,' when you don't share your secrets with me? You've made fun of me three times now, and you still haven't told me what makes you so strong!" ¹⁶She tormented him with her nagging day after day until he was sick to death of it.

¹⁷Finally, Samson shared his secret with her. "My hair has never been cut," he confessed, "for I was dedicated to God as a Nazirite from birth. If my head were shaved, my strength would leave me, and I would become as weak as anyone else."

¹⁸Delilah realized he had finally told her the truth, so she sent for the Philistine rulers. "Come back one more time," she said, "for he has finally told me his secret." So the Philistine rulers returned with the money in their hands.

¹⁹Delilah lulled Samson to sleep with his head in her lap, and then she called in a man to shave off the seven locks of his hair. In this way she began to bring him down,* and his strength left him.

²⁰Then she cried out, "Samson! The Philistines have come to capture you!"

When he woke up, he thought, "I will do as before and shake myself free." But he didn't realize the LORD had left him.

²¹So the Philistines captured him and gouged out his eyes. They took him to Gaza, where he was bound with bronze chains and forced to grind grain in the prison.

²²But before long, his hair began to grow back.

²³The Philistine rulers held a great festival, offering sacrifices and praising their god, Dagon. They said, "Our god has given us victory over our enemy Samson!"

²⁴When the people saw him, they praised their god, saying, "Our god has delivered our enemy to us! The one who killed so many of us is now in our power!"

²⁵Half drunk by now, the people demanded, "Bring out Samson so he can amuse us!" So he was brought from the prison to amuse them, and they had him stand between the pillars supporting the roof.

²⁶Samson said to the young servant who was leading him by the hand, "Place my hands against the pillars that hold up the temple. I want to rest against them."

²⁷Now the temple was completely filled with people. All the Philistine rulers were there, and there were about 3,000 men and women on the roof who were watching as Samson amused them.

²⁸Then Samson prayed to the LORD, "Sovereign LORD, remember me again. O God, please strengthen me just one more time. With one blow let me pay back the Philistines for the loss of my two eyes." ²⁹Then Samson put his hands on the two center pillars that held up the temple. Pushing against them with both hands, ³⁰he prayed, "Let me die with the Philistines." And the temple crashed down on the Philistine rulers and all the

people. So he killed more people when he died than he had during his entire lifetime.

³¹Later his brothers and other relatives went down to get his body. They took him back home and buried him between Zorah and Eshtaol, where his father, Manoah, was buried. Samson had judged Israel for twenty years.

15:17 Hebrew *Ramath-lehi.*   15:19 Hebrew *En-hakkore.*
16:2 As in Greek and Syriac versions and Latin Vulgate; Hebrew lacks *Word soon spread.*   16:5 Hebrew *1,100 shekels,* about 28 pounds or 12.5 kilograms in weight.
16:13-14 As in Greek version and Latin Vulgate; Hebrew lacks *I would become as weak as anyone else. / So while he slept, Delilah wove the seven braids of his hair into the fabric.* ¹⁴*Then she tightened it with the loom shuttle.*
16:19 Or *she began to torment him.* Greek version reads *He began to grow weak.*

JOHN 2:1-25

The next day* there was a wedding celebration in the village of Cana in Galilee. Jesus' mother was there, ²and Jesus and his disciples were also invited to the celebration. ³The wine supply ran out during the festivities, so Jesus' mother told him, "They have no more wine."

⁴"Dear woman, that's not our problem," Jesus replied. "My time has not yet come."

⁵But his mother told the servants, "Do whatever he tells you."

⁶Standing nearby were six stone water jars, used for Jewish ceremonial washing. Each could hold twenty to thirty gallons.* ⁷Jesus told the servants, "Fill the jars with water." When the jars had been filled, ⁸he said, "Now dip some out, and take it to the master of ceremonies." So the servants followed his instructions.

⁹When the master of ceremonies tasted the water that was now wine, not knowing where it had come from (though, of course, the servants knew), he called the bridegroom over. ¹⁰"A host always serves the best wine first," he said. "Then, when everyone has had a lot to drink, he brings out the less expensive wine. But you have kept the best until now!"

¹¹This miraculous sign at Cana in Galilee was the first time Jesus revealed his glory. And his disciples believed in him.

¹²After the wedding he went to Capernaum for a few days with his mother, his brothers, and his disciples.

¹³It was nearly time for the Jewish Passover celebration, so Jesus went to Jerusalem. ¹⁴In the Temple area he saw merchants selling cattle, sheep, and doves for sacrifices; he also saw dealers at tables exchanging foreign money. ¹⁵Jesus made a whip from some ropes and chased them all out of the Temple. He drove out the sheep and cattle, scattered the money changers' coins over the floor, and turned over their tables. ¹⁶Then, going over to the people who sold doves, he told them, "Get these things out of here. Stop turning my Father's house into a marketplace!"

¹⁷Then his disciples remembered this prophecy from the Scriptures: "Passion for God's house will consume me."*

¹⁸But the Jewish leaders demanded, "What are you doing? If God gave you authority to do this, show us a miraculous sign to prove it."

¹⁹"All right," Jesus replied. "Destroy this temple, and in three days I will raise it up."

²⁰"What!" they exclaimed. "It has taken forty-six years to build this Temple, and you can rebuild it in three days?" ²¹But when Jesus said "this temple," he meant his own body. ²²After he was raised from the dead, his disciples remembered he had said this, and they believed both the Scriptures and what Jesus had said.

²³Because of the miraculous signs Jesus did in Jerusalem at the Passover celebration, many began to trust in him. ²⁴But Jesus didn't trust them, because he knew human nature. ²⁵No one needed to tell him what mankind is really like.

2:1 Greek *On the third day;* see 1:35, 43.   2:6 Greek *2 or 3 measures* [75 to 113 liters].   2:17 Or *"Concern for God's house will be my undoing."* Ps 69:9.

PSALM 103:1-22
A psalm of David.

¹ Let all that I am praise the LORD;
  with my whole heart, I will praise
  his holy name.

² Let all that I am praise the LORD;
  may I never forget the good
  things he does for me.
³ He forgives all my sins
  and heals all my diseases.
⁴ He redeems me from death
  and crowns me with love and
  tender mercies.
⁵ He fills my life with good things.
  My youth is renewed like
  the eagle's!

⁶ The LORD gives righteousness
  and justice to all who are treated
  unfairly.

⁷ He revealed his character to Moses
  and his deeds to the people
  of Israel.
⁸ The LORD is compassionate
  and merciful,
  slow to get angry and filled with
  unfailing love.
⁹ He will not constantly accuse us,
  nor remain angry forever.
¹⁰ He does not punish us for all
  our sins;
  he does not deal harshly with us,
  as we deserve.
¹¹ **For his unfailing love toward
  those who fear him
  is as great as the height of the
  heavens above the earth.**
¹² **He has removed our sins as far
  from us
  as the east is from the west.**
¹³ The LORD is like a father to
  his children,
  tender and compassionate to
  those who fear him.
¹⁴ For he knows how weak we are;
  he remembers we are only dust.
¹⁵ Our days on earth are like grass;
  like wildflowers, we bloom
  and die.
¹⁶ The wind blows, and we are gone—
  as though we had never
  been here.
¹⁷ But the love of the LORD remains
  forever
  with those who fear him.
  His salvation extends to the
  children's children

¹⁸   of those who are faithful to his
          covenant,
       of those who obey his
          commandments!

¹⁹ The LORD has made the heavens his
       throne;
       from there he rules over
          everything.

²⁰ Praise the LORD, you angels,
       you mighty ones who carry
          out his plans,
       listening for each of his
          commands.

²¹ Yes, praise the LORD, you armies
       of angels
       who serve him and do his will!

²² Praise the LORD, everything he
       has created,
       everything in all his kingdom.

   Let all that I am praise the LORD.

PROVERBS 14:17-19

Short-tempered people do foolish things, and schemers are hated. □ Simpletons are clothed with foolishness,* but the prudent are crowned with knowledge. □ Evil people will bow before good people; the wicked will bow at the gates of the godly.

14:18 Or *inherit foolishness.*

JUDGES 17:1–18:31

There was a man named Micah, who lived in the hill country of Ephraim. ²One day he said to his mother, "I heard you place a curse on the person who stole 1,100 pieces* of silver from you. Well, I have the money. I was the one who took it."

"The LORD bless you for admitting it," his mother replied. ³He returned the money to her, and she said, "I now dedicate these silver coins to the LORD. In honor of my son, I will have an image carved and an idol cast."

⁴So when he returned the money to his mother, she took 200 silver coins and gave them to a silversmith, who made them into an image and an idol. And these were placed in Micah's house. ⁵Micah set up a shrine for the idol, and he made a sacred ephod and some household idols. Then he installed one of his sons as his personal priest.

⁶In those days Israel had no king; all the people did whatever seemed right in their own eyes.

⁷One day a young Levite, who had been living in Bethlehem in Judah, arrived in that area. ⁸He had left Bethlehem in search of another place to live, and as he traveled, he came to the hill country of Ephraim. He happened to stop at Micah's house as he was traveling through. ⁹"Where are you from?" Micah asked him.

He replied, "I am a Levite from Bethlehem in Judah, and I am looking for a place to live."

¹⁰"Stay here with me," Micah said, "and you can be a father and priest to me. I will give you ten pieces* of silver a year, plus a change of clothes and your food." ¹¹The Levite agreed to this, and the young man became like one of Micah's sons.

¹²So Micah installed the Levite as his personal priest, and he lived in Micah's house. ¹³"I know the LORD will bless me now," Micah said, "because I have a Levite serving as my priest."

¹⁸:¹Now in those days Israel had no king. And the tribe of Dan was trying to find a place where they could settle, for they had not yet moved into the land assigned to them when the land was divided among the tribes of Israel. ²So the men of Dan chose from their clans five capable warriors from the towns of Zorah and Eshtaol to scout out a land for them to settle in.

When these warriors arrived in the hill country of Ephraim, they came to

Micah's house and spent the night there. [3]While at Micah's house, they recognized the young Levite's accent, so they went over and asked him, "Who brought you here, and what are you doing in this place? Why are you here?" [4]He told them about his agreement with Micah and that he had been hired as Micah's personal priest.

[5]Then they said, "Ask God whether or not our journey will be successful."

[6]"Go in peace," the priest replied. "For the LORD is watching over your journey."

[7]So the five men went on to the town of Laish, where they noticed the people living carefree lives, like the Sidonians; they were peaceful and secure.* The people were also wealthy because their land was very fertile. And they lived a great distance from Sidon and had no allies nearby.

[8]When the men returned to Zorah and Eshtaol, their relatives asked them, "What did you find?"

[9]The men replied, "Come on, let's attack them! We have seen the land, and it is very good. What are you waiting for? Don't hesitate to go and take possession of it. [10]When you get there, you will find the people living carefree lives. God has given us a spacious and fertile land, lacking in nothing!"

[11]So 600 men from the tribe of Dan, armed with weapons of war, set out from Zorah and Eshtaol. [12]They camped at a place west of Kiriath-jearim in Judah, which is called Mahaneh-dan* to this day. [13]Then they went on from there into the hill country of Ephraim and came to the house of Micah.

[14]The five men who had scouted out the land around Laish explained to the others, "These buildings contain a sacred ephod, as well as some household idols, a carved image, and a cast idol. What do you think you should do?" [15]Then the five men turned off the road and went over to Micah's house, where the young Levite lived, and greeted him kindly. [16]As the 600 armed warriors from the tribe of Dan stood at the entrance of the gate, [17]the five scouts entered the shrine and removed the carved image, the sacred ephod, the household idols, and the cast idol. Meanwhile, the priest was standing at the gate with the 600 armed warriors.

[18]When the priest saw the men carrying all the sacred objects out of Micah's shrine, he said, "What are you doing?"

[19]"Be quiet and come with us," they said. "Be a father and priest to all of us. Isn't it better to be a priest for an entire tribe and clan of Israel than for the household of just one man?"

[20]The young priest was quite happy to go with them, so he took along the sacred ephod, the household idols, and the carved image. [21]They turned and started on their way again, placing their children, livestock, and possessions in front of them.

[22]When the people from the tribe of Dan were quite a distance from Micah's house, the people who lived near Micah came chasing after them. [23]They were shouting as they caught up with them. The men of Dan turned around and said to Micah, "What's the matter? Why have you called these men together and chased after us like this?"

[24]"What do you mean, 'What's the matter?'" Micah replied. "You've taken away all the gods I have made, and my priest, and I have nothing left!"

[25]The men of Dan said, "Watch what you say! There are some short-tempered men around here who might get angry and kill you and your family." [26]So the men of Dan continued on their way. When Micah saw that there were too many of them for him to attack, he turned around and went home.

[27]Then, with Micah's idols and his priest, the men of Dan came to the town of Laish, whose people were peaceful and secure. They attacked with swords and burned the town to the ground. [28]There was no one to rescue the people, for they lived a great distance from Sidon and had no allies nearby. This happened in the valley near Beth-rehob.

Then the people of the tribe of Dan rebuilt the town and lived there. 29 They renamed the town Dan after their ancestor, Israel's son, but it had originally been called Laish.

30Then they set up the carved image, and they appointed Jonathan son of Gershom, son of Moses,* as their priest. This family continued as priests for the tribe of Dan until the Exile. 31So Micah's carved image was worshiped by the tribe of Dan as long as the Tabernacle of God remained at Shiloh.

17:2 Hebrew *1,100 shekels,* about 28 pounds or 12.5 kilograms in weight.   17:10 Hebrew *10 shekels,* about 4 ounces or 114 grams in weight.   18:7 The meaning of the Hebrew is uncertain.   18:12 *Mahaneh-dan* means "the camp of Dan."   18:30 As in an ancient Hebrew tradition, some Greek manuscripts, and Latin Vulgate; Masoretic Text reads *son of Manasseh.*

JOHN 3:1-21

There was a man named Nicodemus, a Jewish religious leader who was a Pharisee. 2After dark one evening, he came to speak with Jesus. "Rabbi," he said, "we all know that God has sent you to teach us. Your miraculous signs are evidence that God is with you."

3Jesus replied, "I tell you the truth, unless you are born again,* you cannot see the Kingdom of God."

4"What do you mean?" exclaimed Nicodemus. "How can an old man go back into his mother's womb and be born again?"

5Jesus replied, "I assure you, no one can enter the Kingdom of God without being born of water and the Spirit.* 6Humans can reproduce only human life, but the Holy Spirit gives birth to spiritual life.* 7So don't be surprised when I say, 'You* must be born again.' 8The wind blows wherever it wants. Just as you can hear the wind but can't tell where it comes from or where it is going, so you can't explain how people are born of the Spirit."

9"How are these things possible?" Nicodemus asked.

10Jesus replied, "You are a respected Jewish teacher, and yet you don't understand these things? 11I assure you, we tell you what we know and have seen, and yet you won't believe our testimony. 12But if you don't believe me when I tell you about earthly things, how can you possibly believe if I tell you about heavenly things? 13No one has ever gone to heaven and returned. But the Son of Man* has come down from heaven. 14And as Moses lifted up the bronze snake on a pole in the wilderness, so the Son of Man must be lifted up, 15so that everyone who believes in him will have eternal life.*

16**"For God loved the world so much that he gave his one and only Son, so that everyone who believes in him will not perish but have eternal life. 17God sent his Son into the world not to judge the world, but to save the world through him.**

18"There is no judgment against anyone who believes in him. But anyone who does not believe in him has already been judged for not believing in God's one and only Son. 19And the judgment is based on this fact: God's light came into the world, but people loved the darkness more than the light, for their actions were evil. 20All who do evil hate the light and refuse to go near it for fear their sins will be exposed. 21But those who do what is right come to the light so others can see that they are doing what God wants.*"

3:3 Or *born from above;* also in 3:7.   3:5 Or *and spirit.* The Greek word for *Spirit* can also be translated *wind;* see 3:8. 3:6 Greek *what is born of the Spirit is spirit.*   3:7 The Greek word for *you* is plural; also in 3:12.   3:13 Some manuscripts add *who lives in heaven.* "Son of Man" is a title Jesus used for himself.   3:15 Or *everyone who believes will have eternal life in him.*   3:21 Or *can see God at work in what he is doing.*

PSALM 104:1-23

Let all that I am praise the LORD.

O LORD my God, how great you are!
　　You are robed with honor and
　　　　majesty.
2　You are dressed in a robe of light.
　You stretch out the starry curtain
　　　　of the heavens;
3　you lay out the rafters of your
　　　　home in the rain clouds.
　You make the clouds your chariot;
　　you ride upon the wings
　　　　of the wind.

⁴ The winds are your messengers;
     flames of fire are your servants.*

⁵ You placed the world on its
     foundation
     so it would never be moved.
⁶ You clothed the earth with floods
     of water,
     water that covered even the
     mountains.
⁷ At your command, the water fled;
     at the sound of your thunder,
     it hurried away.
⁸ Mountains rose and valleys sank
     to the levels you decreed.
⁹ Then you set a firm boundary
     for the seas,
     so they would never again cover
     the earth.

¹⁰ You make springs pour water into
     the ravines,
     so streams gush down from
     the mountains.
¹¹ They provide water for all
     the animals,
     and the wild donkeys quench
     their thirst.
¹² The birds nest beside the streams
     and sing among the branches
     of the trees.
¹³ You send rain on the mountains
     from your heavenly home,
     and you fill the earth with the
     fruit of your labor.
¹⁴ You cause grass to grow for
     the livestock
     and plants for people to use.
     You allow them to produce food
     from the earth—
¹⁵   wine to make them glad,
     olive oil to soothe their skin,
     and bread to give them strength.
¹⁶ The trees of the Lᴏʀᴅ are well
     cared for—
     the cedars of Lebanon that
     he planted.
¹⁷ There the birds make their nests,
     and the storks make their homes
     in the cypresses.
¹⁸ High in the mountains live the
     wild goats,

and the rocks form a refuge for
     the hyraxes.*

¹⁹ You made the moon to mark
     the seasons,
     and the sun knows when to set.
²⁰ You send the darkness, and it
     becomes night,
     when all the forest animals
     prowl about.
²¹ Then the young lions roar for
     their prey,
     stalking the food provided
     by God.
²² At dawn they slink back
     into their dens to rest.
²³ Then people go off to their work,
     where they labor until evening.

104:4 Greek version reads *He sends his angels like the
winds, / his servants like flames of fire.* Compare Heb 1:7.
104:18 Or *coneys,* or *rock badgers.*

PROVERBS 14:20-21
The poor are despised even by their
neighbors, while the rich have many
"friends." □It is a sin to belittle one's
neighbor; blessed are those who help
the poor.

JUDGES 19:1–20:48
Now in those days Israel had no king.
There was a man from the tribe of Levi
living in a remote area of the hill country of Ephraim. One day he brought
home a woman from Bethlehem in Judah to be his concubine. ²But she became angry with him* and returned to
her father's home in Bethlehem.

After about four months, ³her husband set out for Bethlehem to speak
personally to her and persuade her to
come back. He took with him a servant
and a pair of donkeys. When he arrived
at* her father's house, her father saw

him and welcomed him. ⁴Her father urged him to stay awhile, so he stayed three days, eating, drinking, and sleeping there.

⁵On the fourth day the man was up early, ready to leave, but the woman's father said to his son-in-law, "Have something to eat before you go." ⁶So the two men sat down together and had something to eat and drink. Then the woman's father said, "Please stay another night and enjoy yourself." ⁷The man got up to leave, but his father-in-law kept urging him to stay, so he finally gave in and stayed the night.

⁸On the morning of the fifth day he was up early again, ready to leave, and again the woman's father said, "Have something to eat; then you can leave later this afternoon." So they had another day of feasting. ⁹Later, as the man and his concubine and servant were preparing to leave, his father-in-law said, "Look, it's almost evening. Stay the night and enjoy yourself. Tomorrow you can get up early and be on your way."

¹⁰But this time the man was determined to leave. So he took his two saddled donkeys and his concubine and headed in the direction of Jebus (that is, Jerusalem). ¹¹It was late in the day when they neared Jebus, and the man's servant said to him, "Let's stop at this Jebusite town and spend the night there."

¹²"No," his master said, "we can't stay in this foreign town where there are no Israelites. Instead, we will go on to Gibeah. ¹³Come on, let's try to get as far as Gibeah or Ramah, and we'll spend the night in one of those towns." ¹⁴So they went on. The sun was setting as they came to Gibeah, a town in the land of Benjamin, ¹⁵so they stopped there to spend the night. They rested in the town square, but no one took them in for the night.

¹⁶That evening an old man came home from his work in the fields. He was from the hill country of Ephraim, but he was living in Gibeah, where the people were from the tribe of Benjamin. ¹⁷When he saw the travelers sitting in the town square, he asked them where they were from and where they were going.

¹⁸"We have been in Bethlehem in Judah," the man replied. "We are on our way to a remote area in the hill country of Ephraim, which is my home. I traveled to Bethlehem, and now I'm returning home.* But no one has taken us in for the night, ¹⁹even though we have everything we need. We have straw and feed for our donkeys and plenty of bread and wine for ourselves."

²⁰"You are welcome to stay with me," the old man said. "I will give you anything you might need. But whatever you do, don't spend the night in the square." ²¹So he took them home with him and fed the donkeys. After they washed their feet, they ate and drank together.

²²While they were enjoying themselves, a crowd of troublemakers from the town surrounded the house. They began beating at the door and shouting to the old man, "Bring out the man who is staying with you so we can have sex with him."

²³The old man stepped outside to talk to them. "No, my brothers, don't do such an evil thing. For this man is a guest in my house, and such a thing would be shameful. ²⁴Here, take my virgin daughter and this man's concubine. I will bring them out to you, and you can abuse them and do whatever you like. But don't do such a shameful thing to this man."

²⁵But they wouldn't listen to him. So the Levite took hold of his concubine and pushed her out the door. The men of the town abused her all night, taking turns raping her until morning. Finally, at dawn they let her go. ²⁶At daybreak the woman returned to the house where her husband was staying. She collapsed at the door of the house and lay there until it was light.

²⁷When her husband opened the door to leave, there lay his concubine with her hands on the threshold. ²⁸He said, "Get up! Let's go!" But there was no answer.* So he put her body on his donkey and took her home.

²⁹When he got home, he took a knife and cut his concubine's body into twelve pieces. Then he sent one piece to each tribe throughout all the territory of Israel.

³⁰Everyone who saw it said, "Such a horrible crime has not been committed in all the time since Israel left Egypt. Think about it! What are we going to do? Who's going to speak up?"

²⁰:¹THEN all the Israelites were united as one man, from Dan in the north to Beersheba in the south, including those from across the Jordan in the land of Gilead. The entire community assembled in the presence of the LORD at Mizpah. ²The leaders of all the people and all the tribes of Israel—400,000 warriors armed with swords—took their positions in the assembly of the people of God. ³(Word soon reached the land of Benjamin that the other tribes had gone up to Mizpah.) The Israelites then asked how this terrible crime had happened.

⁴The Levite, the husband of the woman who had been murdered, said, "My concubine and I came to spend the night in Gibeah, a town that belongs to the people of Benjamin. ⁵That night some of the leading citizens of Gibeah surrounded the house, planning to kill me, and they raped my concubine until she was dead. ⁶So I cut her body into twelve pieces and sent the pieces throughout the territory assigned to Israel, for these men have committed a terrible and shameful crime. ⁷Now then, all of you—the entire community of Israel—must decide here and now what should be done about this!"

⁸And all the people rose to their feet in unison and declared, "None of us will return home! No, not even one of us! ⁹Instead, this is what we will do to Gibeah; we will draw lots to decide who will attack it. ¹⁰One tenth of the men* from each tribe will be chosen to supply the warriors with food, and the rest of us will take revenge on Gibeah* of Benjamin for this shameful thing they have done in Israel." ¹¹So all the Israelites were completely united, and they gathered together to attack the town.

¹²The Israelites sent messengers to the tribe of Benjamin, saying, "What a terrible thing has been done among you! ¹³Give up those evil men, those troublemakers from Gibeah, so we can execute them and purge Israel of this evil."

But the people of Benjamin would not listen. ¹⁴Instead, they came from their towns and gathered at Gibeah to fight the Israelites. ¹⁵In all, 26,000 of their warriors armed with swords arrived in Gibeah to join the 700 elite troops who lived there. ¹⁶Among Benjamin's elite troops, 700 were left-handed, and each of them could sling a rock and hit a target within a hairsbreadth without missing. ¹⁷Israel had 400,000 experienced soldiers armed with swords, not counting Benjamin's warriors.

¹⁸Before the battle the Israelites went to Bethel and asked God, "Which tribe should go first to attack the people of Benjamin?"

The LORD answered, "Judah is to go first."

¹⁹So the Israelites left early the next morning and camped near Gibeah. ²⁰Then they advanced toward Gibeah to attack the men of Benjamin. ²¹But Benjamin's warriors, who were defending the town, came out and killed 22,000 Israelites on the battlefield that day.

²²But the Israelites encouraged each other and took their positions again at the same place they had fought the previous day. ²³For they had gone up to Bethel and wept in the presence of the LORD until evening. They had asked the LORD, "Should we fight against our relatives from Benjamin again?"

And the LORD had said, "Go out and fight against them."

²⁴So the next day they went out again to fight against the men of Benjamin, ²⁵but the men of Benjamin killed another 18,000 Israelites, all of whom were experienced with the sword.

²⁶Then all the Israelites went up to Bethel and wept in the presence of the

LORD and fasted until evening. They also brought burnt offerings and peace offerings to the LORD. ²⁷The Israelites went up seeking direction from the LORD. (In those days the Ark of the Covenant of God was in Bethel, ²⁸and Phinehas son of Eleazar and grandson of Aaron was the priest.) The Israelites asked the LORD, "Should we fight against our relatives from Benjamin again, or should we stop?"

The LORD said, "Go! Tomorrow I will hand them over to you."

²⁹So the Israelites set an ambush all around Gibeah. ³⁰They went out on the third day and took their positions at the same place as before. ³¹When the men of Benjamin came out to attack, they were drawn away from the town. And as they had done before, they began to kill the Israelites. About thirty Israelites died in the open fields and along the roads, one leading to Bethel and the other leading back to Gibeah.

³²Then the warriors of Benjamin shouted, "We're defeating them as we did before!" But the Israelites had planned in advance to run away so that the men of Benjamin would chase them along the roads and be drawn away from the town.

³³When the main group of Israelite warriors reached Baal-tamar, they turned and took up their positions. Meanwhile, the Israelites hiding in ambush to the west* of Gibeah jumped up to fight. ³⁴There were 10,000 elite Israelite troops who advanced against Gibeah. The fighting was so heavy that Benjamin didn't realize the impending disaster. ³⁵So the LORD helped Israel defeat Benjamin, and that day the Israelites killed 25,100 of Benjamin's warriors, all of whom were experienced swordsmen. ³⁶Then the men of Benjamin saw that they were beaten.

The Israelites had retreated from Benjamin's warriors in order to give those hiding in ambush more room to maneuver against Gibeah. ³⁷Then those who were hiding rushed in from all sides and killed everyone in the town.

³⁸They had arranged to send up a large cloud of smoke from the town as a signal. ³⁹When the Israelites saw the smoke, they turned and attacked Benjamin's warriors.

By that time Benjamin's warriors had killed about thirty Israelites, and they shouted, "We're defeating them as we did in the first battle!" ⁴⁰But when the warriors of Benjamin looked behind them and saw the smoke rising into the sky from every part of the town, ⁴¹the men of Israel turned and attacked. At this point the men of Benjamin became terrified, because they realized disaster was close at hand. ⁴²So they turned around and fled before the Israelites toward the wilderness. But they couldn't escape the battle, and the people who came out of the nearby towns were also killed.* ⁴³The Israelites surrounded the men of Benjamin and chased them relentlessly, finally overtaking them east of Gibeah.* ⁴⁴That day 18,000 of Benjamin's strongest warriors died in battle. ⁴⁵The survivors fled into the wilderness toward the rock of Rimmon, but Israel killed 5,000 of them along the road. They continued the chase until they had killed another 2,000 near Gidom.

⁴⁶So that day the tribe of Benjamin lost 25,000 strong warriors armed with swords, ⁴⁷leaving only 600 men who escaped to the rock of Rimmon, where they lived for four months. ⁴⁸And the Israelites returned and slaughtered every living thing in all the towns—the people, the livestock, and everything they found. They also burned down all the towns they came to.

19:2 Or *she was unfaithful to him.*   **19:3** As in Greek version; Hebrew reads *When she brought him to.*   **19:18** As in Greek version (see also 19:29); Hebrew reads *now I'm going to the Tabernacle of the LORD.*   **19:28** Greek version adds *for she was dead.*   **20:10a** Hebrew *10 men from every hundred, 100 men from every thousand, and 1,000 men from every 10,000.*   **20:10b** Hebrew *Geba,* in this case a variant spelling of Gibeah; also in 20:33.   **20:33** As in Greek and Syriac versions and Latin Vulgate; Hebrew reads *hiding in the open space.*   **20:42** Or *battle, for the people from the nearby towns also came out and killed them.*   **20:43** The meaning of the Hebrew is uncertain.

JOHN 3:22–4:3

Then Jesus and his disciples left Jerusalem and went into the Judean countryside. Jesus spent some time with them there, baptizing people.

[23]At this time John the Baptist was baptizing at Aenon, near Salim, because there was plenty of water there; and people kept coming to him for baptism. [24](This was before John was thrown into prison.) [25]A debate broke out between John's disciples and a certain Jew* over ceremonial cleansing. [26]So John's disciples came to him and said, "Rabbi, the man you met on the other side of the Jordan River, the one you identified as the Messiah, is also baptizing people. And everybody is going to him instead of coming to us."

[27]John replied, "No one can receive anything unless God gives it from heaven. [28]You yourselves know how plainly I told you, 'I am not the Messiah. I am only here to prepare the way for him.' [29]It is the bridegroom who marries the bride, and the best man is simply glad to stand with him and hear his vows. Therefore, I am filled with joy at his success. [30]He must become greater and greater, and I must become less and less.

[31]"He has come from above and is greater than anyone else. We are of the earth, and we speak of earthly things, but he has come from heaven and is greater than anyone else.* [32]He testifies about what he has seen and heard, but how few believe what he tells them! [33]Anyone who accepts his testimony can affirm that God is true. [34]For he is sent by God. He speaks God's words, for God gives him the Spirit without limit. **[35]The Father loves his Son and has put everything into his hands. [36]And anyone who believes in God's Son has eternal life. Anyone who doesn't obey the Son will never experience eternal life but remains under God's angry judgment."**

[4:1]JESUS* knew the Pharisees had heard that he was baptizing and making more disciples than John [2](though Jesus himself didn't baptize them—his disciples did). [3]So he left Judea and returned to Galilee.

3:25 Some manuscripts read *some Jews*.   3:31 Some manuscripts omit *and is greater than anyone else*.
4:1 Some manuscripts read *The Lord*.

PSALM 104:24-35

⭕ LORD, what a variety of things
   you have made!
   In wisdom you have made
   them all.
   The earth is full of your
   creatures.
[25] Here is the ocean, vast and wide,
   teeming with life of every kind,
   both large and small.
[26] See the ships sailing along,
   and Leviathan,* which you made
   to play in the sea.

[27] They all depend on you
   to give them food as they
   need it.
[28] When you supply it, they gather it.
   You open your hand
   to feed them,
   and they are richly satisfied.
[29] But if you turn away from them,
   they panic.
   When you take away their
   breath,
   they die and turn again to dust.
[30] When you give them your breath,*
   life is created,
   and you renew the face
   of the earth.

[31] May the glory of the LORD continue
   forever!
   The LORD takes pleasure in
   all he has made!
[32] The earth trembles at his glance;
   the mountains smoke
   at his touch.

[33] I will sing to the LORD as long
   as I live.
   I will praise my God to my
   last breath!
[34] May all my thoughts be pleasing
   to him,
   for I rejoice in the LORD.

35 Let all sinners vanish from the face
    of the earth;
   let the wicked disappear forever.

Let all that I am praise the LORD.

Praise the LORD!

104:26 The identification of Leviathan is disputed, ranging
from an earthly creature to a mythical sea monster in
ancient literature.   **104:30** Or *When you send your Spirit.*

PROVERBS 14:22-24
If you plan to do evil, you will be lost; if
you plan to do good, you will receive unfailing love and faithfulness. □ Work
brings profit, but mere talk leads to poverty! □ Wealth is a crown for the wise;
the effort of fools yields only foolishness.

MAY 5

JUDGES 21:1—RUTH 1:22
The Israelites had vowed at Mizpah, "We
will never give our daughters in marriage
to a man from the tribe of Benjamin."
2Now the people went to Bethel and sat
in the presence of God until evening,
weeping loudly and bitterly. 3"O LORD,
God of Israel," they cried out, "why has
this happened in Israel? Now one of our
tribes is missing from Israel!"
   4Early the next morning the people
built an altar and presented their burnt
offerings and peace offerings on it.
5Then they said, "Who among the tribes
of Israel did not join us at Mizpah when
we held our assembly in the presence of
the LORD?" At that time they had taken a
solemn oath in the LORD's presence,
vowing that anyone who refused to
come would be put to death.
   6The Israelites felt sorry for their
brother Benjamin and said, "Today one
of the tribes of Israel has been cut off.
7How can we find wives for the few who
remain, since we have sworn by the

LORD not to give them our daughters in
marriage?"
   8So they asked, "Who among the
tribes of Israel did not join us at Mizpah
when we assembled in the presence of
the LORD?" And they discovered that no
one from Jabesh-gilead had attended
the assembly. 9For after they counted
all the people, no one from Jabesh-
gilead was present.
   10So the assembly sent 12,000 of
their best warriors to Jabesh-gilead with
orders to kill everyone there, including
women and children. 11"This is what you
are to do," they said. "Completely destroy* all the males and every woman
who is not a virgin." 12Among the residents of Jabesh-gilead they found
400 young virgins who had never slept
with a man, and they brought them to
the camp at Shiloh in the land of Canaan.
   13The Israelite assembly sent a peace
delegation to the remaining people of
Benjamin who were living at the rock
of Rimmon. 14Then the men of Benjamin returned to their homes, and the
400 women of Jabesh-gilead who had
been spared were given to them as wives.
But there were not enough women for all
of them.
   15The people felt sorry for Benjamin
because the LORD had made this gap
among the tribes of Israel. 16So the elders of the assembly asked, "How can
we find wives for the few who remain,
since the women of the tribe of Benjamin are dead? 17There must be heirs for
the survivors so that an entire tribe of
Israel is not wiped out. 18But we cannot
give them our own daughters in marriage because we have sworn with a solemn oath that anyone who does this will
fall under God's curse."
   19Then they thought of the annual
festival of the LORD held in Shiloh, south
of Lebonah and north of Bethel, along
the east side of the road that goes from
Bethel to Shechem. 20They told the men
of Benjamin who still needed wives, "Go
and hide in the vineyards. 21When you
see the young women of Shiloh come
out for their dances, rush out from the

vineyards, and each of you can take one of them home to the land of Benjamin to be your wife! 22And when their fathers and brothers come to us in protest, we will tell them, 'Please be sympathetic. Let them have your daughters, for we didn't find wives for all of them when we destroyed Jabesh-gilead. And you are not guilty of breaking the vow since you did not actually give your daughters to them in marriage.'"

23 So the men of Benjamin did as they were told. Each man caught one of the women as she danced in the celebration and carried her off to be his wife. They returned to their own land, and they rebuilt their towns and lived in them.

24Then the people of Israel departed by tribes and families, and they returned to their own homes.

25 In those days Israel had no king; all the people did whatever seemed right in their own eyes.

1:1IN the days when the judges ruled in Israel, a severe famine came upon the land. So a man from Bethlehem in Judah left his home and went to live in the country of Moab, taking his wife and two sons with him. 2The man's name was Elimelech, and his wife was Naomi. Their two sons were Mahlon and Kilion. They were Ephrathites from Bethlehem in the land of Judah. And when they reached Moab, they settled there.

3 Then Elimelech died, and Naomi was left with her two sons. 4The two sons married Moabite women. One married a woman named Orpah, and the other a woman named Ruth. But about ten years later, 5 both Mahlon and Kilion died. This left Naomi alone, without her two sons or her husband.

6Then Naomi heard in Moab that the LORD had blessed his people in Judah by giving them good crops again. So Naomi and her daughters-in-law got ready to leave Moab to return to her homeland. 7 With her two daughters-in-law she set out from the place where she had been living, and they took the road that would lead them back to Judah.

8But on the way, Naomi said to her two daughters-in-law, "Go back to your mothers' homes. And may the LORD reward you for your kindness to your husbands and to me. 9May the LORD bless you with the security of another marriage." Then she kissed them good-bye, and they all broke down and wept.

10"No," they said. "We want to go with you to your people."

11But Naomi replied, "Why should you go on with me? Can I still give birth to other sons who could grow up to be your husbands? 12No, my daughters, return to your parents' homes, for I am too old to marry again. And even if it were possible, and I were to get married tonight and bear sons, then what? 13 Would you wait for them to grow up and refuse to marry someone else? No, of course not, my daughters! Things are far more bitter for me than for you, because the LORD himself has raised his fist against me."

14And again they wept together, and Orpah kissed her mother-in-law good-bye. But Ruth clung tightly to Naomi. 15"Look," Naomi said to her, "your sister-in-law has gone back to her people and to her gods. You should do the same."

16**But Ruth replied, "Don't ask me to leave you and turn back. Wherever you go, I will go; wherever you live, I will live. Your people will be my people, and your God will be my God.** 17 Wherever you die, I will die, and there I will be buried. May the LORD punish me severely if I allow anything but death to separate us!" 18When Naomi saw that Ruth was determined to go with her, she said nothing more.

19So the two of them continued on their journey. When they came to Bethlehem, the entire town was excited by their arrival. "Is it really Naomi?" the women asked.

20"Don't call me Naomi," she responded. "Instead, call me Mara,* for the Almighty has made life very bitter for me. 21I went away full, but the LORD has brought me home empty. Why call me Naomi when the LORD has caused me to suffer* and the Almighty has sent such tragedy upon me?"

²²So Naomi returned from Moab, accompanied by her daughter-in-law Ruth, the young Moabite woman. They arrived in Bethlehem in late spring, at the beginning of the barley harvest.

21:11 The Hebrew term used here refers to the complete consecration of things or people to the LORD, either by destroying them or by giving them as an offering.
1:20 *Naomi* means "pleasant"; *Mara* means "bitter."
1:21 Or *has testified against me.*

JOHN 4:4-42

He [Jesus] had to go through Samaria on the way. ⁵Eventually he came to the Samaritan village of Sychar, near the field that Jacob gave to his son Joseph. ⁶Jacob's well was there; and Jesus, tired from the long walk, sat wearily beside the well about noontime. ⁷Soon a Samaritan woman came to draw water, and Jesus said to her, "Please give me a drink." ⁸He was alone at the time because his disciples had gone into the village to buy some food.

⁹The woman was surprised, for Jews refuse to have anything to do with Samaritans.* She said to Jesus, "You are a Jew, and I am a Samaritan woman. Why are you asking me for a drink?"

¹⁰Jesus replied, "If you only knew the gift God has for you and who you are speaking to, you would ask me, and I would give you living water."

¹¹"But sir, you don't have a rope or a bucket," she said, "and this well is very deep. Where would you get this living water? ¹²And besides, do you think you're greater than our ancestor Jacob, who gave us this well? How can you offer better water than he and his sons and his animals enjoyed?"

¹³Jesus replied, "Anyone who drinks this water will soon become thirsty again. ¹⁴But those who drink the water I give will never be thirsty again. It becomes a fresh, bubbling spring within them, giving them eternal life."

¹⁵"Please, sir," the woman said, "give me this water! Then I'll never be thirsty again, and I won't have to come here to get water."

¹⁶"Go and get your husband," Jesus told her.

¹⁷"I don't have a husband," the woman replied.

Jesus said, "You're right! You don't have a husband—¹⁸for you have had five husbands, and you aren't even married to the man you're living with now. You certainly spoke the truth!"

¹⁹"Sir," the woman said, "you must be a prophet. ²⁰So tell me, why is it that you Jews insist that Jerusalem is the only place of worship, while we Samaritans claim it is here at Mount Gerizim,* where our ancestors worshiped?"

²¹Jesus replied, "Believe me, dear woman, the time is coming when it will no longer matter whether you worship the Father on this mountain or in Jerusalem. ²²You Samaritans know very little about the one you worship, while we Jews know all about him, for salvation comes through the Jews. ²³But the time is coming—indeed it's here now—when true worshipers will worship the Father in spirit and in truth. The Father is looking for those who will worship him that way. ²⁴For God is Spirit, so those who worship him must worship in spirit and in truth."

²⁵The woman said, "I know the Messiah is coming—the one who is called Christ. When he comes, he will explain everything to us."

²⁶Then Jesus told her, "I AM the Messiah!"*

²⁷Just then his disciples came back. They were shocked to find him talking to a woman, but none of them had the nerve to ask, "What do you want with her?" or "Why are you talking to her?" ²⁸The woman left her water jar beside the well and ran back to the village, telling everyone, ²⁹"Come and see a man who told me everything I ever did! Could he possibly be the Messiah?" ³⁰So the people came streaming from the village to see him.

³¹Meanwhile, the disciples were urging Jesus, "Rabbi, eat something."

³²But Jesus replied, "I have a kind of food you know nothing about."

33"Did someone bring him food while we were gone?" the disciples asked each other.

34Then Jesus explained: "My nourishment comes from doing the will of God, who sent me, and from finishing his work. 35You know the saying, 'Four months between planting and harvest.' But I say, wake up and look around. The fields are already ripe* for harvest. 36The harvesters are paid good wages, and the fruit they harvest is people brought to eternal life. What joy awaits both the planter and the harvester alike! 37You know the saying, 'One plants and another harvests.' And it's true. 38I sent you to harvest where you didn't plant; others had already done the work, and now you will get to gather the harvest."

39Many Samaritans from the village believed in Jesus because the woman had said, "He told me everything I ever did!" 40When they came out to see him, they begged him to stay in their village. So he stayed for two days, 41long enough for many more to hear his message and believe. 42Then they said to the woman, "Now we believe, not just because of what you told us, but because we have heard him ourselves. Now we know that he is indeed the Savior of the world."

4:9 Some manuscripts omit this sentence.   **4:20** Greek *on this mountain.*   **4:26** Or *"The 'I Am' is here";* or *"I am the Lord";* Greek reads *"I am, the one speaking to you."* See Exod 3:14.   **4:35** Greek *white.*

PSALM 105:1-15
Give thanks to the Lord and
proclaim his greatness.
Let the whole world know
what he has done.
2 Sing to him; yes, sing his praises.
Tell everyone about his
wonderful deeds.
3 Exult in his holy name;
rejoice, you who worship
the Lord.
4 Search for the Lord and for
his strength;
continually seek him.
5 Remember the wonders he
has performed,

his miracles, and the rulings
he has given,
6 you children of his servant
Abraham,
you descendants of Jacob,
his chosen ones.

7 He is the Lord our God.
His justice is seen throughout
the land.
8 He always stands by his covenant—
the commitment he made to a
thousand generations.
9 This is the covenant he made
with Abraham
and the oath he swore to Isaac.
10 He confirmed it to Jacob as a decree,
and to the people of Israel as a
never-ending covenant:
11 "I will give you the land of Canaan
as your special possession."

12 He said this when they were
few in number,
a tiny group of strangers
in Canaan.
13 They wandered from nation
to nation,
from one kingdom to another.
14 Yet he did not let anyone oppress
them.
He warned kings on their behalf:
15 "Do not touch my chosen people,
and do not hurt my prophets."

PROVERBS 14:25
A truthful witness saves lives, but a false witness is a traitor.

RUTH 2:1–4:22
Now there was a wealthy and influential man in Bethlehem named Boaz, who was a relative of Naomi's husband, Elimelech.

2One day Ruth the Moabite said to

Naomi, "Let me go out into the harvest fields to pick up the stalks of grain left behind by anyone who is kind enough to let me do it."

Naomi replied, "All right, my daughter, go ahead." ³So Ruth went out to gather grain behind the harvesters. And as it happened, she found herself working in a field that belonged to Boaz, the relative of her father-in-law, Elimelech.

⁴While she was there, Boaz arrived from Bethlehem and greeted the harvesters. "The LORD be with you!" he said.

"The LORD bless you!" the harvesters replied.

⁵Then Boaz asked his foreman, "Who is that young woman over there? Who does she belong to?"

⁶And the foreman replied, "She is the young woman from Moab who came back with Naomi. ⁷She asked me this morning if she could gather grain behind the harvesters. She has been hard at work ever since, except for a few minutes' rest in the shelter."

⁸Boaz went over and said to Ruth, "Listen, my daughter. Stay right here with us when you gather grain; don't go to any other fields. Stay right behind the young women working in my field. ⁹See which part of the field they are harvesting, and then follow them. I have warned the young men not to treat you roughly. And when you are thirsty, help yourself to the water they have drawn from the well."

¹⁰Ruth fell at his feet and thanked him warmly. "What have I done to deserve such kindness?" she asked. "I am only a foreigner."

¹¹"Yes, I know," Boaz replied. "But I also know about everything you have done for your mother-in-law since the death of your husband. I have heard how you left your father and mother and your own land to live here among complete strangers. ¹²May the LORD, the God of Israel, under whose wings you have come to take refuge, reward you fully for what you have done."

¹³"I hope I continue to please you, sir," she replied. "You have comforted me by speaking so kindly to me, even though I am not one of your workers."

¹⁴At mealtime Boaz called to her, "Come over here, and help yourself to some food. You can dip your bread in the sour wine." So she sat with his harvesters, and Boaz gave her some roasted grain to eat. She ate all she wanted and still had some left over.

¹⁵When Ruth went back to work again, Boaz ordered his young men, "Let her gather grain right among the sheaves without stopping her. ¹⁶And pull out some heads of barley from the bundles and drop them on purpose for her. Let her pick them up, and don't give her a hard time!"

¹⁷So Ruth gathered barley there all day, and when she beat out the grain that evening, it filled an entire basket.* ¹⁸She carried it back into town and showed it to her mother-in-law. Ruth also gave her the roasted grain that was left over from her meal.

¹⁹"Where did you gather all this grain today?" Naomi asked. "Where did you work? May the LORD bless the one who helped you!"

So Ruth told her mother-in-law about the man in whose field she had worked. She said, "The man I worked with today is named Boaz."

²⁰"May the LORD bless him!" Naomi told her daughter-in-law. "He is showing his kindness to us as well as to your dead husband.* That man is one of our closest relatives, one of our family redeemers."

²¹Then Ruth* said, "What's more, Boaz even told me to come back and stay with his harvesters until the entire harvest is completed."

²²"Good!" Naomi exclaimed. "Do as he said, my daughter. Stay with his young women right through the whole harvest. You might be harassed in other fields, but you'll be safe with him."

²³So Ruth worked alongside the women in Boaz's fields and gathered grain with them until the end of the barley harvest. Then she continued working with them through the wheat

harvest in early summer. And all the while she lived with her mother-in-law.

3:1ONE day Naomi said to Ruth, "My daughter, it's time that I found a permanent home for you, so that you will be provided for. 2Boaz is a close relative of ours, and he's been very kind by letting you gather grain with his young women. Tonight he will be winnowing barley at the threshing floor. 3Now do as I tell you—take a bath and put on perfume and dress in your nicest clothes. Then go to the threshing floor, but don't let Boaz see you until he has finished eating and drinking. 4Be sure to notice where he lies down; then go and uncover his feet and lie down there. He will tell you what to do."

5"I will do everything you say," Ruth replied. 6So she went down to the threshing floor that night and followed the instructions of her mother-in-law.

7After Boaz had finished eating and drinking and was in good spirits, he lay down at the far end of the pile of grain and went to sleep. Then Ruth came quietly, uncovered his feet, and lay down. 8Around midnight Boaz suddenly woke up and turned over. He was surprised to find a woman lying at his feet! 9"Who are you?" he asked.

"I am your servant Ruth," she replied. "Spread the corner of your covering over me, for you are my family redeemer."

10"The LORD bless you, my daughter!" Boaz exclaimed. "You are showing even more family loyalty now than you did before, for you have not gone after a younger man, whether rich or poor. 11Now don't worry about a thing, my daughter. I will do what is necessary, for everyone in town knows you are a virtuous woman. 12But while it's true that I am one of your family redeemers, there is another man who is more closely related to you than I am. 13Stay here tonight, and in the morning I will talk to him. If he is willing to redeem you, very well. Let him marry you. But if he is not willing, then as surely as the LORD lives, I

will redeem you myself! Now lie down here until morning."

14So Ruth lay at Boaz's feet until the morning, but she got up before it was light enough for people to recognize each other. For Boaz had said, "No one must know that a woman was here at the threshing floor." 15Then Boaz said to her, "Bring your cloak and spread it out." He measured six scoops* of barley into the cloak and placed it on her back. Then he* returned to the town.

16When Ruth went back to her mother-in-law, Naomi asked, "What happened, my daughter?"

Ruth told Naomi everything Boaz had done for her, 17and she added, "He gave me these six scoops of barley and said, 'Don't go back to your mother-in-law empty-handed.'"

18Then Naomi said to her, "Just be patient, my daughter, until we hear what happens. The man won't rest until he has settled things today."

4:1BOAZ went to the town gate and took a seat there. Just then the family redeemer he had mentioned came by, so Boaz called out to him, "Come over here and sit down, friend. I want to talk to you." So they sat down together. 2Then Boaz called ten leaders from the town and asked them to sit as witnesses. 3And Boaz said to the family redeemer, "You know Naomi, who came back from Moab. She is selling the land that belonged to our relative Elimelech. 4I thought I should speak to you about it so that you can redeem it if you wish. If you want the land, then buy it here in the presence of these witnesses. But if you don't want it, let me know right away, because I am next in line to redeem it after you."

The man replied, "All right, I'll redeem it."

5Then Boaz told him, "Of course, your purchase of the land from Naomi also requires that you marry Ruth, the Moabite widow. That way she can have children who will carry on her husband's name and keep the land in the family."

⁶"Then I can't redeem it," the family redeemer replied, "because this might endanger my own estate. You redeem the land; I cannot do it."

⁷Now in those days it was the custom in Israel for anyone transferring a right of purchase to remove his sandal and hand it to the other party. This publicly validated the transaction. ⁸So the other family redeemer drew off his sandal as he said to Boaz, "You buy the land."

⁹Then Boaz said to the elders and to the crowd standing around, "You are witnesses that today I have bought from Naomi all the property of Elimelech, Kilion, and Mahlon. ¹⁰And with the land I have acquired Ruth, the Moabite widow of Mahlon, to be my wife. This way she can have a son to carry on the family name of her dead husband and to inherit the family property here in his hometown. You are all witnesses today."

¹¹Then the elders and all the people standing in the gate replied, "We are witnesses! May the LORD make this woman who is coming into your home like Rachel and Leah, from whom all the nation of Israel descended! May you prosper in Ephrathah and be famous in Bethlehem. ¹²And may the LORD give you descendants by this young woman who will be like those of our ancestor Perez, the son of Tamar and Judah."

¹³So Boaz took Ruth into his home, and she became his wife. When he slept with her, the LORD enabled her to become pregnant, and she gave birth to a son. **¹⁴Then the women of the town said to Naomi, "Praise the LORD, who has now provided a redeemer for your family! May this child be famous in Israel. ¹⁵May he restore your youth and care for you in your old age. For he is the son of your daughter-in-law who loves you and has been better to you than seven sons!"**

¹⁶Naomi took the baby and cuddled him to her breast. And she cared for him as if he were her own. ¹⁷The neighbor women said, "Now at last Naomi has a son again!" And they named him Obed. He became the father of Jesse and the grandfather of David.

¹⁸This is the genealogical record of their ancestor Perez:

Perez was the father of Hezron.
¹⁹ Hezron was the father of Ram.
Ram was the father of Amminadab.
²⁰ Amminadab was the father
    of Nahshon.
Nahshon was the father of Salmon.*
²¹ Salmon was the father of Boaz.
Boaz was the father of Obed.
²² Obed was the father of Jesse.
Jesse was the father of David.

2:17 Hebrew *it was about an ephah* [20 quarts or 22 liters]. 2:20 Hebrew *to the living and to the dead.* 2:21 Hebrew *Ruth the Moabite.* 3:15a Hebrew *six measures,* an unknown quantity. 3:15b Most Hebrew manuscripts read *he;* many Hebrew manuscripts, Syriac version, and Latin Vulgate read *she.* 4:20 As in some Greek manuscripts (see also 4:21); Hebrew reads *Salma.*

JOHN 4:43-54

At the end of the two days, Jesus went on to Galilee. ⁴⁴He himself had said that a prophet is not honored in his own hometown. ⁴⁵Yet the Galileans welcomed him, for they had been in Jerusalem at the Passover celebration and had seen everything he did there.

⁴⁶As he traveled through Galilee, he came to Cana, where he had turned the water into wine. There was a government official in nearby Capernaum whose son was very sick. ⁴⁷When he heard that Jesus had come from Judea to Galilee, he went and begged Jesus to come to Capernaum to heal his son, who was about to die.

⁴⁸Jesus asked, "Will you never believe in me unless you see miraculous signs and wonders?"

⁴⁹The official pleaded, "Lord, please come now before my little boy dies."

⁵⁰Then Jesus told him, "Go back home. Your son will live!" And the man believed what Jesus said and started home.

⁵¹While the man was on his way, some of his servants met him with the news that his son was alive and well. ⁵²He asked them when the boy had begun to

get better, and they replied, "Yesterday afternoon at one o'clock his fever suddenly disappeared!" ⁵³Then the father realized that that was the very time Jesus had told him, "Your son will live." And he and his entire household believed in Jesus. ⁵⁴This was the second miraculous sign Jesus did in Galilee after coming from Judea.

PSALM 105:16-36

He [the LORD] called for a famine on
the land of Canaan,
cutting off its food supply.
¹⁷ Then he sent someone to Egypt
ahead of them—
Joseph, who was sold as a slave.
¹⁸ They bruised his feet with fetters
and placed his neck in an
iron collar.
¹⁹ Until the time came to fulfill
his dreams,*
the LORD tested Joseph's
character.
²⁰ Then Pharaoh sent for him and
set him free;
the ruler of the nation opened
his prison door.
²¹ Joseph was put in charge of all the
king's household;
he became ruler over all the
king's possessions.
²² He could instruct the king's aides
as he pleased
and teach the king's advisers.

²³ Then Israel arrived in Egypt;
Jacob lived as a foreigner in the
land of Ham.
²⁴ And the LORD multiplied the
people of Israel
until they became too mighty
for their enemies.
²⁵ Then he turned the Egyptians
against the Israelites,
and they plotted against the
LORD's servants.

²⁶ But the LORD sent his servant Moses,
along with Aaron, whom he
had chosen.
²⁷ They performed miraculous signs
among the Egyptians,

and wonders in the land of Ham.
²⁸ The LORD blanketed Egypt in
darkness,
for they had defied his
commands to let his people go.
²⁹ He turned their water into blood,
poisoning all the fish.
³⁰ Then frogs overran the land
and even invaded the king's
bedrooms.
³¹ When the LORD spoke, flies
descended on the Egyptians,
and gnats swarmed across Egypt.
³² He sent them hail instead of rain,
and lightning flashed over
the land.
³³ He ruined their grapevines and
fig trees
and shattered all the trees.
³⁴ He spoke, and hordes of locusts
came—
young locusts beyond number.
³⁵ They ate up everything green
in the land,
destroying all the crops in
their fields.
³⁶ Then he killed the oldest son
in each Egyptian home,
the pride and joy of each family.

105:19 Hebrew *his word.*

PROVERBS 14:26-27

Those who fear the LORD are secure; he will be a refuge for their children. □ Fear of the LORD is a life-giving fountain; it offers escape from the snares of death.

MAY 7

1 SAMUEL 1:1–2:21

There was a man named Elkanah who lived in Ramah in the region of Zuph* in the hill country of Ephraim. He was the son of Jeroham, son of Elihu, son of Tohu, son of Zuph, of Ephraim. ²Elkanah had two wives, Hannah and Peninnah. Peninnah had children, but Hannah did not.

³Each year Elkanah would travel to Shiloh to worship and sacrifice to the LORD of Heaven's Armies at the Tabernacle. The priests of the LORD at that time were the two sons of Eli—Hophni and Phinehas. ⁴On the days Elkanah presented his sacrifice, he would give portions of the meat to Peninnah and each of her children. ⁵And though he loved Hannah, he would give her only one choice portion* because the LORD had given her no children. ⁶So Peninnah would taunt Hannah and make fun of her because the LORD had kept her from having children. ⁷Year after year it was the same—Peninnah would taunt Hannah as they went to the Tabernacle.* Each time, Hannah would be reduced to tears and would not even eat.

⁸"Why are you crying, Hannah?" Elkanah would ask. "Why aren't you eating? Why be downhearted just because you have no children? You have me—isn't that better than having ten sons?"

⁹Once after a sacrificial meal at Shiloh, Hannah got up and went to pray. Eli the priest was sitting at his customary place beside the entrance of the Tabernacle.* ¹⁰Hannah was in deep anguish, crying bitterly as she prayed to the LORD. ¹¹And she made this vow: "O LORD of Heaven's Armies, if you will look upon my sorrow and answer my prayer and give me a son, then I will give him back to you. He will be yours for his entire lifetime, and as a sign that he has been dedicated to the LORD, his hair will never be cut.*"

¹²As she was praying to the LORD, Eli watched her. ¹³Seeing her lips moving but hearing no sound, he thought she had been drinking. ¹⁴"Must you come here drunk?" he demanded. "Throw away your wine!"

¹⁵"Oh no, sir!" she replied. "I haven't been drinking wine or anything stronger. But I am very discouraged, and I was pouring out my heart to the LORD. ¹⁶Don't think I am a wicked woman! For

I have been praying out of great anguish and sorrow."

¹⁷"In that case," Eli said, "go in peace! May the God of Israel grant the request you have asked of him."

¹⁸"Oh, thank you, sir!" she exclaimed. Then she went back and began to eat again, and she was no longer sad.

¹⁹The entire family got up early the next morning and went to worship the LORD once more. Then they returned home to Ramah. When Elkanah slept with Hannah, the LORD remembered her plea, ²⁰and in due time she gave birth to a son. She named him Samuel,* for she said, "I asked the LORD for him."

²¹The next year Elkanah and his family went on their annual trip to offer a sacrifice to the LORD. ²²But Hannah did not go. She told her husband, "Wait until the boy is weaned. Then I will take him to the Tabernacle and leave him there with the LORD permanently.*"

²³"Whatever you think is best," Elkanah agreed. "Stay here for now, and may the LORD help you keep your promise." So she stayed home and nursed the boy until he was weaned.

²⁴When the child was weaned, Hannah took him to the Tabernacle in Shiloh. They brought along a three-year-old bull* for the sacrifice and a basket* of flour and some wine. ²⁵After sacrificing the bull, they brought the boy to Eli. ²⁶"Sir, do you remember me?" Hannah asked. "I am the woman who stood here several years ago praying to the LORD. ²⁷I asked the LORD to give me this boy, and he has granted my request. ²⁸Now I am giving him to the LORD, and he will belong to the LORD his whole life." And they* worshiped the LORD there.

2:1THEN Hannah prayed:

"My heart rejoices in the LORD!
    The LORD has made me strong.*
Now I have an answer for my
        enemies;
    I rejoice because you rescued me.
² No one is holy like the LORD!
    There is no one besides you;
    there is no Rock like our God.

3 "Stop acting so proud and
  haughty!
    Don't speak with such
      arrogance!
  For the LORD is a God who knows
    what you have done;
    he will judge your actions.
4 The bow of the mighty is now
    broken,
    and those who stumbled are
      now strong.
5 Those who were well fed are
    now starving,
    and those who were starving
      are now full.
  The childless woman now has
    seven children,
    and the woman with many
      children wastes away.
6 The LORD gives both death
    and life;
    he brings some down to the
      grave* but raises others up.
7 The LORD makes some poor and
    others rich;
    he brings some down and lifts
      others up.
8 He lifts the poor from the dust
    and the needy from the garbage
      dump.
  He sets them among princes,
    placing them in seats of honor.
  For all the earth is the LORD's,
    and he has set the world
      in order.

9 "He will protect his faithful ones,
    but the wicked will disappear
      in darkness.
  No one will succeed by strength
    alone.
10   Those who fight against the LORD
        will be shattered.
  He thunders against them
      from heaven;
    the LORD judges throughout
      the earth.
  He gives power to his king;
    he increases the strength*
      of his anointed one."

11Then Elkanah returned home to Ramah without Samuel. And the boy
served the LORD by assisting Eli the
priest.

12Now the sons of Eli were scoundrels who had no respect for the LORD
13or for their duties as priests. Whenever anyone offered a sacrifice, Eli's
sons would send over a servant with a
three-pronged fork. While the meat of
the sacrificed animal was still boiling,
14the servant would stick the fork into
the pot and demand that whatever it
brought up be given to Eli's sons. All the
Israelites who came to worship at Shiloh were treated this way. 15Sometimes
the servant would come even before the
animal's fat had been burned on the altar. He would demand raw meat before
it had been boiled so that it could be
used for roasting.

16The man offering the sacrifice
might reply, "Take as much as you want,
but the fat must be burned first." Then
the servant would demand, "No, give it
to me now, or I'll take it by force." 17So
the sin of these young men was very serious in the LORD's sight, for they treated
the LORD's offerings with contempt.

18But Samuel, though he was only a
boy, served the LORD. He wore a linen
garment like that of a priest.* 19Each
year his mother made a small coat for
him and brought it to him when she
came with her husband for the sacrifice. 20Before they returned home, Eli
would bless Elkanah and his wife and
say, "May the LORD give you other children to take the place of this one she
gave to the LORD.*" 21And the LORD gave
Hannah three sons and two daughters.
Meanwhile, Samuel grew up in the presence of the LORD.

1:1 As in Greek version; Hebrew reads in Ramathaim-
zophim; compare 1:19.   1:5 Or And because he loved
Hannah, he would give her a choice portion. The meaning
of the Hebrew is uncertain.   1:7 Hebrew the house of the
LORD; also in 1:24.   1:9 Hebrew the Temple of the LORD.
1:11 Some manuscripts add He will drink neither wine nor
intoxicants.   1:20 Samuel sounds like the Hebrew term for
"asked of God" or "heard by God."   1:22 Some manuscripts
add I will offer him as a Nazirite for all time.   1:24a As in
Dead Sea Scrolls, Greek and Syriac versions; Masoretic Text
reads three bulls.   1:24b Hebrew and an ephah [20 quarts
or 22 liters].   1:28 Hebrew he.   2:1 Hebrew has exalted
my horn.   2:6 Hebrew to Sheol.   2:10 Hebrew he exalts
the horn.   2:18 Hebrew He wore a linen ephod.   2:20 As
in Dead Sea Scrolls and Greek version; Masoretic Text reads
this one she requested of the LORD in prayer.

JOHN 5:1-23

Afterward Jesus returned to Jerusalem for one of the Jewish holy days. [2]Inside the city, near the Sheep Gate, was the pool of Bethesda,* with five covered porches. [3]Crowds of sick people—blind, lame, or paralyzed—lay on the porches.* [5]One of the men lying there had been sick for thirty-eight years. [6]When Jesus saw him and knew he had been ill for a long time, he asked him, "Would you like to get well?"

[7]"I can't, sir," the sick man said, "for I have no one to put me into the pool when the water bubbles up. Someone else always gets there ahead of me."

[8]Jesus told him, "Stand up, pick up your mat, and walk!"

[9]Instantly, the man was healed! He rolled up his sleeping mat and began walking! But this miracle happened on the Sabbath, [10]so the Jewish leaders objected. They said to the man who was cured, "You can't work on the Sabbath! The law doesn't allow you to carry that sleeping mat!"

[11]But he replied, "The man who healed me told me, 'Pick up your mat and walk.'"

[12]"Who said such a thing as that?" they demanded.

[13]The man didn't know, for Jesus had disappeared into the crowd. [14]But afterward Jesus found him in the Temple and told him, "Now you are well; so stop sinning, or something even worse may happen to you." [15]Then the man went and told the Jewish leaders that it was Jesus who had healed him.

[16]So the Jewish leaders began harassing* Jesus for breaking the Sabbath rules. [17]But Jesus replied, "My Father is always working, and so am I." [18]So the Jewish leaders tried all the harder to find a way to kill him. For he not only broke the Sabbath, he called God his Father, thereby making himself equal with God.

[19]**So Jesus explained, "I tell you the truth, the Son can do nothing by himself. He does only what he sees the Father doing. Whatever the Father does, the Son also does.** [20]For the Father loves the Son and shows him everything he is doing. In fact, the Father will show him how to do even greater works than healing this man. Then you will truly be astonished. [21]For just as the Father gives life to those he raises from the dead, so the Son gives life to anyone he wants. [22]In addition, the Father judges no one. Instead, he has given the Son absolute authority to judge, [23]so that everyone will honor the Son, just as they honor the Father. Anyone who does not honor the Son is certainly not honoring the Father who sent him."

5:2 Other manuscripts read *Beth-zatha;* still others read *Bethsaida.* 5:3 Some manuscripts add *waiting for a certain movement of the water, 'for an angel of the Lord came from time to time and stirred up the water. And the first person to step in after the water was stirred was healed of whatever disease he had.* 5:16 Or *persecuting.*

PSALM 105:37-45

The LORD brought his people
    out of Egypt, loaded with silver
      and gold;
  and not one among the tribes
    of Israel even stumbled.
[38] Egypt was glad when they were gone,
    for they feared them greatly.
[39] The LORD spread a cloud above
    them as a covering
  and gave them a great fire to
    light the darkness.
[40] They asked for meat, and he sent
    them quail;
  he satisfied their hunger with
    manna—bread from heaven.
[41] He split open a rock, and water
    gushed out
  to form a river through the
    dry wasteland.
[42] For he remembered his sacred
    promise
  to his servant Abraham.
[43] So he brought his people out
    of Egypt with joy,
  his chosen ones with rejoicing.
[44] He gave his people the lands
    of pagan nations,
  and they harvested crops that
    others had planted.

⁴⁵ All this happened so they would
       follow his decrees
    and obey his instructions.

Praise the LORD!

PROVERBS 14:28-29

A growing population is a king's glory; a prince without subjects has nothing. □ People with understanding control their anger; a hot temper shows great foolishness.

MAY
8

1 SAMUEL 2:22–4:22

Now Eli was very old, but he was aware of what his sons were doing to the people of Israel. He knew, for instance, that his sons were seducing the young women who assisted at the entrance of the Tabernacle.* ²³Eli said to them, "I have been hearing reports from all the people about the wicked things you are doing. Why do you keep sinning? ²⁴You must stop, my sons! The reports I hear among the LORD's people are not good. ²⁵If someone sins against another person, God* can mediate for the guilty party. But if someone sins against the LORD, who can intercede?" But Eli's sons wouldn't listen to their father, for the LORD was already planning to put them to death.

²⁶Meanwhile, the boy Samuel grew taller and grew in favor with the LORD and with the people.

²⁷One day a man of God came to Eli and gave him this message from the LORD: "I revealed myself* to your ancestors when the people of Israel were slaves in Egypt. ²⁸I chose your ancestor Aaron* from among all the tribes of Israel to be my priest, to offer sacrifices on my altar, to burn incense, and to wear the priestly vest* as he served me. And I assigned the sacrificial offerings

to you priests. ²⁹So why do you scorn my sacrifices and offerings? Why do you give your sons more honor than you give me—for you and they have become fat from the best offerings of my people Israel!

³⁰"Therefore, the LORD, the God of Israel, says: I promised that your branch of the tribe of Levi* would always be my priests. But I will honor those who honor me, and I will despise those who think lightly of me. ³¹The time is coming when I will put an end to your family, so it will no longer serve as my priests. All the members of your family will die before their time. None will reach old age. ³²You will watch with envy as I pour out prosperity on the people of Israel. But no members of your family will ever live out their days. ³³Those who survive will live in sadness and grief, and their children will die a violent death.* ³⁴And to prove that what I have said will come true, I will cause your two sons, Hophni and Phinehas, to die on the same day!

³⁵"Then I will raise up a faithful priest who will serve me and do what I desire. I will establish his family, and they will be priests to my anointed kings forever. ³⁶Then all of your surviving family will bow before him, begging for money and food. 'Please,' they will say, 'give us jobs among the priests so we will have enough to eat.'"

³:¹MEANWHILE, the boy Samuel served the LORD by assisting Eli. Now in those days messages from the LORD were very rare, and visions were quite uncommon.

²One night Eli, who was almost blind by now, had gone to bed. ³The lamp of God had not yet gone out, and Samuel was sleeping in the Tabernacle* near the Ark of God. ⁴Suddenly the LORD called out, "Samuel!"

"Yes?" Samuel replied. "What is it?" ⁵He got up and ran to Eli. "Here I am. Did you call me?"

"I didn't call you," Eli replied. "Go back to bed." So he did.

⁶Then the LORD called out again, "Samuel!"

Again Samuel got up and went to Eli. "Here I am. Did you call me?"

"I didn't call you, my son," Eli said. "Go back to bed."

[7]Samuel did not yet know the LORD because he had never had a message from the LORD before. [8]So the LORD called a third time, and once more Samuel got up and went to Eli. "Here I am. Did you call me?"

Then Eli realized it was the LORD who was calling the boy. [9]So he said to Samuel, "Go and lie down again, and if someone calls again, say, 'Speak, LORD, your servant is listening.'" So Samuel went back to bed.

[10]And the LORD came and called as before, "Samuel! Samuel!"

And Samuel replied, "Speak, your servant is listening."

[11]Then the LORD said to Samuel, "I am about to do a shocking thing in Israel. [12]I am going to carry out all my threats against Eli and his family, from beginning to end. [13]I have warned him that judgment is coming upon his family forever, because his sons are blaspheming God* and he hasn't disciplined them. [14]So I have vowed that the sins of Eli and his sons will never be forgiven by sacrifices or offerings."

[15]Samuel stayed in bed until morning, then got up and opened the doors of the Tabernacle* as usual. He was afraid to tell Eli what the LORD had said to him. [16]But Eli called out to him, "Samuel, my son."

"Here I am," Samuel replied.

[17]"What did the LORD say to you? Tell me everything. And may God strike you and even kill you if you hide anything from me!" [18]So Samuel told Eli everything; he didn't hold anything back. "It is the LORD's will," Eli replied. "Let him do what he thinks best."

[19]As Samuel grew up, the LORD was with him, and everything Samuel said proved to be reliable. [20]And all Israel, from Dan in the north to Beersheba in the south, knew that Samuel was confirmed as a prophet of the LORD. [21]The LORD continued to appear at Shiloh and gave messages to Samuel there at the Tabernacle. [4:1]And Samuel's words went out to all the people of Israel.

[4:1]At that time Israel was at war with the Philistines. The Israelite army was camped near Ebenezer, and the Philistines were at Aphek. [2]The Philistines attacked and defeated the army of Israel, killing 4,000 men. [3]After the battle was over, the troops retreated to their camp, and the elders of Israel asked, "Why did the LORD allow us to be defeated by the Philistines?" Then they said, "Let's bring the Ark of the Covenant of the LORD from Shiloh. If we carry it into battle with us, it* will save us from our enemies."

[4]So they sent men to Shiloh to bring the Ark of the Covenant of the LORD of Heaven's Armies, who is enthroned between the cherubim. Hophni and Phinehas, the sons of Eli, were also there with the Ark of the Covenant of God. [5]When all the Israelites saw the Ark of the Covenant of the LORD coming into the camp, their shout of joy was so loud it made the ground shake!

[6]"What's going on?" the Philistines asked. "What's all the shouting about in the Hebrew camp?" When they were told it was because the Ark of the LORD had arrived, [7]they panicked. "The gods have* come into their camp!" they cried. "This is a disaster! We have never had to face anything like this before! [8]Help! Who can save us from these mighty gods of Israel? They are the same gods who destroyed the Egyptians with plagues when Israel was in the wilderness. [9]Fight as never before, Philistines! If you don't, we will become the Hebrews' slaves just as they have been ours! Stand up like men and fight!"

[10]So the Philistines fought desperately, and Israel was defeated again. The slaughter was great; 30,000 Israelite soldiers died that day. The survivors turned and fled to their tents. [11]The Ark of God was captured, and Hophni and Phinehas, the two sons of Eli, were killed.

[12]A man from the tribe of Benjamin

ran from the battlefield and arrived at Shiloh later that same day. He had torn his clothes and put dust on his head to show his grief. [13]Eli was waiting beside the road to hear the news of the battle, for his heart trembled for the safety of the Ark of God. When the messenger arrived and told what had happened, an outcry resounded throughout the town.

[14]"What is all the noise about?" Eli asked.

The messenger rushed over to Eli, [15]who was ninety-eight years old and blind. [16]He said to Eli, "I have just come from the battlefield—I was there this very day."

"What happened, my son?" Eli demanded.

[17]"Israel has been defeated by the Philistines," the messenger replied. "The people have been slaughtered, and your two sons, Hophni and Phinehas, were also killed. And the Ark of God has been captured."

[18]When the messenger mentioned what had happened to the Ark of God, Eli fell backward from his seat beside the gate. He broke his neck and died, for he was old and overweight. He had been Israel's judge for forty years.

[19]Eli's daughter-in-law, the wife of Phinehas, was pregnant and near her time of delivery. When she heard that the Ark of God had been captured and that her father-in-law and husband were dead, she went into labor and gave birth. [20]She died in childbirth, but before she passed away the midwives tried to encourage her. "Don't be afraid," they said. "You have a baby boy!" But she did not answer or pay attention to them.

[21]She named the child Ichabod (which means "Where is the glory?"), for she said, "Israel's glory is gone." She named him this because the Ark of God had been captured and because her father-in-law and husband were dead. [22]Then she said, "The glory has departed from Israel, for the Ark of God has been captured."

2:22 Hebrew *Tent of Meeting*. Some manuscripts lack this entire sentence. 2:25 Or *the judges*. 2:27 As in Greek and Syriac versions; Hebrew reads *Did I reveal myself*. 2:28a Hebrew *your father*. 2:28b Hebrew *an ephod*. 2:30 Hebrew *that your house and your father's house*. 2:33 As in Dead Sea Scrolls, which read *die by the sword*; Masoretic Text reads *die like mortals*. 3:3 Hebrew *Temple of the Lord*. 3:13 As in Greek version; Hebrew reads *his sons have made themselves contemptible*. 3:15 Hebrew *the house of the Lord*. 4:3 Or *he*. 4:7 Or *A god has*.

JOHN 5:24-47

"I [Jesus] tell you the truth, those who listen to my message and believe in God who sent me have eternal life. They will never be condemned for their sins, but they have already passed from death into life.

[25]"And I assure you that the time is coming, indeed it's here now, when the dead will hear my voice—the voice of the Son of God. And those who listen will live. [26]The Father has life in himself, and he has granted that same life-giving power to his Son. [27]And he has given him authority to judge everyone because he is the Son of Man.* [28]Don't be so surprised! Indeed, the time is coming when all the dead in their graves will hear the voice of God's Son, [29]and they will rise again. Those who have done good will rise to experience eternal life, and those who have continued in evil will rise to experience judgment. [30]I can do nothing on my own. I judge as God tells me. Therefore, my judgment is just, because I carry out the will of the one who sent me, not my own will.

[31]"If I were to testify on my own behalf, my testimony would not be valid. [32]But someone else is also testifying about me, and I assure you that everything he says about me is true. [33]In fact, you sent investigators to listen to John the Baptist, and his testimony about me was true. [34]Of course, I have no need of human witnesses, but I say these things so you might be saved. [35]John was like a burning and shining lamp, and you were excited for a while about his message. [36]But I have a greater witness than John—my teachings and my miracles. The Father gave me these works to accomplish, and they prove that he sent me. [37]And the Father who sent me has

testified about me himself. You have never heard his voice or seen him face to face, 38 and you do not have his message in your hearts, because you do not believe me—the one he sent to you.

39"You search the Scriptures because you think they give you eternal life. But the Scriptures point to me! 40Yet you refuse to come to me to receive this life.

41"Your approval means nothing to me, 42 because I know you don't have God's love within you. 43For I have come to you in my Father's name, and you have rejected me. Yet if others come in their own name, you gladly welcome them. 44No wonder you can't believe! For you gladly honor each other, but you don't care about the honor that comes from the one who alone is God.*

45"Yet it isn't I who will accuse you before the Father. Moses will accuse you! Yes, Moses, in whom you put your hopes. 46If you really believed Moses, you would believe me, because he wrote about me. 47But since you don't believe what he wrote, how will you believe what I say?"

5:27 "Son of Man" is a title Jesus used for himself.
5:44 Some manuscripts read *from the only One.*

PSALM 106:1-12
Praise the LORD!

Give thanks to the LORD, for he
    is good!
His faithful love endures forever.
2 Who can list the glorious miracles
    of the LORD?
Who can ever praise him
    enough?
3 There is joy for those who deal
    justly with others
and always do what is right.

4 Remember me, LORD, when you
    show favor to your people;
come near and rescue me.
5 Let me share in the prosperity
    of your chosen ones.
Let me rejoice in the joy
    of your people;
let me praise you with those who
    are your heritage.

6 Like our ancestors, we have sinned.
    We have done wrong! We have
        acted wickedly!
7 Our ancestors in Egypt
    were not impressed by the
        LORD's miraculous deeds.
They soon forgot his many acts
    of kindness to them.
Instead, they rebelled against him
    at the Red Sea.*
8 Even so, he saved them—
    to defend the honor of his name
    and to demonstrate his
        mighty power.
9 He commanded the Red Sea*
    to dry up.
He led Israel across the sea as
    if it were a desert.
10 So he rescued them from their
        enemies
    and redeemed them from
        their foes.
11 Then the water returned and
        covered their enemies;
    not one of them survived.
12 Then his people believed his
        promises.
    Then they sang his praise.

106:7 Hebrew *at the sea, the sea of reeds.*   106:9 Hebrew *sea of reeds;* also in 106:22.

PROVERBS 14:30-31
A peaceful heart leads to a healthy body; jealousy is like cancer in the bones. □ Those who oppress the poor insult their Maker, but helping the poor honors him.

1 SAMUEL 5:1–7:17
After the Philistines captured the Ark of God, they took it from the battleground at Ebenezer to the town of Ashdod. 2They carried the Ark of God into the temple of Dagon and placed it beside an

idol of Dagon. ³But when the citizens of Ashdod went to see it the next morning, Dagon had fallen with his face to the ground in front of the Ark of the LORD! So they took Dagon and put him in his place again. ⁴But the next morning the same thing happened—Dagon had fallen face down before the Ark of the LORD again. This time his head and hands had broken off and were lying in the doorway. Only the trunk of his body was left intact. ⁵That is why to this day neither the priests of Dagon nor anyone who enters the temple of Dagon in Ashdod will step on its threshold.

⁶Then the LORD's heavy hand struck the people of Ashdod and the nearby villages with a plague of tumors.* ⁷When the people realized what was happening, they cried out, "We can't keep the Ark of the God of Israel here any longer! He is against us! We will all be destroyed along with Dagon, our god." ⁸So they called together the rulers of the Philistine towns and asked, "What should we do with the Ark of the God of Israel?"

The rulers discussed it and replied, "Move it to the town of Gath." So they moved the Ark of the God of Israel to Gath. ⁹But when the Ark arrived at Gath, the LORD's heavy hand fell on its men, young and old; he struck them with a plague of tumors, and there was a great panic.

¹⁰So they sent the Ark of God to the town of Ekron, but when the people of Ekron saw it coming they cried out, "They are bringing the Ark of the God of Israel here to kill us, too!" ¹¹The people summoned the Philistine rulers again and begged them, "Please send the Ark of the God of Israel back to its own country, or it* will kill us all." For the deadly plague from God had already begun, and great fear was sweeping across the town. ¹²Those who didn't die were afflicted with tumors; and the cry from the town rose to heaven.

⁶:¹THE Ark of the LORD remained in Philistine territory seven months in all. ²Then the Philistines called in their priests and diviners and asked them, "What should we do about the Ark of the LORD? Tell us how to return it to its own country."

³"Send the Ark of the God of Israel back with a gift," they were told. "Send a guilt offering so the plague will stop. Then, if you are healed, you will know it was his hand that caused the plague."

⁴"What sort of guilt offering should we send?" they asked.

And they were told, "Since the plague has struck both you and your five rulers, make five gold tumors and five gold rats, just like those that have ravaged your land. ⁵Make these things to show honor to the God of Israel. Perhaps then he will stop afflicting you, your gods, and your land. ⁶Don't be stubborn and rebellious as Pharaoh and the Egyptians were. By the time God was finished with them, they were eager to let Israel go.

⁷"Now build a new cart, and find two cows that have just given birth to calves. Make sure the cows have never been yoked to a cart. Hitch the cows to the cart, but shut their calves away from them in a pen. ⁸Put the Ark of the LORD on the cart, and beside it place a chest containing the gold rats and gold tumors you are sending as a guilt offering. Then let the cows go wherever they want. ⁹If they cross the border of our land and go to Beth-shemesh, we will know it was the LORD who brought this great disaster upon us. If they don't, we will know it was not his hand that caused the plague. It came simply by chance."

¹⁰So these instructions were carried out. Two cows were hitched to the cart, and their newborn calves were shut up in a pen. ¹¹Then the Ark of the LORD and the chest containing the gold rats and gold tumors were placed on the cart. ¹²And sure enough, without veering off in other directions, the cows went straight along the road toward Beth-shemesh, lowing as they went. The Philistine rulers followed them as far as the border of Beth-shemesh.

¹³The people of Beth-shemesh were harvesting wheat in the valley, and

when they saw the Ark, they were over-joyed! [14]The cart came into the field of a man named Joshua and stopped beside a large rock. So the people broke up the wood of the cart for a fire and killed the cows and sacrificed them to the LORD as a burnt offering. [15]Several men of the tribe of Levi lifted the Ark of the LORD and the chest containing the gold rats and gold tumors from the cart and placed them on the large rock. Many sacrifices and burnt offerings were offered to the LORD that day by the people of Beth-shemesh. [16]The five Philistine rulers watched all this and then returned to Ekron that same day.

[17]The five gold tumors sent by the Philistines as a guilt offering to the LORD were gifts from the rulers of Ashdod, Gaza, Ashkelon, Gath, and Ekron. [18]The five gold rats represented the five Philistine towns and their surrounding villages, which were controlled by the five rulers. The large rock at Beth-shemesh, where they set the Ark of the LORD, still stands in the field of Joshua as a witness to what happened there.

[19]But the LORD killed seventy men* from Beth-shemesh because they looked into the Ark of the LORD. And the people mourned greatly because of what the LORD had done. [20]"Who is able to stand in the presence of the LORD, this holy God?" they cried out. "Where can we send the Ark from here?"

[21]So they sent messengers to the people at Kiriath-jearim and told them, "The Philistines have returned the Ark of the LORD. Come here and get it!"

[7:1]So the men of Kiriath-jearim came to get the Ark of the LORD. They took it to the hillside home of Abinadab and ordained Eleazar, his son, to be in charge of it. [2]The Ark remained in Kiriath-jearim for a long time—twenty years in all. During that time all Israel mourned because it seemed the LORD had abandoned them.

[3]Then Samuel said to all the people of Israel, "If you are really serious about wanting to return to the LORD, get rid of your foreign gods and your images of Ashtoreth. Determine to obey only the LORD; then he will rescue you from the Philistines." [4]So the Israelites got rid of their images of Baal and Ashtoreth and worshiped only the LORD.

[5]Then Samuel told them, "Gather all of Israel to Mizpah, and I will pray to the LORD for you." [6]So they gathered at Mizpah and, in a great ceremony, drew water from a well and poured it out before the LORD. They also went without food all day and confessed that they had sinned against the LORD. (It was at Mizpah that Samuel became Israel's judge.)

[7]When the Philistine rulers heard that Israel had gathered at Mizpah, they mobilized their army and advanced. The Israelites were badly frightened when they learned that the Philistines were approaching. [8]"Don't stop pleading with the LORD our God to save us from the Philistines!" they begged Samuel. [9]So Samuel took a young lamb and offered it to the LORD as a whole burnt offering. He pleaded with the LORD to help Israel, and the LORD answered him.

[10]Just as Samuel was sacrificing the burnt offering, the Philistines arrived to attack Israel. But the LORD spoke with a mighty voice of thunder from heaven that day, and the Philistines were thrown into such confusion that the Israelites defeated them. [11]The men of Israel chased them from Mizpah to a place below Beth-car, slaughtering them all along the way.

[12]Samuel then took a large stone and placed it between the towns of Mizpah and Jeshanah.* He named it Ebenezer (which means "the stone of help"), for he said, "Up to this point the LORD has helped us!"

[13]So the Philistines were subdued and didn't invade Israel again for some time. And throughout Samuel's lifetime, the LORD's powerful hand was raised against the Philistines. [14]The Israelite villages near Ekron and Gath that the Philistines had captured were restored to Israel, along with the rest of

the territory that the Philistines had taken. And there was peace between Israel and the Amorites in those days.

15Samuel continued as Israel's judge for the rest of his life. 16Each year he traveled around, setting up his court first at Bethel, then at Gilgal, and then at Mizpah. He judged the people of Israel at each of these places. 17Then he would return to his home at Ramah, and he would hear cases there, too. And Samuel built an altar to the LORD at Ramah.

5:6 Greek version and Latin Vulgate read *tumors; and rats appeared in their land, and death and destruction were throughout the city.*   5:11 Or *he.*   6:19 As in a few Hebrew manuscripts; most Hebrew manuscripts read *70 men, 50,000 men.* Perhaps the text should be understood to read *the LORD killed 70 men and 50 oxen.* 7:12 As in Greek and Syriac versions; Hebrew reads *Shen.*

JOHN 6:1-21

After this, Jesus crossed over to the far side of the Sea of Galilee, also known as the Sea of Tiberias. 2A huge crowd kept following him wherever he went, because they saw his miraculous signs as he healed the sick. 3Then Jesus climbed a hill and sat down with his disciples around him. 4(It was nearly time for the Jewish Passover celebration.) 5Jesus soon saw a huge crowd of people coming to look for him. Turning to Philip, he asked, "Where can we buy bread to feed all these people?" 6He was testing Philip, for he already knew what he was going to do.

7Philip replied, "Even if we worked for months, we wouldn't have enough money* to feed them!"

8Then Andrew, Simon Peter's brother, spoke up. 9"There's a young boy here with five barley loaves and two fish. But what good is that with this huge crowd?"

10"Tell everyone to sit down," Jesus said. So they all sat down on the grassy slopes. (The men alone numbered 5,000.) 11Then Jesus took the loaves, gave thanks to God, and distributed them to the people. Afterward he did the same with the fish. And they all ate as much as they wanted. 12After everyone was full, Jesus told his disciples, "Now gather the leftovers, so that nothing is wasted." 13So they picked up the pieces and filled twelve baskets with scraps left by the people who had eaten from the five barley loaves.

14When the people saw him* do this miraculous sign, they exclaimed, "Surely, he is the Prophet we have been expecting!"* 15When Jesus saw that they were ready to force him to be their king, he slipped away into the hills by himself.

16That evening Jesus' disciples went down to the shore to wait for him. 17But as darkness fell and Jesus still hadn't come back, they got into the boat and headed across the lake toward Capernaum. 18Soon a gale swept down upon them, and the sea grew very rough. 19They had rowed three or four miles* when suddenly they saw Jesus walking on the water toward the boat. They were terrified, 20but he called out to them, "Don't be afraid. I am here!*" 21Then they were eager to let him in the boat, and immediately they arrived at their destination!

6:7 Greek *Two hundred denarii would not be enough.* A denarius was equivalent to a laborer's full day's wage. 6:14a Some manuscripts read *Jesus.*   6:14b See Deut 18:15, 18; Mal 4:5-6.   6:19 Greek *25 or 30 stadia* [4.6 or 5.5 kilometers].   6:20 Or *The 'I AM' is here;* Greek reads *I am.* See Exod 3:14.

PSALM 106:13-31

Yet how quickly they forgot what
    he had done!
    They wouldn't wait for his
      counsel!
14 **In the wilderness their desires
    ran wild,
    testing God's patience in that
      dry wasteland.**
15 So he gave them what they
    asked for,
    but he sent a plague along with it.
16 The people in the camp were jealous
    of Moses
    and envious of Aaron, the LORD's
      holy priest.
17 Because of this, the earth opened up;
    it swallowed Dathan
    and buried Abiram and the
      other rebels.
18 Fire fell upon their followers;
    a flame consumed the wicked.

¹⁹ The people made a calf at
      Mount Sinai*;
   they bowed before an image
      made of gold.
²⁰ They traded their glorious God
      for a statue of a grass-eating
      bull.
²¹ They forgot God, their savior,
   who had done such great things
      in Egypt—
²² such wonderful things in the
      land of Ham,
   such awesome deeds at the
      Red Sea.
²³ So he declared he would destroy
      them.
   But Moses, his chosen one,
      stepped between the LORD
      and the people.
   He begged him to turn from his
      anger and not destroy them.

²⁴ The people refused to enter the
      pleasant land,
   for they wouldn't believe his
      promise to care for them.
²⁵ Instead, they grumbled in
      their tents
   and refused to obey the LORD.
²⁶ Therefore, he solemnly swore
      that he would kill them in
      the wilderness,
²⁷ that he would scatter their
      descendants among
      the nations,
   exiling them to distant lands.

²⁸ Then our ancestors joined in the
      worship of Baal at Peor;
   they even ate sacrifices offered
      to the dead!
²⁹ They angered the LORD with all
      these things,
   so a plague broke out among
      them.
³⁰ But Phinehas had the courage
      to intervene,
   and the plague was stopped.
³¹ So he has been regarded as a
      righteous man
   ever since that time.

106:19 Hebrew *at Horeb*, another name for Sinai.

PROVERBS 14:32-33

The wicked are crushed by disaster, but
the godly have a refuge when they die.
□ Wisdom is enshrined in an understanding heart; wisdom is not* found
among fools.

14:33 As in Greek and Syriac versions; Hebrew lacks *not*.

MAY
10

1 SAMUEL 8:1–9:27

As Samuel grew old, he appointed his
sons to be judges over Israel. ²Joel and
Abijah, his oldest sons, held court in
Beersheba. ³But they were not like their
father, for they were greedy for money.
They accepted bribes and perverted
justice.

⁴Finally, all the elders of Israel met at
Ramah to discuss the matter with Samuel. ⁵"Look," they told him, "you are now
old, and your sons are not like you. Give
us a king to judge us like all the other
nations have."

⁶Samuel was displeased with their
request and went to the LORD for guid-
ance. ⁷"Do everything they say to you,"
the LORD replied, "for it is me they are
rejecting, not you. They don't want me
to be their king any longer. ⁸Ever since I
brought them from Egypt they have
continually abandoned me and followed other gods. And now they are giving you the same treatment. ⁹Do as they
ask, but solemnly warn them about the
way a king will reign over them."

¹⁰So Samuel passed on the LORD's
warning to the people who were asking
him for a king. ¹¹"This is how a king will
reign over you," Samuel said. "The king
will draft your sons and assign them to
his chariots and his charioteers, making
them run before his chariots. ¹²Some
will be generals and captains in his
army,* some will be forced to plow in

his fields and harvest his crops, and some will make his weapons and chariot equipment. ¹³The king will take your daughters from you and force them to cook and bake and make perfumes for him. ¹⁴He will take away the best of your fields and vineyards and olive groves and give them to his own officials. ¹⁵He will take a tenth of your grain and your grape harvest and distribute it among his officers and attendants. ¹⁶He will take your male and female slaves and demand the finest of your cattle* and donkeys for his own use. ¹⁷He will demand a tenth of your flocks, and you will be his slaves. ¹⁸When that day comes, you will beg for relief from this king you are demanding, but then the LORD will not help you."

¹⁹But the people refused to listen to Samuel's warning. "Even so, we still want a king," they said. ²⁰"We want to be like the nations around us. Our king will judge us and lead us into battle."

²¹So Samuel repeated to the LORD what the people had said, ²²and the LORD replied, "Do as they say, and give them a king." Then Samuel agreed and sent the people home.

⁹:¹THERE was a wealthy, influential man named Kish from the tribe of Benjamin. He was the son of Abiel, son of Zeror, son of Becorath, son of Aphiah, of the tribe of Benjamin. ²His son Saul was the most handsome man in Israel—head and shoulders taller than anyone else in the land.

³One day Kish's donkeys strayed away, and he told Saul, "Take a servant with you, and go look for the donkeys." ⁴So Saul took one of the servants and traveled through the hill country of Ephraim, the land of Shalishah, the Shaalim area, and the entire land of Benjamin, but they couldn't find the donkeys anywhere.

⁵Finally, they entered the region of Zuph, and Saul said to his servant, "Let's go home. By now my father will be more worried about us than about the donkeys!"

⁶But the servant said, "I've just thought of something! There is a man of God who lives here in this town. He is held in high honor by all the people because everything he says comes true. Let's go find him. Perhaps he can tell us which way to go."

⁷"But we don't have anything to offer him," Saul replied. "Even our food is gone, and we don't have a thing to give him."

⁸"Well," the servant said, "I have one small silver piece.* We can at least offer it to the man of God and see what happens!" ⁹(In those days if people wanted a message from God, they would say, "Let's go and ask the seer," for prophets used to be called seers.)

¹⁰"All right," Saul agreed, "let's try it!" So they started into the town where the man of God lived.

¹¹As they were climbing the hill to the town, they met some young women coming out to draw water. So Saul and his servant asked, "Is the seer here today?"

¹²"Yes," they replied. "Stay right on this road. He is at the town gates. He has just arrived to take part in a public sacrifice up at the place of worship. ¹³Hurry and catch him before he goes up there to eat. The guests won't begin eating until he arrives to bless the food."

¹⁴So they entered the town, and as they passed through the gates, Samuel was coming out toward them to go up to the place of worship.

¹⁵Now the LORD had told Samuel the previous day, ¹⁶"About this time tomorrow I will send you a man from the land of Benjamin. Anoint him to be the leader of my people, Israel. He will rescue them from the Philistines, for I have looked down on my people in mercy and have heard their cry."

¹⁷When Samuel saw Saul, the LORD said, "That's the man I told you about! He will rule my people."

¹⁸Just then Saul approached Samuel at the gateway and asked, "Can you please tell me where the seer's house is?"

¹⁹"I am the seer!" Samuel replied. "Go up to the place of worship ahead of me.

We will eat there together, and in the morning I'll tell you what you want to know and send you on your way. [20]And don't worry about those donkeys that were lost three days ago, for they have been found. And I am here to tell you that you and your family are the focus of all Israel's hopes."

[21]Saul replied, "But I'm only from the tribe of Benjamin, the smallest tribe in Israel, and my family is the least important of all the families of that tribe! Why are you talking like this to me?"

[22]Then Samuel brought Saul and his servant into the hall and placed them at the head of the table, honoring them above the thirty special guests. [23]Samuel then instructed the cook to bring Saul the finest cut of meat, the piece that had been set aside for the guest of honor. [24]So the cook brought in the meat and placed it before Saul. "Go ahead and eat it," Samuel said. "I was saving it for you even before I invited these others!" So Saul ate with Samuel that day.

[25]When they came down from the place of worship and returned to town, Samuel took Saul up to the roof of the house and prepared a bed for him there.* [26]At daybreak the next morning, Samuel called to Saul, "Get up! It's time you were on your way." So Saul got ready, and he and Samuel left the house together. [27]When they reached the edge of town, Samuel told Saul to send his servant on ahead. After the servant was gone, Samuel said, "Stay here, for I have received a special message for you from God."

8:12 Hebrew *commanders of thousands and commanders of fifties.*   8:16 As in Greek version; Hebrew reads *young men.*   9:8 Hebrew ¼ *shekel of silver,* about 0.1 ounces or 3 grams in weight.   9:25 As in Greek version; Hebrew reads *and talked with him there.*

JOHN 6:22-42

The next day the crowd that had stayed on the far shore saw that the disciples had taken the only boat, and they realized Jesus had not gone with them. [23]Several boats from Tiberias landed near the place where the Lord had blessed the bread and the people had eaten. [24]So when the crowd saw that neither Jesus

nor his disciples were there, they got into the boats and went across to Capernaum to look for him. [25]They found him on the other side of the lake and asked, "Rabbi, when did you get here?"

[26]Jesus replied, "I tell you the truth, you want to be with me because I fed you, not because you understood the miraculous signs. [27]But don't be so concerned about perishable things like food. Spend your energy seeking the eternal life that the Son of Man* can give you. For God the Father has given me the seal of his approval."

[28]They replied, "We want to perform God's works, too. What should we do?"

[29]Jesus told them, "This is the only work God wants from you: Believe in the one he has sent."

[30]They answered, "Show us a miraculous sign if you want us to believe in you. What can you do? [31]After all, our ancestors ate manna while they journeyed through the wilderness! The Scriptures say, 'Moses gave them bread from heaven to eat.'*"

[32]Jesus said, "I tell you the truth, Moses didn't give you bread from heaven. My Father did. And now he offers you the true bread from heaven. [33]The true bread of God is the one who comes down from heaven and gives life to the world."

[34]"Sir," they said, "give us that bread every day."

[35]**Jesus replied, "I am the bread of life. Whoever comes to me will never be hungry again. Whoever believes in me will never be thirsty.** [36]But you haven't believed in me even though you have seen me. [37]However, those the Father has given me will come to me, and I will never reject them. [38]For I have come down from heaven to do the will of God who sent me, not to do my own will. [39]And this is the will of God, that I should not lose even one of all those he has given me, but that I should raise them up at the last day. [40]For it is my Father's will that all who see his Son and believe in him should have eternal life. I will raise them up at the last day."

[41]Then the people* began to murmur

in disagreement because he had said, "I am the bread that came down from heaven." ⁴²They said, "Isn't this Jesus, the son of Joseph? We know his father and mother. How can he say, 'I came down from heaven'?"

6:27 "Son of Man" is a title Jesus used for himself. 6:31 Exod 16:4; Ps 78:24.   6:41 Greek *Jewish people;* also in 6:52.

PSALM 106:32-48
At Meribah, too, they angered
the LORD,
causing Moses serious trouble.
³³ They made Moses angry,*
and he spoke foolishly.

³⁴ Israel failed to destroy the nations
in the land,
as the LORD had commanded
them.
³⁵ Instead, they mingled among
the pagans
and adopted their evil customs.
³⁶ They worshiped their idols,
which led to their downfall.
³⁷ They even sacrificed their sons
and their daughters to
the demons.
³⁸ They shed innocent blood,
the blood of their sons
and daughters.
By sacrificing them to the idols
of Canaan,
they polluted the land
with murder.
³⁹ They defiled themselves by their
evil deeds,
and their love of idols was
adultery in the LORD's sight.

⁴⁰ That is why the LORD's anger
burned against his people,
and he abhorred his own special
possession.
⁴¹ He handed them over to pagan
nations,
and they were ruled by those
who hated them.
⁴² Their enemies crushed them
and brought them under their
cruel power.
⁴³ Again and again he rescued them,

but they chose to rebel
against him,
and they were finally destroyed
by their sin.
⁴⁴ Even so, he pitied them in their
distress
and listened to their cries.
⁴⁵ He remembered his covenant
with them
and relented because of his
unfailing love.
⁴⁶ He even caused their captors
to treat them with kindness.

⁴⁷ Save us, O LORD our God!
Gather us back from among
the nations,
so we can thank your holy name
and rejoice and praise you.

⁴⁸ Praise the LORD, the God of Israel,
who lives from everlasting
to everlasting!
Let all the people say, "Amen!"

Praise the LORD!

106:33 Hebrew *They embittered his spirit.*

PROVERBS 14:34-35
Godliness makes a nation great, but sin is a disgrace to any people. □ A king rejoices in wise servants but is angry with those who disgrace him.

MAY 11

1 SAMUEL 10:1–11:15
Then Samuel took a flask of olive oil and poured it over Saul's head. He kissed Saul and said, "I am doing this because the LORD has appointed you to be the ruler over Israel, his special possession.* ²When you leave me today, you will see two men beside Rachel's tomb at Zelzah, on the border of Benjamin. They will tell you that the donkeys have been found and that your father

has stopped worrying about them and is now worried about you. He is asking, 'Have you seen my son?'

3"When you get to the oak of Tabor, you will see three men coming toward you who are on their way to worship God at Bethel. One will be bringing three young goats, another will have three loaves of bread, and the third will be carrying a wineskin full of wine. 4They will greet you and offer you two of the loaves, which you are to accept.

5"When you arrive at Gibeah of God,* where the garrison of the Philistines is located, you will meet a band of prophets coming down from the place of worship. They will be playing a harp, a tambourine, a flute, and a lyre, and they will be prophesying. 6At that time the Spirit of the Lord will come powerfully upon you, and you will prophesy with them. You will be changed into a different person. 7After these signs take place, do what must be done, for God is with you. 8Then go down to Gilgal ahead of me. I will join you there to sacrifice burnt offerings and peace offerings. You must wait for seven days until I arrive and give you further instructions."

9As Saul turned and started to leave, God gave him a new heart, and all Samuel's signs were fulfilled that day. 10When Saul and his servant arrived at Gibeah, they saw a group of prophets coming toward them. Then the Spirit of God came powerfully upon Saul, and he, too, began to prophesy. 11When those who knew Saul heard about it, they exclaimed, "What? Is even Saul a prophet? How did the son of Kish become a prophet?"

12And one of those standing there said, "Can anyone become a prophet, no matter who his father is?"* So that is the origin of the saying "Is even Saul a prophet?"

13When Saul had finished prophesying, he went up to the place of worship. 14"Where have you been?" Saul's uncle asked him and his servant.

"We were looking for the donkeys," Saul replied, "but we couldn't find them. So we went to Samuel to ask him where they were."

15"Oh? And what did he say?" his uncle asked.

16"He told us that the donkeys had already been found," Saul replied. But Saul didn't tell his uncle what Samuel said about the kingdom.

17Later Samuel called all the people of Israel to meet before the Lord at Mizpah. 18And he said, "This is what the Lord, the God of Israel, has declared: I brought you from Egypt and rescued you from the Egyptians and from all of the nations that were oppressing you. 19But though I have rescued you from your misery and distress, you have rejected your God today and have said, 'No, we want a king instead!' Now, therefore, present yourselves before the Lord by tribes and clans."

20So Samuel brought all the tribes of Israel before the Lord, and the tribe of Benjamin was chosen by lot. 21Then he brought each family of the tribe of Benjamin before the Lord, and the family of the Matrites was chosen. And finally Saul son of Kish was chosen from among them. But when they looked for him, he had disappeared! 22So they asked the Lord, "Where is he?"

And the Lord replied, "He is hiding among the baggage." 23So they found him and brought him out, and he stood head and shoulders above anyone else.

24Then Samuel said to all the people, "This is the man the Lord has chosen as your king. No one in all Israel is like him!"

And all the people shouted, "Long live the king!"

25Then Samuel told the people what the rights and duties of a king were. He wrote them down on a scroll and placed it before the Lord. Then Samuel sent the people home again.

26When Saul returned to his home at Gibeah, a group of men whose hearts God had touched went with him. 27But there were some scoundrels who complained, "How can this man save us?"

And they scorned him and refused to bring him gifts. But Saul ignored them.

[Nahash, king of the Ammonites, had been grievously oppressing the people of Gad and Reuben who lived east of the Jordan River. He gouged out the right eye of each of the Israelites living there, and he didn't allow anyone to come and rescue them. In fact, of all the Israelites east of the Jordan, there wasn't a single one whose right eye Nahash had not gouged out. But there were 7,000 men who had escaped from the Ammonites, and they had settled in Jabesh-gilead.]*

11:1ABOUT a month later,* King Nahash of Ammon led his army against the Israelite town of Jabesh-gilead. But all the citizens of Jabesh asked for peace. "Make a treaty with us, and we will be your servants," they pleaded.

²"All right," Nahash said, "but only on one condition. I will gouge out the right eye of every one of you as a disgrace to all Israel!"

³"Give us seven days to send messengers throughout Israel!" replied the elders of Jabesh. "If no one comes to save us, we will agree to your terms."

⁴When the messengers came to Gibeah of Saul and told the people about their plight, everyone broke into tears. ⁵Saul had been plowing a field with his oxen, and when he returned to town, he asked, "What's the matter? Why is everyone crying?" So they told him about the message from Jabesh.

⁶Then the Spirit of God came powerfully upon Saul, and he became very angry. ⁷He took two oxen and cut them into pieces and sent the messengers to carry them throughout Israel with this message: "This is what will happen to the oxen of anyone who refuses to follow Saul and Samuel into battle!" And the LORD made the people afraid of Saul's anger, and all of them came out together as one. ⁸When Saul mobilized them at Bezek, he found that there were 300,000 men from Israel and 30,000* men from Judah.

⁹So Saul sent the messengers back to Jabesh-gilead to say, "We will rescue you by noontime tomorrow!" There was great joy throughout the town when that message arrived!

¹⁰The men of Jabesh then told their enemies, "Tomorrow we will come out to you, and you can do to us whatever you wish." ¹¹But before dawn the next morning, Saul arrived, having divided his army into three detachments. He launched a surprise attack against the Ammonites and slaughtered them the whole morning. The remnant of their army was so badly scattered that no two of them were left together.

¹²Then the people exclaimed to Samuel, "Now where are those men who said, 'Why should Saul rule over us?' Bring them here, and we will kill them!"

¹³But Saul replied, "No one will be executed today, for today the LORD has rescued Israel!"

¹⁴Then Samuel said to the people, "Come, let us all go to Gilgal to renew the kingdom." ¹⁵So they all went to Gilgal, and in a solemn ceremony before the LORD they made Saul king. Then they offered peace offerings to the LORD, and Saul and all the Israelites were filled with joy.

10:1 Greek version reads *over Israel. And you will rule over the LORD's people and save them from their enemies around them. This will be the sign to you that the LORD has appointed you to be leader over his special possession.* **10:5** Hebrew *Gibeath-elohim.* **10:12** Hebrew *said, "Who is their father?"* **10:27** This paragraph, which is not included in the Masoretic Text, is found in Dead Sea Scroll 4QSamᵃ. **11:1** As in Greek version; Hebrew lacks *About a month later.* **11:8** Dead Sea Scrolls and Greek version read *70,000.*

JOHN 6:43-71

But Jesus replied, "Stop complaining about what I said. ⁴⁴For no one can come to me unless the Father who sent me draws them to me, and at the last day I will raise them up. ⁴⁵As it is written in the Scriptures,* 'They will all be taught by God.' Everyone who listens to the Father and learns from him comes to me. ⁴⁶(Not that anyone has ever seen the Father; only I, who was sent from God, have seen him.)

⁴⁷"I tell you the truth, anyone who believes has eternal life. ⁴⁸Yes, I am the

bread of life! [49] Your ancestors ate manna in the wilderness, but they all died. [50] Anyone who eats the bread from heaven, however, will never die. [51] I am the living bread that came down from heaven. Anyone who eats this bread will live forever; and this bread, which I will offer so the world may live, is my flesh."

[52] Then the people began arguing with each other about what he meant. "How can this man give us his flesh to eat?" they asked.

[53] So Jesus said again, "I tell you the truth, unless you eat the flesh of the Son of Man and drink his blood, you cannot have eternal life within you. [54] But anyone who eats my flesh and drinks my blood has eternal life, and I will raise that person at the last day. [55] For my flesh is true food, and my blood is true drink. [56] Anyone who eats my flesh and drinks my blood remains in me, and I in him. [57] I live because of the living Father who sent me; in the same way, anyone who feeds on me will live because of me. [58] I am the true bread that came down from heaven. Anyone who eats this bread will not die as your ancestors did (even though they ate the manna) but will live forever."

[59] He said these things while he was teaching in the synagogue in Capernaum.

[60] Many of his disciples said, "This is very hard to understand. How can anyone accept it?"

[61] Jesus was aware that his disciples were complaining, so he said to them, "Does this offend you? [62] Then what will you think if you see the Son of Man ascend to heaven again? [63] The Spirit alone gives eternal life. Human effort accomplishes nothing. And the very words I have spoken to you are spirit and life. [64] But some of you do not believe me." (For Jesus knew from the beginning which ones didn't believe, and he knew who would betray him.) [65] Then he said, "That is why I said that people can't come to me unless the Father gives them to me."

[66] At this point many of his disciples turned away and deserted him. [67] **Then Jesus turned to the Twelve and asked, "Are you also going to leave?"**

[68] **Simon Peter replied, "Lord, to whom would we go? You have the words that give eternal life. [69] We believe, and we know you are the Holy One of God.*"**

[70] Then Jesus said, "I chose the twelve of you, but one is a devil." [71] He was speaking of Judas, son of Simon Iscariot, one of the Twelve, who would later betray him.

6:45 Greek *in the prophets.* Isa 54:13.   **6:69** Other manuscripts read *you are the Christ, the Holy One of God;* still others read *you are the Christ, the Son of God;* and still others read *you are the Christ, the Son of the living God.*

PSALM 107:1-43

Give thanks to the LORD, for
    he is good!
    His faithful love endures forever.
2 Has the LORD redeemed you?
    Then speak out!
    Tell others he has redeemed you
      from your enemies.
3 For he has gathered the exiles
    from many lands,
    from east and west,
    from north and south.

4 Some wandered in the wilderness,
    lost and homeless.
5 Hungry and thirsty,
    they nearly died.
6 "LORD, help!" they cried in their
    trouble,
    and he rescued them from their
      distress.
7 He led them straight to safety,
    to a city where they could live.
8 Let them praise the LORD for his
    great love
    and for the wonderful things he
      has done for them.
9 For he satisfies the thirsty
    and fills the hungry with
      good things.

10 Some sat in darkness and deepest
    gloom,
    imprisoned in iron chains
      of misery.

11 They rebelled against the words
        of God,
    scorning the counsel of the
        Most High.
12 That is why he broke them with
        hard labor;
    they fell, and no one was there
        to help them.
13 "LORD, help!" they cried in their
        trouble,
    and he saved them from
        their distress.
14 He led them from the darkness
        and deepest gloom;
    he snapped their chains.
15 Let them praise the LORD for his
        great love
    and for the wonderful things he
        has done for them.
16 For he broke down their prison
        gates of bronze;
    he cut apart their bars of iron.

17 Some were fools; they rebelled
        and suffered for their sins.
18 They couldn't stand the thought
        of food,
    and they were knocking on
        death's door.
19 "LORD, help!" they cried in their
        trouble,
    and he saved them from their
        distress.
20 He sent out his word and healed
        them,
    snatching them from the door
        of death.
21 Let them praise the LORD for his
        great love
    and for the wonderful things
        he has done for them.
22 Let them offer sacrifices of
        thanksgiving
    and sing joyfully about his
        glorious acts.

23 Some went off to sea in ships,
        plying the trade routes of
        the world.
24 They, too, observed the LORD's
        power in action,
    his impressive works on the
        deepest seas.

25 He spoke, and the winds rose,
        stirring up the waves.
26 Their ships were tossed to the
        heavens
    and plunged again to the depths;
        the sailors cringed in terror.
27 They reeled and staggered like
        drunkards
    and were at their wits' end.
28 "LORD, help!" they cried in their
        trouble,
    and he saved them from their
        distress.
29 He calmed the storm to a whisper
        and stilled the waves.
30 What a blessing was that stillness
    as he brought them safely into
        harbor!
31 Let them praise the LORD for
        his great love
    and for the wonderful things he
        has done for them.
32 Let them exalt him publicly before
        the congregation
    and before the leaders of
        the nation.

33 He changes rivers into deserts,
    and springs of water into dry,
        thirsty land.
34 He turns the fruitful land into salty
        wastelands,
    because of the wickedness of
        those who live there.
35 But he also turns deserts into pools
        of water,
    the dry land into springs of water.
36 He brings the hungry to settle there
        and to build their cities.
37 They sow their fields, plant their
        vineyards,
    and harvest their bumper crops.
38 How he blesses them!
    They raise large families there,
        and their herds of livestock
        increase.

39 When they decrease in number and
        become impoverished
    through oppression, trouble,
        and sorrow,
40 the LORD pours contempt on
        their princes,

causing them to wander in
   trackless wastelands.
41 But he rescues the poor from
   trouble
   and increases their families like
   flocks of sheep.
42 The godly will see these things
   and be glad,
   while the wicked are struck silent.
43 Those who are wise will take all this
   to heart;
   they will see in our history the
   faithful love of the LORD.

PROVERBS 15:1-3

A gentle answer deflects anger, but
harsh words make tempers flare. □ The
tongue of the wise makes knowledge
appealing, but the mouth of a fool
belches out foolishness. □ The LORD is
watching everywhere, keeping his eye
on both the evil and the good.

MAY
12

1 SAMUEL 12:1-13:23

Then Samuel addressed all Israel: "I have
done as you asked and given you a king.
2 Your king is now your leader. I stand
here before you—an old, gray-haired
man—and my sons serve you. I have
served as your leader from the time I
was a boy to this very day. 3 Now testify
against me in the presence of the LORD
and before his anointed one. Whose ox
or donkey have I stolen? Have I ever
cheated any of you? Have I ever oppressed you? Have I ever taken a bribe
and perverted justice? Tell me and I will
make right whatever I have done wrong."

4 "No," they replied, "you have never
cheated or oppressed us, and you have
never taken even a single bribe."

5 "The LORD and his anointed one are
my witnesses today," Samuel declared,
"that my hands are clean."

"Yes, he is a witness," they replied.

6 "It was the LORD who appointed
Moses and Aaron," Samuel continued.
"He brought your ancestors out of the
land of Egypt. 7 Now stand here quietly
before the LORD as I remind you of all
the great things the LORD has done for
you and your ancestors.

8 "When the Israelites were* in Egypt
and cried out to the LORD, he sent
Moses and Aaron to rescue them from
Egypt and to bring them into this land.
9 But the people soon forgot about the
LORD their God, so he handed them over
to Sisera, the commander of Hazor's army,
and also to the Philistines and to the king
of Moab, who fought against them.

10 "Then they cried to the LORD again
and confessed, 'We have sinned by
turning away from the LORD and worshiping the images of Baal and Ashtoreth. But we will worship you and you
alone if you will rescue us from our enemies.' 11 Then the LORD sent Gideon,*
Bedan,* Jephthah, and Samuel* to save
you, and you lived in safety.

12 "But when you were afraid of Nahash, the king of Ammon, you came to
me and said that you wanted a king to
reign over you, even though the LORD
your God was already your king. 13 All
right, here is the king you have chosen.
You asked for him, and the LORD has
granted your request.

14 "Now if you fear and worship the
LORD and listen to his voice, and if you
do not rebel against the LORD's commands, then both you and your king will
show that you recognize the LORD as
your God. 15 But if you rebel against the
LORD's commands and refuse to listen
to him, then his hand will be as heavy
upon you as it was upon your ancestors.

16 "Now stand here and see the great
thing the LORD is about to do. 17 You
know that it does not rain at this time of
the year during the wheat harvest. I will
ask the LORD to send thunder and rain
today. Then you will realize how wicked
you have been in asking the LORD for a
king!"

18 So Samuel called to the LORD, and

the LORD sent thunder and rain that day. And all the people were terrified of the LORD and of Samuel. [19]"Pray to the LORD your God for us, or we will die!" they all said to Samuel. "For now we have added to our sins by asking for a king."

[20]"Don't be afraid," Samuel reassured them. "You have certainly done wrong, but make sure now that you worship the LORD with all your heart, and don't turn your back on him. [21]Don't go back to worshiping worthless idols that cannot help or rescue you—they are totally useless! [22]The LORD will not abandon his people, because that would dishonor his great name. For it has pleased the LORD to make you his very own people.

[23]"As for me, I will certainly not sin against the LORD by ending my prayers for you. And I will continue to teach you what is good and right. [24]But be sure to fear the LORD and faithfully serve him. Think of all the wonderful things he has done for you. [25]But if you continue to sin, you and your king will be swept away."

[13:1]SAUL was thirty* years old when he became king, and he reigned for forty-two years.*

[2]Saul selected 3,000 special troops from the army of Israel and sent the rest of the men home. He took 2,000 of the chosen men with him to Micmash and the hill country of Bethel. The other 1,000 went with Saul's son Jonathan to Gibeah in the land of Benjamin.

[3]Soon after this, Jonathan attacked and defeated the garrison of Philistines at Geba. The news spread quickly among the Philistines. So Saul blew the ram's horn throughout the land, saying, "Hebrews, hear this! Rise up in revolt!" [4]All Israel heard the news that Saul had destroyed the Philistine garrison at Geba and that the Philistines now hated the Israelites more than ever. So the entire Israelite army was summoned to join Saul at Gilgal.

[5]The Philistines mustered a mighty army of 3,000* chariots, 6,000 charioteers, and as many warriors as the grains of sand on the seashore! They camped at Micmash east of Beth-aven. [6]The men of Israel saw what a tight spot they were in; and because they were hard pressed by the enemy, they tried to hide in caves, thickets, rocks, holes, and cisterns. [7]Some of them crossed the Jordan River and escaped into the land of Gad and Gilead.

Meanwhile, Saul stayed at Gilgal, and his men were trembling with fear. [8]Saul waited there seven days for Samuel, as Samuel had instructed him earlier, but Samuel still didn't come. Saul realized that his troops were rapidly slipping away. [9]So he demanded, "Bring me the burnt offering and the peace offerings!" And Saul sacrificed the burnt offering himself.

[10]Just as Saul was finishing with the burnt offering, Samuel arrived. Saul went out to meet and welcome him, [11]but Samuel said, "What is this you have done?"

Saul replied, "I saw my men scattering from me, and you didn't arrive when you said you would, and the Philistines are at Micmash ready for battle. [12]So I said, 'The Philistines are ready to march against us at Gilgal, and I haven't even asked for the LORD's help!' So I felt compelled to offer the burnt offering myself before you came."

[13]"How foolish!" Samuel exclaimed. "You have not kept the command the LORD your God gave you. Had you kept it, the LORD would have established your kingdom over Israel forever. [14]But now your kingdom must end, for the LORD has sought out a man after his own heart. The LORD has already appointed him to be the leader of his people, because you have not kept the LORD's command."

[15]Samuel then left Gilgal and went on his way, but the rest of the troops went with Saul to meet the army. They went up from Gilgal to Gibeah in the land of Benjamin.* When Saul counted the men who were still with him, he found only 600 were left! [16]Saul and Jonathan and the troops with them were staying at Geba in the land of Benjamin. The Philis-

tines set up their camp at Micmash. [17]Three raiding parties soon left the camp of the Philistines. One went north toward Ophrah in the land of Shual, [18]another went west to Beth-horon, and the third moved toward the border above the valley of Zeboim near the wilderness.

[19]There were no blacksmiths in the land of Israel in those days. The Philistines wouldn't allow them for fear they would make swords and spears for the Hebrews. [20]So whenever the Israelites needed to sharpen their plowshares, picks, axes, or sickles,* they had to take them to a Philistine blacksmith. [21](The charges were as follows: a quarter of an ounce of silver* for sharpening a plowshare or a pick, and an eighth of an ounce* for sharpening an ax, a sickle, or an ox goad.) [22]So on the day of the battle none of the people of Israel had a sword or spear, except for Saul and Jonathan.

[23]The pass at Micmash had meanwhile been secured by a contingent of the Philistine army.

12:8 Hebrew *When Jacob was*. The names "Jacob" and "Israel" are often interchanged throughout the Old Testament, referring sometimes to the individual patriarch and sometimes to the nation.   12:11a Hebrew *Jerub-baal*, another name for Gideon; see Judg 6:32.   12:11b Greek and Syriac versions read *Barak*.   12:11c Greek and Syriac versions read *Samson*.   13:1a As in a few Greek manuscripts; the number is missing in the Hebrew.   13:1b Hebrew *reigned . . . and two*; the number is incomplete in the Hebrew. Compare Acts 13:21.   13:5 As in Greek and Syriac versions; Hebrew reads *30,000*.   13:15 As in Greek version; Hebrew reads *Samuel then left Gilgal and went to Gibeah in the land of Benjamin*.   13:20 As in Greek version; Hebrew reads *or plowshares*.   13:21a Hebrew *1 pim* [8 grams].   13:21b Hebrew *⅓ of a shekel* [4 grams].

JOHN 7:1-30

After this, Jesus traveled around Galilee. He wanted to stay out of Judea, where the Jewish leaders were plotting his death. [2]But soon it was time for the Jewish Festival of Shelters, [3]and Jesus' brothers said to him, "Leave here and go to Judea, where your followers can see your miracles! [4]You can't become famous if you hide like this! If you can do such wonderful things, show yourself to the world!" [5]For even his brothers didn't believe in him.

[6]Jesus replied, "Now is not the right time for me to go, but you can go any-time. [7]The world can't hate you, but it does hate me because I accuse it of doing evil. [8]You go on. I'm not going* to this festival, because my time has not yet come." [9]After saying these things, Jesus remained in Galilee.

[10]But after his brothers left for the festival, Jesus also went, though secretly, staying out of public view. [11]The Jewish leaders tried to find him at the festival and kept asking if anyone had seen him. [12]There was a lot of grumbling about him among the crowds. Some argued, "He's a good man," but others said, "He's nothing but a fraud who deceives the people." [13]But no one had the courage to speak favorably about him in public, for they were afraid of getting in trouble with the Jewish leaders.

[14]Then, midway through the festival, Jesus went up to the Temple and began to teach. [15]The people* were surprised when they heard him. "How does he know so much when he hasn't been trained?" they asked.

[16]So Jesus told them, "My message is not my own; it comes from God who sent me. [17]Anyone who wants to do the will of God will know whether my teaching is from God or is merely my own. [18]Those who speak for themselves want glory only for themselves, but a person who seeks to honor the one who sent him speaks truth, not lies. [19]Moses gave you the law, but none of you obeys it! In fact, you are trying to kill me."

[20]The crowd replied, "You're demon possessed! Who's trying to kill you?"

[21]Jesus replied, "I did one miracle on the Sabbath, and you were amazed. [22]But you work on the Sabbath, too, when you obey Moses' law of circumcision. (Actually, this tradition of circumcision began with the patriarchs, long before the law of Moses.) [23]For if the correct time for circumcising your son falls on the Sabbath, you go ahead and do it so as not to break the law of Moses. So why should you be angry with me for healing a man on the Sabbath? [24]Look

beneath the surface so you can judge correctly."

²⁵Some of the people who lived in Jerusalem started to ask each other, "Isn't this the man they are trying to kill? ²⁶But here he is, speaking in public, and they say nothing to him. Could our leaders possibly believe that he is the Messiah? ²⁷But how could he be? For we know where this man comes from. When the Messiah comes, he will simply appear; no one will know where he comes from."

²⁸While Jesus was teaching in the Temple, he called out, "Yes, you know me, and you know where I come from. But I'm not here on my own. The one who sent me is true, and you don't know him. ²⁹But I know him because I come from him, and he sent me to you." ³⁰Then the leaders tried to arrest him; but no one laid a hand on him, because his time* had not yet come.

7:8 Some manuscripts read *not yet going.*   7:15 Greek *Jewish people.*   7:30 Greek *his hour.*

PSALM 108:1-13
A song. A psalm of David.

¹ **M**y heart is confident in you, O God;
no wonder I can sing your praises
with all my heart!
² Wake up, lyre and harp!
I will wake the dawn with my
song.
³ I will thank you, Lᴏʀᴅ, among all
the people.
I will sing your praises among
the nations.
⁴ For your unfailing love is higher
than the heavens.
Your faithfulness reaches to
the clouds.
⁵ Be exalted, O God, above the
highest heavens.
May your glory shine over
all the earth.

⁶ Now rescue your beloved people.
Answer and save us by
your power.
⁷ God has promised this by
his holiness*:

"I will divide up Shechem with joy.
I will measure out the valley
of Succoth.
⁸ Gilead is mine,
and Manasseh, too.
Ephraim, my helmet, will produce
my warriors,
and Judah, my scepter, will
produce my kings.
⁹ But Moab, my washbasin, will
become my servant,
and I will wipe my feet on Edom
and shout in triumph over
Philistia."

¹⁰ Who will bring me into the fortified
city?
Who will bring me victory
over Edom?
¹¹ Have you rejected us, O God?
Will you no longer march with
our armies?
¹² Oh, please help us against our
enemies,
for all human help is useless.
¹³ With God's help we will do mighty
things,
for he will trample down our foes.

108:7 Or *in his sanctuary.*

PROVERBS 15:4
Gentle words are a tree of life; a deceitful tongue crushes the spirit.

MAY
13

1 SAMUEL 14:1–52
One day Jonathan said to his armor bearer, "Come on, let's go over to where the Philistines have their outpost." But Jonathan did not tell his father what he was doing.

²Meanwhile, Saul and his 600 men were camped on the outskirts of Gibeah, around the pomegranate tree* at Migron. ³Among Saul's men was Ahijah

the priest, who was wearing the ephod, the priestly vest. Ahijah was the son of Ichabod's brother Ahitub, son of Phinehas, son of Eli, the priest of the LORD who had served at Shiloh.

No one realized that Jonathan had left the Israelite camp. ⁴To reach the Philistine outpost, Jonathan had to go down between two rocky cliffs that were called Bozez and Seneh. ⁵The cliff on the north was in front of Micmash, and the one on the south was in front of Geba. ⁶"Let's go across to the outpost of those pagans," Jonathan said to his armor bearer. "Perhaps the LORD will help us, for nothing can hinder the LORD. He can win a battle whether he has many warriors or only a few!"

⁷"Do what you think is best," the armor bearer replied. "I'm with you completely, whatever you decide."

⁸"All right then," Jonathan told him. "We will cross over and let them see us. ⁹If they say to us, 'Stay where you are or we'll kill you,' then we will stop and not go up to them. ¹⁰But if they say, 'Come on up and fight,' then we will go up. That will be the LORD's sign that he will help us defeat them."

¹¹When the Philistines saw them coming, they shouted, "Look! The Hebrews are crawling out of their holes!" ¹²Then the men from the outpost shouted to Jonathan, "Come on up here, and we'll teach you a lesson!"

"Come on, climb right behind me," Jonathan said to his armor bearer, "for the LORD will help us defeat them!"

¹³So they climbed up using both hands and feet, and the Philistines fell before Jonathan, and his armor bearer killed those who came behind them. ¹⁴They killed some twenty men in all, and their bodies were scattered over about half an acre.*

¹⁵Suddenly, panic broke out in the Philistine army, both in the camp and in the field, including even the outposts and raiding parties. And just then an earthquake struck, and everyone was terrified.

¹⁶Saul's lookouts in Gibeah of Benjamin saw a strange sight—the vast army of Philistines began to melt away in every direction. ¹⁷"Call the roll and find out who's missing," Saul ordered. And when they checked, they found that Jonathan and his armor bearer were gone.

¹⁸Then Saul shouted to Ahijah, "Bring the ephod here!" For at that time Ahijah was wearing the ephod in front of the Israelites.* ¹⁹But while Saul was talking to the priest, the confusion in the Philistine camp grew louder and louder. So Saul said to the priest, "Never mind; let's get going!"*

²⁰Then Saul and all his men rushed out to the battle and found the Philistines killing each other. There was terrible confusion everywhere. ²¹Even the Hebrews who had previously gone over to the Philistine army revolted and joined in with Saul, Jonathan, and the rest of the Israelites. ²²Likewise, the men of Israel who were hiding in the hill country of Ephraim joined the chase when they saw the Philistines running away. ²³So the LORD saved Israel that day, and the battle continued to rage even beyond Beth-aven.

²⁴Now the men of Israel were pressed to exhaustion that day, because Saul had placed them under an oath, saying, "Let a curse fall on anyone who eats before evening—before I have full revenge on my enemies." So no one ate anything all day, ²⁵even though they had all found honeycomb on the ground in the forest. ²⁶They didn't dare touch the honey because they all feared the oath they had taken.

²⁷But Jonathan had not heard his father's command, and he dipped the end of his stick into a piece of honeycomb and ate the honey. After he had eaten it, he felt refreshed.* ²⁸But one of the men saw him and said, "Your father made the army take a strict oath that anyone who eats food today will be cursed. That is why everyone is weary and faint."

²⁹"My father has made trouble for us all!" Jonathan exclaimed. "A command like that only hurts us. See how refreshed I am now that I have eaten this

little bit of honey. 30If the men had been allowed to eat freely from the food they found among our enemies, think how many more Philistines we could have killed!"

31They chased and killed the Philistines all day from Micmash to Aijalon, growing more and more faint. 32That evening they rushed for the battle plunder and butchered the sheep, goats, cattle, and calves, but they ate them without draining the blood. 33Someone reported to Saul, "Look, the men are sinning against the LORD by eating meat that still has blood in it."

"That is very wrong," Saul said. "Find a large stone and roll it over here. 34Then go out among the troops and tell them, 'Bring the cattle, sheep, and goats here to me. Kill them here, and drain the blood before you eat them. Do not sin against the LORD by eating meat with the blood still in it.'"

So that night all the troops brought their animals and slaughtered them there. 35Then Saul built an altar to the LORD; it was the first of the altars he built to the LORD.

36Then Saul said, "Let's chase the Philistines all night and plunder them until sunrise. Let's destroy every last one of them."

His men replied, "We'll do whatever you think is best."

But the priest said, "Let's ask God first."

37So Saul asked God, "Should we go after the Philistines? Will you help us defeat them?" But God made no reply that day.

38Then Saul said to the leaders, "Something's wrong! I want all my army commanders to come here. We must find out what sin was committed today. 39I vow by the name of the LORD who rescued Israel that the sinner will surely die, even if it is my own son Jonathan!" But no one would tell him what the trouble was.

40Then Saul said, "Jonathan and I will stand over here, and all of you stand over there."

And the people responded to Saul, "Whatever you think is best."

41Then Saul prayed, "O LORD, God of Israel, please show us who is guilty and who is innocent.*" Then they cast sacred lots, and Jonathan and Saul were chosen as the guilty ones, and the people were declared innocent.

42Then Saul said, "Now cast lots again and choose between me and Jonathan." And Jonathan was shown to be the guilty one.

43"Tell me what you have done," Saul demanded of Jonathan.

"I tasted a little honey," Jonathan admitted. "It was only a little bit on the end of my stick. Does that deserve death?"

44"Yes, Jonathan," Saul said, "you must die! May God strike me and even kill me if you do not die for this."

45But the people broke in and said to Saul, "Jonathan has won this great victory for Israel. Should he die? Far from it! As surely as the LORD lives, not one hair on his head will be touched, for God helped him do a great deed today." So the people rescued Jonathan, and he was not put to death.

46Then Saul called back the army from chasing the Philistines, and the Philistines returned home.

47Now when Saul had secured his grasp on Israel's throne, he fought against his enemies in every direction—against Moab, Ammon, Edom, the kings of Zobah, and the Philistines. And wherever he turned, he was victorious. 48He performed great deeds and conquered the Amalekites, saving Israel from all those who had plundered them.

49Saul's sons included Jonathan, Ishbosheth,* and Malkishua. He also had two daughters: Merab, who was older, and Michal. 50Saul's wife was Ahinoam, the daughter of Ahimaaz. The commander of Saul's army was Abner, the son of Saul's uncle Ner. 51Saul's father, Kish, and Abner's father, Ner, were both sons of Abiel.

52The Israelites fought constantly with the Philistines throughout Saul's lifetime. So whenever Saul observed a young man who was brave and strong, he drafted him into his army.

14:2 Or *around the rock of Rimmon;* compare Judg 20:45, 47; 21:13.   **14:14** Hebrew *half a yoke;* a "yoke" was the amount of land plowed by a pair of yoked oxen in one day.   **14:18** As in some Greek manuscripts; Hebrew reads *"Bring the Ark of God." For at that time the Ark of God was with the Israelites.*   **14:19** Hebrew *Withdraw your hand.*   **14:27** Or *his eyes brightened;* similarly in 14:29.   **14:41** Greek version adds *If the fault is with me or my son Jonathan, respond with Urim; but if the men of Israel are at fault, respond with Thummim.*   **14:49** Hebrew *Ishvi,* a variant name for Ishbosheth; also known as Esh-baal.

JOHN 7:31-53

Many among the crowds at the Temple believed in him [Jesus]. "After all," they said, "would you expect the Messiah to do more miraculous signs than this man has done?"

32 When the Pharisees heard that the crowds were whispering such things, they and the leading priests sent Temple guards to arrest Jesus. 33 But Jesus told them, "I will be with you only a little longer. Then I will return to the one who sent me. 34 You will search for me but not find me. And you cannot go where I am going."

35 The Jewish leaders were puzzled by this statement. "Where is he planning to go?" they asked. "Is he thinking of leaving the country and going to the Jews in other lands?* Maybe he will even teach the Greeks! 36 What does he mean when he says, 'You will search for me but not find me,' and 'You cannot go where I am going'?"

37 On the last day, the climax of the festival, Jesus stood and shouted to the crowds, "Anyone who is thirsty may come to me! 38 Anyone who believes in me may come and drink! For the Scriptures declare, 'Rivers of living water will flow from his heart.'"* 39 (When he said "living water," he was speaking of the Spirit, who would be given to everyone believing in him. But the Spirit had not yet been given,* because Jesus had not yet entered into his glory.)

40 When the crowds heard him say this, some of them declared, "Surely this man is the Prophet we've been expecting."* 41 Others said, "He is the Messiah." Still others said, "But he can't be!

Will the Messiah come from Galilee? 42 For the Scriptures clearly state that the Messiah will be born of the royal line of David, in Bethlehem, the village where King David was born."* 43 So the crowd was divided about him. 44 Some even wanted him arrested, but no one laid a hand on him.

45 When the Temple guards returned without having arrested Jesus, the leading priests and Pharisees demanded, "Why didn't you bring him in?"

46 "We have never heard anyone speak like this!" the guards responded.

47 "Have you been led astray, too?" the Pharisees mocked. 48 "Is there a single one of us rulers or Pharisees who believes in him? 49 This foolish crowd follows him, but they are ignorant of the law. God's curse is on them!"

50 Then Nicodemus, the leader who had met with Jesus earlier, spoke up. 51 "Is it legal to convict a man before he is given a hearing?" he asked.

52 They replied, "Are you from Galilee, too? Search the Scriptures and see for yourself—no prophet ever comes* from Galilee!"

[The most ancient Greek manuscripts do not include John 7:53–8:11.]

53 Then the meeting broke up, and everybody went home.

7:35 Or *the Jews who live among the Greeks?*   **7:37-38** Or *"Let anyone who is thirsty come to me and drink. 38 For the Scriptures declare, 'Rivers of living water will flow from the heart of anyone who believes in me.'"*   **7:39** Some manuscripts read *But as yet there was no [Holy] Spirit.*   **7:40** See Deut 18:15, 18; Mal 4:5-6.   **7:42** See Mic 5:2.   **7:52** Some manuscripts read *the prophet does not come.*

PSALM 109:1-31

For the choir director: A psalm of David.

1 **O** God, whom I praise,
    don't stand silent and aloof
2 while the wicked slander me
    and tell lies about me.
3 They surround me with hateful words
    and fight against me for
    no reason.
4 I love them, but they try to destroy
    me with accusations

even as I am praying for them!
⁵ They repay evil for good,
    and hatred for my love.

⁶ They say,* "Get an evil person
        to turn against him.
    Send an accuser to bring him
        to trial.
⁷ When his case comes up for
        judgment,
    let him be pronounced guilty.
    Count his prayers as sins.
⁸ Let his years be few;
    let someone else take his position.
⁹ May his children become fatherless,
    and his wife a widow.
¹⁰ May his children wander as beggars
    and be driven from their ruined
        homes.
¹¹ May creditors seize his entire estate,
    and strangers take all he has
        earned.
¹² Let no one be kind to him;
    let no one pity his fatherless
        children.
¹³ May all his offspring die.
    May his family name be blotted
        out in a single generation.
¹⁴ May the LORD never forget the
        sins of his fathers;
    may his mother's sins never be
        erased from the record.
¹⁵ May the LORD always remember
        these sins,
    and may his name disappear
        from human memory.
¹⁶ For he refused all kindness
        to others;
    he persecuted the poor
        and needy,
    and he hounded the
        brokenhearted to death.
¹⁷ He loved to curse others;
    now you curse him.
    He never blessed others;
    now don't you bless him.
¹⁸ Cursing is as natural to him as
        his clothing,
    or the water he drinks,
    or the rich food he eats.
¹⁹ Now may his curses return and
    cling to him like clothing;

may they be tied around him
    like a belt."

²⁰ May those curses become the
        LORD's punishment
    for my accusers who speak evil
        of me.
²¹ But deal well with me,
        O Sovereign LORD,
    for the sake of your own
        reputation!
    Rescue me
        because you are so faithful
        and good.
²² For I am poor and needy,
    and my heart is full of pain.
²³ I am fading like a shadow at dusk;
    I am brushed off like a locust.
²⁴ My knees are weak from fasting,
    and I am skin and bones.
²⁵ I am a joke to people everywhere;
    when they see me, they shake
        their heads in scorn.

²⁶ Help me, O LORD my God!
    Save me because of your
        unfailing love.
²⁷ Let them see that this is your doing,
    that you yourself have done
        it, LORD.
²⁸ Then let them curse me if they like,
    but you will bless me!
    When they attack me, they will
        be disgraced!
    But I, your servant, will go right
        on rejoicing!
²⁹ May my accusers be clothed
        with disgrace;
    may their humiliation cover
        them like a cloak.
**³⁰ But I will give repeated thanks
        to the LORD,
    praising him to everyone.**
**³¹ For he stands beside the needy,
    ready to save them from those
        who condemn them.**

109:6 Hebrew lacks *They say.*

PROVERBS 15:5-7
Only a fool despises a parent's* discipline; whoever learns from correction is wise. □ There is treasure in the house of the godly, but the earnings of the

wicked bring trouble. □ The lips of the wise give good advice; the heart of a fool has none to give.

15:5 Hebrew *father's.*

MAY 14

1 SAMUEL 15:1–16:23

One day Samuel said to Saul, "It was the LORD who told me to anoint you as king of his people, Israel. Now listen to this message from the LORD! ²This is what the LORD of Heaven's Armies has declared: I have decided to settle accounts with the nation of Amalek for opposing Israel when they came from Egypt. ³Now go and completely destroy* the entire Amalekite nation—men, women, children, babies, cattle, sheep, goats, camels, and donkeys."

⁴So Saul mobilized his army at Telaim. There were 200,000 soldiers from Israel and 10,000 men from Judah. ⁵Then Saul and his army went to a town of the Amalekites and lay in wait in the valley. ⁶Saul sent this warning to the Kenites: "Move away from where the Amalekites live, or you will die with them. For you showed kindness to all the people of Israel when they came up from Egypt." So the Kenites packed up and left.

⁷Then Saul slaughtered the Amalekites from Havilah all the way to Shur, east of Egypt. ⁸He captured Agag, the Amalekite king, but completely destroyed everyone else. ⁹Saul and his men spared Agag's life and kept the best of the sheep and goats, the cattle, the fat calves, and the lambs—everything, in fact, that appealed to them. They destroyed only what was worthless or of poor quality.

¹⁰Then the LORD said to Samuel, ¹¹"I am sorry that I ever made Saul king, for he has not been loyal to me and has refused to obey my command." Samuel was so deeply moved when he heard this that he cried out to the LORD all night.

¹²Early the next morning Samuel went to find Saul. Someone told him, "Saul went to the town of Carmel to set up a monument to himself; then he went on to Gilgal."

¹³When Samuel finally found him, Saul greeted him cheerfully. "May the LORD bless you," he said. "I have carried out the LORD's command!"

¹⁴"Then what is all the bleating of sheep and goats and the lowing of cattle I hear?" Samuel demanded.

¹⁵"It's true that the army spared the best of the sheep, goats, and cattle," Saul admitted. "But they are going to sacrifice them to the LORD your God. We have destroyed everything else."

¹⁶Then Samuel said to Saul, "Stop! Listen to what the LORD told me last night!"

"What did he tell you?" Saul asked.

¹⁷And Samuel told him, "Although you may think little of yourself, are you not the leader of the tribes of Israel? The LORD has anointed you king of Israel. ¹⁸And the LORD sent you on a mission and told you, 'Go and completely destroy the sinners, the Amalekites, until they are all dead.' ¹⁹Why haven't you obeyed the LORD? Why did you rush for the plunder and do what was evil in the LORD's sight?"

²⁰"But I did obey the LORD," Saul insisted. "I carried out the mission he gave me. I brought back King Agag, but I destroyed everyone else. ²¹Then my troops brought in the best of the sheep, goats, cattle, and plunder to sacrifice to the LORD your God in Gilgal."

²²But Samuel replied,

"What is more pleasing to the LORD:
    your burnt offerings and
        sacrifices
    or your obedience to his voice?
Listen! Obedience is better
        than sacrifice,
    and submission is better than
        offering the fat of rams.

²³ Rebellion is as sinful as witchcraft,
   and stubbornness as bad as
   worshiping idols.
So because you have rejected the
   command of the LORD,
   he has rejected you as king."

²⁴Then Saul admitted to Samuel, "Yes, I have sinned. I have disobeyed your instructions and the LORD's command, for I was afraid of the people and did what they demanded. ²⁵But now, please forgive my sin and come back with me so that I may worship the LORD."

²⁶But Samuel replied, "I will not go back with you! Since you have rejected the LORD's command, he has rejected you as king of Israel."

²⁷As Samuel turned to go, Saul tried to hold him back and tore the hem of his robe. ²⁸And Samuel said to him, "The LORD has torn the kingdom of Israel from you today and has given it to someone else—one who is better than you. ²⁹And he who is the Glory of Israel will not lie, nor will he change his mind, for he is not human that he should change his mind!"

³⁰Then Saul pleaded again, "I know I have sinned. But please, at least honor me before the elders of my people and before Israel by coming back with me so that I may worship the LORD your God." ³¹So Samuel finally agreed and went back with him, and Saul worshiped the LORD.

³²Then Samuel said, "Bring King Agag to me." Agag arrived full of hope, for he thought, "Surely the worst is over, and I have been spared!"* ³³But Samuel said, "As your sword has killed the sons of many mothers, now your mother will be childless." And Samuel cut Agag to pieces before the LORD at Gilgal.

³⁴Then Samuel went home to Ramah, and Saul returned to his house at Gibeah of Saul. ³⁵Samuel never went to meet with Saul again, but he mourned constantly for him. And the LORD was sorry he had ever made Saul king of Israel.

¹⁶:¹Now the LORD said to Samuel, "You have mourned long enough for Saul. I have rejected him as king of Israel, so fill your flask with olive oil and go to Bethlehem. Find a man named Jesse who lives there, for I have selected one of his sons to be my king."

²But Samuel asked, "How can I do that? If Saul hears about it, he will kill me."

"Take a heifer with you," the LORD replied, "and say that you have come to make a sacrifice to the LORD. ³Invite Jesse to the sacrifice, and I will show you which of his sons to anoint for me."

⁴So Samuel did as the LORD instructed. When he arrived at Bethlehem, the elders of the town came trembling to meet him. "What's wrong?" they asked. "Do you come in peace?"

⁵"Yes," Samuel replied. "I have come to sacrifice to the LORD. Purify yourselves and come with me to the sacrifice." Then Samuel performed the purification rite for Jesse and his sons and invited them to the sacrifice, too.

⁶When they arrived, Samuel took one look at Eliab and thought, "Surely this is the LORD's anointed!"

⁷But the LORD said to Samuel, "Don't judge by his appearance or height, for I have rejected him. The LORD doesn't see things the way you see them. People judge by outward appearance, but the LORD looks at the heart."

⁸Then Jesse told his son Abinadab to step forward and walk in front of Samuel. But Samuel said, "This is not the one the LORD has chosen." ⁹Next Jesse summoned Shimea,* but Samuel said, "Neither is this the one the LORD has chosen." ¹⁰In the same way all seven of Jesse's sons were presented to Samuel. But Samuel said to Jesse, "The LORD has not chosen any of these." ¹¹Then Samuel asked, "Are these all the sons you have?"

"There is still the youngest," Jesse replied. "But he's out in the fields watching the sheep and goats."

"Send for him at once," Samuel said. "We will not sit down to eat until he arrives."

¹²So Jesse sent for him. He was dark and handsome, with beautiful eyes.

And the LORD said, "This is the one; anoint him."

¹³So as David stood there among his brothers, Samuel took the flask of olive oil he had brought and anointed David with the oil. And the Spirit of the LORD came powerfully upon David from that day on. Then Samuel returned to Ramah.

¹⁴Now the Spirit of the LORD had left Saul, and the LORD sent a tormenting spirit* that filled him with depression and fear.

¹⁵Some of Saul's servants said to him, "A tormenting spirit from God is troubling you. ¹⁶Let us find a good musician to play the harp whenever the tormenting spirit troubles you. He will play soothing music, and you will soon be well again."

¹⁷"All right," Saul said. "Find me someone who plays well, and bring him here."

¹⁸One of the servants said to Saul, "One of Jesse's sons from Bethlehem is a talented harp player. Not only that—he is a brave warrior, a man of war, and has good judgment. He is also a fine-looking young man, and the LORD is with him."

¹⁹So Saul sent messengers to Jesse to say, "Send me your son David, the shepherd." ²⁰Jesse responded by sending David to Saul, along with a young goat, a donkey loaded with bread, and a wineskin full of wine.

²¹So David went to Saul and began serving him. Saul loved David very much, and David became his armor bearer.

²²Then Saul sent word to Jesse asking, "Please let David remain in my service, for I am very pleased with him."

²³And whenever the tormenting spirit from God troubled Saul, David would play the harp. Then Saul would feel better, and the tormenting spirit would go away.

15:3 The Hebrew term used here refers to the complete consecration of things or people to the LORD, either by destroying them or by giving them as an offering; also in 15:8, 9, 15, 18, 20, 21.   15:32 Dead Sea Scrolls and Greek version read *Agag arrived hesitantly, for he thought, "Surely this is the bitterness of death."*   16:9 Hebrew *Shammah,* a variant spelling of Shimea; compare 1 Chr 2:13; 20:7.   16:14 Or *an evil spirit;* also in 16:15, 16, 23.

JOHN 8:1-20

Jesus returned to the Mount of Olives, ²but early the next morning he was back again at the Temple. A crowd soon gathered, and he sat down and taught them. ³As he was speaking, the teachers of religious law and the Pharisees brought a woman who had been caught in the act of adultery. They put her in front of the crowd.

⁴"Teacher," they said to Jesus, "this woman was caught in the act of adultery. ⁵The law of Moses says to stone her. What do you say?"

⁶They were trying to trap him into saying something they could use against him, but Jesus stooped down and wrote in the dust with his finger. ⁷They kept demanding an answer, so he stood up again and said, "All right, but let the one who has never sinned throw the first stone!" ⁸Then he stooped down again and wrote in the dust.

⁹When the accusers heard this, they slipped away one by one, beginning with the oldest, until only Jesus was left in the middle of the crowd with the woman. ¹⁰Then Jesus stood up again and said to the woman, "Where are your accusers? Didn't even one of them condemn you?"

¹¹"No, Lord," she said.

And Jesus said, "Neither do I. Go and sin no more."

---

¹²**Jesus spoke to the people once more and said, "I am the light of the world. If you follow me, you won't have to walk in darkness, because you will have the light that leads to life."**

¹³The Pharisees replied, "You are making those claims about yourself! Such testimony is not valid."

¹⁴Jesus told them, "These claims are valid even though I make them about myself. For I know where I came from and where I am going, but you don't know this about me. ¹⁵You judge me by human standards, but I do not judge anyone. ¹⁶And if I did, my judgment would be correct in every respect because I am

not alone. The Father* who sent me is with me. ¹⁷Your own law says that if two people agree about something, their witness is accepted as fact.* ¹⁸I am one witness, and my Father who sent me is the other."

¹⁹"Where is your father?" they asked.

Jesus answered, "Since you don't know who I am, you don't know who my Father is. If you knew me, you would also know my Father." ²⁰Jesus made these statements while he was teaching in the section of the Temple known as the Treasury. But he was not arrested, because his time* had not yet come.

8:16 Some manuscripts read *The One.*   **8:17** See Deut 19:15.   **8:20** Greek *his hour.*

PSALM 110:1-7
A psalm of David.

¹ **T**he LORD said to my Lord,
     "Sit in the place of honor
          at my right hand
     until I humble your enemies,
          making them a footstool under
               your feet."

² The LORD will extend your
          powerful kingdom from
          Jerusalem*;
     you will rule over your enemies.
³ When you go to war,
     your people will serve you
          willingly.
     You are arrayed in holy garments,
     and your strength will be
          renewed each day like the
          morning dew.

⁴ The LORD has taken an oath and
     will not break his vow:
     "You are a priest forever in the
          order of Melchizedek."

⁵ The Lord stands at your right hand
     to protect you.
     He will strike down many kings
          when his anger erupts.
⁶ He will punish the nations
     and fill their lands with
          corpses;
     he will shatter heads over the
          whole earth.

⁷ But he himself will be refreshed
     from brooks along the way.
     He will be victorious.

110:2 Hebrew *Zion.*

PROVERBS 15:8-10
The LORD detests the sacrifice of the wicked, but he delights in the prayers of the upright. □ The LORD detests the way of the wicked, but he loves those who pursue godliness. □ Whoever abandons the right path will be severely disciplined; whoever hates correction will die.

1 SAMUEL 17:1–18:4
The Philistines now mustered their army for battle and camped between Socoh in Judah and Azekah at Ephesdammim. ²Saul countered by gathering his Israelite troops near the valley of Elah. ³So the Philistines and Israelites faced each other on opposite hills, with the valley between them.

⁴Then Goliath, a Philistine champion from Gath, came out of the Philistine ranks to face the forces of Israel. He was over nine feet* tall! ⁵He wore a bronze helmet, and his bronze coat of mail weighed 125 pounds.* ⁶He also wore bronze leg armor, and he carried a bronze javelin on his shoulder. ⁷The shaft of his spear was as heavy and thick as a weaver's beam, tipped with an iron spearhead that weighed 15 pounds.* His armor bearer walked ahead of him carrying a shield.

⁸Goliath stood and shouted a taunt across to the Israelites. "Why are you all coming out to fight?" he called. "I am the Philistine champion, but you are only the servants of Saul. Choose one man to come down here and fight me!

⁹If he kills me, then we will be your slaves. But if I kill him, you will be our slaves! ¹⁰I defy the armies of Israel today! Send me a man who will fight me!" ¹¹When Saul and the Israelites heard this, they were terrified and deeply shaken.

¹²Now David was the son of a man named Jesse, an Ephrathite from Bethlehem in the land of Judah. Jesse was an old man at that time, and he had eight sons. ¹³Jesse's three oldest sons—Eliab, Abinadab, and Shimea*—had already joined Saul's army to fight the Philistines. ¹⁴David was the youngest son. David's three oldest brothers stayed with Saul's army, ¹⁵but David went back and forth so he could help his father with the sheep in Bethlehem.

¹⁶For forty days, every morning and evening, the Philistine champion strutted in front of the Israelite army.

¹⁷One day Jesse said to David, "Take this basket* of roasted grain and these ten loaves of bread, and carry them quickly to your brothers. ¹⁸And give these ten cuts of cheese to their captain. See how your brothers are getting along, and bring back a report on how they are doing.*" ¹⁹David's brothers were with Saul and the Israelite army at the valley of Elah, fighting against the Philistines.

²⁰So David left the sheep with another shepherd and set out early the next morning with the gifts, as Jesse had directed him. He arrived at the camp just as the Israelite army was leaving for the battlefield with shouts and battle cries. ²¹Soon the Israelite and Philistine forces stood facing each other, army against army. ²²David left his things with the keeper of supplies and hurried out to the ranks to greet his brothers. ²³As he was talking with them, Goliath, the Philistine champion from Gath, came out from the Philistine ranks. Then David heard him shout his usual taunt to the army of Israel.

²⁴As soon as the Israelite army saw him, they began to run away in fright. ²⁵"Have you seen the giant?" the men asked. "He comes out each day to defy Israel. The king has offered a huge reward to anyone who kills him. He will give that man one of his daughters for a wife, and the man's entire family will be exempted from paying taxes!"

²⁶David asked the soldiers standing nearby, "What will a man get for killing this Philistine and ending his defiance of Israel? Who is this pagan Philistine anyway, that he is allowed to defy the armies of the living God?"

²⁷And these men gave David the same reply. They said, "Yes, that is the reward for killing him."

²⁸But when David's oldest brother, Eliab, heard David talking to the men, he was angry. "What are you doing around here anyway?" he demanded. "What about those few sheep you're supposed to be taking care of? I know about your pride and deceit. You just want to see the battle!"

²⁹"What have I done now?" David replied. "I was only asking a question!" ³⁰He walked over to some others and asked them the same thing and received the same answer. ³¹Then David's question was reported to King Saul, and the king sent for him.

³²"Don't worry about this Philistine," David told Saul. "I'll go fight him!"

³³"Don't be ridiculous!" Saul replied. "There's no way you can fight this Philistine and possibly win! You're only a boy, and he's been a man of war since his youth."

³⁴But David persisted. "I have been taking care of my father's sheep and goats," he said. "When a lion or a bear comes to steal a lamb from the flock, ³⁵I go after it with a club and rescue the lamb from its mouth. If the animal turns on me, I catch it by the jaw and club it to death. ³⁶I have done this to both lions and bears, and I'll do it to this pagan Philistine, too, for he has defied the armies of the living God! ³⁷The LORD who rescued me from the claws of the lion and the bear will rescue me from this Philistine!"

Saul finally consented. "All right, go

ahead," he said. "And may the LORD be with you!"

38Then Saul gave David his own armor—a bronze helmet and a coat of mail. 39David put it on, strapped the sword over it, and took a step or two to see what it was like, for he had never worn such things before.

"I can't go in these," he protested to Saul. "I'm not used to them." So David took them off again. 40He picked up five smooth stones from a stream and put them into his shepherd's bag. Then, armed only with his shepherd's staff and sling, he started across the valley to fight the Philistine.

41Goliath walked out toward David with his shield bearer ahead of him, 42sneering in contempt at this ruddy-faced boy. 43"Am I a dog," he roared at David, "that you come at me with a stick?" And he cursed David by the names of his gods. 44"Come over here, and I'll give your flesh to the birds and wild animals!" Goliath yelled.

45David replied to the Philistine, "You come to me with sword, spear, and javelin, but I come to you in the name of the LORD of Heaven's Armies—the God of the armies of Israel, whom you have defied. 46Today the LORD will conquer you, and I will kill you and cut off your head. And then I will give the dead bodies of your men to the birds and wild animals, and the whole world will know that there is a God in Israel! 47And everyone assembled here will know that the LORD rescues his people, but not with sword and spear. This is the LORD's battle, and he will give you to us!"

48As Goliath moved closer to attack, David quickly ran out to meet him. 49Reaching into his shepherd's bag and taking out a stone, he hurled it with his sling and hit the Philistine in the forehead. The stone sank in, and Goliath stumbled and fell face down on the ground.

50So David triumphed over the Philistine with only a sling and a stone, for he had no sword. 51Then David ran over

and pulled Goliath's sword from its sheath. David used it to kill him and cut off his head.

When the Philistines saw that their champion was dead, they turned and ran. 52Then the men of Israel and Judah gave a great shout of triumph and rushed after the Philistines, chasing them as far as Gath* and the gates of Ekron. The bodies of the dead and wounded Philistines were strewn all along the road from Shaaraim, as far as Gath and Ekron. 53Then the Israelite army returned and plundered the deserted Philistine camp. 54(David took the Philistine's head to Jerusalem, but he stored the man's armor in his own tent.)

55As Saul watched David go out to fight the Philistine, he asked Abner, the commander of his army, "Abner, whose son is this young man?"

"I really don't know," Abner declared.

56"Well, find out who he is!" the king told him.

57As soon as David returned from killing Goliath, Abner brought him to Saul with the Philistine's head still in his hand. 58"Tell me about your father, young man," Saul said.

And David replied, "His name is Jesse, and we live in Bethlehem."

18:1AFTER David had finished talking with Saul, he met Jonathan, the king's son. There was an immediate bond of love between them, and they became the best of friends. 2From that day on Saul kept David with him and wouldn't let him return home. 3**And Jonathan made a solemn pact with David, because he loved him as he loved himself. 4Jonathan sealed the pact by taking off his robe and giving it to David, together with his tunic, sword, bow, and belt.**

17:4 Hebrew *6 cubits and 1 span* [which totals about 9.75 feet or 3 meters]; Dead Sea Scrolls and Greek version read *4 cubits and 1 span* [which totals about 6.75 feet or 2 meters].   17:5 Hebrew *5,000 shekels* [57 kilograms].   17:7 Hebrew *600 shekels* [6.8 kilograms].   17:13 Hebrew *Shammah*, a variant spelling of Shimea; compare 1 Chr 2:13; 20:7.   17:17 Hebrew *ephah* [20 quarts or 22 liters].   17:18 Hebrew *and take their pledge*.   17:52 As in some Greek manuscripts; Hebrew reads *a valley*.

JOHN 8:21-30

Later Jesus said to them again, "I am going away. You will search for me but will die in your sin. You cannot come where I am going."

22 The people* asked, "Is he planning to commit suicide? What does he mean, 'You cannot come where I am going'?"

23 Jesus continued, "You are from below; I am from above. You belong to this world; I do not. 24 That is why I said that you will die in your sins; for unless you believe that I AM who I claim to be,* you will die in your sins."

25 "Who are you?" they demanded.

Jesus replied, "The one I have always claimed to be.* 26 I have much to say about you and much to condemn, but I won't. For I say only what I have heard from the one who sent me, and he is completely truthful." 27 But they still didn't understand that he was talking about his Father.

28 So Jesus said, "When you have lifted up the Son of Man on the cross, then you will understand that I AM he.* I do nothing on my own but say only what the Father taught me. 29 And the one who sent me is with me—he has not deserted me. For I always do what pleases him." 30 Then many who heard him say these things believed in him.

8:22 Greek *Jewish people;* also in 8:31, 48, 52, 57.
8:24 Greek *unless you believe that I am.* See Exod 3:14.
8:25 Or *Why do I speak to you at all?*   8:28 Greek *When you have lifted up the Son of Man, then you will know that I am.* "Son of Man" is a title Jesus used for himself.

PSALM 111:1-10*

Praise the LORD!

I will thank the LORD with
all my heart
as I meet with his godly people.
2 How amazing are the deeds
of the LORD!
All who delight in him should
ponder them.
3 Everything he does reveals his glory
and majesty.
His righteousness never fails.
4 He causes us to remember his
wonderful works.

How gracious and merciful
is our LORD!
5 He gives food to those who fear him;
he always remembers his
covenant.
6 He has shown his great power
to his people
by giving them the lands
of other nations.
7 All he does is just and good,
and all his commandments
are trustworthy.
8 They are forever true,
to be obeyed faithfully and
with integrity.
9 He has paid a full ransom for
his people.
He has guaranteed his covenant
with them forever.
What a holy, awe-inspiring name
he has!
10 Fear of the LORD is the foundation
of true wisdom.
All who obey his commandments
will grow in wisdom.

Praise him forever!

111 This psalm is a Hebrew acrostic poem; after the introductory note of praise, each line begins with a successive letter of the Hebrew alphabet.

PROVERBS 15:11

Even Death and Destruction* hold no secrets from the LORD. How much more does he know the human heart!

15:11 Hebrew *Sheol and Abaddon.*

MAY 16

1 SAMUEL 18:5–19:24

Whatever Saul asked David to do, David did it successfully. So Saul made him a commander over the men of war, an appointment that was welcomed by the people and Saul's officers alike.

6 When the victorious Israelite army was returning home after David had

killed the Philistine, women from all the towns of Israel came out to meet King Saul. They sang and danced for joy with tambourines and cymbals.* [7]This was their song:

"Saul has killed his thousands,
and David his ten thousands!"

[8]This made Saul very angry. "What's this?" he said. "They credit David with ten thousands and me with only thousands. Next they'll be making him their king!" [9]So from that time on Saul kept a jealous eye on David.

[10]The very next day a tormenting spirit* from God overwhelmed Saul, and he began to rave in his house like a madman. David was playing the harp, as he did each day. But Saul had a spear in his hand, [11]and he suddenly hurled it at David, intending to pin him to the wall. But David escaped him twice.

[12]Saul was then afraid of David, for the LORD was with David and had turned away from Saul. [13]Finally, Saul sent him away and appointed him commander over 1,000 men, and David faithfully led his troops into battle.

[14]David continued to succeed in everything he did, for the LORD was with him. [15]When Saul recognized this, he became even more afraid of him. [16]But all Israel and Judah loved David because he was so successful at leading his troops into battle.

[17]One day Saul said to David, "I am ready to give you my older daughter, Merab, as your wife. But first you must prove yourself to be a real warrior by fighting the LORD's battles." For Saul thought, "I'll send him out against the Philistines and let them kill him rather than doing it myself."

[18]"Who am I, and what is my family in Israel that I should be the king's son-in-law?" David exclaimed. "My father's family is nothing!" [19]So* when the time came for Saul to give his daughter Merab in marriage to David, he gave her instead to Adriel, a man from Meholah.

[20]In the meantime, Saul's daughter Michal had fallen in love with David, and Saul was delighted when he heard about it. [21]"Here's another chance to see him killed by the Philistines!" Saul said to himself. But to David he said, "Today you have a second chance to become my son-in-law!"

[22]Then Saul told his men to say to David, "The king really likes you, and so do we. Why don't you accept the king's offer and become his son-in-law?"

[23]When Saul's men said these things to David, he replied, "How can a poor man from a humble family afford the bride price for the daughter of a king?"

[24]When Saul's men reported this back to the king, [25]he told them, "Tell David that all I want for the bride price is 100 Philistine foreskins! Vengeance on my enemies is all I really want." But what Saul had in mind was that David would be killed in the fight.

[26]David was delighted to accept the offer. Before the time limit expired, [27]he and his men went out and killed 200 Philistines. Then David fulfilled the king's requirement by presenting all their foreskins to him. So Saul gave his daughter Michal to David to be his wife.

[28]When Saul realized that the LORD was with David and how much his daughter Michal loved him, [29]Saul became even more afraid of him, and he remained David's enemy for the rest of his life.

[30]Every time the commanders of the Philistines attacked, David was more successful against them than all the rest of Saul's officers. So David's name became very famous.

19:1SAUL now urged his servants and his son Jonathan to assassinate David. But Jonathan, because of his close friendship with David, [2]told him what his father was planning. "Tomorrow morning," he warned him, "you must find a hiding place out in the fields. [3]I'll ask my father to go out there with me, and I'll talk to him about you. Then I'll tell you everything I can find out."

[4]The next morning Jonathan spoke with his father about David, saying many good things about him. "The king must not sin against his servant David," Jonathan said. "He's never done anything to harm you. He has always helped you in any way he could. [5]Have you forgotten about the time he risked his life to kill the Philistine giant and how the LORD brought a great victory to all Israel as a result? You were certainly happy about it then. Why should you murder an innocent man like David? There is no reason for it at all!"

[6]So Saul listened to Jonathan and vowed, "As surely as the LORD lives, David will not be killed."

[7]Afterward Jonathan called David and told him what had happened. Then he brought David to Saul, and David served in the court as before.

[8]War broke out again after that, and David led his troops against the Philistines. He attacked them with such fury that they all ran away.

[9]But one day when Saul was sitting at home, with spear in hand, the tormenting spirit* from the LORD suddenly came upon him again. As David played his harp, [10]Saul hurled his spear at David. But David dodged out of the way, and leaving the spear stuck in the wall, he fled and escaped into the night.

[11]Then Saul sent troops to watch David's house. They were told to kill David when he came out the next morning. But Michal, David's wife, warned him, "If you don't escape tonight, you will be dead by morning." [12]So she helped him climb out through a window, and he fled and escaped. [13]Then she took an idol* and put it in his bed, covered it with blankets, and put a cushion of goat's hair at its head.

[14]When the troops came to arrest David, she told them he was sick and couldn't get out of bed.

[15]But Saul sent the troops back to get David. He ordered, "Bring him to me in his bed so I can kill him!" [16]But when they came to carry David out, they discovered that it was only an idol in the bed with a cushion of goat's hair at its head.

[17]"Why have you betrayed me like this and let my enemy escape?" Saul demanded of Michal.

"I had to," Michal replied. "He threatened to kill me if I didn't help him."

[18]So David escaped and went to Ramah to see Samuel, and he told him all that Saul had done to him. Then Samuel took David with him to live at Naioth. [19]When the report reached Saul that David was at Naioth in Ramah, [20]he sent troops to capture him. But when they arrived and saw Samuel leading a group of prophets who were prophesying, the Spirit of God came upon Saul's men, and they also began to prophesy. [21]When Saul heard what had happened, he sent other troops, but they, too, prophesied! The same thing happened a third time. [22]Finally, Saul himself went to Ramah and arrived at the great well in Secu. "Where are Samuel and David?" he demanded.

"They are at Naioth in Ramah," someone told him.

[23]But on the way to Naioth in Ramah the Spirit of God came even upon Saul, and he, too, began to prophesy all the way to Naioth! [24]He tore off his clothes and lay naked on the ground all day and all night, prophesying in the presence of Samuel. The people who were watching exclaimed, "What? Is even Saul a prophet?"

18:6 The type of instrument represented by the word *cymbals* is uncertain.   18:10 Or *an evil spirit*.   18:19 Or *But*.   19:9 Or *evil spirit*.   19:13 Hebrew *teraphim;* also in 19:16.

JOHN 8:31-59

Jesus said to the people who believed in him, "You are truly my disciples if you remain faithful to my teachings. [32]And you will know the truth, and the truth will set you free."

[33]"But we are descendants of Abraham," they said. "We have never been slaves to anyone. What do you mean, 'You will be set free'?"

[34]**Jesus replied, "I tell you the truth, everyone who sins is a slave of sin. [35]A slave is not a permanent member of the family, but a son is part of the**

family forever. [36]**So if the Son sets you free, you are truly free.** [37]Yes, I realize that you are descendants of Abraham. And yet some of you are trying to kill me because there's no room in your hearts for my message. [38]I am telling you what I saw when I was with my Father. But you are following the advice of your father."

[39]"Our father is Abraham!" they declared.

"No," Jesus replied, "for if you were really the children of Abraham, you would follow his example.* [40]Instead, you are trying to kill me because I told you the truth, which I heard from God. Abraham never did such a thing. [41]No, you are imitating your real father."

They replied, "We aren't illegitimate children! God himself is our true Father."

[42]Jesus told them, "If God were your Father, you would love me, because I have come to you from God. I am not here on my own, but he sent me. [43]Why can't you understand what I am saying? It's because you can't even hear me! [44]For you are the children of your father the devil, and you love to do the evil things he does. He was a murderer from the beginning. He has always hated the truth, because there is no truth in him. When he lies, it is consistent with his character; for he is a liar and the father of lies. [45]So when I tell the truth, you just naturally don't believe me! [46]Which of you can truthfully accuse me of sin? And since I am telling you the truth, why don't you believe me? [47]Anyone who belongs to God listens gladly to the words of God. But you don't listen because you don't belong to God."

[48]The people retorted, "You Samaritan devil! Didn't we say all along that you were possessed by a demon?"

[49]"No," Jesus said, "I have no demon in me. For I honor my Father—and you dishonor me. [50]And though I have no wish to glorify myself, God is going to glorify me. He is the true judge. [51]I tell you the truth, anyone who obeys my teaching will never die!"

[52]The people said, "Now we know

you are possessed by a demon. Even Abraham and the prophets died, but you say, 'Anyone who obeys my teaching will never die!' [53]Are you greater than our father Abraham? He died, and so did the prophets. Who do you think you are?"

[54]Jesus answered, "If I want glory for myself, it doesn't count. But it is my Father who will glorify me. You say, 'He is our God,' [55]but you don't even know him. I know him. If I said otherwise, I would be as great a liar as you! But I do know him and obey him. [56]Your father Abraham rejoiced as he looked forward to my coming. He saw it and was glad."

[57]The people said, "You aren't even fifty years old. How can you say you have seen Abraham?*"

[58]Jesus answered, "I tell you the truth, before Abraham was even born, I AM!*" [59]At that point they picked up stones to throw at him. But Jesus was hidden from them and left the Temple.

8:39 Some manuscripts read *if you are really the children of Abraham, follow his example.* **8:57** Some manuscripts read *How can you say Abraham has seen you?* **8:58** Or *before Abraham was even born, I have always been alive;* Greek reads *before Abraham was, I am.* See Exod 3:14.

PSALM 112:1-10*
Praise the LORD!

How joyful are those who fear
     the LORD
     and delight in obeying his
        commands.
[2] Their children will be successful
        everywhere;
     an entire generation of godly
        people will be blessed.
[3] They themselves will be wealthy,
     and their good deeds will last
        forever.
[4] Light shines in the darkness for
     the godly.
     They are generous,
        compassionate, and righteous.
[5] Good comes to those who lend
        money generously
     and conduct their business fairly.
[6] Such people will not be overcome
        by evil.

Those who are righteous will be
long remembered.
7 They do not fear bad news;
they confidently trust the LORD
to care for them.
8 They are confident and fearless
and can face their foes
triumphantly.
9 They share freely and give
generously to those in need.
Their good deeds will be
remembered forever.
They will have influence and
honor.
10 The wicked will see this and
be infuriated.
They will grind their teeth
in anger;
they will slink away, their hopes
thwarted.

112 This psalm is a Hebrew acrostic poem; after the
introductory note of praise, each line begins with a
successive letter of the Hebrew alphabet.

PROVERBS 15:12-14
Mockers hate to be corrected, so they
stay away from the wise. □ A glad heart
makes a happy face; a broken heart
crushes the spirit. □ A wise person is
hungry for knowledge, while the fool
feeds on trash.

MAY
17

1 SAMUEL 20:1–21:15
David now fled from Naioth in Ramah
and found Jonathan. "What have I
done?" he exclaimed. "What is my
crime? How have I offended your father
that he is so determined to kill me?"

2"That's not true!" Jonathan protested. "You're not going to die. He always tells me everything he's going to
do, even the little things. I know my father wouldn't hide something like this
from me. It just isn't so!"

3 Then David took an oath before Jonathan and said, "Your father knows perfectly well about our friendship, so he
has said to himself, 'I won't tell Jonathan—why should I hurt him?' But I
swear to you that I am only a step away
from death! I swear it by the LORD and
by your own soul!"

4"Tell me what I can do to help you,"
Jonathan exclaimed.

5David replied, "Tomorrow we celebrate the new moon festival. I've always
eaten with the king on this occasion, but
tomorrow I'll hide in the field and stay
there until the evening of the third day.
6If your father asks where I am, tell him
I asked permission to go home to Bethlehem for an annual family sacrifice. 7If
he says, 'Fine!' you will know all is well.
But if he is angry and loses his temper,
you will know he is determined to kill
me. 8Show me this loyalty as my sworn
friend—for we made a solemn pact before the LORD—or kill me yourself if I
have sinned against your father. But
please don't betray me to him!"

9"Never!" Jonathan exclaimed. "You
know that if I had the slightest notion
my father was planning to kill you, I
would tell you at once."

10Then David asked, "How will I know
whether or not your father is angry?"

11"Come out to the field with me,"
Jonathan replied. And they went out
there together. 12Then Jonathan told
David, "I promise by the LORD, the God
of Israel, that by this time tomorrow, or
the next day at the latest, I will talk to my
father and let you know at once how he
feels about you. If he speaks favorably
about you, I will let you know. 13But if he
is angry and wants you killed, may the
LORD strike me and even kill me if I
don't warn you so you can escape and
live. May the LORD be with you as he
used to be with my father. 14And may
you treat me with the faithful love of the
LORD as long as I live. But if I die, 15treat
my family with this faithful love, even
when the LORD destroys all your enemies from the face of the earth."

16So Jonathan made a solemn pact

with David,* saying, "May the LORD destroy all your enemies!" [17]And Jonathan made David reaffirm his vow of friendship again, for Jonathan loved David as he loved himself.

[18]Then Jonathan said, "Tomorrow we celebrate the new moon festival. You will be missed when your place at the table is empty. [19]The day after tomorrow, toward evening, go to the place where you hid before, and wait there by the stone pile.* [20]I will come out and shoot three arrows to the side of the stone pile as though I were shooting at a target. [21]Then I will send a boy to bring the arrows back. If you hear me tell him, 'They're on this side,' then you will know, as surely as the LORD lives, that all is well, and there is no trouble. [22]But if I tell him, 'Go farther—the arrows are still ahead of you,' then it will mean that you must leave immediately, for the LORD is sending you away. [23]And may the LORD make us keep our promises to each other, for he has witnessed them."

[24]So David hid himself in the field, and when the new moon festival began, the king sat down to eat. [25]He sat at his usual place against the wall, with Jonathan sitting opposite him* and Abner beside him. But David's place was empty. [26]Saul didn't say anything about it that day, for he said to himself, "Something must have made David ceremonially unclean." [27]But when David's place was empty again the next day, Saul asked Jonathan, "Why hasn't the son of Jesse been here for the meal either yesterday or today?"

[28]Jonathan replied, "David earnestly asked me if he could go to Bethlehem. [29]He said, 'Please let me go, for we are having a family sacrifice. My brother demanded that I be there. So please let me get away to see my brothers.' That's why he isn't here at the king's table."

[30]Saul boiled with rage at Jonathan. "You stupid son of a whore!"* he swore at him. "Do you think I don't know that you want him to be king in your place, shaming yourself and your mother? [31]As long as that son of Jesse is alive,

you'll never be king. Now go and get him so I can kill him!"

[32]"But why should he be put to death?" Jonathan asked his father. "What has he done?" [33]Then Saul hurled his spear at Jonathan, intending to kill him. So at last Jonathan realized that his father was really determined to kill David.

[34]Jonathan left the table in fierce anger and refused to eat on that second day of the festival, for he was crushed by his father's shameful behavior toward David.

[35]The next morning, as agreed, Jonathan went out into the field and took a young boy with him to gather his arrows. [36]"Start running," he told the boy, "so you can find the arrows as I shoot them." So the boy ran, and Jonathan shot an arrow beyond him. [37]When the boy had almost reached the arrow, Jonathan shouted, "The arrow is still ahead of you. [38]Hurry, hurry, don't wait." So the boy quickly gathered up the arrows and ran back to his master. [39]He, of course, suspected nothing; only Jonathan and David understood the signal. [40]Then Jonathan gave his bow and arrows to the boy and told him to take them back to town.

[41]As soon as the boy was gone, David came out from where he had been hiding near the stone pile.* Then David bowed three times to Jonathan with his face to the ground. Both of them were in tears as they embraced each other and said good-bye, especially David.

[42]At last Jonathan said to David, "Go in peace, for we have sworn loyalty to each other in the LORD's name. The LORD is the witness of a bond between us and our children forever." Then David left, and Jonathan returned to the town.*

21:1*DAVID went to the town of Nob to see Ahimelech the priest. Ahimelech trembled when he saw him. "Why are you alone?" he asked. "Why is no one with you?"

[2]"The king has sent me on a private matter," David said. "He told me not to

tell anyone why I am here. I have told my men where to meet me later. 3Now, what is there to eat? Give me five loaves of bread or anything else you have."

4"We don't have any regular bread," the priest replied. "But there is the holy bread, which you can have if your young men have not slept with any women recently."

5"Don't worry," David replied. "I never allow my men to be with women when they are on a campaign. And since they stay clean even on ordinary trips, how much more on this one!"

6Since there was no other food available, the priest gave him the holy bread—the Bread of the Presence that was placed before the LORD in the Tabernacle. It had just been replaced that day with fresh bread.

7Now Doeg the Edomite, Saul's chief herdsman, was there that day, having been detained before the LORD.*

8David asked Ahimelech, "Do you have a spear or sword? The king's business was so urgent that I didn't even have time to grab a weapon!"

9"I only have the sword of Goliath the Philistine, whom you killed in the valley of Elah," the priest replied. "It is wrapped in a cloth behind the ephod. Take that if you want it, for there is nothing else here."

"There is nothing like it!" David replied. "Give it to me!"

10So David escaped from Saul and went to King Achish of Gath. 11But the officers of Achish were unhappy about his being there. "Isn't this David, the king of the land?" they asked. "Isn't he the one the people honor with dances, singing,

'Saul has killed his thousands,
    and David his ten thousands'?"

12David heard these comments and was very afraid of what King Achish of Gath might do to him. 13So he pretended to be insane, scratching on doors and drooling down his beard.

14Finally, King Achish said to his men, "Must you bring me a madman? 15We already have enough of them around here! Why should I let someone like this be my guest?"

20:16 Hebrew *with the house of David.*   20:19 Hebrew *the stone Ezel.* The meaning of the Hebrew is uncertain.   20:25 As in Greek version; Hebrew reads *with Jonathan standing.*   20:30 Hebrew *You son of a perverse and rebellious woman.*   20:41 As in Greek version; Hebrew reads *near the south edge.*   20:42 This sentence is numbered 21:1 in Hebrew text.   21:1 Verses 21:1-15 are numbered 21:2-16 in Hebrew text.   21:7 The meaning of the Hebrew is uncertain.

JOHN 9:1-41

As Jesus was walking along, he saw a man who had been blind from birth. 2**"Rabbi," his disciples asked him, "why was this man born blind? Was it because of his own sins or his parents' sins?"**

3**"It was not because of his sins or his parents' sins," Jesus answered. "This happened so the power of God could be seen in him.** 4We must quickly carry out the tasks assigned us by the one who sent us.* The night is coming, and then no one can work. 5But while I am here in the world, I am the light of the world."

6Then he spit on the ground, made mud with the saliva, and spread the mud over the blind man's eyes. 7He told him, "Go wash yourself in the pool of Siloam" (Siloam means "sent"). So the man went and washed and came back seeing!

8His neighbors and others who knew him as a blind beggar asked each other, "Isn't this the man who used to sit and beg?" 9Some said he was, and others said, "No, he just looks like him!"

But the beggar kept saying, "Yes, I am the same one!"

10They asked, "Who healed you? What happened?"

11He told them, "The man they call Jesus made mud and spread it over my eyes and told me, 'Go to the pool of Siloam and wash yourself.' So I went and washed, and now I can see!"

12"Where is he now?" they asked.

"I don't know," he replied.

13Then they took the man who had

been blind to the Pharisees, [14] because it was on the Sabbath that Jesus had made the mud and healed him. [15] The Pharisees asked the man all about it. So he told them, "He put the mud over my eyes, and when I washed it away, I could see!"

[16] Some of the Pharisees said, "This man Jesus is not from God, for he is working on the Sabbath." Others said, "But how could an ordinary sinner do such miraculous signs?" So there was a deep division of opinion among them.

[17] Then the Pharisees again questioned the man who had been blind and demanded, "What's your opinion about this man who healed you?"

The man replied, "I think he must be a prophet."

[18] The Jewish leaders still refused to believe the man had been blind and could now see, so they called in his parents. [19] They asked them, "Is this your son? Was he born blind? If so, how can he now see?"

[20] His parents replied, "We know this is our son and that he was born blind, [21] but we don't know how he can see or who healed him. Ask him. He is old enough to speak for himself." [22] His parents said this because they were afraid of the Jewish leaders, who had announced that anyone saying Jesus was the Messiah would be expelled from the synagogue. [23] That's why they said, "He is old enough. Ask him."

[24] So for the second time they called in the man who had been blind and told him, "God should get the glory for this,* because we know this man Jesus is a sinner."

[25] "I don't know whether he is a sinner," the man replied. "But I know this: I was blind, and now I can see!"

[26] "But what did he do?" they asked. "How did he heal you?"

[27] "Look!" the man exclaimed. "I told you once. Didn't you listen? Why do you want to hear it again? Do you want to become his disciples, too?"

[28] Then they cursed him and said, "You are his disciple, but we are disciples of Moses! [29] We know God spoke to Moses, but we don't even know where this man comes from."

[30] "Why, that's very strange!" the man replied. "He healed my eyes, and yet you don't know where he comes from? [31] We know that God doesn't listen to sinners, but he is ready to hear those who worship him and do his will. [32] Ever since the world began, no one has been able to open the eyes of someone born blind. [33] If this man were not from God, he couldn't have done it."

[34] "You were born a total sinner!" they answered. "Are you trying to teach us?" And they threw him out of the synagogue.

[35] When Jesus heard what had happened, he found the man and asked, "Do you believe in the Son of Man?*"

[36] The man answered, "Who is he, sir? I want to believe in him."

[37] "You have seen him," Jesus said, "and he is speaking to you!"

[38] "Yes, Lord, I believe!" the man said. And he worshiped Jesus.

[39] Then Jesus told him,* "I entered this world to render judgment—to give sight to the blind and to show those who think they see* that they are blind."

[40] Some Pharisees who were standing nearby heard him and asked, "Are you saying we're blind?"

[41] "If you were blind, you wouldn't be guilty," Jesus replied. "But you remain guilty because you claim you can see."

9:4 Other manuscripts read *I must quickly carry out the tasks assigned me by the one who sent me;* still others read *We must quickly carry out the tasks assigned us by the one who sent me.* **9:24** Or *Give glory to God, not to Jesus;* Greek reads *Give glory to God.* **9:35** Some manuscripts read *the Son of God?* "Son of Man" is a title Jesus used for himself. **9:38-39a** Some manuscripts do not include *"Yes, Lord, I believe!" the man said. And he worshiped Jesus. Then Jesus told him.* **9:39b** Greek *those who see.*

PSALM 113:1–114:8

Praise the Lord!

Yes, give praise, O servants
    of the Lord.
Praise the name of the Lord!
[2] Blessed be the name of the Lord
    now and forever.

³ Everywhere—from east to west—
   praise the name of the LORD.
⁴ For the LORD is high above the
      nations;
   his glory is higher than
      the heavens.

⁵ Who can be compared with the
      LORD our God,
   who is enthroned on high?
⁶ He stoops to look down
   on heaven and on earth.
⁷ He lifts the poor from the
      dust
   and the needy from the
      garbage dump.
⁸ He sets them among princes,
   even the princes of his
      own people!
⁹ He gives the childless woman a
      family,
   making her a happy mother.

   Praise the LORD!

¹¹⁴:¹ WHEN the Israelites escaped
      from Egypt—
   when the family of Jacob left that
      foreign land—
² the land of Judah became God's
      sanctuary,
   and Israel became his kingdom.

³ The Red Sea* saw them coming and
      hurried out of their way!
   The water of the Jordan River
      turned away.
⁴ The mountains skipped like rams,
   the hills like lambs!
⁵ What's wrong, Red Sea, that made
      you hurry out of their way?
   What happened, Jordan River,
      that you turned away?
⁶ Why, mountains, did you skip
      like rams?
   Why, hills, like lambs?

⁷ Tremble, O earth, at the presence
      of the Lord,
   at the presence of the God
      of Jacob.
⁸ He turned the rock into a pool
      of water;

   yes, a spring of water flowed from
      solid rock.

114:3 Hebrew *the sea;* also in 114:5.

PROVERBS 15:15-17

For the despondent, every day brings trouble; for the happy heart, life is a continual feast. □Better to have little, with fear for the LORD, than to have great treasure and inner turmoil. □A bowl of vegetables with someone you love is better than steak with someone you hate.

MAY
18

1 SAMUEL 22:1–23:29

So David left Gath and escaped to the cave of Adullam. Soon his brothers and all his other relatives joined him there. ² Then others began coming—men who were in trouble or in debt or who were just discontented—until David was the captain of about 400 men.

³Later David went to Mizpeh in Moab, where he asked the king, "Please allow my father and mother to live here with you until I know what God is going to do for me." ⁴So David's parents stayed in Moab with the king during the entire time David was living in his stronghold.

⁵One day the prophet Gad told David, "Leave the stronghold and return to the land of Judah." So David went to the forest of Hereth.

⁶The news of his arrival in Judah soon reached Saul. At the time, the king was sitting beneath the tamarisk tree on the hill at Gibeah, holding his spear and surrounded by his officers.

⁷"Listen here, you men of Benjamin!" Saul shouted to his officers when he heard the news. "Has that son of Jesse promised every one of you fields and vineyards? Has he promised to make

you all generals and captains in his army?* ⁸Is that why you have conspired against me? For not one of you told me when my own son made a solemn pact with the son of Jesse. You're not even sorry for me. Think of it! My own son—encouraging him to kill me, as he is trying to do this very day!"

⁹Then Doeg the Edomite, who was standing there with Saul's men, spoke up. "When I was at Nob," he said, "I saw the son of Jesse talking to the priest, Ahimelech son of Ahitub. ¹⁰Ahimelech consulted the LORD for him. Then he gave him food and the sword of Goliath the Philistine."

¹¹King Saul immediately sent for Ahimelech and all his family, who served as priests at Nob. ¹²When they arrived, Saul shouted at him, "Listen to me, you son of Ahitub!"

"What is it, my king?" Ahimelech asked.

¹³"Why have you and the son of Jesse conspired against me?" Saul demanded. "Why did you give him food and a sword? Why have you consulted God for him? Why have you encouraged him to kill me, as he is trying to do this very day?"

¹⁴"But sir," Ahimelech replied, "is anyone among all your servants as faithful as David, your son-in-law? Why, he is the captain of your bodyguard and a highly honored member of your household! ¹⁵This was certainly not the first time I had consulted God for him! May the king not accuse me and my family in this matter, for I knew nothing at all of any plot against you."

¹⁶"You will surely die, Ahimelech, along with your entire family!" the king shouted. ¹⁷And he ordered his bodyguards, "Kill these priests of the LORD, for they are allies and conspirators with David! They knew he was running away from me, but they didn't tell me!" But Saul's men refused to kill the LORD's priests.

¹⁸Then the king said to Doeg, "You do it." So Doeg the Edomite turned on them and killed them that day, eighty-five priests in all, still wearing their priestly garments. ¹⁹Then he went to Nob, the town of the priests, and killed the priests' families—men and women, children and babies—and all the cattle, donkeys, sheep, and goats.

²⁰Only Abiathar, one of the sons of Ahimelech, escaped and fled to David. ²¹When he told David that Saul had killed the priests of the LORD, ²²David exclaimed, "I knew it! When I saw Doeg the Edomite there that day, I knew he was sure to tell Saul. Now I have caused the death of all your father's family. ²³Stay here with me, and don't be afraid. I will protect you with my own life, for the same person wants to kill us both."

²³:¹ONE day news came to David that the Philistines were at Keilah stealing grain from the threshing floors. ²David asked the LORD, "Should I go and attack them?"

"Yes, go and save Keilah," the LORD told him.

³But David's men said, "We're afraid even here in Judah. We certainly don't want to go to Keilah to fight the whole Philistine army!"

⁴So David asked the LORD again, and again the LORD replied, "Go down to Keilah, for I will help you conquer the Philistines."

⁵So David and his men went to Keilah. They slaughtered the Philistines and took all their livestock and rescued the people of Keilah. ⁶Now when Abiathar son of Ahimelech fled to David at Keilah, he brought the ephod with him.

⁷Saul soon learned that David was at Keilah. "Good!" he exclaimed. "We've got him now! God has handed him over to me, for he has trapped himself in a walled town!" ⁸So Saul mobilized his entire army to march to Keilah and besiege David and his men.

⁹But David learned of Saul's plan and told Abiathar the priest to bring the ephod and ask the LORD what he should do. ¹⁰Then David prayed, "O LORD, God of Israel, I have heard that Saul is plan-

ning to come and destroy Keilah because I am here. ¹¹Will the leaders of Keilah betray me to him?* And will Saul actually come as I have heard? O LORD, God of Israel, please tell me."

And the LORD said, "He will come."

¹²Again David asked, "Will the leaders of Keilah betray me and my men to Saul?"

And the LORD replied, "Yes, they will betray you."

¹³So David and his men—about 600 of them now—left Keilah and began roaming the countryside. Word soon reached Saul that David had escaped, so he didn't go to Keilah after all. ¹⁴David now stayed in the strongholds of the wilderness and in the hill country of Ziph. Saul hunted him day after day, but God didn't let Saul find him.

¹⁵One day near Horesh, David received the news that Saul was on the way to Ziph to search for him and kill him. ¹⁶Jonathan went to find David and encouraged him to stay strong in his faith in God. ¹⁷"Don't be afraid," Jonathan reassured him. "My father will never find you! You are going to be the king of Israel, and I will be next to you, as my father, Saul, is well aware." ¹⁸So the two of them renewed their solemn pact before the LORD. Then Jonathan returned home, while David stayed at Horesh.

¹⁹But now the men of Ziph went to Saul in Gibeah and betrayed David to him. "We know where David is hiding," they said. "He is in the strongholds of Horesh on the hill of Hakilah, which is in the southern part of Jeshimon. ²⁰Come down whenever you're ready, O king, and we will catch him and hand him over to you!"

²¹"The LORD bless you," Saul said. "At last someone is concerned about me! ²²Go and check again to be sure of where he is staying and who has seen him there, for I know that he is very crafty. ²³Discover his hiding places, and come back when you are sure. Then I'll go with you. And if he is in the area at all, I'll track him down, even if I have to search every hiding place in Judah!"

²⁴So the men of Ziph returned home ahead of Saul.

Meanwhile, David and his men had moved into the wilderness of Maon in the Arabah Valley south of Jeshimon. ²⁵When David heard that Saul and his men were searching for him, he went even farther into the wilderness to the great rock, and he remained there in the wilderness of Maon. But Saul kept after him in the wilderness.

²⁶Saul and David were now on opposite sides of a mountain. Just as Saul and his men began to close in on David and his men, ²⁷an urgent message reached Saul that the Philistines were raiding Israel again. ²⁸So Saul quit chasing David and returned to fight the Philistines. Ever since that time, the place where David was camped has been called the Rock of Escape.* ²⁹*David then went to live in the strongholds of En-gedi.

22:7 Hebrew *commanders of thousands and commanders of hundreds?* 23:11 Some manuscripts lack the first sentence of 23:11. 23:28 Hebrew *Sela-hammahlekoth.* 23:29 Verse 23:29 is numbered 24:1 in Hebrew text.

JOHN 10:1-21

"I [Jesus} tell you the truth, anyone who sneaks over the wall of a sheepfold, rather than going through the gate, must surely be a thief and a robber! ²But the one who enters through the gate is the shepherd of the sheep. ³The gatekeeper opens the gate for him, and the sheep recognize his voice and come to him. He calls his own sheep by name and leads them out. ⁴After he has gathered his own flock, he walks ahead of them, and they follow him because they know his voice. ⁵They won't follow a stranger; they will run from him because they don't know his voice."

⁶Those who heard Jesus use this illustration didn't understand what he meant, ⁷so he explained it to them: "I tell you the truth, I am the gate for the sheep. ⁸All who came before me* were thieves and robbers. But the true sheep did not listen to them. ⁹Yes, I am the gate. Those who come in through me will be saved.* They will come and go freely and will find good pastures.

¹⁰**The thief's purpose is to steal and kill and destroy. My purpose is to give them a rich and satisfying life.**

¹¹"I am the good shepherd. The good shepherd sacrifices his life for the sheep. ¹²A hired hand will run when he sees a wolf coming. He will abandon the sheep because they don't belong to him and he isn't their shepherd. And so the wolf attacks them and scatters the flock. ¹³The hired hand runs away because he's working only for the money and doesn't really care about the sheep.

¹⁴"I am the good shepherd; I know my own sheep, and they know me, ¹⁵just as my Father knows me and I know the Father. So I sacrifice my life for the sheep. ¹⁶I have other sheep, too, that are not in this sheepfold. I must bring them also. They will listen to my voice, and there will be one flock with one shepherd.

¹⁷"The Father loves me because I sacrifice my life so I may take it back again. ¹⁸No one can take my life from me. I sacrifice it voluntarily. For I have the authority to lay it down when I want to and also to take it up again. For this is what my Father has commanded."

¹⁹When he said these things, the people* were again divided in their opinions about him. ²⁰Some said, "He's demon possessed and out of his mind. Why listen to a man like that?" ²¹Others said, "This doesn't sound like a man possessed by a demon! Can a demon open the eyes of the blind?"

10:8 Some manuscripts do not include *before me.* **10:9** Or *will find safety.* **10:19** Greek *Jewish people;* also in 10:24, 31.

PSALM 115:1-18

Not to us, O LORD, not to us,
    but to your name goes all
      the glory
    for your unfailing love and
      faithfulness.
² Why let the nations say,
    "Where is their God?"
³ Our God is in the heavens,
    and he does as he wishes.
⁴ Their idols are merely things
    of silver and gold,

    shaped by human hands.
⁵ They have mouths but cannot speak,
    and eyes but cannot see.
⁶ They have ears but cannot hear,
    and noses but cannot smell.
⁷ They have hands but cannot feel,
    and feet but cannot walk,
    and throats but cannot make
      a sound.
⁸ And those who make idols are
      just like them,
    as are all who trust in them.

⁹ O Israel, trust the LORD!
    He is your helper and your shield.
¹⁰ O priests, descendants of Aaron,
      trust the LORD!
    He is your helper and your shield.
¹¹ All you who fear the LORD, trust
      the LORD!
    He is your helper and your shield.

¹² The LORD remembers us and
      will bless us.
    He will bless the people of Israel
    and bless the priests, the
      descendants of Aaron.
¹³ He will bless those who fear
      the LORD,
    both great and lowly.

¹⁴ May the LORD richly bless
    both you and your children.
¹⁵ May you be blessed by the LORD,
    who made heaven and earth.
¹⁶ The heavens belong to the LORD,
    but he has given the earth
      to all humanity.
¹⁷ The dead cannot sing praises
      to the LORD,
    for they have gone into the
      silence of the grave.
¹⁸ But we can praise the LORD
    both now and forever!

    Praise the LORD!

PROVERBS 15:18-19

A hot-tempered person starts fights; a cool-tempered person stops them. □ A lazy person's way is blocked with briers, but the path of the upright is an open highway.

MAY 19

1 SAMUEL 24:1–25:44

[1]*After Saul returned from fighting the Philistines, he was told that David had gone into the wilderness of En-gedi. [2]So Saul chose 3,000 elite troops from all Israel and went to search for David and his men near the rocks of the wild goats.

[3]At the place where the road passes some sheepfolds, Saul went into a cave to relieve himself. But as it happened, David and his men were hiding farther back in that very cave!

[4]"Now's your opportunity!" David's men whispered to him. "Today the LORD is telling you, 'I will certainly put your enemy into your power, to do with as you wish.'" So David crept forward and cut off a piece of the hem of Saul's robe.

[5]But then David's conscience began bothering him because he had cut Saul's robe. [6]"The LORD knows I shouldn't have done that to my lord the king," he said to his men. "The LORD forbid that I should do this to my lord the king and attack the LORD's anointed one, for the LORD himself has chosen him." [7]So David restrained his men and did not let them kill Saul.

After Saul had left the cave and gone on his way, [8]David came out and shouted after him, "My lord the king!" And when Saul looked around, David bowed low before him.

[9]Then he shouted to Saul, "Why do you listen to the people who say I am trying to harm you? [10]This very day you can see with your own eyes it isn't true. For the LORD placed you at my mercy back there in the cave. Some of my men told me to kill you, but I spared you. For I said, 'I will never harm the king—he is the LORD's anointed one.' [11]Look, my father, at what I have in my hand. It is a piece of the hem of your robe! I cut it off, but I didn't kill you. This proves that I am not trying to harm you and that I have not sinned against you, even though you have been hunting for me to kill me.

[12]"May the LORD judge between us. Perhaps the LORD will punish you for what you are trying to do to me, but I will never harm you. [13]As that old proverb says, 'From evil people come evil deeds.' So you can be sure I will never harm you. [14]Who is the king of Israel trying to catch anyway? Should he spend his time chasing one who is as worthless as a dead dog or a single flea? [15]May the LORD therefore judge which of us is right and punish the guilty one. He is my advocate, and he will rescue me from your power!"

[16]When David had finished speaking, Saul called back, "Is that really you, my son David?" Then he began to cry. [17]And he said to David, "You are a better man than I am, for you have repaid me good for evil. [18]Yes, you have been amazingly kind to me today, for when the LORD put me in a place where you could have killed me, you didn't do it. [19]Who else would let his enemy get away when he had him in his power? May the LORD reward you well for the kindness you have shown me today. [20]And now I realize that you are surely going to be king, and that the kingdom of Israel will flourish under your rule. [21]Now swear to me by the LORD that when that happens you will not kill my family and destroy my line of descendants!"

[22]So David promised this to Saul with an oath. Then Saul went home, but David and his men went back to their stronghold.

[25:1]Now Samuel died, and all Israel gathered for his funeral. They buried him at his house in Ramah.

Then David moved down to the wilderness of Maon.* [2]There was a wealthy man from Maon who owned property near the town of Carmel. He had 3,000 sheep and 1,000 goats, and it was sheep-shearing time. [3]This man's name was Nabal, and his wife, Abigail, was a sensible and beautiful woman. But Nabal, a descendant of Caleb, was crude and mean in all his dealings.

⁴When David heard that Nabal was shearing his sheep, ⁵he sent ten of his young men to Carmel with this message for Nabal: ⁶"Peace and prosperity to you, your family, and everything you own! ⁷I am told that it is sheep-shearing time. While your shepherds stayed among us near Carmel, we never harmed them, and nothing was ever stolen from them. ⁸Ask your own men, and they will tell you this is true. So would you be kind to us, since we have come at a time of celebration? Please share any provisions you might have on hand with us and with your friend David." ⁹David's young men gave this message to Nabal in David's name, and they waited for a reply.

¹⁰"Who is this fellow David?" Nabal sneered to the young men. "Who does this son of Jesse think he is? There are lots of servants these days who run away from their masters. ¹¹Should I take my bread and my water and my meat that I've slaughtered for my shearers and give it to a band of outlaws who come from who knows where?"

¹²So David's young men returned and told him what Nabal had said. ¹³"Get your swords!" was David's reply as he strapped on his own. Then 400 men started off with David, and 200 remained behind to guard their equipment.

¹⁴Meanwhile, one of Nabal's servants went to Abigail and told her, "David sent messengers from the wilderness to greet our master, but he screamed insults at them. ¹⁵These men have been very good to us, and we never suffered any harm from them. Nothing was stolen from us the whole time they were with us. ¹⁶In fact, day and night they were like a wall of protection to us and the sheep. ¹⁷You need to know this and figure out what to do, for there is going to be trouble for our master and his

whole family. He's so ill-tempered that no one can even talk to him!"

¹⁸Abigail wasted no time. She quickly gathered 200 loaves of bread, two wineskins full of wine, five sheep that had been slaughtered, nearly a bushel* of roasted grain, 100 clusters of raisins, and 200 fig cakes. She packed them on donkeys ¹⁹and said to her servants, "Go on ahead. I will follow you shortly." But she didn't tell her husband Nabal what she was doing.

²⁰As she was riding her donkey into a mountain ravine, she saw David and his men coming toward her. ²¹David had just been saying, "A lot of good it did to help this fellow. We protected his flocks in the wilderness, and nothing he owned was lost or stolen. But he has repaid me evil for good. ²²May God strike me and kill me* if even one man of his household is still alive tomorrow morning!"

²³When Abigail saw David, she quickly got off her donkey and bowed low before him. ²⁴She fell at his feet and said, "I accept all blame in this matter, my lord. Please listen to what I have to say. ²⁵I know Nabal is a wicked and ill-tempered man; please don't pay any attention to him. He is a fool, just as his name suggests.* But I never even saw the young men you sent.

²⁶"Now, my lord, as surely as the LORD lives and you yourself live, since the LORD has kept you from murdering and taking vengeance into your own hands, let all your enemies and those who try to harm you be as cursed as Nabal is. ²⁷And here is a present that I, your servant, have brought to you and your young men. ²⁸Please forgive me if I have offended you in any way. The LORD will surely reward you with a lasting dynasty, for you are fighting the LORD's battles. And you have not done wrong throughout your entire life.

²⁹"Even when you are chased by those who seek to kill you, your life is safe in the care of the LORD your God, secure in his treasure pouch! But the lives of your enemies will disappear like stones shot

from a sling! [30]When the LORD has done all he promised and has made you leader of Israel, [31]don't let this be a blemish on your record. Then your conscience won't have to bear the staggering burden of needless bloodshed and vengeance. And when the LORD has done these great things for you, please remember me, your servant!"

[32]David replied to Abigail, "Praise the LORD, the God of Israel, who has sent you to meet me today! [33]Thank God for your good sense! Bless you for keeping me from murder and from carrying out vengeance with my own hands. [34]For I swear by the LORD, the God of Israel, who has kept me from hurting you, that if you had not hurried out to meet me, not one of Nabal's men would still be alive tomorrow morning." [35]Then David accepted her present and told her, "Return home in peace. I have heard what you said. We will not kill your husband."

[36]When Abigail arrived home, she found that Nabal was throwing a big party and was celebrating like a king. He was very drunk, so she didn't tell him anything about her meeting with David until dawn the next day. [37]In the morning when Nabal was sober, his wife told him what had happened. As a result he had a stroke,* and he lay paralyzed on his bed like a stone. [38]About ten days later, the LORD struck him, and he died.

[39]When David heard that Nabal was dead, he said, "Praise the LORD, who has avenged the insult I received from Nabal and has kept me from doing it myself. Nabal has received the punishment for his sin." Then David sent messengers to Abigail to ask her to become his wife.

[40]When the messengers arrived at Carmel, they told Abigail, "David has sent us to take you back to marry him."

[41]She bowed low to the ground and responded, "I, your servant, would be happy to marry David. I would even be willing to become a slave, washing the feet of his servants!" [42]Quickly getting ready, she took along five of her servant girls as attendants, mounted her don-

key, and went with David's messengers. And so she became his wife. [43]David also married Ahinoam from Jezreel, making both of them his wives. [44]Saul, meanwhile, had given his daughter Michal, David's wife, to a man from Gallim named Palti son of Laish.

24:1 Verses 24:1-22 are numbered 24:2-23 in Hebrew text.   25:1 As in Greek version (see also 25:2); Hebrew reads *Paran*.   25:18 Hebrew *5 seahs* [30 liters].   25:22 As in Greek version; Hebrew reads *May God strike and kill the enemies of David*.   25:25 The name *Nabal* means "fool."   25:37 Hebrew *his heart failed him*.

JOHN 10:22-42

It was now winter, and Jesus was in Jerusalem at the time of Hanukkah, the Festival of Dedication. [23]He was in the Temple, walking through the section known as Solomon's Colonnade. [24]The people surrounded him and asked, "How long are you going to keep us in suspense? If you are the Messiah, tell us plainly."

[25]Jesus replied, "I have already told you, and you don't believe me. The proof is the work I do in my Father's name. [26]But you don't believe me because you are not my sheep. [27]**My sheep listen to my voice; I know them, and they follow me. [28]I give them eternal life, and they will never perish. No one can snatch them away from me,** [29]for my Father has given them to me, and he is more powerful than anyone else.* No one can snatch them from the Father's hand. [30]The Father and I are one."

[31]Once again the people picked up stones to kill him. [32]Jesus said, "At my Father's direction I have done many good works. For which one are you going to stone me?"

[33]They replied, "We're stoning you not for any good work, but for blasphemy! You, a mere man, claim to be God."

[34]Jesus replied, "It is written in your own Scriptures* that God said to certain leaders of the people, 'I say, you are gods!'* [35]And you know that the Scriptures cannot be altered. So if those people who received God's message were called 'gods,' [36]why do you call it blasphemy when I say, 'I am the Son of God'?

After all, the Father set me apart and sent me into the world. ³⁷Don't believe me unless I carry out my Father's work. ³⁸But if I do his work, believe in the evidence of the miraculous works I have done, even if you don't believe me. Then you will know and understand that the Father is in me, and I am in the Father."

³⁹Once again they tried to arrest him, but he got away and left them. ⁴⁰He went beyond the Jordan River near the place where John was first baptizing and stayed there awhile. ⁴¹And many followed him. "John didn't perform miraculous signs," they remarked to one another, "but everything he said about this man has come true." ⁴²And many who were there believed in Jesus.

10:29 Other manuscripts read *for what my Father has given me is more powerful than anything;* still others read *for regarding that which my Father has given me, he is greater than all.*   10:34a Greek *your own law.* 10:34b Ps 82:6.

PSALM 116:1-19

I love the LORD because he hears
    my voice
    and my prayer for mercy.
² Because he bends down to listen,
    I will pray as long as I have breath!
³ Death wrapped its ropes around me;
    the terrors of the grave*
        overtook me.
    I saw only trouble and sorrow.
⁴ Then I called on the name
    of the LORD:
    "Please, LORD, save me!"
⁵ How kind the LORD is! How good
    he is!
    So merciful, this God of ours!
⁶ The LORD protects those of
    childlike faith;
    I was facing death, and he
        saved me.
⁷ Let my soul be at rest again,
    for the LORD has been good to me.
⁸ He has saved me from death,
    my eyes from tears,
    my feet from stumbling.
⁹ And so I walk in the LORD's presence
    as I live here on earth!
¹⁰ I believed in you, so I said,
    "I am deeply troubled, LORD."

¹¹ In my anxiety I cried out to you,
    "These people are all liars!"
¹² What can I offer the LORD
    for all he has done for me?
¹³ I will lift up the cup of salvation
    and praise the LORD's name for
        saving me.
¹⁴ I will keep my promises to the LORD
    in the presence of all his people.
¹⁵ The LORD cares deeply
    when his loved ones die.
¹⁶ O LORD, I am your servant;
    yes, I am your servant, born into
        your household;
    you have freed me from my chains.
¹⁷ I will offer you a sacrifice of
        thanksgiving
    and call on the name of the LORD.
¹⁸ I will fulfill my vows to the LORD
    in the presence of all his people—
¹⁹ in the house of the LORD
    in the heart of Jerusalem.

    Praise the LORD!

116:3 Hebrew *of Sheol.*

PROVERBS 15:20-21

Sensible children bring joy to their father; foolish children despise their mother. □ Foolishness brings joy to those with no sense; a sensible person stays on the right path.

MAY
20

1 SAMUEL 26:1-28:25

Now some men from Ziph came to Saul at Gibeah to tell him, "David is hiding on the hill of Hakilah, which overlooks Jeshimon."

²So Saul took 3,000 of Israel's elite troops and went to hunt him down in the wilderness of Ziph. ³Saul camped along the road beside the hill of Hakilah, near Jeshimon, where David was hiding. When David learned that Saul

had come after him into the wilderness, [4]he sent out spies to verify the report of Saul's arrival.

[5]David slipped over to Saul's camp one night to look around. Saul and Abner son of Ner, the commander of his army, were sleeping inside a ring formed by the slumbering warriors. [6]"Who will volunteer to go in there with me?" David asked Ahimelech the Hittite and Abishai son of Zeruiah, Joab's brother.

"I'll go with you," Abishai replied. [7]So David and Abishai went right into Saul's camp and found him asleep, with his spear stuck in the ground beside his head. Abner and the soldiers were lying asleep around him.

[8]"God has surely handed your enemy over to you this time!" Abishai whispered to David. "Let me pin him to the ground with one thrust of the spear; I won't need to strike twice!"

[9]"No!" David said. "Don't kill him. For who can remain innocent after attacking the LORD's anointed one? [10]Surely the LORD will strike Saul down someday, or he will die of old age or in battle. [11]The LORD forbid that I should kill the one he has anointed! But take his spear and that jug of water beside his head, and then let's get out of here!"

[12]So David took the spear and jug of water that were near Saul's head. Then he and Abishai got away without anyone seeing them or even waking up, because the LORD had put Saul's men into a deep sleep.

[13]David climbed the hill opposite the camp until he was at a safe distance. [14]Then he shouted down to the soldiers and to Abner son of Ner, "Wake up, Abner!"

"Who is it?" Abner demanded.

[15]"Well, Abner, you're a great man, aren't you?" David taunted. "Where in all Israel is there anyone as mighty? So why haven't you guarded your master the king when someone came to kill him? [16]This isn't good at all! I swear by the LORD that you and your men deserve to die, because you failed to protect your master, the LORD's anointed! Look around! Where are the king's spear and the jug of water that were beside his head?"

[17]Saul recognized David's voice and called out, "Is that you, my son David?"

And David replied, "Yes, my lord the king. [18]Why are you chasing me? What have I done? What is my crime? [19]But now let my lord the king listen to his servant. If the LORD has stirred you up against me, then let him accept my offering. But if this is simply a human scheme, then may those involved be cursed by the LORD. For they have driven me from my home, so I can no longer live among the LORD's people, and they have said, 'Go, worship pagan gods.' [20]Must I die on foreign soil, far from the presence of the LORD? Why has the king of Israel come out to search for a single flea? Why does he hunt me down like a partridge on the mountains?"

[21]Then Saul confessed, "I have sinned. Come back home, my son, and I will no longer try to harm you, for you valued my life today. I have been a fool and very, very wrong."

[22]"Here is your spear, O king," David replied. "Let one of your young men come over and get it. [23]The LORD gives his own reward for doing good and for being loyal, and I refused to kill you even when the LORD placed you in my power, for you are the LORD's anointed one. [24]Now may the LORD value my life, even as I have valued yours today. May he rescue me from all my troubles."

[25]And Saul said to David, "Blessings on you, my son David. You will do many heroic deeds, and you will surely succeed." Then David went away, and Saul returned home.

[27:1]BUT David kept thinking to himself, "Someday Saul is going to get me. The best thing I can do is escape to the Philistines. Then Saul will stop hunting for me in Israelite territory, and I will finally be safe."

[2]So David took his 600 men and went over and joined Achish son of Maoch, the king of Gath. [3]David and his men and

their families settled there with Achish at Gath. David brought his two wives along with him—Ahinoam from Jezreel and Abigail, Nabal's widow from Carmel. ⁴Word soon reached Saul that David had fled to Gath, so he stopped hunting for him.

⁵One day David said to Achish, "If it is all right with you, we would rather live in one of the country towns instead of here in the royal city."

⁶So Achish gave him the town of Ziklag (which still belongs to the kings of Judah to this day), ⁷and they lived there among the Philistines for a year and four months.

⁸David and his men spent their time raiding the Geshurites, the Girzites, and the Amalekites—people who had lived near Shur, toward the land of Egypt, since ancient times. ⁹David did not leave one person alive in the villages he attacked. He took the sheep, goats, cattle, donkeys, camels, and clothing before returning home to see King Achish.

¹⁰"Where did you make your raid today?" Achish would ask.

And David would reply, "Against the south of Judah, the Jerahmeelites, and the Kenites."

¹¹No one was left alive to come to Gath and tell where he had really been. This happened again and again while he was living among the Philistines. ¹²Achish believed David and thought to himself, "By now the people of Israel must hate him bitterly. Now he will have to stay here and serve me forever!"

28:1 ABOUT that time the Philistines mustered their armies for another war with Israel. King Achish told David, "You and your men will be expected to join me in battle."

²"Very well!" David agreed. "Now you will see for yourself what we can do."

Then Achish told David, "I will make you my personal bodyguard for life."

³Meanwhile, Samuel had died, and all Israel had mourned for him. He was buried in Ramah, his hometown. And Saul had banned from the land of Israel all mediums and those who consult the spirits of the dead.

⁴The Philistines set up their camp at Shunem, and Saul gathered all the army of Israel and camped at Gilboa. ⁵When Saul saw the vast Philistine army, he became frantic with fear. ⁶He asked the LORD what he should do, but the LORD refused to answer him, either by dreams or by sacred lots* or by the prophets. ⁷Saul then said to his advisers, "Find a woman who is a medium, so I can go and ask her what to do."

His advisers replied, "There is a medium at Endor."

⁸So Saul disguised himself by wearing ordinary clothing instead of his royal robes. Then he went to the woman's home at night, accompanied by two of his men.

"I have to talk to a man who has died," he said. "Will you call up his spirit for me?"

⁹"Are you trying to get me killed?" the woman demanded. "You know that Saul has outlawed all the mediums and all who consult the spirits of the dead. Why are you setting a trap for me?"

¹⁰But Saul took an oath in the name of the LORD and promised, "As surely as the LORD lives, nothing bad will happen to you for doing this."

¹¹Finally, the woman said, "Well, whose spirit do you want me to call up?"

"Call up Samuel," Saul replied.

¹²When the woman saw Samuel, she screamed, "You've deceived me! You are Saul!"

¹³"Don't be afraid!" the king told her. "What do you see?"

"I see a god* coming up out of the earth," she said.

¹⁴"What does he look like?" Saul asked.

"He is an old man wrapped in a robe," she replied. Saul realized it was Samuel, and he fell to the ground before him.

¹⁵"Why have you disturbed me by calling me back?" Samuel asked Saul.

"Because I am in deep trouble," Saul replied. "The Philistines are at war with me, and God has left me and won't reply by prophets or dreams. So I have called for you to tell me what to do."

¹⁶But Samuel replied, "Why ask me, since the Lord has left you and has become your enemy? ¹⁷The Lord has done just as he said he would. He has torn the kingdom from you and given it to your rival, David. ¹⁸The Lord has done this to you today because you refused to carry out his fierce anger against the Amalekites. ¹⁹What's more, the Lord will hand you and the army of Israel over to the Philistines tomorrow, and you and your sons will be here with me. The Lord will bring down the entire army of Israel in defeat."

²⁰Saul fell full length on the ground, paralyzed with fright because of Samuel's words. He was also faint with hunger, for he had eaten nothing all day and all night.

²¹When the woman saw how distraught he was, she said, "Sir, I obeyed your command at the risk of my life. ²²Now do what I say, and let me give you a little something to eat so you can regain your strength for the trip back."

²³But Saul refused. The men who were with him also urged him to eat, so he finally yielded and got up from the ground and sat on the couch.

²⁴The woman had been fattening a calf, so she hurried out and killed it. She took some flour, kneaded it into dough and baked unleavened bread. ²⁵She brought the meal to Saul and his men, and they ate it. Then they went out into the night.

28:6 Hebrew *by Urim.* 28:13 Or *gods.*

JOHN 11:1-54

A man named Lazarus was sick. He lived in Bethany with his sisters, Mary and Martha. ²This is the Mary who later poured the expensive perfume on the Lord's feet and wiped them with her hair.* Her brother, Lazarus, was sick. ³So the two sisters sent a message to Jesus telling him, "Lord, your dear friend is very sick."

⁴But when Jesus heard about it he said, "Lazarus's sickness will not end in death. No, it happened for the glory of God so that the Son of God will receive glory from this." ⁵So although Jesus loved Martha, Mary, and Lazarus, ⁶he stayed where he was for the next two days. ⁷Finally, he said to his disciples, "Let's go back to Judea."

⁸But his disciples objected. "Rabbi," they said, "only a few days ago the people* in Judea were trying to stone you. Are you going there again?"

⁹Jesus replied, "There are twelve hours of daylight every day. During the day people can walk safely. They can see because they have the light of this world. ¹⁰But at night there is danger of stumbling because they have no light."

¹¹Then he said, "Our friend Lazarus has fallen asleep, but now I will go and wake him up."

¹²The disciples said, "Lord, if he is sleeping, he will soon get better!" ¹³They thought Jesus meant Lazarus was simply sleeping, but Jesus meant Lazarus had died.

¹⁴So he told them plainly, "Lazarus is dead. ¹⁵And for your sakes, I'm glad I wasn't there, for now you will really believe. Come, let's go see him."

¹⁶Thomas, nicknamed the Twin,* said to his fellow disciples, "Let's go, too—and die with Jesus."

¹⁷When Jesus arrived at Bethany, he was told that Lazarus had already been in his grave for four days. ¹⁸Bethany was only a few miles* down the road from Jerusalem, ¹⁹and many of the people had come to console Martha and Mary in their loss. ²⁰When Martha got word that Jesus was coming, she went to meet him. But Mary stayed in the house. ²¹Martha said to Jesus, "Lord, if only you had been here, my brother would not have died. ²²But even now I know that God will give you whatever you ask."

²³Jesus told her, "Your brother will rise again."

²⁴"Yes," Martha said, "he will rise when everyone else rises, at the last day."

²⁵Jesus told her, "I am the resurrection and the life.* Anyone who believes in me will live, even after

dying. [26]Everyone who lives in me and believes in me will never ever die. Do you believe this, Martha?"

[27]"Yes, Lord," she told him. "I have always believed you are the Messiah, the Son of God, the one who has come into the world from God." [28]Then she returned to Mary. She called Mary aside from the mourners and told her, "The Teacher is here and wants to see you." [29]So Mary immediately went to him.

[30]Jesus had stayed outside the village, at the place where Martha met him. [31]When the people who were at the house consoling Mary saw her leave so hastily, they assumed she was going to Lazarus's grave to weep. So they followed her there. [32]When Mary arrived and saw Jesus, she fell at his feet and said, "Lord, if only you had been here, my brother would not have died."

[33]When Jesus saw her weeping and saw the other people wailing with her, a deep anger welled up within him,* and he was deeply troubled. [34]"Where have you put him?" he asked them.

They told him, "Lord, come and see." [35]Then Jesus wept. [36]The people who were standing nearby said, "See how much he loved him!" [37]But some said, "This man healed a blind man. Couldn't he have kept Lazarus from dying?"

[38]Jesus was still angry as he arrived at the tomb, a cave with a stone rolled across its entrance. [39]"Roll the stone aside," Jesus told them.

But Martha, the dead man's sister, protested, "Lord, he has been dead for four days. The smell will be terrible."

[40]Jesus responded, "Didn't I tell you that you would see God's glory if you believe?" [41]So they rolled the stone aside. Then Jesus looked up to heaven and said, "Father, thank you for hearing me. [42]You always hear me, but I said it out loud for the sake of all these people standing here, so that they will believe you sent me." [43]Then Jesus shouted, "Lazarus, come out!" [44]And the dead man came out, his hands and feet bound in graveclothes, his face wrapped in a headcloth.

Jesus told them, "Unwrap him and let him go!"

[45]Many of the people who were with Mary believed in Jesus when they saw this happen. [46]But some went to the Pharisees and told them what Jesus had done. [47]Then the leading priests and Pharisees called the high council* together. "What are we going to do?" they asked each other. "This man certainly performs many miraculous signs. [48]If we allow him to go on like this, soon everyone will believe in him. Then the Roman army will come and destroy both our Temple* and our nation."

[49]Caiaphas, who was high priest at that time,* said, "You don't know what you're talking about! [50]You don't realize that it's better for you that one man should die for the people than for the whole nation to be destroyed."

[51]He did not say this on his own; as high priest at that time he was led to prophesy that Jesus would die for the entire nation. [52]And not only for that nation, but to bring together and unite all the children of God scattered around the world.

[53]So from that time on, the Jewish leaders began to plot Jesus' death. [54]As a result, Jesus stopped his public ministry among the people and left Jerusalem. He went to a place near the wilderness, to the village of Ephraim, and stayed there with his disciples.

11:2 This incident is recorded in chapter 12.   11:8 Greek *Jewish people;* also in 11:19, 31, 33, 36, 45, 54.
11:16 Greek *Thomas, who was called Didymus.*
11:18 Greek *was about 15 stadia* (about 2.8 kilometers).
11:25 Some manuscripts do not include *and the life.*
11:33 Or *he was angry in his spirit.*   11:47 Greek *the Sanhedrin.*   11:48 Or *our position;* Greek reads *our place.*   11:49 Greek *that year;* also in 11:51.

PSALM 117:1-2

Praise the LORD, all you nations.
    Praise him, all you people of the earth.
[2] For he loves us with unfailing love;
    the LORD's faithfulness endures forever.

Praise the LORD!

PROVERBS 15:22-23

Plans go wrong for lack of advice; many advisers bring success. ☐ Everyone enjoys a fitting reply; it is wonderful to say the right thing at the right time!

MAY
21

1 SAMUEL 29:1–31:13

The entire Philistine army now mobilized at Aphek, and the Israelites camped at the spring in Jezreel. 2As the Philistine rulers were leading out their troops in groups of hundreds and thousands, David and his men marched at the rear with King Achish. 3But the Philistine commanders demanded, "What are these Hebrews doing here?"

And Achish told them, "This is David, the servant of King Saul of Israel. He's been with me for years, and I've never found a single fault in him from the day he arrived until today."

4But the Philistine commanders were angry. "Send him back to the town you've given him!" they demanded. "He can't go into the battle with us. What if he turns against us in battle and becomes our adversary? Is there any better way for him to reconcile himself with his master than by handing our heads over to him? 5Isn't this the same David about whom the women of Israel sing in their dances,

'Saul has killed his thousands,
    and David his ten thousands'?"

6So Achish finally summoned David and said to him, "I swear by the LORD that you have been a trustworthy ally. I think you should go with me into battle, for I've never found a single flaw in you from the day you arrived until today. But the other Philistine rulers won't

hear of it. 7Please don't upset them, but go back quietly."

8"What have I done to deserve this treatment?" David demanded. "What have you ever found in your servant, that I can't go and fight the enemies of my lord the king?"

9But Achish insisted, "As far as I'm concerned, you're as perfect as an angel of God. But the Philistine commanders are afraid to have you with them in the battle. 10Now get up early in the morning, and leave with your men as soon as it gets light."

11So David and his men headed back into the land of the Philistines, while the Philistine army went on to Jezreel.

30:1THREE days later, when David and his men arrived home at their town of Ziklag, they found that the Amalekites had made a raid into the Negev and Ziklag; they had crushed Ziklag and burned it to the ground. 2They had carried off the women and children and everyone else but without killing anyone.

3When David and his men saw the ruins and realized what had happened to their families, 4they wept until they could weep no more. 5David's two wives, Ahinoam from Jezreel and Abigail, the widow of Nabal from Carmel, were among those captured. 6David was now in great danger because all his men were very bitter about losing their sons and daughters, and they began to talk of stoning him. But David found strength in the LORD his God.

7Then he said to Abiathar the priest, "Bring me the ephod!" So Abiathar brought it. 8Then David asked the LORD, "Should I chase after this band of raiders? Will I catch them?"

And the LORD told him, "Yes, go after them. You will surely recover everything that was taken from you!"

9So David and his 600 men set out, and they came to the brook Besor. 10But 200 of the men were too exhausted to cross the brook, so David continued the pursuit with 400 men.

11Along the way they found an

Egyptian man in a field and brought him to David. They gave him some bread to eat and water to drink. ¹²They also gave him part of a fig cake and two clusters of raisins, for he hadn't had anything to eat or drink for three days and nights. Before long his strength returned.

¹³"To whom do you belong, and where do you come from?" David asked him.

"I am an Egyptian—the slave of an Amalekite," he replied. "My master abandoned me three days ago because I was sick. ¹⁴We were on our way back from raiding the Kerethites in the Negev, the territory of Judah, and the land of Caleb, and we had just burned Ziklag."

¹⁵"Will you lead me to this band of raiders?" David asked.

The young man replied, "If you take an oath in God's name that you will not kill me or give me back to my master, then I will guide you to them."

¹⁶So he led David to them, and they found the Amalekites spread out across the fields, eating and drinking and dancing with joy because of the vast amount of plunder they had taken from the Philistines and the land of Judah. ¹⁷David and his men rushed in among them and slaughtered them throughout that night and the entire next day until evening. None of the Amalekites escaped except 400 young men who fled on camels. ¹⁸David got back everything the Amalekites had taken, and he rescued his two wives. ¹⁹Nothing was missing: small or great, son or daughter, nor anything else that had been taken. David brought everything back. ²⁰He also recovered all the flocks and herds, and his men drove them ahead of the other livestock. "This plunder belongs to David!" they said.

²¹Then David returned to the brook Besor and met up with the 200 men who had been left behind because they were too exhausted to go with him. They went out to meet David and his men, and David greeted them joyfully. ²²But some evil troublemakers among David's men said, "They didn't go with

us, so they can't have any of the plunder we recovered. Give them their wives and children, and tell them to be gone."

²³But David said, "No, my brothers! Don't be selfish with what the LORD has given us. He has kept us safe and helped us defeat the band of raiders that attacked us. ²⁴Who will listen when you talk like this? We share and share alike—those who go to battle and those who guard the equipment." ²⁵From then on David made this a decree and regulation for Israel, and it is still followed today.

²⁶When he arrived at Ziklag, David sent part of the plunder to the elders of Judah, who were his friends. "Here is a present for you, taken from the LORD's enemies," he said.

²⁷The gifts were sent to the people of the following towns David had visited: Bethel, Ramoth-negev, Jattir, ²⁸Aroer, Siphmoth, Eshtemoa, ²⁹Racal,* the towns of the Jerahmeelites, the towns of the Kenites, ³⁰Hormah, Bor-ashan, Athach, ³¹Hebron, and all the other places David and his men had visited.

³¹:¹Now the Philistines attacked Israel, and the men of Israel fled before them. Many were slaughtered on the slopes of Mount Gilboa. ²The Philistines closed in on Saul and his sons, and they killed three of his sons—Jonathan, Abinadab, and Malkishua. ³The fighting grew very fierce around Saul, and the Philistine archers caught up with him and wounded him severely.

⁴Saul groaned to his armor bearer, "Take your sword and kill me before these pagan Philistines come to run me through and taunt and torture me."

But his armor bearer was afraid and would not do it. So Saul took his own sword and fell on it. ⁵When his armor bearer realized that Saul was dead, he fell on his own sword and died beside the king. ⁶So Saul, his three sons, his armor bearer, and his troops all died together that same day.

⁷When the Israelites on the other side of the Jezreel Valley and beyond

the Jordan saw that the Israelite army had fled and that Saul and his sons were dead, they abandoned their towns and fled. So the Philistines moved in and occupied their towns.

⁸The next day, when the Philistines went out to strip the dead, they found the bodies of Saul and his three sons on Mount Gilboa. ⁹So they cut off Saul's head and stripped off his armor. Then they proclaimed the good news of Saul's death in their pagan temple and to the people throughout the land of Philistia. ¹⁰They placed his armor in the temple of the Ashtoreths, and they fastened his body to the wall of the city of Beth-shan.

¹¹But when the people of Jabesh-gilead heard what the Philistines had done to Saul, ¹²all their mighty warriors traveled through the night to Beth-shan and took the bodies of Saul and his sons down from the wall. They brought them to Jabesh, where they burned the bodies. ¹³Then they took their bones and buried them beneath the tamarisk tree at Jabesh, and they fasted for seven days.

30:29 Greek version reads *Carmel.*

JOHN 11:55–12:19

It was now almost time for the Jewish Passover celebration, and many people from all over the country arrived in Jerusalem several days early so they could go through the purification ceremony before Passover began. ⁵⁶They kept looking for Jesus, but as they stood around in the Temple, they said to each other, "What do you think? He won't come for Passover, will he?" ⁵⁷Meanwhile, the leading priests and Pharisees had publicly ordered that anyone seeing Jesus must report it immediately so they could arrest him.

12:1Six days before the Passover celebration began, Jesus arrived in Bethany, the home of Lazarus—the man he had raised from the dead. ²A dinner was prepared in Jesus' honor. Martha served, and Lazarus was among those who ate* with him. ³Then Mary took a twelve-ounce jar* of expensive perfume made from essence

of nard, and she anointed Jesus' feet with it, wiping his feet with her hair. The house was filled with the fragrance.

⁴But Judas Iscariot, the disciple who would soon betray him, said, ⁵"That perfume was worth a year's wages.* It should have been sold and the money given to the poor." ⁶Not that he cared for the poor—he was a thief, and since he was in charge of the disciples' money, he often stole some for himself.

⁷Jesus replied, "Leave her alone. She did this in preparation for my burial. ⁸You will always have the poor among you, but you will not always have me."

⁹When all the people* heard of Jesus' arrival, they flocked to see him and also to see Lazarus, the man Jesus had raised from the dead. ¹⁰Then the leading priests decided to kill Lazarus, too, ¹¹for it was because of him that many of the people had deserted them* and believed in Jesus.

¹²The next day, the news that Jesus was on the way to Jerusalem swept through the city. A large crowd of Passover visitors ¹³took palm branches and went down the road to meet him. They shouted,

"Praise God!*
Blessings on the one who comes in
      the name of the LORD!
Hail to the King of Israel!"*

¹⁴Jesus found a young donkey and rode on it, fulfilling the prophecy that said:

¹⁵ "Don't be afraid, people
      of Jerusalem.*
Look, your King is coming,
      riding on a donkey's colt."*

¹⁶His disciples didn't understand at the time that this was a fulfillment of prophecy. But after Jesus entered into his glory, they remembered what had happened and realized that these things had been written about him.

¹⁷Many in the crowd had seen Jesus call Lazarus from the tomb, raising him from the dead, and they were telling others* about it. ¹⁸That was the reason so

many went out to meet him—because they had heard about this miraculous sign. ¹⁹Then the Pharisees said to each other, "There's nothing we can do. Look, everyone* has gone after him!"

12:2 Or *who reclined.*   12:3 Greek *took 1 litra* [327 grams].   12:5 Greek *worth 300 denarii.* A denarius was equivalent to a laborer's full day's wage.   12:9 Greek *Jewish people;* also in 12:11.   12:11 Or *had deserted their traditions;* Greek reads *had deserted.*   12:13a Greek *Hosanna,* an exclamation of praise adapted from a Hebrew expression that means "save now."   12:13b Ps 118:25-26; Zeph 3:15.   12:15a Greek *daughter of Zion.* 12:15b Zech 9:9.   12:17 Greek *were testifying.* 12:19 Greek *the world.*

PSALM 118:1-18

Give thanks to the LORD, for
    he is good!
    His faithful love endures forever.

² Let all Israel repeat:
    "His faithful love endures
        forever."
³ Let Aaron's descendants, the priests,
        repeat:
    "His faithful love endures
        forever."
⁴ Let all who fear the LORD repeat:
    "His faithful love endures forever."

⁵ In my distress I prayed to the LORD,
    and the LORD answered me and
        set me free.
⁶ The LORD is for me, so I will have
        no fear.
    What can mere people do to me?
⁷ Yes, the LORD is for me; he will
        help me.
    I will look in triumph at those
        who hate me.
⁸ **It is better to take refuge**
        in the LORD
    than to trust in people.
⁹ **It is better to take refuge**
        in the LORD
    than to trust in princes.

¹⁰ Though hostile nations surrounded
        me,
    I destroyed them all with the
        authority of the LORD.
¹¹ Yes, they surrounded and
        attacked me,
    but I destroyed them all with the
        authority of the LORD.

¹² They swarmed around me like bees;
    they blazed against me like a
        crackling fire.
    But I destroyed them all with the
        authority of the LORD.
¹³ My enemies did their best to kill
        me,
    but the LORD rescued me.
¹⁴ The LORD is my strength and
        my song;
    he has given me victory.
¹⁵ Songs of joy and victory are sung
        in the camp of the godly.
    The strong right arm of the LORD
        has done glorious things!
¹⁶ The strong right arm of the LORD
        is raised in triumph.
    The strong right arm of the LORD
        has done glorious things!
¹⁷ I will not die; instead, I will live
        to tell what the LORD has done.
¹⁸ The LORD has punished me
        severely,
    but he did not let me die.

PROVERBS 15:24-26

The path of life leads upward for the wise; they leave the grave* behind. □ The LORD tears down the house of the proud, but he protects the property of widows. □ The LORD detests evil plans, but he delights in pure words.

15:24 Hebrew *Sheol.*

MAY 22

2 SAMUEL 1:1–2:11

After the death of Saul, David returned from his victory over the Amalekites and spent two days in Ziklag. ²On the third day a man arrived from Saul's army camp. He had torn his clothes and put dirt on his head to show that he was in mourning. He fell to the ground before David in deep respect.

³"Where have you come from?" David asked.

"I escaped from the Israelite camp," the man replied.

⁴"What happened?" David demanded. "Tell me how the battle went."

The man replied, "Our entire army fled from the battle. Many of the men are dead, and Saul and his son Jonathan are also dead."

⁵"How do you know Saul and Jonathan are dead?" David demanded of the young man.

⁶The man answered, "I happened to be on Mount Gilboa, and there was Saul leaning on his spear with the enemy chariots and charioteers closing in on him. ⁷When he turned and saw me, he cried out for me to come to him. 'How can I help?' I asked him.

⁸"He responded, 'Who are you?'

"'I am an Amalekite,' I told him.

⁹"Then he begged me, 'Come over here and put me out of my misery, for I am in terrible pain and want to die.'

¹⁰"So I killed him," the Amalekite told David, "for I knew he couldn't live. Then I took his crown and his armband, and I have brought them here to you, my lord."

¹¹David and his men tore their clothes in sorrow when they heard the news. ¹²They mourned and wept and fasted all day for Saul and his son Jonathan, and for the LORD's army and the nation of Israel, because they had died by the sword that day.

¹³Then David said to the young man who had brought the news, "Where are you from?"

And he replied, "I am a foreigner, an Amalekite, who lives in your land."

¹⁴"Why were you not afraid to kill the LORD's anointed one?" David asked.

¹⁵Then David said to one of his men, "Kill him!" So the man thrust his sword into the Amalekite and killed him. ¹⁶"You have condemned yourself," David said, "for you yourself confessed that you killed the LORD's anointed one."

¹⁷Then David composed a funeral song for Saul and Jonathan, ¹⁸and he commanded that it be taught to the people of Judah. It is known as the Song of the Bow, and it is recorded in *The Book of Jashar*.*

¹⁹ Your pride and joy, O Israel, lies
     dead on the hills!
  Oh, how the mighty heroes
     have fallen!
²⁰ Don't announce the news in Gath,
     don't proclaim it in the streets
        of Ashkelon,
  or the daughters of the Philistines
     will rejoice
  and the pagans will laugh in
     triumph.

²¹ O mountains of Gilboa,
     let there be no dew or rain
        upon you,
     nor fruitful fields producing
        offerings of grain.*
  For there the shield of the mighty
     heroes was defiled;
  the shield of Saul will no longer
     be anointed with oil.
²² The bow of Jonathan was powerful,
     and the sword of Saul did its
        mighty work.
  They shed the blood of their
     enemies
  and pierced the bodies
     of mighty heroes.

²³ How beloved and gracious were
     Saul and Jonathan!
  They were together in life and
     in death.
  They were swifter than eagles,
     stronger than lions.
²⁴ O women of Israel, weep for Saul,
  for he dressed you in luxurious
     scarlet clothing,
  in garments decorated
     with gold.

²⁵ Oh, how the mighty heroes have
     fallen in battle!
  Jonathan lies dead on the hills.
²⁶ How I weep for you, my brother
     Jonathan!
  Oh, how much I loved you!
  And your love for me was deep,
     deeper than the love of women!

²⁷ Oh, how the mighty heroes
      have fallen!
    Stripped of their weapons,
      they lie dead.

²:¹AFTER this, David asked the LORD, "Should I move back to one of the towns of Judah?"

"Yes," the LORD replied.

Then David asked, "Which town should I go to?"

"To Hebron," the LORD answered.

²David's two wives were Ahinoam from Jezreel and Abigail, the widow of Nabal from Carmel. So David and his wives ³and his men and their families all moved to Judah, and they settled in the villages near Hebron. ⁴Then the men of Judah came to David and crowned him king over the people of Judah.

When David heard that the men of Jabesh-gilead had buried Saul, ⁵he sent them this message: "May the LORD bless you for being so loyal to your master Saul and giving him a decent burial. ⁶May the LORD be loyal to you in return and reward you with his unfailing love! And I, too, will reward you for what you have done. ⁷Now that Saul is dead, I ask you to be my strong and loyal subjects like the people of Judah, who have anointed me as their new king."

⁸But Abner son of Ner, the commander of Saul's army, had already gone to Mahanaim with Saul's son Ishbosheth.* ⁹There he proclaimed Ishbosheth king over Gilead, Jezreel, Ephraim, Benjamin, the land of the Ashurites, and all the rest of Israel.

¹⁰Ishbosheth, Saul's son, was forty years old when he became king, and he ruled from Mahanaim for two years. Meanwhile, the people of Judah remained loyal to David. ¹¹David made Hebron his capital, and he ruled as king of Judah for seven and a half years.

1:18 Or *The Book of the Upright.*   1:21 The meaning of the Hebrew is uncertain.   2:8 *Ishbosheth* is another name for Esh-baal.

JOHN 12:20-50

Some Greeks who had come to Jerusalem for the Passover celebration ²¹paid a visit to Philip, who was from Bethsaida in Galilee. They said, "Sir, we want to meet Jesus." ²²Philip told Andrew about it, and they went together to ask Jesus.

²³**Jesus replied, "Now the time has come for the Son of Man* to enter into his glory. ²⁴I tell you the truth, unless a kernel of wheat is planted in the soil and dies, it remains alone. But its death will produce many new kernels—a plentiful harvest of new lives.** ²⁵Those who love their life in this world will lose it. Those who care nothing for their life in this world will keep it for eternity. ²⁶Anyone who wants to be my disciple must follow me, because my servants must be where I am. And the Father will honor anyone who serves me.

²⁷"Now my soul is deeply troubled. Should I pray, 'Father, save me from this hour'? But this is the very reason I came! ²⁸Father, bring glory to your name."

Then a voice spoke from heaven, saying, "I have already brought glory to my name, and I will do so again." ²⁹When the crowd heard the voice, some thought it was thunder, while others declared an angel had spoken to him.

³⁰Then Jesus told them, "The voice was for your benefit, not mine. ³¹The time for judging this world has come, when Satan, the ruler of this world, will be cast out. ³²And when I am lifted up from the earth, I will draw everyone to myself." ³³He said this to indicate how he was going to die.

³⁴The crowd responded, "We understood from Scripture* that the Messiah would live forever. How can you say the Son of Man will die? Just who is this Son of Man, anyway?"

³⁵Jesus replied, "My light will shine for you just a little longer. Walk in the light while you can, so the darkness will not overtake you. Those who walk in the darkness cannot see where they are going. ³⁶Put your trust in the light while there is still time; then you will become children of the light."

After saying these things, Jesus went away and was hidden from them.

³⁷ But despite all the miraculous signs Jesus had done, most of the people still did not believe in him. ³⁸This is exactly what Isaiah the prophet had predicted:

"LORD, who has believed our
    message?
To whom has the LORD revealed
    his powerful arm?"*

³⁹ But the people couldn't believe, for as Isaiah also said,

⁴⁰ "The Lord has blinded their eyes
    and hardened their hearts—
so that their eyes cannot see,
    and their hearts cannot
        understand,
and they cannot turn to me
    and have me heal them."*

⁴¹Isaiah was referring to Jesus when he said this, because he saw the future and spoke of the Messiah's glory. ⁴²Many people did believe in him, however, including some of the Jewish leaders. But they wouldn't admit it for fear that the Pharisees would expel them from the synagogue. ⁴³For they loved human praise more than the praise of God.

⁴⁴Jesus shouted to the crowds, "If you trust me, you are trusting not only me, but also God who sent me. ⁴⁵For when you see me, you are seeing the one who sent me. ⁴⁶I have come as a light to shine in this dark world, so that all who put their trust in me will no longer remain in the dark. ⁴⁷I will not judge those who hear me but don't obey me, for I have come to save the world and not to judge it. ⁴⁸But all who reject me and my message will be judged on the day of judgment by the truth I have spoken. ⁴⁹I don't speak on my own authority. The Father who sent me has commanded me what to say and how to say it. ⁵⁰And I know his commands lead to eternal life; so I say whatever the Father tells me to say."

12:23 "Son of Man" is a title Jesus used for himself.
12:34 Greek *from the law.*   12:38 Isa 53:1.
12:40 Isa 6:10.

PSALM 118:19-29

Open for me the gates where the
    righteous enter,
and I will go in and thank
    the LORD.
²⁰ These gates lead to the presence
    of the LORD,
and the godly enter there.
²¹ I thank you for answering my prayer
    and giving me victory!

²² The stone that the builders rejected
    has now become the cornerstone.
²³ This is the LORD's doing,
    and it is wonderful to see.
²⁴ This is the day the LORD has made.
    We will rejoice and be glad in it.
²⁵ Please, LORD, please save us.
    Please, LORD, please give us
        success.
²⁶ Bless the one who comes in the
    name of the LORD.
    We bless you from the house
        of the LORD.
²⁷ The LORD is God, shining upon us.
    Take the sacrifice and bind it
        with cords on the altar.
²⁸ You are my God, and I will praise
    you!
    You are my God, and I will exalt
        you!

²⁹ Give thanks to the LORD, for
    he is good!
    His faithful love endures
        forever.

PROVERBS 15:27-28

Greed brings grief to the whole family, but those who hate bribes will live. □The heart of the godly thinks carefully before speaking; the mouth of the wicked overflows with evil words.

MAY 23

2 SAMUEL 2:12–3:39

One day Abner led Ishbosheth's troops from Mahanaim to Gibeon. ¹³About the same time, Joab son of Zeruiah led David's troops out and met them at the pool of Gibeon. The two groups sat down there, facing each other from opposite sides of the pool.

¹⁴Then Abner suggested to Joab, "Let's have a few of our warriors fight hand to hand here in front of us."

"All right," Joab agreed. ¹⁵So twelve men were chosen to fight from each side—twelve men of Benjamin representing Ishbosheth son of Saul, and twelve representing David. ¹⁶Each one grabbed his opponent by the hair and thrust his sword into the other's side so that all of them died. So this place at Gibeon has been known ever since as the Field of Swords.*

¹⁷A fierce battle followed that day, and Abner and the men of Israel were defeated by the forces of David.

¹⁸Joab, Abishai, and Asahel—the three sons of Zeruiah—were among David's forces that day. Asahel could run like a gazelle, ¹⁹and he began chasing Abner. He pursued him relentlessly, not stopping for anything. ²⁰When Abner looked back and saw him coming, he called out, "Is that you, Asahel?"

"Yes, it is," he replied.

²¹"Go fight someone else!" Abner warned. "Take on one of the younger men, and strip him of his weapons." But Asahel kept right on chasing Abner.

²²Again Abner shouted to him, "Get away from here! I don't want to kill you. How could I ever face your brother Joab again?"

²³But Asahel refused to turn back, so Abner thrust the butt end of his spear through Asahel's stomach, and the spear came out through his back. He stumbled to the ground and died there.

And everyone who came by that spot stopped and stood still when they saw Asahel lying there.

²⁴When Joab and Abishai found out what had happened, they set out after Abner. The sun was just going down as they arrived at the hill of Ammah near Giah, along the road to the wilderness of Gibeon. ²⁵Abner's troops from the tribe of Benjamin regrouped there at the top of the hill to take a stand.

²⁶Abner shouted down to Joab, "Must we always be killing each other? Don't you realize that bitterness is the only result? When will you call off your men from chasing their Israelite brothers?"

²⁷Then Joab said, "God only knows what would have happened if you hadn't spoken, for we would have chased you all night if necessary." ²⁸So Joab blew the ram's horn, and his men stopped chasing the troops of Israel.

²⁹All that night Abner and his men retreated through the Jordan Valley.* They crossed the Jordan River, traveling all through the morning,* and didn't stop until they arrived at Mahanaim.

³⁰Meanwhile, Joab and his men also returned home. When Joab counted his casualties, he discovered that only 19 men were missing in addition to Asahel. ³¹But 360 of Abner's men had been killed, all from the tribe of Benjamin. ³²Joab and his men took Asahel's body to Bethlehem and buried him there in his father's tomb. Then they traveled all night and reached Hebron at daybreak.

³:¹THAT was the beginning of a long war between those who were loyal to Saul and those loyal to David. As time passed David became stronger and stronger, while Saul's dynasty became weaker and weaker.

²These are the sons who were born to David in Hebron:

The oldest was Amnon, whose mother was Ahinoam from Jezreel.
³ The second was Daniel,* whose

mother was Abigail, the widow of Nabal from Carmel.

The third was Absalom, whose mother was Maacah, the daughter of Talmai, king of Geshur.

⁴ The fourth was Adonijah, whose mother was Haggith.

The fifth was Shephatiah, whose mother was Abital.

⁵ The sixth was Ithream, whose mother was Eglah, David's wife.

These sons were all born to David in Hebron.

⁶As the war between the house of Saul and the house of David went on, Abner became a powerful leader among those loyal to Saul. ⁷One day Ishbosheth,* Saul's son, accused Abner of sleeping with one of his father's concubines, a woman named Rizpah, daughter of Aiah.

⁸Abner was furious. "Am I some Judean dog to be kicked around like this?" he shouted. "After all I have done for your father, Saul, and his family and friends by not handing you over to David, is this my reward—that you find fault with me about this woman? ⁹May God strike me and even kill me if I don't do everything I can to help David get what the Lord has promised him! ¹⁰I'm going to take Saul's kingdom and give it to David. I will establish the throne of David over Israel as well as Judah, all the way from Dan in the north to Beersheba in the south." ¹¹Ishbosheth didn't dare say another word because he was afraid of what Abner might do.

¹²Then Abner sent messengers to David, saying, "Doesn't the entire land belong to you? Make a solemn pact with me, and I will help turn over all of Israel to you."

¹³"All right," David replied, "but I will not negotiate with you unless you bring back my wife Michal, Saul's daughter, when you come."

¹⁴David then sent this message to Ishbosheth, Saul's son: "Give me back my wife Michal, for I bought her with the lives* of 100 Philistines."

¹⁵So Ishbosheth took Michal away from her husband, Palti* son of Laish. ¹⁶Palti followed along behind her as far as Bahurim, weeping as he went. Then Abner told him, "Go back home!" So Palti returned.

¹⁷Meanwhile, Abner had consulted with the elders of Israel. "For some time now," he told them, "you have wanted to make David your king. ¹⁸Now is the time! For the Lord has said, 'I have chosen David to save my people Israel from the hands of the Philistines and from all their other enemies.'" ¹⁹Abner also spoke with the men of Benjamin. Then he went to Hebron to tell David that all the people of Israel and Benjamin had agreed to support him.

²⁰When Abner and twenty of his men came to Hebron, David entertained them with a great feast. ²¹Then Abner said to David, "Let me go and call an assembly of all Israel to support my lord the king. They will make a covenant with you to make you their king, and you will rule over everything your heart desires." So David sent Abner safely on his way.

²²But just after David had sent Abner away in safety, Joab and some of David's troops returned from a raid, bringing much plunder with them. ²³When Joab arrived, he was told that Abner had just been there visiting the king and had been sent away in safety.

²⁴Joab rushed to the king and demanded, "What have you done? What do you mean by letting Abner get away? ²⁵You know perfectly well that he came to spy on you and find out everything you're doing!"

²⁶Joab then left David and sent messengers to catch up with Abner, asking him to return. They found him at the well of Sirah and brought him back, though David knew nothing about it. ²⁷When Abner arrived back at Hebron, Joab took him aside at the gateway as if to speak with him privately. But then he stabbed Abner in the stomach and killed him in revenge for killing his brother Asahel.

²⁸When David heard about it, he declared, "I vow by the Lord that I and my kingdom are forever innocent of this

crime against Abner son of Ner. ²⁹Joab and his family are the guilty ones. May the family of Joab be cursed in every generation with a man who has open sores or leprosy* or who walks on crutches* or dies by the sword or begs for food!"

³⁰So Joab and his brother Abishai killed Abner because Abner had killed their brother Asahel at the battle of Gibeon.

³¹Then David said to Joab and all those who were with him, "Tear your clothes and put on burlap. Mourn for Abner." And King David himself walked behind the procession to the grave. ³²They buried Abner in Hebron, and the king and all the people wept at his graveside. ³³Then the king sang this funeral song for Abner:

"Should Abner have died as
    fools die?
³⁴ Your hands were not bound;
    your feet were not chained.
No, you were murdered—
    the victim of a wicked plot."

All the people wept again for Abner. ³⁵David had refused to eat anything on the day of the funeral, and now everyone begged him to eat. But David had made a vow, saying, "May God strike me and even kill me if I eat anything before sundown."

³⁶This pleased the people very much. In fact, everything the king did pleased them! ³⁷So everyone in Judah and all Israel understood that David was not responsible for Abner's murder.

³⁸Then King David said to his officials, "Don't you realize that a great commander has fallen today in Israel? ³⁹And even though I am the anointed king, these two sons of Zeruiah—Joab and Abishai—are too strong for me to control. So may the LORD repay these evil men for their evil deeds."

2:16 Hebrew *Helkath-hazzurim.*   2:29a Hebrew *the Arabah.*   2:29b Or *continued on through the Bithron.* The meaning of the Hebrew is uncertain.   3:3 As in parallel text at 1 Chr 3:1 (see also Greek version, which reads *Daluia,* and Dead Sea Scrolls, which read *Dan[iel]);* Hebrew reads *Kileab.*   3:7 *Ishbosheth* is another name for Esh-baal.   3:14 Hebrew *the foreskins.*   3:15 As in 1 Sam 25:44; Hebrew reads *Paltiel,* a variant spelling of Palti.   3:29a Or

or a contagious skin disease. The Hebrew word used here can describe various skin diseases.   3:29b Or *who is effeminate;* Hebrew reads *who handles a spindle.*

JOHN 13:1-30

Before the Passover celebration, Jesus knew that his hour had come to leave this world and return to his Father. He had loved his disciples during his ministry on earth, and now he loved them to the very end.* ²It was time for supper, and the devil had already prompted Judas,* son of Simon Iscariot, to betray Jesus. ³Jesus knew that the Father had given him authority over everything and that he had come from God and would return to God. ⁴So he got up from the table, took off his robe, wrapped a towel around his waist, ⁵and poured water into a basin. Then he began to wash the disciples' feet, drying them with the towel he had around him.

⁶When Jesus came to Simon Peter, Peter said to him, "Lord, are you going to wash my feet?"

⁷Jesus replied, "You don't understand now what I am doing, but someday you will."

⁸"No," Peter protested, "you will never ever wash my feet!"

Jesus replied, "Unless I wash you, you won't belong to me."

⁹Simon Peter exclaimed, "Then wash my hands and head as well, Lord, not just my feet!"

¹⁰Jesus replied, "A person who has bathed all over does not need to wash, except for the feet,* to be entirely clean. And you disciples are clean, but not all of you." ¹¹For Jesus knew who would betray him. That is what he meant when he said, "Not all of you are clean."

¹²After washing their feet, he put on his robe again and sat down and asked, "Do you understand what I was doing? ¹³You call me 'Teacher' and 'Lord,' and you are right, because that's what I am. ¹⁴**And since I, your Lord and Teacher, have washed your feet, you ought to wash each other's feet. ¹⁵I have given you an example to follow. Do as I have done to you.** ¹⁶I tell you the truth, slaves are not greater than their master.

Nor is the messenger more important than the one who sends the message. 17Now that you know these things, God will bless you for doing them.

18"I am not saying these things to all of you; I know the ones I have chosen. But this fulfills the Scripture that says, 'The one who eats my food has turned against me.'* 19I tell you this beforehand, so that when it happens you will believe that I Am the Messiah.* 20I tell you the truth, anyone who welcomes my messenger is welcoming me, and anyone who welcomes me is welcoming the Father who sent me."

21Now Jesus was deeply troubled,* and he exclaimed, "I tell you the truth, one of you will betray me!"

22The disciples looked at each other, wondering whom he could mean. 23The disciple Jesus loved was sitting next to Jesus at the table.* 24Simon Peter motioned to him to ask, "Who's he talking about?" 25So that disciple leaned over to Jesus and asked, "Lord, who is it?"

26Jesus responded, "It is the one to whom I give the bread I dip in the bowl." And when he had dipped it, he gave it to Judas, son of Simon Iscariot. 27When Judas had eaten the bread, Satan entered into him. Then Jesus told him, "Hurry and do what you're going to do." 28None of the others at the table knew what Jesus meant. 29Since Judas was their treasurer, some thought Jesus was telling him to go and pay for the food or to give some money to the poor. 30So Judas left at once, going out into the night.

13:1 Or *he showed them the full extent of his love.* 13:2 Or *the devil had already intended for Judas.* 13:10 Some manuscripts do not include *except for the feet.* 13:18 Ps 41:9. 13:19 Or *that the 'I Am' has come;* or *that I am the Lord;* Greek reads *that I am.* See Exod 3:14. 13:21 Greek *was troubled in his spirit.* 13:23 Greek *was reclining on Jesus' bosom.* The "disciple Jesus loved" was probably John.

PSALM 119:1-16

Aleph*

1 **J**oyful are people of integrity,
    who follow the instructions
    of the Lord.
2 Joyful are those who obey his laws

and search for him with
    all their hearts.
3 They do not compromise with evil,
    and they walk only in his paths.
4 You have charged us
    to keep your commandments
    carefully.
5 Oh, that my actions would
    consistently
    reflect your decrees!
6 Then I will not be ashamed
    when I compare my life with
    your commands.
7 As I learn your righteous
    regulations,
    I will thank you by living
    as I should!
8 I will obey your decrees.
    Please don't give up on me!

Beth
9 How can a young person stay
    pure?
    By obeying your word.
10 I have tried hard to find you—
    don't let me wander from your
    commands.
11 I have hidden your word in my heart,
    that I might not sin against you.
12 I praise you, O Lord;
    teach me your decrees.
13 I have recited aloud
    all the regulations you have
    given us.
14 I have rejoiced in your laws
    as much as in riches.
15 I will study your commandments
    and reflect on your ways.
16 I will delight in your decrees
    and not forget your word.

119 This psalm is a Hebrew acrostic poem; there are twenty-two stanzas, one for each successive letter of the Hebrew alphabet. Each of the eight verses within each stanza begins with the Hebrew letter named in its heading.

PROVERBS 15:29-30

The Lord is far from the wicked, but he hears the prayers of the righteous. □A cheerful look brings joy to the heart; good news makes for good health.

MAY 24

2 SAMUEL 4:1–6:23

When Ishbosheth,* Saul's son, heard about Abner's death at Hebron, he lost all courage, and all Israel became paralyzed with fear. ²Now there were two brothers, Baanah and Recab, who were captains of Ishbosheth's raiding parties. They were sons of Rimmon, a member of the tribe of Benjamin who lived in Beeroth. The town of Beeroth is now part of Benjamin's territory ³because the original people of Beeroth fled to Gittaim, where they still live as foreigners.

⁴(Saul's son Jonathan had a son named Mephibosheth,* who was crippled as a child. He was five years old when the report came from Jezreel that Saul and Jonathan had been killed in battle. When the child's nurse heard the news, she picked him up and fled. But as she hurried away, she dropped him, and he became crippled.)

⁵One day Recab and Baanah, the sons of Rimmon from Beeroth, went to Ishbosheth's house around noon as he was taking his midday rest. ⁶The doorkeeper, who had been sifting wheat, became drowsy and fell asleep. So Recab and Baanah slipped past her.* ⁷They went into the house and found Ishbosheth sleeping on his bed. They struck and killed him and cut off his head. Then, taking his head with them, they fled across the Jordan Valley* through the night. ⁸When they arrived at Hebron, they presented Ishbosheth's head to David. "Look!" they exclaimed to the king. "Here is the head of Ishbosheth, the son of your enemy Saul who tried to kill you. Today the LORD has given my lord the king revenge on Saul and his entire family!"

⁹But David said to Recab and Baanah, "The LORD, who saves me from all my enemies, is my witness. ¹⁰Someone once told me, 'Saul is dead,' thinking he was bringing me good news. But I seized him and killed him at Ziklag. That's the reward I gave him for his news! ¹¹How much more should I reward evil men who have killed an innocent man in his own house and on his own bed? Shouldn't I hold you responsible for his blood and rid the earth of you?"

¹²So David ordered his young men to kill them, and they did. They cut off their hands and feet and hung their bodies beside the pool in Hebron. Then they took Ishbosheth's head and buried it in Abner's tomb in Hebron.

⁵:¹THEN all the tribes of Israel went to David at Hebron and told him, "We are your own flesh and blood. ²In the past,* when Saul was our king, you were the one who really led the forces of Israel. And the LORD told you, 'You will be the shepherd of my people Israel. You will be Israel's leader.'"

³So there at Hebron, King David made a covenant before the LORD with all the elders of Israel. And they anointed him king of Israel.

⁴David was thirty years old when he began to reign, and he reigned forty years in all. ⁵He had reigned over Judah from Hebron for seven years and six months, and from Jerusalem he reigned over all Israel and Judah for thirty-three years.

⁶David then led his men to Jerusalem to fight against the Jebusites, the original inhabitants of the land who were living there. The Jebusites taunted David, saying, "You'll never get in here! Even the blind and lame could keep you out!" For the Jebusites thought they were safe. ⁷But David captured the fortress of Zion, which is now called the City of David.

⁸On the day of the attack, David said to his troops, "I hate those 'lame' and 'blind' Jebusites.* Whoever attacks them should strike by going into the city through the water tunnel.*" That is the origin of the saying, "The blind and the lame may not enter the house."*

⁹So David made the fortress his home, and he called it the City of David. He extended the city, starting at the supporting terraces* and working inward. ¹⁰And David became more and more powerful, because the LORD God of Heaven's Armies was with him.

¹¹Then King Hiram of Tyre sent messengers to David, along with cedar timber and carpenters and stonemasons, and they built David a palace. ¹²And David realized that the LORD had confirmed him as king over Israel and had blessed his kingdom for the sake of his people Israel.

¹³After moving from Hebron to Jerusalem, David married more concubines and wives, and they had more sons and daughters. ¹⁴These are the names of David's sons who were born in Jerusalem: Shammua, Shobab, Nathan, Solomon, ¹⁵Ibhar, Elishua, Nepheg, Japhia, ¹⁶Elishama, Eliada, and Eliphelet.

¹⁷When the Philistines heard that David had been anointed king of Israel, they mobilized all their forces to capture him. But David was told they were coming, so he went into the stronghold. ¹⁸The Philistines arrived and spread out across the valley of Rephaim. ¹⁹So David asked the LORD, "Should I go out to fight the Philistines? Will you hand them over to me?"

The LORD replied to David, "Yes, go ahead. I will certainly hand them over to you."

²⁰So David went to Baal-perazim and defeated the Philistines there. "The LORD did it!" David exclaimed. "He burst through my enemies like a raging flood!" So he named that place Baal-perazim (which means "the Lord who bursts through"). ²¹The Philistines had abandoned their idols there, so David and his men confiscated them.

²²But after a while the Philistines returned and again spread out across the valley of Rephaim. ²³And again David asked the LORD what to do. "Do not attack them straight on," the LORD replied. "Instead, circle around behind and attack them near the poplar* trees.

²⁴When you hear a sound like marching feet in the tops of the poplar trees, be on the alert! That will be the signal that the LORD is moving ahead of you to strike down the Philistine army." ²⁵So David did what the LORD commanded, and he struck down the Philistines all the way from Gibeon* to Gezer.

6:1THEN David again gathered all the elite troops in Israel, 30,000 in all. ²He led them to Baalah of Judah* to bring back the Ark of God, which bears the name of the LORD of Heaven's Armies,* who is enthroned between the cherubim. ³They placed the Ark of God on a new cart and brought it from Abinadab's house, which was on a hill. Uzzah and Ahio, Abinadab's sons, were guiding the cart as it left the house, ⁴carrying the Ark of God. Ahio walked in front of the Ark. ⁵David and all the people of Israel were celebrating before the LORD, singing songs* and playing all kinds of musical instruments—lyres, harps, tambourines, castanets, and cymbals.

⁶But when they arrived at the threshing floor of Nacon, the oxen stumbled, and Uzzah reached out his hand and steadied the Ark of God. ⁷Then the LORD's anger was aroused against Uzzah, and God struck him dead because of this.* So Uzzah died right there beside the Ark of God.

⁸David was angry because the LORD's anger had burst out against Uzzah. He named that place Perez-uzzah (which means "to burst out against Uzzah"), as it is still called today.

⁹David was now afraid of the LORD, and he asked, "How can I ever bring the Ark of the LORD back into my care?" ¹⁰So David decided not to move the Ark of the LORD into the City of David. Instead, he took it to the house of Obed-edom of Gath. ¹¹The Ark of the LORD remained there in Obed-edom's house for three months, and the LORD blessed Obed-edom and his entire household.

¹²Then King David was told, "The LORD has blessed Obed-edom's household and everything he has because of

the Ark of God." So David went there and brought the Ark of God from the house of Obed-edom to the City of David with a great celebration. [13]After the men who were carrying the Ark of the LORD had gone six steps, David sacrificed a bull and a fattened calf. [14]And David danced before the LORD with all his might, wearing a priestly garment.* [15]So David and all the people of Israel brought up the Ark of the LORD with shouts of joy and the blowing of rams' horns.

[16]But as the Ark of the LORD entered the City of David, Michal, the daughter of Saul, looked down from her window. When she saw King David leaping and dancing before the LORD, she was filled with contempt for him.

[17]They brought the Ark of the LORD and set it in its place inside the special tent David had prepared for it. And David sacrificed burnt offerings and peace offerings to the LORD. [18]When he had finished his sacrifices, David blessed the people in the name of the LORD of Heaven's Armies. [19]Then he gave to every Israelite man and woman in the crowd a loaf of bread, a cake of dates,* and a cake of raisins. Then all the people returned to their homes.

[20]When David returned home to bless his own family, Michal, the daughter of Saul, came out to meet him. She said in disgust, "How distinguished the king of Israel looked today, shamelessly exposing himself to the servant girls like any vulgar person might do!"

[21]David retorted to Michal, "I was dancing before the LORD, who chose me above your father and all his family! He appointed me as the leader of Israel, the people of the LORD, so I celebrate before the LORD. [22]Yes, and I am willing to look even more foolish than this, even to be humiliated in my own eyes! But those servant girls you mentioned will indeed think I am distinguished!" [23]So Michal, the daughter of Saul, remained childless throughout her entire life.

4:1 *Ishbosheth* is another name for Esh-baal.
4:4 *Mephibosheth* is another name for Merib-baal.   4:6 As in Greek version; Hebrew reads *So they went into the*

house pretending to fetch wheat, but they stabbed him in the stomach. Then Recab and Baanah escaped.
4:7 Hebrew *the Arabah.*   5:2 Or *For some time.*   5:8a Or *Those 'lame' and 'blind' Jebusites hate me.*   5:8b Or *with scaling hooks.* The meaning of the Hebrew is uncertain.
5:8c The meaning of this saying is uncertain.   5:9 Hebrew *the millo.* The meaning of the Hebrew is uncertain.
5:23 Or *aspen,* or *balsam;* also in 5:24. The exact identification of this tree is uncertain.   5:25 As in Greek version (see also 1 Chr 14:16); Hebrew reads *Geba.*
6:2a *Baalah of Judah* is another name for Kiriath-jearim; compare 1 Chr 13:6.   6:2b Or *the Ark of God where the Name is proclaimed—the name of the LORD of Heaven's Armies.*   6:5 As in Greek version (see also 1 Chr 13:8); Hebrew reads *before the LORD with all manner of cypress trees.*   6:7 As in Dead Sea Scrolls; Masoretic Text reads *because of his irreverence.*   6:14 Hebrew *a linen ephod.*   6:19 Or *a portion of meat.* The meaning of the Hebrew is uncertain.

JOHN 13:31–14:14

As soon as Judas left the room, Jesus said, "The time has come for the Son of Man* to enter into his glory, and God will be glorified because of him. [32]And since God receives glory because of the Son,* he will soon give glory to the Son. [33]Dear children, I will be with you only a little longer. And as I told the Jewish leaders, you will search for me, but you can't come where I am going. [34]**So now I am giving you a new commandment: Love each other. Just as I have loved you, you should love each other.** [35]**Your love for one another will prove to the world that you are my disciples."**

[36]Simon Peter asked, "Lord, where are you going?"

And Jesus replied, "You can't go with me now, but you will follow me later."

[37]"But why can't I come now, Lord?" he asked. "I'm ready to die for you."

[38]Jesus answered, "Die for me? I tell you the truth, Peter—before the rooster crows tomorrow morning, you will deny three times that you even know me.

14:1"DON'T let your hearts be troubled. Trust in God, and trust also in me. [2]There is more than enough room in my Father's home.* If this were not so, would I have told you that I am going to prepare a place for you?* [3]When everything is ready, I will come and get you, so that you will always be with me where I am. [4]And you know the way to where I am going."

[5]"No, we don't know, Lord," Thomas

said. "We have no idea where you are going, so how can we know the way?"

6 Jesus told him, "I am the way, the truth, and the life. No one can come to the Father except through me. 7 If you had really known me, you would know who my Father is.* From now on, you do know him and have seen him!"

8 Philip said, "Lord, show us the Father, and we will be satisfied."

9 Jesus replied, "Have I been with you all this time, Philip, and yet you still don't know who I am? Anyone who has seen me has seen the Father! So why are you asking me to show him to you? 10 Don't you believe that I am in the Father and the Father is in me? The words I speak are not my own, but my Father who lives in me does his work through me. 11 Just believe that I am in the Father and the Father is in me. Or at least believe because of the work you have seen me do.

12 "I tell you the truth, anyone who believes in me will do the same works I have done, and even greater works, because I am going to be with the Father. 13 You can ask for anything in my name, and I will do it, so that the Son can bring glory to the Father. 14 Yes, ask me for anything in my name, and I will do it!

13:31 "Son of Man" is a title Jesus used for himself. 13:32 Some manuscripts omit *And since God receives glory because of the Son.* 14:2a Or *There are many rooms in my Father's house.* 14:2b Or *If this were not so, I would have told you that I am going to prepare a place for you.* Some manuscripts read *If this were not so, I would have told you. I am going to prepare a place for you.* 14:7 Some manuscripts read *If you have really known me, you will know who my Father is.*

PSALM 119:17-32

Gimel
17 **B**e good to your servant,
  that I may live and obey
  your word.
18 Open my eyes to see
  the wonderful truths in your
  instructions.
19 I am only a foreigner in the land.
  Don't hide your commands
  from me!
20 I am always overwhelmed
  with a desire for your regulations.

21 You rebuke the arrogant;
  those who wander from your
  commands are cursed.
22 Don't let them scorn and
  insult me,
  for I have obeyed your laws.
23 Even princes sit and speak
  against me,
  but I will meditate on your
  decrees.
24 Your laws please me;
  they give me wise advice.

Daleth
25 I lie in the dust;
  revive me by your word.
26 I told you my plans, and you
  answered.
  Now teach me your decrees.
27 Help me understand the meaning
  of your commandments,
  and I will meditate on your
  wonderful deeds.
28 I weep with sorrow;
  encourage me by your word.
29 Keep me from lying to myself;
  give me the privilege of knowing
  your instructions.
30 I have chosen to be faithful;
  I have determined to live by
  your regulations.
31 I cling to your laws.
  LORD, don't let me be put
  to shame!
32 I will pursue your commands,
  for you expand my
  understanding.

PROVERBS 15:31-32
If you listen to constructive criticism, you will be at home among the wise. □ If you reject discipline, you only harm yourself; but if you listen to correction, you grow in understanding.

MAY
25

2 SAMUEL 7:1–8:18

When King David was settled in his palace and the LORD had given him rest from all the surrounding enemies, [2]the king summoned Nathan the prophet. "Look," David said, "I am living in a beautiful cedar palace,* but the Ark of God is out there in a tent!"

[3]Nathan replied to the king, "Go ahead and do whatever you have in mind, for the LORD is with you."

[4]But that same night the LORD said to Nathan,

[5]"Go and tell my servant David, 'This is what the LORD has declared: Are you the one to build a house for me to live in? [6]I have never lived in a house, from the day I brought the Israelites out of Egypt until this very day. I have always moved from one place to another with a tent and a Tabernacle as my dwelling. [7]Yet no matter where I have gone with the Israelites, I have never once complained to Israel's tribal leaders, the shepherds of my people Israel. I have never asked them, "Why haven't you built me a beautiful cedar house?"'

[8]"Now go and say to my servant David, 'This is what the LORD of Heaven's Armies has declared: I took you from tending sheep in the pasture and selected you to be the leader of my people Israel. [9]I have been with you wherever you have gone, and I have destroyed all your enemies before your eyes. Now I will make your name as famous as anyone who has ever lived on the earth! [10]And I will provide a homeland for my people Israel, planting them in a secure place where they will never be disturbed. Evil nations won't oppress them as

they've done in the past, [11]starting from the time I appointed judges to rule my people Israel. And I will give you rest from all your enemies.

"'Furthermore, the LORD declares that he will make a house for you—a dynasty of kings! [12]For when you die and are buried with your ancestors, I will raise up one of your descendants, your own offspring, and I will make his kingdom strong. [13]He is the one who will build a house—a temple—for my name. And I will secure his royal throne forever. [14]I will be his father, and he will be my son. If he sins, I will correct and discipline him with the rod, like any father would do. [15]But my favor will not be taken from him as I took it from Saul, whom I removed from your sight. [16]Your house and your kingdom will continue before me* for all time, and your throne will be secure forever.'"

[17]So Nathan went back to David and told him everything the LORD had said in this vision.

[18]Then King David went in and sat before the LORD and prayed,

"Who am I, O Sovereign LORD, and what is my family, that you have brought me this far? [19]And now, Sovereign LORD, in addition to everything else, you speak of giving your servant a lasting dynasty! Do you deal with everyone this way, O Sovereign LORD?*

[20]"What more can I say to you? You know what your servant is really like, Sovereign LORD. [21]Because of your promise and according to your will, you have done all these great things and have made them known to your servant.

[22]"How great you are, O Sovereign LORD! There is no one like you. We have never even heard of another God like you! [23]What other nation on earth is like your people Israel? What other nation, O God, have you redeemed from slavery to be your

own people? You made a great name for yourself when you redeemed your people from Egypt. You performed awesome miracles and drove out the nations and gods that stood in their way.* 24You made Israel your very own people forever, and you, O Lord, became their God.

25"And now, O Lord God, I am your servant; do as you have promised concerning me and my family. Confirm it as a promise that will last forever. 26And may your name be honored forever so that everyone will say, 'The Lord of Heaven's Armies is God over Israel!' And may the house of your servant David continue before you forever.

27"O Lord of Heaven's Armies, God of Israel, I have been bold enough to pray this prayer to you because you have revealed all this to your servant, saying, 'I will build a house for you—a dynasty of kings!' 28For you are God, O Sovereign Lord. Your words are truth, and you have promised these good things to your servant. 29And now, may it please you to bless the house of your servant, so that it may continue forever before you. For you have spoken, and when you grant a blessing to your servant, O Sovereign Lord, it is an eternal blessing!"

8:1After this, David defeated and subdued the Philistines by conquering Gath, their largest town.* 2David also conquered the land of Moab. He made the people lie down on the ground in a row, and he measured them off in groups with a length of rope. He measured off two groups to be executed for every one group to be spared. The Moabites who were spared became David's subjects and paid him tribute money.

3David also destroyed the forces of Hadadezer son of Rehob, king of Zobah, when Hadadezer marched out to strengthen his control along the Euphrates River. 4David captured 1,700 charioteers* and 20,000 foot soldiers.

He crippled all the chariot horses except enough for 100 chariots.

5When Arameans from Damascus arrived to help King Hadadezer, David killed 22,000 of them. 6Then he placed several army garrisons in Damascus, the Aramean capital, and the Arameans became David's subjects and paid him tribute money. So the Lord made David victorious wherever he went.

7David brought the gold shields of Hadadezer's officers to Jerusalem, 8along with a large amount of bronze from Hadadezer's towns of Tebah* and Berothai.

9When King Toi of Hamath heard that David had destroyed the entire army of Hadadezer, 10he sent his son Joram to congratulate King David for his successful campaign. Hadadezer and Toi had been enemies and were often at war. Joram presented David with many gifts of silver, gold, and bronze.

11King David dedicated all these gifts to the Lord, as he did with the silver and gold from the other nations he had defeated—12from Edom,* Moab, Ammon, Philistia, and Amalek—and from Hadadezer son of Rehob, king of Zobah.

13So David became very famous. After his return he destroyed 18,000 Edomites* in the Valley of Salt. 14He placed army garrisons throughout Edom, and all the Edomites became David's subjects. In fact, the Lord made David victorious wherever he went.

15So David reigned over all Israel and did what was just and right for all his people. 16Joab son of Zeruiah was commander of the army. Jehoshaphat son of Ahilud was the royal historian. 17Zadok son of Ahitub and Ahimelech son of Abiathar were the priests. Seraiah was the court secretary. 18Benaiah son of Jehoiada was captain of the king's bodyguard.* And David's sons served as priestly leaders.*

7:2 Hebrew a house of cedar.   7:16 As in Greek version and some Hebrew manuscripts; Masoretic text reads before you.   7:19 Or This is your instruction for all humanity, O Sovereign Lord.   7:23 As in Greek version (see also 1 Chr 17:21); Hebrew reads You made a great name for yourself and performed awesome miracles for your land. You did *this in the sight of your people, whom you redeemed from Egypt, from nations and their gods.* **8:1** Hebrew *by conquering Metheg-ammah,* a name that means "the bridle," possibly referring to the size of the town or the tribute money taken from it. Compare 1 Chr 18:1. **8:4** Greek version reads *1,000 chariots and 7,000 charioteers;* compare 1 Chr 18:4. **8:8** As in some Greek manuscripts (see also 1 Chr 18:8); Hebrew reads *Betah.* **8:12** As in a few Hebrew manuscripts and Greek and Syriac versions (see also 8:14; 1 Chr 18:11); most Hebrew manuscripts read *Aram.* **8:13** As in a few Hebrew manuscripts and Greek and Syriac versions (see also 8:14; 1 Chr 18:12); most Hebrew manuscripts read *Arameans.* **8:18a** Hebrew *of the Kerethites and Pelethites.* **8:18b** Hebrew *David's sons were priests;* compare parallel text at 1 Chr 18:17.

JOHN 14:15-31

"**I**f you love me [Jesus], obey* my commandments. [16]And I will ask the Father, and he will give you another Advocate,* who will never leave you. [17]He is the Holy Spirit, who leads into all truth. The world cannot receive him, because it isn't looking for him and doesn't recognize him. But you know him, because he lives with you now and later will be in you.* [18]No, I will not abandon you as orphans—I will come to you. [19]Soon the world will no longer see me, but you will see me. Since I live, you also will live. [20]When I am raised to life again, you will know that I am in my Father, and you are in me, and I am in you. [21]Those who accept my commandments and obey them are the ones who love me. And because they love me, my Father will love them. And I will love them and reveal myself to each of them."

[22]Judas (not Judas Iscariot, but the other disciple with that name) said to him, "Lord, why are you going to reveal yourself only to us and not to the world at large?"

[23]Jesus replied, "All who love me will do what I say. My Father will love them, and we will come and make our home with each of them. [24]Anyone who doesn't love me will not obey me. And remember, my words are not my own. What I am telling you is from the Father who sent me. [25]I am telling you these things now while I am still with you. [26]But when the Father sends the Advocate as my representative—that is, the Holy Spirit—he will teach you everything

and will remind you of everything I have told you.

[27]"I am leaving you with a gift—peace of mind and heart. And the peace I give is a gift the world cannot give. So don't be troubled or afraid. [28]Remember what I told you: I am going away, but I will come back to you again. If you really loved me, you would be happy that I am going to the Father, who is greater than I am. [29]I have told you these things before they happen so that when they do happen, you will believe.

[30]"I don't have much more time to talk to you, because the ruler of this world approaches. He has no power over me, [31]but I will do what the Father requires of me, so that the world will know that I love the Father. Come, let's be going."

14:15 Other manuscripts read *you will obey;* still others read *you should obey.* **14:16** Or *Comforter,* or *Encourager,* or *Counselor.* Greek reads *Paraclete;* also in 14:26. **14:17** Some manuscripts read *and is in you.*

PSALM 119:33-48

He

[33] **T**each me your decrees, O LORD;
  I will keep them to the end.
[34] Give me understanding and I will
    obey your instructions;
  I will put them into practice
    with all my heart.
[35] Make me walk along the path
    of your commands,
  for that is where my happiness
    is found.
[36] **Give me an eagerness for your**
    laws
  rather than a love for money!
[37] **Turn my eyes from worthless**
    things,
  and give me life through
    your word.*
[38] Reassure me of your promise,
    made to those who fear you.
[39] Help me abandon my shameful
    ways;
  for your regulations are good.
[40] I long to obey your commandments!
  Renew my life with your
    goodness.

Waw

⁴¹ Lᴏʀᴅ, give me your unfailing love,
    the salvation that you
        promised me.
⁴² Then I can answer those who
        taunt me,
    for I trust in your word.
⁴³ Do not snatch your word of truth
        from me,
    for your regulations are my
        only hope.
⁴⁴ I will keep on obeying your
        instructions
    forever and ever.
⁴⁵ I will walk in freedom,
    for I have devoted myself
        to your commandments.
⁴⁶ I will speak to kings about your laws,
    and I will not be ashamed.
⁴⁷ How I delight in your commands!
    How I love them!
⁴⁸ I honor and love your commands.
    I meditate on your decrees.

119:37 Some manuscripts read *in your ways.*

PROVERBS 15:33

Fear of the Lᴏʀᴅ teaches wisdom; humility precedes honor.

MAY 26

2 SAMUEL 9:1–11:27

One day David asked, "Is anyone in Saul's family still alive—anyone to whom I can show kindness for Jonathan's sake?" ²He summoned a man named Ziba, who had been one of Saul's servants. "Are you Ziba?" the king asked.

"Yes sir, I am," Ziba replied.

³The king then asked him, "Is anyone still alive from Saul's family? If so, I want to show God's kindness to them."

Ziba replied, "Yes, one of Jonathan's sons is still alive. He is crippled in both feet."

⁴"Where is he?" the king asked.

"In Lo-debar," Ziba told him, "at the home of Makir son of Ammiel."

⁵So David sent for him and brought him from Makir's home. ⁶His name was Mephibosheth*; he was Jonathan's son and Saul's grandson. When he came to David, he bowed low to the ground in deep respect. David said, "Greetings, Mephibosheth."

Mephibosheth replied, "I am your servant."

⁷"Don't be afraid!" David said. "I intend to show kindness to you because of my promise to your father, Jonathan. I will give you all the property that once belonged to your grandfather Saul, and you will eat here with me at the king's table!"

⁸Mephibosheth bowed respectfully and exclaimed, "Who is your servant, that you should show such kindness to a dead dog like me?"

⁹Then the king summoned Saul's servant Ziba and said, "I have given your master's grandson everything that belonged to Saul and his family. ¹⁰You and your sons and servants are to farm the land for him to produce food for your master's household.* But Mephibosheth, your master's grandson, will eat here at my table." (Ziba had fifteen sons and twenty servants.)

Ziba replied, ¹¹"Yes, my lord the king; I am your servant, and I will do all that you have commanded." And from that time on, Mephibosheth ate regularly at David's table,* like one of the king's own sons.

¹²Mephibosheth had a young son named Mica. From then on, all the members of Ziba's household were Mephibosheth's servants. ¹³And Mephibosheth, who was crippled in both feet, lived in Jerusalem and ate regularly at the king's table.

¹⁰:¹Some time after this, King Nahash* of the Ammonites died, and his son Hanun became king. ²David said, "I am going to show loyalty to Hanun just as his father, Nahash, was always loyal to me."

So David sent ambassadors to express sympathy to Hanun about his father's death.

But when David's ambassadors arrived in the land of Ammon, [3] the Ammonite commanders said to Hanun, their master, "Do you really think these men are coming here to honor your father? No! David has sent them to spy out the city so they can come in and conquer it!" [4] So Hanun seized David's ambassadors and shaved off half of each man's beard, cut off their robes at the buttocks, and sent them back to David in shame.

[5] When David heard what had happened, he sent messengers to tell the men, "Stay at Jericho until your beards grow out, and then come back." For they felt deep shame because of their appearance.

[6] When the people of Ammon realized how seriously they had angered David, they sent and hired 20,000 Aramean foot soldiers from the lands of Beth-rehob and Zobah, 1,000 from the king of Maacah, and 12,000 from the land of Tob. [7] When David heard about this, he sent Joab and all his warriors to fight them. [8] The Ammonite troops came out and drew up their battle lines at the entrance of the city gate, while the Arameans from Zobah and Rehob and the men from Tob and Maacah positioned themselves to fight in the open fields.

[9] When Joab saw that he would have to fight on both the front and the rear, he chose some of Israel's elite troops and placed them under his personal command to fight the Arameans in the fields. [10] He left the rest of the army under the command of his brother Abishai, who was to attack the Ammonites. [11] "If the Arameans are too strong for me, then come over and help me," Joab told his brother. "And if the Ammonites are too strong for you, I will come and help you. [12] Be courageous! Let us fight bravely for our people and the cities of our God. May the LORD's will be done."

[13] When Joab and his troops attacked, the Arameans began to run away. [14] And when the Ammonites saw the Arameans running, they ran from Abishai and retreated into the city. After the battle was over, Joab returned to Jerusalem.

[15] The Arameans now realized that they were no match for Israel. So when they regrouped, [16] they were joined by additional Aramean troops summoned by Hadadezer from the other side of the Euphrates River.* These troops arrived at Helam under the command of Shobach, the commander of Hadadezer's forces.

[17] When David heard what was happening, he mobilized all Israel, crossed the Jordan River, and led the army to Helam. The Arameans positioned themselves in battle formation and fought against David. [18] But again the Arameans fled from the Israelites. This time David's forces killed 700 charioteers and 40,000 foot soldiers,* including Shobach, the commander of their army. [19] When all the kings allied with Hadadezer saw that they had been defeated by Israel, they surrendered to Israel and became their subjects. After that, the Arameans were afraid to help the Ammonites.

11:1 IN the spring of the year,* when kings normally go out to war, David sent Joab and the Israelite army to fight the Ammonites. They destroyed the Ammonite army and laid siege to the city of Rabbah. However, David stayed behind in Jerusalem.

[2] Late one afternoon, after his midday rest, David got out of bed and was walking on the roof of the palace. As he looked out over the city, he noticed a woman of unusual beauty taking a bath. [3] He sent someone to find out who she was, and he was told, "She is Bathsheba, the daughter of Eliam and the wife of Uriah the Hittite." [4] Then David sent messengers to get her; and when she came to the palace, he slept with her. She had just completed the purification rites after having her menstrual period. Then she returned home. [5] Later, when

Bathsheba discovered that she was pregnant, she sent a message, saying, "I'm pregnant."

6Then David sent word to Joab: "Send me Uriah the Hittite." So Joab sent him to David. 7When Uriah arrived, David asked him how Joab and the army were getting along and how the war was progressing. 8Then he told Uriah, "Go on home and relax.*" David even sent a gift to Uriah after he had left the palace. 9But Uriah didn't go home. He slept that night at the palace entrance with the king's palace guard.

10When David heard that Uriah had not gone home, he summoned him and asked, "What's the matter? Why didn't you go home last night after being away for so long?"

11Uriah replied, "The Ark and the armies of Israel and Judah are living in tents,* and Joab and my master's men are camping in the open fields. How could I go home to wine and dine and sleep with my wife? I swear that I would never do such a thing."

12"Well, stay here today," David told him, "and tomorrow you may return to the army." So Uriah stayed in Jerusalem that day and the next. 13Then David invited him to dinner and got him drunk. But even then he couldn't get Uriah to go home to his wife. Again he slept at the palace entrance with the king's palace guard.

14So the next morning David wrote a letter to Joab and gave it to Uriah to deliver. 15The letter instructed Joab, "Station Uriah on the front lines where the battle is fiercest. Then pull back so that he will be killed." 16So Joab assigned Uriah to a spot close to the city wall where he knew the enemy's strongest men were fighting. 17And when the enemy soldiers came out of the city to fight, Uriah the Hittite was killed along with several other Israelite soldiers.

18Then Joab sent a battle report to David. 19He told his messenger, "Report all the news of the battle to the king. 20But he might get angry and ask, 'Why did the troops go so close to the city?

Didn't they know there would be shooting from the walls? 21Wasn't Abimelech son of Gideon* killed at Thebez by a woman who threw a millstone down on him from the wall? Why would you get so close to the wall?' Then tell him, 'Uriah the Hittite was killed, too.'"

22So the messenger went to Jerusalem and gave a complete report to David. 23"The enemy came out against us in the open fields," he said. "And as we chased them back to the city gate, 24the archers on the wall shot arrows at us. Some of the king's men were killed, including Uriah the Hittite."

25"Well, tell Joab not to be discouraged," David said. "The sword devours this one today and that one tomorrow! Fight harder next time, and conquer the city!"

26When Uriah's wife heard that her husband was dead, she mourned for him. 27When the period of mourning was over, David sent for her and brought her to the palace, and she became one of his wives. Then she gave birth to a son. But the LORD was displeased with what David had done.

9:6 *Mephibosheth* is another name for Merib-baal. 9:10 As in Greek version; Hebrew reads *your master's grandson.* 9:11 As in Greek version; Hebrew reads *my table.* 10:1 As in parallel text at 1 Chr 19:1; Hebrew reads *the king.* 10:16 Hebrew *the river.* 10:18 As in some Greek manuscripts (see also 1 Chr 19:18); Hebrew reads *charioteers.* 11:1 Hebrew *At the turn of the year.* The first day of the year in the ancient Hebrew lunar calendar occurred in March or April. 11:8 Hebrew *and wash your feet,* an expression that may also have a connotation of ritualistic washing. 11:11 Or *at Succoth.* 11:21 Hebrew *son of Jerub-besheth.* Jerub-besheth is a variation on the name Jerub-baal, which is another name for Gideon; see Judg 6:32.

JOHN 15:1-27

"I [Jesus] am the true grapevine, and my Father is the gardener. 2He cuts off every branch of mine that doesn't produce fruit, and he prunes the branches that do bear fruit so they will produce even more. 3You have already been pruned and purified by the message I have given you. 4Remain in me, and I will remain in you. For a branch cannot produce fruit if it is severed from the vine, and you cannot be fruitful unless you remain in me.

[5]"Yes, I am the vine; you are the branches. Those who remain in me, and I in them, will produce much fruit. For apart from me you can do nothing. [6]Anyone who does not remain in me is thrown away like a useless branch and withers. Such branches are gathered into a pile to be burned. [7]But if you remain in me and my words remain in you, you may ask for anything you want, and it will be granted! [8]When you produce much fruit, you are my true disciples. This brings great glory to my Father.

[9]"I have loved you even as the Father has loved me. Remain in my love. [10]When you obey my commandments, you remain in my love, just as I obey my Father's commandments and remain in his love. [11]I have told you these things so that you will be filled with my joy. Yes, your joy will overflow! [12]This is my commandment: Love each other in the same way I have loved you. [13]There is no greater love than to lay down one's life for one's friends. [14]You are my friends if you do what I command. [15]I no longer call you slaves, because a master doesn't confide in his slaves. Now you are my friends, since I have told you everything the Father told me. [16]You didn't choose me. I chose you. I appointed you to go and produce lasting fruit, so that the Father will give you whatever you ask for, using my name. [17]This is my command: Love each other.

[18]"If the world hates you, remember that it hated me first. [19]The world would love you as one of its own if you belonged to it, but you are no longer part of the world. I chose you to come out of the world, so it hates you. [20]Do you remember what I told you? 'A slave is not greater than the master.' Since they persecuted me, naturally they will persecute you. And if they had listened to me, they would listen to you. [21]They will do all this to you because of me, for they have rejected the One who sent me. [22]They would not be guilty if I had not come and spoken to them. But now they have no excuse for their sin.

[23]Anyone who hates me also hates my Father. [24]If I hadn't done such miraculous signs among them that no one else could do, they would not be guilty. But as it is, they have seen everything I did, yet they still hate me and my Father. [25]This fulfills what is written in their Scriptures:* 'They hated me without cause.'

[26]"But I will send you the Advocate*—the Spirit of truth. He will come to you from the Father and will testify all about me. [27]And you must also testify about me because you have been with me from the beginning of my ministry."

15:25 Greek *in their law.* Pss 35:19; 69:4. **15:26** Or *Comforter,* or *Encourager,* or *Counselor.* Greek reads *Paraclete.*

PSALM 119:49-64

Zayin
[49] **R**emember your promise to me;
   it is my only hope.
[50] Your promise revives me;
   it comforts me in all my troubles.
[51] The proud hold me in utter
      contempt,
   but I do not turn away from your
      instructions.
[52] I meditate on your age-old
      regulations;
   O Lord, they comfort me.
[53] I become furious with the wicked,
   because they reject your
      instructions.
[54] Your decrees have been the theme
      of my songs
   wherever I have lived.
[55] I reflect at night on who you are,
      O Lord;
   therefore, I obey your
      instructions.
[56] This is how I spend my life:
   obeying your commandments.

Heth
[57] Lord, you are mine!
   I promise to obey your words!
[58] With all my heart I want your
      blessings.
   Be merciful as you promised.
[59] I pondered the direction of my life,
   and I turned to follow your laws.

⁶⁰ I will hurry, without delay,
　　to obey your commands.
⁶¹ Evil people try to drag me into sin,
　　but I am firmly anchored to your
　　instructions.
⁶² I rise at midnight to thank you
　　for your just regulations.
⁶³ I am a friend to anyone who
　　fears you—
　　anyone who obeys your
　　commandments.
⁶⁴ O LORD, your unfailing love fills
　　the earth;
　　teach me your decrees.

PROVERBS 16:1-3

We can make our own plans, but the LORD gives the right answer. □People may be pure in their own eyes, but the LORD examines their motives. □Commit your actions to the LORD, and your plans will succeed.

MAY 27

2 SAMUEL 12:1-31

So the LORD sent Nathan the prophet to tell David this story: "There were two men in a certain town. One was rich, and one was poor. ²The rich man owned a great many sheep and cattle. ³The poor man owned nothing but one little lamb he had bought. He raised that little lamb, and it grew up with his children. It ate from the man's own plate and drank from his cup. He cuddled it in his arms like a baby daughter. ⁴One day a guest arrived at the home of the rich man. But instead of killing an animal from his own flock or herd, he took the poor man's lamb and killed it and prepared it for his guest."

⁵David was furious. "As surely as the LORD lives," he vowed, "any man who would do such a thing deserves to die! ⁶He must repay four lambs to the poor

man for the one he stole and for having no pity."

⁷Then Nathan said to David, "You are that man! The LORD, the God of Israel, says: I anointed you king of Israel and saved you from the power of Saul. ⁸I gave you your master's house and his wives and the kingdoms of Israel and Judah. And if that had not been enough, I would have given you much, much more. ⁹Why, then, have you despised the word of the LORD and done this horrible deed? For you have murdered Uriah the Hittite with the sword of the Ammonites and stolen his wife. ¹⁰From this time on, your family will live by the sword because you have despised me by taking Uriah's wife to be your own.

¹¹"This is what the LORD says: Because of what you have done, I will cause your own household to rebel against you. I will give your wives to another man before your very eyes, and he will go to bed with them in public view. ¹²You did it secretly, but I will make this happen to you openly in the sight of all Israel."

¹³Then David confessed to Nathan, "I have sinned against the LORD."

Nathan replied, "Yes, but the LORD has forgiven you, and you won't die for this sin. ¹⁴Nevertheless, because you have shown utter contempt for the LORD* by doing this, your child will die."

¹⁵After Nathan returned to his home, the LORD sent a deadly illness to the child of David and Uriah's wife. ¹⁶David begged God to spare the child. He went without food and lay all night on the bare ground. ¹⁷The elders of his household pleaded with him to get up and eat with them, but he refused.

¹⁸Then on the seventh day the child died. David's advisers were afraid to tell him. "He wouldn't listen to reason while the child was ill," they said. "What drastic thing will he do when we tell him the child is dead?"

¹⁹When David saw them whispering, he realized what had happened. "Is the child dead?" he asked.

"Yes," they replied, "he is dead."

²⁰Then David got up from the ground,

washed himself, put on lotions,* and changed his clothes. He went to the Tabernacle and worshiped the LORD. After that, he returned to the palace and was served food and ate.

²¹His advisers were amazed. "We don't understand you," they told him. "While the child was still living, you wept and refused to eat. But now that the child is dead, you have stopped your mourning and are eating again."

²²David replied, "I fasted and wept while the child was alive, for I said, 'Perhaps the LORD will be gracious to me and let the child live.' ²³But why should I fast when he is dead? Can I bring him back again? I will go to him one day, but he cannot return to me."

²⁴Then David comforted Bathsheba, his wife, and slept with her. She became pregnant and gave birth to a son, and they named him Solomon. The LORD loved the child ²⁵and sent word through Nathan the prophet that they should name him Jedidiah (which means "beloved of the LORD"), as the LORD had commanded.*

²⁶Meanwhile, Joab was fighting against Rabbah, the capital of Ammon, and he captured the royal fortifications.* ²⁷Joab sent messengers to tell David, "I have fought against Rabbah and captured its water supply.* ²⁸Now bring the rest of the army and capture the city. Otherwise, I will capture it and get credit for the victory."

²⁹So David gathered the rest of the army and went to Rabbah, and he fought against it and captured it. ³⁰David removed the crown from the king's head,* and it was placed on his own head. The crown was made of gold and set with gems, and it weighed seventy-five pounds.* David took a vast amount of plunder from the city. ³¹He also made slaves of the people of Rabbah and forced them to labor with* saws, iron picks, and iron axes, and to work in the brick kilns.* That is how he dealt with the people of all the Ammonite towns. Then David and all the army returned to Jerusalem.

12:14 As in Dead Sea Scrolls; Masoretic Text reads *the LORD's enemies.*   12:20 Hebrew *anointed himself.*   12:25 As in Greek version; Hebrew reads *because of the LORD.*   12:26 Or *the royal city.*   12:27 Or *captured the city of water.*   12:30a Or *from the head of Milcom* (as in Greek version). Milcom, also called Molech, was the god of the Ammonites.   12:30b Hebrew *1 talent* [34 kilograms].   12:31a Or *He also brought out the people of Rabbah and put them under.*   12:31b Or *and he made them pass through the brick kilns.*

JOHN 16:1-33

"I [Jesus] have told you these things so that you won't abandon your faith. ²For you will be expelled from the synagogues, and the time is coming when those who kill you will think they are doing a holy service for God. ³This is because they have never known the Father or me. ⁴Yes, I'm telling you these things now, so that when they happen, you will remember my warning. I didn't tell you earlier because I was going to be with you for a while longer.

⁵"But now I am going away to the One who sent me, and not one of you is asking where I am going. ⁶Instead, you grieve because of what I've told you. ⁷But in fact, it is best for you that I go away, because if I don't, the Advocate* won't come. If I do go away, then I will send him to you. ⁸And when he comes, he will convict the world of its sin, and of God's righteousness, and of the coming judgment. ⁹The world's sin is that it refuses to believe in me. ¹⁰Righteousness is available because I go to the Father, and you will see me no more. ¹¹Judgment will come because the ruler of this world has already been judged.

¹²"There is so much more I want to tell you, but you can't bear it now. ¹³When the Spirit of truth comes, he will guide you into all truth. He will not speak on his own but will tell you what he has heard. He will tell you about the future. ¹⁴He will bring me glory by telling you whatever he receives from me. ¹⁵All that belongs to the Father is mine; this is why I said, 'The Spirit will tell you whatever he receives from me.'

¹⁶"In a little while you won't see me anymore. But a little while after that, you will see me again."

¹⁷Some of the disciples asked each

other, "What does he mean when he says, 'In a little while you won't see me, but then you will see me,' and 'I am going to the Father'? [18]And what does he mean by 'a little while'? We don't understand."

[19]Jesus realized they wanted to ask him about it, so he said, "Are you asking yourselves what I meant? I said in a little while you won't see me, but a little while after that you will see me again. [20]I tell you the truth, you will weep and mourn over what is going to happen to me, but the world will rejoice. You will grieve, but your grief will suddenly turn to wonderful joy. [21]It will be like a woman suffering the pains of labor. When her child is born, her anguish gives way to joy because she has brought a new baby into the world. [22]So you have sorrow now, but I will see you again; then you will rejoice, and no one can rob you of that joy. [23]At that time you won't need to ask me for anything. I tell you the truth, you will ask the Father directly, and he will grant your request because you use my name. [24]You haven't done this before. Ask, using my name, and you will receive, and you will have abundant joy.

[25]"I have spoken of these matters in figures of speech, but soon I will stop speaking figuratively and will tell you plainly all about the Father. [26]Then you will ask in my name. I'm not saying I will ask the Father on your behalf, [27]for the Father himself loves you dearly because you love me and believe that I came from God. [28]Yes, I came from the Father into the world, and now I will leave the world and return to the Father."

[29]Then his disciples said, "At last you are speaking plainly and not figuratively. [30]Now we understand that you know everything, and there's no need to question you. From this we believe that you came from God."

[31]Jesus asked, "Do you finally believe? [32]But the time is coming—indeed it's here now—when you will be scattered, each one going his own way, leaving me alone. Yet I am not alone because the Father is with me. [33]**I have told you all this so that you may have peace in me. Here on earth you will have many trials and sorrows. But take heart, because I have overcome the world."**

16:7 Or *Comforter*, or *Encourager*, or *Counselor*. Greek reads *Paraclete*.

PSALM 119:65-80

Teth

[65] **Y**ou have done many good things for me, LORD,
  just as you promised.
[66] I believe in your commands;
  now teach me good judgment
  and knowledge.
[67] I used to wander off until you
  disciplined me;
  but now I closely follow
  your word.
[68] You are good and do only good;
  teach me your decrees.
[69] Arrogant people smear me with lies,
  but in truth I obey your
  commandments with all
  my heart.
[70] Their hearts are dull and stupid,
  but I delight in your instructions.
[71] My suffering was good for me,
  for it taught me to pay attention
  to your decrees.
[72] Your instructions are more valuable
  to me
  than millions in gold and silver.

Yodh

[73] You made me; you created me.
  Now give me the sense to follow
  your commands.
[74] May all who fear you find in me a
  cause for joy,
  for I have put my hope in your
  word.
[75] I know, O LORD, that your
  regulations are fair;
  you disciplined me because
  I needed it.
[76] Now let your unfailing love comfort
  me,
  just as you promised me, your
  servant.
[77] Surround me with your tender
  mercies so I may live,

for your instructions are
my delight.
78 Bring disgrace upon the arrogant
people who lied about me;
meanwhile, I will concentrate on
your commandments.
79 Let me be united with all who
fear you,
with those who know your laws.
80 May I be blameless in keeping your
decrees;
then I will never be ashamed.

PROVERBS 16:4-5

The LORD has made everything for his own purposes, even the wicked for a day of disaster. ☐ The LORD detests the proud; they will surely be punished.

MAY 28

2 SAMUEL 13:1-39

Now David's son Absalom had a beautiful sister named Tamar. And Amnon, her half brother, fell desperately in love with her. 2Amnon became so obsessed with Tamar that he became ill. She was a virgin, and Amnon thought he could never have her.

3But Amnon had a very crafty friend—his cousin Jonadab. He was the son of David's brother Shimea.* 4One day Jonadab said to Amnon, "What's the trouble? Why should the son of a king look so dejected morning after morning?"

So Amnon told him, "I am in love with Tamar, my brother Absalom's sister."

5"Well," Jonadab said, "I'll tell you what to do. Go back to bed and pretend you are ill. When your father comes to see you, ask him to let Tamar come and prepare some food for you. Tell him you'll feel better if she prepares it as you watch and feeds you with her own hands."

6So Amnon lay down and pretended to be sick. And when the king came to see him, Amnon asked him, "Please let my sister Tamar come and cook my favorite dish* as I watch. Then I can eat it from her own hands." 7So David agreed and sent Tamar to Amnon's house to prepare some food for him.

8When Tamar arrived at Amnon's house, she went to the place where he was lying down so he could watch her mix some dough. Then she baked his favorite dish for him. 9But when she set the serving tray before him, he refused to eat. "Everyone get out of here," Amnon told his servants. So they all left.

10Then he said to Tamar, "Now bring the food into my bedroom and feed it to me here." So Tamar took his favorite dish to him. 11But as she was feeding him, he grabbed her and demanded, "Come to bed with me, my darling sister."

12"No, my brother!" she cried. "Don't be foolish! Don't do this to me! Such wicked things aren't done in Israel. 13Where could I go in my shame? And you would be called one of the greatest fools in Israel. Please, just speak to the king about it, and he will let you marry me."

14But Amnon wouldn't listen to her, and since he was stronger than she was, he raped her. 15Then suddenly Amnon's love turned to hate, and he hated her even more than he had loved her. "Get out of here!" he snarled at her.

16"No, no!" Tamar cried. "Sending me away now is worse than what you've already done to me."

But Amnon wouldn't listen to her. 17He shouted for his servant and demanded, "Throw this woman out, and lock the door behind her!"

18So the servant put her out and locked the door behind her. She was wearing a long, beautiful robe,* as was the custom in those days for the king's virgin daughters. 19But now Tamar tore her robe and put ashes on her head. And then, with her face in her hands, she went away crying.

20Her brother Absalom saw her and asked, "Is it true that Amnon has been with you? Well, my sister, keep quiet for now, since he's your brother. Don't you worry about it." So Tamar lived as a desolate woman in her brother Absalom's house.

21When King David heard what had happened, he was very angry.* 22And though Absalom never spoke to Amnon about this, he hated Amnon deeply because of what he had done to his sister.

23Two years later, when Absalom's sheep were being sheared at Baal-hazor near Ephraim, Absalom invited all the king's sons to come to a feast. 24He went to the king and said, "My sheep-shearers are now at work. Would the king and his servants please come to celebrate the occasion with me?"

25The king replied, "No, my son. If we all came, we would be too much of a burden on you." Absalom pressed him, but the king would not come, though he gave Absalom his blessing.

26"Well, then," Absalom said, "if you can't come, how about sending my brother Amnon with us?"

"Why Amnon?" the king asked. 27But Absalom kept on pressing the king until he finally agreed to let all his sons attend, including Amnon. So Absalom prepared a feast fit for a king.*

28Absalom told his men, "Wait until Amnon gets drunk; then at my signal, kill him! Don't be afraid. I'm the one who has given the command. Take courage and do it!" 29So at Absalom's signal they murdered Amnon. Then the other sons of the king jumped on their mules and fled.

30As they were on the way back to Jerusalem, this report reached David: "Absalom has killed all the king's sons; not one is left alive!" 31The king got up, tore his robe, and threw himself on the ground. His advisers also tore their clothes in horror and sorrow.

32But just then Jonadab, the son of David's brother Shimea, arrived and said, "No, don't believe that all the king's sons have been killed! It was only Amnon! Absalom has been plotting this ever since Amnon raped his sister Tamar. 33No, my lord the king, your sons aren't all dead! It

was only Amnon." 34Meanwhile Absalom escaped.

Then the watchman on the Jerusalem wall saw a great crowd coming toward the city from the west. He ran to tell the king, "I see a crowd of people coming from the Horonaim road* along the side of the hill."

35"Look!" Jonadab told the king. "There they are now! The king's sons are coming, just as I said."

36They soon arrived, weeping and sobbing, and the king and all his servants wept bitterly with them. 37And David mourned many days for his son Amnon.

Absalom fled to his grandfather, Talmai son of Ammihud, the king of Geshur. 38He stayed there in Geshur for three years. 39And King David, now reconciled to Amnon's death, longed to be reunited with his son Absalom.*

13:3 Hebrew *Shimeah* (also in 13:32), a variant spelling of Shimea; compare 1 Chr 2:13.   13:6 Or *a couple of cakes;* also in 13:8, 10.   13:18 Or *a robe with sleeves,* or *an ornamented robe.* The meaning of the Hebrew is uncertain. 13:21 Dead Sea Scrolls and Greek version add *But he did not punish his son Amnon, because he loved him, for he was his firstborn.*   13:27 As in Greek and Latin versions (compare also Dead Sea Scrolls); the Hebrew text omits this sentence.   13:34 As in Greek version; Hebrew reads *from the road behind him.*   13:39 Or *no longer felt a need to go out after Absalom.*

JOHN 17:1-26

After saying all these things, Jesus looked up to heaven and said, "Father, the hour has come. Glorify your Son so he can give glory back to you. 2For you have given him authority over everyone. He gives eternal life to each one you have given him. 3And this is the way to have eternal life—to know you, the only true God, and Jesus Christ, the one you sent to earth. 4I brought glory to you here on earth by completing the work you gave me to do. 5Now, Father, bring me into the glory we shared before the world began.

6"I have revealed you* to the ones you gave me from this world. They were always yours. You gave them to me, and they have kept your word. 7Now they know that everything I have is a gift from you, 8for I have passed on to them the message you gave me. They accepted it and know that I came from you, and they believe you sent me.

9"My prayer is not for the world, but for those you have given me, because they belong to you. 10All who are mine belong to you, and you have given them to me, so they bring me glory. 11Now I am departing from the world; they are staying in this world, but I am coming to you. Holy Father, you have given me your name;* now protect them by the power of your name so that they will be united just as we are. 12During my time here, I protected them by the power of the name you gave me.* I guarded them so that not one was lost, except the one headed for destruction, as the Scriptures foretold.

13"Now I am coming to you. I told them many things while I was with them in this world so they would be filled with my joy. 14I have given them your word. And the world hates them because they do not belong to the world, just as I do not belong to the world. 15I'm not asking you to take them out of the world, but to keep them safe from the evil one. 16They do not belong to this world any more than I do. 17Make them holy by your truth; teach them your word, which is truth. 18Just as you sent me into the world, I am sending them into the world. 19And I give myself as a holy sacrifice for them so they can be made holy by your truth.

20"I am praying not only for these disciples but also for all who will ever believe in me through their message. 21I **pray that they will all be one, just as you and I are one—as you are in me, Father, and I am in you. And may they be in us so that the world will believe you sent me.**

22"I have given them the glory you gave me, so they may be one as we are one. 23I am in them and you are in me. May they experience such perfect unity that the world will know that you sent me and that you love them as much as you love me. 24Father, I want these whom you have given me to be with me

where I am. Then they can see all the glory you gave me because you loved me even before the world began!

25"O righteous Father, the world doesn't know you, but I do; and these disciples know you sent me. 26I have revealed you to them, and I will continue to do so. Then your love for me will be in them, and I will be in them."

17:6 Greek *have revealed your name;* also in 17:26.
17:11 Some manuscripts read *you have given me these [disciples].* 17:12 Some manuscripts read *I protected those you gave me, by the power of your name.*

PSALM 119:81-96

Kaph

81 I am worn out waiting for
        your rescue,
      but I have put my hope in
        your word.
82 My eyes are straining to see your
        promises come true.
      When will you comfort me?
83 I am shriveled like a wineskin
        in the smoke,
      but I have not forgotten to obey
        your decrees.
84 How long must I wait?
      When will you punish those
        who persecute me?
85 These arrogant people who hate
        your instructions
      have dug deep pits to trap me.
86 All your commands are trustworthy.
      Protect me from those who hunt
        me down without cause.
87 They almost finished me off,
      but I refused to abandon your
        commandments.
88 In your unfailing love, spare my life;
      then I can continue to obey
        your laws.

Lamedh

89 Your eternal word, O LORD,
      stands firm in heaven.
90 Your faithfulness extends to every
        generation,
      as enduring as the earth you
        created.
91 Your regulations remain true
        to this day,
      for everything serves your plans.

92 If your instructions hadn't sustained
        me with joy,
    I would have died in my misery.
93 I will never forget your
        commandments,
    for by them you give me life.
94 I am yours; rescue me!
    For I have worked hard at obeying
        your commandments.
95 Though the wicked hide along the
        way to kill me,
    I will quietly keep my mind on
        your laws.
96 Even perfection has its limits,
    but your commands have no limit.

PROVERBS 16:6-7
Unfailing love and faithfulness make
atonement for sin. By fearing the LORD,
people avoid evil. □ When people's lives
please the LORD, even their enemies are
at peace with them.

MAY
29

2 SAMUEL 14:1–15:22
Joab realized how much the king
longed to see Absalom. 2 So he sent for a
woman from Tekoa who had a reputation for great wisdom. He said to her,
"Pretend you are in mourning; wear
mourning clothes and don't put on lotions.* Act like a woman who has been
mourning for the dead for a long time.
3 Then go to the king and tell him the
story I am about to tell you." Then Joab
told her what to say.

4 When the woman from Tekoa approached the king, she bowed with her
face to the ground in deep respect and
cried out, "O king! Help me!"

5 "What's the trouble?" the king asked.

"Alas, I am a widow!" she replied. "My
husband is dead. 6 My two sons had a
fight out in the field. And since no one
was there to stop it, one of them was

killed. 7 Now the rest of the family is demanding, 'Let us have your son. We will
execute him for murdering his brother.
He doesn't deserve to inherit his family's property.' They want to extinguish
the only coal I have left, and my husband's name and family will disappear
from the face of the earth."

8 "Leave it to me," the king told her.
"Go home, and I'll see to it that no one
touches him."

9 "Oh, thank you, my lord the king,"
the woman from Tekoa replied. "If you
are criticized for helping me, let the
blame fall on me and on my father's
house, and let the king and his throne
be innocent."

10 "If anyone objects," the king said,
"bring him to me. I can assure you he
will never complain again!"

11 Then she said, "Please swear to me
by the LORD your God that you won't let
anyone take vengeance against my son.
I want no more bloodshed."

"As surely as the LORD lives," he replied, "not a hair on your son's head will
be disturbed!"

12 "Please allow me to ask one more
thing of my lord the king," she said.

"Go ahead and speak," he responded.

13 She replied, "Why don't you do as
much for the people of God as you have
promised to do for me? You have con-
victed yourself in making this decision,
because you have refused to bring
home your own banished son. 14 All of
us must die eventually. Our lives are like
water spilled out on the ground, which
cannot be gathered up again. But God
does not just sweep life away; instead,
he devises ways to bring us back when
we have been separated from him.

15 "I have come to plead with my lord
the king because people have threatened
me. I said to myself, 'Perhaps the king
will listen to me 16 and rescue us from
those who would cut us off from the inheritance* God has given us. 17 Yes, my
lord the king will give us peace of mind
again.' I know that you are like an angel
of God in discerning good from evil. May
the LORD your God be with you."

¹⁸"I must know one thing," the king replied, "and tell me the truth."

"Yes, my lord the king," she responded.

¹⁹"Did Joab put you up to this?"

And the woman replied, "My lord the king, how can I deny it? Nobody can hide anything from you. Yes, Joab sent me and told me what to say. ²⁰He did it to place the matter before you in a different light. But you are as wise as an angel of God, and you understand everything that happens among us!"

²¹So the king sent for Joab and told him, "All right, go and bring back the young man Absalom."

²²Joab bowed with his face to the ground in deep respect and said, "At last I know that I have gained your approval, my lord the king, for you have granted me this request!"

²³Then Joab went to Geshur and brought Absalom back to Jerusalem. ²⁴But the king gave this order: "Absalom may go to his own house, but he must never come into my presence." So Absalom did not see the king.

²⁵Now Absalom was praised as the most handsome man in all Israel. He was flawless from head to foot. ²⁶He cut his hair only once a year, and then only because it was so heavy. When he weighed it out, it came to five pounds!* ²⁷He had three sons and one daughter. His daughter's name was Tamar, and she was very beautiful.

²⁸Absalom lived in Jerusalem for two years, but he never got to see the king. ²⁹Then Absalom sent for Joab to ask him to intercede for him, but Joab refused to come. Absalom sent for him a second time, but again Joab refused to come. ³⁰So Absalom said to his servants, "Go and set fire to Joab's barley field, the field next to mine." So they set his field on fire, as Absalom had commanded.

³¹Then Joab came to Absalom at his house and demanded, "Why did your servants set my field on fire?"

³²And Absalom replied, "Because I wanted you to ask the king why he brought me back from Geshur if he didn't intend to see me. I might as well have stayed there. Let me see the king; if he finds me guilty of anything, then let him kill me."

³³So Joab told the king what Absalom had said. Then at last David summoned Absalom, who came and bowed low before the king, and the king kissed him.

¹⁵:¹AFTER this, Absalom bought a chariot and horses, and he hired fifty bodyguards to run ahead of him. ²He got up early every morning and went out to the gate of the city. When people brought a case to the king for judgment, Absalom would ask where in Israel they were from, and they would tell him their tribe. ³Then Absalom would say, "You've really got a strong case here! It's too bad the king doesn't have anyone to hear it. ⁴I wish I were the judge. Then everyone could bring their cases to me for judgment, and I would give them justice!"

⁵When people tried to bow before him, Absalom wouldn't let them. Instead, he took them by the hand and embraced them. ⁶Absalom did this with everyone who came to the king for judgment, and so he stole the hearts of all the people of Israel.

⁷After four years,* Absalom said to the king, "Let me go to Hebron to offer a sacrifice to the LORD and fulfill a vow I made to him. ⁸For while your servant was at Geshur in Aram, I promised to sacrifice to the LORD in Hebron* if he would bring me back to Jerusalem."

⁹"All right," the king told him. "Go and fulfill your vow."

So Absalom went to Hebron. ¹⁰But while he was there, he sent secret messengers to all the tribes of Israel to stir up a rebellion against the king. "As soon as you hear the ram's horn," his message read, "you are to say, 'Absalom has been crowned king in Hebron.'" ¹¹He took 200 men from Jerusalem with him as guests, but they knew nothing of his intentions. ¹²While Absalom was offering the sacrifices, he sent for Ahithophel, one of David's counselors who lived in

Giloh. Soon many others also joined Absalom, and the conspiracy gained momentum.

¹³A messenger soon arrived in Jerusalem to tell David, "All Israel has joined Absalom in a conspiracy against you!"

¹⁴"Then we must flee at once, or it will be too late!" David urged his men. "Hurry! If we get out of the city before Absalom arrives, both we and the city of Jerusalem will be spared from disaster."

¹⁵"We are with you," his advisers replied. "Do what you think is best."

¹⁶So the king and all his household set out at once. He left no one behind except ten of his concubines to look after the palace. ¹⁷The king and all his people set out on foot, pausing at the last house ¹⁸to let all the king's men move past to lead the way. There were 600 men from Gath who had come with David, along with the king's bodyguard.*

¹⁹Then the king turned and said to Ittai, a leader of the men from Gath, "Why are you coming with us? Go on back to King Absalom, for you are a guest in Israel, a foreigner in exile. ²⁰You arrived only recently, and should I force you today to wander with us? I don't even know where we will go. Go on back and take your kinsmen with you, and may the LORD show you his unfailing love and faithfulness.*"

²¹But Ittai said to the king, "I vow by the LORD and by your own life that I will go wherever my lord the king goes, no matter what happens—whether it means life or death."

²²David replied, "All right, come with us." So Ittai and all his men and their families went along.

14:2 Hebrew *don't anoint yourself with oil.*   14:16 Or *the property;* or *the people.*   14:26 Hebrew *200 shekels* [2.3 kilograms] *by the royal standard.*   15:7 As in Greek and Syriac versions; Hebrew reads *forty years.*   15:8 As in some Greek manuscripts; Hebrew lacks *in Hebron.* 15:18 Hebrew *the Kerethites and Pelethites.*   15:20 As in Greek version; Hebrew reads *and may unfailing love and faithfulness go with you.*

JOHN 18:1-24

After saying these things, Jesus crossed the Kidron Valley with his disciples and entered a grove of olive trees. ²Judas, the betrayer, knew this place, because Jesus had often gone there with his disciples. ³The leading priests and Pharisees had given Judas a contingent of Roman soldiers and Temple guards to accompany him. Now with blazing torches, lanterns, and weapons, they arrived at the olive grove.

⁴Jesus fully realized all that was going to happen to him, so he stepped forward to meet them. "Who are you looking for?" he asked.

⁵"Jesus the Nazarene,"* they replied.

"I AM he,"* Jesus said. (Judas, who betrayed him, was standing with them.) ⁶As Jesus said "I AM he," they all drew back and fell to the ground! ⁷Once more he asked them, "Who are you looking for?"

And again they replied, "Jesus the Nazarene."

⁸"I told you that I AM he," Jesus said. "And since I am the one you want, let these others go." ⁹He did this to fulfill his own statement: "I did not lose a single one of those you have given me."*

¹⁰Then Simon Peter drew a sword and slashed off the right ear of Malchus, the high priest's slave. ¹¹But Jesus said to Peter, "Put your sword back into its sheath. Shall I not drink from the cup of suffering the Father has given me?"

¹²So the soldiers, their commanding officer, and the Temple guards arrested Jesus and tied him up. ¹³First they took him to Annas, the father-in-law of Caiaphas, the high priest at that time.* ¹⁴Caiaphas was the one who had told the other Jewish leaders, "It's better that one man should die for the people."

¹⁵Simon Peter followed Jesus, as did another of the disciples. That other disciple was acquainted with the high priest, so he was allowed to enter the high priest's courtyard with Jesus. ¹⁶Peter had to stay outside the gate. Then the disciple who knew the high priest spoke to the woman watching at the gate, and she let Peter in. ¹⁷The woman asked Peter, "You're not one of that man's disciples, are you?"

"No," he said, "I am not."

[18]Because it was cold, the household servants and the guards had made a charcoal fire. They stood around it, warming themselves, and Peter stood with them, warming himself.

[19]Inside, the high priest began asking Jesus about his followers and what he had been teaching them. [20]Jesus replied, "Everyone knows what I teach. I have preached regularly in the synagogues and the Temple, where the people* gather. I have not spoken in secret. [21]Why are you asking me this question? Ask those who heard me. They know what I said."

[22]Then one of the Temple guards standing nearby slapped Jesus across the face. "Is that the way to answer the high priest?" he demanded.

[23]Jesus replied, "If I said anything wrong, you must prove it. But if I'm speaking the truth, why are you beating me?"

[24]Then Annas bound Jesus and sent him to Caiaphas, the high priest.

18:5a Or *Jesus of Nazareth;* also in 18:7.   **18:5b** Or *"The 'I Am' is here";* or *"I am the Lord";* Greek reads *I am;* also in 18:6, 8. See Exod 3:14.   **18:9** See John 6:39 and 17:12.   **18:13** Greek *that year.*   **18:20** Greek *Jewish people;* also in 18:38.

PSALM 119:97-112

Mem

[97] **O**h, how I love your instructions!
   I think about them all day long.
[98] Your commands make me wiser
      than my enemies,
   for they are my constant guide.
[99] Yes, I have more insight than
      my teachers,
   for I am always thinking
      of your laws.
[100]I am even wiser than my elders,
   for I have kept your
      commandments.
[101]I have refused to walk on any
      evil path,
   so that I may remain obedient
      to your word.
[102]I haven't turned away from
      your regulations,
   for you have taught me well.
[103]How sweet your words taste to me;

   they are sweeter than honey.
[104]Your commandments give me
      understanding;
   no wonder I hate every false
      way of life.

Nun

[105]**Your word is a lamp to guide
      my feet
   and a light for my path.**
[106]**I've promised it once, and I'll
      promise it again:
   I will obey your righteous
      regulations.**
[107]I have suffered much, O Lord;
   restore my life again as you
      promised.
[108]Lord, accept my offering of praise,
   and teach me your regulations.
[109]My life constantly hangs in the
      balance,
   but I will not stop obeying
      your instructions.
[110]The wicked have set their traps
      for me,
   but I will not turn from your
      commandments.
[111]Your laws are my treasure;
   they are my heart's delight.
[112]I am determined to keep
      your decrees
   to the very end.

PROVERBS 16:8-9

Better to have little, with godliness, than to be rich and dishonest. □ We can make our plans, but the Lord determines our steps.

MAY 30

2 SAMUEL 15:23–16:23

Everyone cried loudly as the king and his followers passed by. They crossed the Kidron Valley and then went out toward the wilderness.

²⁴Zadok and all the Levites also came along, carrying the Ark of the Covenant of God. They set down the Ark of God, and Abiathar offered sacrifices* until everyone had passed out of the city.

²⁵Then the king instructed Zadok to take the Ark of God back into the city. "If the LORD sees fit," David said, "he will bring me back to see the Ark and the Tabernacle* again. ²⁶But if he is through with me, then let him do what seems best to him."

²⁷The king also told Zadok the priest, "Look,* here is my plan. You and Abiathar* should return quietly to the city with your son Ahimaaz and Abiathar's son Jonathan. ²⁸I will stop at the shallows of the Jordan River* and wait there for a report from you." ²⁹So Zadok and Abiathar took the Ark of God back to the city and stayed there.

³⁰David walked up the road to the Mount of Olives, weeping as he went. His head was covered and his feet were bare as a sign of mourning. And the people who were with him covered their heads and wept as they climbed the hill. ³¹When someone told David that his adviser Ahithophel was now backing Absalom, David prayed, "O LORD, let Ahithophel give Absalom foolish advice!"

³²When David reached the summit of the Mount of Olives where people worshiped God, Hushai the Arkite was waiting there for him. Hushai had torn his clothing and put dirt on his head as a sign of mourning. ³³But David told him, "If you go with me, you will only be a burden. ³⁴Return to Jerusalem and tell Absalom, 'I will now be your adviser, O king, just as I was your father's adviser in the past.' Then you can frustrate and counter Ahithophel's advice. ³⁵Zadok and Abiathar, the priests, will be there. Tell them about the plans being made in the king's palace, ³⁶and they will send their sons Ahimaaz and Jonathan to tell me what is going on."

³⁷So David's friend Hushai returned to Jerusalem, getting there just as Absalom arrived.

¹⁶:¹WHEN David had gone a little beyond the summit of the Mount of Olives, Ziba, the servant of Mephibosheth,* was waiting there for him. He had two donkeys loaded with 200 loaves of bread, 100 clusters of raisins, 100 bunches of summer fruit, and a wineskin full of wine.

²"What are these for?" the king asked Ziba.

Ziba replied, "The donkeys are for the king's people to ride on, and the bread and summer fruit are for the young men to eat. The wine is for those who become exhausted in the wilderness."

³"And where is Mephibosheth, Saul's grandson?" the king asked him.

"He stayed in Jerusalem," Ziba replied. "He said, 'Today I will get back the kingdom of my grandfather Saul.'"

⁴"In that case," the king told Ziba, "I give you everything Mephibosheth owns."

"I bow before you," Ziba replied. "May I always be pleasing to you, my lord the king."

⁵As King David came to Bahurim, a man came out of the village cursing them. It was Shimei son of Gera, from the same clan as Saul's family. ⁶He threw stones at the king and the king's officers and all the mighty warriors who surrounded him. ⁷"Get out of here, you murderer, you scoundrel!" he shouted at David. ⁸"The LORD is paying you back for all the bloodshed in Saul's clan. You stole his throne, and now the LORD has given it to your son Absalom. At last you will taste some of your own medicine, for you are a murderer!"

⁹"Why should this dead dog curse my lord the king?" Abishai son of Zeruiah demanded. "Let me go over and cut off his head!"

¹⁰"No!" the king said. "Who asked your opinion, you sons of Zeruiah! If the LORD has told him to curse me, who are you to stop him?"

¹¹Then David said to Abishai and to all his servants, "My own son is trying to kill me. Doesn't this relative of Saul* have even more reason to do so? Leave him

alone and let him curse, for the LORD has told him to do it. [12]And perhaps the LORD will see that I am being wronged and will bless me because of these curses today." [13]So David and his men continued down the road, and Shimei kept pace with them on a nearby hillside, cursing as he went and throwing stones at David and tossing dust into the air.

[14]The king and all who were with him grew weary along the way, so they rested when they reached the Jordan River.*

[15]Meanwhile, Absalom and all the army of Israel arrived at Jerusalem, accompanied by Ahithophel. [16]When David's friend Hushai the Arkite arrived, he went immediately to see Absalom. "Long live the king!" he exclaimed. "Long live the king!"

[17]"Is this the way you treat your friend David?" Absalom asked him. "Why aren't you with him?"

[18]"I'm here because I belong to the man who is chosen by the LORD and by all the men of Israel," Hushai replied. [19]"And anyway, why shouldn't I serve you? Just as I was your father's adviser, now I will be your adviser!"

[20]Then Absalom turned to Ahithophel and asked him, "What should I do next?"

[21]Ahithophel told him, "Go and sleep with your father's concubines, for he has left them here to look after the palace. Then all Israel will know that you have insulted your father beyond hope of reconciliation, and they will throw their support to you." [22]So they set up a tent on the palace roof where everyone could see it, and Absalom went in and had sex with his father's concubines.

[23]Absalom followed Ahithophel's advice, just as David had done. For every word Ahithophel spoke seemed as wise as though it had come directly from the mouth of God.

15:24 Or *Abiathar went up.*   15:25 Hebrew *and his dwelling place.*   15:27a As in Greek version; Hebrew reads *Are you a seer?* or *Do you see?*   15:27b Hebrew lacks *and Abiathar;* compare 15:29.   15:28 Hebrew *at the crossing points of the wilderness.*   16:1 *Mephibosheth* is another name for Merib-baal.   16:11 Hebrew *this Benjaminite.*   16:14 As in Greek version (see also 17:16); Hebrew reads *when they reached their destination.*

JOHN 18:25–19:22

Meanwhile, as Simon Peter was standing by the fire, they asked him again, "You're not one of his disciples, are you?"

He denied it, saying, "No, I am not."

[26]But one of the household slaves of the high priest, a relative of the man whose ear Peter had cut off, asked, "Didn't I see you out there in the olive grove with Jesus?" [27]Again Peter denied it. And immediately a rooster crowed.

[28]Jesus' trial before Caiaphas ended in the early hours of the morning. Then he was taken to the headquarters of the Roman governor.* His accusers didn't go inside because it would defile them, and they wouldn't be allowed to celebrate the Passover. [29]So Pilate, the governor, went out to them and asked, "What is your charge against this man?"

[30]"We wouldn't have handed him over to you if he weren't a criminal!" they retorted.

[31]"Then take him away and judge him by your own law," Pilate told them.

"Only the Romans are permitted to execute someone," the Jewish leaders replied. [32](This fulfilled Jesus' prediction about the way he would die.*)

[33]Then Pilate went back into his headquarters and called for Jesus to be brought to him. "Are you the king of the Jews?" he asked him.

[34]Jesus replied, "Is this your own question, or did others tell you about me?"

[35]"Am I a Jew?" Pilate retorted. "Your own people and their leading priests brought you to me for trial. Why? What have you done?"

[36]**Jesus answered, "My Kingdom is not an earthly kingdom. If it were, my followers would fight to keep me from being handed over to the Jewish leaders. But my Kingdom is not of this world."**

[37]Pilate said, "So you are a king?"

Jesus responded, "You say I am a king. Actually, I was born and came into the world to testify to the truth. All who love the truth recognize that what I say is true."

38"What is truth?" Pilate asked. Then he went out again to the people and told them, "He is not guilty of any crime. 39But you have a custom of asking me to release one prisoner each year at Passover. Would you like me to release this 'King of the Jews'?"

40But they shouted back, "No! Not this man. We want Barabbas!" (Barabbas was a revolutionary.)

19:1THEN Pilate had Jesus flogged with a lead-tipped whip. 2The soldiers wove a crown of thorns and put it on his head, and they put a purple robe on him. 3"Hail! King of the Jews!" they mocked, as they slapped him across the face.

4Pilate went outside again and said to the people, "I am going to bring him out to you now, but understand clearly that I find him not guilty." 5Then Jesus came out wearing the crown of thorns and the purple robe. And Pilate said, "Look, here is the man!"

6When they saw him, the leading priests and Temple guards began shouting, "Crucify him! Crucify him!"

"Take him yourselves and crucify him," Pilate said. "I find him not guilty."

7The Jewish leaders replied, "By our law he ought to die because he called himself the Son of God."

8When Pilate heard this, he was more frightened than ever. 9He took Jesus back into the headquarters* again and asked him, "Where are you from?" But Jesus gave no answer. 10"Why don't you talk to me?" Pilate demanded. "Don't you realize that I have the power to release you or crucify you?"

11Then Jesus said, "You would have no power over me at all unless it were given to you from above. So the one who handed me over to you has the greater sin."

12Then Pilate tried to release him, but the Jewish leaders shouted, "If you release this man, you are no 'friend of Caesar.'* Anyone who declares himself a king is a rebel against Caesar."

13When they said this, Pilate brought Jesus out to them again. Then Pilate sat down on the judgment seat on the platform that is called the Stone Pavement (in Hebrew, *Gabbatha*). 14It was now about noon on the day of preparation for the Passover. And Pilate said to the people,* "Look, here is your king!"

15"Away with him," they yelled. "Away with him! Crucify him!"

"What? Crucify your king?" Pilate asked.

"We have no king but Caesar," the leading priests shouted back.

16Then Pilate turned Jesus over to them to be crucified.

So they took Jesus away. 17Carrying the cross by himself, he went to the place called Place of the Skull (in Hebrew, *Golgotha*). 18There they nailed him to the cross. Two others were crucified with him, one on either side, with Jesus between them. 19And Pilate posted a sign over him that read, "Jesus of Nazareth,* the King of the Jews." 20The place where Jesus was crucified was near the city, and the sign was written in Hebrew, Latin, and Greek, so that many people could read it.

21Then the leading priests objected and said to Pilate, "Change it from 'The King of the Jews' to 'He said, I am King of the Jews.'"

22Pilate replied, "No, what I have written, I have written."

18:28 Greek *to the Praetorium;* also in 18:33.   18:32 See John 12:32-33.   19:9 Greek *the Praetorium.* 19:12 "Friend of Caesar" is a technical term that refers to an ally of the emperor.   19:14 Greek *Jewish people;* also in 19:20.   19:19 Or *Jesus the Nazarene.*

PSALM 119:113-128

Samekh

113 I hate those with divided loyalties,
    but I love your instructions.
114 You are my refuge and my shield;
    your word is my source of hope.
115 Get out of my life, you evil-minded
        people,
    for I intend to obey the
        commands of my God.
116 LORD, sustain me as you promised,
        that I may live!
    Do not let my hope be crushed.

117 Sustain me, and I will be rescued;
     then I will meditate continually
          on your decrees.
118 But you have rejected all who stray
     from your decrees.
     They are only fooling themselves.
119 You skim off the wicked of the
          earth like scum;
     no wonder I love to obey your laws!
120 I tremble in fear of you;
     I stand in awe of your regulations.

Ayin

121 Don't leave me to the mercy
          of my enemies,
     for I have done what is just
          and right.
122 Please guarantee a blessing for me.
     Don't let the arrogant oppress me!
123 My eyes strain to see your rescue,
     to see the truth of your promise
          fulfilled.
124 I am your servant; deal with me
          in unfailing love,
     and teach me your decrees.
125 Give discernment to me,
          your servant;
     then I will understand your laws.
126 LORD, it is time for you to act,
     for these evil people have violated
          your instructions.
127 Truly, I love your commands
     more than gold, even the
          finest gold.
128 Each of your commandments
          is right.
     That is why I hate every false way.

PROVERBS 16:10-11

The king speaks with divine wisdom; he must never judge unfairly. □ The LORD demands accurate scales and balances; he sets the standards for fairness.

MAY
31

2 SAMUEL 17:1-29

Now Ahithophel urged Absalom, "Let me choose 12,000 men to start out after David tonight. 2I will catch up with him while he is weary and discouraged. He and his troops will panic, and everyone will run away. Then I will kill only the king, 3and I will bring all the people back to you as a bride returns to her husband. After all, it is only one man's life that you seek.* Then you will be at peace with all the people." 4This plan seemed good to Absalom and to all the elders of Israel.

5But then Absalom said, "Bring in Hushai the Arkite. Let's see what he thinks about this." 6When Hushai arrived, Absalom told him what Ahithophel had said. Then he asked, "What is your opinion? Should we follow Ahithophel's advice? If not, what do you suggest?"

7"Well," Hushai replied to Absalom, "this time Ahithophel has made a mistake. 8You know your father and his men; they are mighty warriors. Right now they are as enraged as a mother bear who has been robbed of her cubs. And remember that your father is an experienced man of war. He won't be spending the night among the troops. 9He has probably already hidden in some pit or cave. And when he comes out and attacks and a few of your men fall, there will be panic among your troops, and the word will spread that Absalom's men are being slaughtered. 10Then even the bravest soldiers, though they have the heart of a lion, will be paralyzed with fear. For all Israel knows what a mighty warrior your father is and how courageous his men are.

11"I recommend that you mobilize the entire army of Israel, bringing them from as far away as Dan in the north and Beersheba in the south. That way you will have an army as numerous as the sand on the seashore. And I advise that you personally lead the troops. [12]When we find David, we'll fall on him like dew that falls on the ground. Then neither he nor any of his men will be left alive. [13]And if David were to escape into some town, you will have all Israel there at your command. Then we can take ropes and drag the walls of the town into the nearest valley until every stone is torn down."

[14]Then Absalom and all the men of Israel said, "Hushai's advice is better than Ahithophel's." For the LORD had determined to defeat the counsel of Ahithophel, which really was the better plan, so that he could bring disaster on Absalom!

[15]Hushai told Zadok and Abiathar, the priests, what Ahithophel had said to Absalom and the elders of Israel and what he himself had advised instead. [16]"Quick!" he told them. "Find David and urge him not to stay at the shallows of the Jordan River* tonight. He must go across at once into the wilderness beyond. Otherwise he will die and his entire army with him."

[17]Jonathan and Ahimaaz had been staying at En-rogel so as not to be seen entering and leaving the city. Arrangements had been made for a servant girl to bring them the message they were to take to King David. [18]But a boy spotted them at En-rogel, and he told Absalom about it. So they quickly escaped to Bahurim, where a man hid them down inside a well in his courtyard. [19]The man's wife put a cloth over the top of the well and scattered grain on it to dry in the sun; so no one suspected they were there.

[20]When Absalom's men arrived, they asked her, "Have you seen Ahimaaz and Jonathan?"

The woman replied, "They were here, but they crossed over the brook." Absalom's men looked for them without success and returned to Jerusalem.

[21]Then the two men crawled out of the well and hurried on to King David.

"Quick!" they told him, "cross the Jordan tonight!" And they told him how Ahithophel had advised that he be captured and killed. [22]So David and all the people with him went across the Jordan River during the night, and they were all on the other bank before dawn.

[23]When Ahithophel realized that his advice had not been followed, he saddled his donkey, went to his hometown, set his affairs in order, and hanged himself. He died there and was buried in the family tomb.

[24]David soon arrived at Mahanaim. By now, Absalom had mobilized the entire army of Israel and was leading his troops across the Jordan River. [25]Absalom had appointed Amasa as commander of his army, replacing Joab, who had been commander under David. (Amasa was Joab's cousin. His father was Jether,* an Ishmaelite.* His mother, Abigail daughter of Nahash, was the sister of Joab's mother, Zeruiah.) [26]Absalom and the Israelite army set up camp in the land of Gilead.

[27]When David arrived at Mahanaim, he was warmly greeted by Shobi son of Nahash, who came from Rabbah of the Ammonites, and by Makir son of Ammiel from Lo-debar, and by Barzillai of Gilead from Rogelim. [28]They brought sleeping mats, cooking pots, serving bowls, wheat and barley, flour and roasted grain, beans, lentils, [29]honey, butter, sheep, goats, and cheese for David and those who were with him. For they said, "You must all be very hungry and tired and thirsty after your long march through the wilderness."

17:3 As in Greek version; Hebrew reads *like the return of all is the man whom you seek.* 17:16 Hebrew *at the crossing points of the wilderness.* 17:25a Hebrew *Ithra,* a variant spelling of Jether. 17:25b As in some Greek manuscripts (see also 1 Chr 2:17); Hebrew reads *an Israelite.*

JOHN 19:23-42

When the soldiers had crucified Jesus, they divided his clothes among the four of them. They also took his robe, but it was seamless, woven in one piece from top to bottom. [24]So they said, "Rather than tearing it apart, let's throw dice* for it. This fulfilled the Scripture that says, "They divided my garments among themselves and threw dice for my clothing."* So that is what they did.

25 Standing near the cross were Jesus' mother, and his mother's sister, Mary (the wife of Clopas), and Mary Magdalene. 26 When Jesus saw his mother standing there beside the disciple he loved, he said to her, "Dear woman, here is your son." 27 And he said to this disciple, "Here is your mother." And from then on this disciple took her into his home.

28 Jesus knew that his mission was now finished, and to fulfill Scripture he said, "I am thirsty."* 29 A jar of sour wine was sitting there, so they soaked a sponge in it, put it on a hyssop branch, and held it up to his lips. 30 When Jesus had tasted it, he said, "It is finished!" Then he bowed his head and released his spirit.

31 It was the day of preparation, and the Jewish leaders didn't want the bodies hanging there the next day, which was the Sabbath (and a very special Sabbath, because it was the Passover). So they asked Pilate to hasten their deaths by ordering that their legs be broken. Then their bodies could be taken down. 32 So the soldiers came and broke the legs of the two men crucified with Jesus. 33 But when they came to Jesus, they saw that he was already dead, so they didn't break his legs. 34 One of the soldiers, however, pierced his side with a spear, and immediately blood and water flowed out. 35 (This report is from an eyewitness giving an accurate account. He speaks the truth so that you also can believe.*) 36 These things happened in fulfillment of the Scriptures that say, "Not one of his bones will be broken,"* 37 and "They will look on the one they pierced."*

38 Afterward Joseph of Arimathea, who had been a secret disciple of Jesus (because he feared the Jewish leaders), asked Pilate for permission to take down Jesus' body. When Pilate gave permission, Joseph came and took the body away. 39 With him came Nicodemus, the man who had come to Jesus at night. He brought seventy-five pounds* of perfumed ointment made from myrrh and aloes. 40 Following Jewish burial custom, they wrapped Jesus' body with the spices in long sheets of linen cloth. 41 The place of crucifixion was near a garden, where there was a new tomb, never used before. 42 And so, because it was the day of preparation for the Jewish Passover* and since the tomb was close at hand, they laid Jesus there.

19:24a Greek *cast lots.*   19:24b Ps 22:18.   19:28 See Pss 22:15; 69:21.   19:35 Some manuscripts read *can continue to believe.*   19:36 Exod 12:46; Num 9:12; Ps 34:20. 19:37 Zech 12:10.   19:39 Greek *100 litras* [32.7 kilograms].   19:42 Greek *because of the Jewish day of preparation.*

PSALM 119:129-152

Pe

129 Your laws are wonderful.
No wonder I obey them!
130 The teaching of your word
gives light,
so even the simple can
understand.
131 I pant with expectation,
longing for your commands.
132 Come and show me your mercy,
as you do for all who love your
name.
133 Guide my steps by your word,
so I will not be overcome
by evil.
134 Ransom me from the oppression
of evil people;
then I can obey your
commandments.
135 Look upon me with love;
teach me your decrees.
136 Rivers of tears gush from my eyes
because people disobey your
instructions.

Tsadhe

137 **O Lord, you are righteous,
and your regulations are fair.**
138 **Your laws are perfect
and completely trustworthy.**
139 I am overwhelmed with indignation,

for my enemies have disregarded
your words.
140 Your promises have been
thoroughly tested;
that is why I love them so much.
141 I am insignificant and despised,
but I don't forget your
commandments.
142 Your justice is eternal,
and your instructions are
perfectly true.
143 As pressure and stress bear down
on me,
I find joy in your commands.
144 Your laws are always right;
help me to understand them
so I may live.

Qoph
145 I pray with all my heart; answer
me, LORD!
I will obey your decrees.
146 I cry out to you; rescue me,
that I may obey your laws.

147 I rise early, before the sun is up;
I cry out for help and put my
hope in your words.
148 I stay awake through the night,
thinking about your promise.
149 In your faithful love, O LORD,
hear my cry;
let me be revived by following
your regulations.
150 Lawless people are coming to
attack me;
they live far from your
instructions.
151 But you are near, O LORD,
and all your commands are true.
152 I have known from my earliest days
that your laws will last forever.

PROVERBS 16:12-13
A king detests wrongdoing, for his rule
is built on justice. □ The king is pleased
with words from righteous lips; he loves
those who speak honestly.

JUNE
1

2 SAMUEL 18:1–19:10

David now mustered the men who were with him and appointed generals and captains* to lead them. ²He sent the troops out in three groups, placing one group under Joab, one under Joab's brother Abishai son of Zeruiah, and one under Ittai, the man from Gath. The king told his troops, "I am going out with you."

³But his men objected strongly. "You must not go," they urged. "If we have to turn and run—and even if half of us die—it will make no difference to Absalom's troops; they will be looking only for you. You are worth 10,000 of us,* and it is better that you stay here in the town and send help if we need it."

⁴"If you think that's the best plan, I'll do it," the king answered. So he stood alongside the gate of the town as all the troops marched out in groups of hundreds and of thousands.

⁵And the king gave this command to Joab, Abishai, and Ittai: "For my sake, deal gently with young Absalom." And all the troops heard the king give this order to his commanders.

⁶So the battle began in the forest of Ephraim, ⁷and the Israelite troops were beaten back by David's men. There was a great slaughter that day, and 20,000 men laid down their lives. ⁸The battle raged all across the countryside, and more men died because of the forest than were killed by the sword.

⁹During the battle, Absalom happened to come upon some of David's men. He tried to escape on his mule, but as he rode beneath the thick branches of a great tree, his hair* got caught in the tree. His mule kept going and left him dangling in the air. ¹⁰One of David's men saw what had happened and told Joab, "I saw Absalom dangling from a great tree."

¹¹"What?" Joab demanded. "You saw him there and didn't kill him? I would have rewarded you with ten pieces of silver* and a hero's belt!"

¹²"I would not kill the king's son for even a thousand pieces of silver,*" the man replied to Joab. "We all heard the king say to you and Abishai and Ittai, 'For my sake, please spare young Absalom.' ¹³And if I had betrayed the king by killing his son—and the king would certainly find out who did it—you yourself would be the first to abandon me."

¹⁴"Enough of this nonsense," Joab said. Then he took three daggers and plunged them into Absalom's heart as he dangled, still alive, in the great tree. ¹⁵Ten of Joab's young armor bearers then surrounded Absalom and killed him.

¹⁶Then Joab blew the ram's horn, and his men returned from chasing the army of Israel. ¹⁷They threw Absalom's body into a deep pit in the forest and piled a great heap of stones over it. And all Israel fled to their homes.

¹⁸During his lifetime, Absalom had built a monument to himself in the King's Valley, for he said, "I have no son to carry on my name." He named the monument after himself, and it is known as Absalom's Monument to this day.

¹⁹Then Zadok's son Ahimaaz said, "Let me run to the king with the good news that the LORD has rescued him from his enemies."

²⁰"No," Joab told him, "it wouldn't be good news to the king that his son is dead. You can be my messenger another time, but not today."

²¹Then Joab said to a man from Ethiopia,* "Go tell the king what you have seen." The man bowed and ran off.

²²But Ahimaaz continued to plead with Joab, "Whatever happens, please let me go, too."

"Why should you go, my son?" Joab replied. "There will be no reward for your news."

²³"Yes, but let me go anyway," he begged.

Joab finally said, "All right, go ahead." So Ahimaaz took the less demanding route by way of the plain and ran to Mahanaim ahead of the Ethiopian.

²⁴While David was sitting between the inner and outer gates of the town, the watchman climbed to the roof of the gateway by the wall. As he looked, he saw a lone man running toward them. ²⁵He shouted the news down to David, and the king replied, "If he is alone, he has news."

As the messenger came closer, ²⁶the watchman saw another man running toward them. He shouted down, "Here comes another one!"

The king replied, "He also will have news."

²⁷"The first man runs like Ahimaaz son of Zadok," the watchman said.

"He is a good man and comes with good news," the king replied.

²⁸Then Ahimaaz cried out to the king, "Everything is all right!" He bowed before the king with his face to the ground and said, "Praise to the LORD your God, who has handed over the rebels who dared to stand against my lord the king."

²⁹"What about young Absalom?" the king demanded. "Is he all right?"

Ahimaaz replied, "When Joab told me to come, there was a lot of commotion. But I didn't know what was happening."

³⁰"Wait here," the king told him. So Ahimaaz stepped aside.

³¹Then the man from Ethiopia arrived and said, "I have good news for my lord the king. Today the LORD has rescued you from all those who rebelled against you."

³²"What about young Absalom?" the king demanded. "Is he all right?"

And the Ethiopian replied, "May all of your enemies, my lord the king, both now and in the future, share the fate of that young man!"

³³*The king was overcome with emotion. He went up to the room over the gateway and burst into tears. And as he went, he cried, "O my son Absalom! My son, my son Absalom! If only I had died instead of you! O Absalom, my son, my son."

19:1*WORD soon reached Joab that the king was weeping and mourning for Absalom. ²As all the people heard of the king's deep grief for his son, the joy of that day's victory was turned into deep sadness. ³They crept back into the town that day as though they were ashamed and had deserted in battle. ⁴The king covered his face with his hands and kept on crying, "O my son Absalom! O Absalom, my son, my son!"

⁵Then Joab went to the king's room and said to him, "We saved your life today and the lives of your sons, your daughters, and your wives and concubines. Yet you act like this, making us feel ashamed of ourselves. ⁶You seem to love those who hate you and hate those who love you. You have made it clear today that your commanders and troops mean nothing to you. It seems that if Absalom had lived and all of us had died, you would be pleased. ⁷Now go out there and congratulate your troops, for I swear by the LORD that if you don't go out, not a single one of them will remain here tonight. Then you will be worse off than ever before."

⁸So the king went out and took his seat at the town gate, and as the news spread throughout the town that he was there, everyone went to him.

Meanwhile, the Israelites who had supported Absalom fled to their homes. ⁹And throughout all the tribes of Israel there was much discussion and argument going on. The people were saying, "The king rescued us from our enemies and saved us from the Philistines, but Absalom chased him out of the country.

¹⁰Now Absalom, whom we anointed to rule over us, is dead. Why not ask David to come back and be our king again?"

18:1 Hebrew *appointed commanders of thousands and commanders of hundreds.*   18:3 As in two Hebrew manuscripts and some Greek and Latin manuscripts; most Hebrew manuscripts read *Now there are 10,000 like us.* 18:9 Hebrew *his head.*   18:11 Hebrew *10 shekels of silver,* about 4 ounces or 114 grams in weight.   18:12 Hebrew *1,000 shekels,* about 25 pounds or 11.4 kilograms in weight.   18:21 Hebrew *from Cush;* similarly in 18:23, 31, 32.   18:33 Verse 18:33 is numbered 19:1 in Hebrew text.   19:1 Verses 19:1-43 are numbered 19:2-44 in Hebrew text.

JOHN 20:1-31

Early on Sunday morning,* while it was still dark, Mary Magdalene came to the tomb and found that the stone had been rolled away from the entrance. ²She ran and found Simon Peter and the other disciple, the one whom Jesus loved. She said, "They have taken the Lord's body out of the tomb, and we don't know where they have put him!"

³Peter and the other disciple started out for the tomb. ⁴They were both running, but the other disciple outran Peter and reached the tomb first. ⁵He stooped and looked in and saw the linen wrappings lying there, but he didn't go in. ⁶Then Simon Peter arrived and went inside. He also noticed the linen wrappings lying there, ⁷while the cloth that had covered Jesus' head was folded up and lying apart from the other wrappings. ⁸Then the disciple who had reached the tomb first also went in, and he saw and believed—⁹for until then they still hadn't understood the Scriptures that said Jesus must rise from the dead. ¹⁰Then they went home.

¹¹Mary was standing outside the tomb crying, and as she wept, she stooped and looked in. ¹²She saw two white-robed angels, one sitting at the head and the other at the foot of the place where the body of Jesus had been lying. ¹³"Dear woman, why are you crying?" the angels asked her.

"Because they have taken away my Lord," she replied, "and I don't know where they have put him."

¹⁴She turned to leave and saw someone standing there. It was Jesus, but she didn't recognize him. ¹⁵"Dear woman, why are you crying?" Jesus asked her. "Who are you looking for?"

She thought he was the gardener. "Sir," she said, "if you have taken him away, tell me where you have put him, and I will go and get him."

¹⁶"Mary!" Jesus said.

She turned to him and cried out, "Rabboni!" (which is Hebrew for "Teacher").

¹⁷"Don't cling to me," Jesus said, "for I haven't yet ascended to the Father. But go find my brothers and tell them that I am ascending to my Father and your Father, to my God and your God."

¹⁸Mary Magdalene found the disciples and told them, "I have seen the Lord!" Then she gave them his message.

¹⁹That Sunday evening* the disciples were meeting behind locked doors because they were afraid of the Jewish leaders. Suddenly, Jesus was standing there among them! "Peace be with you," he said. ²⁰As he spoke, he showed them the wounds in his hands and his side. They were filled with joy when they saw the Lord! ²¹Again he said, "Peace be with you. As the Father has sent me, so I am sending you." ²²Then he breathed on them and said, "Receive the Holy Spirit. ²³If you forgive anyone's sins, they are forgiven. If you do not forgive them, they are not forgiven."

²⁴One of the disciples, Thomas (nicknamed the Twin),* was not with the others when Jesus came. ²⁵They told him, "We have seen the Lord!"

But he replied, "I won't believe it unless I see the nail wounds in his hands, put my fingers into them, and place my hand into the wound in his side."

²⁶Eight days later the disciples were together again, and this time Thomas was with them. The doors were locked; but suddenly, as before, Jesus was standing among them. "Peace be with you," he said. ²⁷Then he said to Thomas, "Put your finger here, and look at my hands. Put your hand into the wound in my side. Don't be faithless any longer. Believe!"

[28]"My Lord and my God!" Thomas exclaimed.

[29]Then Jesus told him, "You believe because you have seen me. Blessed are those who believe without seeing me."

[30]**The disciples saw Jesus do many other miraculous signs in addition to the ones recorded in this book.** [31]**But these are written so that you may continue to believe* that Jesus is the Messiah, the Son of God, and that by believing in him you will have life by the power of his name.**

20:1 Greek *On the first day of the week.* 20:19 Greek *In the evening of that day, the first day of the week.* 20:24 Greek *Thomas, who was called Didymus.* 20:31 Some manuscripts read *that you may believe.*

PSALM 119:153-176

Resh

[153]**L**ook upon my suffering and rescue me,
for I have not forgotten your instructions.
[154]Argue my case; take my side!
Protect my life as you promised.
[155]The wicked are far from rescue,
for they do not bother with your decrees.
[156]LORD, how great is your mercy;
let me be revived by following your regulations.
[157]Many persecute and trouble me,
yet I have not swerved from your laws.
[158]Seeing these traitors makes me sick at heart,
because they care nothing for your word.
[159]See how I love your commandments, LORD.
Give back my life because of your unfailing love.
[160]The very essence of your words is truth;
all your just regulations will stand forever.

Shin

[161]Powerful people harass me without cause,
but my heart trembles only at your word.

[162]I rejoice in your word
like one who discovers a great treasure.
[163]I hate and abhor all falsehood,
but I love your instructions.
[164]I will praise you seven times a day
because all your regulations are just.
[165]Those who love your instructions have great peace
and do not stumble.
[166]I long for your rescue, LORD,
so I have obeyed your commands.
[167]I have obeyed your laws,
for I love them very much.
[168]Yes, I obey your commandments and laws
because you know everything I do.

Taw

[169]O LORD, listen to my cry;
give me the discerning mind you promised.
[170]Listen to my prayer;
rescue me as you promised.
[171]Let praise flow from my lips,
for you have taught me your decrees.
[172]Let my tongue sing about your word,
for all your commands are right.
[173]Give me a helping hand,
for I have chosen to follow your commandments.
[174]O LORD, I have longed for your rescue,
and your instructions are my delight.
[175]Let me live so I can praise you,
and may your regulations help me.
[176]I have wandered away like a lost sheep;
come and find me,
for I have not forgotten your commands.

PROVERBS 16:14-15

The anger of the king is a deadly threat; the wise will try to appease it. ☐When the king smiles, there is life; his favor refreshes like a spring rain.

JUNE 2

2 SAMUEL 19:11–20:13

Then King David sent Zadok and Abiathar, the priests, to say to the elders of Judah, "Why are you the last ones to welcome back the king into his palace? For I have heard that all Israel is ready. ¹²You are my relatives, my own tribe, my own flesh and blood! So why are you the last ones to welcome back the king?" ¹³And David told them to tell Amasa, "Since you are my own flesh and blood, like Joab, may God strike me and even kill me if I do not appoint you as commander of my army in his place."

¹⁴Then Amasa* convinced all the men of Judah, and they responded unanimously. They sent word to the king, "Return to us, and bring back all who are with you."

¹⁵So the king started back to Jerusalem. And when he arrived at the Jordan River, the people of Judah came to Gilgal to meet him and escort him across the river. ¹⁶Shimei son of Gera, the man from Bahurim in Benjamin, hurried across with the men of Judah to welcome King David. ¹⁷A thousand other men from the tribe of Benjamin were with him, including Ziba, the chief servant of the house of Saul, and Ziba's fifteen sons and twenty servants. They rushed down to the Jordan to meet the king. ¹⁸They crossed the shallows of the Jordan to bring the king's household across the river, helping him in every way they could.

As the king was about to cross the river, Shimei fell down before him. ¹⁹"My lord the king, please forgive me," he pleaded. "Forget the terrible thing your servant did when you left Jerusalem. May the king put it out of his mind. ²⁰I know how much I sinned. That is why I have come here today, the very first person in all Israel* to greet my lord the king."

²¹Then Abishai son of Zeruiah said,

"Shimei should die, for he cursed the LORD's anointed king!"

²²"Who asked your opinion, you sons of Zeruiah!" David exclaimed. "Why have you become my adversary* today? This is not a day for execution but for celebration! Today I am once again the king of Israel!" ²³Then, turning to Shimei, David vowed, "Your life will be spared."

²⁴Now Mephibosheth,* Saul's grandson, came down from Jerusalem to meet the king. He had not cared for his feet, trimmed his beard, or washed his clothes since the day the king left Jerusalem. ²⁵"Why didn't you come with me, Mephibosheth?" the king asked him.

²⁶Mephibosheth replied, "My lord the king, my servant Ziba deceived me. I told him, 'Saddle my donkey* so I can go with the king.' For as you know I am crippled. ²⁷Ziba has slandered me by saying that I refused to come. But I know that my lord the king is like an angel of God, so do what you think is best. ²⁸All my relatives and I could expect only death from you, my lord, but instead you have honored me by allowing me to eat at your own table! What more can I ask?"

²⁹"You've said enough," David replied. "I've decided that you and Ziba will divide your land equally between you."

³⁰"Give him all of it," Mephibosheth said. "I am content just to have you safely back again, my lord the king!"

³¹Barzillai of Gilead had come down from Rogelim to escort the king across the Jordan. ³²He was very old, about eighty, and very wealthy. He was the one who had provided food for the king during his stay in Mahanaim. ³³"Come across with me and live in Jerusalem," the king said to Barzillai. "I will take care of you there."

³⁴"No," he replied, "I am far too old to go with the king to Jerusalem. ³⁵I am eighty years old today, and I can no longer enjoy anything. Food and wine are no longer tasty, and I cannot hear the singers as they sing. I would only be a burden to my lord the king. ³⁶Just to go

across the Jordan River with the king is all the honor I need! ³⁷Then let me return again to die in my own town, where my father and mother are buried. But here is your servant, my son Kimham. Let him go with my lord the king and receive whatever you want to give him."

³⁸"Good," the king agreed. "Kimham will go with me, and I will help him in any way you would like. And I will do for you anything you want." ³⁹So all the people crossed the Jordan with the king. After David had blessed and embraced him, Barzillai returned to his own home.

⁴⁰The king then crossed over to Gilgal, taking Kimham with him. All the troops of Judah and half the troops of Israel escorted the king on his way.

⁴¹But all the men of Israel complained to the king, "The men of Judah stole the king and didn't give us the honor of helping take you, your household, and all your men across the Jordan."

⁴²The men of Judah replied, "The king is one of our own kinsmen. Why should this make you angry? We haven't eaten any of the king's food or received any special favors!"

⁴³"But there are ten tribes in Israel," the others replied. "So we have ten times as much right to the king as you do. What right do you have to treat us with such contempt? Weren't we the first to speak of bringing him back to be our king again?" The argument continued back and forth, and the men of Judah spoke even more harshly than the men of Israel.

²⁰:¹THERE happened to be a troublemaker there named Sheba son of Bicri, a man from the tribe of Benjamin. Sheba blew a ram's horn and began to chant:

"Down with the dynasty of David!
    We have no interest in the
        son of Jesse.
Come on, you men of Israel,
    back to your homes!"

²So all the men of Israel deserted David and followed Sheba son of Bicri. But the men of Judah stayed with their king

and escorted him from the Jordan River to Jerusalem.

³When David came to his palace in Jerusalem, he took the ten concubines he had left to look after the palace and placed them in seclusion. Their needs were provided for, but he no longer slept with them. So each of them lived like a widow until she died.

⁴Then the king told Amasa, "Mobilize the army of Judah within three days, and report back at that time." ⁵So Amasa went out to notify Judah, but it took him longer than the time he had been given.

⁶Then David said to Abishai, "Sheba son of Bicri is going to hurt us more than Absalom did. Quick, take my troops and chase after him before he gets into a fortified town where we can't reach him."

⁷So Abishai and Joab,* together with the king's bodyguard* and all the mighty warriors, set out from Jerusalem to go after Sheba. ⁸As they arrived at the great stone in Gibeon, Amasa met them. Joab was wearing his military tunic with a dagger strapped to his belt. As he stepped forward to greet Amasa, he slipped the dagger from its sheath.*

⁹"How are you, my cousin?" Joab said and took him by the beard with his right hand as though to kiss him. ¹⁰Amasa didn't notice the dagger in his left hand, and Joab stabbed him in the stomach with it so that his insides gushed out onto the ground. Joab did not need to strike again, and Amasa soon died. Joab and his brother Abishai left him lying there and continued after Sheba.

¹¹One of Joab's young men shouted to Amasa's troops, "If you are for Joab and David, come and follow Joab." ¹²But Amasa lay in his blood in the middle of the road, and Joab's man saw that everyone was stopping to stare at him. So he pulled him off the road into a field and threw a cloak over him. ¹³With Amasa's body out of the way, everyone went on with Joab to capture Sheba son of Bicri.

19:14 As in Greek version; Hebrew reads *he.*
19:20 Hebrew *in the house of Joseph.*   19:22 Or *my prosecutor.*   19:24 *Mephibosheth* is another name for Merib-baal.   19:26 As in Greek, Syriac, and Latin versions;

Hebrew reads *I will saddle a donkey for myself.*
20:7a Hebrew *So Joab's men.*   **20:7b** Hebrew *the
Kerethites and Pelethites;* also in 20:23.   **20:8** Hebrew *As
he stepped forward, it fell out.*

JOHN 21:1-25

Later, Jesus appeared again to the disciples beside the Sea of Galilee.* This is
how it happened. ²Several of the disciples were there—Simon Peter, Thomas
(nicknamed the Twin),* Nathanael
from Cana in Galilee, the sons of Zebe-
dee, and two other disciples.

³Simon Peter said, "I'm going fish-
ing."

"We'll come, too," they all said. So they
went out in the boat, but they caught
nothing all night.

⁴At dawn Jesus was standing on the
beach, but the disciples couldn't see
who he was. ⁵He called out, "Fellows,*
have you caught any fish?"

"No," they replied.

⁶Then he said, "Throw out your net
on the right-hand side of the boat, and
you'll get some!" So they did, and they
couldn't haul in the net because there
were so many fish in it.

⁷Then the disciple Jesus loved said to
Peter, "It's the Lord!" When Simon Peter
heard that it was the Lord, he put on his
tunic (for he had stripped for work),
jumped into the water, and headed to
shore. ⁸The others stayed with the boat
and pulled the loaded net to the shore,
for they were only about a hundred
yards* from shore. ⁹When they got
there, they found breakfast waiting for
them—fish cooking over a charcoal fire,
and some bread.

¹⁰"Bring some of the fish you've just
caught," Jesus said. ¹¹So Simon Peter
went aboard and dragged the net to the
shore. There were 153 large fish, and
yet the net hadn't torn.

¹²"Now come and have some breakfast!" Jesus said. None of the disciples
dared to ask him, "Who are you?" They
knew it was the Lord. ¹³Then Jesus
served them the bread and the fish.
¹⁴This was the third time Jesus had appeared to his disciples since he had
been raised from the dead.

¹⁵After breakfast Jesus asked Simon
Peter, "Simon son of John, do you love
me more than these?*"

"Yes, Lord," Peter replied, "you know
I love you."

"Then feed my lambs," Jesus told him.

¹⁶Jesus repeated the question: "Simon son of John, do you love me?"

"Yes, Lord," Peter said, "you know I
love you."

"Then take care of my sheep," Jesus
said.

¹⁷A third time he asked him, "Simon
son of John, do you love me?"

Peter was hurt that Jesus asked the
question a third time. He said, "Lord,
you know everything. You know that I
love you."

Jesus said, "Then feed my sheep.

¹⁸"I tell you the truth, when you were
young, you were able to do as you liked;
you dressed yourself and went wherever you wanted to go. But when you are
old, you will stretch out your hands, and
others* will dress you and take you
where you don't want to go." ¹⁹Jesus
said this to let him know by what kind
of death he would glorify God. Then
Jesus told him, "Follow me."

²⁰Peter turned around and saw behind them the disciple Jesus loved—the
one who had leaned over to Jesus during supper and asked, "Lord, who will
betray you?" ²¹Peter asked Jesus, "What
about him, Lord?"

²²Jesus replied, "If I want him to remain alive until I return, what is that to
you? As for you, follow me." ²³So the ru-
mor spread among the community of
believers* that this disciple wouldn't
die. But that isn't what Jesus said at all.
He only said, "If I want him to remain
alive until I return, what is that to you?"

²⁴This disciple is the one who testifies to these events and has recorded
them here. And we know that his account of these things is accurate.

²⁵**Jesus also did many other things.
If they were all written down, I suppose the whole world could not contain the books that would be written.**

21:1 Greek *Sea of Tiberias,* another name for the Sea of Galilee.   21:2 Greek *Thomas, who was called Didymus.*   21:5 Greek *Children.*   21:8 Greek *200 cubits* [90 meters].   21:15 Or *more than these others do?*   21:18 Some manuscripts read *and another one.*   21:23 Greek *the brothers.*

PSALM 120:1-7
A song for pilgrims ascending to Jerusalem.

¹ I took my troubles to the LORD;
   I cried out to him, and he
      answered my prayer.
² Rescue me, O LORD, from liars
      and from all deceitful people.
³ O deceptive tongue, what will God
      do to you?
   How will he increase your
      punishment?
⁴ You will be pierced with sharp
      arrows
   and burned with glowing coals.

⁵ How I suffer in far-off Meshech.
   It pains me to live in distant
      Kedar.
⁶ I am tired of living
      among people who hate peace.
⁷ I search for peace;
      but when I speak of peace, they
         want war!

PROVERBS 16:16-17
How much better to get wisdom than gold, and good judgment than silver! □ The path of the virtuous leads away from evil; whoever follows that path is safe.

JUNE 3

2 SAMUEL 20:14–21:22
Meanwhile, Sheba traveled through all the tribes of Israel and eventually came to the town of Abel-beth-maacah. All the members of his own clan, the Bicrites,* assembled for battle and followed him into the town. ¹⁵When Joab's forces arrived, they attacked Abel-beth-maacah. They built a siege ramp against the town's fortifications and began battering down the wall. ¹⁶But a wise woman in the town called out to Joab, "Listen to me, Joab. Come over here so I can talk to you." ¹⁷As he approached, the woman asked, "Are you Joab?"

"I am," he replied.

So she said, "Listen carefully to your servant."

"I'm listening," he said.

¹⁸Then she continued, "There used to be a saying, 'If you want to settle an argument, ask advice at the town of Abel.' ¹⁹I am one who is peace loving and faithful in Israel. But you are destroying an important town in Israel.* Why do you want to devour what belongs to the LORD?"

²⁰And Joab replied, "Believe me, I don't want to devour or destroy your town! ²¹That's not my purpose. All I want is a man named Sheba son of Bicri from the hill country of Ephraim, who has revolted against King David. If you hand over this one man to me, I will leave the town in peace."

"All right," the woman replied, "we will throw his head over the wall to you." ²²Then the woman went to all the people with her wise advice, and they cut off Sheba's head and threw it out to Joab. So he blew the ram's horn and called his troops back from the attack. They all returned to their homes, and Joab returned to the king at Jerusalem.

²³Now Joab was the commander of the army of Israel. Benaiah son of Jehoiada was captain of the king's bodyguard. ²⁴Adoniram* was in charge of the labor force. Jehoshaphat son of Ahilud was the royal historian. ²⁵Sheva was the court secretary. Zadok and Abiathar were the priests. ²⁶And Ira, a descendant of Jair, was David's personal priest.

²¹:¹THERE was a famine during David's reign that lasted for three years, so David asked the LORD about it. And the LORD said, "The famine has come because Saul and his family are guilty of murdering the Gibeonites."

²So the king summoned the Gibeon-

ites. They were not part of Israel but were all that was left of the nation of the Amorites. The people of Israel had sworn not to kill them, but Saul, in his zeal for Israel and Judah, had tried to wipe them out. ³David asked them, "What can I do for you? How can I make amends so that you will bless the Lord's people again?"

⁴"Well, money can't settle this matter between us and the family of Saul," the Gibeonites replied. "Neither can we demand the life of anyone in Israel."

"What can I do then?" David asked. "Just tell me and I will do it for you."

⁵Then they replied, "It was Saul who planned to destroy us, to keep us from having any place at all in the territory of Israel. ⁶So let seven of Saul's sons be handed over to us, and we will execute them before the Lord at Gibeon, on the mountain of the Lord.*"

"All right," the king said, "I will do it." ⁷The king spared Jonathan's son Mephibosheth,* who was Saul's grandson, because of the oath David and Jonathan had sworn before the Lord. ⁸But he gave them Saul's two sons Armoni and Mephibosheth, whose mother was Rizpah daughter of Aiah. He also gave them the five sons of Saul's daughter Merab,* the wife of Adriel son of Barzillai from Meholah. ⁹The men of Gibeon executed them on the mountain before the Lord. So all seven of them died together at the beginning of the barley harvest.

¹⁰Then Rizpah daughter of Aiah, the mother of two of the men, spread burlap on a rock and stayed there the entire harvest season. She prevented the scavenger birds from tearing at their bodies during the day and stopped wild animals from eating them at night. ¹¹When David learned what Rizpah, Saul's concubine, had done, ¹²he went to the people of Jabesh-gilead and retrieved the bones of Saul and his son Jonathan. (When the Philistines had killed Saul and Jonathan on Mount Gilboa, the people of Jabesh-gilead stole their bodies from the public square of Beth-shan, where the Philistines had hung them.) ¹³So David obtained the bones of Saul and Jonathan, as

well as the bones of the men the Gibeonites had executed.

¹⁴Then the king ordered that they bury the bones in the tomb of Kish, Saul's father, at the town of Zela in the land of Benjamin. After that, God ended the famine in the land.

¹⁵Once again the Philistines were at war with Israel. And when David and his men were in the thick of battle, David became weak and exhausted. ¹⁶Ishbibenob was a descendant of the giants*; his bronze spearhead weighed more than seven pounds,* and he was armed with a new sword. He had cornered David and was about to kill him. ¹⁷But Abishai son of Zeruiah came to David's rescue and killed the Philistine. Then David's men declared, "You are not going out to battle with us again! Why risk snuffing out the light of Israel?"

¹⁸After this, there was another battle against the Philistines at Gob. As they fought, Sibbecai from Hushah killed Saph, another descendant of the giants.

¹⁹During another battle at Gob, Elhanan son of Jair* from Bethlehem killed the brother of Goliath of Gath.* The handle of his spear was as thick as a weaver's beam!

²⁰In another battle with the Philistines at Gath, they encountered a huge man with six fingers on each hand and six toes on each foot, twenty-four in all, who was also a descendant of the giants. ²¹But when he defied and taunted Israel, he was killed by Jonathan, the son of David's brother Shimea.*

²²These four Philistines were descendants of the giants of Gath, but David and his warriors killed them.

20:14 As in Greek and Latin versions; Hebrew reads *All the Berites.*   20:19 Hebrew *a town that is a mother in Israel.*
20:24 As in Greek version (see also 1 Kgs 4:6; 5:14); Hebrew reads *Adoram.*   21:6 As in Greek version (see also 21:9); Hebrew reads *at Gibeah of Saul, the chosen of the Lord.*
21:7 *Mephibosheth* is another name for Merib-baal.
21:8 As in a few Hebrew and Greek manuscripts and Syriac version (see also 1 Sam 18:19); most Hebrew manuscripts read *Michal.*   21:16a As in Greek version; Hebrew reads *a descendant of the Rephaites;* also in 21:18, 20, 22.
21:16b Hebrew *300 shekels* [3.4 kilograms].   21:19a As in parallel text at 1 Chr 20:5; Hebrew reads *son of Jaare-oregim.*   21:19b As in parallel text at 1 Chr 20:5; Hebrew reads *killed Goliath of Gath.*   21:21 As in parallel text at 1 Chr 20:7; Hebrew reads *Shimei,* a variant spelling of Shimea.

ACTS 1:1-26

In my first book* I told you, Theophilus, about everything Jesus began to do and teach [2] until the day he was taken up to heaven after giving his chosen apostles further instructions through the Holy Spirit. [3] During the forty days after his crucifixion, he appeared to the apostles from time to time, and he proved to them in many ways that he was actually alive. And he talked to them about the Kingdom of God.

[4] Once when he was eating with them, he commanded them, "Do not leave Jerusalem until the Father sends you the gift he promised, as I told you before. [5] John baptized with* water, but in just a few days you will be baptized with the Holy Spirit."

[6] So when the apostles were with Jesus, they kept asking him, "Lord, has the time come for you to free Israel and restore our kingdom?"

[7] He replied, "The Father alone has the authority to set those dates and times, and they are not for you to know. [8] But you will receive power when the Holy Spirit comes upon you. And you will be my witnesses, telling people about me everywhere—in Jerusalem, throughout Judea, in Samaria, and to the ends of the earth."

[9] After saying this, he was taken up into a cloud while they were watching, and they could no longer see him. [10] As they strained to see him rising into heaven, two white-robed men suddenly stood among them. [11] "Men of Galilee," they said, "why are you standing here staring into heaven? Jesus has been taken from you into heaven, but someday he will return from heaven in the same way you saw him go!"

[12] Then the apostles returned to Jerusalem from the Mount of Olives, a distance of half a mile.* [13] When they arrived, they went to the upstairs room of the house where they were staying.

Here are the names of those who were present: Peter, John, James, Andrew, Philip, Thomas, Bartholomew, Matthew, James (son of Alphaeus), Simon (the Zealot), and Judas (son of James). [14] They all met together and were constantly united in prayer, along with Mary the mother of Jesus, several other women, and the brothers of Jesus.

[15] During this time, when about 120 believers* were together in one place, Peter stood up and addressed them. [16] "Brothers," he said, "the Scriptures had to be fulfilled concerning Judas, who guided those who arrested Jesus. This was predicted long ago by the Holy Spirit, speaking through King David. [17] Judas was one of us and shared in the ministry with us."

[18] (Judas had bought a field with the money he received for his treachery. Falling headfirst there, his body split open, spilling out all his intestines. [19] The news of his death spread to all the people of Jerusalem, and they gave the place the Aramaic name *Akeldama,* which means "Field of Blood.")

[20] Peter continued, "This was written in the book of Psalms, where it says, 'Let his home become desolate, with no one living in it.' It also says, 'Let someone else take his position.'*

[21] "So now we must choose a replacement for Judas from among the men who were with us the entire time we were traveling with the Lord Jesus— [22] from the time he was baptized by John until the day he was taken from us. Whoever is chosen will join us as a witness of Jesus' resurrection."

[23] So they nominated two men: Joseph called Barsabbas (also known as Justus) and Matthias. [24] Then they all prayed, "O Lord, you know every heart. Show us which of these men you have chosen [25] as an apostle to replace Judas in this ministry, for he has deserted us and gone where he belongs." [26] Then they cast lots, and Matthias was selected to become an apostle with the other eleven.

1:1 The reference is to the Gospel of Luke.   **1:5** Or *in;* also in 1:5b.   **1:12** Greek *a Sabbath day's journey.* **1:15** Greek *brothers.*   **1:20** Pss 69:25; 109:8.

PSALM 121:1-8
A song for pilgrims ascending to Jerusalem.

¹ **I look up to the mountains—
   does my help come from there?**
² **My help comes from the LORD,
   who made heaven and earth!**

³ **He will not let you stumble;
   the one who watches over you
   will not slumber.**
⁴ Indeed, he who watches over Israel
   never slumbers or sleeps.

⁵ The LORD himself watches over you!
   The LORD stands beside you as
   your protective shade.
⁶ The sun will not harm you by day,
   nor the moon at night.

⁷ The LORD keeps you from all harm
   and watches over your life.
⁸ The LORD keeps watch over you as
   you come and go,
   both now and forever.

PROVERBS 16:18
Pride goes before destruction, and
haughtiness before a fall.

JUNE
4

2 SAMUEL 22:1–23:23
David sang this song to the LORD on the
day the LORD rescued him from all his
enemies and from Saul. ²He sang:

"The LORD is my rock, my fortress,
   and my savior;
³   my God is my rock, in whom
   I find protection.
He is my shield, the power that
   saves me,
   and my place of safety.
He is my refuge, my savior,
   the one who saves me from
   violence.

⁴ I called on the LORD, who is worthy
   of praise,
   and he saved me from
   my enemies.

⁵ "The waves of death overwhelmed
   me;
   floods of destruction swept
   over me.
⁶ The grave* wrapped its ropes
   around me;
   death laid a trap in my path.
⁷ But in my distress I cried out
   to the LORD;
   yes, I cried to my God for help.
He heard me from his sanctuary;
   my cry reached his ears.

⁸ "Then the earth quaked and
   trembled.
   The foundations of the heavens
   shook;
   they quaked because of his anger.
⁹ Smoke poured from his nostrils;
   fierce flames leaped from
   his mouth.
   Glowing coals blazed forth
   from him.
¹⁰ He opened the heavens and
   came down;
   dark storm clouds were beneath
   his feet.
¹¹ Mounted on a mighty angelic
   being,* he flew,
   soaring* on the wings
   of the wind.
¹² He shrouded himself in darkness,
   veiling his approach with dense
   rain clouds.
¹³ A great brightness shone around
   him,
   and burning coals* blazed forth.
¹⁴ The LORD thundered from heaven;
   the voice of the Most High
   resounded.
¹⁵ He shot arrows and scattered
   his enemies;
   his lightning flashed, and they
   were confused.
¹⁶ Then at the command of the LORD,
   at the blast of his breath,
   the bottom of the sea could be seen,

and the foundations of the earth
were laid bare.

¹⁷ "He reached down from heaven
and rescued me;
he drew me out of deep
waters.
¹⁸ He rescued me from my powerful
enemies,
from those who hated me and
were too strong for me.
¹⁹ They attacked me at a moment
when I was in distress,
but the LORD supported me.
²⁰ He led me to a place of safety;
he rescued me because he
delights in me.
²¹ The LORD rewarded me for
doing right;
he restored me because
of my innocence.
²² For I have kept the ways of the LORD;
I have not turned from my God
to follow evil.
²³ I have followed all his regulations;
I have never abandoned his
decrees.
²⁴ I am blameless before God;
I have kept myself from sin.
²⁵ The LORD rewarded me for
doing right.
He has seen my innocence.

²⁶ "To the faithful you show yourself
faithful;
to those with integrity you
show integrity.
²⁷ To the pure you show yourself pure,
but to the wicked you show
yourself hostile.
²⁸ You rescue the humble,
but your eyes watch the proud
and humiliate them.
²⁹ O LORD, you are my lamp.
The LORD lights up my darkness.
³⁰ In your strength I can crush an army;
with my God I can scale any wall.

³¹ "God's way is perfect.
All the LORD's promises
prove true.
He is a shield for all who look to
him for protection.

³² For who is God except the LORD?
Who but our God is a solid rock?
³³ **God is my strong fortress,**
and he makes my way perfect.
³⁴ **He makes me as surefooted**
as a deer,
enabling me to stand on
mountain heights.
³⁵ He trains my hands for battle;
he strengthens my arm to draw
a bronze bow.
³⁶ You have given me your shield
of victory;
your help* has made me great.
³⁷ You have made a wide path
for my feet
to keep them from slipping.

³⁸ "I chased my enemies and
destroyed them;
I did not stop until they were
conquered.
³⁹ I consumed them;
I struck them down so they did
not get up;
they fell beneath my feet.
⁴⁰ You have armed me with strength
for the battle;
you have subdued my enemies
under my feet.
⁴¹ You placed my foot on their necks.
I have destroyed all who
hated me.
⁴² They looked for help, but no one
came to their rescue.
They even cried to the LORD,
but he refused to answer.
⁴³ I ground them as fine as the dust
of the earth;
I trampled them* in the gutter
like dirt.

⁴⁴ "You gave me victory over my
accusers.
You preserved me as the ruler
over nations;
people I don't even know now
serve me.
⁴⁵ Foreign nations cringe before me;
as soon as they hear of me, they
submit.
⁴⁶ They all lose their courage

and come trembling* from their
strongholds.

47 "The Lord lives! Praise to my Rock!
May God, the Rock of my
salvation, be exalted!
48 He is the God who pays back those
who harm me;
he brings down the nations
under me
49 and delivers me from my enemies.
You hold me safe beyond the reach
of my enemies;
you save me from violent
opponents.
50 For this, O Lord, I will praise you
among the nations;
I will sing praises to your name.
51 You give great victories to your king;
you show unfailing love to your
anointed,
to David and all his descendants
forever."

23:1 These are the last words of David:

"David, the son of Jesse, speaks—
David, the man who was raised
up so high,
David, the man anointed by the
God of Jacob,
David, the sweet psalmist
of Israel.*

2 "The Spirit of the Lord speaks
through me;
his words are upon my tongue.
3 The God of Israel spoke.
The Rock of Israel said to me:
'The one who rules righteously,
who rules in the fear of God,
4 is like the light of morning at
sunrise,
like a morning without clouds,
like the gleaming of the sun
on new grass after rain.'

5 "Is it not my family God has chosen?
Yes, he has made an everlasting
covenant with me.
His agreement is arranged and
guaranteed in every detail.
He will ensure my safety
and success.

6 But the godless are like thorns
to be thrown away,
for they tear the hand that
touches them.
7 One must use iron tools to chop
them down;
they will be totally consumed
by fire."

8 These are the names of David's
mightiest warriors. The first was Jasho-
beam the Hacmonite,* who was leader
of the Three*—the three mightiest warriors among David's men. He once used
his spear to kill 800 enemy warriors in a
single battle.*

9 Next in rank among the Three was
Eleazar son of Dodai, a descendant of
Ahoah. Once Eleazar and David stood
together against the Philistines when
the entire Israelite army had fled. 10 He
killed Philistines until his hand was too
tired to lift his sword, and the Lord gave
him a great victory that day. The rest of
the army did not return until it was time
to collect the plunder!

11 Next in rank was Shammah son of
Agee from Harar. One time the Philistines gathered at Lehi and attacked the
Israelites in a field full of lentils. The Israelite army fled, 12 but Shammah* held
his ground in the middle of the field
and beat back the Philistines. So the
Lord brought about a great victory.

13 Once during the harvest, when David was at the cave of Adullam, the Philistine army was camped in the valley of
Rephaim. The Three (who were among
the Thirty—an elite group among David's fighting men) went down to meet
him there. 14 David was staying in the
stronghold at the time, and a Philistine
detachment had occupied the town of
Bethlehem.

15 David remarked longingly to his
men, "Oh, how I would love some of that
good water from the well by the gate in
Bethlehem." 16 So the Three broke
through the Philistine lines, drew some
water from the well by the gate in Bethlehem, and brought it back to David. But
he refused to drink it. Instead, he poured

it out as an offering to the LORD. ¹⁷"The LORD forbid that I should drink this!" he exclaimed. "This water is as precious as the blood of these men* who risked their lives to bring it to me." So David did not drink it. These are examples of the exploits of the Three.

¹⁸Abishai son of Zeruiah, the brother of Joab, was the leader of the Thirty.* He once used his spear to kill 300 enemy warriors in a single battle. It was by such feats that he became as famous as the Three. ¹⁹Abishai was the most famous of the Thirty* and was their commander, though he was not one of the Three.

²⁰There was also Benaiah son of Jehoiada, a valiant warrior* from Kabzeel. He did many heroic deeds, which included killing two champions* of Moab. Another time, on a snowy day, he chased a lion down into a pit and killed it. ²¹Once, armed only with a club, he killed a great Egyptian warrior who was armed with a spear. Benaiah wrenched the spear from the Egyptian's hand and killed him with it. ²²Deeds like these made Benaiah as famous as the Three mightiest warriors. ²³He was more honored than the other members of the Thirty, though he was not one of the Three. And David made him captain of his bodyguard.

22:6 Hebrew *Sheol.*   22:11a Hebrew *a cherub.*
22:11b As in some Hebrew manuscripts (see also Ps 18:10); other Hebrew manuscripts read *appearing.*   22:13 Or *and lightning bolts.*   22:36 As in Dead Sea Scrolls (see also Ps 18:35); Masoretic Text reads *your answering.*
22:43 As in Dead Sea Scrolls (see also Ps 18:42); Masoretic Text reads *I crushed and trampled them.*   22:46 As in parallel text at Ps 18:45; Hebrew reads *come girding themselves.*   23:1 Or *the favorite subject of the songs of Israel;* or *the favorite of the Strong One of Israel.*   23:8a As in parallel text at 1 Chr 11:11; Hebrew reads *Josheb-basshebeth the Tahkemonite.*   23:8b As in Greek and Latin versions (see also 1 Chr 11:11); the meaning of the Hebrew is uncertain.   23:8c As in some Greek manuscripts (see also 1 Chr 11:11); the meaning of the Hebrew is uncertain, though it might be rendered *the Three. It was Adino the Eznite who killed 800 men at one time.*   23:12 Hebrew *he.*   23:17 Hebrew *Shall I drink the blood of these men?*   23:18 As in a few Hebrew manuscripts and Syriac version; most Hebrew manuscripts read *the Three.*   23:19 As in Syriac version; Hebrew reads *the Three.*   23:20a Or *son of Jehoiada, son of Ish-hai.*   23:20b Or *two sons of Ariel.*

ACTS 2:1-47

❶On the day of Pentecost* all the believers were meeting together in one place. ²Suddenly, there was a sound from heaven like the roaring of a mighty windstorm, and it filled the house where they were sitting. ³Then, what looked like flames or tongues of fire appeared and settled on each of them. ⁴And everyone present was filled with the Holy Spirit and began speaking in other languages,* as the Holy Spirit gave them this ability.

⁵At that time there were devout Jews from every nation living in Jerusalem. ⁶When they heard the loud noise, everyone came running, and they were bewildered to hear their own languages being spoken by the believers.

⁷They were completely amazed. "How can this be?" they exclaimed. "These people are all from Galilee, ⁸and yet we hear them speaking in our own native languages! ⁹Here we are—Parthians, Medes, Elamites, people from Mesopotamia, Judea, Cappadocia, Pontus, the province of Asia, ¹⁰Phrygia, Pamphylia, Egypt, and the areas of Libya around Cyrene, visitors from Rome (both Jews and converts to Judaism), ¹¹Cretans, and Arabs. And we all hear these people speaking in our own languages about the wonderful things God has done!" ¹²They stood there amazed and perplexed. "What can this mean?" they asked each other.

¹³But others in the crowd ridiculed them, saying, "They're just drunk, that's all!"

¹⁴Then Peter stepped forward with the eleven other apostles and shouted to the crowd, "Listen carefully, all of you, fellow Jews and residents of Jerusalem! Make no mistake about this. ¹⁵These people are not drunk, as some of you are assuming. Nine o'clock in the morning is much too early for that. ¹⁶No, what you see was predicted long ago by the prophet Joel:

¹⁷ 'In the last days,' God says,
     'I will pour out my Spirit upon
          all people.
     Your sons and daughters will
          prophesy.
          Your young men will see visions,
          and your old men will dream
               dreams.

¹⁸ In those days I will pour out
     my Spirit
     even on my servants—men and
     women alike—
     and they will prophesy.
¹⁹ And I will cause wonders in the
     heavens above
     and signs on the earth below—
     blood and fire and clouds
     of smoke.
²⁰ The sun will become dark,
     and the moon will turn blood red
     before that great and glorious
     day of the LORD arrives.
²¹ But everyone who calls on the
     name of the LORD
     will be saved.'*

²²"People of Israel, listen! God publicly endorsed Jesus the Nazarene* by
doing powerful miracles, wonders, and
signs through him, as you well know.
²³But God knew what would happen,
and his prearranged plan was carried
out when Jesus was betrayed. With the
help of lawless Gentiles, you nailed him
to a cross and killed him. ²⁴But God released him from the horrors of death
and raised him back to life, for death
could not keep him in its grip. ²⁵King
David said this about him:

'I see that the LORD is always
     with me.
     I will not be shaken, for he is
     right beside me.
²⁶ No wonder my heart is glad,
     and my tongue shouts his praises!
     My body rests in hope.
²⁷ For you will not leave my soul
     among the dead*
     or allow your Holy One to rot in
     the grave.
²⁸ You have shown me the way of life,
     and you will fill me with the joy
     of your presence.'*

²⁹"Dear brothers, think about this!
You can be sure that the patriarch David
wasn't referring to himself, for he died
and was buried, and his tomb is still
here among us. ³⁰But he was a prophet,
and he knew God had promised with an

oath that one of David's own descendants would sit on his throne. ³¹David
was looking into the future and speaking of the Messiah's resurrection. He
was saying that God would not leave
him among the dead or allow his body
to rot in the grave.

³²"God raised Jesus from the dead,
and we are all witnesses of this. ³³Now he
is exalted to the place of highest honor
in heaven, at God's right hand. And the
Father, as he had promised, gave him the
Holy Spirit to pour out upon us, just as
you see and hear today. ³⁴For David himself never ascended into heaven, yet he
said,

'The LORD said to my Lord,
     "Sit in the place of honor
     at my right hand
³⁵ until I humble your enemies,
     making them a footstool under
     your feet."'*

³⁶"So let everyone in Israel know for
certain that God has made this Jesus,
whom you crucified, to be both Lord
and Messiah!"

³⁷Peter's words pierced their hearts,
and they said to him and to the other
apostles, "Brothers, what should we do?"

³⁸Peter replied, "Each of you must repent of your sins, turn to God, and be
baptized in the name of Jesus Christ to
show that you have received forgiveness
for your sins. Then you will receive the
gift of the Holy Spirit. ³⁹This promise is
to you, and to your children, and even to
the Gentiles*—all who have been called
by the Lord our God." ⁴⁰Then Peter continued preaching for a long time,
strongly urging all his listeners, "Save
yourselves from this crooked generation!"

⁴¹Those who believed what Peter said
were baptized and added to the church
that day—about 3,000 in all.

⁴²All the believers devoted themselves
to the apostles' teaching, and to fellowship, and to sharing in meals (including
the Lord's Supper*), and to prayer.

⁴³A deep sense of awe came over them
all, and the apostles performed many

miraculous signs and wonders. [44]And all the believers met together in one place and shared everything they had. [45]They sold their property and possessions and shared the money with those in need. [46]They worshiped together at the Temple each day, met in homes for the Lord's Supper, and shared their meals with great joy and generosity*—[47]all the while praising God and enjoying the goodwill of all the people. And each day the Lord added to their fellowship those who were being saved.

2:1 The Festival of Pentecost came 50 days after Passover (when Jesus was crucified).   2:4 Or *in other tongues.*   2:17-21 Joel 2:28-32.   2:22 Or *Jesus of Nazareth.*   2:27 Greek *in Hades;* also in 2:31.   2:25-28 Ps 16:8-11 (Greek version).   2:34-35 Ps 110:1.   2:39 Or *and to people far in the future;* Greek reads *and to those far away.*   2:42 Greek *the breaking of bread;* also in 2:46.   2:46 Or *and sincere hearts.*

PSALM 122:1-9

A song for pilgrims ascending to Jerusalem. A psalm of David.

[1] I was glad when they said to me,
"Let us go to the house
of the LORD."
[2] And now here we are,
standing inside your gates,
O Jerusalem.
[3] Jerusalem is a well-built city;
its seamless walls cannot be
breached.
[4] All the tribes of Israel—the LORD's
people—
make their pilgrimage here.
They come to give thanks to the
name of the LORD,
as the law requires of Israel.
[5] Here stand the thrones where
judgment is given,
the thrones of the dynasty
of David.

[6] Pray for peace in Jerusalem.
May all who love this city prosper.
[7] O Jerusalem, may there be peace
within your walls
and prosperity in your palaces.
[8] For the sake of my family and
friends, I will say,
"May you have peace."

[9] For the sake of the house of the
LORD our God,
I will seek what is best for you,
O Jerusalem.

PROVERBS 16:19-20

Better to live humbly with the poor than to share plunder with the proud. □Those who listen to instruction will prosper; those who trust the LORD will be joyful.

JUNE 5

2 SAMUEL 23:24–24:25

Other members of the Thirty included:

Asahel, Joab's brother;
Elhanan son of Dodo from
Bethlehem;
[25] Shammah from Harod;
Elika from Harod;
[26] Helez from Pelon*;
Ira son of Ikkesh from Tekoa;
[27] Abiezer from Anathoth;
Sibbecai* from Hushah;
[28] Zalmon from Ahoah;
Maharai from Netophah;
[29] Heled* son of Baanah from
Netophah;
Ithai* son of Ribai from Gibeah
(in the land of Benjamin);
[30] Benaiah from Pirathon;
Hurai* from Nahale-gaash*;
[31] Abi-albon from Arabah;
Azmaveth from Bahurim;
[32] Eliahba from Shaalbon;
the sons of Jashen;
[33] Jonathan son of Shagee* from
Harar;
Ahiam son of Sharar from Harar;
[34] Eliphelet son of Ahasbai from
Maacah;
Eliam son of Ahithophel from Giloh;
[35] Hezro from Carmel;
Paarai from Arba;

³⁶ Igal son of Nathan from Zobah;
Bani from Gad;

³⁷ Zelek from Ammon;
Naharai from Beeroth, Joab's
armor bearer;

³⁸ Ira from Jattir;
Gareb from Jattir;

³⁹ Uriah the Hittite.

There were thirty-seven in all.

²⁴:¹ONCE again the anger of the LORD burned against Israel, and he caused David to harm them by taking a census. "Go and count the people of Israel and Judah," the LORD told him.

²So the king said to Joab and the commanders* of the army, "Take a census of all the tribes of Israel—from Dan in the north to Beersheba in the south—so I may know how many people there are."

³But Joab replied to the king, "May the LORD your God let you live to see a hundred times as many people as there are now! But why, my lord the king, do you want to do this?"

⁴But the king insisted that they take the census, so Joab and the commanders of the army went out to count the people of Israel. ⁵First they crossed the Jordan and camped at Aroer, south of the town in the valley, in the direction of Gad. Then they went on to Jazer, ⁶then to Gilead in the land of Tahtim-hodshi* and to Dan-jaan and around to Sidon. ⁷Then they came to the stronghold of Tyre, and all the towns of the Hivites and Canaanites. Finally, they went south to Judah* as far as Beersheba.

⁸Having gone through the entire land for nine months and twenty days, they returned to Jerusalem. ⁹Joab reported the number of people to the king. There were 800,000 capable warriors in Israel who could handle a sword, and 500,000 in Judah.

¹⁰But after he had taken the census, David's conscience began to bother him. And he said to the LORD, "I have sinned greatly by taking this census. Please forgive my guilt, LORD, for doing this foolish thing."

¹¹The next morning the word of the LORD came to the prophet Gad, who was David's seer. This was the message: ¹²"Go and say to David, 'This is what the LORD says: I will give you three choices. Choose one of these punishments, and I will inflict it on you.'"

¹³So Gad came to David and asked him, "Will you choose three* years of famine throughout your land, three months of fleeing from your enemies, or three days of severe plague throughout your land? Think this over and decide what answer I should give the LORD who sent me."

¹⁴"I'm in a desperate situation!" David replied to Gad. "But let us fall into the hands of the LORD, for his mercy is great. Do not let me fall into human hands."

¹⁵So the LORD sent a plague upon Israel that morning, and it lasted for three days.* A total of 70,000 people died throughout the nation, from Dan in the north to Beersheba in the south. ¹⁶But as the angel was preparing to destroy Jerusalem, the LORD relented and said to the death angel, "Stop! That is enough!" At that moment the angel of the LORD was by the threshing floor of Araunah the Jebusite.

¹⁷When David saw the angel, he said to the LORD, "I am the one who has sinned and done wrong! But these people are as innocent as sheep—what have they done? Let your anger fall against me and my family."

¹⁸That day Gad came to David and said to him, "Go up and build an altar to the LORD on the threshing floor of Araunah the Jebusite."

¹⁹So David went up to do what the LORD had commanded him. ²⁰When Araunah saw the king and his men coming toward him, he came and bowed before the king with his face to the ground. ²¹"Why have you come, my lord the king?" Araunah asked.

David replied, "I have come to buy your threshing floor and to build an altar to the LORD there, so that he will stop the plague."

²²"Take it, my lord the king, and use it

as you wish," Araunah said to David. "Here are oxen for the burnt offering, and you can use the threshing boards and ox yokes for wood to build a fire on the altar. ²³I will give it all to you, Your Majesty, and may the LORD your God accept your sacrifice."

²⁴But the king replied to Araunah, "No, I insist on buying it, for I will not present burnt offerings to the LORD my God that have cost me nothing." So David paid him fifty pieces of silver* for the threshing floor and the oxen.

²⁵David built an altar there to the LORD and sacrificed burnt offerings and peace offerings. And the LORD answered his prayer for the land, and the plague on Israel was stopped.

23:26 As in parallel text at 1 Chr 11:27 (see also 1 Chr 27:10); Hebrew reads *from Palti.*   23:27 As in some Greek manuscripts (see also 1 Chr 11:29); Hebrew reads *Mebunnai.*   23:29a As in some Hebrew manuscripts (see also 1 Chr 11:30); most Hebrew manuscripts read *Heleb.*   23:29b As in parallel text at 1 Chr 11:31; Hebrew reads *Ittai.*   23:30a As in some Greek manuscripts (see also 1 Chr 11:32); Hebrew reads *Hiddai.*   23:30b Or *from the ravines of Gaash.*   23:33 As in parallel text at 1 Chr 11:34; Hebrew reads *Jonathan, Shammah;* some Greek manuscripts read *Jonathan son of Shammah.*   24:2 As in Greek version (see also 24:4 and 1 Chr 21:2); Hebrew reads *Joab the commander.*   24:6 Greek version reads *to Gilead and to Kadesh in the land of the Hittites.*   24:7 Or *they went to the Negev of Judah.*   24:13 As in Greek version (see also 1 Chr 21:12); Hebrew reads *seven.*   24:15 Hebrew *for the designated time.*   24:24 Hebrew *50 shekels of silver,* about 20 ounces or 570 grams in weight.

ACTS 3:1-26

Peter and John went to the Temple one afternoon to take part in the three o'clock prayer service. ²As they approached the Temple, a man lame from birth was being carried in. Each day he was put beside the Temple gate, the one called the Beautiful Gate, so he could beg from the people going into the Temple. ³When he saw Peter and John about to enter, he asked them for some money.

⁴Peter and John looked at him intently, and Peter said, "Look at us!" ⁵The lame man looked at them eagerly, expecting some money. ⁶But Peter said, "I don't have any silver or gold for you. But I'll give you what I have. In the name of Jesus Christ the Nazarene,* get up and walk!"

⁷Then Peter took the lame man by the right hand and helped him up. And as he did, the man's feet and ankles were instantly healed and strengthened. ⁸He jumped up, stood on his feet, and began to walk! Then, walking, leaping, and praising God, he went into the Temple with them.

⁹All the people saw him walking and heard him praising God. ¹⁰When they realized he was the lame beggar they had seen so often at the Beautiful Gate, they were absolutely astounded! ¹¹They all rushed out in amazement to Solomon's Colonnade, where the man was holding tightly to Peter and John.

¹²Peter saw his opportunity and addressed the crowd. "People of Israel," he said, "what is so surprising about this? And why stare at us as though we had made this man walk by our own power or godliness? ¹³For it is the God of Abraham, Isaac, and Jacob—the God of all our ancestors—who has brought glory to his servant Jesus by doing this. This is the same Jesus whom you handed over and rejected before Pilate, despite Pilate's decision to release him. ¹⁴You rejected this holy, righteous one and instead demanded the release of a murderer. ¹⁵You killed the author of life, but God raised him from the dead. And we are witnesses of this fact!

¹⁶"Through faith in the name of Jesus, this man was healed—and you know how crippled he was before. Faith in Jesus' name has healed him before your very eyes.

¹⁷"Friends,* I realize that what you and your leaders did to Jesus was done in ignorance. ¹⁸But God was fulfilling what all the prophets had foretold about the Messiah—that he must suffer these things. ¹⁹Now repent of your sins and turn to God, so that your sins may be wiped away. ²⁰Then times of refreshment will come from the presence of the Lord, and he will again send you Jesus, your appointed Messiah. ²¹For he must remain in heaven until the time for the final restoration of all things, as God promised long ago through his holy prophets. ²²Moses said, 'The LORD

your God will raise up for you a Prophet like me from among your own people. Listen carefully to everything he tells you.'* ²³Then Moses said, 'Anyone who will not listen to that Prophet will be completely cut off from God's people.'*

²⁴"Starting with Samuel, every prophet spoke about what is happening today. ²⁵You are the children of those prophets, and you are included in the covenant God promised to your ancestors. For God said to Abraham, 'Through your descendants all the families on earth will be blessed.'* ²⁶When God raised up his servant, Jesus, he sent him first to you people of Israel, to bless you by turning each of you back from your sinful ways."

3:6 Or *Jesus Christ of Nazareth.*   **3:17** Greek *Brothers.*   **3:22** Deut 18:15.   **3:23** Deut 18:19; Lev 23:29.   **3:25** Gen 12:3; 22:18.

PSALM 123:1-4
A song for pilgrims ascending to Jerusalem.

¹ I lift my eyes to you,
   O God, enthroned in heaven.
² **We keep looking to the L**ORD **our
      God for his mercy,
   just as servants keep their eyes
      on their master,
   as a slave girl watches her
      mistress for the slightest
      signal.**
³ Have mercy on us, LORD, have mercy,
   for we have had our fill of
      contempt.
⁴ We have had more than our fill of
      the scoffing of the proud
   and the contempt of the arrogant.

PROVERBS 16:21-23
The wise are known for their understanding, and pleasant words are persuasive. □ Discretion is a life-giving fountain to those who possess it, but discipline is wasted on fools. □ From a wise mind comes wise speech; the words of the wise are persuasive.

JUNE 6

1 KINGS 1:1-53
King David was now very old, and no matter how many blankets covered him, he could not keep warm. ²So his advisers told him, "Let us find a young virgin to wait on you and look after you, my lord. She will lie in your arms and keep you warm."

³So they searched throughout the land of Israel for a beautiful girl, and they found Abishag from Shunem and brought her to the king. ⁴The girl was very beautiful, and she looked after the king and took care of him. But the king had no sexual relations with her.

⁵About that time David's son Adonijah, whose mother was Haggith, began boasting, "I will make myself king." So he provided himself with chariots and charioteers and recruited fifty men to run in front of him. ⁶Now his father, King David, had never disciplined him at any time, even by asking, "Why are you doing that?" Adonijah had been born next after Absalom, and he was very handsome.

⁷Adonijah took Joab son of Zeruiah and Abiathar the priest into his confidence, and they agreed to help him become king. ⁸But Zadok the priest, Benaiah son of Jehoiada, Nathan the prophet, Shimei, Rei, and David's personal bodyguard refused to support Adonijah.

⁹Adonijah went to the Stone of Zoheleth* near the spring of En-rogel, where he sacrificed sheep, cattle, and fattened calves. He invited all his brothers—the other sons of King David—and all the royal officials of Judah. ¹⁰But he did not invite Nathan the prophet or Benaiah or the king's bodyguard or his brother Solomon.

¹¹Then Nathan went to Bathsheba, Solomon's mother, and asked her, "Haven't you heard that Haggith's son, Adonijah, has made himself king, and

our lord David doesn't even know about it? ¹²If you want to save your own life and the life of your son Solomon, follow my advice. ¹³Go at once to King David and say to him, 'My lord the king, didn't you make a vow and say to me, "Your son Solomon will surely be the next king and will sit on my throne"? Why then has Adonijah become king?' ¹⁴And while you are still talking with him, I will come and confirm everything you have said."

¹⁵So Bathsheba went into the king's bedroom. (He was very old now, and Abishag was taking care of him.) ¹⁶Bathsheba bowed down before the king.

"What can I do for you?" he asked her.

¹⁷She replied, "My lord, you made a vow before the LORD your God when you said to me, 'Your son Solomon will surely be the next king and will sit on my throne.' ¹⁸But instead, Adonijah has made himself king, and my lord the king does not even know about it. ¹⁹He has sacrificed many cattle, fattened calves, and sheep, and he has invited all the king's sons to attend the celebration. He also invited Abiathar the priest and Joab, the commander of the army. But he did not invite your servant Solomon. ²⁰And now, my lord the king, all Israel is waiting for you to announce who will become king after you. ²¹If you do not act, my son Solomon and I will be treated as criminals as soon as my lord the king has died."

²²While she was still speaking with the king, Nathan the prophet arrived. ²³The king's officials told him, "Nathan the prophet is here to see you."

Nathan went in and bowed before the king with his face to the ground. ²⁴Nathan asked, "My lord the king, have you decided that Adonijah will be the next king and that he will sit on your throne? ²⁵Today he has sacrificed many cattle, fattened calves, and sheep, and he has invited all the king's sons to attend the celebration. He also invited the commanders of the army and Abiathar the priest. They are feasting and drink-

ing with him and shouting, 'Long live King Adonijah!' ²⁶But he did not invite me or Zadok the priest or Benaiah or your servant Solomon. ²⁷Has my lord the king really done this without letting any of his officials know who should be the next king?"

²⁸King David responded, "Call Bathsheba!" So she came back in and stood before the king. ²⁹And the king repeated his vow: "As surely as the LORD lives, who has rescued me from every danger, ³⁰your son Solomon will be the next king and will sit on my throne this very day, just as I vowed to you before the LORD, the God of Israel."

³¹Then Bathsheba bowed down with her face to the ground before the king and exclaimed, "May my lord King David live forever!"

³²Then King David ordered, "Call Zadok the priest, Nathan the prophet, and Benaiah son of Jehoiada." When they came into the king's presence, ³³the king said to them, "Take Solomon and my officials down to Gihon Spring. Solomon is to ride on my own mule. ³⁴There Zadok the priest and Nathan the prophet are to anoint him king over Israel. Blow the ram's horn and shout, 'Long live King Solomon!' ³⁵Then escort him back here, and he will sit on my throne. He will succeed me as king, for I have appointed him to be ruler over Israel and Judah."

³⁶"Amen!" Benaiah son of Jehoiada replied. "May the LORD, the God of my lord the king, decree that it happen. ³⁷And may the LORD be with Solomon as he has been with you, my lord the king, and may he make Solomon's reign even greater than yours!"

³⁸So Zadok the priest, Nathan the prophet, Benaiah son of Jehoiada, and the king's bodyguard* took Solomon down to Gihon Spring, with Solomon riding on King David's own mule. ³⁹There Zadok the priest took the flask of olive oil from the sacred tent and anointed Solomon with the oil. Then they sounded the ram's horn and all the people shouted, "Long live King Solo-

mon!" ⁴⁰And all the people followed Solomon into Jerusalem, playing flutes and shouting for joy. The celebration was so joyous and noisy that the earth shook with the sound.

⁴¹Adonijah and his guests heard the celebrating and shouting just as they were finishing their banquet. When Joab heard the sound of the ram's horn, he asked, "What's going on? Why is the city in such an uproar?"

⁴²And while he was still speaking, Jonathan son of Abiathar the priest arrived. "Come in," Adonijah said to him, "for you are a good man. You must have good news."

⁴³"Not at all!" Jonathan replied. "Our lord King David has just declared Solomon king! ⁴⁴The king sent him down to Gihon Spring with Zadok the priest, Nathan the prophet, and Benaiah son of Jehoiada, protected by the king's bodyguard. They had him ride on the king's own mule, ⁴⁵and Zadok and Nathan have anointed him at Gihon Spring as the new king. They have just returned, and the whole city is celebrating and rejoicing. That's what all the noise is about. ⁴⁶What's more, Solomon is now sitting on the royal throne as king. ⁴⁷And all the royal officials have gone to King David and congratulated him, saying, 'May your God make Solomon's fame even greater than your own, and may Solomon's reign be even greater than yours!' Then the king bowed his head in worship as he lay in his bed, ⁴⁸and he said, 'Praise the Lᴏʀᴅ, the God of Israel, who today has chosen a successor to sit on my throne while I am still alive to see it.'"

⁴⁹Then all of Adonijah's guests jumped up in panic from the banquet table and quickly scattered. ⁵⁰Adonijah was afraid of Solomon, so he rushed to the sacred tent and grabbed onto the horns of the altar. ⁵¹Word soon reached Solomon that Adonijah had seized the horns of the altar in fear, and that he was pleading, "Let King Solomon swear today that he will not kill me!"

⁵²Solomon replied, "If he proves himself to be loyal, not a hair on his head will be touched. But if he makes trouble, he will die." ⁵³So King Solomon summoned Adonijah, and they brought him down from the altar. He came and bowed respectfully before King Solomon, who dismissed him, saying, "Go on home."

1:9 Or *to the Serpent's Stone;* Greek version supports reading *Zoheleth* as a proper name.   **1:38** Hebrew *the Kerethites and Pelethites;* also in 1:44.

ACTS 4:1-37

While Peter and John were speaking to the people, they were confronted by the priests, the captain of the Temple guard, and some of the Sadducees. ²These leaders were very disturbed that Peter and John were teaching the people that through Jesus there is a resurrection of the dead. ³They arrested them and, since it was already evening, put them in jail until morning. ⁴But many of the people who heard their message believed it, so the number of believers now totaled about 5,000 men, not counting women and children.*

⁵The next day the council of all the rulers and elders and teachers of religious law met in Jerusalem. ⁶Annas the high priest was there, along with Caiaphas, John, Alexander, and other relatives of the high priest. ⁷They brought in the two disciples and demanded, "By what power, or in whose name, have you done this?"

⁸Then Peter, filled with the Holy Spirit, said to them, "Rulers and elders of our people, ⁹are we being questioned today because we've done a good deed for a crippled man? Do you want to know how he was healed? ¹⁰Let me clearly state to all of you and to all the people of Israel that he was healed by the powerful name of Jesus Christ the Nazarene,* the man you crucified but whom God raised from the dead. ¹¹For Jesus is the one referred to in the Scriptures, where it says,

'The stone that you builders rejected
     has now become the
         cornerstone.'*

12There is salvation in no one else! God has given no other name under heaven by which we must be saved."

13The members of the council were amazed when they saw the boldness of Peter and John, for they could see that they were ordinary men with no special training in the Scriptures. They also recognized them as men who had been with Jesus. 14But since they could see the man who had been healed standing right there among them, there was nothing the council could say. 15So they ordered Peter and John out of the council chamber* and conferred among themselves.

16"What should we do with these men?" they asked each other. "We can't deny that they have performed a miraculous sign, and everybody in Jerusalem knows about it. 17But to keep them from spreading their propaganda any further, we must warn them not to speak to anyone in Jesus' name again." 18So they called the apostles back in and commanded them never again to speak or teach in the name of Jesus.

19But Peter and John replied, "Do you think God wants us to obey you rather than him? 20We cannot stop telling about everything we have seen and heard."

21The council then threatened them further, but they finally let them go because they didn't know how to punish them without starting a riot. For everyone was praising God 22for this miraculous sign—the healing of a man who had been lame for more than forty years.

23As soon as they were freed, Peter and John returned to the other believers and told them what the leading priests and elders had said. 24When they heard the report, all the believers lifted their voices together in prayer to God: "O Sovereign Lord, Creator of heaven and earth, the sea, and everything in them—25you spoke long ago by the Holy Spirit through our ancestor David, your servant, saying,

'Why were the nations so angry?
    Why did they waste their time
        with futile plans?

26 The kings of the earth prepared
        for battle;
    the rulers gathered together
against the LORD
    and against his Messiah.'*

27"In fact, this has happened here in this very city! For Herod Antipas, Pontius Pilate the governor, the Gentiles, and the people of Israel were all united against Jesus, your holy servant, whom you anointed. 28But everything they did was determined beforehand according to your will. 29And now, O Lord, hear their threats, and give us, your servants, great boldness in preaching your word. 30Stretch out your hand with healing power; may miraculous signs and wonders be done through the name of your holy servant Jesus."

31After this prayer, the meeting place shook, and they were all filled with the Holy Spirit. Then they preached the word of God with boldness.

32All the believers were united in heart and mind. And they felt that what they owned was not their own, so they shared everything they had. 33The apostles testified powerfully to the resurrection of the Lord Jesus, and God's great blessing was upon them all. 34There were no needy people among them, because those who owned land or houses would sell them 35and bring the money to the apostles to give to those in need.

36For instance, there was Joseph, the one the apostles nicknamed Barnabas (which means "Son of Encouragement"). He was from the tribe of Levi and came from the island of Cyprus. 37He sold a field he owned and brought the money to the apostles.

4:4 Greek 5,000 adult males. 4:10 Or Jesus Christ of Nazareth. 4:11 Ps 118:22. 4:15 Greek the Sanhedrin. 4:25-26 Or his anointed one; or his Christ. Ps 2:1-2.

PSALM 124:1-8
A song for pilgrims ascending to Jerusalem. A psalm of David.

1 **W**hat if the LORD had not been
        on our side?
    Let all Israel repeat:

² What if the LORD had not been
      on our side
   when people attacked us?
³ They would have swallowed us alive
   in their burning anger.
⁴ The waters would have engulfed us;
      a torrent would have
      overwhelmed us.
⁵ Yes, the raging waters of their fury
      would have overwhelmed our
      very lives.

⁶ **Praise the LORD,**
   who did not let their teeth tear
   us apart!
⁷ **We escaped like a bird from**
   a hunter's trap.
   The trap is broken, and we
   are free!
⁸ Our help is from the LORD,
   who made heaven and earth.

PROVERBS 16:24
Kind words are like honey—sweet to
the soul and healthy for the body.

JUNE
7

1 KINGS 2:1–3:2
As the time of King David's death ap-
proached, he gave this charge to his son
Solomon:

²"I am going where everyone on earth
must someday go. Take courage and be a
man. ³Observe the requirements of the
LORD your God, and follow all his ways.
Keep the decrees, commands, regulations, and laws written in the Law of Moses so that you will be successful in all
you do and wherever you go. ⁴If you do
this, then the LORD will keep the promise
he made to me. He told me, 'If your descendants live as they should and follow
me faithfully with all their heart and
soul, one of them will always sit on the
throne of Israel.'

⁵"And there is something else. You
know what Joab son of Zeruiah did to me
when he murdered my two army commanders, Abner son of Ner and Amasa
son of Jether. He pretended that it was an
act of war, but it was done in a time of
peace,* staining his belt and sandals with
innocent blood.* ⁶Do with him what you
think best, but don't let him grow old and
go to his grave in peace.*

⁷"Be kind to the sons of Barzillai of
Gilead. Make them permanent guests at
your table, for they took care of me
when I fled from your brother Absalom.

⁸"And remember Shimei son of Gera,
the man from Bahurim in Benjamin. He
cursed me with a terrible curse as I was
fleeing to Mahanaim. When he came
down to meet me at the Jordan River, I
swore by the LORD that I would not kill
him. ⁹But that oath does not make him
innocent. You are a wise man, and you
will know how to arrange a bloody
death for him.*"

¹⁰Then David died and was buried
with his ancestors in the City of David.
¹¹David had reigned over Israel for forty
years, seven of them in Hebron and
thirty-three in Jerusalem. ¹²Solomon
became king and sat on the throne of
David his father, and his kingdom was
firmly established.

¹³One day Adonijah, whose mother
was Haggith, came to see Bathsheba, Solomon's mother. "Have you come with
peaceful intentions?" she asked him.

"Yes," he said, "I come in peace. ¹⁴In
fact, I have a favor to ask of you."

"What is it?" she asked.

¹⁵He replied, "As you know, the king-
dom was rightfully mine; all Israel
wanted me to be the next king. But the
tables were turned, and the kingdom
went to my brother instead; for that is
the way the LORD wanted it. ¹⁶So now I
have just one favor to ask of you. Please
don't turn me down."

"What is it?" she asked.

¹⁷He replied, "Speak to King Solo-
mon on my behalf, for I know he will do
anything you request. Ask him to let me
marry Abishag, the girl from Shunem."

¹⁸"All right," Bathsheba replied. "I will speak to the king for you."

¹⁹So Bathsheba went to King Solomon to speak on Adonijah's behalf. The king rose from his throne to meet her, and he bowed down before her. When he sat down on his throne again, the king ordered that a throne be brought for his mother, and she sat at his right hand.

²⁰"I have one small request to make of you," she said. "I hope you won't turn me down."

"What is it, my mother?" he asked. "You know I won't refuse you."

²¹"Then let your brother Adonijah marry Abishag, the girl from Shunem," she replied.

²²"How can you possibly ask me to give Abishag to Adonijah?" King Solomon demanded. "You might as well ask me to give him the kingdom! You know that he is my older brother, and that he has Abiathar the priest and Joab son of Zeruiah on his side."

²³Then King Solomon made a vow before the LORD: "May God strike me and even kill me if Adonijah has not sealed his fate with this request. ²⁴The LORD has confirmed me and placed me on the throne of my father, David; he has established my dynasty as he promised. So as surely as the LORD lives, Adonijah will die this very day!" ²⁵So King Solomon ordered Benaiah son of Jehoiada to execute him, and Adonijah was put to death.

²⁶Then the king said to Abiathar the priest, "Go back to your home in Anathoth. You deserve to die, but I will not kill you now, because you carried the Ark of the Sovereign LORD for David my father and you shared all his hardships." ²⁷So Solomon deposed Abiathar from his position as priest of the LORD, thereby fulfilling the prophecy the LORD had given at Shiloh concerning the descendants of Eli.

²⁸Joab had not joined Absalom's earlier rebellion, but he had joined Adonijah's rebellion. So when Joab heard about Adonijah's death, he ran to the sacred tent of the LORD and grabbed onto the horns of the altar. ²⁹When this was reported to King Solomon, he sent Benaiah son of Jehoiada to execute him.

³⁰Benaiah went to the sacred tent of the LORD and said to Joab, "The king orders you to come out!"

But Joab answered, "No, I will die here."

So Benaiah returned to the king and told him what Joab had said.

³¹"Do as he said," the king replied. "Kill him there beside the altar and bury him. This will remove the guilt of Joab's senseless murders from me and from my father's family. ³²The LORD will repay him* for the murders of two men who were more righteous and better than he. For my father knew nothing about the deaths of Abner son of Ner, commander of the army of Israel, and of Amasa son of Jether, commander of the army of Judah. ³³May their blood be on Joab and his descendants forever, and may the LORD grant peace forever to David, his descendants, his dynasty, and his throne."

³⁴So Benaiah son of Jehoiada returned to the sacred tent and killed Joab, and he was buried at his home in the wilderness. ³⁵Then the king appointed Benaiah to command the army in place of Joab, and he installed Zadok the priest to take the place of Abiathar.

³⁶The king then sent for Shimei and told him, "Build a house here in Jerusalem and live there. But don't step outside the city to go anywhere else. ³⁷On the day you so much as cross the Kidron Valley, you will surely die; and your blood will be on your own head."

³⁸Shimei replied, "Your sentence is fair; I will do whatever my lord the king commands." So Shimei lived in Jerusalem for a long time.

³⁹But three years later two of Shimei's slaves ran away to King Achish son of Maacah of Gath. When Shimei learned where they were, ⁴⁰he saddled his donkey and went to Gath to search for them. When he found them, he brought them back to Jerusalem.

⁴¹Solomon heard that Shimei had left Jerusalem and had gone to Gath and re-

turned. ⁴²So the king sent for Shimei and demanded, "Didn't I make you swear by the LORD and warn you not to go anywhere else or you would surely die? And you replied, 'The sentence is fair; I will do as you say.' ⁴³Then why haven't you kept your oath to the LORD and obeyed my command?"

⁴⁴The king also said to Shimei, "You certainly remember all the wicked things you did to my father, David. May the LORD now bring that evil on your own head. ⁴⁵But may I, King Solomon, receive the LORD's blessings, and may one of David's descendants always sit on this throne in the presence of the LORD."

⁴⁶Then, at the king's command, Benaiah son of Jehoiada took Shimei outside and killed him.

So the kingdom was now firmly in Solomon's grip.

³:¹SOLOMON made an alliance with Pharaoh, the king of Egypt, and married one of his daughters. He brought her to live in the City of David until he could finish building his palace and the Temple of the LORD and the wall around the city. ²At that time the people of Israel sacrificed their offerings at local places of worship, for a temple honoring the name of the LORD had not yet been built.

2:5a Or *He murdered them during a time of peace as revenge for deaths they had caused in time of war.* **2:5b** As in some Greek and Old Latin manuscripts; Hebrew reads *with the blood of war.* **2:6** Hebrew *don't let his white head go down to Sheol in peace.* **2:9** Hebrew *how to bring his white head down to Sheol in blood.* **2:32** Hebrew *will return his blood on his own head.*

ACTS 5:1-42

But there was a certain man named Ananias who, with his wife, Sapphira, sold some property. ²He brought part of the money to the apostles, claiming it was the full amount. With his wife's consent, he kept the rest.

³Then Peter said, "Ananias, why have you let Satan fill your heart? You lied to the Holy Spirit, and you kept some of the money for yourself. ⁴The property was yours to sell or not sell, as you wished. And after selling it, the money was also yours to give away. How could

you do a thing like this? You weren't lying to us but to God!"

⁵As soon as Ananias heard these words, he fell to the floor and died. Everyone who heard about it was terrified. ⁶Then some young men got up, wrapped him in a sheet, and took him out and buried him.

⁷About three hours later his wife came in, not knowing what had happened. ⁸Peter asked her, "Was this the price you and your husband received for your land?"

"Yes," she replied, "that was the price."

⁹And Peter said, "How could the two of you even think of conspiring to test the Spirit of the Lord like this? The young men who buried your husband are just outside the door, and they will carry you out, too."

¹⁰Instantly, she fell to the floor and died. When the young men came in and saw that she was dead, they carried her out and buried her beside her husband. ¹¹Great fear gripped the entire church and everyone else who heard what had happened.

¹²The apostles were performing many miraculous signs and wonders among the people. And all the believers were meeting regularly at the Temple in the area known as Solomon's Colonnade. ¹³But no one else dared to join them, even though all the people had high regard for them. ¹⁴Yet more and more people believed and were brought to the Lord—crowds of both men and women. ¹⁵As a result of the apostles' work, sick people were brought out into the streets on beds and mats so that Peter's shadow might fall across some of them as he went by. ¹⁶Crowds came from the villages around Jerusalem, bringing their sick and those possessed by evil* spirits, and they were all healed.

¹⁷The high priest and his officials, who were Sadducees, were filled with jealousy. ¹⁸They arrested the apostles and put them in the public jail. ¹⁹But an angel of the Lord came at night, opened the gates of the jail, and brought them out. Then he told them, ²⁰"Go to the

Temple and give the people this message of life!"

²¹So at daybreak the apostles entered the Temple, as they were told, and immediately began teaching.

When the high priest and his officials arrived, they convened the high council*—the full assembly of the elders of Israel. Then they sent for the apostles to be brought from the jail for trial. ²²But when the Temple guards went to the jail, the men were gone. So they returned to the council and reported, ²³"The jail was securely locked, with the guards standing outside, but when we opened the gates, no one was there!"

²⁴When the captain of the Temple guard and the leading priests heard this, they were perplexed, wondering where it would all end. ²⁵Then someone arrived with startling news: "The men you put in jail are standing in the Temple, teaching the people!"

²⁶The captain went with his Temple guards and arrested the apostles, but without violence, for they were afraid the people would stone them. ²⁷Then they brought the apostles before the high council, where the high priest confronted them. ²⁸"Didn't we tell you never again to teach in this man's name?" he demanded. "Instead, you have filled all Jerusalem with your teaching about him, and you want to make us responsible for his death!"

²⁹But Peter and the apostles replied, "We must obey God rather than any human authority. ³⁰The God of our ancestors raised Jesus from the dead after you killed him by hanging him on a cross.* ³¹Then God put him in the place of honor at his right hand as Prince and Savior. He did this so the people of Israel would repent of their sins and be forgiven. ³²We are witnesses of these things and so is the Holy Spirit, who is given by God to those who obey him."

³³When they heard this, the high council was furious and decided to kill them. ³⁴But one member, a Pharisee named Gamaliel, who was an expert in religious law and respected by all the people, stood up and ordered that the men be sent outside the council chamber for a while. ³⁵Then he said to his colleagues, "Men of Israel, take care what you are planning to do to these men! ³⁶Some time ago there was that fellow Theudas, who pretended to be someone great. About 400 others joined him, but he was killed, and all his followers went their various ways. The whole movement came to nothing. ³⁷After him, at the time of the census, there was Judas of Galilee. He got people to follow him, but he was killed, too, and all his followers were scattered.

³⁸**"So my advice is, leave these men alone. Let them go. If they are planning and doing these things merely on their own, it will soon be overthrown. ³⁹But if it is from God, you will not be able to overthrow them. You may even find yourselves fighting against God!"**

⁴⁰The others accepted his advice. They called in the apostles and had them flogged. Then they ordered them never again to speak in the name of Jesus, and they let them go.

⁴¹The apostles left the high council rejoicing that God had counted them worthy to suffer disgrace for the name of Jesus.* ⁴²And every day, in the Temple and from house to house, they continued to teach and preach this message: "Jesus is the Messiah."

5:16 Greek *unclean.*   5:21 Greek *Sanhedrin;* also in 5:27, 41.   5:30 Greek *on a tree.*   5:41 Greek *for the name.*

PSALM 125:1-5
A song for pilgrims ascending to Jerusalem.

¹ **T**hose who trust in the LORD are as
      secure as Mount Zion;
    they will not be defeated but will
      endure forever.
² Just as the mountains surround
      Jerusalem,
    so the LORD surrounds his people,
      both now and forever.
³ The wicked will not rule the land
      of the godly,
    for then the godly might be
      tempted to do wrong.

⁴ O Lᴏʀᴅ, do good to those who are
good,
whose hearts are in tune with you.
⁵ But banish those who turn to
crooked ways, O Lᴏʀᴅ.
Take them away with those who
do evil.

May Israel have peace!

PROVERBS 16:25
There is a path before each person that
seems right, but it ends in death.

JUNE
8

1 KINGS 3:3–4:34
Solomon loved the Lᴏʀᴅ and followed
all the decrees of his father, David, except
that Solomon, too, offered sacrifices and
burned incense at the local places of
worship. ⁴The most important of these
places of worship was at Gibeon, so the
king went there and sacrificed 1,000
burnt offerings. ⁵That night the Lᴏʀᴅ appeared to Solomon in a dream, and God
said, "What do you want? Ask, and I will
give it to you!"

⁶Solomon replied, "You showed
faithful love to your servant my father,
David, because he was honest and true
and faithful to you. And you have continued your faithful love to him today
by giving him a son to sit on his throne.
⁷"Now, O Lᴏʀᴅ my God, you have
made me king instead of my father, David, but I am like a little child who doesn't
know his way around. ⁸And here I am in
the midst of your own chosen people, a
nation so great and numerous they cannot be counted! ⁹**Give me an understanding heart so that I can govern
your people well and know the difference between right and wrong. For
who by himself is able to govern this
great people of yours?"**

¹⁰**The Lord was pleased that Solomon had asked for wisdom.** ¹¹So God
replied, "Because you have asked for wisdom in governing my people with justice
and have not asked for a long life or
wealth or the death of your enemies—¹²I
will give you what you asked for! I will
give you a wise and understanding heart
such as no one else has had or ever will
have! ¹³And I will also give you what you
did not ask for—riches and fame! No
other king in all the world will be compared to you for the rest of your life!
¹⁴And if you follow me and obey my decrees and my commands as your father,
David, did, I will give you a long life."

¹⁵Then Solomon woke up and realized it had been a dream. He returned
to Jerusalem and stood before the Ark
of the Lᴏʀᴅ's Covenant, where he sacrificed burnt offerings and peace offerings. Then he invited all his officials to a
great banquet.

¹⁶Some time later two prostitutes
came to the king to have an argument
settled. ¹⁷"Please, my lord," one of them
began, "this woman and I live in the same
house. I gave birth to a baby while she
was with me in the house. ¹⁸Three days
later this woman also had a baby. We
were alone; there were only two of us in
the house.

¹⁹"But her baby died during the night
when she rolled over on it. ²⁰Then she
got up in the night and took my son
from beside me while I was asleep. She
laid her dead child in my arms and took
mine to sleep beside her. ²¹And in the
morning when I tried to nurse my son,
he was dead! But when I looked more
closely in the morning light, I saw that it
wasn't my son at all."

²²Then the other woman inter-
rupted, "It certainly was your son, and
the living child is mine."

"No," the first woman said, "the living
child is mine, and the dead one is yours."
And so they argued back and forth before the king.

²³Then the king said, "Let's get the
facts straight. Both of you claim the living child is yours, and each says that the

dead one belongs to the other. ²⁴All right, bring me a sword." So a sword was brought to the king.

²⁵Then he said, "Cut the living child in two, and give half to one woman and half to the other!"

²⁶Then the woman who was the real mother of the living child, and who loved him very much, cried out, "Oh no, my lord! Give her the child—please do not kill him!"

But the other woman said, "All right, he will be neither yours nor mine; divide him between us!"

²⁷Then the king said, "Do not kill the child, but give him to the woman who wants him to live, for she is his mother!"

²⁸When all Israel heard the king's decision, the people were in awe of the king, for they saw the wisdom God had given him for rendering justice.

⁴:¹KING Solomon now ruled over all Israel, ²and these were his high officials:

Azariah son of Zadok was the priest.
³ Elihoreph and Ahijah, the sons of Shisha, were court secretaries.
Jehoshaphat son of Ahilud was the royal historian.
⁴ Benaiah son of Jehoiada was commander of the army.
Zadok and Abiathar were priests.
⁵ Azariah son of Nathan was in charge of the district governors.
Zabud son of Nathan, a priest, was a trusted adviser to the king.
⁶ Ahishar was manager of the palace property.
Adoniram son of Abda was in charge of the labor force.

⁷Solomon also had twelve district governors who were over all Israel. They were responsible for providing food for the king's household. Each of them arranged provisions for one month of the year. ⁸These are the names of the twelve governors:

Ben-hur, in the hill country of Ephraim.
⁹ Ben-deker, in Makaz, Shaalbim,

Beth-shemesh, and Elon-bethhanan.
¹⁰ Ben-hesed, in Arubboth, including Socoh and all the land of Hepher.
¹¹ Ben-abinadab, in all of Naphoth-dor.* (He was married to Taphath, one of Solomon's daughters.)
¹² Baana son of Ahilud, in Taanach and Megiddo, all of Beth-shan* near Zarethan below Jezreel, and all the territory from Beth-shan to Abel-meholah and over to Jokmeam.
¹³ Ben-geber, in Ramoth-gilead, including the Towns of Jair (named for Jair of the tribe of Manasseh*) in Gilead, and in the Argob region of Bashan, including sixty large fortified towns with bronze bars on their gates.
¹⁴ Ahinadab son of Iddo, in Mahanaim.
¹⁵ Ahimaaz, in Naphtali. (He was married to Basemath, another of Solomon's daughters.)
¹⁶ Baana son of Hushai, in Asher and in Aloth.
¹⁷ Jehoshaphat son of Paruah, in Issachar.
¹⁸ Shimei son of Ela, in Benjamin.
¹⁹ Geber son of Uri, in the land of Gilead,* including the territories of King Sihon of the Amorites and King Og of Bashan.
There was also one governor over the land of Judah.*

²⁰The people of Judah and Israel were as numerous as the sand on the seashore. They were very contented, with plenty to eat and drink. ²¹*Solomon ruled over all the kingdoms from the Euphrates River* in the north to the land of the Philistines and the border of Egypt in the south. The conquered peoples of those lands sent tribute money to Solomon and continued to serve him throughout his lifetime.

²²The daily food requirements for Solomon's palace were 150 bushels of choice flour and 300 bushels of meal*; ²³also 10 oxen from the fattening pens,

20 pasture-fed cattle, 100 sheep or goats, as well as deer, gazelles, roe deer, and choice poultry.*

24Solomon's dominion extended over all the kingdoms west of the Euphrates River, from Tiphsah to Gaza. And there was peace on all his borders. 25During the lifetime of Solomon, all of Judah and Israel lived in peace and safety. And from Dan in the north to Beersheba in the south, each family had its own home and garden.*

26Solomon had 4,000* stalls for his chariot horses, and he had 12,000 horses.*

27The district governors faithfully provided food for King Solomon and his court; each made sure nothing was lacking during the month assigned to him. 28They also brought the necessary barley and straw for the royal horses in the stables.

29God gave Solomon very great wisdom and understanding, and knowledge as vast as the sands of the seashore. 30In fact, his wisdom exceeded that of all the wise men of the East and the wise men of Egypt. 31He was wiser than anyone else, including Ethan the Ezrahite and the sons of Mahol—Heman, Calcol, and Darda. His fame spread throughout all the surrounding nations. 32He composed some 3,000 proverbs and wrote 1,005 songs. 33He could speak with authority about all kinds of plants, from the great cedar of Lebanon to the tiny hyssop that grows from cracks in a wall. He could also speak about animals, birds, small creatures, and fish. 34And kings from every nation sent their ambassadors to listen to the wisdom of Solomon.

4:11 Hebrew Naphath-dor, a variant spelling of Naphoth-dor.   4:12 Hebrew Beth-shean, a variant spelling of Beth-shan; also in 4:12b.   4:13 Hebrew Jair son of Manasseh; compare 1 Chr 2:22.   4:19a Greek version reads of Gad; compare 4:13.   4:19b As in some Greek manuscripts; Hebrew lacks of Judah. The meaning of the Hebrew is uncertain.   4:21a Verses 4:21-34 are numbered 5:1-14 in Hebrew text.   4:21b Hebrew the river; also in 4:24.   4:22 Hebrew 30 cors [5.5 kiloliters] of choice flour and 60 cors [11 kiloliters] of meal.   4:23 Or and fattened geese.   4:25 Hebrew each family lived under its own grapevine and under its own fig tree.   4:26a As in some Greek manuscripts (see also 2 Chr 9:25); Hebrew reads 40,000.   4:26b Or 12,000 charioteers.

ACTS 6:1-15

But as the believers* rapidly multiplied, there were rumblings of discontent. The Greek-speaking believers complained about the Hebrew-speaking believers, saying that their widows were being discriminated against in the daily distribution of food.

2So the Twelve called a meeting of all the believers. They said, "We apostles should spend our time teaching the word of God, not running a food program. 3And so, brothers, select seven men who are well respected and are full of the Spirit and wisdom. We will give them this responsibility. 4Then we apostles can spend our time in prayer and teaching the word."

5Everyone liked this idea, and they chose the following: Stephen (a man full of faith and the Holy Spirit), Philip, Procorus, Nicanor, Timon, Parmenas, and Nicolas of Antioch (an earlier convert to the Jewish faith). 6These seven were presented to the apostles, who prayed for them as they laid their hands on them.

7So God's message continued to spread. The number of believers greatly increased in Jerusalem, and many of the Jewish priests were converted, too.

8Stephen, a man full of God's grace and power, performed amazing miracles and signs among the people. 9But one day some men from the Synagogue of Freed Slaves, as it was called, started to debate with him. They were Jews from Cyrene, Alexandria, Cilicia, and the province of Asia. 10None of them could stand against the wisdom and the Spirit with which Stephen spoke.

11So they persuaded some men to lie about Stephen, saying, "We heard him blaspheme Moses, and even God." 12This roused the people, the elders, and the teachers of religious law. So they arrested Stephen and brought him before the high council.* 13The lying witnesses said, "This man is always speaking against the holy Temple and against the law of Moses. 14We have heard him say that this Jesus of Nazareth* will destroy the Temple and change the customs Moses handed down to us."

¹⁵At this point everyone in the high council stared at Stephen, because his face became as bright as an angel's.

6:1 Greek *disciples;* also in 6:2, 7.   6:12 Greek *Sanhedrin;* also in 6:15.   6:14 Or *Jesus the Nazarene.*

PSALM 126:1-6
A song for pilgrims ascending to Jerusalem.

¹ **W**hen the LORD brought back
his exiles to Jerusalem,*
it was like a dream!
² We were filled with laughter,
and we sang for joy.
And the other nations said,
"What amazing things the LORD
has done for them."
³ Yes, the LORD has done amazing
things for us!
What joy!

⁴ Restore our fortunes, LORD,
as streams renew the desert.
⁵ Those who plant in tears
will harvest with shouts of joy.
⁶ They weep as they go to plant
their seed,
but they sing as they return
with the harvest.

126:1 Hebrew *Zion.*

PROVERBS 16:26-27
It is good for workers to have an appetite; an empty stomach drives them on. □ Scoundrels create trouble; their words are a destructive blaze.

JUNE 9

1 KINGS 5:1–6:38
¹***K**ing Hiram of Tyre had always been a loyal friend of David. When Hiram learned that David's son Solomon was the new king of Israel, he sent ambassadors to congratulate him.

²Then Solomon sent this message back to Hiram:

³"You know that my father, David, was not able to build a Temple to honor the name of the LORD his God because of the many wars waged against him by surrounding nations. He could not build until the LORD gave him victory over all his enemies. ⁴But now the LORD my God has given me peace on every side; I have no enemies, and all is well. ⁵So I am planning to build a Temple to honor the name of the LORD my God, just as he had instructed my father, David. For the LORD told him, 'Your son, whom I will place on your throne, will build the Temple to honor my name.'

⁶"Therefore, please command that cedars from Lebanon be cut for me. Let my men work alongside yours, and I will pay your men whatever wages you ask. As you know, there is no one among us who can cut timber like you Sidonians!"

⁷When Hiram received Solomon's message, he was very pleased and said, "Praise the LORD today for giving David a wise son to be king of the great nation of Israel." ⁸Then he sent this reply to Solomon:

"I have received your message, and I will supply all the cedar and cypress timber you need. ⁹My servants will bring the logs from the Lebanon mountains to the Mediterranean Sea* and make them into rafts and float them along the coast to whatever place you choose. Then we will break the rafts apart so you can carry the logs away. You can pay me by supplying me with food for my household."

¹⁰So Hiram supplied as much cedar and cypress timber as Solomon desired. ¹¹In return, Solomon sent him an annual payment of 100,000 bushels* of wheat for his household and 110,000

gallons* of pure olive oil. ¹²So the Lord gave wisdom to Solomon, just as he had promised. And Hiram and Solomon made a formal alliance of peace.

¹³Then King Solomon conscripted a labor force of 30,000 men from all Israel. ¹⁴He sent them to Lebanon in shifts, 10,000 every month, so that each man would be one month in Lebanon and two months at home. Adoniram was in charge of this labor force. ¹⁵Solomon also had 70,000 common laborers, 80,000 quarry workers in the hill country, ¹⁶and 3,600* foremen to supervise the work. ¹⁷At the king's command, they quarried large blocks of high-quality stone and shaped them to make the foundation of the Temple. ¹⁸Men from the city of Gebal helped Solomon's and Hiram's builders prepare the timber and stone for the Temple.

⁶:¹It was in midspring, in the month of Ziv,* during the fourth year of Solomon's reign, that he began to construct the Temple of the Lord. This was 480 years after the people of Israel were rescued from their slavery in the land of Egypt.

²The Temple that King Solomon built for the Lord was 90 feet long, 30 feet wide, and 45 feet high.* ³The entry room at the front of the Temple was 30 feet* wide, running across the entire width of the Temple. It projected outward 15 feet* from the front of the Temple. ⁴Solomon also made narrow recessed windows throughout the Temple.

⁵He built a complex of rooms against the outer walls of the Temple, all the way around the sides and rear of the building. ⁶The complex was three stories high, the bottom floor being 7½ feet wide, the second floor 9 feet wide, and the top floor 10½ feet wide.* The rooms were connected to the walls of the Temple by beams resting on ledges built out from the wall. So the beams were not inserted into the walls themselves.

⁷The stones used in the construction of the Temple were finished at the quarry, so there was no sound of hammer, ax, or any other iron tool at the building site.

⁸The entrance to the bottom floor* was on the south side of the Temple. There were winding stairs going up to the second floor, and another flight of stairs between the second and third floors. ⁹After completing the Temple structure, Solomon put in a ceiling made of cedar beams and planks. ¹⁰As already stated, he built a complex of rooms on three sides of the building, attached to the Temple walls by cedar timbers. Each story of the complex was 7½ feet* high.

¹¹Then the Lord gave this message to Solomon: ¹²"Concerning this Temple you are building, if you keep all my decrees and regulations and obey all my commands, I will fulfill through you the promise I made to your father, David. ¹³I will live among the Israelites and will never abandon my people Israel."

¹⁴So Solomon finished building the Temple. ¹⁵The entire inside, from floor to ceiling, was paneled with wood. He paneled the walls and ceilings with cedar, and he used planks of cypress for the floors. ¹⁶He partitioned off an inner sanctuary—the Most Holy Place—at the far end of the Temple. It was 30 feet deep and was paneled with cedar from floor to ceiling. ¹⁷The main room of the Temple, outside the Most Holy Place, was 60 feet* long. ¹⁸Cedar paneling completely covered the stone walls throughout the Temple, and the paneling was decorated with carvings of gourds and open flowers.

¹⁹He prepared the inner sanctuary at the far end of the Temple, where the Ark of the Lord's Covenant would be placed. ²⁰This inner sanctuary was 30 feet long, 30 feet wide, and 30 feet high. He overlaid the inside with solid gold. He also overlaid the altar made of cedar.* ²¹Then Solomon overlaid the rest of the Temple's interior with solid gold, and he made gold chains to protect the entrance* to the Most Holy Place. ²²So he finished overlaying the entire Temple with gold, including the

altar that belonged to the Most Holy Place.

²³He made two cherubim of wild olive* wood, each 15 feet* tall, and placed them in the inner sanctuary. ²⁴The wingspan of each of the cherubim was 15 feet, each wing being 7½ feet* long. ²⁵The two cherubim were identical in shape and size; ²⁶each was 15 feet tall. ²⁷He placed them side by side in the inner sanctuary of the Temple. Their outspread wings reached from wall to wall, while their inner wings touched at the center of the room. ²⁸He overlaid the two cherubim with gold.

²⁹He decorated all the walls of the inner sanctuary and the main room with carvings of cherubim, palm trees, and open flowers. ³⁰He overlaid the floor in both rooms with gold.

³¹For the entrance to the inner sanctuary, he made double doors of wild olive wood with five-sided doorposts.* ³²These double doors were decorated with carvings of cherubim, palm trees, and open flowers. The doors, including the decorations of cherubim and palm trees, were overlaid with gold.

³³Then he made four-sided doorposts of wild olive wood for the entrance to the Temple. ³⁴There were two folding doors of cypress wood, and each door was hinged to fold back upon itself. ³⁵These doors were decorated with carvings of cherubim, palm trees, and open flowers—all overlaid evenly with gold.

³⁶The walls of the inner courtyard were built so that there was one layer of cedar beams between every three layers of finished stone.

³⁷The foundation of the LORD's Temple was laid in midspring, in the month of Ziv,* during the fourth year of Solomon's reign. ³⁸The entire building was completed in every detail by midautumn, in the month of Bul,* during the eleventh year of his reign. So it took seven years to build the Temple.

5:1 Verses 5:1-18 are numbered 5:15-32 in Hebrew text. 5:9 Hebrew *the sea.* 5:11a Hebrew *20,000 cors* [3,640 kiloliters]. 5:11b As in Greek version, which reads *20,000 baths* [420 kiloliters] (see also 2 Chr 2:10); Hebrew reads *20 cors*, about 800 gallons or 3.6 kiloliters in volume.

5:16 As in some Greek manuscripts (see also 2 Chr 2:2, 18); Hebrew reads *3,300.* 6:1 Hebrew *It was in the month of Ziv, which is the second month.* This month of the ancient Hebrew lunar calendar usually occurs within the months of April and May. 6:2 Hebrew *60 cubits* [27.6 meters] *long, 20 cubits* [9.2 meters] *wide, and 30 cubits* [13.8 meters] *high.* 6:3a Hebrew *20 cubits* [9.2 meters]; also in 6:16, 20. 6:3b Hebrew *10 cubits* [4.6 meters]. 6:6 Hebrew *the bottom floor being 5 cubits* [2.3 meters] *wide, the second floor 6 cubits* [2.8 meters] *wide, and the top floor 7 cubits* [3.2 meters] *wide.* 6:8 As in Greek version; Hebrew reads *middle floor.* 6:10 Hebrew *5 cubits* [2.3 meters]. 6:17 Hebrew *40 cubits* [18.4 meters]. 6:20 Or *overlaid the altar with cedar.* The meaning of the Hebrew is uncertain. 6:21 Or *to draw curtains across.* The meaning of the Hebrew is uncertain. 6:23a Or *pine;* Hebrew reads *oil tree;* also in 6:31, 33. 6:23b Hebrew *10 cubits* [4.6 meters]; also in 6:24, 25. 6:24 Hebrew *5 cubits* [2.3 meters]. 6:31 The meaning of the Hebrew is uncertain. 6:37 Hebrew *was laid in the month of Ziv.* This month of the ancient Hebrew lunar calendar usually occurs within the months of April and May. 6:38 Hebrew *by the month of Bul, which is the eighth month.* This month of the ancient Hebrew lunar calendar usually occurs within the months of October and November.

ACTS 7:1-29

Then the high priest asked Stephen, "Are these accusations true?"

²This was Stephen's reply: "Brothers and fathers, listen to me. Our glorious God appeared to our ancestor Abraham in Mesopotamia before he settled in Haran.* ³God told him, 'Leave your native land and your relatives, and come into the land that I will show you.'* ⁴So Abraham left the land of the Chaldeans and lived in Haran until his father died. Then God brought him here to the land where you now live.

⁵"But God gave him no inheritance here, not even one square foot of land. God did promise, however, that eventually the whole land would belong to Abraham and his descendants—even though he had no children yet. ⁶God also told him that his descendants would live in a foreign land, where they would be oppressed as slaves for 400 years. ⁷'But I will punish the nation that enslaves them,' God said, 'and in the end they will come out and worship me here in this place.'*

⁸"God also gave Abraham the covenant of circumcision at that time. So when Abraham became the father of Isaac, he circumcised him on the eighth day. And the practice was continued when Isaac became the father of Jacob, and when Jacob became the father of

the twelve patriarchs of the Israelite nation.

9"These patriarchs were jealous of their brother Joseph, and they sold him to be a slave in Egypt. But God was with him 10and rescued him from all his troubles. And God gave him favor before Pharaoh, king of Egypt. God also gave Joseph unusual wisdom, so that Pharaoh appointed him governor over all of Egypt and put him in charge of the palace.

11"But a famine came upon Egypt and Canaan. There was great misery, and our ancestors ran out of food. 12Jacob heard that there was still grain in Egypt, so he sent his sons—our ancestors—to buy some. 13The second time they went, Joseph revealed his identity to his brothers,* and they were introduced to Pharaoh. 14Then Joseph sent for his father, Jacob, and all his relatives to come to Egypt, seventy-five persons in all. 15So Jacob went to Egypt. He died there, as did our ancestors. 16Their bodies were taken to Shechem and buried in the tomb Abraham had bought for a certain price from Hamor's sons in Shechem.

17"As the time drew near when God would fulfill his promise to Abraham, the number of our people in Egypt greatly increased. 18But then a new king came to the throne of Egypt who knew nothing about Joseph. 19This king exploited our people and oppressed them, forcing parents to abandon their newborn babies so they would die.

20"At that time Moses was born—a beautiful child in God's eyes. His parents cared for him at home for three months. 21When they had to abandon him, Pharaoh's daughter adopted him and raised him as her own son. 22Moses was taught all the wisdom of the Egyptians, and he was powerful in both speech and action.

23"One day when Moses was forty years old, he decided to visit his relatives, the people of Israel. 24He saw an Egyptian mistreating an Israelite. So Moses came to the man's defense and avenged him, killing the Egyptian.

25Moses assumed his fellow Israelites would realize that God had sent him to rescue them, but they didn't.

26"The next day he visited them again and saw two men of Israel fighting. He tried to be a peacemaker. 'Men,' he said, 'you are brothers. Why are you fighting each other?'

27"But the man in the wrong pushed Moses aside. 'Who made you a ruler and judge over us?' he asked. 28'Are you going to kill me as you killed that Egyptian yesterday?' 29When Moses heard that, he fled the country and lived as a foreigner in the land of Midian. There his two sons were born."

7:2 *Mesopotamia* was the region now called Iraq. *Haran* was a city in what is now called Syria. **7:3** Gen 12:1. **7:5-7** Gen 12:7; 15:13-14; Exod 3:12. **7:13** Other manuscripts read *Joseph was recognized by his brothers.*

PSALM 127:1-5

A song for pilgrims ascending to Jerusalem. A psalm of Solomon.

1 **Unless the LORD builds a house,**
　　the work of the builders is
　　wasted.
Unless the LORD protects a city,
　　guarding it with sentries will
　　do no good.
2 It is useless for you to work so hard
　　from early morning until late
　　　at night,
　anxiously working for food to eat;
　　for God gives rest to his
　　　loved ones.

3 Children are a gift from the LORD;
　　they are a reward from him.
4 Children born to a young man
　　are like arrows in a warrior's
　　　hands.
5 How joyful is the man whose quiver
　　is full of them!
　He will not be put to shame when
　　he confronts his accusers
　　　at the city gates.

PROVERBS 16:28-30

A troublemaker plants seeds of strife; gossip separates the best of friends. □ Violent people mislead their companions, leading them down a harmful path. □With narrowed eyes, people plot evil; with a smirk, they plan their mischief.

JUNE
10

1 KINGS 7:1-51

Solomon also built a palace for himself, and it took him thirteen years to complete the construction.

²One of Solomon's buildings was called the Palace of the Forest of Lebanon. It was 150 feet long, 75 feet wide, and 45 feet high.* There were four rows of cedar pillars, and great cedar beams rested on the pillars. ³The hall had a cedar roof. Above the beams on the pillars were forty-five side rooms,* arranged in three tiers of fifteen each. ⁴On each end of the long hall were three rows of windows facing each other. ⁵All the doorways and doorposts* had rectangular frames and were arranged in sets of three, facing each other.

⁶Solomon also built the Hall of Pillars, which was 75 feet long and 45 feet wide.* There was a porch in front, along with a canopy supported by pillars.

⁷Solomon also built the throne room, known as the Hall of Justice, where he sat to hear legal matters. It was paneled with cedar from floor to ceiling.* ⁸Solomon's living quarters surrounded a courtyard behind this hall, and they were constructed the same way. He also built similar living quarters for Pharaoh's daughter, whom he had married.

⁹From foundation to eaves, all these buildings were built from huge blocks of high-quality stone, cut with saws and trimmed to exact measure on all sides. ¹⁰Some of the huge foundation stones were 15 feet long, and some were 12 feet* long. ¹¹The blocks of high-quality stone used in the walls were also

cut to measure, and cedar beams were also used. ¹²The walls of the great courtyard were built so that there was one layer of cedar beams between every three layers of finished stone, just like the walls of the inner courtyard of the LORD's Temple with its entry room.

¹³King Solomon then asked for a man named Huram* to come from Tyre. ¹⁴He was half Israelite, since his mother was a widow from the tribe of Naphtali, and his father had been a craftsman in bronze from Tyre. Huram was extremely skillful and talented in any work in bronze, and he came to do all the metal work for King Solomon.

¹⁵Huram cast two bronze pillars, each 27 feet tall and 18 feet in circumference.* ¹⁶For the tops of the pillars he cast bronze capitals, each 7½ feet* tall. ¹⁷Each capital was decorated with seven sets of latticework and interwoven chains. ¹⁸He also encircled the latticework with two rows of pomegranates to decorate the capitals over the pillars. ¹⁹The capitals on the columns inside the entry room were shaped like water lilies, and they were six feet* tall. ²⁰The capitals on the two pillars had 200 pomegranates in two rows around them, beside the rounded surface next to the latticework. ²¹Huram set the pillars at the entrance of the Temple, one toward the south and one toward the north. He named the one on the south Jakin, and the one on the north Boaz.* ²²The capitals on the pillars were shaped like water lilies. And so the work on the pillars was finished.

²³Then Huram cast a great round basin, 15 feet across from rim to rim, called the Sea. It was 7½ feet deep and about 45 feet in circumference.* ²⁴It was encircled just below its rim by two rows of decorative gourds. There were about six gourds per foot* all the way around, and they were cast as part of the basin.

²⁵The Sea was placed on a base of twelve bronze oxen,* all facing outward. Three faced north, three faced west, three faced south, and three faced east, and the Sea rested on them. ²⁶The walls

of the Sea were about three inches* thick, and its rim flared out like a cup and resembled a water lily blossom. It could hold about 11,000 gallons* of water.

27Huram also made ten bronze water carts, each 6 feet long, 6 feet wide, and 4½ feet tall.* 28They were constructed with side panels braced with crossbars. 29Both the panels and the crossbars were decorated with carved lions, oxen, and cherubim. Above and below the lions and oxen were wreath decorations. 30Each of these carts had four bronze wheels and bronze axles. There were supporting posts for the bronze basins at the corners of the carts; these supports were decorated on each side with carvings of wreaths. 31The top of each cart had a rounded frame for the basin. It projected 1½ feet* above the cart's top like a round pedestal, and its opening was 2¼ feet* across; it was decorated on the outside with carvings of wreaths. The panels of the carts were square, not round. 32Under the panels were four wheels that were connected to axles that had been cast as one unit with the cart. The wheels were 2¼ feet in diameter 33and were similar to chariot wheels. The axles, spokes, rims, and hubs were all cast from molten bronze.

34There were handles at each of the four corners of the carts, and these, too, were cast as one unit with the cart. 35Around the top of each cart was a rim nine inches wide.* The corner supports and side panels were cast as one unit with the cart. 36Carvings of cherubim, lions, and palm trees decorated the panels and corner supports wherever there was room, and there were wreaths all around. 37All ten water carts were the same size and were made alike, for each was cast from the same mold.

38Huram also made ten smaller bronze basins, one for each cart. Each basin was six feet across and could hold 220 gallons* of water. 39He set five water carts on the south side of the Temple and five on the north side. The great bronze basin called the Sea was placed near the southeast corner of the Tem-

ple. 40He also made the necessary washbasins, shovels, and bowls.

So at last Huram completed everything King Solomon had assigned him to make for the Temple of the LORD:

41 the two pillars;
   the two bowl-shaped capitals
      on top of the pillars;
   the two networks of interwoven
      chains that decorated the capitals;
42 the 400 pomegranates that hung
      from the chains on the capitals
      (two rows of pomegranates for
      each of the chain networks that
      decorated the capitals on top of
      the pillars);
43 the ten water carts holding the
      ten basins;
44 the Sea and the twelve oxen under it;
45 the ash buckets, the shovels, and
      the bowls.

Huram made all these things of burnished bronze for the Temple of the LORD, just as King Solomon had directed. 46The king had them cast in clay molds in the Jordan Valley between Succoth and Zarethan. 47Solomon did not weigh all these things because there were so many; the weight of the bronze could not be measured.

48Solomon also made all the furnishings of the Temple of the LORD:

   the gold altar;
   the gold table for the Bread of the
      Presence;
49 the lampstands of solid gold, five on
      the south and five on the north,
      in front of the Most Holy Place;
   the flower decorations, lamps, and
      tongs—all of gold;
50 the small bowls, lamp snuffers,
      bowls, dishes, and incense
      burners—all of solid gold;
   the doors for the entrances to the
      Most Holy Place and the main
      room of the Temple, with their
      fronts overlaid with gold.

51So King Solomon finished all his work on the Temple of the LORD. Then he brought all the gifts his father, David, had dedicated—the silver, the gold, and the various articles—and he stored them in the treasuries of the LORD's Temple.

7:2 Hebrew *100 cubits* [46 meters] *long, 50 cubits* [23 meters] *wide, and 30 cubits* [13.5 meters] *high.* 7:3 Or *45 rafters,* or *45 beams,* or *45 pillars.* The architectural details in 7:2-6 can be interpreted in many different ways. 7:5 Greek version reads *windows.* 7:6 Hebrew *50 cubits* [23 meters] *long and 30 cubits* [13.8 meters] *wide.* 7:7 As in Syriac version and Latin Vulgate; Hebrew reads *from floor to floor.* 7:10 Hebrew *10 cubits* [4.6 meters] . . . *8 cubits* [3.7 meters]. 7:13 Hebrew *Hiram* (also in 7:40, 45); compare 2 Chr 2:13. This is not the same person mentioned in 5:1. 7:15 Hebrew *18 cubits* [8.3 meters] *tall and 12 cubits* [5.5 meters] *in circumference.* 7:16 Hebrew *5 cubits* [2.3 meters]. 7:19 Hebrew *4 cubits* [1.8 meters]; also in 7:38. 7:21 *Jakin* probably means "he establishes"; *Boaz* probably means "in him is strength." 7:23 Hebrew *10 cubits* [4.6 meters] *across. . . . 5 cubits* [2.3 meters] *deep and 30 cubits* [13.8 meters] *in circumference.* 7:24 Or *20 gourds per meter;* Hebrew reads *10 per cubit.* 7:25 Hebrew *12 oxen;* compare 2 Kgs 16:17, which specifies *bronze oxen.* 7:26a Hebrew *a handbreadth* [8 centimeters]. 7:26b Hebrew *2,000 baths* [42 kiloliters]. 7:27 Hebrew *4 cubits* [1.8 meters] *long, 4 cubits wide, and 3 cubits* [1.4 meters] *high.* 7:31a Hebrew *a cubit* [46 centimeters]. 7:31b Hebrew *1½ cubits* [69 centimeters]; also in 7:32. 7:35 Hebrew *half a cubit wide* [23 centimeters]. 7:38 Hebrew *40 baths* [840 liters].

ACTS 7:30-50

"**F**orty years later, in the desert near Mount Sinai, an angel appeared to Moses in the flame of a burning bush. ³¹When Moses saw it, he was amazed at the sight. As he went to take a closer look, the voice of the LORD called out to him, ³²'I am the God of your ancestors—the God of Abraham, Isaac, and Jacob.' Moses shook with terror and did not dare to look.

³³"Then the LORD said to him, 'Take off your sandals, for you are standing on holy ground. ³⁴I have certainly seen the oppression of my people in Egypt. I have heard their groans and have come down to rescue them. Now go, for I am sending you back to Egypt.'*

³⁵"So God sent back the same man his people had previously rejected when they demanded, 'Who made you a ruler and judge over us?' Through the angel who appeared to him in the burning bush, God sent Moses to be their ruler and savior. ³⁶And by means of many wonders and miraculous signs, he led them out of Egypt, through the Red Sea, and through the wilderness for forty years.

³⁷"Moses himself told the people of Israel, 'God will raise up for you a Prophet like me from among your own people.'* ³⁸Moses was with our ancestors, the assembly of God's people in the wilderness, when the angel spoke to him at Mount Sinai. And there Moses received life-giving words to pass on to us.*

³⁹"But our ancestors refused to listen to Moses. They rejected him and wanted to return to Egypt. ⁴⁰They told Aaron, 'Make us some gods who can lead us, for we don't know what has become of this Moses, who brought us out of Egypt.' ⁴¹So they made an idol shaped like a calf, and they sacrificed to it and celebrated over this thing they had made. ⁴²Then God turned away from them and abandoned them to serve the stars of heaven as their gods! In the book of the prophets it is written,

'Was it to me you were bringing
    sacrifices and offerings
during those forty years in the
    wilderness, Israel?
⁴³ No, you carried your pagan
    gods—
    the shrine of Molech,
    the star of your god Rephan,
    and the images you made to
        worship them.
So I will send you into exile
    as far away as Babylon.'*

⁴⁴"Our ancestors carried the Tabernacle* with them through the wilderness. It was constructed according to the plan God had shown to Moses. ⁴⁵Years later, when Joshua led our ancestors in battle against the nations that God drove out of this land, the Tabernacle was taken with them into their new territory. And it stayed there until the time of King David.

⁴⁶"David found favor with God and asked for the privilege of building a permanent Temple for the God of Jacob.* ⁴⁷But it was Solomon who actually built it. ⁴⁸However, the Most High doesn't live in temples made by human hands. As the prophet says,

⁴⁹ 'Heaven is my throne,
    and the earth is my footstool.
Could you build me a temple as good
    as that?'
    asks the LORD.
'Could you build me such a resting
    place?
⁵⁰ Didn't my hands make both
    heaven and earth?'*

7:31-34 Exod 3:5-10.   7:37 Deut 18:15.   7:38 Some
manuscripts read *to you*.   7:42-43 Amos 5:25-27 (Greek
version).   7:44 Greek *the tent of witness*.   7:46 Some
manuscripts read *the house of Jacob*.   7:49-50 Isa 66:1-2.

PSALM 128:1-6
A song for pilgrims ascending to Jerusalem.

¹ **How joyful are those who fear
    the LORD—**
    all who follow his ways!
² **You will enjoy the fruit of your
    labor.**
    **How joyful and prosperous
    you will be!**
³ Your wife will be like a fruitful
    grapevine,
    flourishing within your home.
Your children will be like vigorous
    young olive trees
    as they sit around your table.
⁴ That is the LORD's blessing
    for those who fear him.

⁵ May the LORD continually bless
    you from Zion.
May you see Jerusalem prosper
    as long as you live.
⁶ May you live to enjoy your
    grandchildren.
    May Israel have peace!

PROVERBS 16:31-33
Gray hair is a crown of glory; it is gained
by living a godly life. ☐ Better to be patient than powerful; better to have self-
control than to conquer a city. ☐ We
may throw the dice, but the LORD determines how they fall.

JUNE 11

1 KINGS 8:1-66
Solomon then summoned to Jerusalem
the elders of Israel and all the heads of
the tribes—the leaders of the ancestral
families of the Israelites. They were to
bring the Ark of the LORD's Covenant to
the Temple from its location in the City
of David, also known as Zion. ²So all the
men of Israel assembled before King
Solomon at the annual Festival of Shelters, which is held in early autumn in
the month of Ethanim.*

³When all the elders of Israel arrived,
the priests picked up the Ark. ⁴The
priests and Levites brought up the Ark
of the LORD along with the special tent*
and all the sacred items that had been in
it. ⁵There, before the Ark, King Solomon and the entire community of Israel
sacrificed so many sheep, goats, and
cattle that no one could keep count!
⁶Then the priests carried the Ark of
the LORD's Covenant into the inner sanctuary of the Temple—the Most Holy
Place—and placed it beneath the wings
of the cherubim. ⁷The cherubim spread
their wings over the Ark, forming a canopy over the Ark and its carrying poles.
⁸These poles were so long that their ends
could be seen from the Temple's main
room—the Holy Place—but not from the
outside. They are still there to this day.
⁹Nothing was in the Ark except the two
stone tablets that Moses had placed in it
at Mount Sinai,* where the LORD made a
covenant with the people of Israel when
they left the land of Egypt.
¹⁰When the priests came out of the
Holy Place, a thick cloud filled the Temple of the LORD. ¹¹The priests could not
continue their service because of the
cloud, for the glorious presence of the
LORD filled the Temple.
¹²Then Solomon prayed, "O LORD, you
have said that you would live in a thick
cloud of darkness. ¹³Now I have built a

glorious Temple for you, a place where you can live forever!*"

¹⁴Then the king turned around to the entire community of Israel standing before him and gave this blessing: ¹⁵"Praise the LORD, the God of Israel, who has kept the promise he made to my father, David. For he told my father, ¹⁶'From the day I brought my people Israel out of Egypt, I have never chosen a city among any of the tribes of Israel as the place where a Temple should be built to honor my name. But I have chosen David to be king over my people Israel.'"

¹⁷Then Solomon said, "My father, David, wanted to build this Temple to honor the name of the LORD, the God of Israel. ¹⁸But the LORD told him, 'You wanted to build the Temple to honor my name. Your intention is good, ¹⁹but you are not the one to do it. One of your own sons will build the Temple to honor me.'

²⁰And now the LORD has fulfilled the promise he made, for I have become king in my father's place, and I now sit on the throne of Israel, just as the LORD promised. I have built this Temple to honor the name of the LORD, the God of Israel. ²¹And I have prepared a place there for the Ark, which contains the covenant that the LORD made with our ancestors when he brought them out of Egypt."

²²Then Solomon stood before the altar of the LORD in front of the entire community of Israel. He lifted his hands toward heaven, ²³and he prayed,

"O LORD, God of Israel, there is no God like you in all of heaven above or on the earth below. You keep your covenant and show unfailing love to all who walk before you in wholehearted devotion. ²⁴You have kept your promise to your servant David, my father. You made that promise with your own mouth, and with your own hands you have fulfilled it today.

²⁵"And now, O LORD, God of Israel, carry out the additional promise you made to your servant David, my father. For you said to him, 'If your descendants guard their behavior and faithfully follow me as you have done, one of them will always sit on the throne of Israel.' ²⁶Now, O God of Israel, fulfill this promise to your servant David, my father.

²⁷"But will God really live on earth? Why, even the highest heavens cannot contain you. How much less this Temple I have built! ²⁸Nevertheless, listen to my prayer and my plea, O LORD my God. Hear the cry and the prayer that your servant is making to you today. ²⁹May you watch over this Temple night and day, this place where you have said, 'My name will be there.' May you always hear the prayers I make toward this place. ³⁰May you hear the humble and earnest requests from me and your people Israel when we pray toward this place. Yes, hear us from heaven where you live, and when you hear, forgive.

³¹"If someone wrongs another person and is required to take an oath of innocence in front of your altar in this Temple, ³²then hear from heaven and judge between your servants—the accuser and the accused. Punish the guilty as they deserve. Acquit the innocent because of their innocence.

³³"If your people Israel are defeated by their enemies because they have sinned against you, and if they turn to you and acknowledge your name and pray to you here in this Temple, ³⁴then hear from heaven and forgive the sin of your people Israel and return them to this land you gave their ancestors.

³⁵"If the skies are shut up and there is no rain because your people have sinned against you, and if they pray toward this Temple and acknowledge your name and turn from their sins because you have punished them, ³⁶then hear from

heaven and forgive the sins of your servants, your people Israel. Teach them to follow the right path, and send rain on your land that you have given to your people as their special possession.

37"If there is a famine in the land or a plague or crop disease or attacks of locusts or caterpillars, or if your people's enemies are in the land besieging their towns— whatever disaster or disease there is—38 and if your people Israel pray about their troubles, raising their hands toward this Temple, 39 then hear from heaven where you live, and forgive. Give your people what their actions deserve, for you alone know each human heart. 40Then they will fear you as long as they live in the land you gave to our ancestors.

41"In the future, foreigners who do not belong to your people Israel will hear of you. They will come from distant lands because of your name, 42 for they will hear of your great name and your strong hand and your powerful arm. And when they pray toward this Temple, 43 then hear from heaven where you live, and grant what they ask of you. In this way, all the people of the earth will come to know and fear you, just as your own people Israel do. They, too, will know that this Temple I have built honors your name.

44"If your people go out where you send them to fight their enemies, and if they pray to the LORD by turning toward this city you have chosen and toward this Temple I have built to honor your name, 45 then hear their prayers from heaven and uphold their cause.

46"If they sin against you—and who has never sinned?—you might become angry with them and let their enemies conquer them and take them captive to their land far away or near. 47 But in that land of

exile, they might turn to you in repentance and pray, 'We have sinned, done evil, and acted wickedly.' 48If they turn to you with their whole heart and soul in the land of their enemies and pray toward the land you gave to their ancestors—toward this city you have chosen, and toward this Temple I have built to honor your name— 49 then hear their prayers and their petition from heaven where you live, and uphold their cause. 50Forgive your people who have sinned against you. Forgive all the offenses they have committed against you. Make their captors merciful to them, 51 for they are your people— your special possession—whom you brought out of the iron-smelting furnace of Egypt.

52"May your eyes be open to my requests and to the requests of your people Israel. May you hear and answer them whenever they cry out to you. 53For when you brought our ancestors out of Egypt, O Sovereign LORD, you told your servant Moses that you had set Israel apart from all the nations of the earth to be your own special possession."

54When Solomon finished making these prayers and petitions to the LORD, he stood up in front of the altar of the LORD, where he had been kneeling with his hands raised toward heaven. 55He stood and in a loud voice blessed the entire congregation of Israel:

56"Praise the LORD who has given rest to his people Israel, just as he promised. Not one word has failed of all the wonderful promises he gave through his servant Moses. 57**May the LORD our God be with us as he was with our ancestors; may he never leave us or abandon us. 58May he give us the desire to do his will in everything and to obey all the commands, decrees, and regulations that he gave our ancestors. 59And may these words that I have prayed in the presence of the LORD be** before him constantly, day and night, so that the LORD our God may give justice to me and to his people Israel, according to each day's needs. [60]Then people all over the earth will know that the LORD alone is God and there is no other. [61]And may you be completely faithful to the LORD our God. May you always obey his decrees and commands, just as you are doing today."

[62]Then the king and all Israel with him offered sacrifices to the LORD. [63]Solomon offered to the LORD a peace offering of 22,000 cattle and 120,000 sheep and goats. And so the king and all the people of Israel dedicated the Temple of the LORD.

[64]That same day the king consecrated the central area of the courtyard in front of the LORD's Temple. He offered burnt offerings, grain offerings, and the fat of peace offerings there, because the bronze altar in the LORD's presence was too small to hold all the burnt offerings, grain offerings, and the fat of the peace offerings.

[65]Then Solomon and all Israel celebrated the Festival of Shelters* in the presence of the LORD our God. A large congregation had gathered from as far away as Lebo-hamath in the north and the Brook of Egypt in the south. The celebration went on for fourteen days in all—seven days for the dedication of the altar and seven days for the Festival of Shelters.* [66]After the festival was over,* Solomon sent the people home. They blessed the king and went to their homes joyful and glad because the LORD had been good to his servant David and to his people Israel.

8:2 Hebrew *at the festival in the month Ethanim, which is the seventh month.* The Festival of Shelters began on the fifteenth day of the seventh month of the ancient Hebrew lunar calendar. This day occurred in late September, October, or early November. 8:4 Hebrew *the Tent of Meeting;* i.e., the tent mentioned in 2 Sam 6:17 and 1 Chr 16:1. 8:9 Hebrew *at Horeb,* another name for Sinai.
8:13 Some Greek texts add the line *Is this not written in the Book of Jashar?* 8:65a Hebrew *the festival;* see note on 8:2. 8:65b Hebrew *seven days and seven days, fourteen days;* compare parallel text at 2 Chr 7:8-10. 8:66 Hebrew *On the eighth day,* probably referring to the day following the seven-day Festival of Shelters; compare parallel text at 2 Chr 7:9-10.

ACTS 7:51–8:13

"**Y**ou stubborn people! You are heathen* at heart and deaf to the truth. Must you forever resist the Holy Spirit? That's what your ancestors did, and so do you! [52]Name one prophet your ancestors didn't persecute! They even killed the ones who predicted the coming of the Righteous One—the Messiah whom you betrayed and murdered. [53]You deliberately disobeyed God's law, even though you received it from the hands of angels."

[54]The Jewish leaders were infuriated by Stephen's accusation, and they shook their fists at him in rage.* [55]But Stephen, full of the Holy Spirit, gazed steadily into heaven and saw the glory of God, and he saw Jesus standing in the place of honor at God's right hand. [56]And he told them, "Look, I see the heavens opened and the Son of Man standing in the place of honor at God's right hand!"

[57]Then they put their hands over their ears and began shouting. They rushed at him [58]and dragged him out of the city and began to stone him. His accusers took off their coats and laid them at the feet of a young man named Saul.*

[59]As they stoned him, Stephen prayed, "Lord Jesus, receive my spirit." [60]He fell to his knees, shouting, "Lord, don't charge them with this sin!" And with that, he died.

[8:1]SAUL was one of the witnesses, and he agreed completely with the killing of Stephen.

A great wave of persecution began that day, sweeping over the church in Jerusalem; and all the believers except the apostles were scattered through the regions of Judea and Samaria. [2](Some devout men came and buried Stephen with great mourning.) [3]But Saul was going everywhere to destroy the church. He went from house to house, dragging out both men and women to throw them into prison.

[4]But the believers who were scattered preached the Good News about Jesus wherever they went. [5]Philip, for example, went to the city of Samaria

and told the people there about the Messiah. ⁶Crowds listened intently to Philip because they were eager to hear his message and see the miraculous signs he did. ⁷Many evil* spirits were cast out, screaming as they left their victims. And many who had been paralyzed or lame were healed. ⁸So there was great joy in that city.

⁹A man named Simon had been a sorcerer there for many years, amazing the people of Samaria and claiming to be someone great. ¹⁰Everyone, from the least to the greatest, often spoke of him as "the Great One—the Power of God." ¹¹They listened closely to him because for a long time he had astounded them with his magic.

¹²But now the people believed Philip's message of Good News concerning the Kingdom of God and the name of Jesus Christ. As a result, many men and women were baptized. ¹³Then Simon himself believed and was baptized. He began following Philip wherever he went, and he was amazed by the signs and great miracles Philip performed.

7:51 Greek *uncircumcised.*   7:54 Greek *they were grinding their teeth against him.*   7:58 *Saul* is later called Paul; see 13:9.   8:7 Greek *unclean.*

PSALM 129:1-8

A song for pilgrims ascending to Jerusalem.

¹ From my earliest youth my enemies
    have persecuted me.
    Let all Israel repeat this:
² From my earliest youth my enemies
    have persecuted me,
    but they have never defeated
    me.
³ My back is covered with cuts,
    as if a farmer had plowed long
    furrows.
⁴ But the LORD is good;
    he has cut me free from the ropes
    of the ungodly.

⁵ May all who hate Jerusalem*
    be turned back in shameful
    defeat.
⁶ May they be as useless as grass
    on a rooftop,

    turning yellow when only half
        grown,
⁷ ignored by the harvester,
    despised by the binder.
⁸ And may those who pass by
    refuse to give them this blessing:
    "The LORD bless you;
    we bless you in the LORD's name."

129:5 Hebrew *Zion.*

PROVERBS 17:1

Better a dry crust eaten in peace than a house filled with feasting—and conflict.

JUNE
12

1 KINGS 9:1–10:29

So Solomon finished building the Temple of the LORD, as well as the royal palace. He completed everything he had planned to do. ²Then the LORD appeared to Solomon a second time, as he had done before at Gibeon. ³The LORD said to him,

"I have heard your prayer and your petition. I have set this Temple apart to be holy—this place you have built where my name will be honored forever. I will always watch over it, for it is dear to my heart.

⁴"As for you, if you will follow me with integrity and godliness, as David your father did, obeying all my commands, decrees, and regulations, ⁵then I will establish the throne of your dynasty over Israel forever. For I made this promise to your father, David: 'One of your descendants will always sit on the throne of Israel.'

⁶"But if you or your descendants abandon me and disobey the commands and decrees I have given you, and if you serve and worship

other gods, [7] then I will uproot Israel from this land that I have given them. I will reject this Temple that I have made holy to honor my name. I will make Israel an object of mockery and ridicule among the nations. [8] And though this Temple is impressive now, all who pass by will be appalled and will shake their heads in amazement. They will ask, 'Why did the LORD do such terrible things to this land and to this Temple?'

[9] "And the answer will be, 'Because his people abandoned the LORD their God, who brought their ancestors out of Egypt, and they worshiped other gods instead and bowed down to them. That is why the LORD has brought all these disasters on them.'"

[10] It took Solomon twenty years to build the LORD's Temple and his own royal palace. At the end of that time, [11] he gave twenty towns in the land of Galilee to King Hiram of Tyre. (Hiram had previously provided all the cedar and cypress timber and gold that Solomon had requested.) [12] But when Hiram came from Tyre to see the towns Solomon had given him, he was not at all pleased with them. [13] "What kind of towns are these, my brother?" he asked. So Hiram called that area Cabul (which means "worthless"), as it is still known today. [14] Nevertheless, Hiram paid* Solomon 9,000 pounds* of gold.

[15] This is the account of the forced labor that King Solomon conscripted to build the LORD's Temple, the royal palace, the supporting terraces,* the wall of Jerusalem, and the cities of Hazor, Megiddo, and Gezer. [16] (Pharaoh, the king of Egypt, had attacked and captured Gezer, killing the Canaanite population and burning it down. He gave the city to his daughter as a wedding gift when she married Solomon. [17] So Solomon rebuilt the city of Gezer.) He also built up the towns of Lower Beth-horon, [18] Baalath, and Tamar* in the wilderness

within his land. [19] He built towns as supply centers and constructed towns where his chariots and horses* could be stationed. He built everything he desired in Jerusalem and Lebanon and throughout his entire realm.

[20] There were still some people living in the land who were not Israelites, including Amorites, Hittites, Perizzites, Hivites, and Jebusites. [21] These were descendants of the nations whom the people of Israel had not completely destroyed.* So Solomon conscripted them for his labor force, and they serve in the labor force to this day. [22] But Solomon did not conscript any of the Israelites for forced labor. Instead, he assigned them to serve as fighting men, government officials, officers and captains in his army, commanders of his chariots, and charioteers. [23] Solomon appointed 550 of them to supervise the people working on his various projects.

[24] Solomon moved his wife, Pharaoh's daughter, from the City of David to the new palace he had built for her. Then he constructed the supporting terraces.

[25] Three times each year Solomon presented burnt offerings and peace offerings on the altar he had built for the LORD. He also burned incense to the LORD. And so he finished the work of building the Temple.

[26] King Solomon also built a fleet of ships at Ezion-geber, a port near Elath* in the land of Edom, along the shore of the Red Sea.* [27] Hiram sent experienced crews of sailors to sail the ships with Solomon's men. [28] They sailed to Ophir and brought back to Solomon some sixteen tons* of gold.

[10:1] WHEN the queen of Sheba heard of Solomon's fame, which brought honor to the name of the LORD,* she came to test him with hard questions. [2] She arrived in Jerusalem with a large group of attendants and a great caravan of camels loaded with spices, large quantities of gold, and precious jewels. When she met with Solomon, she talked with him about everything she had on her mind.

³Solomon had answers for all her questions; nothing was too hard for the king to explain to her. ⁴When the queen of Sheba realized how very wise Solomon was, and when she saw the palace he had built, ⁵she was overwhelmed. She was also amazed at the food on his tables, the organization of his officials and their splendid clothing, the cupbearers, and the burnt offerings Solomon made at the Temple of the LORD.

⁶She exclaimed to the king, "Everything I heard in my country about your achievements* and wisdom is true! ⁷I didn't believe what was said until I arrived here and saw it with my own eyes. In fact, I had not heard the half of it! Your wisdom and prosperity are far beyond what I was told. ⁸How happy your people* must be! What a privilege for your officials to stand here day after day, listening to your wisdom! ⁹Praise the LORD your God, who delights in you and has placed you on the throne of Israel. Because of the LORD's eternal love for Israel, he has made you king so you can rule with justice and righteousness."

¹⁰Then she gave the king a gift of 9,000 pounds* of gold, great quantities of spices, and precious jewels. Never again were so many spices brought in as those the queen of Sheba gave to King Solomon.

¹¹(In addition, Hiram's ships brought gold from Ophir, and they also brought rich cargoes of red sandalwood* and precious jewels. ¹²The king used the sandalwood to make railings for the Temple of the LORD and the royal palace, and to construct lyres and harps for the musicians. Never before or since has there been such a supply of sandalwood.)

¹³King Solomon gave the queen of Sheba whatever she asked for, besides all the customary gifts he had so generously given. Then she and all her attendants returned to their own land.

¹⁴Each year Solomon received about 25 tons* of gold. ¹⁵This did not include the additional revenue he received from merchants and traders, all the kings of Arabia, and the governors of the land.

¹⁶King Solomon made 200 large shields of hammered gold, each weighing more than fifteen pounds.* ¹⁷He also made 300 smaller shields of hammered gold, each weighing nearly four pounds.* The king placed these shields in the Palace of the Forest of Lebanon.

¹⁸Then the king made a huge throne, decorated with ivory and overlaid with fine gold. ¹⁹The throne had six steps and a rounded back. There were armrests on both sides of the seat, and the figure of a lion stood on each side of the throne. ²⁰There were also twelve other lions, one standing on each end of the six steps. No other throne in all the world could be compared with it!

²¹All of King Solomon's drinking cups were solid gold, as were all the utensils in the Palace of the Forest of Lebanon. They were not made of silver, for silver was considered worthless in Solomon's day!

²²The king had a fleet of trading ships* that sailed with Hiram's fleet. Once every three years the ships returned, loaded with gold, silver, ivory, apes, and peacocks.*

²³So King Solomon became richer and wiser than any other king on earth. ²⁴People from every nation came to consult him and to hear the wisdom God had given him. ²⁵Year after year everyone who visited brought him gifts of silver and gold, clothing, weapons, spices, horses, and mules.

²⁶Solomon built up a huge force of chariots and horses.* He had 1,400 chariots and 12,000 horses. He stationed some of them in the chariot cities and some near him in Jerusalem. ²⁷The king made silver as plentiful in Jerusalem as stone. And valuable cedar timber was as common as the sycamore-fig trees that grow in the foothills of Judah.* ²⁸Solomon's horses were imported from Egypt* and from Cilicia*; the king's traders acquired them from Cilicia at the standard price. ²⁹At that time chariots

from Egypt could be purchased for 600 pieces of silver,* and horses for 150 pieces of silver.* They were then exported to the kings of the Hittites and the kings of Aram.

9:14a Or *For Hiram had paid.*   9:14b Hebrew *120 talents* [4,000 kilograms].   9:15 Hebrew *the millo;* also in 9:24. The meaning of the Hebrew is uncertain.   9:18 An alternate reading in the Masoretic Text reads *Tadmor.*
9:19 Or *and charioteers.*   9:21 The Hebrew term used here refers to the complete consecration of things or people to the LORD, either by destroying them or by giving them as an offering.   9:26a As in Greek version (see also 2 Kgs 14:22; 16:6); Hebrew reads *Eloth,* a variant spelling of Elath.   9:26b Hebrew *sea of reeds.*   9:28 Hebrew *420 talents* [14 metric tons].   10:1 Or *which was due to the name of the LORD.* The meaning of the Hebrew is uncertain.   10:6 Hebrew *your words.*   10:8 Greek and Syriac versions and Latin Vulgate read *your wives.*
10:10 Hebrew *120 talents* [4,000 kilograms].
10:11 Hebrew *almug wood;* also in 10:12.   10:14 Hebrew *666 talents* [23 metric tons].   10:16 Hebrew *600 shekels* [6.8 kilograms].   10:17 Hebrew *3 minas* [1.8 kilograms].
10:22a Hebrew *fleet of ships of Tarshish.*   10:22b Or *and baboons.*   10:26 Or *charioteers;* also in 10:26b.
10:27 Hebrew *the Shephelah.*   10:28a Possibly *Muzur,* a district near Cilicia; also in 10:29.   10:28b Hebrew *Kue,* probably another name for Cilicia.   10:29a Hebrew *600 shekels of silver,* about 15 pounds or 6.8 kilograms in weight.   10:29b Hebrew *150 [shekels],* about 3.8 pounds or 1.7 kilograms in weight.

ACTS 8:14-40

When the apostles in Jerusalem heard that the people of Samaria had accepted God's message, they sent Peter and John there. 15As soon as they arrived, they prayed for these new believers to receive the Holy Spirit. 16The Holy Spirit had not yet come upon any of them, for they had only been baptized in the name of the Lord Jesus. 17Then Peter and John laid their hands upon these believers, and they received the Holy Spirit.

18When Simon saw that the Spirit was given when the apostles laid their hands on people, he offered them money to buy this power. 19"Let me have this power, too," he exclaimed, "so that when I lay my hands on people, they will receive the Holy Spirit!"

20But Peter replied, "May your money be destroyed with you for thinking God's gift can be bought! 21You can have no part in this, for your heart is not right with God. 22Repent of your wickedness and pray to the Lord. Perhaps he will forgive your evil thoughts, 23for I can see that you are full of bitter jealousy and are held captive by sin."

24"Pray to the Lord for me," Simon exclaimed, "that these terrible things you've said won't happen to me!"

25After testifying and preaching the word of the Lord in Samaria, Peter and John returned to Jerusalem. And they stopped in many Samaritan villages along the way to preach the Good News.

26As for Philip, an angel of the Lord said to him, "Go south* down the desert road that runs from Jerusalem to Gaza." 27So he started out, and he met the treasurer of Ethiopia, a eunuch of great authority under the Kandake, the queen of Ethiopia. The eunuch had gone to Jerusalem to worship, 28and he was now returning. Seated in his carriage, he was reading aloud from the book of the prophet Isaiah.

29The Holy Spirit said to Philip, "Go over and walk along beside the carriage."

30Philip ran over and heard the man reading from the prophet Isaiah. Philip asked, "Do you understand what you are reading?"

31The man replied, "How can I, unless someone instructs me?" And he urged Philip to come up into the carriage and sit with him.

32The passage of Scripture he had been reading was this:

"He was led like a sheep to the
    slaughter.
And as a lamb is silent before
    the shearers,
he did not open his mouth.
33 He was humiliated and received
    no justice.
Who can speak of his
    descendants?
For his life was taken
    from the earth."*

34The eunuch asked Philip, "Tell me, was the prophet talking about himself or someone else?" 35So beginning with this same Scripture, Philip told him the Good News about Jesus.

36As they rode along, they came to some water, and the eunuch said, "Look! There's some water! Why can't I be baptized?"* 38He ordered the carriage to stop, and they went down into the water, and Philip baptized him.

³⁹When they came up out of the water, the Spirit of the Lord snatched Philip away. The eunuch never saw him again but went on his way rejoicing. ⁴⁰Meanwhile, Philip found himself farther north at the town of Azotus. He preached the Good News there and in every town along the way until he came to Caesarea.

8:26 Or *Go at noon.*   8:32-33 Isa 53:7-8 (Greek version). 8:36 Some manuscripts add verse 37, *"You can," Philip answered, "if you believe with all your heart." And the eunuch replied, "I believe that Jesus Christ is the Son of God."*

PSALM 130:1-8
A song for pilgrims ascending to Jerusalem.

¹ From the depths of despair,
    O Lord,
    I call for your help.
² Hear my cry, O Lord.
    Pay attention to my prayer.

³ Lord, if you kept a record
    of our sins,
    who, O Lord, could ever
    survive?
⁴ But you offer forgiveness,
    that we might learn to
    fear you.

⁵ I am counting on the Lord;
    yes, I am counting on him.
    I have put my hope in
    his word.
⁶ I long for the Lord
    more than sentries long
    for the dawn,
    yes, more than sentries long
    for the dawn.

⁷ O Israel, hope in the Lord;
    for with the Lord there is
    unfailing love.
    His redemption overflows.
⁸ He himself will redeem Israel
    from every kind of sin.

PROVERBS 17:2-3
A wise servant will rule over the master's disgraceful son and will share the inheritance of the master's children.
□ Fire tests the purity of silver and gold, but the Lord tests the heart.

JUNE 13

1 KINGS 11:1–12:19
Now King Solomon loved many foreign women. Besides Pharaoh's daughter, he married women from Moab, Ammon, Edom, Sidon, and from among the Hittites. ²The Lord had clearly instructed the people of Israel, 'You must not marry them, because they will turn your hearts to their gods.' Yet Solomon insisted on loving them anyway. ³He had 700 wives of royal birth and 300 concubines. And in fact, they did turn his heart away from the Lord.

⁴In Solomon's old age, they turned his heart to worship other gods instead of being completely faithful to the Lord his God, as his father, David, had been. ⁵Solomon worshiped Ashtoreth, the goddess of the Sidonians, and Molech,* the detestable god of the Ammonites. ⁶In this way, Solomon did what was evil in the Lord's sight; he refused to follow the Lord completely, as his father, David, had done.

⁷On the Mount of Olives, east of Jerusalem,* he even built a pagan shrine for Chemosh, the detestable god of Moab, and another for Molech, the detestable god of the Ammonites. ⁸Solomon built such shrines for all his foreign wives to use for burning incense and sacrificing to their gods.

⁹The Lord was very angry with Solomon, for his heart had turned away from the Lord, the God of Israel, who had appeared to him twice. ¹⁰He had warned Solomon specifically about worshiping other gods, but Solomon did not listen to the Lord's command. ¹¹So now the Lord

said to him, "Since you have not kept my covenant and have disobeyed my decrees, I will surely tear the kingdom away from you and give it to one of your servants. [12]But for the sake of your father, David, I will not do this while you are still alive. I will take the kingdom away from your son. [13]And even so, I will not take away the entire kingdom; I will let him be king of one tribe, for the sake of my servant David and for the sake of Jerusalem, my chosen city."

[14]Then the LORD raised up Hadad the Edomite, a member of Edom's royal family, to be Solomon's adversary. [15]Years before, David had defeated Edom. Joab, his army commander, had stayed to bury some of the Israelite soldiers who had died in battle. While there, they killed every male in Edom. [16]Joab and the army of Israel had stayed there for six months, killing them.

[17]But Hadad and a few of his father's royal officials escaped and headed for Egypt. (Hadad was just a boy at the time.) [18]They set out from Midian and went to Paran, where others joined them. Then they traveled to Egypt and went to Pharaoh, who gave them a home, food, and some land. [19]Pharaoh grew very fond of Hadad, and he gave him his wife's sister in marriage—the sister of Queen Tahpenes. [20]She bore him a son named Genubath. Tahpenes raised him* in Pharaoh's palace among Pharaoh's own sons.

[21]When the news reached Hadad in Egypt that David and his commander Joab were both dead, he said to Pharaoh, "Let me return to my own country."

[22]"Why?" Pharaoh asked him. "What do you lack here that makes you want to go home?"

"Nothing," he replied. "But even so, please let me return home."

[23]God also raised up Rezon son of Eliada as Solomon's adversary. Rezon had fled from his master, King Hadadezer of Zobah, [24]and had become the leader of a gang of rebels. After David conquered Hadadezer, Rezon and his men fled to Damascus, where he became

king. [25]Rezon was Israel's bitter adversary for the rest of Solomon's reign, and he made trouble, just as Hadad did. Rezon hated Israel intensely and continued to reign in Aram.

[26]Another rebel leader was Jeroboam son of Nebat, one of Solomon's own officials. He came from the town of Zeredah in Ephraim, and his mother was Zeruah, a widow.

[27]This is the story behind his rebellion. Solomon was rebuilding the supporting terraces* and repairing the walls of the city of his father, David. [28]Jeroboam was a very capable young man, and when Solomon saw how industrious he was, he put him in charge of the labor force from the tribes of Ephraim and Manasseh, the descendants of Joseph.

[29]One day as Jeroboam was leaving Jerusalem, the prophet Ahijah from Shiloh met him along the way. Ahijah was wearing a new cloak. The two of them were alone in a field, [30]and Ahijah took hold of the new cloak he was wearing and tore it into twelve pieces. [31]Then he said to Jeroboam, "Take ten of these pieces, for this is what the LORD, the God of Israel, says: 'I am about to tear the kingdom from the hand of Solomon, and I will give ten of the tribes to you! [32]But I will leave him one tribe for the sake of my servant David and for the sake of Jerusalem, which I have chosen out of all the tribes of Israel. [33]For Solomon has* abandoned me and worshiped Ashtoreth, the goddess of the Sidonians; Chemosh, the god of Moab; and Molech, the god of the Ammonites. He has not followed my ways and done what is pleasing in my sight. He has not obeyed my decrees and regulations as David his father did.

[34]'But I will not take the entire kingdom from Solomon at this time. For the sake of my servant David, the one whom I chose and who obeyed my commands and decrees, I will keep Solomon as leader for the rest of his life. [35]But I will take the kingdom away from his son and give ten of the tribes to you. [36]His son will have one tribe so that the de-

scendants of David my servant will continue to reign, shining like a lamp in Jerusalem, the city I have chosen to be the place for my name. ³⁷And I will place you on the throne of Israel, and you will rule over all that your heart desires. ³⁸If you listen to what I tell you and follow my ways and do whatever I consider to be right, and if you obey my decrees and commands, as my servant David did, then I will always be with you. I will establish an enduring dynasty for you as I did for David, and I will give Israel to you. ³⁹Because of Solomon's sin I will punish the descendants of David—though not forever.'"

⁴⁰Solomon tried to kill Jeroboam, but he fled to King Shishak of Egypt and stayed there until Solomon died.

⁴¹The rest of the events in Solomon's reign, including all his deeds and his wisdom, are recorded in *The Book of the Acts of Solomon.* ⁴²Solomon ruled in Jerusalem over all Israel for forty years. ⁴³When he died, he was buried in the City of David, named for his father. Then his son Rehoboam became the next king.

^{12:1}REHOBOAM went to Shechem, where all Israel had gathered to make him king. ²When Jeroboam son of Nebat heard of this, he returned from Egypt,* for he had fled to Egypt to escape from King Solomon. ³The leaders of Israel summoned him, and Jeroboam and the whole assembly of Israel went to speak with Rehoboam. ⁴"Your father was a hard master," they said. "Lighten the harsh labor demands and heavy taxes that your father imposed on us. Then we will be your loyal subjects."

⁵Rehoboam replied, "Give me three days to think this over. Then come back for my answer." So the people went away.

⁶Then King Rehoboam discussed the matter with the older men who had counseled his father, Solomon. "What is your advice?" he asked. "How should I answer these people?"

⁷The older counselors replied, "If you

are willing to be a servant to these people today and give them a favorable answer, they will always be your loyal subjects."

⁸But Rehoboam rejected the advice of the older men and instead asked the opinion of the young men who had grown up with him and were now his advisers. ⁹"What is your advice?" he asked them. "How should I answer these people who want me to lighten the burdens imposed by my father?"

¹⁰The young men replied, "This is what you should tell those complainers who want a lighter burden: 'My little finger is thicker than my father's waist! ¹¹Yes, my father laid heavy burdens on you, but I'm going to make them even heavier! My father beat you with whips, but I will beat you with scorpions!'"

¹²Three days later Jeroboam and all the people returned to hear Rehoboam's decision, just as the king had ordered. ¹³But Rehoboam spoke harshly to the people, for he rejected the advice of the older counselors ¹⁴and followed the counsel of his younger advisers. He told the people, "My father laid heavy burdens on you, but I'm going to make them even heavier! My father beat you with whips, but I will beat you with scorpions!"

¹⁵So the king paid no attention to the people. This turn of events was the will of the LORD, for it fulfilled the LORD's message to Jeroboam son of Nebat through the prophet Ahijah from Shiloh.

¹⁶When all Israel realized that the king had refused to listen to them, they responded,

> "Down with the dynasty of David!
>   We have no interest in the
>   son of Jesse.
> Back to your homes, O Israel!
>   Look out for your own house,
>   O David!"

So the people of Israel returned home. ¹⁷But Rehoboam continued to rule over the Israelites who lived in the towns of Judah.

¹⁸King Rehoboam sent Adoniram,* who was in charge of the labor force, to

restore order, but the people of Israel stoned him to death. When this news reached King Rehoboam, he quickly jumped into his chariot and fled to Jerusalem. ¹⁹And to this day the northern tribes of Israel have refused to be ruled by a descendant of David.

11:5 Hebrew *Milcom*, a variant spelling of Molech; also in 11:33.   11:7 Hebrew *On the mountain east of Jerusalem.*   11:20 As in Greek version; Hebrew reads *weaned him.*   11:27 Hebrew *the millo.* The meaning of the Hebrew is uncertain.   11:33 As in Greek, Syriac, and Latin Vulgate; Hebrew reads *For they have.*   12:2 As in Greek version and Latin Vulgate (see also 2 Chr 10:2); Hebrew reads *he lived in Egypt.*   12:18 As in some Greek manuscripts and Syriac version (see also 4:6; 5:14); Hebrew reads *Adoram.*

ACTS 9:1-25

Meanwhile, Saul was uttering threats with every breath and was eager to kill the Lord's followers.* So he went to the high priest. ²He requested letters addressed to the synagogues in Damascus, asking for their cooperation in the arrest of any followers of the Way he found there. He wanted to bring them—both men and women—back to Jerusalem in chains.

³As he was approaching Damascus on this mission, a light from heaven suddenly shone down around him. ⁴He fell to the ground and heard a voice saying to him, "Saul! Saul! Why are you persecuting me?"

⁵"Who are you, lord?" Saul asked.

And the voice replied, "I am Jesus, the one you are persecuting! ⁶Now get up and go into the city, and you will be told what you must do."

⁷The men with Saul stood speechless, for they heard the sound of someone's voice but saw no one! ⁸Saul picked himself up off the ground, but when he opened his eyes he was blind. So his companions led him by the hand to Damascus. ⁹He remained there blind for three days and did not eat or drink.

¹⁰Now there was a believer* in Damascus named Ananias. The Lord spoke to him in a vision, calling, "Ananias!"

"Yes, Lord!" he replied.

¹¹The Lord said, "Go over to Straight Street, to the house of Judas. When you get there, ask for a man from Tarsus named Saul. He is praying to me right now. ¹²I have shown him a vision of a man named Ananias coming in and laying hands on him so he can see again."

¹³"But Lord," exclaimed Ananias, "I've heard many people talk about the terrible things this man has done to the believers in Jerusalem! ¹⁴And he is authorized by the leading priests to arrest everyone who calls upon your name."

¹⁵**But the Lord said, "Go, for Saul is my chosen instrument to take my message to the Gentiles and to kings, as well as to the people of Israel. ¹⁶And I will show him how much he must suffer for my name's sake."**

¹⁷So Ananias went and found Saul. He laid his hands on him and said, "Brother Saul, the Lord Jesus, who appeared to you on the road, has sent me so that you might regain your sight and be filled with the Holy Spirit." ¹⁸Instantly something like scales fell from Saul's eyes, and he regained his sight. Then he got up and was baptized. ¹⁹Afterward he ate some food and regained his strength.

Saul stayed with the believers* in Damascus for a few days. ²⁰And immediately he began preaching about Jesus in the synagogues, saying, "He is indeed the Son of God!"

²¹All who heard him were amazed. "Isn't this the same man who caused such devastation among Jesus' followers in Jerusalem?" they asked. "And didn't he come here to arrest them and take them in chains to the leading priests?"

²²Saul's preaching became more and more powerful, and the Jews in Damascus couldn't refute his proofs that Jesus was indeed the Messiah. ²³After a while some of the Jews plotted together to kill him. ²⁴They were watching for him day and night at the city gate so they could murder him, but Saul was told about their plot. ²⁵So during the night, some of the other believers* lowered him in a large basket through an opening in the city wall.

9:1 Greek *disciples.*   9:10 Greek *disciple;* also in 9:26, 36.   9:19 Greek *disciples;* also in 9:26, 38.   9:25 Greek *his disciples.*

PSALM 131:1-3
A song for pilgrims ascending to Jerusalem.
A psalm of David.

¹ LORD, my heart is not proud;
   my eyes are not haughty.
I don't concern myself with matters
   too great
   or too awesome for me to grasp.
² Instead, I have calmed and quieted
   myself,
   like a weaned child who no longer
   cries for its mother's milk.
   Yes, like a weaned child is my
   soul within me.

³ O Israel, put your hope in the LORD—
   now and always.

PROVERBS 17:4-5
Wrongdoers eagerly listen to gossip;
liars pay close attention to slander.
□ Those who mock the poor insult their
Maker; those who rejoice at the misfortune of others will be punished.

JUNE
14

1 KINGS 12:20–13:34
When the people of Israel learned of
Jeroboam's return from Egypt, they
called an assembly and made him king
over all Israel. So only the tribe of Judah
remained loyal to the family of David.

²¹When Rehoboam arrived at Jerusalem, he mobilized the men of Judah and
the tribe of Benjamin—180,000 select
troops—to fight against the men of Israel and to restore the kingdom to himself.

²²But God said to Shemaiah, the man
of God, ²³"Say to Rehoboam son of Solomon, king of Judah, and to all the people
of Judah and Benjamin, and to the rest of
the people, ²⁴'This is what the LORD says:
Do not fight against your relatives, the Israelites. Go back home, for what has

happened is my doing!'" So they obeyed
the message of the LORD and went home,
as the LORD had commanded.

²⁵Jeroboam then built up the city of
Shechem in the hill country of Ephraim,
and it became his capital. Later he went
and built up the town of Peniel.*

²⁶Jeroboam thought to himself, "Unless I am careful, the kingdom will return to the dynasty of David. ²⁷When
these people go to Jerusalem to offer
sacrifices at the Temple of the LORD,
they will again give their allegiance to
King Rehoboam of Judah. They will kill
me and make him their king instead."

²⁸So on the advice of his counselors,
the king made two gold calves. He said
to the people,* "It is too much trouble
for you to worship in Jerusalem. Look,
Israel, these are the gods who brought
you out of Egypt!"

²⁹He placed these calf idols in Bethel
and in Dan—at either end of his kingdom. ³⁰But this became a great sin, for
the people worshiped the idols, traveling as far north as Dan to worship the
one there.

³¹Jeroboam also erected buildings at
the pagan shrines and ordained priests
from the common people—those who
were not from the priestly tribe of Levi.
³²And Jeroboam instituted a religious
festival in Bethel, held on the fifteenth
day of the eighth month,* in imitation
of the annual Festival of Shelters in Judah. There at Bethel he himself offered
sacrifices to the calves he had made,
and he appointed priests for the pagan
shrines he had made. ³³So on the fifteenth day of the eighth month, a day
that he himself had designated, Jeroboam offered sacrifices on the altar at
Bethel. He instituted a religious festival
for Israel, and he went up to the altar to
burn incense.

¹³:¹At the LORD's command, a man of
God from Judah went to Bethel, arriving
there just as Jeroboam was approaching
the altar to burn incense. ²Then at the
LORD's command, he shouted, "O altar,
altar! This is what the LORD says: A child

named Josiah will be born into the dynasty of David. On you he will sacrifice the priests from the pagan shrines who come here to burn incense, and human bones will be burned on you." ³That same day the man of God gave a sign to prove his message. He said, "The LORD has promised to give this sign: This altar will split apart, and its ashes will be poured out on the ground."

⁴When King Jeroboam heard the man of God speaking against the altar at Bethel, he pointed at him and shouted, "Seize that man!" But instantly the king's hand became paralyzed in that position, and he couldn't pull it back. ⁵At the same time a wide crack appeared in the altar, and the ashes poured out, just as the man of God had predicted in his message from the LORD.

⁶The king cried out to the man of God, "Please ask the LORD your God to restore my hand again!" So the man of God prayed to the LORD, and the king's hand was restored and he could move it again.

⁷Then the king said to the man of God, "Come to the palace with me and have something to eat, and I will give you a gift."

⁸But the man of God said to the king, "Even if you gave me half of everything you own, I would not go with you. I would not eat or drink anything in this place. ⁹For the LORD gave me this command: 'You must not eat or drink anything while you are there, and do not return to Judah by the same way you came.' " ¹⁰So he left Bethel and went home another way.

¹¹As it happened, there was an old prophet living in Bethel, and his sons* came home and told him what the man of God had done in Bethel that day. They also told their father what the man had said to the king. ¹²The old prophet asked them, "Which way did he go?" So they showed their father* which road the man of God had taken. ¹³"Quick, saddle the donkey," the old man said. So they saddled the donkey for him, and he mounted it.

¹⁴Then he rode after the man of God and found him sitting under a great tree. The old prophet asked him, "Are you the man of God who came from Judah?"

"Yes, I am," he replied.

¹⁵Then he said to the man of God, "Come home with me and eat some food."

¹⁶"No, I cannot," he replied. "I am not allowed to eat or drink anything here in this place. ¹⁷For the LORD gave me this command: 'You must not eat or drink anything while you are there, and do not return to Judah by the same way you came.' "

¹⁸But the old prophet answered, "I am a prophet, too, just as you are. And an angel gave me this command from the LORD: 'Bring him home with you so he can have something to eat and drink.' " But the old man was lying to him. ¹⁹So they went back together, and the man of God ate and drank at the prophet's home.

²⁰Then while they were sitting at the table, a command from the LORD came to the old prophet. ²¹He cried out to the man of God from Judah, "This is what the LORD says: You have defied the word of the LORD and have disobeyed the command the LORD your God gave you. ²²You came back to this place and ate and drank where he told you not to eat or drink. Because of this, your body will not be buried in the grave of your ancestors."

²³After the man of God had finished eating and drinking, the old prophet saddled his own donkey for him, ²⁴and the man of God started off again. But as he was traveling along, a lion came out and killed him. His body lay there on the road, with the donkey and the lion standing beside it. ²⁵People who passed by saw the body lying in the road and the lion standing beside it, and they went and reported it in Bethel, where the old prophet lived.

²⁶When the prophet heard the report, he said, "It is the man of God who disobeyed the LORD's command. The

LORD has fulfilled his word by causing the lion to attack and kill him."

²⁷Then the prophet said to his sons, "Saddle a donkey for me." So they saddled a donkey, ²⁸and he went out and found the body lying in the road. The donkey and lion were still standing there beside it, for the lion had not eaten the body nor attacked the donkey. ²⁹So the prophet laid the body of the man of God on the donkey and took it back to the town to mourn over him and bury him. ³⁰He laid the body in his own grave, crying out in grief, "Oh, my brother!"

³¹Afterward the prophet said to his sons, "When I die, bury me in the grave where the man of God is buried. Lay my bones beside his bones. ³²For the message the LORD told him to proclaim against the altar in Bethel and against the pagan shrines in the towns of Samaria will certainly come true."

³³But even after this, Jeroboam did not turn from his evil ways. He continued to choose priests from the common people. He appointed anyone who wanted to become a priest for the pagan shrines. ³⁴This became a great sin and resulted in the utter destruction of Jeroboam's dynasty from the face of the earth.

12:25 Hebrew *Penuel,* a variant spelling of Peniel.
12:28 Hebrew *to them.*   12:32 This day of the ancient Hebrew lunar calendar occurred in late October or early November, exactly one month after the annual Festival of Shelters in Judah (see Lev 23:34).   13:11 As in Greek version; Hebrew reads *son.*   13:12 As in Greek version; Hebrew reads *They had seen.*

ACTS 9:26-43

When Saul arrived in Jerusalem, he tried to meet with the believers, but they were all afraid of him. They did not believe he had truly become a believer! ²⁷Then Barnabas brought him to the apostles and told them how Saul had seen the Lord on the way to Damascus and how the Lord had spoken to Saul. He also told them that Saul had preached boldly in the name of Jesus in Damascus.

²⁸So Saul stayed with the apostles and went all around Jerusalem with them, preaching boldly in the name of the Lord. ²⁹He debated with some Greek-speaking Jews, but they tried to murder him. ³⁰When the believers* heard about this, they took him down to Caesarea and sent him away to Tarsus, his hometown.

³¹**The church then had peace throughout Judea, Galilee, and Samaria, and it became stronger as the believers lived in the fear of the Lord. And with the encouragement of the Holy Spirit, it also grew in numbers.**

³²Meanwhile, Peter traveled from place to place, and he came down to visit the believers in the town of Lydda. ³³There he met a man named Aeneas, who had been paralyzed and bedridden for eight years. ³⁴Peter said to him, "Aeneas, Jesus Christ heals you! Get up, and roll up your sleeping mat!" And he was healed instantly. ³⁵Then the whole population of Lydda and Sharon saw Aeneas walking around, and they turned to the Lord.

³⁶There was a believer in Joppa named Tabitha (which in Greek is Dorcas*). She was always doing kind things for others and helping the poor. ³⁷About this time she became ill and died. Her body was washed for burial and laid in an upstairs room. ³⁸But the believers had heard that Peter was nearby at Lydda, so they sent two men to beg him, "Please come as soon as possible!"

³⁹So Peter returned with them; and as soon as he arrived, they took him to the upstairs room. The room was filled with widows who were weeping and showing him the coats and other clothes Dorcas had made for them. ⁴⁰But Peter asked them all to leave the room; then he knelt and prayed. Turning to the body he said, "Get up, Tabitha." And she opened her eyes! When she saw Peter, she sat up! ⁴¹He gave her his hand and helped her up. Then he called in the widows and all the believers, and he presented her to them alive.

⁴²The news spread through the whole town, and many believed in the Lord. ⁴³And Peter stayed a long time in Joppa, living with Simon, a tanner of hides.

9:30 Greek *brothers.*   9:36 The names *Tabitha* in Aramaic and *Dorcas* in Greek both mean "gazelle."

PSALM 132:1-18

A song for pilgrims ascending to Jerusalem.

¹ **L**ORD, remember David
and all that he suffered.
² He made a solemn promise
to the LORD.
He vowed to the Mighty One
of Israel,*
³ "I will not go home;
I will not let myself rest.
⁴ I will not let my eyes sleep
nor close my eyelids in slumber
⁵ until I find a place to build a house
for the LORD,
a sanctuary for the Mighty One
of Israel."

⁶ We heard that the Ark was
in Ephrathah;
then we found it in the distant
countryside of Jaar.
⁷ Let us go to the sanctuary of
the LORD;
let us worship at the footstool
of his throne.
⁸ Arise, O LORD, and enter your
resting place,
along with the Ark, the symbol
of your power.
⁹ May your priests be clothed
in godliness;
may your loyal servants sing
for joy.
¹⁰ For the sake of your servant David,
do not reject the king you have
anointed.
¹¹ The LORD swore an oath to David
with a promise he will never
take back:
"I will place one of your descendants
on your throne.
¹² If your descendants obey the terms
of my covenant
and the laws that I teach them,
then your royal line
will continue forever and ever."

¹³ For the LORD has chosen Jerusalem*;
he has desired it for his home.
¹⁴ "This is my resting place
forever," he said.

"I will live here, for this is the
home I desired.
¹⁵ I will bless this city and make
it prosperous;
I will satisfy its poor with food.
¹⁶ I will clothe its priests with
godliness;
its faithful servants will sing
for joy.
¹⁷ Here I will increase the power
of David;
my anointed one will be a light
for my people.
¹⁸ I will clothe his enemies with shame,
but he will be a glorious king."

132:2 Hebrew *of Jacob;* also in 132:5. See note on 44:4.
132:13 Hebrew *Zion.*

PROVERBS 17:6

Grandchildren are the crowning glory
of the aged; parents* are the pride of
their children.

17:6 Hebrew *fathers.*

JUNE 15

1 KINGS 14:1–15:24

At that time Jeroboam's son Abijah became very sick. ²So Jeroboam told his
wife, "Disguise yourself so that no one
will recognize you as my wife. Then go
to the prophet Ahijah at Shiloh—the
man who told me I would become king.
³Take him a gift of ten loaves of bread,
some cakes, and a jar of honey, and ask
him what will happen to the boy."

⁴So Jeroboam's wife went to Ahijah's
home at Shiloh. He was an old man now
and could no longer see. ⁵But the LORD
had told Ahijah, "Jeroboam's wife will
come here, pretending to be someone
else. She will ask you about her son, for
he is very sick. Give her the answer I give
you."

⁶So when Ahijah heard her footsteps
at the door, he called out, "Come in, wife

of Jeroboam! Why are you pretending to be someone else?" Then he told her, "I have bad news for you. ⁷Give your husband, Jeroboam, this message from the LORD, the God of Israel: 'I promoted you from the ranks of the common people and made you ruler over my people Israel. ⁸I ripped the kingdom away from the family of David and gave it to you. But you have not been like my servant David, who obeyed my commands and followed me with all his heart and always did whatever I wanted. ⁹You have done more evil than all who lived before you. You have made other gods for yourself and have made me furious with your gold calves. And since you have turned your back on me, ¹⁰I will bring disaster on your dynasty and will destroy every one of your male descendants, slave and free alike, anywhere in Israel. I will burn up your royal dynasty as one burns up trash until it is all gone. ¹¹The members of Jeroboam's family who die in the city will be eaten by dogs, and those who die in the field will be eaten by vultures. I, the LORD, have spoken.'"

¹²Then Ahijah said to Jeroboam's wife, "Go on home, and when you enter the city, the child will die. ¹³All Israel will mourn for him and bury him. He is the only member of your family who will have a proper burial, for this child is the only good thing that the LORD, the God of Israel, sees in the entire family of Jeroboam.

¹⁴"In addition, the LORD will raise up a king over Israel who will destroy the family of Jeroboam. This will happen today, even now! ¹⁵Then the LORD will shake Israel like a reed whipped about in a stream. He will uproot the people of Israel from this good land that he gave their ancestors and will scatter them beyond the Euphrates River,* for they have angered the LORD with the Asherah poles they have set up for worship. ¹⁶He will abandon Israel because Jeroboam sinned and made Israel sin along with him."

¹⁷So Jeroboam's wife returned to Tirzah, and the child died just as she walked through the door of her home. ¹⁸And all Israel buried him and mourned for him, as the LORD had promised through the prophet Ahijah.

¹⁹The rest of the events in Jeroboam's reign, including all his wars and how he ruled, are recorded in *The Book of the History of the Kings of Israel.* ²⁰Jeroboam reigned in Israel twenty-two years. When Jeroboam died, his son Nadab became the next king.

²¹Meanwhile, Rehoboam son of Solomon was king in Judah. He was forty-one years old when he became king, and he reigned seventeen years in Jerusalem, the city the LORD had chosen from among all the tribes of Israel as the place to honor his name. Rehoboam's mother was Naamah, an Ammonite woman.

²²During Rehoboam's reign, the people of Judah did what was evil in the LORD's sight, provoking his anger with their sin, for it was even worse than that of their ancestors. ²³For they also built for themselves pagan shrines and set up sacred pillars and Asherah poles on every high hill and under every green tree. ²⁴There were even male and female shrine prostitutes throughout the land. The people imitated the detestable practices of the pagan nations the LORD had driven from the land ahead of the Israelites.

²⁵In the fifth year of King Rehoboam's reign, King Shishak of Egypt came up and attacked Jerusalem. ²⁶He ransacked the treasuries of the LORD's Temple and the royal palace; he stole everything, including all the gold shields Solomon had made. ²⁷King Rehoboam later replaced them with bronze shields as substitutes, and he entrusted them to the care of the commanders of the guard who protected the entrance to the royal palace. ²⁸Whenever the king went to the Temple of the LORD, the guards would also take the shields and then return them to the guardroom.

²⁹The rest of the events in Rehoboam's reign and everything he did are recorded in *The Book of the History of the Kings of Judah.* ³⁰There was constant war between Rehoboam and Jeroboam.

³¹When Rehoboam died, he was buried among his ancestors in the City of David. His mother was Naamah, an Ammonite woman. Then his son Abijam* became the next king.

¹⁵:¹ABIJAM* began to rule over Judah in the eighteenth year of Jeroboam's reign in Israel. ²He reigned in Jerusalem three years. His mother was Maacah, the daughter of Absalom.*

³He committed the same sins as his father before him, and he was not faithful to the LORD his God, as his ancestor David had been. ⁴But for David's sake, the LORD his God allowed his descendants to continue ruling, shining like a lamp, and he gave Abijam a son to rule after him in Jerusalem. ⁵For David had done what was pleasing in the LORD's sight and had obeyed the LORD's commands throughout his life, except in the affair concerning Uriah the Hittite.

⁶There was war between Abijam and Jeroboam* throughout Abijam's reign. ⁷The rest of the events in Abijam's reign and everything he did are recorded in *The Book of the History of the Kings of Judah.* There was constant war between Abijam and Jeroboam. ⁸When Abijam died, he was buried in the City of David. Then his son Asa became the next king.

⁹Asa began to rule over Judah in the twentieth year of Jeroboam's reign in Israel. ¹⁰He reigned in Jerusalem forty-one years. His grandmother* was Maacah, the daughter of Absalom.

¹¹Asa did what was pleasing in the LORD's sight, as his ancestor David had done. ¹²He banished the male and female shrine prostitutes from the land and got rid of all the idols* his ancestors had made. ¹³He even deposed his grandmother Maacah from her position as queen mother because she had made an obscene Asherah pole. He cut down her obscene pole and burned it in the Kidron Valley. ¹⁴Although the pagan shrines were not removed, Asa's heart remained completely faithful to the LORD throughout his life. ¹⁵He brought into the Temple of the LORD the silver and gold and the various items that he and his father had dedicated.

¹⁶There was constant war between King Asa of Judah and King Baasha of Israel. ¹⁷King Baasha of Israel invaded Judah and fortified Ramah in order to prevent anyone from entering or leaving King Asa's territory in Judah.

¹⁸Asa responded by removing all the silver and gold that was left in the treasuries of the Temple of the LORD and the royal palace. He sent it with some of his officials to Ben-hadad son of Tabrimmon, son of Hezion, the king of Aram, who was ruling in Damascus, along with this message:

¹⁹"Let there be a treaty* between you and me like the one between your father and my father. See, I am sending you a gift of silver and gold. Break your treaty with King Baasha of Israel so that he will leave me alone."

²⁰Ben-hadad agreed to King Asa's request and sent the commanders of his army to attack the towns of Israel. They conquered the towns of Ijon, Dan, Abel-beth-maacah, and all Kinnereth, and all the land of Naphtali. ²¹As soon as Baasha of Israel heard what was happening, he abandoned his project of fortifying Ramah and withdrew to Tirzah. ²²Then King Asa sent an order throughout Judah, requiring that everyone, without exception, help to carry away the building stones and timbers that Baasha had been using to fortify Ramah. Asa used these materials to fortify the town of Geba in Benjamin and the town of Mizpah.

²³The rest of the events in Asa's reign—the extent of his power, everything he did, and the names of the cities he built—are recorded in *The Book of the History of the Kings of Judah.* In his old age his feet became diseased. ²⁴When Asa died, he was buried with his ancestors in the City of David.

Then Jehoshaphat, Asa's son, became the next king.

14:15 Hebrew *the river.*   14:31 Also known as *Abijah.*
15:1 Also known as *Abijah.*   15:2 Hebrew *Abishalom*

(also in 15:10), a variant spelling of Absalom; compare
2 Chr 11:20.   15:6 As in a few Hebrew and Greek
manuscripts; most Hebrew manuscripts read *between
Rehoboam and Jeroboam.*   15:10 Or *The queen mother;*
Hebrew reads *His mother* (also in 15:13); compare 15:2.
15:12 The Hebrew term (literally *round things*) probably
alludes to dung.   15:19 As in Greek version; Hebrew reads
There is a treaty.

ACTS 10:1-23

In Caesarea there lived a Roman army officer* named Cornelius, who was a captain of the Italian Regiment. ²He was a devout, God-fearing man, as was everyone in his household. He gave generously to the poor and prayed regularly to God. ³One afternoon about three o'clock, he had a vision in which he saw an angel of God coming toward him. "Cornelius!" the angel said.

⁴Cornelius stared at him in terror. "What is it, sir?" he asked the angel.

And the angel replied, "Your prayers and gifts to the poor have been received by God as an offering! ⁵Now send some men to Joppa, and summon a man named Simon Peter. ⁶He is staying with Simon, a tanner who lives near the seashore."

⁷As soon as the angel was gone, Cornelius called two of his household servants and a devout soldier, one of his personal attendants. ⁸He told them what had happened and sent them off to Joppa.

⁹The next day as Cornelius's messengers were nearing the town, Peter went up on the flat roof to pray. It was about noon, ¹⁰and he was hungry. But while a meal was being prepared, he fell into a trance. ¹¹He saw the sky open, and something like a large sheet was let down by its four corners. ¹²In the sheet were all sorts of animals, reptiles, and birds. ¹³Then a voice said to him, "Get up, Peter; kill and eat them."

¹⁴"No, Lord," Peter declared. "I have never eaten anything that our Jewish laws have declared impure and unclean.*"

¹⁵But the voice spoke again: "Do not call something unclean if God has made it clean." ¹⁶The same vision was repeated three times. Then the sheet was suddenly pulled up to heaven.

¹⁷Peter was very perplexed. What could the vision mean? Just then the men sent by Cornelius found Simon's house. Standing outside the gate, ¹⁸they asked if a man named Simon Peter was staying there.

¹⁹Meanwhile, as Peter was puzzling over the vision, the Holy Spirit said to him, "Three men have come looking for you. ²⁰Get up, go downstairs, and go with them without hesitation. Don't worry, for I have sent them."

²¹So Peter went down and said, "I'm the man you are looking for. Why have you come?"

²²They said, "We were sent by Cornelius, a Roman officer. He is a devout and God-fearing man, well respected by all the Jews. A holy angel instructed him to summon you to his house so that he can hear your message." ²³So Peter invited the men to stay for the night. The next day he went with them, accompanied by some of the brothers from Joppa.

10:1 Greek *a centurion;* similarly in 10:22.   10:14 Greek
anything common and unclean.

PSALM 133:1-3

*A song for pilgrims ascending to Jerusalem.
A psalm of David.*

¹ **How wonderful and pleasant
        it is
    when brothers live together
        in harmony!**
² **For harmony is as precious as the
        anointing oil
    that was poured over Aaron's
        head,
    that ran down his beard
    and onto the border of
        his robe.**
³ Harmony is as refreshing as
        the dew from Mount Hermon
    that falls on the mountains
        of Zion.
  And there the LORD has pronounced
        his blessing,
    even life everlasting.

PROVERBS 17:7-8

Eloquent words are not fitting for a fool; even less are lies fitting for a ruler.

□ A bribe is like a lucky charm; whoever gives one will prosper!

JUNE 16

1 KINGS 15:25–17:24

Nadab son of Jeroboam began to rule over Israel in the second year of King Asa's reign in Judah. He reigned in Israel two years. ²⁶But he did what was evil in the LORD's sight and followed the example of his father, continuing the sins that Jeroboam had led Israel to commit.

²⁷Then Baasha son of Ahijah, from the tribe of Issachar, plotted against Nadab and assassinated him while he and the Israelite army were laying siege to the Philistine town of Gibbethon. ²⁸Baasha killed Nadab in the third year of King Asa's reign in Judah, and he became the next king of Israel.

²⁹He immediately slaughtered all the descendants of King Jeroboam, so that not one of the royal family was left, just as the LORD had promised concerning Jeroboam by the prophet Ahijah from Shiloh. ³⁰This was done because Jeroboam had provoked the anger of the LORD, the God of Israel, by the sins he had committed and the sins he had led Israel to commit.

³¹The rest of the events in Nadab's reign and everything he did are recorded in *The Book of the History of the Kings of Israel.*

³²There was constant war between King Asa of Judah and King Baasha of Israel. ³³Baasha son of Ahijah began to rule over all Israel in the third year of King Asa's reign in Judah. Baasha reigned in Tirzah twenty-four years. ³⁴But he did what was evil in the LORD's sight and followed the example of Jeroboam, continuing the sins that Jeroboam had led Israel to commit.

¹⁶:¹THIS message from the LORD was delivered to King Baasha by the prophet Jehu son of Hanani: ²"I lifted you out of the dust to make you ruler of my people Israel, but you have followed the evil example of Jeroboam. You have provoked my anger by causing my people Israel to sin. ³So now I will destroy you and your family, just as I destroyed the descendants of Jeroboam son of Nebat. ⁴The members of Baasha's family who die in the city will be eaten by dogs, and those who die in the field will be eaten by vultures."

⁵The rest of the events in Baasha's reign and the extent of his power are recorded in *The Book of the History of the Kings of Israel.* ⁶When Baasha died, he was buried in Tirzah. Then his son Elah became the next king.

⁷The message from the LORD against Baasha and his family came through the prophet Jehu son of Hanani. It was delivered because Baasha had done what was evil in the LORD's sight (just as the family of Jeroboam had done), and also because Baasha had destroyed the family of Jeroboam. The LORD's anger was provoked by Baasha's sins.

⁸Elah son of Baasha began to rule over Israel in the twenty-sixth year of King Asa's reign in Judah. He reigned in the city of Tirzah for two years.

⁹Then Zimri, who commanded half of the royal chariots, made plans to kill him. One day in Tirzah, Elah was getting drunk at the home of Arza, the supervisor of the palace. ¹⁰Zimri walked in and struck him down and killed him. This happened in the twenty-seventh year of King Asa's reign in Judah. Then Zimri became the next king.

¹¹Zimri immediately killed the entire royal family of Baasha, leaving him not even a single male child. He even destroyed distant relatives and friends. ¹²So Zimri destroyed the dynasty of Baasha as the LORD had promised through the prophet Jehu. ¹³This happened because of all the sins Baasha and his son Elah had committed, and because of the sins they led Israel to commit. They pro-

voked the anger of the LORD, the God of Israel, with their worthless idols.

¹⁴The rest of the events in Elah's reign and everything he did are recorded in *The Book of the History of the Kings of Israel.*

¹⁵Zimri began to rule over Israel in the twenty-seventh year of King Asa's reign in Judah, but his reign in Tirzah lasted only seven days. The army of Israel was then attacking the Philistine town of Gibbethon. ¹⁶When they heard that Zimri had committed treason and had assassinated the king, that very day they chose Omri, commander of the army, as the new king of Israel. ¹⁷So Omri led the entire army of Israel up from Gibbethon to attack Tirzah, Israel's capital. ¹⁸When Zimri saw that the city had been taken, he went into the citadel of the palace and burned it down over himself and died in the flames. ¹⁹For he, too, had done what was evil in the LORD's sight. He followed the example of Jeroboam in all the sins he had committed and led Israel to commit.

²⁰The rest of the events in Zimri's reign and his conspiracy are recorded in *The Book of the History of the Kings of Israel.*

²¹But now the people of Israel were split into two factions. Half the people tried to make Tibni son of Ginath their king, while the other half supported Omri. ²²But Omri's supporters defeated the supporters of Tibni. So Tibni was killed, and Omri became the next king.

²³Omri began to rule over Israel in the thirty-first year of King Asa's reign in Judah. He reigned twelve years in all, six of them in Tirzah. ²⁴Then Omri bought the hill now known as Samaria from its owner, Shemer, for 150 pounds of silver.* He built a city on it and called the city Samaria in honor of Shemer.

²⁵But Omri did what was evil in the LORD's sight, even more than any of the kings before him. ²⁶He followed the example of Jeroboam son of Nebat in all the sins he had committed and led Israel to commit. The people provoked the

anger of the LORD, the God of Israel, with their worthless idols.

²⁷The rest of the events in Omri's reign, the extent of his power, and everything he did are recorded in *The Book of the History of the Kings of Israel.* ²⁸When Omri died, he was buried in Samaria. Then his son Ahab became the next king.

²⁹Ahab son of Omri began to rule over Israel in the thirty-eighth year of King Asa's reign in Judah. He reigned in Samaria twenty-two years. ³⁰But Ahab son of Omri did what was evil in the LORD's sight, even more than any of the kings before him. ³¹And as though it were not enough to follow the example of Jeroboam, he married Jezebel, the daughter of King Ethbaal of the Sidonians, and he began to bow down in worship of Baal. ³²First Ahab built a temple and an altar for Baal in Samaria. ³³Then he set up an Asherah pole. He did more to provoke the anger of the LORD, the God of Israel, than any of the other kings of Israel before him.

³⁴It was during his reign that Hiel, a man from Bethel, rebuilt Jericho. When he laid its foundations, it cost him the life of his oldest son, Abiram. And when he completed it and set up its gates, it cost him the life of his youngest son, Segub.* This all happened according to the message from the LORD concerning Jericho spoken by Joshua son of Nun.

¹⁷:¹Now Elijah, who was from Tishbe in Gilead, told King Ahab, "As surely as the LORD, the God of Israel, lives—the God I serve—there will be no dew or rain during the next few years until I give the word!"

²Then the LORD said to Elijah, ³"Go to the east and hide by Kerith Brook, near where it enters the Jordan River. ⁴Drink from the brook and eat what the ravens bring you, for I have commanded them to bring you food."

⁵So Elijah did as the LORD told him and camped beside Kerith Brook, east of the Jordan. ⁶The ravens brought him bread and meat each morning and

evening, and he drank from the brook. [7]But after a while the brook dried up, for there was no rainfall anywhere in the land.

[8]Then the LORD said to Elijah, [9]"Go and live in the village of Zarephath, near the city of Sidon. I have instructed a widow there to feed you."

[10]So he went to Zarephath. As he arrived at the gates of the village, he saw a widow gathering sticks, and he asked her, "Would you please bring me a little water in a cup?" [11]As she was going to get it, he called to her, "Bring me a bite of bread, too."

[12]But she said, "I swear by the LORD your God that I don't have a single piece of bread in the house. And I have only a handful of flour left in the jar and a little cooking oil in the bottom of the jug. I was just gathering a few sticks to cook this last meal, and then my son and I will die."

[13]But Elijah said to her, "Don't be afraid! Go ahead and do just what you've said, but make a little bread for me first. Then use what's left to prepare a meal for yourself and your son. [14]For this is what the LORD, the God of Israel, says: There will always be flour and olive oil left in your containers until the time when the LORD sends rain and the crops grow again!"

[15]So she did as Elijah said, and she and Elijah and her son continued to eat for many days. [16]There was always enough flour and olive oil left in the containers, just as the LORD had promised through Elijah.

[17]Some time later the woman's son became sick. He grew worse and worse, and finally he died. [18]Then she said to Elijah, "O man of God, what have you done to me? Have you come here to point out my sins and kill my son?"

[19]But Elijah replied, "Give me your son." And he took the child's body from her arms, carried him up the stairs to the room where he was staying, and laid the body on his bed. [20]Then Elijah cried out to the LORD, "O LORD my God, why have you brought tragedy to this widow

who has opened her home to me, causing her son to die?"

[21]And he stretched himself out over the child three times and cried out to the LORD, "O LORD my God, please let this child's life return to him." [22]The LORD heard Elijah's prayer, and the life of the child returned, and he revived! [23]Then Elijah brought him down from the upper room and gave him to his mother. "Look!" he said. "Your son is alive!"

[24]Then the woman told Elijah, "Now I know for sure that you are a man of God, and that the LORD truly speaks through you."

16:24 Hebrew *for 2 talents* [68 kilograms] *of silver.*
16:34 An ancient Hebrew scribal tradition reads *He killed his oldest son when he laid its foundations, and he killed his youngest son when he set up its gates.*

ACTS 10:24-48

They [Peter and the other believers] arrived in Caesarea the following day. Cornelius was waiting for them and had called together his relatives and close friends. [25]As Peter entered his home, Cornelius fell at his feet and worshiped him. [26]But Peter pulled him up and said, "Stand up! I'm a human being just like you!" [27]So they talked together and went inside, where many others were assembled.

[28]Peter told them, "You know it is against our laws for a Jewish man to enter a Gentile home like this or to associate with you. But God has shown me that I should no longer think of anyone as impure or unclean. [29]So I came without objection as soon as I was sent for. Now tell me why you sent for me."

[30]Cornelius replied, "Four days ago I was praying in my house about this same time, three o'clock in the afternoon. Suddenly, a man in dazzling clothes was standing in front of me. [31]He told me, 'Cornelius, your prayer has been heard, and your gifts to the poor have been noticed by God! [32]Now send messengers to Joppa, and summon a man named Simon Peter. He is staying in the home of Simon, a tanner who lives near the seashore.' [33]So I sent for you at once, and it was good of you to come. Now we are all

here, waiting before God to hear the message the Lord has given you."

³⁴Then Peter replied, "I see very clearly that God shows no favoritism. ³⁵In every nation he accepts those who fear him and do what is right. ³⁶This is the message of Good News for the people of Israel—that there is peace with God through Jesus Christ, who is Lord of all. ³⁷You know what happened throughout Judea, beginning in Galilee, after John began preaching his message of baptism. ³⁸And you know that God anointed Jesus of Nazareth with the Holy Spirit and with power. Then Jesus went around doing good and healing all who were oppressed by the devil, for God was with him.

³⁹"And we apostles are witnesses of all he did throughout Judea and in Jerusalem. They put him to death by hanging him on a cross,* ⁴⁰but God raised him to life on the third day. Then God allowed him to appear, ⁴¹not to the general public,* but to us whom God had chosen in advance to be his witnesses. We were those who ate and drank with him after he rose from the dead. ⁴²And he ordered us to preach everywhere and to testify that Jesus is the one appointed by God to be the judge of all—the living and the dead. ⁴³He is the one all the prophets testified about, saying that everyone who believes in him will have their sins forgiven through his name."

⁴⁴Even as Peter was saying these things, the Holy Spirit fell upon all who were listening to the message. ⁴⁵The Jewish believers* who came with Peter were amazed that the gift of the Holy Spirit had been poured out on the Gentiles, too. ⁴⁶For they heard them speaking in tongues and praising God.

Then Peter asked, ⁴⁷"Can anyone object to their being baptized, now that they have received the Holy Spirit just as we did?" ⁴⁸So he gave orders for them to be baptized in the name of Jesus Christ. Afterward Cornelius asked him to stay with them for several days.

10:39 Greek *on a tree.*   10:41 Greek *the people.*
10:45 Greek *The faithful ones of the circumcision.*

PSALM 134:1-3
A song for pilgrims ascending to Jerusalem.

¹ **O**h, praise the Lord, all you
        servants of the Lord,
    you who serve at night in the
        house of the Lord.
² Lift up holy hands in prayer,
        and praise the Lord.

³ May the Lord, who made heaven
        and earth,
    bless you from Jerusalem.*
134:3 Hebrew *Zion.*

PROVERBS 17:9-11
Love prospers when a fault is forgiven, but dwelling on it separates close friends. □ A single rebuke does more for a person of understanding than a hundred lashes on the back of a fool. □ Evil people are eager for rebellion, but they will be severely punished.

JUNE
17

1 KINGS 18:1-46
Later on, in the third year of the drought, the Lord said to Elijah, "Go and present yourself to King Ahab. Tell him that I will soon send rain!" ²So Elijah went to appear before Ahab.

Meanwhile, the famine had become very severe in Samaria. ³So Ahab summoned Obadiah, who was in charge of the palace. (Obadiah was a devoted follower of the Lord. ⁴Once when Jezebel had tried to kill all the Lord's prophets, Obadiah had hidden 100 of them in two caves. He put fifty prophets in each cave and supplied them with food and water.) ⁵Ahab said to Obadiah, "We must check every spring and valley in the land to see if we can find enough grass to save at least some of my horses and mules." ⁶So they divided the land between them. Ahab went one way by himself, and Obadiah went another way by himself.

⁷As Obadiah was walking along, he suddenly saw Elijah coming toward him. Obadiah recognized him at once and bowed low to the ground before him. "Is it really you, my lord Elijah?" he asked.

⁸"Yes, it is," Elijah replied. "Now go and tell your master, 'Elijah is here.'"

⁹"Oh, sir," Obadiah protested, "what harm have I done to you that you are sending me to my death at the hands of Ahab? ¹⁰For I swear by the LORD your God that the king has searched every nation and kingdom on earth from end to end to find you. And each time he was told, 'Elijah isn't here,' King Ahab forced the king of that nation to swear to the truth of his claim. ¹¹And now you say, 'Go and tell your master, "Elijah is here."' ¹²But as soon as I leave you, the Spirit of the LORD will carry you away to who knows where. When Ahab comes and cannot find you, he will kill me. Yet I have been a true servant of the LORD all my life. ¹³Has no one told you, my lord, about the time when Jezebel was trying to kill the LORD's prophets? I hid 100 of them in two caves and supplied them with food and water. ¹⁴And now you say, 'Go and tell your master, "Elijah is here."' Sir, if I do that, Ahab will certainly kill me."

¹⁵But Elijah said, "I swear by the LORD Almighty, in whose presence I stand, that I will present myself to Ahab this very day."

¹⁶So Obadiah went to tell Ahab that Elijah had come, and Ahab went out to meet Elijah. ¹⁷When Ahab saw him, he exclaimed, "So, is it really you, you troublemaker of Israel?"

¹⁸"I have made no trouble for Israel," Elijah replied. "You and your family are the troublemakers, for you have refused to obey the commands of the LORD and have worshiped the images of Baal instead. ¹⁹Now summon all Israel to join me at Mount Carmel, along with the 450 prophets of Baal and the

400 prophets of Asherah who are supported by Jezebel.*"

²⁰So Ahab summoned all the people of Israel and the prophets to Mount Carmel. ²¹Then Elijah stood in front of them and said, "How much longer will you waver, hobbling between two opinions? If the LORD is God, follow him! But if Baal is God, then follow him!" But the people were completely silent.

²²Then Elijah said to them, "I am the only prophet of the LORD who is left, but Baal has 450 prophets. ²³Now bring two bulls. The prophets of Baal may choose whichever one they wish and cut it into pieces and lay it on the wood of their altar, but without setting fire to it. I will prepare the other bull and lay it on the wood on the altar, but not set fire to it. ²⁴Then call on the name of your god, and I will call on the name of the LORD. The god who answers by setting fire to the wood is the true God!" And all the people agreed.

²⁵Then Elijah said to the prophets of Baal, "You go first, for there are many of you. Choose one of the bulls, and prepare it and call on the name of your god. But do not set fire to the wood."

²⁶So they prepared one of the bulls and placed it on the altar. Then they called on the name of Baal from morning until noontime, shouting, "O Baal, answer us!" But there was no reply of any kind. Then they danced, hobbling around the altar they had made.

²⁷About noontime Elijah began mocking them. "You'll have to shout louder," he scoffed, "for surely he is a god! Perhaps he is daydreaming, or is relieving himself.* Or maybe he is away on a trip, or is asleep and needs to be wakened!"

²⁸So they shouted louder, and following their normal custom, they cut themselves with knives and swords until the blood gushed out. ²⁹They raved all afternoon until the time of the evening sacrifice, but still there was no sound, no reply, no response.

³⁰Then Elijah called to the people, "Come over here!" They all crowded around him as he repaired the altar of

the Lord that had been torn down. ³¹He took twelve stones, one to represent each of the tribes of Israel,* ³²and he used the stones to rebuild the altar in the name of the Lord. Then he dug a trench around the altar large enough to hold about three gallons.* ³³He piled wood on the altar, cut the bull into pieces, and laid the pieces on the wood.

Then he said, "Fill four large jars with water, and pour the water over the offering and the wood."

³⁴After they had done this, he said, "Do the same thing again!" And when they were finished, he said, "Now do it a third time!" So they did as he said, ³⁵and the water ran around the altar and even filled the trench.

³⁶At the usual time for offering the evening sacrifice, Elijah the prophet walked up to the altar and prayed, "O Lord, God of Abraham, Isaac, and Jacob,* prove today that you are God in Israel and that I am your servant. Prove that I have done all this at your command. ³⁷O Lord, answer me! Answer me so these people will know that you, O Lord, are God and that you have brought them back to yourself."

³⁸Immediately the fire of the Lord flashed down from heaven and burned up the young bull, the wood, the stones, and the dust. It even licked up all the water in the trench! ³⁹And when all the people saw it, they fell face down on the ground and cried out, "The Lord—he is God! Yes, the Lord is God!"

⁴⁰Then Elijah commanded, "Seize all the prophets of Baal. Don't let a single one escape!" So the people seized them all, and Elijah took them down to the Kishon Valley and killed them there.

⁴¹Then Elijah said to Ahab, "Go get something to eat and drink, for I hear a mighty rainstorm coming!"

⁴²So Ahab went to eat and drink. But Elijah climbed to the top of Mount Carmel and bowed low to the ground and prayed with his face between his knees.

⁴³Then he said to his servant, "Go and look out toward the sea."

The servant went and looked, then returned to Elijah and said, "I didn't see anything."

Seven times Elijah told him to go and look. ⁴⁴Finally the seventh time, his servant told him, "I saw a little cloud about the size of a man's hand rising from the sea."

Then Elijah shouted, "Hurry to Ahab and tell him, 'Climb into your chariot and go back home. If you don't hurry, the rain will stop you!'"

⁴⁵And soon the sky was black with clouds. A heavy wind brought a terrific rainstorm, and Ahab left quickly for Jezreel. ⁴⁶Then the Lord gave special strength to Elijah. He tucked his cloak into his belt* and ran ahead of Ahab's chariot all the way to the entrance of Jezreel.

18:19 Hebrew *who eat at Jezebel's table.*   **18:27** Or *is busy somewhere else, or is engaged in business.*   **18:31** Hebrew *each of the tribes of the sons of Jacob to whom the Lord had said, "Your name will be Israel."*   **18:32** Hebrew *2 seahs* [12 liters] *of seed.*   **18:36** Hebrew *and Israel.* The names "Jacob" and "Israel" are often interchanged throughout the Old Testament, referring sometimes to the individual patriarch and sometimes to the nation.   **18:46** Hebrew *He bound up his loins.*

ACTS 11:1-30

Soon the news reached the apostles and other believers* in Judea that the Gentiles had received the word of God. ²But when Peter arrived back in Jerusalem, the Jewish believers* criticized him. ³"You entered the home of Gentiles* and even ate with them!" they said.

⁴Then Peter told them exactly what had happened. ⁵"I was in the town of Joppa," he said, "and while I was praying, I went into a trance and saw a vision. Something like a large sheet was let down by its four corners from the sky. And it came right down to me. ⁶When I looked inside the sheet, I saw all sorts of small animals, wild animals, reptiles, and birds. ⁷And I heard a voice say, 'Get up, Peter; kill and eat them.'

⁸"'No, Lord,' I replied. 'I have never eaten anything that our Jewish laws have declared impure or unclean.*'

⁹"But the voice from heaven spoke again: 'Do not call something unclean if God has made it clean.' ¹⁰This

happened three times before the sheet and all it contained was pulled back up to heaven.

11"Just then three men who had been sent from Caesarea arrived at the house where we were staying. 12The Holy Spirit told me to go with them and not to worry that they were Gentiles. These six brothers here accompanied me, and we soon entered the home of the man who had sent for us. 13He told us how an angel had appeared to him in his home and had told him, 'Send messengers to Joppa, and summon a man named Simon Peter. 14He will tell you how you and everyone in your household can be saved!'

15"As I began to speak," Peter continued, "the Holy Spirit fell on them, just as he fell on us at the beginning. 16Then I thought of the Lord's words when he said, 'John baptized with* water, but you will be baptized with the Holy Spirit.' 17And since God gave these Gentiles the same gift he gave us when we believed in the Lord Jesus Christ, who was I to stand in God's way?"

18When the others heard this, they stopped objecting and began praising God. They said, "We can see that God has also given the Gentiles the privilege of repenting of their sins and receiving eternal life."

19Meanwhile, the believers who had been scattered during the persecution after Stephen's death traveled as far as Phoenicia, Cyprus, and Antioch of Syria. They preached the word of God, but only to Jews. 20However, some of the believers who went to Antioch from Cyprus and Cyrene began preaching to the Gentiles* about the Lord Jesus. 21The power of the Lord was with them, and a large number of these Gentiles believed and turned to the Lord.

22When the church at Jerusalem heard what had happened, they sent Barnabas to Antioch. 23When he arrived and saw this evidence of God's blessing, he was filled with joy, and he encouraged the believers to stay true to the Lord. 24Barnabas was a good man, full of the Holy Spirit and strong in faith. And many people were brought to the Lord.

25Then Barnabas went on to Tarsus to look for Saul. 26When he found him, he brought him back to Antioch. Both of them stayed there with the church for a full year, teaching large crowds of people. (It was at Antioch that the believers* were first called Christians.)

27During this time some prophets traveled from Jerusalem to Antioch. 28One of them named Agabus stood up in one of the meetings and predicted by the Spirit that a great famine was coming upon the entire Roman world. (This was fulfilled during the reign of Claudius.) 29So the believers in Antioch decided to send relief to the brothers and sisters* in Judea, everyone giving as much as they could. 30This they did, entrusting their gifts to Barnabas and Saul to take to the elders of the church in Jerusalem.

11:1 Greek brothers.   11:2 Greek those of the circumcision.   11:3 Greek of uncircumcised men.   11:8 Greek anything common or unclean.   11:16 Or in; also in 11:16b.   11:20 Greek the Hellenists (i.e., those who speak Greek); other manuscripts read the Greeks.   11:26 Greek disciples; also in 11:29.   11:29 Greek the brothers.

PSALM 135:1-21

Praise the LORD!

Praise the name of the LORD!
  Praise him, you who serve
    the LORD,
2 you who serve in the house of
    the LORD,
  in the courts of the house
    of our God.

3 Praise the LORD, for the LORD
    is good;
  celebrate his lovely name
    with music.
4 For the LORD has chosen Jacob
    for himself,
  Israel for his own special
    treasure.

5 I know the greatness of
    the LORD—
  that our Lord is greater than any
    other god.

⁶ The Lord does whatever pleases
him
throughout all heaven and
earth,
and on the seas and in their
depths.
⁷ He causes the clouds to rise over
the whole earth.
He sends the lightning with
the rain
and releases the wind from
his storehouses.

⁸ He destroyed the firstborn in
each Egyptian home,
both people and animals.
⁹ He performed miraculous signs
and wonders in Egypt
against Pharaoh and all
his people.
¹⁰ He struck down great nations
and slaughtered mighty
kings—
¹¹ Sihon king of the Amorites,
Og king of Bashan,
and all the kings of Canaan.
¹² He gave their land as an inheritance,
a special possession to his
people Israel.

¹³ **Your name, O Lord, endures**
forever;
your fame, O Lord, is known
to every generation.
¹⁴ **For the Lord will give justice**
to his people
and have compassion on
his servants.

¹⁵ The idols of the nations are merely
things of silver and gold,
shaped by human hands.
¹⁶ They have mouths but cannot
speak,
and eyes but cannot see.
¹⁷ They have ears but cannot hear,
and noses but cannot smell.
¹⁸ And those who make idols are just
like them,
as are all who trust in them.

¹⁹ O Israel, praise the Lord!
O priests—descendants of
Aaron—praise the Lord!

²⁰ O Levites, praise the Lord!
All you who fear the Lord, praise
the Lord!
²¹ The Lord be praised from Zion,
for he lives here in Jerusalem.

Praise the Lord!

PROVERBS 17:12-13
It is safer to meet a bear robbed of her
cubs than to confront a fool caught in
foolishness. □ If you repay good with
evil, evil will never leave your house.

JUNE
18

1 KINGS 19:1-21
When Ahab got home, he told Jezebel
everything Elijah had done, including
the way he had killed all the prophets of
Baal. ²So Jezebel sent this message to
Elijah: "May the gods strike me and even
kill me if by this time tomorrow I have
not killed you just as you killed them."

³Elijah was afraid and fled for his life.
He went to Beersheba, a town in Judah,
and he left his servant there. ⁴Then he
went on alone into the wilderness, traveling all day. He sat down under a solitary
broom tree and prayed that he might die.
"I have had enough, Lord," he said. "Take
my life, for I am no better than my ancestors who have already died."

⁵Then he lay down and slept under the
broom tree. But as he was sleeping, an angel touched him and told him, "Get up
and eat!" ⁶He looked around and there
beside his head was some bread baked
on hot stones and a jar of water! So he ate
and drank and lay down again.

⁷Then the angel of the Lord came
again and touched him and said, "Get
up and eat some more, or the journey
ahead will be too much for you."

⁸So he got up and ate and drank, and
the food gave him enough strength to

travel forty days and forty nights to Mount Sinai,* the mountain of God. ⁹There he came to a cave, where he spent the night.

But the LORD said to him, "What are you doing here, Elijah?"

¹⁰Elijah replied, "I have zealously served the LORD God Almighty. But the people of Israel have broken their covenant with you, torn down your altars, and killed every one of your prophets. I am the only one left, and now they are trying to kill me, too."

¹¹"Go out and stand before me on the mountain," the LORD told him. And as Elijah stood there, the LORD passed by, and a mighty windstorm hit the mountain. It was such a terrible blast that the rocks were torn loose, but the LORD was not in the wind. After the wind there was an earthquake, but the LORD was not in the earthquake. ¹²And after the earthquake there was a fire, but the LORD was not in the fire. And after the fire there was the sound of a gentle whisper. ¹³When Elijah heard it, he wrapped his face in his cloak and went out and stood at the entrance of the cave.

And a voice said, "What are you doing here, Elijah?"

¹⁴He replied again, "I have zealously served the LORD God Almighty. But the people of Israel have broken their covenant with you, torn down your altars, and killed every one of your prophets. I am the only one left, and now they are trying to kill me, too."

¹⁵Then the LORD told him, "Go back the same way you came, and travel to the wilderness of Damascus. When you arrive there, anoint Hazael to be king of Aram. ¹⁶Then anoint Jehu son of Nimshi to be king of Israel, and anoint Elisha son of Shaphat from the town of Abelmeholah to replace you as my prophet. ¹⁷Anyone who escapes from Hazael will be killed by Jehu, and those who escape Jehu will be killed by Elisha! ¹⁸Yet I will preserve 7,000 others in Israel who have never bowed down to Baal or kissed him!"

¹⁹So Elijah went and found Elisha son of Shaphat plowing a field. There were twelve teams of oxen in the field, and Elisha was plowing with the twelfth team. Elijah went over to him and threw his cloak across his shoulders and then walked away. ²⁰Elisha left the oxen standing there, ran after Elijah, and said to him, "First let me go and kiss my father and mother good-bye, and then I will go with you!"

Elijah replied, "Go on back, but think about what I have done to you."

²¹So Elisha returned to his oxen and slaughtered them. He used the wood from the plow to build a fire to roast their flesh. He passed around the meat to the townspeople, and they all ate. Then he went with Elijah as his assistant.

19:8 Hebrew *to Horeb,* another name for Sinai.

ACTS 12:1-23

About that time King Herod Agrippa* began to persecute some believers in the church. ²He had the apostle James (John's brother) killed with a sword. ³When Herod saw how much this pleased the Jewish people, he also arrested Peter. (This took place during the Passover celebration.*) ⁴Then he imprisoned him, placing him under the guard of four squads of four soldiers each. Herod intended to bring Peter out for public trial after the Passover. ⁵But while Peter was in prison, the church prayed very earnestly for him.

⁶The night before Peter was to be placed on trial, he was asleep, fastened with two chains between two soldiers. Others stood guard at the prison gate. ⁷Suddenly, there was a bright light in the cell, and an angel of the Lord stood before Peter. The angel struck him on the side to awaken him and said, "Quick! Get up!" And the chains fell off his wrists. ⁸Then the angel told him, "Get dressed and put on your sandals." And he did. "Now put on your coat and follow me," the angel ordered.

⁹So Peter left the cell, following the angel. But all the time he thought it was a vision. He didn't realize it was actually happening. ¹⁰They passed the first and

second guard posts and came to the iron gate leading to the city, and this opened for them all by itself. So they passed through and started walking down the street, and then the angel suddenly left him.

¹¹Peter finally came to his senses. "It's really true!" he said. "The Lord has sent his angel and saved me from Herod and from what the Jewish leaders* had planned to do to me!"

¹²When he realized this, he went to the home of Mary, the mother of John Mark, where many were gathered for prayer. ¹³He knocked at the door in the gate, and a servant girl named Rhoda came to open it. ¹⁴When she recognized Peter's voice, she was so overjoyed that, instead of opening the door, she ran back inside and told everyone, "Peter is standing at the door!"

¹⁵"You're out of your mind!" they said. When she insisted, they decided, "It must be his angel."

¹⁶Meanwhile, Peter continued knocking. When they finally opened the door and saw him, they were amazed. ¹⁷He motioned for them to quiet down and told them how the Lord had led him out of prison. "Tell James and the other brothers what happened," he said. And then he went to another place.

¹⁸At dawn there was a great commotion among the soldiers about what had happened to Peter. ¹⁹Herod Agrippa ordered a thorough search for him. When he couldn't be found, Herod interrogated the guards and sentenced them to death. Afterward Herod left Judea to stay in Caesarea for a while.

²⁰Now Herod was very angry with the people of Tyre and Sidon. So they sent a delegation to make peace with him because their cities were dependent upon Herod's country for food. The delegates won the support of Blastus, Herod's personal assistant, ²¹and an appointment with Herod was granted. When the day arrived, Herod put on his royal robes, sat on his throne, and made a speech to them. ²²The people gave him a great ovation, shouting, "It's the voice of a god, not of a man!"

²³Instantly, an angel of the Lord struck Herod with a sickness, because he accepted the people's worship instead of giving the glory to God. So he was consumed with worms and died.

12:1 Greek *Herod the king.* He was the nephew of Herod Antipas and a grandson of Herod the Great.   12:3 Greek *the days of unleavened bread.*   12:11 Or *the Jewish people.*

PSALM 136:1-26

Give thanks to the Lord, for
    he is good!
His faithful love endures forever.
² Give thanks to the God of gods.
His faithful love endures forever.
³ Give thanks to the Lord of lords.
His faithful love endures forever.

⁴ Give thanks to him who alone does
    mighty miracles.
His faithful love endures forever.
⁵ Give thanks to him who made the
    heavens so skillfully.
His faithful love endures forever.
⁶ Give thanks to him who placed the
    earth among the waters.
His faithful love endures forever.
⁷ Give thanks to him who made the
    heavenly lights—
His faithful love endures forever.
⁸ the sun to rule the day,
His faithful love endures forever.
⁹ and the moon and stars to rule
    the night.
His faithful love endures forever.

¹⁰ Give thanks to him who killed the
    firstborn of Egypt.
His faithful love endures forever.
¹¹ He brought Israel out of Egypt.
His faithful love endures forever.
¹² He acted with a strong hand and
    powerful arm.
His faithful love endures forever.
¹³ Give thanks to him who parted the
    Red Sea.*
His faithful love endures forever.
¹⁴ He led Israel safely through,
His faithful love endures forever.
¹⁵ but he hurled Pharaoh and his army
    into the Red Sea.

His faithful love endures forever.
16 Give thanks to him who led his
     people through the wilderness.
     His faithful love endures forever.

17 Give thanks to him who struck down
     mighty kings.
     His faithful love endures forever.
18 He killed powerful kings—
     His faithful love endures forever.
19 Sihon king of the Amorites,
     His faithful love endures forever.
20 and Og king of Bashan.
     His faithful love endures forever.
21 God gave the land of these kings as
     an inheritance—
     His faithful love endures forever.
22 a special possession to his servant
     Israel.
     His faithful love endures forever.

23 He remembered us in our weakness.
     His faithful love endures forever.
24 He saved us from our enemies.
     His faithful love endures forever.
25 He gives food to every living thing.
     His faithful love endures forever.
26 Give thanks to the God of heaven.
     His faithful love endures forever.

136:13 Hebrew *sea of reeds;* also in 136:15.

PROVERBS 17:14-15

Starting a quarrel is like opening a floodgate, so stop before a dispute breaks out. □ Acquitting the guilty and condemning the innocent—both are detestable to the LORD.

JUNE 19

1 KINGS 20:1–21:29

About that time King Ben-hadad of Aram mobilized his army, supported by the chariots and horses of thirty-two allied kings. They went to besiege Samaria, the capital of Israel, and launched attacks against it. 2Ben-hadad sent messengers into the city to relay this message to King Ahab of Israel: "This is what Ben-hadad says: 3'Your silver and gold are mine, and so are your wives and the best of your children!'"

4"All right, my lord the king," Israel's king replied. "All that I have is yours!"

5Soon Ben-hadad's messengers returned again and said, "This is what Ben-hadad says: 'I have already demanded that you give me your silver, gold, wives, and children. 6But about this time tomorrow I will send my officials to search your palace and the homes of your people. They will take away everything you consider valuable!'"

7Then Ahab summoned all the elders of the land and said to them, "Look how this man is stirring up trouble! I already agreed with his demand that I give him my wives and children and silver and gold."

8"Don't give in to any more demands," all the elders and the people advised.

9So Ahab told the messengers from Ben-hadad, "Say this to my lord the king: 'I will give you everything you asked for the first time, but I cannot accept this last demand of yours.'" So the messengers returned to Ben-hadad with that response.

10Then Ben-hadad sent this message to Ahab: "May the gods strike me and even kill me if there remains enough dust from Samaria to provide even a handful for each of my soldiers."

11The king of Israel sent back this answer: "A warrior putting on his sword for battle should not boast like a warrior who has already won."

12Ahab's reply reached Ben-hadad and the other kings as they were drinking in their tents.* "Prepare to attack!" Ben-hadad commanded his officers. So they prepared to attack the city.

13Then a certain prophet came to see King Ahab of Israel and told him, "This is what the LORD says: Do you see all these enemy forces? Today I will hand them all over to you. Then you will know that I am the LORD."

¹⁴Ahab asked, "How will he do it?"

And the prophet replied, "This is what the LORD says: The troops of the provincial commanders will do it."

"Should we attack first?" Ahab asked.

"Yes," the prophet answered.

¹⁵So Ahab mustered the troops of the 232 provincial commanders. Then he called out the rest of the army of Israel, some 7,000 men. ¹⁶About noontime, as Ben-hadad and the thirty-two allied kings were still in their tents drinking themselves into a stupor, ¹⁷the troops of the provincial commanders marched out of the city as the first contingent.

As they approached, Ben-hadad's scouts reported to him, "Some troops are coming from Samaria."

¹⁸"Take them alive," Ben-hadad commanded, "whether they have come for peace or for war."

¹⁹But Ahab's provincial commanders and the entire army had now come out to fight. ²⁰Each Israelite soldier killed his Aramean opponent, and suddenly the entire Aramean army panicked and fled. The Israelites chased them, but King Ben-hadad and a few of his charioteers escaped on horses. ²¹However, the king of Israel destroyed the other horses and chariots and slaughtered the Arameans.

²²Afterward the prophet said to King Ahab, "Get ready for another attack. Begin making plans now, for the king of Aram will come back next spring.*"

²³After their defeat, Ben-hadad's officers said to him, "The Israelite gods are gods of the hills; that is why they won. But we can beat them easily on the plains. ²⁴Only this time replace the kings with field commanders! ²⁵Recruit another army like the one you lost. Give us the same number of horses, chariots, and men, and we will fight against them on the plains. There's no doubt that we will beat them." So King Ben-hadad did as they suggested.

²⁶The following spring he called up the Aramean army and marched out against Israel, this time at Aphek. ²⁷Israel then mustered its army, set up supply lines, and marched out for battle. But the Israelite army looked like two little flocks of goats in comparison to the vast Aramean forces that filled the countryside!

²⁸Then the man of God went to the king of Israel and said, "This is what the LORD says: The Arameans have said, 'The LORD is a god of the hills and not of the plains.' So I will defeat this vast army for you. Then you will know that I am the LORD."

²⁹The two armies camped opposite each other for seven days, and on the seventh day the battle began. The Israelites killed 100,000 Aramean foot soldiers in one day. ³⁰The rest fled into the town of Aphek, but the wall fell on them and killed another 27,000. Ben-hadad fled into the town and hid in a secret room.

³¹Ben-hadad's officers said to him, "Sir, we have heard that the kings of Israel are merciful. So let's humble ourselves by wearing burlap around our waists and putting ropes on our heads, and surrender to the king of Israel. Then perhaps he will let you live."

³²So they put on burlap and ropes, and they went to the king of Israel and begged, "Your servant Ben-hadad says, 'Please let me live!'"

The king of Israel responded, "Is he still alive? He is my brother!"

³³The men took this as a good sign and quickly picked up on his words. "Yes," they said, "your brother Ben-hadad!"

"Go and get him," the king of Israel told them. And when Ben-hadad arrived, Ahab invited him up into his chariot.

³⁴Ben-hadad told him, "I will give back the towns my father took from your father, and you may establish places of trade in Damascus, as my father did in Samaria."

Then Ahab said, "I will release you under these conditions." So they made a new treaty, and Ben-hadad was set free.

³⁵Meanwhile, the LORD instructed one of the group of prophets to say to another man, "Hit me!" But the man

refused to hit the prophet. ³⁶Then the prophet told him, "Because you have not obeyed the voice of the Lord, a lion will kill you as soon as you leave me." And when he had gone, a lion did attack and kill him.

³⁷Then the prophet turned to another man and said, "Hit me!" So he struck the prophet and wounded him.

³⁸The prophet placed a bandage over his eyes to disguise himself and then waited beside the road for the king. ³⁹As the king passed by, the prophet called out to him, "Sir, I was in the thick of battle, and suddenly a man brought me a prisoner. He said, 'Guard this man; if for any reason he gets away, you will either die or pay a fine of seventy-five pounds* of silver!' ⁴⁰But while I was busy doing something else, the prisoner disappeared!"

"Well, it's your own fault," the king replied. "You have brought the judgment on yourself."

⁴¹Then the prophet quickly pulled the bandage from his eyes, and the king of Israel recognized him as one of the prophets. ⁴²The prophet said to him, "This is what the Lord says: Because you have spared the man I said must be destroyed,* now you must die in his place, and your people will die instead of his people." ⁴³So the king of Israel went home to Samaria angry and sullen.

²¹:¹Now there was a man named Naboth, from Jezreel, who owned a vineyard in Jezreel beside the palace of King Ahab of Samaria. ²One day Ahab said to Naboth, "Since your vineyard is so convenient to my palace, I would like to buy it to use as a vegetable garden. I will give you a better vineyard in exchange, or if you prefer, I will pay you for it."

³But Naboth replied, "The Lord forbid that I should give you the inheritance that was passed down by my ancestors."

⁴So Ahab went home angry and sullen because of Naboth's answer. The king went to bed with his face to the wall and refused to eat!

⁵"What's the matter?" his wife Jeze-

bel asked him. "What's made you so upset that you're not eating?"

⁶"I asked Naboth to sell me his vineyard or trade it, but he refused!" Ahab told her.

⁷"Are you the king of Israel or not?" Jezebel demanded. "Get up and eat something, and don't worry about it. I'll get you Naboth's vineyard!"

⁸So she wrote letters in Ahab's name, sealed them with his seal, and sent them to the elders and other leaders of the town where Naboth lived. ⁹In her letters she commanded: "Call the citizens together for fasting and prayer, and give Naboth a place of honor. ¹⁰And then seat two scoundrels across from him who will accuse him of cursing God and the king. Then take him out and stone him to death."

¹¹So the elders and other town leaders followed the instructions Jezebel had written in the letters. ¹²They called for a fast and put Naboth at a prominent place before the people. ¹³Then the two scoundrels came and sat down across from him. And they accused Naboth before all the people, saying, "He cursed God and the king." So he was dragged outside the town and stoned to death. ¹⁴The town leaders then sent word to Jezebel, "Naboth has been stoned to death."

¹⁵When Jezebel heard the news, she said to Ahab, "You know the vineyard Naboth wouldn't sell you? Well, you can have it now! He's dead!" ¹⁶So Ahab immediately went down to the vineyard of Naboth to claim it.

¹⁷But the Lord said to Elijah,* ¹⁸"Go down to meet King Ahab of Israel, who rules in Samaria. He will be at Naboth's vineyard in Jezreel, claiming it for himself. ¹⁹Give him this message: 'This is what the Lord says: Wasn't it enough that you killed Naboth? Must you rob him, too? Because you have done this, dogs will lick your blood at the very place where they licked the blood of Naboth!'"

²⁰"So, my enemy, you have found me!" Ahab exclaimed to Elijah.

"Yes," Elijah answered, "I have come

because you have sold yourself to what is evil in the LORD's sight. ²¹So now the LORD says, 'I will bring disaster on you and consume you. I will destroy every one of your male descendants, slave and free alike, anywhere in Israel! ²²I am going to destroy your family as I did the family of Jeroboam son of Nebat and the family of Baasha son of Ahijah, for you have made me very angry and have led Israel into sin.'

²³"And regarding Jezebel, the LORD says, 'Dogs will eat Jezebel's body at the plot of land in Jezreel.*'

²⁴"The members of Ahab's family who die in the city will be eaten by dogs, and those who die in the field will be eaten by vultures."

²⁵(No one else so completely sold himself to what was evil in the LORD's sight as Ahab did under the influence of his wife Jezebel. ²⁶His worst outrage was worshiping idols* just as the Amorites had done—the people whom the LORD had driven out from the land ahead of the Israelites.)

²⁷But when Ahab heard this message, he tore his clothing, dressed in burlap, and fasted. He even slept in burlap and went about in deep mourning.

²⁸Then another message from the LORD came to Elijah: ²⁹"Do you see how Ahab has humbled himself before me? Because he has done this, I will not do what I promised during his lifetime. It will happen to his sons; I will destroy his dynasty."

20:12 Or *in Succoth;* also in 20:16.　20:22 Hebrew *at the turn of the year;* similarly in 20:26. The first day of the year in the ancient Hebrew lunar calendar occurred in March or April.　20:39 Hebrew *1 talent* [34 kilograms].　20:42 The Hebrew term used here refers to the complete consecration of things or people to the LORD, either by destroying them or by giving them as an offering.　21:17 Hebrew *Elijah the Tishbite;* also in 21:28.　21:23 As in several Hebrew manuscripts, Syriac, and Latin Vulgate (see also 2 Kgs 9:26, 36); most Hebrew manuscripts read *at the city wall.* 21:26 The Hebrew term (literally *round things*) probably alludes to dung.

ACTS 12:24–13:15

Meanwhile, the word of God continued to spread, and there were many new believers.

²⁵When Barnabas and Saul had fin-
ished their mission to Jerusalem, they returned,* taking John Mark with them.

¹³:¹AMONG the prophets and teachers of the church at Antioch of Syria were Barnabas, Simeon (called "the black man"*), Lucius (from Cyrene), Manaen (the childhood companion of King Herod Antipas*), and Saul. **²One day as these men were worshiping the Lord and fasting, the Holy Spirit said, "Dedicate Barnabas and Saul for the special work to which I have called them." ³So after more fasting and prayer, the men laid their hands on them and sent them on their way.**

⁴So Barnabas and Saul were sent out by the Holy Spirit. They went down to the seaport of Seleucia and then sailed for the island of Cyprus. ⁵There, in the town of Salamis, they went to the Jewish synagogues and preached the word of God. John Mark went with them as their assistant.

⁶Afterward they traveled from town to town across the entire island until finally they reached Paphos, where they met a Jewish sorcerer, a false prophet named Bar-Jesus. ⁷He had attached himself to the governor, Sergius Paulus, who was an intelligent man. The governor invited Barnabas and Saul to visit him, for he wanted to hear the word of God. ⁸But Elymas, the sorcerer (as his name means in Greek), interfered and urged the governor to pay no attention to what Barnabas and Saul said. He was trying to keep the governor from believing.

⁹Saul, also known as Paul, was filled with the Holy Spirit, and he looked the sorcerer in the eye. ¹⁰Then he said, "You son of the devil, full of every sort of deceit and fraud, and enemy of all that is good! Will you never stop perverting the true ways of the Lord? ¹¹Watch now, for the Lord has laid his hand of punishment upon you, and you will be struck blind. You will not see the sunlight for some time." Instantly mist and darkness came over the man's eyes, and he began groping around begging for someone to take his hand and lead him.

¹²When the governor saw what had happened, he became a believer, for he was astonished at the teaching about the Lord.

¹³Paul and his companions then left Paphos by ship for Pamphylia, landing at the port town of Perga. There John Mark left them and returned to Jerusalem. ¹⁴But Paul and Barnabas traveled inland to Antioch of Pisidia.*

On the Sabbath they went to the synagogue for the services. ¹⁵After the usual readings from the books of Moses* and the prophets, those in charge of the service sent them this message: "Brothers, if you have any word of encouragement for the people, come and give it."

12:25 Or *mission, they returned to Jerusalem.* Other manuscripts read *mission, they returned from Jerusalem;* still others read *mission, they returned from Jerusalem to Antioch.*   **13:1a** Greek *who was called Niger.* **13:1b** Greek *Herod the tetrarch.* **13:13-14** *Pamphylia* and *Pisidia* were districts in what is now Turkey. **13:15** Greek *from the law.*

PSALM 137:1-9

Beside the rivers of Babylon,
 we sat and wept
 as we thought of Jerusalem.*
² We put away our harps,
 hanging them on the branches
 of poplar trees.
³ For our captors demanded a song
 from us.
 Our tormentors insisted
 on a joyful hymn:
 "Sing us one of those songs
 of Jerusalem!"
⁴ But how can we sing the songs
 of the LORD
 while in a pagan land?

⁵ If I forget you, O Jerusalem,
 let my right hand forget how
 to play the harp.
⁶ May my tongue stick to the roof
 of my mouth
 if I fail to remember you,
 if I don't make Jerusalem my
 greatest joy.

⁷ O LORD, remember what the
 Edomites did
 on the day the armies of Babylon
 captured Jerusalem.

"Destroy it!" they yelled.
 "Level it to the ground!"
⁸ O Babylon, you will be destroyed.
 Happy is the one who pays you
 back
 for what you have done to us.
⁹ Happy is the one who takes
 your babies
 and smashes them against
 the rocks!

137:1 Hebrew *Zion;* also in 137:3.

PROVERBS 17:16

It is senseless to pay tuition to educate a fool, since he has no heart for learning.

JUNE
20

1 KINGS 22:1-53

For three years there was no war between Aram and Israel. ²Then during the third year, King Jehoshaphat of Judah went to visit King Ahab of Israel. ³During the visit, the king of Israel said to his officials, "Do you realize that the town of Ramoth-gilead belongs to us? And yet we've done nothing to recapture it from the king of Aram!"

⁴Then he turned to Jehoshaphat and asked, "Will you join me in battle to recover Ramoth-gilead?"

Jehoshaphat replied to the king of Israel, "Why, of course! You and I are as one. My troops are your troops, and my horses are your horses." ⁵Then Jehoshaphat added, "But first let's find out what the LORD says."

⁶So the king of Israel summoned the prophets, about 400 of them, and asked them, "Should I go to war against Ramoth-gilead, or should I hold back?"

They all replied, "Yes, go right ahead! The Lord will give the king victory."

⁷But Jehoshaphat asked, "Is there not also a prophet of the LORD here? We should ask him the same question."

⁸The king of Israel replied to Jehoshaphat, "There is one more man who could consult the LORD for us, but I hate him. He never prophesies anything but trouble for me! His name is Micaiah son of Imlah."

Jehoshaphat replied, "That's not the way a king should talk! Let's hear what he has to say."

⁹So the king of Israel called one of his officials and said, "Quick! Bring Micaiah son of Imlah."

¹⁰King Ahab of Israel and King Jehoshaphat of Judah, dressed in their royal robes, were sitting on thrones at the threshing floor near the gate of Samaria. All of Ahab's prophets were prophesying there in front of them. ¹¹One of them, Zedekiah son of Kenaanah, made some iron horns and proclaimed, "This is what the LORD says: With these horns you will gore the Arameans to death!"

¹²All the other prophets agreed. "Yes," they said, "go up to Ramoth-gilead and be victorious, for the LORD will give the king victory!"

¹³Meanwhile, the messenger who went to get Micaiah said to him, "Look, all the prophets are promising victory for the king. Be sure that you agree with them and promise success."

¹⁴But Micaiah replied, "As surely as the LORD lives, I will say only what the LORD tells me to say."

¹⁵When Micaiah arrived before the king, Ahab asked him, "Micaiah, should we go to war against Ramoth-gilead, or should we hold back?"

Micaiah replied sarcastically, "Yes, go up and be victorious, for the LORD will give the king victory!"

¹⁶But the king replied sharply, "How many times must I demand that you speak only the truth to me when you speak for the LORD?"

¹⁷Then Micaiah told him, "In a vision I saw all Israel scattered on the mountains, like sheep without a shepherd. And the LORD said, 'Their master has been killed.* Send them home in peace.'"

¹⁸"Didn't I tell you?" the king of Israel exclaimed to Jehoshaphat. "He never prophesies anything but trouble for me."

¹⁹Then Micaiah continued, "Listen to what the LORD says! I saw the LORD sitting on his throne with all the armies of heaven around him, on his right and on his left. ²⁰And the LORD said, 'Who can entice Ahab to go into battle against Ramoth-gilead so he can be killed?'

"There were many suggestions, ²¹and finally a spirit approached the LORD and said, 'I can do it!'

²²"'How will you do this?' the LORD asked.

"And the spirit replied, 'I will go out and inspire all of Ahab's prophets to speak lies.'

"'You will succeed,' said the LORD. 'Go ahead and do it.'

²³"So you see, the LORD has put a lying spirit in the mouths of all your prophets. For the LORD has pronounced your doom."

²⁴Then Zedekiah son of Kenaanah walked up to Micaiah and slapped him across the face. "Since when did the Spirit of the LORD leave me to speak to you?" he demanded.

²⁵And Micaiah replied, "You will find out soon enough when you are trying to hide in some secret room!"

²⁶"Arrest him!" the king of Israel ordered. "Take him back to Amon, the governor of the city, and to my son Joash. ²⁷Give them this order from the king: 'Put this man in prison, and feed him nothing but bread and water until I return safely from the battle!'"

²⁸But Micaiah replied, "If you return safely, it will mean that the LORD has not spoken through me!" Then he added to those standing around, "Everyone mark my words!"

²⁹So King Ahab of Israel and King Jehoshaphat of Judah led their armies against Ramoth-gilead. ³⁰The king of Israel said to Jehoshaphat, "As we go into battle, I will disguise myself so no one will recognize me, but you wear

your royal robes." So the king of Israel disguised himself, and they went into battle.

³¹Meanwhile, the king of Aram had issued these orders to his thirty-two chariot commanders: "Attack only the king of Israel. Don't bother with anyone else!" ³²So when the Aramean chariot commanders saw Jehoshaphat in his royal robes, they went after him. "There is the king of Israel!" they shouted. But when Jehoshaphat called out, ³³the chariot commanders realized he was not the king of Israel, and they stopped chasing him.

³⁴An Aramean soldier, however, randomly shot an arrow at the Israelite troops and hit the king of Israel between the joints of his armor. "Turn the horses* and get me out of here!" Ahab groaned to the driver of his chariot. "I'm badly wounded!"

³⁵The battle raged all that day, and the king remained propped up in his chariot facing the Arameans. The blood from his wound ran down to the floor of his chariot, and as evening arrived he died. ³⁶Just as the sun was setting, the cry ran through his troops: "We're done for! Run for your lives!"

³⁷So the king died, and his body was taken to Samaria and buried there. ³⁸Then his chariot was washed beside the pool of Samaria, and dogs came and licked his blood at the place where the prostitutes bathed,* just as the LORD had promised.

³⁹The rest of the events in Ahab's reign and everything he did, including the story of the ivory palace and the towns he built, are recorded in *The Book of the History of the Kings of Israel.* ⁴⁰So Ahab died, and his son Ahaziah became the next king.

⁴¹Jehoshaphat son of Asa began to rule over Judah in the fourth year of King Ahab's reign in Israel. ⁴²Jehoshaphat was thirty-five years old when he became king, and he reigned in Jerusalem twenty-five years. His mother was Azubah, the daughter of Shilhi.

⁴³Jehoshaphat was a good king, following the example of his father, Asa. He did what was pleasing in the LORD's sight. *During his reign, however, he failed to remove all the pagan shrines, and the people still offered sacrifices and burned incense there. ⁴⁴Jehoshaphat also made peace with the king of Israel.

⁴⁵The rest of the events in Jehoshaphat's reign, the extent of his power, and the wars he waged are recorded in *The Book of the History of the Kings of Judah.* ⁴⁶He banished from the land the rest of the male and female shrine prostitutes, who still continued their practices from the days of his father, Asa.

⁴⁷(There was no king in Edom at that time, only a deputy.)

⁴⁸Jehoshaphat also built a fleet of trading ships* to sail to Ophir for gold. But the ships never set sail, for they met with disaster in their home port of Ezion-geber. ⁴⁹At one time Ahaziah son of Ahab had proposed to Jehoshaphat, "Let my men sail with your men in the ships." But Jehoshaphat refused the request.

⁵⁰When Jehoshaphat died, he was buried with his ancestors in the City of David. Then his son Jehoram became the next king.

⁵¹Ahaziah son of Ahab began to rule over Israel in the seventeenth year of King Jehoshaphat's reign in Judah. He reigned in Samaria two years. ⁵²But he did what was evil in the LORD's sight, following the example of his father and mother and the example of Jeroboam son of Nebat, who had led Israel to sin. ⁵³He served Baal and worshiped him, provoking the anger of the LORD, the God of Israel, just as his father had done.

22:17 Hebrew *These people have no master.*
22:34 Hebrew *Turn your hand.*   **22:38** Or *his blood, and the prostitutes bathed [in it];* or *his blood, and they washed his armor.*   **22:43** Verses 22:43b-53 are numbered 22:44-54 in Hebrew text.   **22:48** Hebrew *fleet of ships of Tarshish.*

ACTS 13:16-41

So Paul stood, lifted his hand to quiet them [those in the synagogue], and started speaking. "Men of Israel," he said, "and you God-fearing Gentiles, listen to me.

[17]"The God of this nation of Israel chose our ancestors and made them multiply and grow strong during their stay in Egypt. Then with a powerful arm he led them out of their slavery. [18]He put up with them* through forty years of wandering in the wilderness. [19]Then he destroyed seven nations in Canaan and gave their land to Israel as an inheritance. [20]All this took about 450 years.

"After that, God gave them judges to rule until the time of Samuel the prophet. [21]Then the people begged for a king, and God gave them Saul son of Kish, a man of the tribe of Benjamin, who reigned for forty years. [22]But God removed Saul and replaced him with David, a man about whom God said, 'I have found David son of Jesse, a man after my own heart. He will do everything I want him to do.'*

[23]"And it is one of King David's descendants, Jesus, who is God's promised Savior of Israel! [24]Before he came, John the Baptist preached that all the people of Israel needed to repent of their sins and turn to God and be baptized. [25]As John was finishing his ministry he asked, 'Do you think I am the Messiah? No, I am not! But he is coming soon—and I'm not even worthy to be his slave and untie the sandals on his feet.'

[26]"Brothers—you sons of Abraham, and also you God-fearing Gentiles—this message of salvation has been sent to us! [27]The people in Jerusalem and their leaders did not recognize Jesus as the one the prophets had spoken about. Instead, they condemned him, and in doing this they fulfilled the prophets' words that are read every Sabbath. [28]They found no legal reason to execute him, but they asked Pilate to have him killed anyway.

[29]"When they had done all that the prophecies said about him, they took him down from the cross* and placed him in a tomb. [30]But God raised him from the dead! [31]And over a period of many days he appeared to those who had gone with him from Galilee to Jerusalem. They are now his witnesses to the people of Israel.

[32]"And now we are here to bring you this Good News. The promise was made to our ancestors, [33]and God has now fulfilled it for us, their descendants, by raising Jesus. This is what the second psalm says about Jesus:

'You are my Son.
    Today I have become
        your Father.*'

[34]For God had promised to raise him from the dead, not leaving him to rot in the grave. He said, 'I will give you the sacred blessings I promised to David.'* [35]Another psalm explains it more fully: 'You will not allow your Holy One to rot in the grave.'* [36]This is not a reference to David, for after David had done the will of God in his own generation, he died and was buried with his ancestors, and his body decayed. [37]No, it was a reference to someone else—someone whom God raised and whose body did not decay.

[38]*"Brothers, listen! We are here to proclaim that through this man Jesus there is forgiveness for your sins. [39]Everyone who believes in him is declared right with God—something the law of Moses could never do. [40]Be careful! Don't let the prophets' words apply to you. For they said,

[41] 'Look, you mockers,
        be amazed and die!
    For I am doing something in your
        own day,
    something you wouldn't believe
        even if someone told you
        about it.*'"

13:18 Some manuscripts read *He cared for them;* compare Deut 1:31.   13:22 1 Sam 13:14.   13:29 Greek *from the tree.*   13:33 Or *Today I reveal you as my Son.* Ps 2:7.   13:34 Isa 55:3.   13:35 Ps 16:10.   13:38 English translations divide verses 38 and 39 in various ways.   13:41 Hab 1:5 (Greek version).

PSALM 138:1-8
A psalm of David.

[1] I give you thanks, O LORD, with
    all my heart;

I will sing your praises before
the gods.
² I bow before your holy Temple
as I worship.
I praise your name for your
unfailing love and
faithfulness;
for your promises are backed
by all the honor of your name.
³ As soon as I pray, you answer me;
you encourage me by giving me
strength.

⁴ Every king in all the earth will
thank you, LORD,
for all of them will hear your
words.
⁵ Yes, they will sing about the
LORD's ways,
for the glory of the LORD is
very great.
⁶ Though the LORD is great, he cares
for the humble,
but he keeps his distance from
the proud.

⁷ Though I am surrounded by
troubles,
you will protect me from the
anger of my enemies.
You reach out your hand,
and the power of your right
hand saves me.
⁸ The LORD will work out his plans
for my life—
for your faithful love, O LORD,
endures forever.
Don't abandon me, for you
made me.

PROVERBS 17:17-18

A friend is always loyal, and a brother is
born to help in time of need. □ It's poor
judgment to guarantee another person's
debt or put up security for a friend.

JUNE 21

2 KINGS 1:1–2:25

After King Ahab's death, the land of
Moab rebelled against Israel.

²One day Israel's new king, Ahaziah,
fell through the latticework of an upper
room at his palace in Samaria and was
seriously injured. So he sent messengers to the temple of Baal-zebub, the
god of Ekron, to ask whether he would
recover.

³But the angel of the LORD told Elijah,
who was from Tishbe, "Go and confront
the messengers of the king of Samaria
and ask them, 'Is there no God in Israel?
Why are you going to Baal-zebub, the god
of Ekron, to ask whether the king will recover? ⁴Now, therefore, this is what the
LORD says: You will never leave the bed
you are lying on; you will surely die.'" So
Elijah went to deliver the message.

⁵When the messengers returned to
the king, he asked them, "Why have you
returned so soon?"

⁶They replied, "A man came up to us
and told us to go back to the king and
give him this message. 'This is what the
LORD says: Is there no God in Israel? Why
are you sending men to Baal-zebub, the
god of Ekron, to ask whether you will recover? Therefore, because you have
done this, you will never leave the bed
you are lying on; you will surely die.'"

⁷"What sort of man was he?" the king
demanded. "What did he look like?"

⁸They replied, "He was a hairy man,*
and he wore a leather belt around his
waist."

"Elijah from Tishbe!" the king exclaimed.

⁹Then he sent an army captain with
fifty soldiers to arrest him. They found
him sitting on top of a hill. The captain
said to him, "Man of God, the king has
commanded you to come down with us."

¹⁰But Elijah replied to the captain, "If
I am a man of God, let fire come down

from heaven and destroy you and your fifty men!" Then fire fell from heaven and killed them all.

11So the king sent another captain with fifty men. The captain said to him, "Man of God, the king demands that you come down at once."

12Elijah replied, "If I am a man of God, let fire come down from heaven and destroy you and your fifty men!" And again the fire of God fell from heaven and killed them all.

13Once more the king sent a third captain with fifty men. But this time the captain went up the hill and fell to his knees before Elijah. He pleaded with him, "O man of God, please spare my life and the lives of these, your fifty servants. 14See how the fire from heaven came down and destroyed the first two groups. But now please spare my life!"

15Then the angel of the LORD said to Elijah, "Go down with him, and don't be afraid of him." So Elijah got up and went with him to the king.

16And Elijah said to the king, "This is what the LORD says: Why did you send messengers to Baal-zebub, the god of Ekron, to ask whether you will recover? Is there no God in Israel to answer your question? Therefore, because you have done this, you will never leave the bed you are lying on; you will surely die."

17So Ahaziah died, just as the LORD had promised through Elijah. Since Ahaziah did not have a son to succeed him, his brother Joram* became the next king. This took place in the second year of the reign of Jehoram son of Jehoshaphat, king of Judah.

18The rest of the events in Ahaziah's reign are recorded in *The Book of the History of the Kings of Israel.*

2:1WHEN the LORD was about to take Elijah up to heaven in a whirlwind, Elijah and Elisha were traveling from Gilgal. 2And Elijah said to Elisha, "Stay here, for the LORD has told me to go to Bethel."

But Elisha replied, "As surely as the LORD lives and you yourself live, I will never leave you!" So they went down together to Bethel.

3The group of prophets from Bethel came to Elisha and asked him, "Did you know that the LORD is going to take your master away from you today?"

"Of course I know," Elisha answered. "But be quiet about it."

4Then Elijah said to Elisha, "Stay here, for the LORD has told me to go to Jericho."

But Elisha replied again, "As surely as the LORD lives and you yourself live, I will never leave you." So they went on together to Jericho.

5Then the group of prophets from Jericho came to Elisha and asked him, "Did you know that the LORD is going to take your master away from you today?"

"Of course I know," Elisha answered. "But be quiet about it."

6Then Elijah said to Elisha, "Stay here, for the LORD has told me to go to the Jordan River."

But again Elisha replied, "As surely as the LORD lives and you yourself live, I will never leave you." So they went on together.

7Fifty men from the group of prophets also went and watched from a distance as Elijah and Elisha stopped beside the Jordan River. 8Then Elijah folded his cloak together and struck the water with it. The river divided, and the two of them went across on dry ground!

9When they came to the other side, Elijah said to Elisha, "Tell me what I can do for you before I am taken away."

And Elisha replied, "Please let me inherit a double share of your spirit and become your successor."

10"You have asked a difficult thing," Elijah replied. "If you see me when I am taken from you, then you will get your request. But if not, then you won't."

11As they were walking along and talking, suddenly a chariot of fire appeared, drawn by horses of fire. It drove between the two men, separating them, and Elijah was carried by a whirlwind into heaven. 12Elisha saw it and cried out, "My father! My father! I see the chariots and charioteers of Israel!" And as they disappeared from sight, Elisha tore his clothes in distress.

13Elisha picked up Elijah's cloak, which had fallen when he was taken up. Then Elisha returned to the bank of the Jordan River. 14He struck the water with Elijah's cloak and cried out, "Where is the LORD, the God of Elijah?" Then the river divided, and Elisha went across.

15When the group of prophets from Jericho saw from a distance what happened, they exclaimed, "Elijah's spirit rests upon Elisha!" And they went to meet him and bowed to the ground before him. 16"Sir," they said, "just say the word and fifty of our strongest men will search the wilderness for your master. Perhaps the Spirit of the LORD has left him on some mountain or in some valley."

"No," Elisha said, "don't send them." 17But they kept urging him until they shamed him into agreeing, and he finally said, "All right, send them." So fifty men searched for three days but did not find Elijah. 18Elisha was still at Jericho when they returned. "Didn't I tell you not to go?" he asked.

19One day the leaders of the town of Jericho visited Elisha. "We have a problem, my lord," they told him. "This town is located in pleasant surroundings, as you can see. But the water is bad, and the land is unproductive."

20Elisha said, "Bring me a new bowl with salt in it." So they brought it to him. 21Then he went out to the spring that supplied the town with water and threw the salt into it. And he said, "This is what the LORD says: I have purified this water. It will no longer cause death or infertility.*" 22And the water has remained pure ever since, just as Elisha said.

23Elisha left Jericho and went up to Bethel. As he was walking along the road, a group of boys from the town began mocking and making fun of him. "Go away, baldy!" they chanted. "Go away, baldy!" 24Elisha turned around and looked at them, and he cursed them in the name of the LORD. Then two bears came out of the woods and mauled forty-two of them. 25From there Elisha went to Mount Carmel and finally returned to Samaria.

1:8 Or He was wearing clothing made of hair.
1:17 Hebrew Jehoram, a variant spelling of Joram.
2:21 Or or make the land unproductive; Hebrew reads or barrenness.

ACTS 13:42–14:7

As Paul and Barnabas left the synagogue that day, the people begged them to speak about these things again the next week. 43Many Jews and devout converts to Judaism followed Paul and Barnabas, and the two men urged them to continue to rely on the grace of God.

44The following week almost the entire city turned out to hear them preach the word of the Lord. 45But when some of the Jews saw the crowds, they were jealous; so they slandered Paul and argued against whatever he said.

46Then Paul and Barnabas spoke out boldly and declared, "It was necessary that we first preach the word of God to you Jews. But since you have rejected it and judged yourselves unworthy of eternal life, we will offer it to the Gentiles. 47For the Lord gave us this command when he said,

'I have made you a light to
     the Gentiles,
  to bring salvation to the
     farthest corners of
     the earth.'*"

48When the Gentiles heard this, they were very glad and thanked the Lord for his message; and all who were chosen for eternal life became believers. 49So the Lord's message spread throughout that region.

50Then the Jews stirred up the influential religious women and the leaders of the city, and they incited a mob against Paul and Barnabas and ran them out of town. 51So they shook the dust from their feet as a sign of rejection and went to the town of Iconium. 52And the believers* were filled with joy and with the Holy Spirit.

14:1THE same thing happened in Iconium.* Paul and Barnabas went to the Jewish synagogue and preached with such power that a great number of both Jews and Greeks became believers. 2Some of the Jews, however, spurned God's message and poisoned the minds of the Gentiles against Paul and Barnabas. 3But the apostles stayed there a long time, preaching boldly about the grace of the Lord. And the Lord proved their message was true by giving them power to do miraculous signs and wonders. 4But the people of the town were divided in their opinion about them. Some sided with the Jews, and some with the apostles.

5Then a mob of Gentiles and Jews, along with their leaders, decided to attack and stone them. 6When the apostles learned of it, they fled to the region of Lycaonia—to the towns of Lystra and Derbe and the surrounding area. 7And there they preached the Good News.

13:47 Isa 49:6.   13:52 Greek *the disciples.*
14:1 *Iconium,* as well as *Lystra* and *Derbe* (14:6), were towns in what is now Turkey.

PSALM 139:1-24
For the choir director: A psalm of David.

1 ⬤ LORD, you have examined my heart
    and know everything about me.
2 You know when I sit down
    or stand up.
  You know my thoughts even
    when I'm far away.
3 You see me when I travel
    and when I rest at home.
  You know everything I do.
4 You know what I am going to say
    even before I say it, LORD.
5 You go before me and follow me.
    You place your hand of blessing
    on my head.
6 Such knowledge is too wonderful
    for me,
    too great for me to understand!

7 I can never escape from your Spirit!
    I can never get away from your
    presence!
8 If I go up to heaven, you are there;

if I go down to the grave,* you
    are there.
9 If I ride the wings of the morning,
    if I dwell by the farthest oceans,
10 even there your hand will guide me,
    and your strength will support
    me.
11 I could ask the darkness to hide me
    and the light around me to
    become night—
12 but even in darkness I cannot
    hide from you.
  To you the night shines as bright
    as day.
  Darkness and light are the same
    to you.

13 **You made all the delicate, inner
    parts of my body
    and knit me together in my
    mother's womb.**
14 **Thank you for making me so
    wonderfully complex!
    Your workmanship is
    marvelous—how well
    I know it.**
15 You watched me as I was being
    formed in utter seclusion,
    as I was woven together in the
    dark of the womb.
16 You saw me before I was born.
    Every day of my life was recorded
    in your book.
  Every moment was laid out
    before a single day had passed.

17 How precious are your thoughts
    about me,* O God.
    They cannot be numbered!
18 I can't even count them;
    they outnumber the grains
    of sand!
  And when I wake up,
    you are still with me!

19 O God, if only you would destroy
    the wicked!
    Get out of my life, you murderers!
20 They blaspheme you;
    your enemies misuse your
    name.
21 O LORD, shouldn't I hate those who
    hate you?

Shouldn't I despise those who
oppose you?
²² Yes, I hate them with total hatred,
for your enemies are my enemies.

²³ Search me, O God, and know
my heart;
test me and know my anxious
thoughts.
²⁴ Point out anything in me that
offends you,
and lead me along the path
of everlasting life.

139:8 Hebrew *to Sheol.*   **139:17** Or *How precious to me
are your thoughts.*

PROVERBS 17:19-21

Anyone who loves to quarrel loves sin;
anyone who trusts in high walls invites
disaster. ☐ The crooked heart will not
prosper; the lying tongue tumbles into
trouble. ☐ It is painful to be the parent
of a fool; there is no joy for the father of
a rebel.

JUNE
22

2 KINGS 3:1-4:17

Ahab's son Joram* began to rule over
Israel in the eighteenth year of King Jehoshaphat's reign in Judah. He reigned
in Samaria twelve years. ²He did what
was evil in the LORD's sight, but not to
the same extent as his father and
mother. He at least tore down the sacred pillar of Baal that his father had set
up. ³Nevertheless, he continued in the
sins that Jeroboam son of Nebat had
committed and led the people of Israel
to commit.
⁴King Mesha of Moab was a sheep
breeder. He used to pay the king of Israel an annual tribute of 100,000 lambs
and the wool of 100,000 rams. ⁵But after Ahab's death, the king of Moab rebelled against the king of Israel. ⁶So

King Joram promptly mustered the
army of Israel and marched from Samaria. ⁷On the way, he sent this message to King Jehoshaphat of Judah: "The
king of Moab has rebelled against me.
Will you join me in battle against him?"
And Jehoshaphat replied, "Why, of
course! You and I are as one. My troops
are your troops, and my horses are your
horses." ⁸Then Jehoshaphat asked,
"What route will we take?"
"We will attack from the wilderness
of Edom," Joram replied.
⁹The king of Edom and his troops
joined them, and all three armies traveled along a roundabout route through
the wilderness for seven days. But there
was no water for the men or their animals.
¹⁰"What should we do?" the king of
Israel cried out. "The LORD has brought
the three of us here to let the king of
Moab defeat us."
¹¹But King Jehoshaphat of Judah
asked, "Is there no prophet of the LORD
with us? If there is, we can ask the LORD
what to do through him."
One of King Joram's officers replied,
"Elisha son of Shaphat is here. He used
to be Elijah's personal assistant.*"
¹²Jehoshaphat said, "Yes, the LORD
speaks through him." So the kings of Israel, Judah, and Edom went to consult
with Elisha.
¹³"Why are you coming to me?"* Elisha asked the king of Israel. "Go to the
pagan prophets of your father and
mother!"
But King Joram of Israel said, "No! For
it was the LORD who called us three
kings here—only to be defeated by the
king of Moab!"
¹⁴Elisha replied, "As surely as the
LORD Almighty lives, whom I serve, I
wouldn't even bother with you except
for my respect for King Jehoshaphat of
Judah. ¹⁵Now bring me someone who
can play the harp."
While the harp was being played, the
power* of the LORD came upon Elisha,
¹⁶and he said, "This is what the LORD
says: This dry valley will be filled with

pools of water! ¹⁷You will see neither wind nor rain, says the LORD, but this valley will be filled with water. You will have plenty for yourselves and your cattle and other animals. ¹⁸But this is only a simple thing for the LORD, for he will make you victorious over the army of Moab! ¹⁹You will conquer the best of their towns, even the fortified ones. You will cut down all their good trees, stop up all their springs, and ruin all their good land with stones."

²⁰The next day at about the time when the morning sacrifice was offered, water suddenly appeared! It was flowing from the direction of Edom, and soon there was water everywhere.

²¹Meanwhile, when the people of Moab heard about the three armies marching against them, they mobilized every man who was old enough to strap on a sword, and they stationed themselves along their border. ²²But when they got up the next morning, the sun was shining across the water, making it appear red to the Moabites—like blood. ²³"It's blood!" the Moabites exclaimed. "The three armies must have attacked and killed each other! Let's go, men of Moab, and collect the plunder!"

²⁴But when the Moabites arrived at the Israelite camp, the army of Israel rushed out and attacked them until they turned and ran. The army of Israel chased them into the land of Moab, destroying everything as they went.* ²⁵They destroyed the towns, covered their good land with stones, stopped up all the springs, and cut down all the good trees. Finally, only Kir-hareseth and its stone walls were left, but men with slings surrounded and attacked it.

²⁶When the king of Moab saw that he was losing the battle, he led 700 of his swordsmen in a desperate attempt to break through the enemy lines near the king of Edom, but they failed. ²⁷Then the king of Moab took his oldest son, who would have been the next king, and sacrificed him as a burnt offering on the wall. So there was great anger

against Israel,* and the Israelites withdrew and returned to their own land.

⁴:¹ONE day the widow of a member of the group of prophets came to Elisha and cried out, "My husband who served you is dead, and you know how he feared the LORD. But now a creditor has come, threatening to take my two sons as slaves."

²"What can I do to help you?" Elisha asked. "Tell me, what do you have in the house?"

"Nothing at all, except a flask of olive oil," she replied.

³And Elisha said, "Borrow as many empty jars as you can from your friends and neighbors. ⁴Then go into your house with your sons and shut the door behind you. Pour olive oil from your flask into the jars, setting each one aside when it is filled."

⁵So she did as she was told. Her sons kept bringing jars to her, and she filled one after another. ⁶Soon every container was full to the brim!

"Bring me another jar," she said to one of her sons.

"There aren't any more!" he told her. And then the olive oil stopped flowing.

⁷When she told the man of God what had happened, he said to her, "Now sell the olive oil and pay your debts, and you and your sons can live on what is left over."

⁸One day Elisha went to the town of Shunem. A wealthy woman lived there, and she urged him to come to her home for a meal. After that, whenever he passed that way, he would stop there for something to eat.

⁹She said to her husband, "I am sure this man who stops in from time to time is a holy man of God. ¹⁰Let's build a small room for him on the roof and furnish it with a bed, a table, a chair, and a lamp. Then he will have a place to stay whenever he comes by."

¹¹One day Elisha returned to Shunem, and he went up to this upper room to rest. ¹²He said to his servant Gehazi, "Tell the woman from Shunem I want to

speak to her." When she appeared, [13]Elisha said to Gehazi, "Tell her, 'We appreciate the kind concern you have shown us. What can we do for you? Can we put in a good word for you to the king or to the commander of the army?'"

"No," she replied, "my family takes good care of me."

[14]Later Elisha asked Gehazi, "What can we do for her?"

Gehazi replied, "She doesn't have a son, and her husband is an old man."

[15]"Call her back again," Elisha told him. When the woman returned, Elisha said to her as she stood in the doorway, [16]"Next year at this time you will be holding a son in your arms!"

"No, my lord!" she cried. "O man of God, don't deceive me and get my hopes up like that."

[17]But sure enough, the woman soon became pregnant. And at that time the following year she had a son, just as Elisha had said.

3:1 Hebrew *Jehoram,* a variant spelling of Joram; also in 3:6.
3:11 Hebrew *He used to pour water on the hands of Elijah.*
3:13 Hebrew *What is there in common between you and me?*   3:15 Hebrew *the hand.*   3:24 The meaning of the Hebrew is uncertain.   3:27 Or *So Israel's anger was great.* The meaning of the Hebrew is uncertain.

ACTS 14:8-28

While they were at Lystra, Paul and Barnabas came upon a man with crippled feet. He had been that way from birth, so he had never walked. He was sitting [9]and listening as Paul preached. Looking straight at him, Paul realized he had faith to be healed. [10]So Paul called to him in a loud voice, "Stand up!" And the man jumped to his feet and started walking.

[11]When the crowd saw what Paul had done, they shouted in their local dialect, "These men are gods in human form!" [12]They decided that Barnabas was the Greek god Zeus and that Paul was Hermes, since he was the chief speaker. [13]Now the temple of Zeus was located just outside the town. So the priest of the temple and the crowd brought bulls and wreaths of flowers to the town gates, and they prepared to offer sacrifices to the apostles.

[14]But when Barnabas and Paul heard what was happening, they tore their clothing in dismay and ran out among the people, shouting, [15]"Friends,* why are you doing this? We are merely human beings—just like you! We have come to bring you the Good News that you should turn from these worthless things and turn to the living God, who made heaven and earth, the sea, and everything in them. [16]In the past he permitted all the nations to go their own ways, [17]but he never left them without evidence of himself and his goodness. For instance, he sends you rain and good crops and gives you food and joyful hearts." [18]But even with these words, Paul and Barnabas could scarcely restrain the people from sacrificing to them.

[19]Then some Jews arrived from Antioch and Iconium and won the crowds to their side. They stoned Paul and dragged him out of town, thinking he was dead. [20]But as the believers* gathered around him, he got up and went back into the town. The next day he left with Barnabas for Derbe.

[21]After preaching the Good News in Derbe and making many disciples, Paul and Barnabas returned to Lystra, Iconium, and Antioch of Pisidia, [22]where they strengthened the believers. They encouraged them to continue in the faith, reminding them that we must suffer many hardships to enter the Kingdom of God. [23]Paul and Barnabas also appointed elders in every church. With prayer and fasting, they turned the elders over to the care of the Lord, in whom they had put their trust. [24]Then they traveled back through Pisidia to Pamphylia. [25]They preached the word in Perga, then went down to Attalia.

[26]Finally, they returned by ship to Antioch of Syria, where their journey had begun. The believers there had entrusted them to the grace of God to do the work they had now completed. [27]Upon arriving in Antioch, they called the church together and reported everything God had done through them and how he had opened the door of faith to the Gentiles,

too. ²⁸And they stayed there with the believers for a long time.

14:15 Greek *Men.*   **14:20** Greek *disciples;* also in 14:22, 28.

PSALM 140:1-13
For the choir director: A psalm of David.

¹ **O** LORD, rescue me from evil people.
Protect me from those who
are violent,
² those who plot evil in their hearts
and stir up trouble all day long.
³ Their tongues sting like a snake;
the venom of a viper drips from
their lips.   *Interlude*

⁴ O LORD, keep me out of the hands
of the wicked.
Protect me from those who
are violent,
for they are plotting against me.
⁵ The proud have set a trap to
catch me;
they have stretched out a net;
they have placed traps all along
the way.   *Interlude*

⁶ I said to the LORD, "You are my God!"
Listen, O LORD, to my cries
for mercy!
⁷ O Sovereign LORD, the strong one
who rescued me,
you protected me on the day
of battle.
⁸ LORD, do not let evil people have
their way.
Do not let their evil schemes
succeed,
or they will become proud.
                    Interlude

⁹ Let my enemies be destroyed
by the very evil they have
planned for me.
¹⁰ Let burning coals fall down on
their heads.
Let them be thrown into the fire
or into watery pits from which
they can't escape.
¹¹ Don't let liars prosper here in our
land.
Cause great disasters to fall
on the violent.

¹² But I know the LORD will help
those they persecute;
he will give justice to the poor.
¹³ Surely righteous people are
praising your name;
the godly will live in your
presence.

PROVERBS 17:22
A cheerful heart is good medicine, but a broken spirit saps a person's strength.

JUNE 23

2 KINGS 4:18–5:27
One day when her child was older, he went out to help his father, who was working with the harvesters. ¹⁹Suddenly he cried out, "My head hurts! My head hurts!"

His father said to one of the servants, "Carry him home to his mother."

²⁰So the servant took him home, and his mother held him on her lap. But around noontime he died. ²¹She carried him up and laid him on the bed of the man of God, then shut the door and left him there. ²²She sent a message to her husband: "Send one of the servants and a donkey so that I can hurry to the man of God and come right back."

²³"Why go today?" he asked. "It is neither a new moon festival nor a Sabbath."

But she said, "It will be all right."

²⁴So she saddled the donkey and said to the servant, "Hurry! Don't slow down unless I tell you to."

²⁵As she approached the man of God at Mount Carmel, Elisha saw her in the distance. He said to Gehazi, "Look, the woman from Shunem is coming. ²⁶Run out to meet her and ask her, 'Is everything all right with you, your husband, and your child?'"

"Yes," the woman told Gehazi, "everything is fine."

27 But when she came to the man of God at the mountain, she fell to the ground before him and caught hold of his feet. Gehazi began to push her away, but the man of God said, "Leave her alone. She is deeply troubled, but the LORD has not told me what it is."

28 Then she said, "Did I ask you for a son, my lord? And didn't I say, 'Don't deceive me and get my hopes up'?"

29 Then Elisha said to Gehazi, "Get ready to travel*; take my staff and go! Don't talk to anyone along the way. Go quickly and lay the staff on the child's face."

30 But the boy's mother said, "As surely as the LORD lives and you yourself live, I won't go home unless you go with me." So Elisha returned with her.

31 Gehazi hurried on ahead and laid the staff on the child's face, but nothing happened. There was no sign of life. He returned to meet Elisha and told him, "The child is still dead."

32 When Elisha arrived, the child was indeed dead, lying there on the prophet's bed. 33 He went in alone and shut the door behind him and prayed to the LORD. 34 Then he lay down on the child's body, placing his mouth on the child's mouth, his eyes on the child's eyes, and his hands on the child's hands. And as he stretched out on him, the child's body began to grow warm again! 35 Elisha got up, walked back and forth across the room once, and then stretched himself out again on the child. This time the boy sneezed seven times and opened his eyes!

36 Then Elisha summoned Gehazi. "Call the child's mother!" he said. And when she came in, Elisha said, "Here, take your son!" 37 She fell at his feet and bowed before him, overwhelmed with gratitude. Then she took her son in her arms and carried him downstairs.

38 Elisha now returned to Gilgal, and there was a famine in the land. One day as the group of prophets was seated before him, he said to his servant, "Put a large pot on the fire, and make some stew for the rest of the group."

39 One of the young men went out into the field to gather herbs and came back with a pocketful of wild gourds. He shredded them and put them into the pot without realizing they were poisonous. 40 Some of the stew was served to the men. But after they had eaten a bite or two they cried out, "Man of God, there's poison in this stew!" So they would not eat it.

41 Elisha said, "Bring me some flour." Then he threw it into the pot and said, "Now it's all right; go ahead and eat." And then it did not harm them.

42 One day a man from Baal-shalishah brought the man of God a sack of fresh grain and twenty loaves of barley bread made from the first grain of his harvest. Elisha said, "Give it to the people so they can eat."

43 "What?" his servant exclaimed. "Feed a hundred people with only this?"

But Elisha repeated, "Give it to the people so they can eat, for this is what the LORD says: Everyone will eat, and there will even be some left over!" 44 And when they gave it to the people, there was plenty for all and some left over, just as the LORD had promised.

5:1 THE king of Aram had great admiration for Naaman, the commander of his army, because through him the LORD had given Aram great victories. But though Naaman was a mighty warrior, he suffered from leprosy.*

2 At this time Aramean raiders had invaded the land of Israel, and among their captives was a young girl who had been given to Naaman's wife as a maid. 3 One day the girl said to her mistress, "I wish my master would go to see the prophet in Samaria. He would heal him of his leprosy."

4 So Naaman told the king what the young girl from Israel had said. 5 "Go and visit the prophet," the king of Aram told him. "I will send a letter of introduction for you to take to the king of Israel." So Naaman started out, carrying as gifts

750 pounds of silver, 150 pounds of gold,* and ten sets of clothing. ⁶The letter to the king of Israel said: "With this letter I present my servant Naaman. I want you to heal him of his leprosy."

⁷When the king of Israel read the letter, he tore his clothes in dismay and said, "This man sends me a leper to heal! Am I God, that I can give life and take it away? I can see that he's just trying to pick a fight with me."

⁸But when Elisha, the man of God, heard that the king of Israel had torn his clothes in dismay, he sent this message to him: "Why are you so upset? Send Naaman to me, and he will learn that there is a true prophet here in Israel."

⁹So Naaman went with his horses and chariots and waited at the door of Elisha's house. ¹⁰But Elisha sent a messenger out to him with this message: "Go and wash yourself seven times in the Jordan River. Then your skin will be restored, and you will be healed of your leprosy."

¹¹But Naaman became angry and stalked away. "I thought he would certainly come out to meet me!" he said. "I expected him to wave his hand over the leprosy and call on the name of the LORD his God and heal me! ¹²Aren't the rivers of Damascus, the Abana and the Pharpar, better than any of the rivers of Israel? Why shouldn't I wash in them and be healed?" So Naaman turned and went away in a rage.

¹³But his officers tried to reason with him and said, "Sir,* if the prophet had told you to do something very difficult, wouldn't you have done it? So you should certainly obey him when he says simply, 'Go and wash and be cured!'" ¹⁴So Naaman went down to the Jordan River and dipped himself seven times, as the man of God had instructed him. And his skin became as healthy as the skin of a young child's, and he was healed!

¹⁵Then Naaman and his entire party went back to find the man of God. They stood before him, and Naaman said, "Now I know that there is no God in all the world except in Israel. So please accept a gift from your servant."

¹⁶But Elisha replied, "As surely as the LORD lives, whom I serve, I will not accept any gifts." And though Naaman urged him to take the gift, Elisha refused.

¹⁷Then Naaman said, "All right, but please allow me to load two of my mules with earth from this place, and I will take it back home with me. From now on I will never again offer burnt offerings or sacrifices to any other god except the LORD. ¹⁸However, may the LORD pardon me in this one thing: When my master the king goes into the temple of the god Rimmon to worship there and leans on my arm, may the LORD pardon me when I bow, too."

¹⁹"Go in peace," Elisha said. So Naaman started home again.

²⁰But Gehazi, the servant of Elisha, the man of God, said to himself, "My master should not have let this Aramean get away without accepting any of his gifts. As surely as the LORD lives, I will chase after him and get something from him." ²¹So Gehazi set off after Naaman.

When Naaman saw Gehazi running after him, he climbed down from his chariot and went to meet him. "Is everything all right?" Naaman asked.

²²"Yes," Gehazi said, "but my master has sent me to tell you that two young prophets from the hill country of Ephraim have just arrived. He would like 75 pounds* of silver and two sets of clothing to give to them."

²³"By all means, take twice as much* silver," Naaman insisted. He gave him two sets of clothing, tied up the money in two bags, and sent two of his servants to carry the gifts for Gehazi. ²⁴But when they arrived at the citadel,* Gehazi took the gifts from the servants and sent the men back. Then he went and hid the gifts inside the house.

²⁵When he went in to his master, Elisha asked him, "Where have you been, Gehazi?"

"I haven't been anywhere," he replied.

[26] But Elisha asked him, "Don't you realize that I was there in spirit when Naaman stepped down from his chariot to meet you? Is this the time to receive money and clothing, olive groves and vineyards, sheep and cattle, and male and female servants? [27] Because you have done this, you and your descendants will suffer from Naaman's leprosy forever." When Gehazi left the room, he was covered with leprosy; his skin was white as snow.

4:29 Hebrew *Bind up your loins.* 5:1 Or *from a contagious skin disease.* The Hebrew word used here and throughout this passage can describe various skin diseases. 5:5 Hebrew *10 talents* [340 kilograms] *of silver, 6,000 shekels* [68 kilograms] *of gold.* 5:13 Hebrew *My father.* 5:22 Hebrew *1 talent* [34 kilograms]. 5:23 Hebrew *take 2 talents* [68 kilograms]. 5:24 Hebrew *the Ophel.*

ACTS 15:1-35

While Paul and Barnabas were at Antioch of Syria, some men from Judea arrived and began to teach the believers*: "Unless you are circumcised as required by the law of Moses, you cannot be saved." [2] Paul and Barnabas disagreed with them, arguing vehemently. Finally, the church decided to send Paul and Barnabas to Jerusalem, accompanied by some local believers, to talk to the apostles and elders about this question. [3] The church sent the delegates to Jerusalem, and they stopped along the way in Phoenicia and Samaria to visit the believers. They told them—much to everyone's joy—that the Gentiles, too, were being converted.

[4] When they arrived in Jerusalem, Barnabas and Paul were welcomed by the whole church, including the apostles and elders. They reported everything God had done through them. [5] But then some of the believers who belonged to the sect of the Pharisees stood up and insisted, "The Gentile converts must be circumcised and required to follow the law of Moses."

[6] So the apostles and elders met together to resolve this issue. [7] At the meeting, after a long discussion, Peter stood and addressed them as follows: "Brothers, you all know that God chose me from among you some time ago to preach to the Gentiles so that they could hear the Good News and believe. [8] God knows people's hearts, and he confirmed that he accepts Gentiles by giving them the Holy Spirit, just as he did to us. [9] He made no distinction between us and them, for he cleansed their hearts through faith. [10] So why are you now challenging God by burdening the Gentile believers* with a yoke that neither we nor our ancestors were able to bear? [11] We believe that we are all saved the same way, by the undeserved grace of the Lord Jesus."

[12] Everyone listened quietly as Barnabas and Paul told about the miraculous signs and wonders God had done through them among the Gentiles.

[13] When they had finished, James stood and said, "Brothers, listen to me. [14] Peter* has told you about the time God first visited the Gentiles to take from them a people for himself. [15] And this conversion of Gentiles is exactly what the prophets predicted. As it is written:

[16] 'Afterward I will return
        and restore the fallen house*
        of David.
   I will rebuild its ruins
        and restore it,
[17] so that the rest of humanity might
        seek the LORD,
        including the Gentiles—
        all those I have called to be mine.
   The LORD has spoken—
[18]   he who made these things
        known so long ago.'*

[19] "And so my judgment is that we should not make it difficult for the Gentiles who are turning to God. [20] Instead, we should write and tell them to abstain from eating food offered to idols, from sexual immorality, from eating the meat of strangled animals, and from consuming blood. [21] For these laws of Moses have been preached in Jewish synagogues in every city on every Sabbath for many generations."

[22] Then the apostles and elders together with the whole church in Jerusalem chose delegates, and they sent them

to Antioch of Syria with Paul and Barnabas to report on this decision. The men chosen were two of the church leaders*—Judas (also called Barsabbas) and Silas. 23 This is the letter they took with them:

"This letter is from the apostles and elders, your brothers in Jerusalem.

It is written to the Gentile believers in Antioch, Syria, and Cilicia. Greetings!

24"We understand that some men from here have troubled you and upset you with their teaching, but we did not send them! 25 So we decided, having come to complete agreement, to send you official representatives, along with our beloved Barnabas and Paul, 26 who have risked their lives for the name of our Lord Jesus Christ. 27 We are sending Judas and Silas to confirm what we have decided concerning your question.

28"For it seemed good to the Holy Spirit and to us to lay no greater burden on you than these few requirements: 29 You must abstain from eating food offered to idols, from consuming blood or the meat of strangled animals, and from sexual immorality. If you do this, you will do well. Farewell."

30The messengers went at once to Antioch, where they called a general meeting of the believers and delivered the letter. 31And there was great joy throughout the church that day as they read this encouraging message.

32Then Judas and Silas, both being prophets, spoke at length to the believers, encouraging and strengthening their faith. 33They stayed for a while, and then the believers sent them back to the church in Jerusalem with a blessing of peace.* 35Paul and Barnabas stayed in Antioch. They and many others taught and preached the word of the Lord there.

15:1 Greek *brothers;* also in 15:3, 23, 32, 33, 36, 40. 15:10 Greek *disciples.* 15:14 Greek *Symeon.*

15:16 Or *kingdom;* Greek reads *tent.* 15:16-18 Amos 9:11-12 (Greek version); Isa 45:21. 15:22 Greek *were leaders among the brothers.* 15:33 Some manuscripts add verse 34, *But Silas decided to stay there.*

PSALM 141:1-10
A psalm of David.

1 ○ LORD, I am calling to you.
    Please hurry!
    Listen when I cry to you for help!
2 Accept my prayer as incense
        offered to you,
    and my upraised hands as an
        evening offering.

3 **Take control of what I say, O LORD,**
    and guard my lips.
4 **Don't let me drift toward evil**
    or take part in acts
        of wickedness.
Don't let me share in the
    delicacies
    of those who do wrong.

5 Let the godly strike me!
    It will be a kindness!
If they correct me, it is soothing
    medicine.
    Don't let me refuse it.

But I pray constantly
    against the wicked and their
        deeds.
6 When their leaders are thrown
        down from a cliff,
    the wicked will listen to my
        words and find them true.
7 Like rocks brought up by a plow,
    the bones of the wicked will lie
        scattered without burial.*

8 I look to you for help,
        O Sovereign LORD.
    You are my refuge; don't let
        them kill me.
9 Keep me from the traps they have
        set for me,
    from the snares of those who
        do wrong.
10 Let the wicked fall into their
        own nets,
    but let me escape.

141:7 Hebrew *scattered at the mouth of Sheol.*

PROVERBS 17:23
The wicked take secret bribes to pervert the course of justice.

JUNE
24

2 KINGS 6:1–7:20
One day the group of prophets came to Elisha and told him, "As you can see, this place where we meet with you is too small. ²Let's go down to the Jordan River, where there are plenty of logs. There we can build a new place for us to meet."

"All right," he told them, "go ahead."

³"Please come with us," someone suggested.

"I will," he said. ⁴So he went with them.

When they arrived at the Jordan, they began cutting down trees. ⁵But as one of them was cutting a tree, his ax head fell into the river. "Oh, sir!" he cried. "It was a borrowed ax!"

⁶"Where did it fall?" the man of God asked. When he showed him the place, Elisha cut a stick and threw it into the water at that spot. Then the ax head floated to the surface. ⁷"Grab it," Elisha said. And the man reached out and grabbed it.

⁸When the king of Aram was at war with Israel, he would confer with his officers and say, "We will mobilize our forces at such and such a place."

⁹But immediately Elisha, the man of God, would warn the king of Israel, "Do not go near that place, for the Arameans are planning to mobilize their troops there." ¹⁰So the king of Israel would send word to the place indicated by the man of God. Time and again Elisha warned the king, so that he would be on the alert there.

¹¹The king of Aram became very upset over this. He called his officers together and demanded, "Which of you is the traitor? Who has been informing the king of Israel of my plans?"

¹²"It's not us, my lord the king," one of the officers replied. "Elisha, the prophet in Israel, tells the king of Israel even the words you speak in the privacy of your bedroom!"

¹³"Go and find out where he is," the king commanded, "so I can send troops to seize him."

And the report came back: "Elisha is at Dothan." ¹⁴So one night the king of Aram sent a great army with many chariots and horses to surround the city.

¹⁵When the servant of the man of God got up early the next morning and went outside, there were troops, horses, and chariots everywhere. "Oh, sir, what will we do now?" the young man cried to Elisha.

¹⁶"Don't be afraid!" Elisha told him. "For there are more on our side than on theirs!" ¹⁷Then Elisha prayed, "O LORD, open his eyes and let him see!" The LORD opened the young man's eyes, and when he looked up, he saw that the hillside around Elisha was filled with horses and chariots of fire.

¹⁸As the Aramean army advanced toward him, Elisha prayed, "O LORD, please make them blind." So the LORD struck them with blindness as Elisha had asked.

¹⁹Then Elisha went out and told them, "You have come the wrong way! This isn't the right city! Follow me, and I will take you to the man you are looking for." And he led them to the city of Samaria.

²⁰As soon as they had entered Samaria, Elisha prayed, "O LORD, now open their eyes and let them see." So the LORD opened their eyes, and they discovered that they were in the middle of Samaria.

²¹When the king of Israel saw them, he shouted to Elisha, "My father, should I kill them? Should I kill them?"

²²"Of course not!" Elisha replied. "Do we kill prisoners of war? Give them food and drink and send them home again to their master."

²³So the king made a great feast for

them and then sent them home to their master. After that, the Aramean raiders stayed away from the land of Israel.

²⁴Some time later, however, King Ben-hadad of Aram mustered his entire army and besieged Samaria. ²⁵As a result, there was a great famine in the city. The siege lasted so long that a donkey's head sold for eighty pieces of silver, and a cup of dove's dung sold for five pieces* of silver.

²⁶One day as the king of Israel was walking along the wall of the city, a woman called to him, "Please help me, my lord the king!"

²⁷He answered, "If the LORD doesn't help you, what can I do? I have neither food from the threshing floor nor wine from the press to give you." ²⁸But then the king asked, "What is the matter?"

She replied, "This woman said to me: 'Come on, let's eat your son today, then we will eat my son tomorrow.' ²⁹So we cooked my son and ate him. Then the next day I said to her, 'Kill your son so we can eat him,' but she has hidden her son."

³⁰When the king heard this, he tore his clothes in despair. And as the king walked along the wall, the people could see that he was wearing burlap under his robe next to his skin.* ³¹"May God strike me and even kill me if I don't separate Elisha's head from his shoulders this very day," the king vowed.

³²Elisha was sitting in his house with the elders of Israel when the king sent a messenger to summon him. But before the messenger arrived, Elisha said to the elders, "A murderer has sent a man to cut off my head. When he arrives, shut the door and keep him out. We will soon hear his master's steps following him."

³³While Elisha was still saying this, the messenger arrived. And the king* said, "All this misery is from the LORD! Why should I wait for the LORD any longer?"

⁷:¹ELISHA replied, "Listen to this message from the LORD! This is what the LORD says: By this time tomorrow in the markets of Samaria, five quarts of choice flour will cost only one piece of silver,* and ten quarts of barley grain will cost only one piece of silver.*"

²The officer assisting the king said to the man of God, "That couldn't happen even if the LORD opened the windows of heaven!"

But Elisha replied, "You will see it happen with your own eyes, but you won't be able to eat any of it!"

³Now there were four men with leprosy* sitting at the entrance of the city gates. "Why should we sit here waiting to die?" they asked each other. ⁴"We will starve if we stay here, but with the famine in the city, we will starve if we go back there. So we might as well go out and surrender to the Aramean army. If they let us live, so much the better. But if they kill us, we would have died anyway."

⁵So at twilight they set out for the camp of the Arameans. But when they came to the edge of the camp, no one was there! ⁶For the Lord had caused the Aramean army to hear the clatter of speeding chariots and the galloping of horses and the sounds of a great army approaching. "The king of Israel has hired the Hittites and Egyptians* to attack us!" they cried to one another. ⁷So they panicked and ran into the night, abandoning their tents, horses, donkeys, and everything else, as they fled for their lives.

⁸When the lepers arrived at the edge of the camp, they went into one tent after another, eating and drinking wine; and they carried off silver and gold and clothing and hid it. ⁹Finally, they said to each other, "This is not right. This is a day of good news, and we aren't sharing it with anyone! If we wait until morning, some calamity will certainly fall upon us. Come on, let's go back and tell the people at the palace."

¹⁰So they went back to the city and told the gatekeepers what had happened. "We went out to the Aramean camp," they said, "and no one was there!

The horses and donkeys were tethered and the tents were all in order, but there wasn't a single person around!" [11]Then the gatekeepers shouted the news to the people in the palace.

[12]The king got out of bed in the middle of the night and told his officers, "I know what has happened. The Arameans know we are starving, so they have left their camp and have hidden in the fields. They are expecting us to leave the city, and then they will take us alive and capture the city."

[13]One of his officers replied, "We had better send out scouts to check into this. Let them take five of the remaining horses. If something happens to them, it will be no worse than if they stay here and die with the rest of us."

[14]So two chariots with horses were prepared, and the king sent scouts to see what had happened to the Aramean army. [15]They went all the way to the Jordan River, following a trail of clothing and equipment that the Arameans had thrown away in their mad rush to escape. The scouts returned and told the king about it. [16]Then the people of Samaria rushed out and plundered the Aramean camp. So it was true that five quarts of choice flour were sold that day for one piece of silver, and ten quarts of barley grain were sold for one piece of silver, just as the Lord had promised. [17]The king appointed his officer to control the traffic at the gate, but he was knocked down and trampled to death as the people rushed out.

So everything happened exactly as the man of God had predicted when the king came to his house. [18]The man of God had said to the king, "By this time tomorrow in the markets of Samaria, five quarts of choice flour will cost one piece of silver, and ten quarts of barley grain will cost one piece of silver."

[19]The king's officer had replied, "That couldn't happen even if the Lord opened the windows of heaven!" And the man of God had said, "You will see it happen with your own eyes, but you won't be able to eat any of it!" [20]And so it

was, for the people trampled him to death at the gate!

6:25 Hebrew *sold for 80 shekels* [2 pounds, or 0.9 kilograms] *of silver, and ¼ of a cab* [0.3 liters] *of dove's dung sold for 5 shekels* [2 ounces, or 57 grams]. *Dove's dung* may be a variety of wild vegetable.   **6:30** As in Greek version; Hebrew reads *wearing burlap next to his skin from the house.*   **6:33** Hebrew *he.*   **7:1a** Hebrew *1 seah* [6 liters] *of choice flour will cost 1 shekel* [0.4 ounces, or 11 grams]; also in 7:16, 18.   **7:1b** Hebrew *2 seahs* [12 liters] *of barley grain will cost 1 shekel* [0.4 ounces, or 11 grams]; also in 7:16, 18.   **7:3** Or *with a contagious skin disease.* The Hebrew word used here and throughout this passage can describe various skin diseases.   **7:6** Possibly *and the people of Muzur,* a district near Cilicia.

ACTS 15:36–16:15

After some time Paul said to Barnabas, "Let's go back and visit each city where we previously preached the word of the Lord, to see how the new believers are doing." [37]Barnabas agreed and wanted to take along John Mark. [38]But Paul disagreed strongly, since John Mark had deserted them in Pamphylia and had not continued with them in their work. [39]Their disagreement was so sharp that they separated. Barnabas took John Mark with him and sailed for Cyprus. [40]Paul chose Silas, and as he left, the believers entrusted him to the Lord's gracious care. [41]Then he traveled throughout Syria and Cilicia, strengthening the churches there.

[16:1]PAUL went first to Derbe and then to Lystra, where there was a young disciple named Timothy. His mother was a Jewish believer, but his father was a Greek. [2]Timothy was well thought of by the believers* in Lystra and Iconium, [3]so Paul wanted him to join them on their journey. In deference to the Jews of the area, he arranged for Timothy to be circumcised before they left, for everyone knew that his father was a Greek. [4]Then they went from town to town, instructing the believers to follow the decisions made by the apostles and elders in Jerusalem. [5]So the churches were strengthened in their faith and grew larger every day.

[6]Next Paul and Silas traveled through the area of Phrygia and Galatia, because the Holy Spirit had prevented them from preaching the word in the province of Asia at that time. [7]Then

coming to the borders of Mysia, they headed north for the province of Bithynia,* but again the Spirit of Jesus did not allow them to go there. ⁸So instead, they went on through Mysia to the seaport of Troas.

⁹That night Paul had a vision: A man from Macedonia in northern Greece was standing there, pleading with him, "Come over to Macedonia and help us!" ¹⁰So we* decided to leave for Macedonia at once, having concluded that God was calling us to preach the Good News there.

¹¹We boarded a boat at Troas and sailed straight across to the island of Samothrace, and the next day we landed at Neapolis. ¹²From there we reached Philippi, a major city of that district of Macedonia and a Roman colony. And we stayed there several days.

¹³On the Sabbath we went a little way outside the city to a riverbank, where we thought people would be meeting for prayer, and we sat down to speak with some women who had gathered there. ¹⁴One of them was Lydia from Thyatira, a merchant of expensive purple cloth, who worshiped God. As she listened to us, the Lord opened her heart, and she accepted what Paul was saying. ¹⁵She was baptized along with other members of her household, and she asked us to be her guests. "If you agree that I am a true believer in the Lord," she said, "come and stay at my home." And she urged us until we agreed.

16:2 Greek *brothers;* also in 16:40.   16:6-7 *Phrygia, Galatia, Asia, Mysia,* and *Bithynia* were all districts in what is now Turkey.   16:10 Luke, the writer of this book, here joined Paul and accompanied him on his journey.

PSALM 142:1-7
A psalm of David, regarding his experience in the cave. A prayer.*

¹ I cry out to the LORD;
    I plead for the LORD's mercy.
² I pour out my complaints
        before him
    and tell him all my troubles.
³ When I am overwhelmed,

    you alone know the way
        I should turn.
Wherever I go,
    my enemies have set traps for me.
⁴ I look for someone to come and
        help me,
    but no one gives me a passing
        thought!
No one will help me;
    no one cares a bit what happens
        to me.
⁵ Then I pray to you, O LORD.
    I say, "You are my place of refuge.
    You are all I really want in life.
⁶ Hear my cry,
    for I am very low.
Rescue me from my persecutors,
    for they are too strong for me.
⁷ Bring me out of prison
    so I can thank you.
The godly will crowd around me,
    for you are good to me."

142:TITLE Hebrew *maskil.* This may be a literary or musical term.

PROVERBS 17:24-25
Sensible people keep their eyes glued on wisdom, but a fool's eyes wander to the ends of the earth. □Foolish children* bring grief to their father and bitterness to the one who gave them birth.

17:25 Hebrew *A foolish son.*

JUNE
25

2 KINGS 8:1–9:13
Elisha had told the woman whose son he had brought back to life, "Take your family and move to some other place, for the LORD has called for a famine on Israel that will last for seven years." ²So the woman did as the man of God instructed. She took her family and settled in the land of the Philistines for seven years.

³After the famine ended she returned

from the land of the Philistines, and she went to see the king about getting back her house and land. 4As she came in, the king was talking with Gehazi, the servant of the man of God. The king had just said, "Tell me some stories about the great things Elisha has done." 5And Gehazi was telling the king about the time Elisha had brought a boy back to life. At that very moment, the mother of the boy walked in to make her appeal to the king about her house and land.

"Look, my lord the king!" Gehazi exclaimed. "Here is the woman now, and this is her son—the very one Elisha brought back to life!"

6"Is this true?" the king asked her. And she told him the story. So he directed one of his officials to see that everything she had lost was restored to her, including the value of any crops that had been harvested during her absence.

7Elisha went to Damascus, the capital of Aram, where King Ben-hadad lay sick. When someone told the king that the man of God had come, 8the king said to Hazael, "Take a gift to the man of God. Then tell him to ask the LORD, 'Will I recover from this illness?'"

9So Hazael loaded down forty camels with the finest products of Damascus as a gift for Elisha. He went to him and said, "Your servant Ben-hadad, the king of Aram, has sent me to ask, 'Will I recover from this illness?'"

10And Elisha replied, "Go and tell him, 'You will surely recover.' But actually the LORD has shown me that he will surely die!" 11Elisha stared at Hazael* with a fixed gaze until Hazael became uneasy.* Then the man of God started weeping.

12"What's the matter, my lord?" Hazael asked him.

Elisha replied, "I know the terrible things you will do to the people of Israel. You will burn their fortified cities, kill their young men with the sword, dash their little children to the ground, and rip open their pregnant women!"

13Hazael responded, "How could a

nobody like me* ever accomplish such great things?"

Elisha answered, "The LORD has shown me that you are going to be the king of Aram."

14When Hazael left Elisha and went back, the king asked him, "What did Elisha tell you?"

And Hazael replied, "He told me that you will surely recover."

15But the next day Hazael took a blanket, soaked it in water, and held it over the king's face until he died. Then Hazael became the next king of Aram.

16Jehoram son of King Jehoshaphat of Judah began to rule over Judah in the fifth year of the reign of Joram son of Ahab, king of Israel. 17Jehoram was thirty-two years old when he became king, and he reigned in Jerusalem eight years. 18But Jehoram followed the example of the kings of Israel and was as wicked as King Ahab, for he had married one of Ahab's daughters. So Jehoram did what was evil in the LORD's sight. 19But the LORD did not want to destroy Judah, for he had made a covenant with David and promised that his descendants would continue to rule, shining like a lamp forever.

20During Jehoram's reign, the Edomites revolted against Judah and crowned their own king. 21So Jehoram* went with all his chariots to attack the town of Zair.* The Edomites surrounded him and his chariot commanders, but he went out at night and attacked them* under cover of darkness. But Jehoram's army deserted him and fled to their homes. 22So Edom has been independent from Judah to this day. The town of Libnah also revolted about that same time.

23The rest of the events in Jehoram's reign and everything he did are recorded in *The Book of the History of the Kings of Judah.* 24When Jehoram died, he was buried with his ancestors in the City of David. Then his son Ahaziah became the next king.

25Ahaziah son of Jehoram began to rule over Judah in the twelfth year of the reign of Joram son of Ahab, king of Israel.

²⁶Ahaziah was twenty-two years old when he became king, and he reigned in Jerusalem one year. His mother was Athaliah, a granddaughter of King Omri of Israel. ²⁷Ahaziah followed the evil example of King Ahab's family. He did what was evil in the LORD's sight, just as Ahab's family had done, for he was related by marriage to the family of Ahab.

²⁸Ahaziah joined Joram son of Ahab, the king of Israel, in his war against King Hazael of Aram at Ramoth-gilead. When the Arameans wounded King Joram in the battle, ²⁹he returned to Jezreel to recover from the wounds he had received at Ramoth.* Because Joram was wounded, King Ahaziah of Judah went to Jezreel to visit him.

⁹:¹MEANWHILE, Elisha the prophet had summoned a member of the group of prophets. "Get ready to travel,"* he told him, "and take this flask of olive oil with you. Go to Ramoth-gilead, ²and find Jehu son of Jehoshaphat, son of Nimshi. Call him into a private room away from his friends, ³and pour the oil over his head. Say to him, 'This is what the LORD says: I anoint you to be the king over Israel.' Then open the door and run for your life!"

⁴So the young prophet did as he was told and went to Ramoth-gilead. ⁵When he arrived there, he found Jehu sitting around with the other army officers. "I have a message for you, Commander," he said.

"For which one of us?" Jehu asked.

"For you, Commander," he replied.

⁶So Jehu left the others and went into the house. Then the young prophet poured the oil over Jehu's head and said, "This is what the LORD, the God of Israel, says: I anoint you king over the LORD's people, Israel. ⁷You are to destroy the family of Ahab, your master. In this way, I will avenge the murder of my prophets and all the LORD's servants who were killed by Jezebel. ⁸The entire family of Ahab must be wiped out. I will destroy

every one of his male descendants, slave and free alike, anywhere in Israel. ⁹I will destroy the family of Ahab as I destroyed the families of Jeroboam son of Nebat and of Baasha son of Ahijah. ¹⁰Dogs will eat Ahab's wife Jezebel at the plot of land in Jezreel, and no one will bury her." Then the young prophet opened the door and ran.

¹¹Jehu went back to his fellow officers, and one of them asked him, "What did that madman want? Is everything all right?"

"You know how a man like that babbles on," Jehu replied.

¹²"You're hiding something," they said. "Tell us."

So Jehu told them, "He said to me, 'This is what the LORD says: I have anointed you to be king over Israel.'"

¹³Then they quickly spread out their cloaks on the bare steps and blew the ram's horn, shouting, "Jehu is king!"

8:11a Hebrew *He stared at him.*   8:11b The meaning of the Hebrew is uncertain.   8:13 Hebrew *a dog.*
8:21a Hebrew *Joram,* a variant spelling of Jehoram; also in 8:23, 24.   8:21b Greek version reads *Seir.*   8:21c Or *he went out and escaped.* The meaning of the Hebrew is uncertain.   8:29 Hebrew *Ramah,* a variant spelling of Ramoth.   9:1 Hebrew *Bind up your loins.*

ACTS 16:16-40

One day as we [Luke, Paul, and their companions] were going down to the place of prayer, we met a demon-possessed slave girl. She was a fortune-teller who earned a lot of money for her masters. ¹⁷She followed Paul and the rest of us, shouting, "These men are servants of the Most High God, and they have come to tell you how to be saved."

¹⁸This went on day after day until Paul got so exasperated that he turned and said to the demon within her, "I command you in the name of Jesus Christ to come out of her." And instantly it left her.

¹⁹Her masters' hopes of wealth were now shattered, so they grabbed Paul and Silas and dragged them before the authorities at the marketplace. ²⁰"The whole city is in an uproar because of these Jews!" they shouted to the city officials. ²¹"They are teaching customs

that are illegal for us Romans to practice."

²²A mob quickly formed against Paul and Silas, and the city officials ordered them stripped and beaten with wooden rods. ²³They were severely beaten, and then they were thrown into prison. The jailer was ordered to make sure they didn't escape. ²⁴So the jailer put them into the inner dungeon and clamped their feet in the stocks.

²⁵**Around midnight Paul and Silas were praying and singing hymns to God, and the other prisoners were listening.** ²⁶Suddenly, there was a massive earthquake, and the prison was shaken to its foundations. All the doors immediately flew open, and the chains of every prisoner fell off! ²⁷The jailer woke up to see the prison doors wide open. He assumed the prisoners had escaped, so he drew his sword to kill himself. ²⁸But Paul shouted to him, "Stop! Don't kill yourself! We are all here!"

²⁹The jailer called for lights and ran to the dungeon and fell down trembling before Paul and Silas. ³⁰Then he brought them out and asked, "Sirs, what must I do to be saved?"

³¹They replied, "Believe in the Lord Jesus and you will be saved, along with everyone in your household." ³²And they shared the word of the Lord with him and with all who lived in his household. ³³Even at that hour of the night, the jailer cared for them and washed their wounds. Then he and everyone in his household were immediately baptized. ³⁴He brought them into his house and set a meal before them, and he and his entire household rejoiced because they all believed in God.

³⁵The next morning the city officials sent the police to tell the jailer, "Let those men go!" ³⁶So the jailer told Paul, "The city officials have said you and Silas are free to leave. Go in peace."

³⁷But Paul replied, "They have publicly beaten us without a trial and put us in prison—and we are Roman citizens. So now they want us to leave secretly? Certainly not! Let them come themselves to release us!"

³⁸When the police reported this, the city officials were alarmed to learn that Paul and Silas were Roman citizens. ³⁹So they came to the jail and apologized to them. Then they brought them out and begged them to leave the city. ⁴⁰When Paul and Silas left the prison, they returned to the home of Lydia. There they met with the believers and encouraged them once more. Then they left town.

PSALM 143:1-12
A psalm of David.

¹ **H**ear my prayer, O LORD;
  listen to my plea!
  Answer me because you are
    faithful and righteous.
² Don't put your servant on trial,
  for no one is innocent before you.
³ My enemy has chased me.
  He has knocked me to the ground
  and forces me to live in darkness
    like those in the grave.
⁴ I am losing all hope;
  I am paralyzed with fear.
⁵ I remember the days of old.
  I ponder all your great works
  and think about what you have
    done.
⁶ I lift my hands to you in prayer.
  I thirst for you as parched land
    thirsts for rain.   *Interlude*

⁷ Come quickly, LORD, and answer me,
  for my depression deepens.
  Don't turn away from me,
    or I will die.
⁸ Let me hear of your unfailing love
    each morning,
  for I am trusting you.
  Show me where to walk,
    for I give myself to you.
⁹ Rescue me from my enemies, LORD;
  I run to you to hide me.
¹⁰ Teach me to do your will,
  for you are my God.
  May your gracious Spirit lead
    me forward
  on a firm footing.

¹¹ For the glory of your name, O LORD,
   preserve my life.
   Because of your faithfulness,
   bring me out of this distress.
¹² In your unfailing love, silence
   all my enemies
   and destroy all my foes,
   for I am your servant.

PROVERBS 17:26
It is wrong to punish the godly for being good or to flog leaders for being honest.

JUNE 26

2 KINGS 9:14–10:31

So Jehu son of Jehoshaphat, son of Nimshi, led a conspiracy against King Joram. (Now Joram had been with the army at Ramoth-gilead, defending Israel against the forces of King Hazael of Aram. ¹⁵ But King Joram* was wounded in the fighting and returned to Jezreel to recover from his wounds.) So Jehu told the men with him, "If you want me to be king, don't let anyone leave town and go to Jezreel to report what we have done."

¹⁶ Then Jehu got into a chariot and rode to Jezreel to find King Joram, who was lying there wounded. King Ahaziah of Judah was there, too, for he had gone to visit him. ¹⁷ The watchman on the tower of Jezreel saw Jehu and his company approaching, so he shouted to Joram, "I see a company of troops coming!"

"Send out a rider to ask if they are coming in peace," King Joram ordered.

¹⁸ So a horseman went out to meet Jehu and said, "The king wants to know if you are coming in peace."

Jehu replied, "What do you know about peace? Fall in behind me!"

The watchman called out to the king, "The messenger has met them, but he's not returning."

¹⁹ So the king sent out a second horseman. He rode up to them and said, "The king wants to know if you come in peace."

Again Jehu answered, "What do you know about peace? Fall in behind me!"

²⁰ The watchman exclaimed, "The messenger has met them, but he isn't returning either! It must be Jehu son of Nimshi, for he's driving like a madman."

²¹ "Quick! Get my chariot ready!" King Joram commanded.

Then King Joram of Israel and King Ahaziah of Judah rode out in their chariots to meet Jehu. They met him at the plot of land that had belonged to Naboth of Jezreel. ²² King Joram demanded, "Do you come in peace, Jehu?"

Jehu replied, "How can there be peace as long as the idolatry and witchcraft of your mother, Jezebel, are all around us?"

²³ Then King Joram turned the horses around* and fled, shouting to King Ahaziah, "Treason, Ahaziah!" ²⁴ But Jehu drew his bow and shot Joram between the shoulders. The arrow pierced his heart, and he sank down dead in his chariot.

²⁵ Jehu said to Bidkar, his officer, "Throw him into the plot of land that belonged to Naboth of Jezreel. Do you remember when you and I were riding along behind his father, Ahab? The LORD pronounced this message against him: ²⁶ 'I solemnly swear that I will repay him here on this plot of land, says the LORD, for the murder of Naboth and his sons that I saw yesterday.' So throw him out on Naboth's property, just as the LORD said."

²⁷ When King Ahaziah of Judah saw what was happening, he fled along the road to Beth-haggan. Jehu rode after him, shouting, "Shoot him, too!" So they shot Ahaziah in his chariot at the Ascent of Gur, near Ibleam. He was able to go on as far as Megiddo, but he died there. ²⁸ His servants took him by chariot to Jerusalem, where they buried him with his ancestors in the City of David. ²⁹ Ahaziah had become king over Judah

in the eleventh year of the reign of Joram son of Ahab.

30When Jezebel, the queen mother, heard that Jehu had come to Jezreel, she painted her eyelids and fixed her hair and sat at a window. 31When Jehu entered the gate of the palace, she shouted at him, "Have you come in peace, you murderer? You're just like Zimri, who murdered his master!"*

32Jehu looked up and saw her at the window and shouted, "Who is on my side?" And two or three eunuchs looked out at him. 33"Throw her down!" Jehu yelled. So they threw her out the window, and her blood spattered against the wall and on the horses. And Jehu trampled her body under his horses' hooves.

34Then Jehu went into the palace and ate and drank. Afterward he said, "Someone go and bury this cursed woman, for she is the daughter of a king." 35But when they went out to bury her, they found only her skull, her feet, and her hands.

36When they returned and told Jehu, he stated, "This fulfills the message from the LORD, which he spoke through his servant Elijah from Tishbe: 'At the plot of land in Jezreel, dogs will eat Jezebel's body. 37Her remains will be scattered like dung on the plot of land in Jezreel, so that no one will be able to recognize her.'"

10:1Ahab had seventy sons living in the city of Samaria. So Jehu wrote letters and sent them to Samaria, to the elders and officials of the city,* and to the guardians of King Ahab's sons. He said, 2"The king's sons are with you, and you have at your disposal chariots, horses, a fortified city, and weapons. As soon as you receive this letter, 3select the best qualified of your master's sons to be your king, and prepare to fight for Ahab's dynasty."

4But they were paralyzed with fear and said, "We've seen that two kings couldn't stand against this man! What can we do?"

5So the palace and city administrators, together with the elders and the guardians of the king's sons, sent this message to Jehu: "We are your servants and will do anything you tell us. We will not make anyone king; do whatever you think is best."

6Jehu responded with a second letter: "If you are on my side and are going to obey me, bring the heads of your master's sons to me at Jezreel by this time tomorrow." Now the seventy sons of the king were being cared for by the leaders of Samaria, where they had been raised since childhood. 7When the letter arrived, the leaders killed all seventy of the king's sons. They placed their heads in baskets and presented them to Jehu at Jezreel.

8A messenger went to Jehu and said, "They have brought the heads of the king's sons."

So Jehu ordered, "Pile them in two heaps at the entrance of the city gate, and leave them there until morning."

9In the morning he went out and spoke to the crowd that had gathered around them. "You are not to blame," he told them. "I am the one who conspired against my master and killed him. But who killed all these? 10You can be sure that the message of the LORD that was spoken concerning Ahab's family will not fail. The LORD declared through his servant Elijah that this would happen." 11Then Jehu killed all who were left of Ahab's relatives living in Jezreel and all his important officials, his personal friends, and his priests. So Ahab was left without a single survivor.

12Then Jehu set out for Samaria. Along the way, while he was at Betheked of the Shepherds, 13he met some relatives of King Ahaziah of Judah. "Who are you?" he asked them.

And they replied, "We are relatives of King Ahaziah. We are going to visit the sons of King Ahab and the sons of the queen mother."

14"Take them alive!" Jehu shouted to his men. And they captured all forty-two of them and killed them at the well of Beth-eked. None of them escaped.

15When Jehu left there, he met Jehonadab son of Recab, who was coming to meet him. After they had greeted each other, Jehu said to him, "Are you as loyal to me as I am to you?"

"Yes, I am," Jehonadab replied.

"If you are," Jehu said, "then give me your hand." So Jehonadab put out his hand, and Jehu helped him into the chariot. 16Then Jehu said, "Now come with me, and see how devoted I am to the LORD." So Jehonadab rode along with him.

17When Jehu arrived in Samaria, he killed everyone who was left there from Ahab's family, just as the LORD had promised through Elijah.

18Then Jehu called a meeting of all the people of the city and said to them, "Ahab's worship of Baal was nothing compared to the way I will worship him! 19Therefore, summon all the prophets and worshipers of Baal, and call together all his priests. See to it that every one of them comes, for I am going to offer a great sacrifice to Baal. Anyone who fails to come will be put to death." But Jehu's cunning plan was to destroy all the worshipers of Baal.

20Then Jehu ordered, "Prepare a solemn assembly to worship Baal!" So they did. 21He sent messengers throughout all Israel summoning those who worshiped Baal. They all came—not a single one remained behind—and they filled the temple of Baal from one end to the other. 22And Jehu instructed the keeper of the wardrobe, "Be sure that every worshiper of Baal wears one of these robes." So robes were given to them.

23Then Jehu went into the temple of Baal with Jehonadab son of Recab. Jehu said to the worshipers of Baal, "Make sure no one who worships the LORD is here—only those who worship Baal." 24So they were all inside the temple to offer sacrifices and burnt offerings. Now Jehu had stationed eighty of his men outside the building and had

warned them, "If you let anyone escape, you will pay for it with your own life."

25As soon as Jehu had finished sacrificing the burnt offering, he commanded his guards and officers, "Go in and kill all of them. Don't let a single one escape!" So they killed them all with their swords, and the guards and officers dragged their bodies outside.* Then Jehu's men went into the innermost fortress* of the temple of Baal. 26They dragged out the sacred pillar* used in the worship of Baal and burned it. 27They smashed the sacred pillar and wrecked the temple of Baal, converting it into a public toilet, as it remains to this day.

28In this way, Jehu destroyed every trace of Baal worship from Israel. 29He did not, however, destroy the gold calves at Bethel and Dan, with which Jeroboam son of Nebat had caused Israel to sin.

30Nonetheless the LORD said to Jehu, "You have done well in following my instructions to destroy the family of Ahab. Therefore, your descendants will be kings of Israel down to the fourth generation." 31But Jehu did not obey the Law of the LORD, the God of Israel, with all his heart. He refused to turn from the sins that Jeroboam had led Israel to commit.

9:15 Hebrew *Jehoram,* a variant spelling of Joram; also in 9:17, 21, 22, 23, 24.   9:23 Hebrew *turned his hands.* 9:31 See 1 Kgs 16:9-10, where Zimri killed his master, King Elah.   10:1 As in some Greek manuscripts and Latin Vulgate (see also 10:6); Hebrew reads *of Jezreel.* 10:25a Or *they left their bodies lying there;* or *they threw them out into the outermost court.*   10:25b Hebrew *city.* 10:26 As in Greek and Syriac versions and Latin Vulgate; Hebrew reads *sacred pillars.*

ACTS 17:1-34

Paul and Silas then traveled through the towns of Amphipolis and Apollonia and came to Thessalonica, where there was a Jewish synagogue. 2As was Paul's custom, he went to the synagogue service, and for three Sabbaths in a row he used the Scriptures to reason with the people. 3He explained the prophecies and proved that the Messiah must suffer and rise from the dead. He said,

"This Jesus I'm telling you about is the Messiah." ⁴Some of the Jews who listened were persuaded and joined Paul and Silas, along with many God-fearing Greek men and quite a few prominent women.*

⁵But some of the Jews were jealous, so they gathered some troublemakers from the marketplace to form a mob and start a riot. They attacked the home of Jason, searching for Paul and Silas so they could drag them out to the crowd.* ⁶Not finding them there, they dragged out Jason and some of the other believers* instead and took them before the city council. "Paul and Silas have caused trouble all over the world," they shouted, "and now they are here disturbing our city, too. ⁷And Jason has welcomed them into his home. They are all guilty of treason against Caesar, for they profess allegiance to another king, named Jesus."

⁸The people of the city, as well as the city council, were thrown into turmoil by these reports. ⁹So the officials forced Jason and the other believers to post bond, and then they released them.

¹⁰That very night the believers sent Paul and Silas to Berea. When they arrived there, they went to the Jewish synagogue. ¹¹And the people of Berea were more open-minded than those in Thessalonica, and they listened eagerly to Paul's message. They searched the Scriptures day after day to see if Paul and Silas were teaching the truth. ¹²As a result, many Jews believed, as did many of the prominent Greek women and men.

¹³But when some Jews in Thessalonica learned that Paul was preaching the word of God in Berea, they went there and stirred up trouble. ¹⁴The believers acted at once, sending Paul on to the coast, while Silas and Timothy remained behind. ¹⁵Those escorting Paul went with him all the way to Athens; then they returned to Berea with instructions for Silas and Timothy to hurry and join him.

¹⁶While Paul was waiting for them in Athens, he was deeply troubled by all the idols he saw everywhere in the city. ¹⁷He went to the synagogue to reason with the Jews and the God-fearing Gentiles, and he spoke daily in the public square to all who happened to be there.

¹⁸He also had a debate with some of the Epicurean and Stoic philosophers. When he told them about Jesus and his resurrection, they said, "What's this babbler trying to say with these strange ideas he's picked up?" Others said, "He seems to be preaching about some foreign gods."

¹⁹Then they took him to the high council of the city.* "Come and tell us about this new teaching," they said. ²⁰"You are saying some rather strange things, and we want to know what it's all about." ²¹(It should be explained that all the Athenians as well as the foreigners in Athens seemed to spend all their time discussing the latest ideas.)

²²So Paul, standing before the council,* addressed them as follows: "Men of Athens, I notice that you are very religious in every way, ²³for as I was walking along I saw your many shrines. And one of your altars had this inscription on it: 'To an Unknown God.' This God, whom you worship without knowing, is the one I'm telling you about.

²⁴"He is the God who made the world and everything in it. Since he is Lord of heaven and earth, he doesn't live in man-made temples, ²⁵and human hands can't serve his needs—for he has no needs. He himself gives life and breath to everything, and he satisfies every need. ²⁶From one man* he created all the nations throughout the whole earth. He decided beforehand when they should rise and fall, and he determined their boundaries.

²⁷"His purpose was for the nations to seek after God and perhaps feel their way toward him and find him—though he is not far from any one of us. ²⁸For in him we live and move and exist. As some of your* own poets have said, 'We are his offspring.' ²⁹And since this is true, we shouldn't think of God as an

idol designed by craftsmen from gold or silver or stone.

30"God overlooked people's ignorance about these things in earlier times, but now he commands everyone everywhere to repent of their sins and turn to him. 31For he has set a day for judging the world with justice by the man he has appointed, and he proved to everyone who this is by raising him from the dead."

32When they heard Paul speak about the resurrection of the dead, some laughed in contempt, but others said, "We want to hear more about this later." 33That ended Paul's discussion with them, 34but some joined him and became believers. Among them were Dionysius, a member of the council,* a woman named Damaris, and others with them.

17:4 Some manuscripts read *quite a few of the wives of the leading men.* 17:5 Or *the city council.* 17:6 Greek *brothers;* also in 17:10, 14. 17:19 Or *the most learned society of philosophers in the city.* Greek reads *the Areopagus.* 17:22 Traditionally rendered *standing in the middle of Mars Hill;* Greek reads *standing in the middle of the Areopagus.* 17:26 Greek *From one;* other manuscripts read *From one blood.* 17:28 Some manuscripts read *our.* 17:34 Greek *an Areopagite.*

PSALM 144:1-15
A psalm of David.

1 Praise the LORD, who is
      my rock.
   He trains my hands for war
   and gives my fingers skill
      for battle.
2 He is my loving ally and
      my fortress,
   my tower of safety, my rescuer.
   He is my shield, and I take
      refuge in him.
   He makes the nations* submit
      to me.

3 O LORD, who are we that you
      should notice us,
      mere mortals that you should
      care for us?
4 For we are like a breath
      of air;
      our days are like a passing
      shadow.

5 Open the heavens, LORD, and
      come down.
   Touch the mountains so they
      billow smoke.
6 Hurl your lightning bolts and scatter
      your enemies!
   Shoot your arrows and confuse
      them!
7 Reach down from heaven and
      rescue me;
   rescue me from deep waters,
   from the power of my enemies.
8 Their mouths are full of lies;
   they swear to tell the truth, but
      they lie instead.

9 I will sing a new song to you, O God!
   I will sing your praises with
      a ten-stringed harp.
10 For you grant victory to kings!
   You rescued your servant David
      from the fatal sword.
11 Save me!
   Rescue me from the power
      of my enemies.
   Their mouths are full of lies;
   they swear to tell the truth, but
      they lie instead.

12 May our sons flourish in their
      youth
   like well-nurtured plants.
   May our daughters be like graceful
      pillars,
   carved to beautify a palace.
13 May our barns be filled
   with crops of every kind.
   May the flocks in our fields
      multiply by the thousands,
   even tens of thousands,
14   and may our oxen be loaded
      down with produce.
   May there be no enemy breaking
      through our walls,
   no going into captivity,
   no cries of alarm in our town
      squares.
15 Yes, joyful are those who live
      like this!
   Joyful indeed are those whose
      God is the LORD.

144:2 Some manuscripts read *my people.*

PROVERBS 17:27-28

A truly wise person uses few words; a person with understanding is even-tempered. □ Even fools are thought wise when they keep silent; with their mouths shut, they seem intelligent.

JUNE 27

2 KINGS 10:32–12:21

At about that time the LORD began to cut down the size of Israel's territory. King Hazael conquered several sections of the country ³³east of the Jordan River, including all of Gilead, Gad, Reuben, and Manasseh. He conquered the area from the town of Aroer by the Arnon Gorge to as far north as Gilead and Bashan.

³⁴The rest of the events in Jehu's reign—everything he did and all his achievements—are recorded in *The Book of the History of the Kings of Israel.*

³⁵When Jehu died, he was buried in Samaria. Then his son Jehoahaz became the next king. ³⁶In all, Jehu reigned over Israel from Samaria for twenty-eight years.

¹¹:¹WHEN Athaliah, the mother of King Ahaziah of Judah, learned that her son was dead, she began to destroy the rest of the royal family. ²But Ahaziah's sister Jehosheba, the daughter of King Jehoram,* took Ahaziah's infant son, Joash, and stole him away from among the rest of the king's children, who were about to be killed. She put Joash and his nurse in a bedroom to hide him from Athaliah, so the child was not murdered. ³Joash remained hidden in the Temple of the LORD for six years while Athaliah ruled over the land.

⁴In the seventh year of Athaliah's reign, Jehoiada the priest summoned the commanders, the Carite mercenaries, and the palace guards to come to the Temple of the LORD. He made a solemn pact with them and made them swear an oath of loyalty there in the LORD's Temple; then he showed them the king's son.

⁵Jehoiada told them, "This is what you must do. A third of you who are on duty on the Sabbath are to guard the royal palace itself. ⁶Another third of you are to stand guard at the Sur Gate. And the final third must stand guard behind the palace guard. These three groups will all guard the palace. ⁷The other two units who are off duty on the Sabbath must stand guard for the king at the LORD's Temple. ⁸Form a bodyguard around the king and keep your weapons in hand. Kill anyone who tries to break through. Stay with the king wherever he goes."

⁹So the commanders did everything as Jehoiada the priest ordered. The commanders took charge of the men reporting for duty that Sabbath, as well as those who were going off duty. They brought them all to Jehoiada the priest, ¹⁰and he supplied them with the spears and small shields that had once belonged to King David and were stored in the Temple of the LORD. ¹¹The palace guards stationed themselves around the king, with their weapons ready. They formed a line from the south side of the Temple around to the north side and all around the altar.

¹²Then Jehoiada brought out Joash, the king's son, placed the crown on his head, and presented him with a copy of God's laws.* They anointed him and proclaimed him king, and everyone clapped their hands and shouted, "Long live the king!"

¹³When Athaliah heard all the noise made by the palace guards and the people, she hurried to the LORD's Temple to see what was happening. ¹⁴When she arrived, she saw the newly crowned king standing in his place of authority by the pillar, as was the custom at times of coronation. The commanders and trumpeters were surrounding him, and

people from all over the land were rejoicing and blowing trumpets. When Athaliah saw all this, she tore her clothes in despair and shouted, "Treason! Treason!"

15 Then Jehoiada the priest ordered the commanders who were in charge of the troops, "Take her to the soldiers in front of the Temple,* and kill anyone who tries to rescue her." For the priest had said, "She must not be killed in the Temple of the LORD." 16 So they seized her and led her out to the gate where horses enter the palace grounds, and she was killed there.

17 Then Jehoiada made a covenant between the LORD and the king and the people that they would be the LORD's people. He also made a covenant between the king and the people. 18 And all the people of the land went over to the temple of Baal and tore it down. They demolished the altars and smashed the idols to pieces, and they killed Mattan the priest of Baal in front of the altars.

Jehoiada the priest stationed guards at the Temple of the LORD. 19 Then the commanders, the Carite mercenaries, the palace guards, and all the people of the land escorted the king from the Temple of the LORD. They went through the gate of the guards and into the palace, and the king took his seat on the royal throne. 20 So all the people of the land rejoiced, and the city was peaceful because Athaliah had been killed at the king's palace.

21 *Joash* was seven years old when he became king.

12:1 *JOASH* began to rule over Judah in the seventh year of King Jehu's reign in Israel. He reigned in Jerusalem forty years. His mother was Zibiah from Beersheba. 2 All his life Joash did what was pleasing in the LORD's sight because Jehoiada the priest instructed him. 3 Yet even so, he did not destroy the pagan shrines, and the people still offered sacrifices and burned incense there.

4 One day King Joash said to the priests, "Collect all the money brought as a sacred offering to the LORD's Temple, whether it is a regular assessment, a payment of vows, or a voluntary gift. 5 Let the priests take some of that money to pay for whatever repairs are needed at the Temple."

6 But by the twenty-third year of Joash's reign, the priests still had not repaired the Temple. 7 So King Joash called for Jehoiada and the other priests and asked them, "Why haven't you repaired the Temple? Don't use any more money for your own needs. From now on, it must all be spent on Temple repairs." 8 So the priests agreed not to accept any more money from the people, and they also agreed to let others take responsibility for repairing the Temple.

9 Then Jehoiada the priest bored a hole in the lid of a large chest and set it on the right-hand side of the altar at the entrance of the Temple of the LORD. The priests guarding the entrance put all of the people's contributions into the chest. 10 Whenever the chest became full, the court secretary and the high priest counted the money that had been brought to the LORD's Temple and put it into bags. 11 Then they gave the money to the construction supervisors, who used it to pay the people working on the LORD's Temple—the carpenters, the builders, 12 the masons, and the stonecutters. They also used the money to buy the timber and the finished stone needed for repairing the LORD's Temple, and they paid any other expenses related to the Temple's restoration.

13 The money brought to the Temple was not used for making silver bowls, lamp snuffers, basins, trumpets, or other articles of gold or silver for the Temple of the LORD. 14 It was paid to the workmen, who used it for the Temple repairs. 15 No accounting of this money was required from the construction supervisors, because they were honest and trustworthy men. 16 However, the money that was contributed for guilt offerings and sin offerings was not brought into the LORD's Temple. It was given to the priests for their own use.

¹⁷About this time King Hazael of Aram went to war against Gath and captured it. Then he turned to attack Jerusalem. ¹⁸King Joash collected all the sacred objects that Jehoshaphat, Jehoram, and Ahaziah, the previous kings of Judah, had dedicated, along with what he himself had dedicated. He sent them all to Hazael, along with all the gold in the treasuries of the LORD's Temple and the royal palace. So Hazael called off his attack on Jerusalem.

¹⁹The rest of the events in Joash's reign and everything he did are recorded in *The Book of the History of the Kings of Judah*.

²⁰Joash's officers plotted against him and assassinated him at Beth-millo on the road to Silla. ²¹The assassins were Jozacar* son of Shimeath and Jehozabad son of Shomer—both trusted advisers. Joash was buried with his ancestors in the City of David. Then his son Amaziah became the next king.

11:2 Hebrew *Joram,* a variant spelling of Jehoram.
11:12 Or *a copy of the covenant.* 11:15 Or *Bring her out from between the ranks;* or *Take her out of the Temple precincts.* The meaning of the Hebrew is uncertain.
11:21a Verse 11:21 is numbered 12:1 in Hebrew text.
11:21b Hebrew *Jehoash,* a variant spelling of Joash.
12:1a Verses 12:1-21 are numbered 12:2-22 in Hebrew text. 12:1b Hebrew *Jehoash,* a variant spelling of Joash; also in 12:2, 4, 6, 7, 18. 12:21 As in Greek and Syriac versions; Hebrew reads *Jozabad.*

ACTS 18:1-22

Then Paul left Athens and went to Corinth.* ²There he became acquainted with a Jew named Aquila, born in Pontus, who had recently arrived from Italy with his wife, Priscilla. They had left Italy when Claudius Caesar deported all Jews from Rome. ³Paul lived and worked with them, for they were tentmakers* just as he was.

⁴Each Sabbath found Paul at the synagogue, trying to convince the Jews and Greeks alike. ⁵And after Silas and Timothy came down from Macedonia, Paul spent all his time preaching the word. He testified to the Jews that Jesus was the Messiah. ⁶But when they opposed and insulted him, Paul shook the dust from his clothes and said, "Your blood is upon your own heads—I am innocent.

From now on I will go preach to the Gentiles."

⁷Then he left and went to the home of Titius Justus, a Gentile who worshiped God and lived next door to the synagogue. ⁸Crispus, the leader of the synagogue, and everyone in his household believed in the Lord. Many others in Corinth also heard Paul, became believers, and were baptized.

⁹One night the Lord spoke to Paul in a vision and told him, "Don't be afraid! Speak out! Don't be silent! ¹⁰For I am with you, and no one will attack and harm you, for many people in this city belong to me." ¹¹So Paul stayed there for the next year and a half, teaching the word of God.

¹²But when Gallio became governor of Achaia, some Jews rose up together against Paul and brought him before the governor for judgment. ¹³They accused Paul of "persuading people to worship God in ways that are contrary to our law."

¹⁴But just as Paul started to make his defense, Gallio turned to Paul's accusers and said, "Listen, you Jews, if this were a case involving some wrongdoing or a serious crime, I would have a reason to accept your case. ¹⁵But since it is merely a question of words and names and your Jewish law, take care of it yourselves. I refuse to judge such matters." ¹⁶And he threw them out of the courtroom.

¹⁷The crowd* then grabbed Sosthenes, the leader of the synagogue, and beat him right there in the courtroom. But Gallio paid no attention.

¹⁸Paul stayed in Corinth for some time after that, then said good-bye to the brothers and sisters* and went to nearby Cenchrea. There he shaved his head according to Jewish custom, marking the end of a vow. Then he set sail for Syria, taking Priscilla and Aquila with him.

¹⁹They stopped first at the port of Ephesus, where Paul left the others behind. While he was there, he went to the synagogue to reason with the Jews. ²⁰They asked him to stay longer, but he declined. ²¹As he left, however, he said,

"I will come back later,* God willing."
Then he set sail from Ephesus. ²²The
next stop was at the port of Caesarea.
From there he went up and visited the
church at Jerusalem* and then went
back to Antioch.

18:1 *Athens* and *Corinth* were major cities in Achaia, the region in the southern portion of the Greek peninsula. 18:3 Or *leatherworkers.* 18:17 Greek *Everyone;* other manuscripts read *All the Greeks.* 18:18 Greek *brothers;* also in 18:27. 18:21 Some manuscripts read *"I must by all means be at Jerusalem for the upcoming festival, but I will come back later."* 18:22 Greek *the church.*

PSALM 145:1-21*
A psalm of praise of David.

¹ **I** will exalt you, my God and
      King,
    and praise your name forever
      and ever.
² I will praise you every day;
    yes, I will praise you forever.
³ Great is the LORD! He is most
      worthy of praise!
    No one can measure his
      greatness.

⁴ Let each generation tell its children
      of your mighty acts;
    let them proclaim your power.
⁵ I will meditate* on your majestic,
      glorious splendor
    and your wonderful miracles.
⁶ Your awe-inspiring deeds will be
      on every tongue;
    I will proclaim your greatness.
⁷ Everyone will share the story
      of your wonderful goodness;
    they will sing with joy about
      your righteousness.

⁸ **The LORD is merciful and
      compassionate,
    slow to get angry and filled
      with unfailing love.**
⁹ **The LORD is good to everyone.
    He showers compassion
      on all his creation.**
¹⁰ All of your works will thank
      you, LORD,
    and your faithful followers will
      praise you.
¹¹ They will speak of the glory
      of your kingdom;

    they will give examples
      of your power.
¹² They will tell about your mighty
      deeds
    and about the majesty and glory
      of your reign.
¹³ For your kingdom is an everlasting
      kingdom.
    You rule throughout all
      generations.

    The LORD always keeps his
      promises;
    he is gracious in all he does.*
¹⁴ The LORD helps the fallen
    and lifts those bent beneath
      their loads.
¹⁵ The eyes of all look to you
      in hope;
    you give them their food as they
      need it.
¹⁶ When you open your hand,
    you satisfy the hunger and thirst
      of every living thing.
¹⁷ The LORD is righteous in everything
      he does;
    he is filled with kindness.
¹⁸ The LORD is close to all who call
      on him,
    yes, to all who call on him
      in truth.
¹⁹ He grants the desires of those who
      fear him;
    he hears their cries for help and
      rescues them.
²⁰ The LORD protects all those who
      love him,
    but he destroys the wicked.

²¹ I will praise the LORD,
    and may everyone on earth bless
      his holy name
    forever and ever.

145 This psalm is a Hebrew acrostic poem; each verse (including 13b) begins with a successive letter of the Hebrew alphabet. 145:5 Some manuscripts read *They will speak.* 145:13 The last two lines of 145:13 are not found in many of the ancient manuscripts.

PROVERBS 18:1
Unfriendly people care only about
themselves; they lash out at common
sense.

JUNE
28

2 KINGS 13:1–14:29

Jehoahaz son of Jehu began to rule over Israel in the twenty-third year of King Joash's reign in Judah. He reigned in Samaria seventeen years. ²But he did what was evil in the LORD's sight. He followed the example of Jeroboam son of Nebat, continuing the sins that Jeroboam had led Israel to commit. ³So the LORD was very angry with Israel, and he allowed King Hazael of Aram and his son Benhadad to defeat them repeatedly.

⁴Then Jehoahaz prayed for the LORD's help, and the LORD heard his prayer, for he could see how severely the king of Aram was oppressing Israel. ⁵So the LORD provided someone to rescue the Israelites from the tyranny of the Arameans. Then Israel lived in safety again as they had in former days.

⁶But they continued to sin, following the evil example of Jeroboam. They also allowed the Asherah pole in Samaria to remain standing. ⁷Finally, Jehoahaz's army was reduced to 50 charioteers, 10 chariots, and 10,000 foot soldiers. The king of Aram had killed the others, trampling them like dust under his feet.

⁸The rest of the events in Jehoahaz's reign—everything he did and the extent of his power—are recorded in *The Book of the History of the Kings of Israel.* ⁹When Jehoahaz died, he was buried in Samaria. Then his son Jehoash* became the next king.

¹⁰Jehoash son of Jehoahaz began to rule over Israel in the thirty-seventh year of King Joash's reign in Judah. He reigned in Samaria sixteen years. ¹¹But he did what was evil in the LORD's sight. He refused to turn from the sins that Jeroboam son of Nebat had led Israel to commit.

¹²The rest of the events in Jehoash's reign and everything he did, including the extent of his power and his war with King Amaziah of Judah, are recorded in *The Book of the History of the Kings of Israel.* ¹³When Jehoash died, he was buried in Samaria with the kings of Israel. Then his son Jeroboam II became the next king.

¹⁴When Elisha was in his last illness, King Jehoash of Israel visited him and wept over him. "My father! My father! I see the chariots and charioteers of Israel!" he cried.

¹⁵Elisha told him, "Get a bow and some arrows." And the king did as he was told. ¹⁶Elisha told him, "Put your hand on the bow," and Elisha laid his own hands on the king's hands.

¹⁷Then he commanded, "Open that eastern window," and he opened it. Then he said, "Shoot!" So he shot an arrow. Elisha proclaimed, "This is the LORD's arrow, an arrow of victory over Aram, for you will completely conquer the Arameans at Aphek.

¹⁸Then he said, "Now pick up the other arrows and strike them against the ground." So the king picked them up and struck the ground three times. ¹⁹But the man of God was angry with him. "You should have struck the ground five or six times!" he exclaimed. "Then you would have beaten Aram until it was entirely destroyed. Now you will be victorious only three times."

²⁰Then Elisha died and was buried.

Groups of Moabite raiders used to invade the land each spring. ²¹Once when some Israelites were burying a man, they spied a band of these raiders. So they hastily threw the corpse into the tomb of Elisha and fled. But as soon as the body touched Elisha's bones, the dead man revived and jumped to his feet!

²²King Hazael of Aram had oppressed Israel during the entire reign of King Jehoahaz. ²³But the LORD was gracious and merciful to the people of Israel, and they were not totally destroyed. He pitied them because of his covenant with Abraham, Isaac, and Jacob. And to this day he still has not completely destroyed them or banished them from his presence.

²⁴King Hazael of Aram died, and his son Ben-hadad became the next king. ²⁵Then Jehoash son of Jehoahaz recaptured from Ben-hadad son of Hazael the towns that had been taken from Jehoash's father, Jehoahaz. Jehoash defeated Ben-hadad on three occasions, and he recovered the Israelite towns.

¹⁴:¹AMAZIAH son of Joash began to rule over Judah in the second year of the reign of King Jehoash* of Israel. ²Amaziah was twenty-five years old when he became king, and he reigned in Jerusalem twenty-nine years. His mother was Jehoaddin from Jerusalem. ³Amaziah did what was pleasing in the LORD's sight, but not like his ancestor David. Instead, he followed the example of his father, Joash. ⁴Amaziah did not destroy the pagan shrines, and the people still offered sacrifices and burned incense there.

⁵When Amaziah was well established as king, he executed the officials who had assassinated his father. ⁶However, he did not kill the children of the assassins, for he obeyed the command of the LORD as written by Moses in the Book of the Law: "Parents must not be put to death for the sins of their children, nor children for the sins of their parents. Those deserving to die must be put to death for their own crimes."*

⁷Amaziah also killed 10,000 Edomites in the Valley of Salt. He also conquered Sela and changed its name to Joktheel, as it is called to this day.

⁸One day Amaziah sent messengers with this challenge to Israel's king Jehoash, the son of Jehoahaz and grandson of Jehu: "Come and meet me in battle!"*

⁹But King Jehoash of Israel replied to King Amaziah of Judah with this story: "Out in the Lebanon mountains, a thistle sent a message to a mighty cedar tree: 'Give your daughter in marriage to my son.' But just then a wild animal of Lebanon came by and stepped on the thistle, crushing it!

¹⁰"You have indeed defeated Edom, and you are very proud of it. But be con-

tent with your victory and stay at home! Why stir up trouble that will only bring disaster on you and the people of Judah?"

¹¹But Amaziah refused to listen, so King Jehoash of Israel mobilized his army against King Amaziah of Judah. The two armies drew up their battle lines at Beth-shemesh in Judah. ¹²Judah was routed by the army of Israel, and its army scattered and fled for home. ¹³King Jehoash of Israel captured Judah's king, Amaziah son of Joash and grandson of Ahaziah, at Beth-shemesh. Then he marched to Jerusalem, where he demolished 600 feet* of Jerusalem's wall, from the Ephraim Gate to the Corner Gate. ¹⁴He carried off all the gold and silver and all the articles from the Temple of the LORD. He also seized the treasures from the royal palace, along with hostages, and then returned to Samaria.

¹⁵The rest of the events in Jehoash's reign and everything he did, including the extent of his power and his war with King Amaziah of Judah, are recorded in *The Book of the History of the Kings of Israel.* ¹⁶When Jehoash died, he was buried in Samaria with the kings of Israel. And his son Jeroboam II became the next king.

¹⁷King Amaziah of Judah lived for fifteen years after the death of King Jehoash of Israel. ¹⁸The rest of the events in Amaziah's reign are recorded in *The Book of the History of the Kings of Judah.*

¹⁹There was a conspiracy against Amaziah's life in Jerusalem, and he fled to Lachish. But his enemies sent assassins after him, and they killed him there. ²⁰They brought his body back to Jerusalem on a horse, and he was buried with his ancestors in the City of David.

²¹All the people of Judah had crowned Amaziah's sixteen-year-old son, Uzziah,* as king in place of his father, Amaziah. ²²After his father's death, Uzziah rebuilt the town of Elath and restored it to Judah.

²³Jeroboam II, the son of Jehoash, began to rule over Israel in the fifteenth

year of King Amaziah's reign in Judah. Jeroboam reigned in Samaria forty-one years. 24He did what was evil in the LORD's sight. He refused to turn from the sins that Jeroboam son of Nebat had led Israel to commit. 25Jeroboam II recovered the territories of Israel between Lebo-hamath and the Dead Sea,* just as the LORD, the God of Israel, had promised through Jonah son of Amittai, the prophet from Gath-hepher.

26For the LORD saw the bitter suffering of everyone in Israel, and that there was no one in Israel, slave or free, to help them. 27And because the LORD had not said he would blot out the name of Israel completely, he used Jeroboam II, the son of Jehoash, to save them.

28The rest of the events in the reign of Jeroboam II and everything he did—including the extent of his power, his wars, and how he recovered for Israel both Damascus and Hamath, which had belonged to Judah*—are recorded in *The Book of the History of the Kings of Israel.* 29When Jeroboam II died, he was buried in Samaria* with the kings of Israel. Then his son Zechariah became the next king.

13:9 Hebrew *Joash,* a variant spelling of Jehoash; also in 13:10, 12, 13, 14, 25. 14:1 Hebrew *Joash,* a variant spelling of Jehoash; also in 14:13, 23, 27. 14:6 Deut 24:16. 14:8 Hebrew *Come, let us look one another in the face.* 14:13 Hebrew *400 cubits* [180 meters]. 14:21 Hebrew *Azariah,* a variant spelling of Uzziah. 14:25 Hebrew *the sea of the Arabah.* 14:28 Or *to Yaudi.* The meaning of the Hebrew is uncertain. 14:29 As in some Greek manuscripts; Hebrew omits *in Samaria.*

ACTS 18:23–19:12

After spending some time in Antioch, Paul went back through Galatia and Phrygia, visiting and strengthening all the believers.*

24Meanwhile, a Jew named Apollos, an eloquent speaker who knew the Scriptures well, had arrived in Ephesus from Alexandria in Egypt. 25He had been taught the way of the Lord, and he taught others about Jesus with an enthusiastic spirit* and with accuracy. However, he knew only about John's baptism. 26When Priscilla and Aquila heard him preaching boldly in the synagogue, they took him aside and explained the way of God even more accurately.

27Apollos had been thinking about going to Achaia, and the brothers and sisters in Ephesus encouraged him to go. They wrote to the believers in Achaia, asking them to welcome him. When he arrived there, he proved to be of great benefit to those who, by God's grace, had believed. 28He refuted the Jews with powerful arguments in public debate. Using the Scriptures, he explained to them that Jesus was the Messiah.

19:1WHILE Apollos was in Corinth, Paul traveled through the interior regions until he reached Ephesus, on the coast, where he found several believers.* 2"Did you receive the Holy Spirit when you believed?" he asked them.

"No," they replied, "we haven't even heard that there is a Holy Spirit."

3"Then what baptism did you experience?" he asked.

And they replied, "The baptism of John."

4Paul said, "John's baptism called for repentance from sin. But John himself told the people to believe in the one who would come later, meaning Jesus."

5As soon as they heard this, they were baptized in the name of the Lord Jesus. 6Then when Paul laid his hands on them, the Holy Spirit came on them, and they spoke in other tongues and prophesied. 7There were about twelve men in all.

8Then Paul went to the synagogue and preached boldly for the next three months, arguing persuasively about the Kingdom of God. 9But some became stubborn, rejecting his message and publicly speaking against the Way. So Paul left the synagogue and took the believers with him. Then he held daily discussions at the lecture hall of Tyrannus. 10This went on for the next two years, so that people throughout the province of Asia—both Jews and Greeks—heard the word of the Lord.

11God gave Paul the power to per-

form unusual miracles. ¹²When hand-
kerchiefs or aprons that had merely
touched his skin were placed on sick
people, they were healed of their diseases, and evil spirits were expelled.

18:23 Greek *disciples;* also in 18:27.   18:25 Or *with
enthusiasm in the Spirit.*   19:1 Greek *disciples;* also in
19:9, 30.

PSALM 146:1-10
Praise the LORD!

Let all that I am praise the LORD.
² I will praise the LORD as long
as I live.
I will sing praises to my God with
my dying breath.

³ Don't put your confidence in
powerful people;
there is no help for you there.
⁴ When they breathe their last, they
return to the earth,
and all their plans die with them.
⁵ **But joyful are those who have the
God of Israel* as their helper,
whose hope is in the LORD
their God.**
⁶ **He made heaven and earth,
the sea, and everything in them.
He keeps every promise
forever.**
⁷ He gives justice to the oppressed
and food to the hungry.
The LORD frees the prisoners.
⁸ The LORD opens the eyes
of the blind.
The LORD lifts up those who are
weighed down.
The LORD loves the godly.
⁹ The LORD protects the foreigners
among us.
He cares for the orphans
and widows,
but he frustrates the plans
of the wicked.

¹⁰ The LORD will reign forever.
He will be your God,
O Jerusalem,* throughout
the generations.

Praise the LORD!

146:5 Hebrew *of Jacob.* See note on 44:4.   146:10 Hebrew
Zion.

PROVERBS 18:2-3
Fools have no interest in understanding; they only want to air their own
opinions. □ Doing wrong leads to disgrace, and scandalous behavior brings
contempt.

JUNE 29

2 KINGS 15:1–16:20
Uzziah* son of Amaziah began to rule
over Judah in the twenty-seventh year
of the reign of King Jeroboam II of Israel. ²He was sixteen years old when he
became king, and he reigned in Jerusalem fifty-two years. His mother was Jec-
oliah from Jerusalem.

³He did what was pleasing in the
LORD's sight, just as his father, Amaziah,
had done. ⁴But he did not destroy the pagan shrines, and the people still offered
sacrifices and burned incense there.
⁵The LORD struck the king with leprosy,*
which lasted until the day he died. He
lived in isolation in a separate house. The
king's son Jotham was put in charge of
the royal palace, and he governed the
people of the land.

⁶The rest of the events in Uzziah's
reign and everything he did are recorded in *The Book of the History of the
Kings of Judah.* ⁷When Uzziah died, he
was buried with his ancestors in the City
of David. And his son Jotham became
the next king.

⁸Zechariah son of Jeroboam II began
to rule over Israel in the thirty-eighth
year of King Uzziah's reign in Judah. He
reigned in Samaria six months. ⁹Zecha-
riah did what was evil in the LORD's sight,
as his ancestors had done. He refused to
turn from the sins that Jeroboam son of
Nebat had led Israel to commit. ¹⁰Then
Shallum son of Jabesh conspired against

Zechariah, assassinated him in public,*
and became the next king.

¹¹The rest of the events in Zechariah's reign are recorded in *The Book of the History of the Kings of Israel.* ¹²So the LORD's message to Jehu came true: "Your descendants will be kings of Israel down to the fourth generation."

¹³Shallum son of Jabesh began to rule over Israel in the thirty-ninth year of King Uzziah's reign in Judah. Shallum reigned in Samaria only one month. ¹⁴Then Menahem son of Gadi went to Samaria from Tirzah and assassinated him, and he became the next king.

¹⁵The rest of the events in Shallum's reign, including his conspiracy, are recorded in *The Book of the History of the Kings of Israel.*

¹⁶At that time Menahem destroyed the town of Tappuah* and all the surrounding countryside as far as Tirzah, because its citizens refused to surrender the town. He killed the entire population and ripped open the pregnant women.

¹⁷Menahem son of Gadi began to rule over Israel in the thirty-ninth year of King Uzziah's reign in Judah. He reigned in Samaria ten years. ¹⁸But Menahem did what was evil in the LORD's sight. During his entire reign, he refused to turn from the sins that Jeroboam son of Nebat had led Israel to commit.

¹⁹Then King Tiglath-pileser* of Assyria invaded the land. But Menahem paid him thirty-seven tons* of silver to gain his support in tightening his grip on royal power. ²⁰Menahem extorted the money from the rich of Israel, demanding that each of them pay fifty pieces* of silver to the king of Assyria. So the king of Assyria turned from attacking Israel and did not stay in the land.

²¹The rest of the events in Menahem's reign and everything he did are recorded in *The Book of the History of the Kings of Israel.* ²²When Menahem died, his son Pekahiah became the next king.

²³Pekahiah son of Menahem began to rule over Israel in the fiftieth year of King Uzziah's reign in Judah. He reigned in Samaria two years. ²⁴But Pekahiah did what was evil in the LORD's sight. He refused to turn from the sins that Jeroboam son of Nebat had led Israel to commit.

²⁵Then Pekah son of Remaliah, the commander of Pekahiah's army, conspired against him. With fifty men from Gilead, Pekah assassinated the king, along with Argob and Arieh, in the citadel of the palace at Samaria. And Pekah reigned in his place.

²⁶The rest of the events in Pekahiah's reign and everything he did are recorded in *The Book of the History of the Kings of Israel.*

²⁷Pekah son of Remaliah began to rule over Israel in the fifty-second year of King Uzziah's reign in Judah. He reigned in Samaria twenty years. ²⁸But Pekah did what was evil in the LORD's sight. He refused to turn from the sins that Jeroboam son of Nebat had led Israel to commit.

²⁹During Pekah's reign, King Tiglath-pileser of Assyria attacked Israel again, and he captured the towns of Ijon, Abel-beth-maacah, Janoah, Kedesh, and Hazor. He also conquered the regions of Gilead, Galilee, and all of Naphtali, and he took the people to Assyria as captives. ³⁰Then Hoshea son of Elah conspired against Pekah and assassinated him. He began to rule over Israel in the twentieth year of Jotham son of Uzziah.

³¹The rest of the events in Pekah's reign and everything he did are recorded in *The Book of the History of the Kings of Israel.*

³²Jotham son of Uzziah began to rule over Judah in the second year of King Pekah's reign in Israel. ³³He was twenty-five years old when he became king, and he reigned in Jerusalem sixteen years. His mother was Jerusha, the daughter of Zadok.

³⁴Jotham did what was pleasing in the LORD's sight. He did everything his father, Uzziah, had done. ³⁵But he did not destroy the pagan shrines, and the people still offered sacrifices and burned incense there. He rebuilt the upper gate of the Temple of the LORD.

³⁶The rest of the events in Jotham's

reign and everything he did are recorded in *The Book of the History of the Kings of Judah.* ³⁷In those days the LORD began to send King Rezin of Aram and King Pekah of Israel to attack Judah. ³⁸When Jotham died, he was buried with his ancestors in the City of David. And his son Ahaz became the next king.

¹⁶:¹AHAZ son of Jotham began to rule over Judah in the seventeenth year of King Pekah's reign in Israel. ²Ahaz was twenty years old when he became king, and he reigned in Jerusalem sixteen years. He did not do what was pleasing in the sight of the LORD his God, as his ancestor David had done. ³Instead, he followed the example of the kings of Israel, even sacrificing his own son in the fire.* In this way, he followed the detestable practices of the pagan nations the LORD had driven from the land ahead of the Israelites. ⁴He offered sacrifices and burned incense at the pagan shrines and on the hills and under every green tree.

⁵Then King Rezin of Aram and King Pekah of Israel came up to attack Jerusalem. They besieged Ahaz but could not conquer him. ⁶At that time the king of Edom* recovered the town of Elath for Edom.* He drove out the people of Judah and sent Edomites* to live there, as they do to this day.

⁷King Ahaz sent messengers to King Tiglath-pileser of Assyria with this message: "I am your servant and your vassal.* Come up and rescue me from the attacking armies of Aram and Israel." ⁸Then Ahaz took the silver and gold from the Temple of the LORD and the palace treasury and sent it as a payment to the Assyrian king. ⁹So the king of Assyria attacked the Aramean capital of Damascus and led its population away as captives, resettling them in Kir. He also killed King Rezin.

¹⁰King Ahaz then went to Damascus to meet with King Tiglath-pileser of Assyria. While he was there, he took special note of the altar. Then he sent a model of the altar to Uriah the priest, along with its design in full detail. ¹¹Uri-

ah followed the king's instructions and built an altar just like it, and it was ready before the king returned from Damascus. ¹²When the king returned, he inspected the altar and made offerings on it. ¹³He presented a burnt offering and a grain offering, he poured out a liquid offering, and he sprinkled the blood of peace offerings on the altar.

¹⁴Then King Ahaz removed the old bronze altar from its place in front of the LORD's Temple, between the entrance and the new altar, and placed it on the north side of the new altar. ¹⁵He told Uriah the priest, "Use the new altar* for the morning sacrifices of burnt offering, the evening grain offering, the king's burnt offering and grain offering, and the burnt offerings of all the people, as well as their grain offerings and liquid offerings. Sprinkle the blood from all the burnt offerings and sacrifices on the new altar. The bronze altar will be for my personal use only." ¹⁶Uriah the priest did just as King Ahaz commanded him.

¹⁷Then the king removed the side panels and basins from the portable water carts. He also removed the great bronze basin called the Sea from the backs of the bronze oxen and placed it on the stone pavement. ¹⁸In deference to the king of Assyria, he also removed the canopy that had been constructed inside the palace for use on the Sabbath day,* as well as the king's outer entrance to the Temple of the LORD.

¹⁹The rest of the events in Ahaz's reign and everything he did are recorded in *The Book of the History of the Kings of Judah.* ²⁰When Ahaz died, he was buried with his ancestors in the City of David. Then his son Hezekiah became the next king.

15:1 Hebrew *Azariah,* a variant spelling of Uzziah; also in 15:6, 7, 8, 17, 23, 27.   15:5 Or *with a contagious skin disease.* The Hebrew word used here and throughout this passage can describe various skin diseases.
15:10 Or *at Ibleam.*   15:16 As in some Greek manuscripts; other Greek manuscripts read *at Ibleam.* Hebrew reads *Tiphsah.*   15:19a Hebrew *Pul,* another name for Tiglath-pileser.   15:19b Hebrew *1,000 talents* [34 metric tons].
15:20 Hebrew *50 shekels* [20 ounces, or 570 grams].
16:3 Or *even making his son pass through the fire.*
16:6a As in Latin Vulgate; Hebrew reads *Rezin king of Aram.*   16:6b As in Latin Vulgate; Hebrew reads *Aram.*
16:6c As in Greek version, Latin Vulgate, and an alternate

reading of the Masoretic Text; the other alternate reads
Arameans. **16:7** Hebrew *your son.* **16:15** Hebrew *the*
great altar. **16:18** The meaning of the Hebrew is uncertain.

ACTS 19:13-41

A group of Jews was traveling from town to town casting out evil spirits. They tried to use the name of the Lord Jesus in their incantation, saying, "I command you in the name of Jesus, whom Paul preaches, to come out!" 14Seven sons of Sceva, a leading priest, were doing this. 15But one time when they tried it, the evil spirit replied, "I know Jesus, and I know Paul, but who are you?" 16Then the man with the evil spirit leaped on them, overpowered them, and attacked them with such violence that they fled from the house, naked and battered.

17 The story of what happened spread quickly all through Ephesus, to Jews and Greeks alike. A solemn fear descended on the city, and the name of the Lord Jesus was greatly honored. 18Many who became believers confessed their sinful practices. 19A number of them who had been practicing sorcery brought their incantation books and burned them at a public bonfire. The value of the books was several million dollars.* 20So the message about the Lord spread widely and had a powerful effect.

21Afterward Paul felt compelled by the Spirit* to go over to Macedonia and Achaia before going to Jerusalem. "And after that," he said, "I must go on to Rome!" 22He sent his two assistants, Timothy and Erastus, ahead to Macedonia while he stayed awhile longer in the province of Asia.

23About that time, serious trouble developed in Ephesus concerning the Way. 24It began with Demetrius, a silversmith who had a large business manufacturing silver shrines of the Greek goddess Artemis.* He kept many craftsmen busy. 25He called them together, along with others employed in similar trades, and addressed them as follows:

"Gentlemen, you know that our wealth comes from this business. 26But as you have seen and heard, this man Paul has persuaded many people that handmade gods aren't really gods at all. And he's done this not only here in Ephesus but throughout the entire province! 27Of course, I'm not just talking about the loss of public respect for our business. I'm also concerned that the temple of the great goddess Artemis will lose its influence and that Artemis—this magnificent goddess worshiped throughout the province of Asia and all around the world—will be robbed of her great prestige!"

28At this their anger boiled, and they began shouting, "Great is Artemis of the Ephesians!" 29Soon the whole city was filled with confusion. Everyone rushed to the amphitheater, dragging along Gaius and Aristarchus, who were Paul's traveling companions from Macedonia. 30Paul wanted to go in, too, but the believers wouldn't let him. 31Some of the officials of the province, friends of Paul, also sent a message to him, begging him not to risk his life by entering the amphitheater.

32Inside, the people were all shouting, some one thing and some another. Everything was in confusion. In fact, most of them didn't even know why they were there. 33The Jews in the crowd pushed Alexander forward and told him to explain the situation. He motioned for silence and tried to speak. 34But when the crowd realized he was a Jew, they started shouting again and kept it up for two hours: "Great is Artemis of the Ephesians! Great is Artemis of the Ephesians!"

35At last the mayor was able to quiet them down enough to speak. "Citizens of Ephesus," he said. "Everyone knows that Ephesus is the official guardian of the temple of the great Artemis, whose image fell down to us from heaven. 36Since this is an undeniable fact, you should stay calm and not do anything rash. 37You have brought these men here, but they have stolen nothing from the temple and have not spoken against our goddess.

38"If Demetrius and the craftsmen have a case against them, the courts are in session and the officials can hear the case at once. Let them make formal charges. 39And if there are complaints about other matters, they can be settled in a legal assembly. [40]I am afraid we are in danger of being charged with rioting by the Roman government, since there is no cause for all this commotion. And if Rome demands an explanation, we won't know what to say." [41]Then he dismissed them, and they dispersed.

19:19 Greek *50,000 pieces of silver,* each of which was the equivalent of a day's wage.   19:21 Or *decided in his spirit.*   19:24 *Artemis* is otherwise known as Diana.

PSALM 147:1-20
Praise the Lord!

How good to sing praises to
    our God!
How delightful and how fitting!
[2] The Lord is rebuilding Jerusalem
    and bringing the exiles back
        to Israel.
[3] He heals the brokenhearted
    and bandages their wounds.
[4] He counts the stars
    and calls them all by name.
[5] How great is our Lord! His power
    is absolute!
His understanding is beyond
    comprehension!
[6] The Lord supports the humble,
    but he brings the wicked down
        into the dust.

[7] Sing out your thanks to the Lord;
    sing praises to our God
        with a harp.
[8] He covers the heavens with clouds,
    provides rain for the earth,
    and makes the grass grow in
        mountain pastures.
[9] He gives food to the wild animals
    and feeds the young ravens when
        they cry.
[10] **He takes no pleasure in the
    strength of a horse
    or in human might.**
[11] **No, the Lord's delight is in those
    who fear him,
    those who put their hope
        in his unfailing love.**

[12] Glorify the Lord, O Jerusalem!
    Praise your God, O Zion!

[13] For he has strengthened the
    bars of your gates
    and blessed your children within
        your walls.
[14] He sends peace across your nation
    and satisfies your hunger
        with the finest wheat.
[15] He sends his orders to the world—
    how swiftly his word flies!
[16] He sends the snow like white wool;
    he scatters frost upon the ground
        like ashes.
[17] He hurls the hail like stones.*
    Who can stand against his
        freezing cold?
[18] Then, at his command, it all melts.
    He sends his winds, and
        the ice thaws.
[19] He has revealed his words to Jacob,
    his decrees and regulations
        to Israel.
[20] He has not done this for any
    other nation;
    they do not know his regulations.

Praise the Lord!

147:17 Hebrew *like bread crumbs.*

PROVERBS 18:4-5
Wise words are like deep waters; wisdom flows from the wise like a bubbling brook. □ It is not right to acquit the guilty or deny justice to the innocent.

JUNE 30

2 KINGS 17:1–18:12
Hoshea son of Elah began to rule over Israel in the twelfth year of King Ahaz's reign in Judah. He reigned in Samaria nine years. [2]He did what was evil in the Lord's sight, but not to the same extent as the kings of Israel who ruled before him.

[3]King Shalmaneser of Assyria attacked King Hoshea, so Hoshea was

forced to pay heavy tribute to Assyria. 4But Hoshea stopped paying the annual tribute and conspired against the king of Assyria by asking King So of Egypt* to help him shake free of Assyria's power. When the king of Assyria discovered this treachery, he seized Hoshea and put him in prison.

5Then the king of Assyria invaded the entire land, and for three years he besieged the city of Samaria. 6Finally, in the ninth year of King Hoshea's reign, Samaria fell, and the people of Israel were exiled to Assyria. They were settled in colonies in Halah, along the banks of the Habor River in Gozan, and in the cities of the Medes.

7This disaster came upon the people of Israel because they worshiped other gods. They sinned against the LORD their God, who had brought them safely out of Egypt and had rescued them from the power of Pharaoh, the king of Egypt. 8They had followed the practices of the pagan nations the LORD had driven from the land ahead of them, as well as the practices the kings of Israel had introduced. 9The people of Israel had also secretly done many things that were not pleasing to the LORD their God. They built pagan shrines for themselves in all their towns, from the smallest outpost to the largest walled city. 10They set up sacred pillars and Asherah poles at the top of every hill and under every green tree. 11They offered sacrifices on all the hilltops, just like the nations the LORD had driven from the land ahead of them. So the people of Israel had done many evil things, arousing the LORD's anger. 12Yes, they worshiped idols,* despite the LORD's specific and repeated warnings.

13Again and again the LORD had sent his prophets and seers to warn both Israel and Judah: "Turn from all your evil ways. Obey my commands and decrees—the entire law that I commanded your ancestors to obey, and that I gave you through my servants the prophets."

14But the Israelites would not listen. They were as stubborn as their ancestors who had refused to believe in the LORD

their God. 15They rejected his decrees and the covenant he had made with their ancestors, and they despised all his warnings. They worshiped worthless idols, so they became worthless themselves. They followed the example of the nations around them, disobeying the LORD's command not to imitate them.

16They rejected all the commands of the LORD their God and made two calves from metal. They set up an Asherah pole and worshiped Baal and all the forces of heaven. 17They even sacrificed their own sons and daughters in the fire.* They consulted fortune-tellers and practiced sorcery and sold themselves to evil, arousing the LORD's anger.

18Because the LORD was very angry with Israel, he swept them away from his presence. Only the tribe of Judah remained in the land. 19But even the people of Judah refused to obey the commands of the LORD their God, for they followed the evil practices that Israel had introduced. 20The LORD rejected all the descendants of Israel. He punished them by handing them over to their attackers until he had banished Israel from his presence.

21For when the LORD* tore Israel away from the kingdom of David, they chose Jeroboam son of Nebat as their king. But Jeroboam drew Israel away from following the LORD and made them commit a great sin. 22And the people of Israel persisted in all the evil ways of Jeroboam. They did not turn from these sins 23until the LORD finally swept them away from his presence, just as all his prophets had warned. So Israel was exiled from their land to Assyria, where they remain to this day.

24The king of Assyria transported groups of people from Babylon, Cuthah, Avva, Hamath, and Sepharvaim and resettled them in the towns of Samaria, replacing the people of Israel. They took possession of Samaria and lived in its towns. 25But since these foreign settlers did not worship the LORD when they first arrived, the LORD sent lions among them, which killed some of them.

[26]So a message was sent to the king of Assyria: "The people you have sent to live in the towns of Samaria do not know the religious customs of the God of the land. He has sent lions among them to destroy them because they have not worshiped him correctly."

[27]The king of Assyria then commanded, "Send one of the exiled priests back to Samaria. Let him live there and teach the new residents the religious customs of the God of the land." [28]So one of the priests who had been exiled from Samaria returned to Bethel and taught the new residents how to worship the LORD.

[29]But these various groups of foreigners also continued to worship their own gods. In town after town where they lived, they placed their idols at the pagan shrines that the people of Samaria had built. [30]Those from Babylon worshiped idols of their god Succoth-benoth. Those from Cuthah worshiped their god Nergal. And those from Hamath worshiped Ashima. [31]The Avvites worshiped their gods Nibhaz and Tartak. And the people from Sepharvaim even burned their own children as sacrifices to their gods Adrammelech and Anammelech.

[32]These new residents worshiped the LORD, but they also appointed from among themselves all sorts of people as priests to offer sacrifices at their places of worship. [33]And though they worshiped the LORD, they continued to follow their own gods according to the religious customs of the nations from which they came. [34]And this is still going on today. They continue to follow their former practices instead of truly worshiping the LORD and obeying the decrees, regulations, instructions, and commands he gave the descendants of Jacob, whose name he changed to Israel.

[35]For the LORD had made a covenant with the descendants of Jacob and commanded them: "Do not worship any other gods or bow before them or serve them or offer sacrifices to them. [36]But worship only the LORD, who brought you out of Egypt with great strength and a powerful arm. Bow down to him alone, and offer sacrifices only to him. [37]Be careful at all times to obey the decrees, regulations, instructions, and commands that he wrote for you. You must not worship other gods. [38]Do not forget the covenant I made with you, and do not worship other gods. [39]You must worship only the LORD your God. He is the one who will rescue you from all your enemies."

[40]But the people would not listen and continued to follow their former practices. [41]So while these new residents worshiped the LORD, they also worshiped their idols. And to this day their descendants do the same.

[18:1]HEZEKIAH son of Ahaz began to rule over Judah in the third year of King Hoshea's reign in Israel. [2]He was twenty-five years old when he became king, and he reigned in Jerusalem twenty-nine years. His mother was Abijah,* the daughter of Zechariah. [3]He did what was pleasing in the LORD's sight, just as his ancestor David had done. [4]He removed the pagan shrines, smashed the sacred pillars, and cut down the Asherah poles. He broke up the bronze serpent that Moses had made, because the people of Israel had been offering sacrifices to it. The bronze serpent was called Nehushtan.*

[5]Hezekiah trusted in the LORD, the God of Israel. There was no one like him among all the kings of Judah, either before or after his time. [6]He remained faithful to the LORD in everything, and he carefully obeyed all the commands the LORD had given Moses. [7]So the LORD was with him, and Hezekiah was successful in everything he did. He revolted against the king of Assyria and refused to pay him tribute. [8]He also conquered the Philistines as far distant as Gaza and its territory, from their smallest outpost to their largest walled city.

[9]During the fourth year of Hezekiah's reign, which was the seventh year of King Hoshea's reign in Israel, King Shalmaneser of Assyria attacked the city of Samaria and began a siege

against it. ¹⁰Three years later, during the sixth year of King Hezekiah's reign and the ninth year of King Hoshea's reign in Israel, Samaria fell. ¹¹At that time the king of Assyria exiled the Israelites to Assyria and placed them in colonies in Halah, along the banks of the Habor River in Gozan, and in the cities of the Medes. ¹²For they refused to listen to the LORD their God and obey him. Instead, they violated his covenant—all the laws that Moses the LORD's servant had commanded them to obey.

17:4 Or *by asking the king of Egypt at Sais.*   17:12 The Hebrew term (literally *round things*) probably alludes to dung.   17:17 Or *They even made their sons and daughters pass through the fire.*   17:21 Hebrew *he;* compare 1 Kgs 11:31-32.   18:2 As in parallel text at 2 Chr 29:1; Hebrew reads *Abi,* a variant spelling of Abijah.   18:4 *Nehushtan* sounds like the Hebrew terms that mean "snake," "bronze," and "unclean thing."

ACTS 20:1-38

When the uproar was over, Paul sent for the believers* and encouraged them. Then he said good-bye and left for Macedonia. ²While there, he encouraged the believers in all the towns he passed through. Then he traveled down to Greece, ³where he stayed for three months. He was preparing to sail back to Syria when he discovered a plot by some Jews against his life, so he decided to return through Macedonia.

⁴Several men were traveling with him. They were Sopater son of Pyrrhus from Berea; Aristarchus and Secundus from Thessalonica; Gaius from Derbe; Timothy; and Tychicus and Trophimus from the province of Asia. ⁵They went on ahead and waited for us at Troas. ⁶After the Passover* ended, we boarded a ship at Philippi in Macedonia and five days later joined them in Troas, where we stayed a week.

⁷On the first day of the week, we gathered with the local believers to share in the Lord's Supper.* Paul was preaching to them, and since he was leaving the next day, he kept talking until midnight. ⁸The upstairs room where we met was lighted with many flickering lamps. ⁹As Paul spoke on and on, a young man named Eutychus, sitting on the window-

sill, became very drowsy. Finally, he fell sound asleep and dropped three stories to his death below. ¹⁰Paul went down, bent over him, and took him into his arms. "Don't worry," he said, "he's alive!" ¹¹Then they all went back upstairs, shared in the Lord's Supper,* and ate together. Paul continued talking to them until dawn, and then he left. ¹²Meanwhile, the young man was taken home unhurt, and everyone was greatly relieved.

¹³Paul went by land to Assos, where he had arranged for us to join him, while we traveled by ship. ¹⁴He joined us there, and we sailed together to Mitylene. ¹⁵The next day we sailed past the island of Kios. The following day we crossed to the island of Samos, and* a day later we arrived at Miletus.

¹⁶Paul had decided to sail on past Ephesus, for he didn't want to spend any more time in the province of Asia. He was hurrying to get to Jerusalem, if possible, in time for the Festival of Pentecost. ¹⁷But when we landed at Miletus, he sent a message to the elders of the church at Ephesus, asking them to come and meet him.

¹⁸When they arrived he declared, "You know that from the day I set foot in the province of Asia until now ¹⁹I have done the Lord's work humbly and with many tears. I have endured the trials that came to me from the plots of the Jews. ²⁰I never shrank back from telling you what you needed to hear, either publicly or in your homes. ²¹I have had one message for Jews and Greeks alike—the necessity of repenting from sin and turning to God, and of having faith in our Lord Jesus.

²²"And now I am bound by the Spirit* to go to Jerusalem. I don't know what awaits me, ²³except that the Holy Spirit tells me in city after city that jail and suffering lie ahead. ²⁴But my life is worth nothing to me unless I use it for finishing the work assigned me by the Lord Jesus—the work of telling others the Good News about the wonderful grace of God.

²⁵"And now I know that none of you to whom I have preached the Kingdom will ever see me again. ²⁶I declare today

that I have been faithful. If anyone suffers eternal death, it's not my fault,* ²⁷for I didn't shrink from declaring all that God wants you to know.

²⁸"So guard yourselves and God's people. Feed and shepherd God's flock—his church, purchased with his own blood*—over which the Holy Spirit has appointed you as elders.* ²⁹I know that false teachers, like vicious wolves, will come in among you after I leave, not sparing the flock. ³⁰Even some men from your own group will rise up and distort the truth in order to draw a following. ³¹Watch out! Remember the three years I was with you—my constant watch and care over you night and day, and my many tears for you.

³²"And now I entrust you to God and the message of his grace that is able to build you up and give you an inheritance with all those he has set apart for himself. ³³I have never coveted anyone's silver or gold or fine clothes. ³⁴You know that these hands of mine have worked to supply my own needs and even the needs of those who were with me. ³⁵And I have been a constant example of how you can help those in need by working hard. You should remember the words of the Lord Jesus: 'It is more blessed to give than to receive.'"

³⁶When he had finished speaking, he knelt and prayed with them. ³⁷They all cried as they embraced and kissed him good-bye. ³⁸They were sad most of all because he had said that they would never see him again. Then they escorted him down to the ship.

20:1 Greek *disciples.*   20:6 Greek *the days of unleavened bread.*   20:7 Greek *to break bread.*   20:11 Greek *broke the bread.*   20:15 Some manuscripts read *and having stayed at Trogyllium.*   20:22 Or *by my spirit,* or *by an inner compulsion;* Greek reads *by the spirit.*   20:26 Greek *I am innocent of the blood of all.*   20:28a Or *with the blood of his own (Son).*   20:28b Greek *overseers.*

PSALM 148:1-14

Praise the LORD!

Praise the LORD from the heavens!
    Praise him from the skies!

² Praise him, all his angels!
    Praise him, all the armies
        of heaven!
³ Praise him, sun and moon!
    Praise him, all you twinkling
        stars!
⁴ Praise him, skies above!
    Praise him, vapors high
        above the clouds!
⁵ Let every created thing give
        praise to the LORD,
    for he issued his command, and
        they came into being.
⁶ He set them in place forever
        and ever.
    His decree will never be
        revoked.

⁷ Praise the LORD from the earth,
    you creatures of the ocean
        depths,
⁸ fire and hail, snow and clouds,*
    wind and weather that obey him,
⁹ mountains and all hills,
    fruit trees and all cedars,
¹⁰ wild animals and all livestock,
    small scurrying animals
        and birds,
¹¹ kings of the earth and all people,
    rulers and judges of the earth,
¹² young men and young women,
    old men and children.

¹³ **Let them all praise the name
        of the LORD.
    For his name is very great;
    his glory towers over the
        earth and heaven!**
¹⁴ He has made his people strong,
    honoring his faithful ones—
    the people of Israel who are
        close to him.

Praise the LORD!

148:8 Or *mist,* or *smoke.*

PROVERBS 18:6-7

Fools' words get them into constant quarrels; they are asking for a beating. □The mouths of fools are their ruin; they trap themselves with their lips.